ECONOMICS FOR POLICYMAKING

ECONOMICS FOR POLICYMAKING

Selected Essays of Arthur M. Okun

Edited by
Joseph A. Pechman

The MIT Press
Cambridge, Massachusetts
London, England

Publication of this volume was made possible in part by a grant from the Alfred P. Sloan Foundation.

This book was set in Times New Roman by Asco Trade Typesetting Ltd., Hong Kong, and printed and bound by Murray Printing Co. in the United States of America.

Library of Congress Cataloging in Publication Data

Okun, Arthur M.
Economics for policymaking.

Bibliography: p.
Includes index.
1. Economics—Addresses, essays, lectures. 2. Economic policy—Addresses, essays, lectures. 3. Inflation (Finance)—Addresses, essays, lectures. 4. United States—Economic conditions—1945– —Addresses, essays, lectures. 5. Economic forecasting—Addresses, essays, lectures. I. Pechman, Joseph A., 1918– II. Title.
HB171.038 1983 330 82-21706
ISBN 0-262-15025-5

Contents

Editor's Preface

The essays in this volume represent the work of a truly gifted economist. Arthur M. Okun, who died suddenly at the age of 51, was one of the few members of his profession who could apply technical economic analysis to difficult policy problems, devise practical solutions to these problems, and explain his results to opinion leaders and the public in language they can understand. The essays collected here include his articles in widely read periodicals as well as his contributions to the technical journals.

Arthur Okun was born in New Jersey, went to Columbia University for his undergraduate and graduate work, and received his doctorate in economics in 1956. He was elected to Phi Beta Kappa in his junior year and received the Kasher E. Green Prize for the highest scholastic average in his college class. He was the Godkin Lecturer at Harvard University in 1974 and received the 1979 Frank E. Seidman Award in political economy. He reached the rank of full professor at Yale University at the age of thirty-five.

Okun taught at Yale University from 1952 to 1960. He first came to Washington with James Tobin in 1961 when Tobin was asked to join Walter W. Heller and Kermit Gordon on President John F. Kennedy's memorable Council of Economic Advisers. Okun returned to Yale in 1963, but was soon called back by Gardner Ackley to become a member of the council in late 1964. He was appointed chairman of the council

I wish to acknowledge with gratitude the assistance of Henry J. Aaron, Julie A. Carr, and Ralph C. Bryant in the preparation of this preface. Miss Carr also assisted in the selection of the articles for this volume.

in February 1968. He came to the Brookings Institution in January 1969, where he remained for the remainder of his career.

Okun's major preoccupation as an economist was to devise methods of achieving economic growth with price stability. He understood that in the modern industrial economy, there is a danger that rapid economic growth stimulates inflation. He therefore supported macroeconomic policies to maintain a steady and sustainable rate of economic growth and also urged the adoption of wage-price guidelines or other forms of incomes policies to minimize inflation. In the last years of his life, Okun was grappling with stagflation—the coexistence of high inflation and high unemployment; he felt that this problem would undermine the US economy unless brought under control. The manuscript he left, *Prices and Quantities: A Macroeconomic Analysis* (Brookings, 1981), will be studied by students and policymakers alike for many years to come.

Okun's ability as a writer and phrase maker greatly added to his effectiveness as a policy analyst. Artful figures of speech adorn his articles, addresses, and congressional testimony. Among others, he invented these terms:

the discomfort index: the sum of the unemployment rate and the inflation rate;

the leaky bucket: the loss in economic efficiency accompanying programs to help low-income people;

the invisible handshake: the implicit contract between employers and workers, which is an important element in the wage-price spiral;

expensive easy money: a condition in which credit is amply available at high interest rates.

Arthur Okun was a compassionate man as well as a fine economist. His monograph *Equality and Efficiency* (Brookings, 1975), which was based on his Godkin lectures at Harvard, is a reasoned explanation of why the pursuit of too much equality can generate unacceptable efficiency losses and why the single-minded pursuit of efficiency can produce gross injustice. He believed that methods can be devised to achieve social betterment without sacrificing too much economic efficiency.

Okun was a prolific writer. The essays chosen for this volume illustrate the wide range of issues he addressed, his technical prowess in economic analysis, and his ability to communicate his thinking to lay audiences. They should be read in conjunction with his three books, *The Political*

Economy of Prosperity (Brookings, 1970), *Equality and Efficiency*, and *Prices and Quantities*, to obtain a thorough understanding of his views.

The following is a brief introduction to Okun's views on the major issues covered in this volume:

I Inflation. Unlike many economists, Okun refused to accept the proposition that inflation is essentially harmless. He believed that inflation imposes intolerable real costs on society and also undermines the usefulness of money as a yardstick in commodity, labor, and financial markets. The cost of stopping stagflation through traditional fiscal and monetary policies are enormous. Okun believed that as much as 90 percent of any reductions in gross national product resulting from a policy of disinflation could be reflected in reduced output, with as little as 10 percent in reduced prices. To cut the losses from disinflation, he urged a combination of cost-reducing measures (such as cutting sales and excise taxes and eliminating unnecessary regulations) and some form of incomes policies to slow the growth of wages and prices.

II Implicit Contracts. The onset of stagflation in the 1970s and the absence of a theory to explain it led to Okun's work on the invisible handshake. According to Okun's theory of implicit contracts, businesses enter into long-term relations with their employees and customers, thereby lowering the costs of searching incurred by workers and buyers. Such contracts, although they reduce the sensitivity of wages and prices to short-run changes in demand for labor and goods, are sensible and efficient when markets are not competitive and when uncertainty and potential surprises are brought into the picture. The idea of implicit contracts helps to explain why monetary and fiscal restraint alone has so little immediate effect on prices and wages.

III Output, Employment, and Unemployment. Early in his career, Okun observed that the economy grew by about 3 percentage points as the unemployment rate was reduced by 1 percentage point. This relation, which became known as Okun's law, held for many years; numerous scholars are trying to explain why it broke down in the late 1970s. Okun emphasized repeatedly that it would be difficult to achieve the conflicting goals of high employment and price stability and spent much of his career trying to develop methods of improving the trade-off between them.

IV Fiscal and Monetary Policy. Okun believed in the efficacy of both monetary policy and fiscal policy for stabilization purposes, but he did not have any ideological preconceptions about which was the preferred instrument. He felt that the unresolved policy debates dividing the economics profession were essentially quantitative. He made considerable efforts to estimate the effect of particular policy actions on spending, saving, investment, and interest rates. He argued that economic policy should be based on an eclectic theory of macroeconomics and that to be effective, economic policy should be activist and flexible. He opposed slavish adherence to a fixed growth path for the money stock and urged instead that officials be guided by use of interest rates as well as the money supply in seeking to achieve their macroeconomic objectives.

V Economic Performance, 1960–1980. Okun was a careful observer of the economic scene, and his analysis was invariably insightful and illuminating. In examining the impact of the 1964 tax cut, he found confirmation of the effectiveness of fiscal policy in stimulating economic activity. He attributed the long and uninterrupted economic expansion of the 1960s to the active and consistent use of the tools of economic policy. He blamed the poor economic performance of 1969–1971 on the adoption of what he called a policy of "decisive inaction" and argued that monetary and fiscal actions were needed to moderate the impact on the economy of the oil shocks and other surprises in the mid- and late 1970s. In his assessment of economic performance, he concluded that countercyclical policy since the end of World War II had been on the whole successful but that insufficient attention had been paid to the problem of chronic inflation.

VI Economic Forecasting. Okun was himself an excellent forecaster. He did his work with a blend of analytical relations and judgments rather than a large-scale econometric model. He was nonetheless sympathetic to the development of models and was always ready to assist those engaged in this work. He used relatively simple but effective criteria for appraising the predictive value of economic forecasts. For example, he would compare the performance of a forecast with forecasts derived from various naive models and used the number of forecast months with the wrong sign to judge predictions of cyclical turning points. To make large-scale models more useful for analysis and policy formulation, he urged modelers to analyze the accuracy of individual equations as well as the overall performance of the models, to formalize decision rules on when to use judgment and to refit or update equations, and to make available enough information to permit others to reproduce the forecasts.

VII Economic Policy Formulation. Okun had definite views about the role of the economist and the economics profession in the policymaking process. He believed that the economist must deal with social values, assess and make judgments about trade-offs, and set priorities. Yet he also believed that the president's economic adviser, to be effective, must be sensitive to the president's aims and values and exhibit a considerable degree of loyalty, particularly in public statements. Though a presidential adviser cannot be a spokesman for the economics profession as well as the incumbent administration, Okun believed that the adviser can represent the views of the profession *within* the administration. He also believed that the public and Congress should be made aware of the profession's view when a consensus on a particular issue exists.

VIII Equality and Efficiency. Although his primary professional interest was macroeconomics, Okun wandered from this familiar turf to examine the socioeconomic trade-off between equality and efficiency. Okun saw contemporary America as a split-level society, one of equal rights but unequal incomes. He believed that this system is sensible and beneficial, but recognized that there is a trade-off between the objectives of equality and productive efficiency. Okun valued the market as a decentralizer and regarded it as an efficient economic institution, but he insisted that the results produced by the market need to be modified to protect the poor and the disadvantaged. Ideally, remedial measures would be taken to the point where the costs of inefficiency equal the benefits of equality. He believed that the shortcomings of the system could best be remedied from within the system by such means as progressive taxation, transfer payments, job programs, improved equality of opportunity, elimination of racial and sexual discrimination, and lowering barriers to access to capital. Okun was convinced that democracy and capitalism need each other "to put some reality into equality and some humanity into efficiency."

As this summary suggests, Arthur Okun was not an ivory-tower economist. He was interested in not only solving economic problems but also improving economic welfare. In *The Political Economy of Prosperity*, he explained why it is difficult to be a successful political economist: "To convey the professional view effectively requires the talents of a missionary, an outstanding pedagogue, and a supersalesman; it also takes skillful and sympathetic understanding of the opposition views and, especially, of noneconomic considerations in policy choices." Okun himself possessed these qualifications, and they enabled him to make major contributions to economic analysis and policy.

The US economy would now be better off if policymakers had paid more attention to what Arthur Okun was saying. It is still not too late to benefit from his insights and wisdom.

I INFLATION: CAUSES AND CURES

Inflation: The Problems and Prospects before Us

Like the weather, inflation is a lot easier to talk about than to do something about. My former colleague Henry Fowler and I can testify to that from personal experience. I welcome the comfortable position here on the sidelines. I wish I had better answers to the big questions about inflation. But as a private citizen I enjoy kicking them around even when I can't answer them. And perhaps I can contribute to your education by showing why easy answers are likely to be wrong answers.

What Is Inflation?

At the primer level, inflation may be defined as a condition of generally rising prices. For the United States, we rely on two general price indices as our basic measuring rods—the Consumer Price Index and the over-all deflator of gross national product (GNP). The former keeps tabs on the prices paid by a typical urban wage-earning family for its market basket of goods and services. The GNP deflator covers all newly produced goods and services—investment goods and items bought by government as well as consumption—but it excludes items which are not newly produced such as used cars and land. If inflation referred to all periods in which these yardsticks registered increases, we would conclude that inflation has been virtually constant for the past 36 years. The only years since 1933 in which both indices declined were 1938, 1939, and 1949.[1]

Clearly, that is not what we mean by inflation either in everyday parlance or in technical discussions. Rather, in our general usage, inflation is a condition of *significantly* or *substantially* rising prices. Since World War II, both measuring rods have risen less than 1.75 per cent in the following 11 years: 1949, 1950, 1953 to 1955, and 1959 through 1964.

Those are noninflationary years by general acclaim. On the other hand, both indices rose at least 2.75 per cent in 9 postwar years: 1946 through 1948, 1951, 1957, and 1966 through 1969. Everybody would call these inflationary; by American standards any rate close to 3 per cent a year is inflation. A few years fall into an intermediate category with price increases between 1.75 and 2.75 per cent, at least by one of the yardsticks: 1952, 1956, 1958, and 1965.[2]

The agreement on the semantics of inflation is understandable. The acceptance of rates of price increase up to 1.75 per cent is, in part, a compromise with realism. For the postwar period, even a very weak economy has meant a slow advance of prices at a rate of more than 1 per cent. Moreover, the tolerance is heightened by new products and new features of old products that give us more for our money even though they are not registered as declines in our price indices. You and I would not want to shop in the drug store of a decade ago—we wouldn't find our current brand of razor blades or shaving cream, or the hair spray our wives use, nor could we fill many of the prescriptions that our doctors write. Nobody knows how to quantify the amount of "bias" resulting from the omission of such elements from our price indices. But it could be as much as 1.5 per cent a year.

When prices are moving up at a 1.5 per cent annual rate, the consumer has little cause to regret that he didn't do his shopping last year. Nor will any firm hold excess inventories or accelerate scheduled investment outlays in order to beat general price increases of this magnitude. Obviously, stockpiling of particular commodities may occur, based on expected major changes in individual prices—but in a noninflationary period, commodities as a group will normally creep up even less than general price indices. In the early sixties, for example, nearly the entire increase in the general price level was attributable to services and to distribution, both areas of slow productivity gains. For industrial commodities at wholesale, prices were virtually horizontal.

If a 1.5 per cent rate of advance in prices is tolerable, then what makes 3 per cent qualitatively different? Perhaps again history conditions our normative standards; 3 per cent looks excessive because we have in fact achieved lower rates for most years. More important, 3 per cent is a big number relative to gains in productivity and to "normal" levels of nominal interest rates—at least to the levels we used to consider normal. When wage increases parallel the average economy-wide gain in productivity, a 3 per cent price rise is big enough to wipe out any gain in real income. When savings accounts and Government bonds yield 4 per cent, a 3 per cent price increase cancels most of the real return from saving. In this situation, price increases are big enough to worry about, to hedge against, and to speculate on. They become a factor in business decision making and a source of uncertainty to borrowers and lenders. Approximately the same rate of price increase that triggers price-oriented behavior by the financial and business executive also evokes the anguished cry of the housewife.

Thus inflation is a situation in which prices rise rapidly enough to become an important influence on economic welfare and decision making. Please don't press me on exactly where to draw the boundary line in the no man's land between 1.75 and 2.75 per cent.

Causes and Cures

The anonymous author who first expressed the cause of inflation as too much money chasing too few goods still holds the prize for the best simple-minded truth on this subject. When the dollar value of what the nation is trying to spend exceeds the value of our capacity output, prices are bid up. Excess demands strain our resources, normally both labor and plant capacity. The relative degree of pinch on these two main types of resources varies; in our recent inflation, labor has clearly been the bottleneck factor.

The main cause of the excessive spending may vary among inflationary periods; it can reflect a spurt in private demand or an overly expansionary fiscal-monetary policy. The inflation of the late forties was caused by the enormous buoyancy of private demand, which in turn stemmed from the shortages of goods and the build-up of liquidity that took place during the war. The last vestiges of these pent-up demands also contributed to the 1956–57 pressures on prices. On the other hand, the Korean inflation and the Vietnam inflation both resulted from mighty swings to stimulus in the Federal budget.

In a sense, of course, stabilization policy can be blamed for any inflation. Whatever the pressures, fiscal-monetary policies can head off inflation if they do their job perfectly. But that standard of perfection simply cannot be achieved in practice. Indeed, one particular stabilization tool—such as monetary policy—can get all the blame all the time for not holding the lid down on aggregate demand. But it takes a strained view of the world to attribute inflation to the failure to use the monetary brakes when private demand or the budget presses the accelerator to the floorboard. Surely, in any meaningful sense, the Federal budget was the engine of the inflation in the period from 1966 to 1968.

The basic cure for inflation is to remove or offset its cause: Cut aggregate demand by fiscal and/or monetary policy sufficiently so that money spending will no longer exceed the value of goods. History tells us that, once inflation has a firm foothold, no reduction in aggregate spending will stop prices dead in their tracks. Today's price rises reflect yesterday's increases in wages and material costs; and today's wage advances reflect yesterday's increases in the cost of living. Thus, a rise in prices develops momentum; even after the accelerator is released and a shift to the brakes is accomplished, prices continue to coast uphill for a while. Even during the severe recession of 1957–58, the momentum of cost pressures continued to push the price level upward at an inflationary rate for some time.

Apart from the lag, however, inflation is easy to cure. Every economist knows a sure and completely reliable remedy. If fiscal-monetary policy is set so tight as to create a recession, we can be assured of price stability. When markets are exceedingly weak, no businessman will dare raise his prices for fear of losing his markets, and no workers—organized or unorganized—will demand significant wage increases for fear of losing their jobs. The problem of curing inflation is difficult and challenging only because the nation will not take this decapitation cure for the headache of rising prices. We are concerned about employment, production, consumer living standards, and business investment for economic growth. It is the conflict of these objectives with the objective of price stability that gives the economist an opportunity to write papers.

It also gives the economist the obligation of telling the nation a most unhappy fact of life: If the American public insists on a better price performance than it got in 1969, it must accept some extra unemployment and some sacrifice of output and real income. Unfortunately, we must say: "Yes, Virginia, there is a trade-off between employment and price stability." Just as we'd love to make omelets without breaking eggs, so we would love to correct our current price performance with no increase in unemployment. But no one in the world has a recipe for doing that. Everything we know about the performance of our economy suggests that the 3.3 per cent unemployment rate that prevailed early in 1969 was totally inconsistent with an improving price record.

Costs of a Slowdown

Curbing inflation involves important costs. Let me offer some *illustrative* arithmetic of what "gradual disinflation" might involve, underlining that my purpose here is not to make a forecast for 1970. Suppose that we experience slow growth of output and employment and an accompanying retreat in the unemployment rate from the 3.7 per cent of the third quarter of 1969 to 4.4 per cent in the spring of 1970. Suppose we then resume growth at a stronger—but not "boomy"—pace, and thus stay at that unemployment rate. Suppose further that this pattern of economic activity successfully produces a gradual deceleration in prices. What will we have paid for this slowdown in output and incomes?

In line with historical evidence that a 1 point increase in the unemployment rate means about a 3 per cent sacrifice of real GNP,[3] a rise in the unemployment rate from 3.7 per cent to 4.4 per cent would cost us about $20 billion in the annual rate of real GNP, measured in today's prices. Obviously, that also means a $20 billion shortfall in real incomes. These costs are measured *relative* to performance along a growth path at a steady unemployment rate of 3.7 per cent; the figures do not imply that real GNP or aggregate real income would actually decline during the period. Corporate profits are particularly vulnerable incomes; while they amount to only about 10 per cent of our gross national product, they absorb about one-third of any shortfall. Thus, about $7 billion of the $20 billion cost in real income would come out of corporate profits (before tax). Owners of small businesses, farmers, and self-employed professionals would absorb a couple of billion dollars of the cost. Roughly $10 billion of the toll would be paid by recipients of wages and salaries.

The assumed increase of unemployment would amount to nearly 600,000 people. In addition, because of the reduced tightness of the labor market, about 300,000 current members of the labor force would eventually stop participating; many women, teen-agers, and older men who lose jobs and do not readily find others stop hunting for work. In addition, a decline in overtime work and an increase in part-time work would take place. All in all, the cost would exceed 1,000,000 man-years of labor. As much as one-fifth of this loss of labor time might be experienced by black workers. To be sure, many of the workers, white and black, whose job opportunities were curtailed would not be the principal breadwinners of their families. Many would experience only an extra week or two of unemployment. Even at a 4.4 per cent rate, relatively few of the jobless would suffer very long unbroken stretches of unemployment.

But the real incomes of a great many additional families would be seriously affected by unemployment. I think it's fair to say that workers are seriously affected if they suffer 5 weeks or more of unemployment during a year; that means their annual real incomes are clipped by at least 10 per cent as a result of unemployment. The number of seriously affected workers would be expected to increase by $1\frac{1}{4}$ to $1\frac{1}{2}$ million if average unemployment rose 600,000.[4] Some interesting, although highly hazardous, calculations made by Metcalf and Mooney[5] also suggest that an increase in the unemployment rate of 0.7 per cent would push about 700,000 people below the line of poverty income. It is important to look at this side of the ledger squarely and to recognize the sacrifice associated with disinflation, no matter how gradual and how well executed it may be.

Costs of Inflation

Now let me turn to the other side of the ledger. What do we get by achieving price stability?

One obvious dividend comes in our balance-of-payments position. Even though we have been inflating only slightly more rapidly than our major trading partners, the U.S. surplus on trade account has suffered enormously from the rapid growth and accelerating prices of recent years. Our trade surplus was \$5 billion in 1965; it was under \$1 billion in 1968 and has begun to improve only in the past few months. The composition of U.S. trade is such that our price performance must be better than that of our trading partners if we are merely to hold our own. To be sure, the major deterioration in our trade position in recent years has not hurt the world role of the dollar. But that result has depended on a series of strokes of good luck—like the shift of the big surplus from gold-hungry de Gaulle to dollar-happy West Germany—and a series of ingenious U.S. policy actions—including unhappy stopgaps of controls and forward-looking innovations like SDR's.

Still, the balance of payments has only limited political appeal as a rationale for price stability in the United States. To be sure, in early 1968, after the devaluation of sterling, the threat of a world financial crisis was a handy argument for Secretary Fowler and the rest of us to invoke in pleading for a program of fiscal restraint that the country needed desperately for our own good. The specter of an international financial crisis really frightened Congress; even to people who didn't know what "the downfall of the dollar" meant, it sounded a lot more serious than a few additional points on interest rates or price indices. But this episode was certainly the exception. In 1951 and 1956–57, the United States was fighting inflation because it was unacceptable at home, even though our inflation would have helped to restore world equilibrium and alleviate the dollar shortage. The gut issues about inflation are those of household finance, not world finance.

The costs on the home front are elusive. Because economists do not have good, solid ways to evaluate the costs, they are tempted either to get moralistic about price stability or else, at the other extreme, to dismiss the problem of inflation as an optical illusion. I don't have good answers either, but I pledge utmost effort neither to moralize nor to dismiss the problem. Instead, let me do some arithmetic on the domestic costs of our recent inflation, in terms of the distribution of real incomes and the impact on balance sheets. Prices in the third quarter of 1969 were about 7 per cent higher than they would have been had we followed a path of 2 per cent annual increases since mid-1965. Let us use that as a rough measure of our recent inflation. Meanwhile, total real incomes and output in the latest quarter may be guessed as roughly 1 to 2 per cent higher than if we had followed a noninflationary track.

Income Effects

It is remarkably difficult to determine who gained and who got hurt in terms of real income. The retired aged are the only major specific demographic group of Americans that I can confidently identify as income losers. Since 1964, benefits under the Federal Civil Service Retirement system have had a cost-of-living escalator providing full adjustment—but this is a rare exception. Only a very few private pension plans have any escalator provision, although benefits to retirees in some industries have been scaled up as the outcome of explicit collective bargaining agreements.

Social security retirement benefits were increased through new legislation by 13 per cent in 1968, and a further increase is slated for 1970. While these legislative actions have undoubtedly been influenced to a degree by the rate of increase of consumer prices, it is doubtful that the benefit increases and price movements have been closely correlated. The nation wished to share the current benefits of prosperity with the retired aged, and it probably would have provided nearly as large money gains (and hence larger real increases) if the price level had been more stable.

All in all, retired Americans must have lost at least 4 per cent of their real pension incomes as a result of the 7 per cent inflation. Greater job opportunities for the aged have cushioned the blow to a degree; for example, the fraction of men over 65 still working rose in 1967 and 1968 for the first time in more than a decade. But the extra labor income cannot be any more than 1 or 2 per cent of the total real incomes of the aged.

For those earning incomes from the productive process, an arithmetic identity assures that for every extra dollar that a buyer must pay as a result of price increases, an extra dollar's worth of income is generated for some seller. Thus, price increases *per se* cannot create an aggregate net gain or net loss of before-tax incomes for sellers of productive services.

For after-tax incomes, a slight qualification is in order. Price increases add more than proportionately to Federal income tax bills because of the graduated character of the tax. The income-elasticity of the Federal personal income tax is nearly 1.3—liabilities go up 1.3 per cent for each 1 per cent rise in money income. For a typical middle-income American household, Federal income taxes are about one-eighth of before-tax income. Thus, if the before-tax income of a family just keeps pace with prices, its after-tax income will lag a bit behind—it can be shown that the elasticity of after-tax income would amount to .96. An inflation totaling 7 per cent thus puts a small dent of one-fourth of 1 per cent in the real after-tax income of such a family.

Because it stepped up employment and tightened labor markets, inflationary excess demand clearly added to the aggregate real income of wage-and-salary earners. Their share of personal income expanded: total wages and salaries, net of social insurance contributions, rose 44 per cent from the second quarter of 1965 to the third quarter of 1969, while the remainder of personal income rose 40 per cent. Disposable (i.e., after-tax) personal income per capita in real terms—our best measure of the purchasing power of the average household—advanced by an unusually strong 15 per cent over the period, and real disposable wage-and-salary income per capita must have scored a slightly larger gain—perhaps 17 per cent.

The most important groups of beneficiaries were those who could gain from the availability of more jobs and steadier jobs. The shortfalls in annual incomes due to unemployment diminished. Many families got an extra paycheck from wives or teen-agers who went to work.

Substantial gains were also made by the many people who were upgraded—for example, by shifting from farm to nonfarm employment or from lower paying jobs in services to higher paying jobs in manufacturing. The tightening of the labor market also tended to narrow percentage wage-differentials between unskilled and skilled workers. In general, the reduced unemployment, greater upgrading, and narrowed differentials all tended to be especially favorable to the working poor. Those who had formerly been at the back of the hiring line generally benefited as a result of inflationary excess demand.[6]

Many middle- and upper-level wage groups also fared particularly well. Building tradesmen were one group of skilled workers with outstanding gains. Many families, however, could not benefit from the new developments in the labor market. Men who had steady jobs in 1965 and are still holding those same jobs (and whose wives have not entered the labor force) have generally been squeezed. In particular, for the average factory worker, real spendable take-home pay stagnated on a plateau after 1965 in contrast to its steady rise during the early sixties.

In light of such dispersions, it is easy to understand the current militancy of veteran union members who have been at the same job for years. It is easy to understand the causes of discontent in many quarters. The large advances of the aggregates do not tell the whole story. Higher prices have raised money incomes in a haphazard, seemingly arbitrary way. Such a reshuffling of real incomes is, in the view of most Americans, unjust—and it does not even seem to create desirable incentives to shift production or to move resources.

Moreover, the effects of inflation in raising money incomes may be less visible than the higher prices. Everybody knows that higher prices in our supermarkets and department stores are the result of inflation. When money incomes go up, however, the cause is not so obvious. When the man of the house brings home an 8 per cent wage increase, he and his wife are confident that he earned and deserved that raise. If prices subsequently go up by 4 per cent, the family is not happy with the 4 per cent gain in real income; rather it feels cheated that the wage gain was cut in half by inflation. In point of fact, of course, the husband's 8 per cent wage increase may have occurred only because of inflation. Nonetheless, nearly everybody feels that inflation leaves him with the short end of the stick. It is thus divisive and disruptive; and these social consequences are in themselves important.

At the same time, one must be careful about interpreting the public's expression of concern about inflation. We all gripe about our financial positions and our difficulties in stretching incomes to meet aspirations. When the income side of the balance is rising, complaints about difficulties of making ends meet get focused on the outgo side—on high prices. My barber was busily defending his latest price increase, noting all the higher prices he had to pay. In that list, he reported that his electric bill at home had doubled over the past year. When I commented that public utility rates hadn't increased, he replied: "You're right, but I installed central air conditioning."

Let me cite one interesting barometer of public attitudes. The University of Michigan's Survey Research Center asks people at the start of each year to evaluate their current financial situation compared to a year earlier. Recession years stick out like sore thumbs in the post-Korean record, with a peak of 31 per cent of the respondents feeling worse off both in 1954 and 1958. But inflation leaves no visible scars. The most favorable appraisals in the 1950's (23 per cent felt worse off) came in 1956 and 1957, years of high employment and rising prices. Every January-February survey since 1965—including January 1969—has yielded more favorable appraisals ("worse off" no higher than 20 per cent) than any year prior to 1965. In two interim surveys during the spring and summer of 1969 (and two in the summer and fall of 1966), however, "worse off" jumped to 25 per cent; perhaps it is the cooling off and not the heating up that creates discomfort. Despite the nagging problems of income redistribution, the American public apparently does not consider itself pressed to the financial wall when rising prices are accompanied by rapidly rising incomes.

Balance-Sheet Effects

In my judgment, the impact of inflation on balance sheets is considerably more serious than that on income statements. In the first place, inflation deprives people of the opportunity to save in a form that gives them a predictable command over future consumption goods. In a noninflationary environment, people can acquire various liquid assets, earn a reasonable return on them, and count on them as the means to acquire a basket of consumer goods in the event of especially large needs or declines in income. To be sure, they can never get a guarantee of future tuition costs, or the prospective price tag on their retirement home, or charges for large medical needs. But these risks are much less serious than those associated with general inflation.

When over-all prices are rising rapidly, their exact course is bound to be unpredictable. If we all knew that 4 per cent a year inflation would last through the next decade, nominal interest rates would probably become adjusted to levels offering a reasonable real return, and people would know how much of a consumer market basket their savings accounts could command in 1980. But there simply can't be great confidence that the price level will rise *steadily* at any substantial rate, such as 4 per cent. Only if the Government is committed to limit the rise to a creep not much above 2 per cent can there be reasonable predictability.

The opportunity for safe saving is lost in a period of sizable and unpredictable price increases. Some assets offer a degree of protection against inflation in the sense that their values are likely to move up as consumer prices rise. But no asset shows a good year-by-year correlation with prices; even corporate equities and real estate are not good anti-inflationary hedges by this test. They may actually tend to outpace the price level on the average in the long run, but only with wide swings and great uncertainty.

Our financial system ought to serve both investors who want to earn maximum returns (and are willing to take substantial risks) and holders of reasonably safe assets who view their saving largely as deferred consumption. The latter are not accommodated during inflation; we thereby lose "savers' surplus." Inflation creates in this way an unhappy division of savers into "sharpies" and "suckers," if I may borrow some nontechnical terminology. The former make sophisticated choices and often reap gains on inflation which do not seem to reflect any real contribution to economic growth. On the other hand, the unsophisticated saver who is merely preparing for the proverbial rainy day becomes a sucker.

The loss of the opportunity to hold a reliable store of value may be costly even for a person who has never suffered a real capital loss on a bond or deposit. But people have suffered substantial real losses in 1965–69 and these must be taken into account. Some have been compensated, at least in part, by higher nominal interest yields. Furthermore, most claims of Americans have their counterparts as debts of other Americans, and the changing real value is a transfer from lender to borrower. However, in the case of the $300 billion net debt of the Federal Government, the lender is made worse off with no corresponding gain on the part of the borrower, since presumably Uncle Sam doesn't really feel relieved by the reduced real value of the public debt. Our 7 per cent of inflation has lowered the real value of that debt by about $21 billion. In September 1969, the average interest rate on Federal marketable debt was about 1.7

percentage points higher than in mid-1965. Over the whole period, the compensatory rise in interest rates may have neutralized as much as half of the decline in real value, but the net loss is still a tidy sum.

Even when the losses of lenders are matched by real gains of borrowers, these do not necessarily cancel out from a social point of view. For good reasons, many borrowers do not feel much better off when the real value of their debt shrinks. Few mayors or governors have had cause to celebrate the $7 billion decline of real value on their $100 billion of outstanding debt. Many homeowners feel no exhilaration about the benefits from the declining real value of their mortgages until and unless they are selling their homes. Finally, the transfers between sharpies and suckers is a matter of concern to society. The most significant real losses are probably incurred by the sizable group of families in middle and upper-middle income brackets whose liquid assets are substantial and often not offset by large mortgages. The aged seem especially vulnerable on capital account, just as they are on income account. Except for the aged, few low-income families have large holdings of liquid assets; hence the poor are not particularly vulnerable to the loss of real value.[7]

Inflationary distortions of balance sheets have important implications for the entire financial system. The efficiency of investment in physical capital is enhanced by a system that allows investors to borrow and thus to acquire real capital beyond their net worth. But opportunities to borrow depend upon incentives to lend, and these in turn are jeopardized when the predictability of the real value of claims disappears. Our financial system shows remarkable ingenuity in a time of inflation; witness the veritable revolution of 1968–69 in the financing of apartment houses through "equity kickers," special features of mortgages that make them resemble convertible bonds. But there is no complete escape from the important negative impact of an inflationary environment on debt markets.

Lessons of the Tally Sheet

Both the costs of inflation and the costs of curing it are significant and serious. We learn to hate that trade-off and wish it would go away. Still, the concrete evidence would not warrant the prediction that another half year of inflation will turn the financial district of lower Manhattan into a desert, or that a half-point rise in the unemployment rate will generate rioting in the streets uptown. The stabilization policy choices we face are indeed important, but they don't have quite the drama that is sometimes attributed to them.

The tally sheet reveals excellent reasons why the American public will not accept inflation as a way of life. Implicitly or explicitly, the Government is obliged to set some ceiling on the tolerable rate of price increase, and it will be guided by the general agreement I noted at the outset: we tolerate rates of price increase of at least 1.5 per cent, while those approaching 3 per cent or more are considered intolerable. When we start from an inflationary position, the Government need not decide exactly where the wheel should stop. Rather it must get a deceleration of prices firmly under way, observe how the trade-off operates, and see how public attitudes respond. By testing the terrain, we can hope to come out with a socially tolerable compromise on rates of unemployment and rates of price increase.

Our policies must recognize the danger that very rapid rates of price rise may feed on themselves and accelerate over time. This danger has been highlighted in some recent research.[8] Under some assumptions about the workings of markets, the extra employment and output associated with excess total demand will either vanish ultimately or else be accompanied by accelerating prices. Assuming that society will not accept ever faster rates of price increase, it cannot maintain the bonus of output and jobs permanently. Thus, in the long run, the trade-off disappears. Given the institutional structure, society cannot opt for a maintained unemployment rate below some "natural" minimum.

This model surely has *some* relevance to the real world. Many of the beneficial side effects associated with excess demand seem to depend on surprising, cheating, and frustrating people. Once the "suckers" learn their lesson, a tendency must emerge toward accelerating prices or retreating rates of utilization. This is the fatal flaw in proposals designed to help us live with inflation by alleviating its worst redistributional effects. Tying money incomes to cost-of-living escalators, selling cost-of-living bonds, etc., might well either speed up inflation or jeopardize the bonus of output and employment. A comprehensive effort to provide insulation against inflation could prevent the cooking as well as the burning.

In my judgment, however, the nonacceleration criterion is not a dependable guide. The long run seems too long to be particularly relevant. It is apparently a matter of decades rather than years. As Milton Friedman has said, ". . . there are many examples in history when you have had several decades of generally rising prices or of generally falling prices without the price rise accelerating or the price decline turning into a collapse."[9]

All in all, the main reason to curb 4 per cent inflation is not that it may ultimately turn into 8 per cent, but rather that 4 per cent is already a source of serious distortion.

Structural Policies

The tally sheet underlines the high premium on any anti-inflationary policies which can improve the terms of the trade-off. Obviously, fiscal-monetary policies must be our main line of defense against inflation. But they can be reinforced by other measures which may ease price pressures without sacrificing growth and employment. The precise terms of the trade-off depend on our institutional framework: the intensity of competition, the mobility of resources, and their adaptability to alternative uses. These factors, in turn, are influenced by a host of decisions and developments in the private economy and by a multitude of Government policies. The Government can aid the trade-off by tailoring its manpower programs to improve the flow of jobless men into unmanned jobs; it can help break bottlenecks in particular industries like construction and health care. It can reverse policies which now add significantly to costs and prices in many areas. It would not be hard to design a legislative program that would knock a full percentage point off our price indices by restructuring a number of government programs. My candidates would include: repeal of enabling legislation for "fair trade," elimination of Government-imposed floors on rates in transportation industries, an overhaul of the oil import quota program, and a restructuring of agricultural programs which pass the cost of the subsidy to the farmer into the consumer's food bill.

Finally, a comprehensive program to achieve noninflationary prosperity should include a major effort to enlist the voluntary cooperation of large firms and labor unions with substantial market power. Prices and wages in the American economy reflect both market competition and market power. In many important areas, management and labor have a good deal of discretion over prices and wages. How they exercise that discretion can be influenced by the attitudes of the Federal Government. When at the start of the Nixon administration, the President expressed his strong opposition to the use of the jawbone, his words were interpreted as a declaration of open season for price and wage increases. That judgment was reflected in the prices of many concentrated industries (as shown in the Appendix). The price record during 1969 of gasoline, automobiles, steel, copper, and other metals has been far worse than that of 1968. The controlled experiment of 1969 gives me confidence in concluding that, even during the excess demand inflation of 1968, White House persuasion had a favorable impact on administered prices.

Once the Government began to carry out properly its job of fiscal-monetary restraint, it moved into an excellent position to ask for help from private decision makers. To capitalize on that opportunity, we need a new program of voluntary restraint. I believe the essential ingredients for such a system can be spelled out in light of the experiences—and the mistakes—of the Kennedy and Johnson administrations.

First, in seeking cooperation from private decision makers, the government must carefully ensure that its actions promote a noninflationary environment. Discipline in fiscal and monetary policy is the first requirement. The structural policies that influence prices and costs must also be in harmony. To take a notable example, the government cannot reasonably ask private workers to restrain their wage demands if the pay scales of government employees are shooting ahead.

Second, the appeal for restraint must be based on ground rules that spell out what private decision makers are being asked to do. "Drive carefully" is just not an effective substitute for a posted speed limit. Speed limits on wages and prices will inevitably share some of the imperfections of posted speed limits on the highways. They will contain an element of arbitrariness, just as a fifty-mile speed limit is arbitrary in the sense that it is not demonstrably superior to forty-nine or fifty-one. Just as a passing lane is needed on the highways, so a "passing lane" must be provided for wages and prices, allowing relative shifts over time in response to the signals of the market. Just as some speeders will escape the eyes of the traffic patrol, so some violators of the price and wage standards will not be identified. Despite their imperfections, posted speed limits on the highways serve the nation well and so can speed limits on prices and wages.

Third, the standards should be developed only after the fullest consultation with business and labor. Private interest groups should have every opportunity to express their views and to identify problems which might not otherwise be recognized. Persuasion can be most effective if it is coupled with representation.

Fourth, the one sanction essential and appropriate in a voluntary restraint program is the force of public opinion. Flagrant violations of the standards must be exposed to public scrutiny. Except for the glare of the spotlight, violators should have impunity. The one issue that may pose some difficult questions is the appropriate use of procurement, stockpiles, tax and foreign trade policies to serve the public interest of price stability.

Fifth, because many price and wage decisions are complex, some responsible and competent authority must call foul balls. But to minimize shouting matches, the umpire should be at least an arm's length away from the President of the United States—and that means farther away than his Council of Economic Advisers. In my opinion, the ideal umpire would be a small special advisory board on price and wage standards, such as Congressman Henry Reuss has proposed. Its members should be experienced in the decision process of the collective bargaining table and the top management meeting, but should not be active partisans at the time of their appointment. Some of our labor mediators and arbitrators and some of our business school deans could carry out this assignment with distinction. The group should be appointed by the President and should consult with executive agencies as well as private and congressional groups. It should be explicitly authorized to issue public statements and reports without clearing them through the administration.

I cannot be confident that such a system would function effectively. But I am confident that an experiment along these lines is worth the effort. By not trying hard enough currently, we are handicapping our efforts to reconcile prosperity and price stability. And we cannot afford even a small handicap in this vital and difficult contest.

In endorsing structural approaches, let me emphasize that mandatory controls on prices and wages do not belong on the list of acceptable remedies. Mandatory wage and price controls ensnare the market in a web of bureaucratic red tape. They ask government officials to carry out the impossible assignment of substituting for our market mechanism in making judgments about relative movements of wages and prices. They are bound to lead to bare shelves and quality deterioration, if they are really effective in holding down prices. Although controls may be popular when they are not in effect, the housewife would find that she disliked their consequences even more than rising prices. Controls were never seriously regarded as a meaningful alternative during the Johnson administration; and they aren't, I am sure, any more popular in the

Nixon administration. They deserve the total scorn and rejection informed opinion.

Obligations to the Poor

The tally sheet underlines the problems of the poor in a period of disinflation. To be sure, some of the poor have a stake in price stability: the aged, recipients of public assistance, and those few with substantial holdings of liquid assets. By any reasonable assessment of the total impact, however, these costs of inflation are swamped by the benefits to the poor of a strained labor market where a job beats a path to their door.

Let me emphasize, however, that inflation is an inefficient antipoverty program; certainly we can design better ones at less total cost to the nation. Society has a special debt to the poor to emphasize antipoverty-program efforts when the economy is being slowed down deliberately to cure inflation. Improvements in unemployment compensation benefits to the innocent victims of economic slowdown can help pay part of that debt. More generally, we need not tolerate either poverty or persistent inflation. The shame of poverty can be eliminated in ways consistent with stability for the entire economy.

The Case for Gradualism

Finally, the tally sheet supports the case for restoring price stability without destroying high-employment prosperity. Gradual disinflation was a basic commitment made by the Nixon administration at the outset, and it has maintained that position faithfully. Undoubtedly, that very commitment made the task of curbing inflation all the more difficult. When the administration first articulated its strategy, it sounded to the business community like nine parts gradualism and one part disinflation. Many observers had expected a new Republican administration to put price stability above all other economic objectives and to take significant risks of sacrificing prosperity through a massive restriction of demand. Both those who had hoped it would do this and those who had feared that it would were surprised that it didn't.

In my view, the commitment to continued prosperity has been the best news on economic policy of 1969. Even though the gradualist strategy has tested our faith and our patience at times, it has been a valuable investment. And I believe that the message is finally getting through that the U.S. Government puts equal weight on the two parts of the gradual disinflation formula.

Because of our imperfect wisdom, any policy that seeks the middle of the road runs some danger of going off the road on either side. We can't be sure that a policy of economic slowdown will in fact properly curb inflation or that it will in fact avoid recession. All we can do is balance the risks and remember the costs on both sides. It is especially difficult to balance them objectively when our memories of recession have become dim while our experiences of inflation are vivid. If over the next year unemployment were to rise to 7 per cent as it did during the 1957–58 and 1960–61 recessions, the illustrative costs of the slowdown as set forth above would have to be multiplied by nearly five: nearly $100 billion of output and real incomes; roughly $30 billion of before-tax profits; more than 3 million people pushed below the poverty line; and 6 million workers seriously affected by unemployment. By any reasonable standard, such an episode would impose far greater costs on the nation than those of the entire recent four years of inflation. It is terribly important to lick inflation without sinking into recession.

I find many analogies between accepting anti-inflation policies as a nation and going on a diet as an individual. Overeating is lots of fun and fundamentally enjoyable. Going on a diet is painful, and it brings few results in the short run. Procrastinating is never terribly serious; for the next bite will never kill you. And there is no clear-cut boundary line between normal weight and overweight. But the more we overindulge and the longer we procrastinate, the more serious the risk becomes. Once we get the message, we are tempted to go to the other extreme and adopt a starvation diet. The choices are never easy and they demand a great deal of maturity. We haven't yet demonstrated whether we have the maturity to adopt a sensible diet as a nation.

The Road to Noninflationary Prosperity

We don't know exactly how much of an economic slowdown for how long is required to cure inflation. But past experience gives us some guides and some understanding of the links between economic activity and prices.

Nonrecessionary Slowdown

Do we know that it is possible to lick inflation without taking a recession in the process? I think we do. Because we used to have recessions very frequently, we slipped into recession shortly after nearly every inflationary period. But there is simply no evidence that the recession was required to end the inflation (or that it was an inevitable consequence of the previous inflation). In the few instances when a nonrecessionary economic slowdown has been sustained for any period of time, it has significantly influenced prices and wages. To put it another way, we have never had a nonrecessionary economic slowdown which failed to produce a deceleration of prices and wages. Inflation did come to a halt in 1951–52, when the economy slowed down, and I do not believe that the mandatory controls on prices and wages were essential elements in that result.

More recently and more pertinently, the experience of 1966–67 was encouraging. In 1966, a massive dose of monetary restraint offset fiscal stimulus and halted the boom. The Consumer Price Index, which had risen at an annual rate of 4.3 per cent between January and October 1966, advanced at a much slower rate of 2.3 per cent in the next nine months. Aided by a downward correction in raw material prices, industrial wholesale prices plateaued—creeping up at an annual rate of less than 1 per cent between July 1966 and July 1967. That reversal of an inflationary price performance was achieved without a recession, without a major increase in unemployment, with only a minor and brief dip in profits. It gave us an excellent second chance to get on the track of noninflationary prosperity during the summer of 1967. That chance was booted when President Johnson's prescription for fiscal restraint was not promptly applied. It could have served as excellent preventive medicine but, by the time fiscal action was actually taken nearly a year later, the task had become cure rather than prevention. Inflation had developed great momentum and private demand had become exceptionally buoyant.

The Disappointing Record of 1968–69

Reflecting that momentum, our 1968–69 experience has been less favorable than that of 1966–67 in two ways: (1) the pace of the economy has shown less response to the dosage of fiscal and monetary restraint, and (2) our price and wage performance has responded less favorably to a slowdown in economic activity.

So far as we can now judge, consumers have curtailed their spending less and correspondingly have reduced saving more than normally in response to the 1968 tax increase. The surcharge has had less bang-for-a-buck than was to be expected on the basis of past experience. Similarly, the public has reacted to tighter money by economizing on cash balances and liquidity to a much greater extent than in 1966. For example, the path of the money supply between July 1968 and October 1969 was very similar to that in the fifteen months following mid-1965. In the 1965–66 period, the impact of tight money on economic activity was evident by April 1966 and dramatic by September. This time, private spending has been far more obstinate.

In retrospect, it is easy to judge that the dose of fiscal restraint should have been even larger in mid-1968 and that it should have been backed up immediately by monetary restraint. Still it is important to note that policy actions worked in the right direction. Economic activity did change pace when the fiscal program was enacted. GNP, which had advanced $43 billion in the first two quarters of 1968, rose $34 billion in the next two quarters. If it had advanced as rapidly in the five quarters after the enactment of the tax increase as it had in the preceding two quarters, our GNP would have been $965 billion rather than $942 billion in the third quarter of 1969. The moderation in the growth of real output was even more marked—from 6.5 per cent in the first half of 1968 to 3.5 per cent in the second half and 2.5 per cent in the first half of 1969.

Given the change of pace in economic activity, the price record of 1969 has been disappointing. With the marked slowdown in real growth, it is surprising to find an actual acceleration of prices this year. Between December 1968 and October 1969, the Consumer Price Index rose at an annual rate of 6 per cent—more than one percentage point faster than during 1968. And the GNP deflator has been moving up at a 5 per cent rate, again topping the 1968 experience by about 1 percentage point. Some of this stubbornness of prices reflects bad breaks: the huge jump in meat prices has been only remotely related to general developments in the economy; the escalation of mortgage interest rates, which gets a big weight in the Consumer Price Index, results from the monetary restraint administered to curb the boom as well as the potency of inflationary pressures.

The main element in the stubborn climb of prices and wages through most of 1969 was the enormous strength of demand for labor. After years of operating in a tight labor market, businessmen hired aggressively both to catch up and get ahead. They added far more workers to their payrolls than would have been dictated merely by shortrun needs. Between mid-1968 and mid-1969, for example, wholesale and retail trade added 600,000 employees or a 4.5 per cent rise in their work force, while the volume of real goods flowing through trade barely increased. Such personnel policies get reflected in sagging productivity, a substantial addition to unit labor costs, and continued tightness in labor markets; the result is more inflationary pressure on both prices and wages.

Employment increases slowed down markedly after mid-1969. This development points toward a relaxation of upward pressures on wages and of the upward pressure of costs on prices. As a result, I believe the deceleration of prices will become visible at long last. In the first half of 1970, we should see some improvement in our price performance—perhaps small, shaky, and spotty at first. Under no circumstances will the 1970 price record look good; but any deceleration visible to the naked eye will be a great victory. The demonstration that price increases are slowing down can make the essential difference in the expectations and attitudes of the American public. Once things get moving in the right direction, the momentum will start working for us rather than against us. Each round of price increases will reflect smaller cost increases behind them, and each round of wage increases will reflect smaller advances in the cost of living that need to be made up.

I would expect collective bargaining wage settlements to be the last to slow down, just as they were the last to speed up. A substantial acceleration of wages centered in unorganized areas in late 1965 and during 1966 before collective bargaining settlements hopped onto the inflationary bandwagon. Similarly, the wage deceleration bandwagon can get rolling before union settlements climb aboard. The balance of power at the bargaining table will ultimately reflect the economic atmosphere. More squeeze on profits and less squeeze on capacity—which means less cost of a strike—both can stiffen management resistance to inflationary wage demands.

We sometimes hear the contention that nothing short of recession will decelerate prices. That assertion rests on the view that inflationary psychology is so deeply rooted that it can be shaken out only by an upheaval in the economic environment. I have trouble following that argument, and I suspect immodestly that the fault lies in the argument rather than in me. Economists know pitifully little about how price expectations are formed and how they influence other economic decisions. We do know that private demand has been especially buoyant in the past year. No doubt price expectations must have been important in triggering off some spending decisions, particularly in construction projects where costs were moving up rapidly. But the lofty levels of market interest rates—as also affected by price expectations—should have offset much of the incentive to beat rising prices to the punch. Moreover, the behavior of inventories suggests that inflationary expectations could not have generally dominated business decision making. It is surely easier to hedge against or speculate on price rises by holding added inventories of materials and supplies than by rescheduling capital projects; yet inventory demand was geared conservatively to business needs during the boom. In any case, the key fact is that over-all demand is no longer surging ahead. Demand has been brought under control, even though inflationary psychology has not been uprooted, as far as we can tell.

Quite apart from any influence on aggregate demand, inflationary expectations could still give the nation trouble by influencing wage and price decisions. But I strongly doubt that these are based heavily on long-term forecasts. Labor's case for substantial wage hikes rests on looking backward to the cost-of-living increases of the past—not on projecting the future. Businessmen find the basis for price increases in past rises of costs and in current and near-term markets. It seems quite likely that price behavior will be less stubborn than price expectations, and that inflationary performance will improve before inflationary psychology is cured. Once prices begin to slow down, we may get extra help from the shift in psychology.

It is important to distinguish between inflationary expectations and prosperity expectations. To be sure, both may have added to aggregate demand and complicated the task of disinflation in 1969. For the long run, however, prosperity expectations are as desirable as inflationary expectations are undesirable. Confidence by businessmen, consumers, and workers in the health and strength of the American economy can contribute to our economic efficiency, and enhance the willingness to innovate and to provide the capacity for growth. Major uncertainties about economic activity add to business costs and require inefficient hedges against recession. We want the kind of economy in which Americans have justified confidence in reasonably steady and sustained growth.

The Long-Term Compromise

As I read our historical record, it supports the optimistic judgment that the gradual cure of inflation will not require a prolonged period of economic sluggishness or a major retreat in utilization rates. The American economy has already demonstrated in the sixties its capacity to support noninflationary prosperity with an unemployment rate no higher than 4.5 per cent. In July 1965, when Vietnam first became a significant economic force, the unemployment rate was 4.5 per cent. Both consumer prices and the GNP price deflator were about 1.75 per cent above their levels of a year earlier.

Labor costs were remarkably stable in both organized and unorganized areas. In the spring of 1965, unit labor costs in both the total nonfinancial corporate sector of the economy and in manufacturing were actually *below* their levels of a year earlier. Productivity advanced briskly and wage rates rose only modestly; thus unit labor costs behaved very well, even though the amount of work paid for at premium overtime rates had expanded significantly.

The average of wholesale industrial prices was within 1 per cent of its level at the beginning of 1961. It had risen 0.5 per cent during the course of 1964, mostly because of nonferrous metals prices which were pushed up by world supply problems. During the first half of 1965, industrial wholesale prices rose 0.6 per cent, with increases more widely dispersed. In manufacturing industries with rapidly rising productivity, price declines, which had previously been common, were going out of style. Yet very few large firms with market power were raising prices to widen profit margins; and there had been no further confrontation between business and Government like that in April 1962 when President Kennedy had strongly condemned an increase in steel prices.

To be sure, the price record of 1964 and the first half of 1965 was distinctly different from that of earlier years. But it had been recognized all along that the achievement of a high-employment economy would necessarily involve some retreat from the exceptional price stability of the early sixties. When the slack in resource utilization was taken up, it was no surprise to find a departure from the virtually absolute stability of industrial wholesale prices that had ruled in earlier years. The deterioration in our price performance was relatively small and readily tolerable. This was not inflation, by any standard I know.

Yet, this is a matter of some controversy: Arthur Burns has said "inflation had already taken hold and become widespread many months before Vietnam began adding appreciably to aggregate monetary demand."[10] This historical issue has critical implications for the future. If it were true that we got into the inflationary soup in 1964 when unemployment exceeded 5 per cent, it would be hard to imagine how we could now get out of that soup without retreating to a similarly high unemployment rate. That would mean doubling the illustrative figures I presented at the outset on the costs of the required slowdown.

As of mid-1965, it was my best judgment that we could continue a well-balanced advance with unemployment gradually declining further to a 4 per cent rate in 1967 with an annual rate of price increase close to 2 per cent. That looked like a tolerable and feasible compromise in the agonizing balance between growth and price stability. Unfortunately, that scenario could not be tested. The initial impact of the Vietnam escalation in the second half of 1965—both directly and through its stimulus to business investment—generated a disruptive boom. The growth rate of real output accelerated dramatically from 5.5 per cent in the first half of 1965 to 8.5 per cent in the next three quarters. This was obviously faster than anyone expected or wished. Our price performance was unhinged by the speed at which we proceeded as well as the low levels of utilization that we reached. The economy had especial difficulty adapting to the breakneck advance, running into limitations on the speed of adjustments of supply in raw materials, and limitations on the speed with which manpower training and upgrading could take place. In a smoother advance, we could have done better.

If we look beyond the immediate problem of correcting inflation, the achievement of a 4–2 combination is, I would concede, on the optimistic end of the plausible range, given our existing institutions. If, however, we reinforce an effective and disciplined fiscal-monetary policy with vigorous and courageous structural policies, I believe that combination can be made realistic—and that over time we can even improve on it. The pessimistic end of the plausible range, in my judgment, is still not a vast distance away. I would be surprised if the feasible combination over the long run proved to be worse than an unemployment rate of 4.5 per cent and a rate of price increase of 2.5 per cent.

The experience of recent years has generated excessive pessimism about the trade-off, in my view. I have been told that, in their planning models, some business and financial executives are projecting an average annual rate of price increase of 4 per cent for the whole decade of the 1970's. I would remind them of the long-term forecasts made early in the sixties which envisioned years and years of continued slow growth, sluggishness, rising unemployment, terrifying consequences of automation, stagnant investment, and sagging profits. But the nation woke up to the costs of a slack economy; and we grew and grew—sometimes not wisely, but all to well.

When the seriousness of an economic problem gets fully recognized in our political process and the nation becomes determined to solve it, we usually succeed. (To be sure, the solution may create or aggravate other problems.) The United States is now alert to the problem of reconciling reasonable price stability with high-employment prosperity. Just as the great victory of economic policy and performance of the sixties was to establish prosperity as the normal state of affairs in the American economy, I would predict that the seventies will witness a tolerable reconciliation of that prosperity with reasonable price stability.

Appendix: The Controlled Experiment of 1969

In January, 1969, President Nixon made clear his intention not to attempt to influence particular price (and wage) decisions in the private economy. This pronouncement represented a discrete shift from the policies of the Johnson administration. During 1969, a very marked acceleration of prices took place in those industries which had been responsive to Government appeals and criticism from 1966 to 1968. According to the evidence set forth below, somewhere between $\frac{1}{2}$ and 1 per cent of extra inflation in the industrial wholesale price index may be attributed to the shift in policy. Since the index of industrial wholesale prices rose 4.0 per cent during 1969 as compared with 2.5 per cent during 1968, that extra price increase represents between one-third and two-thirds of the *acceleration.*

In the table, I have listed those published components of the wholesale industrial price index which I believe were directly responsive to administration persuasion in one or more specific instances during the 1966 to 1968 period. Obviously, some judgment was required to compile that list, but inclusion or exclusion of borderline cases does not change the results appreciably. The big items—steel, copper, aluminum, petroleum, automobiles—are not on the borderline. Specific instances of White House appeals for restraint to these industries and several others are on the public record. Naturally, I was aware that 1969 price performance was not an appropriate criterion for inclusion. Nonetheless, I wish I had formulated the list (and had it notarized!) in January, 1969. For lack of a better term, I shall call these "responsive prices"—that is, responsive to White House persuasion, from 1966 to 1968.

The list of responsive prices is confined to "jawbone" cases; it excludes such items as lumber and hides where prices were influenced, in my judgment, by other structural policies. Finally, the list is limited to the

Table 1 Changes in wholesale prices of selected industrial commodities (1969 compared with prior periods)

	Relative importance[a] (per cent)	(Annual rate) per cent change[b] 1969	1966–1968	1968	1967	1966	1961–1965
Selected petroleum products							
Gasoline	2.772	3.5	−.6	−.9	−3.6	2.8	−.9
Crude	.843	4.8	1.0	.7	.9	1.2	−.1
Middle distillate	1.053	3.7	2.0	−1.3	5.9	1.6	.4
Sulfur products							
Sulfur	.104	−33.3	18.1	7.7	39.3	9.8	1.6
Sulfuric acid	.085	0	9.9	3.7	21.0	6.0	1.7
Tires and tubes	1.221	2.2	3.0	1.7	4.2	3.1	−.2
Paperboard	.669	5.0	−1.8	−2.8	−3.3	.7	−.1
Glass containers	.375	5.3	3.3	9.1	0	1.1	.6
Cigarettes	.890	6.6	3.6	1.6	5.0	4.2	.8
Newsprint, standard	.426	3.3	2.2	0	2.1	4.6	−.3
Photographic supplies	.346	3.4	2.2	2.0	5.1	−.5	.8
Passenger cars	5.818	1.9	1.2	1.2	1.9	.3	−.7
Tin cans	.301	2.7	2.3	3.0	4.1	0	2.3
Laundry equipment	.242	1.2	1.7	2.4	2.8	−.1	−1.3
Selected steel products							
Finished	4.247	6.8	1.6	2.2	1.3	1.3	.4
Semi-finished	.272	5.7	1.4	.3	2.9	1.0	.3
Selected nonferrous metals							
Aluminum ingot	.143	8.7	1.7	3.0	2.0	0	−1.2
Aluminum ingot, alloyed	.058	7.2	2.5	4.6	1.9	1.0	—
Aluminum shapes	.660	6.7	1.2	2.4	1.1	.2	−2.5
Copper wirebar	.386	24.3	5.3	10.2	5.9	0	3.7
Copper and brass shapes	.743	27.9	4.1	−4.2	5.7	11.5	3.6
Wire and cable	.809	22.2	1.7	−3.8	2.3	7.0	3.5
Listed items	22.463	6.0	1.7	1.0	1.9	2.1	0.1
All other (nonlisted) industrials	77.537	3.5	2.3	2.9	1.9	2.3	0.5
All industrials	100.0	4.0	2.2	2.5	1.9	2.2	0.4

a. Fraction of *industrial* wholesale price index in December, 1968, accounted for by commodity.
b. Year figure represents change *during* year—e.g., 1969 is period from December, 1968, to December, 1969, and 1966–1968 is thus December, 1965, to December, 1968.

product prices that were responsive in a fairly direct manner. For example, I did not include machinery made of steel, although its price is affected indirectly by steel prices.

The responsive list accounted in December, 1968, for 22.5 per cent of the total weight in the index of *industrial* wholesale prices, or 16.5 per cent of the comprehensive wholesale price index (which includes farm, food, and feed products as well as industrials). The relative importance of the listed items varies greatly—passenger cars get 100 times the weight of alloyed aluminum ingot.

From 1961 to 1965, prices of the responsive group were especially stable. Between December, 1960, and December, 1965, the index for the responsive group rose only 0.1 per cent a year, on average, while the index for all other (i.e., nonlisted) industrials crept up at an average annual rate of 0.5 per cent. No clear inference about the impact of price guideposts can be drawn directly from this differential in over-all price performance.[11] The responsive group is not a typical or random selection of industrial products in any sense; and their prices, as a group, cannot be expected to behave exactly like other industrials. During the early sixties, some of the listed products displayed exceptional productivity advances, which could account for the better price record. The appeals from the Government during the period were broad rather than pinpointed, apart from the celebrated episode of April, 1962, involving steel prices.

During the inflation of the next three years, 1966 to 1968, the price index of the responsive group rose at an annual rate of 1.7 per cent; meanwhile all other industrials advanced at an annual rate of 2.3 per cent. In each of those three years, the percentage increase of the price index of the responsive group was no more than that of all other industrials, even though demand grew especially strongly for many of the listed items. Again, the over-all differential cannot be reliably attributed to Government appeals for restraint, although several specific rollbacks and reversals of announced price increases provided evidence of some stabilizing impact.

The events of 1969 provide a much better basis for making a judgment. The distinct shift in White House posture produced a situation about as close to a controlled experiment as we are ever likely to find in observing the inherently complex relationship between private decisions on prices and the attitudes of Government officials. In light of the three—indeed eight—previous years of experience, anyone who believed that the responsive prices, as a group, had not been influenced by White House persuasion should have expected them to rise no more rapidly than other industrials in 1969.

However, during 1969, they advanced 6.0 per cent, substantially faster than the 3.5 per cent average increase of all other industrials. The acceleration of prices for the responsive group was 4.3 per cent over the average of the 1966 to 1968 period, while that for all other industrials was only 1.2 per cent. To put it another way, the index of responsive prices rose $3\frac{1}{2}$ times as rapidly during 1969 as during 1966 to 1968, while the index for other industrials increased $1\frac{1}{2}$ times as fast as previously. And the pattern of marked acceleration was widespread, extending to petroleum, steel, copper, aluminum, passenger cars, glass containers, cigarettes, newsprint, photographic supplies, and paperboard. The exceptions were sulfur products, tires, tin cans, and laundry equipment. There were exceedingly few new wage settlements that could have accounted for any acceleration. To be sure, special supply forces encouraged price rises in some areas—just as they generated a major decline in sulfur. But the pronounced and pervasive pattern cannot be reasonably explained as resulting from "bad breaks."

I have heard it conjectured that moral suasion was beginning to lose its grip in any event before the change of administration. The facts of 1968 do not fit that conjecture. During 1968, the differential between the responsive group and other industrials was especially wide: the former rose 1.0 per cent while the latter advanced 2.9 per cent. Surely, the 1968 result was atypical—benefiting particularly from price declines in important petroleum and copper products, when supply eased. But any reading of the 1968 record will reveal no emerging tendency for the price performance of the responsive group to deteriorate relative to other industrial products.

Indeed, in light of the facts of 1968, skeptics may be tempted to embrace an alternative hypothesis, which I have never heard so far. It would conjecture that 1968 was an unusually "lucky" year in the price performance of the responsive group, and that the 1969 acceleration represented an unwinding of favorable transitory factors. But on that hypothesis, the acceleration in 1969 should have been concentrated in those commodities whose price performance had been especially favorable in 1968. It was not.

I conclude that the shift in Government policy is central and crucial to the explanation of the especially large speedup of the responsive prices during 1969.[12]

It is exceedingly difficult—and yet essential—to convert this judgment into an estimate of the effect on the over-all level of industrial prices. Obviously, the issue is whether and how much over-all inflation was stimulated by the shift in policy. Paul McCracken has said: "We are concerned with restraining the average level of prices, and restraining even a significant number of individual prices and wages may not restrain the average level but may only divert inflationary pressure and make other wages and prices rise more."[13]

One can, indeed, conceive of full diversion of inflationary pressure as an extreme possibility. But I suggest that *no* diversion of inflationary pressure is a much more realistic working assumption.

First of all, *no* spillover of spending will occur unless, as a result of price restraint for some items, fewer dollars are spent on those products (and hence some part of a given total of spending is diverted elsewhere). Fewer dollars will be spent on the items with restrained prices only if either (a) the price restraint makes it unprofitable for suppliers to meet demands; or (b) demand is price-inelastic so that quantities demanded respond less than proportionately to lower prices of the listed items. Copper and sulfur were the only ones, to the best of my knowledge, which fit condition (a)—they showed excess demand at times in recent years. Elsewhere suppliers continued to meet and greet all demands for their products, indicating that prices still exceeded costs on the margin. Hence, sales and output were stimulated because prices were held down.

Cigarettes are the one item on the list where I am aware of statistical research demonstrating that (b) applies, i.e., demand is price-inelastic. It would be most hazardous to judge that the listed items have, on the average, price-inelastic demands. And only on such a judgment would there be a presumption that *any* spillover of spending occurs.

Even if some spending spilled over onto other industries, that diverted spending would add to output and employment as well as to prices in those areas, so long as firms were not operating at an absolute ceiling of their productive capacity. The full benefit of the restraint would then be split between some favorable net movement in over-all prices and some more favorable path of output and employment.

Finally and most important, any undesired spillover can, in principle, be mopped up by fiscal-monetary action. Whatever the ideal criteria for monetary policy may be in a period of gradual disinflation, an effective program of restraining some prices allows the Federal Reserve to aim for a slightly lower level of aggregate dollar spending than otherwise, without any greater sacrifice of output and employment. A selective program of restraint will generate a "trade-off dividend"; just how that dividend is divided between lower prices and more output depends on monetary-fiscal decisions.

An assessment of the over-all effect must take into account several forces which tend to magnify or multiply the direct benefits of restraint on the responsive prices. As I noted above, many industries not on my list use steel, copper, aluminum, and other responsive items as inputs; their costs, and presumably their average prices, would have been lower if the responsive prices had been restrained. Similarly, because wage increases are influenced by the cost of living, restraint on selected prices will tend to hold down average wage costs, and hence other prices. Furthermore, a policy of seeking restraint in price decisions can be accompanied by, and reinforced by, an effort to restrain wage settlements. Finally, concern with public opinion and with the public interest may exert a deterrent effect on the pricing decisions of some industries which are never identified as responsive to appeals. I am prepared to judge that, if the responsive prices had been restrained, the other industrial prices would probably have risen somewhat less than they actually did during 1969.

In summary, while I would not hazard a pinpointed estimate of the over-all cost of the policy change, I can reasonably offer a plausible lower and upper limit. To get the lower end of the range, let me suppose that, if the policy of Government persuasion had continued:

a. the nonlisted prices would not have been affected at all during 1969—even though I believe they would have been favorably affected, on balance; and

b. prices in the responsive group would have matched the pace of other industrials—even though they had consistently risen less rapidly prior to 1969.

Under those conditions, the industrial wholesale price index would have risen 3.5 per cent (rather than 4.0 per cent) during 1969, reflecting a 3.5 per cent rise of nonlisted prices (as actually occurred) and a matching 3.5 per cent advance of the responsive group (rather than 6.0 per cent).

I regard this half of a per cent as a reasonable lower limit. It seems equally plausible on the higher side that a continued policy of persuasion might have held down the rise in the industrial wholesale price index by a full percentage point; a 3.0 per cent advance would have resulted if

a. prices in the nonlisted group had increased 3.2 per cent, improving by 0.3 per cent as a result of somewhat lower material and wage costs and some deterrent influence, and
b. responsive prices had risen 2.4 per cent, maintaining their average 1966 to 1968 relationship to the increases in other industrial prices.

Whether the better estimate is 0.5 or 1.0 per cent or something in between, it represents a significant handicap in our vital national effort to achieve noninflationary prosperity. And that handicap is continuing and influencing prices and wages generally as 1970 begins.

Notes

I am indebted to William Rutledge for assisting in the research.

1. The Consumer Price Index also dipped in 1955.

2. While it is convenient and customary to rely on annual averages, such statistics may not significantly reflect new price trends within the year. This is most pronounced for 1950—price increases from the end of 1949 to the end of 1950 are clearly of inflationary size, but the annual averages for 1950 are only modestly higher than those for 1949. Likewise, as measured from the end of 1955 to the end of 1956, the year 1956 would be classed as inflationary.

3. Arthur M. Okun, "Potential GNP: Its Measurement and Significance," 1962 Proceedings of the Business and Economic Statistics Section of the American Statistical Association, pp. 98–104.

4. *Statistics on Manpower, Supplement to the Manpower Report of the President*, March 1969. These calculations are based on Table B-17, p. 47.

5. C. E. Metcalf and J. D. Mooney, "Aggregate Demand Model," unpublished working paper for the Office of Economic Opportunity, 1965.

6. For an interesting discussion of these shifts and some illuminating facts and figures, see Andrew F. Brimmer, "Inflation and Income Distribution in the United States," Paper presented to the Conference on *Input-Output, 1969*, December 2, 1969 (processed), especially pp. 13–16 and Tables 3–6.

7. See Robinson G. Hollister and John L. Palmer, "The Impact of Inflation on the Poor," University of Wisconsin, Institute for Research on Poverty—1969, pp. 40–47; and Dorothy S. Projector and Gertrude S. Weiss, "Survey of Financial Characteristics of Consumers," Federal Reserve Technical Papers—1966, especially pp. 37–41.

8. See Milton Friedman, "The Role of Monetary Policy," in *American Economic*

Review, Vol. 58 (March 1968), pp. 1–17; Edmund S. Phelps, "The New Microeconomics in Inflation and Employment Theory," in American Economic Association, *Papers and Proceedings of the Eighty-First Annual Meeting, 1968* (*American Economic Review*, Vol. 59, May 1969), pp. 147–60.

9. Milton Friedman, *Inflation: Causes and Consequences* (New York: Asia Publishing House, 1963), p. 20.

10. Arthur F. Burns, *The Business Cycle in a Changing World* (Columbia University Press for the National Bureau of Economic Research, 1969), pp. 287–88.

11. In the case of wage behavior, however, the strong evidence of a guidepost influence during the 1962–1965 period is presented by George L. Perry, "Wages and the Guideposts," *American Economic Review*, LVII (September, 1967), 897–904.

12. Of course, the especially inflationary performance of the responsive group during 1969 may not be typical of the longer run. The abandonment of the jawbone may have unloosed a particular flurry of price increases that had been contained by persuasion. That would merely demonstrate the effectiveness of the persuasion, so long as it was maintained.

13. Statement of Paul W. McCracken, Chairman, Council of Economic Advisers, before the Executive and Legislative Reorganization Subcommittee of the Committee on Government Operations, House of Representatives, September 23, 1969.

The Mirage of Steady Inflation

Developments within the economy and the profession in recent years have generated a marked swing toward pessimism in the appraisal of the tradeoff between inflation and unemployment. During the fifties and the sixties, a 4 percent unemployment rate was generally accepted as a target for full employment. At that time, it was expected that it might be accompanied by an inflation rate of 2 or, at most, 3 percent.[1] In contrast, some recent readings of the Phillips curve reported in this journal suggest that, under present circumstances, a 4 percent unemployment rate means as much as 5 percent inflation for the long run, while holding the inflation rate down to 2 percent would require an unemployment rate of $5\frac{1}{2}$ percent.[2] Some economists have responded to this unhappy news by espousing either "brake riding" or "gas pumping," as I have characterized these positions elsewhere.[3]

The brake rider would accept a higher unemployment rate. Although some brake riders have urged actions to ameliorate the adverse human and redistributive impact of unemployment, their program still involves large social costs and a significant reduction of total output and real income. Given that reduction, I find it politically unrealistic to believe that society will become even more generous in compensating the victims of economic adversity. Moreover, I believe—admittedly without strong empirical evidence—that firm labor markets have a significant catalytic value in breaking down arbitrary hiring standards, opening avenues to promotion and career ladders, and generating valuable on-the-job training for low-skilled workers. Hence I cannot accept the brake-riding strategy, in general,[4] and reject it in particular as a rationale for inaction at a time when the unemployment rate is 6 percent.

The gas pumper, on the other hand, would tolerate the higher rate of inflation that now seems required in order to achieve full employment. I am tempted by that argument, and for that very reason wish to spell out some reservations. The case for tolerating a high rate of inflation that I shall characterize—and try not to caricature—is really part of an oral tradition that has gained momentum, along with inflation itself, during the past five years. It has been presented to me most often across the luncheon table, sometimes as an argument for strongly stimulative fiscal-monetary policies but more often as a brief against the need to develop wage-price policies. Only in 1971 has the thesis been advanced in sophisticated fashion by professional economists writing in a policy-oriented context.[5]

The Welfare Economics of Inflation

Brake riders and gas pumpers agree that significant social costs and distortions are created by an inflation that develops out of a tranquil environment of price stability. In the short run, nearly all recipients of pensions, interest, and rents; most salaried employees; and many wage earners are essentially on fixed incomes. Thus sudden inflation redistributes income in inequitable and inefficient ways. It also impacts strongly on balance sheets, reducing liquid wealth in real value and enhancing leveraged portfolios containing real assets partially offset by debt.[6]

Similarly, a highly variable and uncertain state of price movement imposes significant costs by exposing individuals to large risks with respect to the value of their wealth and their incomes. In a defensive response to these risks, people may take the very steps most costly in a period of inflation—adding to their holdings of liquid assets and forgoing the purchase of goods in order to hedge against possible failure of their incomes and wealth to keep pace with the price level.[7]

The gas pumper stresses that these social costs stem from potential or actual *acceleration* of the price level. If, however, a steady rate of price increase were maintained year after year, the seriousness of these costs would diminish. Nominal interest rates would ultimately reflect the pace of inflation; salaries and other sticky incomes and the entire institutional framework would be increasingly adjusted.

The gas pumper concedes that even a perfectly steady, fully anticipated, and completely reliable rate of inflation would impair the use of the pecuniary yardstick in cost and income calculations; it might exacerbate balance-of-payments problems in a world of fixed exchange rates; and it would add to the cost of economizing on cash balances. At extremely high rates of inflation, the high real cost of holding cash can destroy a money economy. But at completely steady inflation rates of 5 or even 10 percent a year, the toll of social costs would amount to a minor annoyance rather than a major disaster. A predictably steady inflation rate of 5 percent is not significantly inferior to a rate of 2 percent; and if it permits the unemployment rate to be lower by as much as $1\frac{1}{2}$ points, the 5 percent inflation rate seems a small price to pay. And even if it yielded no *permanent* reduction in unemployment, as an "accelerationist" would contend, acceptance of inflation near the current rate of 5 percent would save the nation from the needless agony of the prolonged transition period of high unemployment required to wind down the inflation rate.[8]

Public Policy and Inflationary Expectations

I agree that, if there were such an economic state as steady, fully anticipated inflation, it would impose only minor social costs. But I would emphasize that such a state has never existed and can never be attained. The adoption of a public policy designed to yield steady, fully anticipated inflation would commit the government to an impossible goal. Economic policy making is a highly imperfect art and it cannot produce steady inflation any more than it can produce steady unemployment or a steady price level. Moreover, the very acceptance by government of a higher, though hopefully steady, inflation rate would influence expectations in such a way as to make prices rise more rapidly and less steadily. In short, the case for accepting steady inflation fails to recognize both the imperfect capability of public policy and its influence on price expectations.

Pathetically little is known about how people form their expectations about the variability and the trend of future inflation. Nonetheless, it seems reasonable to assume that (1) what the government does (and says) about inflation is one important influence on the inflationary expectations of the private sector; and (2) an increase in expected inflation has *some* tendency to worsen the tradeoff and thus make a higher rate of actual inflation accompany any given unemployment rate.[9]

The words and deeds of policy makers reveal that they believe the first proposition. Whenever inflation is a threat or reality, the nation is flooded by vigorous and highly moralistic official pronouncements excoriating inflation and expressing determination to defeat it. These verbal efforts are far more energetic than any devoted to "talking up" aggregate demand in a slump through bright forecasts or diagnoses of prosperity.

It is also rather striking that American presidents have been willing to specify 4 percent as a target rate of unemployment, thus expressly indicating that they would tolerate that much of that bad thing; on the other hand, so far as I know, no U.S. administration has ever explicitly defined its level of tolerance for inflation. At least in part, this asymmetry seems to reflect concern that a display of equanimity about any degree of price increase would encourage expectations of inflation. Hence, the government is not willing to concede publicly even the first point or two on the inflation rate. Apparently, a "credible neurosis" about inflation is expected to ease the stabilization task by holding down inflationary expectations. In recent years, this posture has become less and less credible—nobody could believe that the government would wage a battle for unconditional surrender of inflation without any regard to the high and lasting toll of unemployment that such a battle would levy.

But neither has anyone had reason to believe that the government would accept a sustained inflation rate as high as 5 percent. Whatever the extent of inflationary expectations embodied in the recent tradeoff (prior to August 15), it could not have assumed that much tolerance for inflation. If, instead of the program he announced, the President had told the nation on August 15 that he was now prepared to accept 5 percent inflation, surely his statement would have been followed by a most dismal day in the bond market.

Moreover, once the government's strategy raises the expected inflation rate, the second proposition above becomes operative, and the tradeoff is worsened. If the statistically estimated Phillips curves are right and 5 percent inflation was required to achieve full employment when the government was expected to battle against that much inflation, then a somewhat higher rate would be required when it became clear that the government had decided to tolerate 5 percent inflation.

Moreover, the change in the target of public policy is bound to raise questions about how the government will respond when the inflation rate goes above target. The one safe forecast about the inflation rate is that it will fluctuate; and the government's response to unforeseen inflationary spurts is subject to uncertainty and indeed to warranted suspicion. The historical record illustrates the political difficulties of invoking restrictive measures when unanticipated excess demand emerges from either a spurt in private spending or, more often, from prior decisions of government made for military or other nonstabilization purposes. In such a case, the required medicine is very unpleasant—squeezing credit, raising interest rates, hiking taxes, or cutting back public services. The basic social question is whose demand should be cut, and the answer is bound to be politically painful. Hence, it is tempting to let inflation make the decision.

Because such tendencies to escape hard choices appeared historically and were recognized, countervailing taboos and myths developed, such as the balance-of-payments and balanced budget disciplines. These were poor safeguards for a democratic society, first and foremost because they misled the public, and also because they were applied unwisely, sometimes, as in 1958–63, swinging the balance too far. On the other hand, the built-in tendencies toward political paralysis in anti-inflationary policy were demonstrated anew in 1965–68. The stabilization choices of that period did not reflect anybody's wish to operate the economy at such high pressure; rather, they revealed the impotence of the fiscal decision process in allocating the costs of Vietnam. Who paid for the war was determined by the marketplace through an inflation that had uneven effects on the purchasing power of income and wealth for various individuals. The extra output and employment that resulted constituted a slight, undesired, and almost irrelevant consolation prize for the temporary breakdown of the democratic process.

Fortunately, the nation does not get frequent readings on the response of public policy to major inflationary surprises, and we can hope that such instances will be even rarer in the future. But the very infrequency may make the government response particularly influential on long-run expectations about future responses. Those in the fifties and the sixties who espoused a 4 percent target for the unemployment rate did not expect an accompanying inflation rate as high as 5 percent. Indeed, many would have thought that 3 percent unemployment could be achieved by accepting that much inflation and yet found that alternative less attractive. A willingness to take 5 percent inflation now that the tradeoff seems less favorable would indicate that the social preference function had been made of Jello.

Would not such a shift in policy have to be read as indicative of future action? Can a government that shifts its inflation tolerance level from 2 to 5 percent convince anyone that it will vigorously combat 8 percent inflation in the event of unforeseen excess demand or another unfavorable surprise in the Phillips curve? Of course, the next surprise may be a favorable one and perhaps it will right the balance. But perhaps that opportunity will be used to shoot for lower unemployment and to carve up the resulting fiscal dividend. There are grounds for suspicion that the government's strategy is asymmetrical and will let the inflation rate accelerate over the long run, even though no accelerationist mechanism exists in the private economy. If my introspection has any resemblance to the way the public would react, then a decision to live with inflation would trigger off expectations of larger and more variable rates of price increase. That consideration need not be decisive, but neither should it be ignored.

Cushions against Inflation

The adjustments of a steady, fully anticipated inflation that are predicted by comforting analytical theorems have little resemblance to the actual experience of the recent inflationary period. Even after three years of fairly steady inflation at a rate close to 5 percent, the U.S. economy is nowhere in sight of fully anticipated inflation. One of the defining characteristics of such a state, as R. J. Gordon points out below, is that holders of bonds would be fully protected against inflation. In fact, the bond market has undergone enormous, virtually unprecedented fluctuations from the summer of 1970 to that of 1971. How much of the big swings represents a change in inflation premiums and how much a change in real interest rates is impossible to determine. But the bond holder is clearly not protected against inflation or anything else when the new issue yield on prime corporate bonds is riding a roller coaster between 9.4 percent and 6.8 percent. Another characteristic of steady, fully anticipated inflation is that holders of equities are assured of capital gains; but a characteristic of the past six years of inflation is the disappearance of such gains. Interest rates on thrift accounts have barely moved upward in response to inflation, partly—but only partly—because of federal controls. Life insurance premiums have not readily adjusted. The property tax and specific excise systems of state and local governments have not been reformed. Private pensions have shown very little adjustment.

Because the dollar is a standard that is embedded in our institutions, protection against inflation develops only very slowly in response to the natural forces of a real-world inflation. Hence any serious program of living with inflation should include public policy action to provide increased cost-of-living protection, as Tobin and Ross have espoused.[10] Once the government issues cost-of-living escalated bonds, private financial institutions can hold these assets as a hedge; and they, in turn, can make promises to pay in "real" terms. Only when such assets are readily available can individuals who worry about inflation be assured of the means to protect their wealth.

Nonetheless, a number of caveats must be registered about the introduction of cost-of-living cushions into bonds, pay, or pensions. First, the announcement of such government-sponsored innovations may be read as evidence that the government has raised its tolerance level of inflation or perhaps even given up the fight against inflation. This announcement effect is hard to appraise and perhaps easy to exaggerate. By analogy, one could argue that seatbelts will make drivers careless and hence frighten, rather than reassure, passengers. But the announcement effect is bound to be somewhat adverse. Second, it is quite rational to expect that the more effectively the government can minimize the social costs of inflation, the more inflation it will accept. If inflation becomes relatively less costly, the unemployment target "should" be shifted downward and the inflation tolerance level upward.[11] As a result, the more effective the cushions look, the more they are likely to raise the expected inflation rate.

Third, the proposed federal cushions against inflation would be automatic destabilizers, in contrast with cushions against unemployment, which have favorable aggregate effects as well as favorable distributive effects. Insulating the victims of unemployment from some of the impact of lower earned income bolsters aggregate demand in a slump and thereby serves as an automatic stabilizer. Insulating the victims of inflation against its costs raises their ability to command goods and services during a boom and is thus destabilizing. To the extent that cost-of-living escalators in government pay, social security benefits, and bonds swell federal outlays in inflation, the fiscal system is saddled with an automatic destabilizing element. Or, to put it another way, to the extent that reductions in the real value of liquid assets or of disposable income help to restrain private expenditures during an inflationary boom, this automatic stabilizer of the private economy is impaired by cost-of-living protection. The cushion against inflation for the individual becomes a spur to inflation for the society.

More generally, to the extent that cost-of-living escalation becomes a feature of the economic system, any development of excess demand is transmitted into costs and prices more rapidly—the lags that sometimes save us from intense inflation are shortened. Where stabilization and equity objectives conflict, the stabilization objectives are not overriding.

A nation with cost-of-living protection may be a better society, but it also tends to be a more inflationary society. Moreover, that prospect is likely to be read properly by the public when the institutions are introduced.

Inflation in a Stop-Go World

Western industrialized countries have not really faced up squarely to the tradeoff problem. Rather than aiming at some feasible combination of utilization and inflation rates, nations have tended to operate a more adaptive type of stabilization policy. While demand management has been normally conducive to growth and economic expansion, the brakes have been applied whenever inflation seemed to be a more serious problem (in domestic or balance-of-payments terms) than idle resources. Such fiscal-monetary "stop" have produced the characteristic stop-go pattern of the economic time series in Western nations.

The stop-go pattern can be roughly approximated by the following model: A vehicle is traveling along a road that contains substantial and uneven amounts of bumpiness as well as some uphill and downhill stretches. The vehicle has a single forward setting on its throttle and is equipped with brakes. The driver cares about both speed and bumpiness. The faster he travels over any bump, the more discomfort he feels; and he can reduce the impact by applying the brakes. A driver who is relatively sensitive to the discomfort of the bumps (compared with the benefits of speed) will make more use of his brakes, thus holding down "bump discomfort" but also, of course, sacrificing speed. A driver who cares relatively less about bumpiness and relatively more about speed will obviously average greater speed and greater bumpiness. But, a little less obviously, the bumpiness of his ride will also be more variable. Like the other driver, he will have some fairly smooth stretches, but he will tolerate greater bumpiness before moving to the brakes. In a sense, he applies a more permissive quality control standard in deciding whether to accept or reject a given amount of bumpiness. That raises not only the average, but also the variability.

If speed represents economic expansion and growth, while bumpiness is interpreted as inflation, and if the driver is identified as the maker of fiscal, monetary, and wage-price policies, this model suggests that countries with high inflation rates would also experience more variable inflation rates. I formulated that hypothesis before looking at time series data on industrialized countries, and the data confirmed my conjecture. In

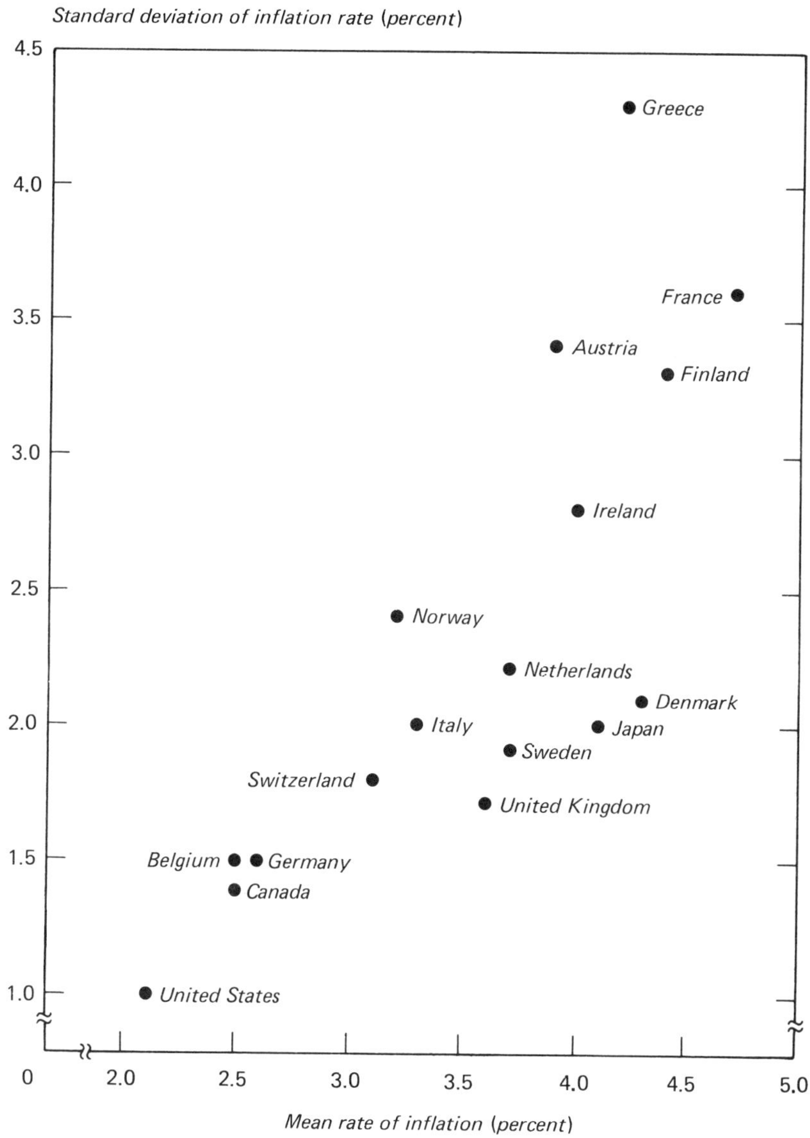

Source: Derived from data in Organisation for Economic Co-operation and Development, *National Accounts Statistics, 1950–1968* (Paris: OECD), pp. 366–415.

Figure 1 Average and variability of percentage changes of GNP deflators, seventeen OECD countries, 1951–68.

the period covered by data from the Organisation for Economic Co-operation and Development for most industrial countries (1951–68), those with high average rates of inflation have had more widely fluctuating rates from year to year. This finding is shown in Figure 1, which uses, as the measure of variability for each country, the standard deviation of the annual increase in the GNP deflator from the average rate of increase. During that period, the United States had the lowest average inflation rate—2.1 percent, and also the lowest standard deviation of annual changes—1.0 percent. The other three countries with average inflation rates below 3 percent (Belgium, Germany, and Canada) had standard deviations of about $1\frac{1}{2}$ percent. For any country with an inflation rate above 3 percent, however, the lowest standard deviation was 1.7 percent.

A number of mechanisms other than the particular model set forth above could account for this relationship. For example, suppose simply that countries are equally able to control the time-path of money GNP within some given percentage range; for those operating in the steep, high-inflation part of the Phillips curve, more of the variation in money GNP would take the form of unsteady price movements, while for those in the low and flat end of the Phillips curve, there would be less variability in prices (and more in real output). Whatever the explanation, however, if the United States were to accept a higher inflation rate, Americans would have an excellent basis from world experience to expect a more variable inflation rate in the future.

It would be interesting to inspect the other side of the coin to determine whether the nations that have tolerated more rapid and more variable inflation have, in fact, been more successful in economic expansion and utilization. But I see no way to get that information out of the time series data. While rates of price increase are reasonably comparable among nations, unemployment rates are not. And while average real growth rates for the longer run tell us much about the supply side of various economies, they do not illuminate the record of demand management: Fiscal-monetary strategy surely is not the source of the difference between the 10 percent growth rate of Japan and the 3 percent growth rate of the United Kingdom.

There may be some interest in the relationship between the variability of the inflation rate and the variability of the growth rate, country by country. If fluctuations in the inflation rate are caused primarily by changes in private demand moving along a given Phillips curve (the

Table 1 Annual percentage changes in real gross national product and GNP implicit price deflators, most industrialized OECD countries, 1951–68[a]

	Real GNP			GNP deflator		
Country	Average	Standard deviation	Mean deviation	Average	Standard deviation	Mean deviation
Canada	4.5	3.0	2.5	2.5	1.4	1.1
United States	3.7	2.5	2.1	2.1	1.0	0.8
Japan[b]	9.6	3.6	3.0	4.1	2.0	1.4
Austria	4.8	2.7	1.9	3.9	3.4	1.9
Belgium[c]	3.7	1.9	1.3	2.5	1.5	1.4
Denmark	4.1	2.3	2.0	4.3	2.1	1.7
Finland	4.3	3.2	2.7	4.4	3.3	2.8
France	4.9	1.5	1.1	4.7	3.6	2.5
Germany	6.0	2.7	2.1	2.6	1.5	1.2
Greece	6.4	3.3	2.6	4.2	4.3	3.1
Ireland[d]	2.4	2.0	1.7	4.0	2.8	2.1
Italy	5.6	1.3	1.1	3.3	2.0	1.4
Netherlands	5.0	2.4	2.1	3.7	2.2	1.5
Norway[d]	4.1	1.5	1.2	3.2	2.4	1.6
Sweden	4.1	1.4	1.2	3.7	1.9	1.5
Switzerland	4.2	2.3	1.7	3.1	1.8	1.5
United Kingdom	2.8	1.6	1.2	3.6	1.7	1.3

Source: Derived from data in Organisation for Economic Co-operation and Development, *National Accounts Statistics, 1950–1968* (Paris: OECD), pp. 366–415.

a. Data on the following OECD countries are not included either because the observations on the GNP deflator were extreme or because data were unavailable for a substantial part of the period. The three values for the GNP deflator—average, standard deviation, and mean deviation—are, respectively:

Luxembourg (1960–67)	2.7	2.5	2.0
Iceland	9.4	4.7	3.5
Portugal (1956–68)	2.3	1.7	1.4
Spain (1958–68)	5.4	2.9	2.1
Turkey	7.9	5.3	4.2

b. Data are for 1952–68.

c. Data are for 1953–68.

d. Data are for 1951–67.

equivalent of changes in speed over uphill and downhill stretches of the road), countries that tolerate wider swings in the inflation rate should also be found to experience wider swings in utilization. If, on the other hand, the primary source of fluctuation stems from shifts in the Phillips curve (the equivalent of changes in bumpiness along the road), countries that held down and stabilized the inflation rate would experience greater variability in real growth. As Table 1 suggests, the relationship is weak in the aggregate.[12] But some interesting pair-wise comparisons emerge. The three large countries with the steadiest and lowest inflation rates—the United States, Canada, and Germany—all have above-average variability in real growth. In contrast to those three countries, France and Italy have greater stability of real growth, while their inflation rates are substantially higher in speed and variability. Basically, the results confirm casual observations that the United States and Germany have really cared about inflation—enough to stabilize its rate as well as to hold it down. On the other hand, countries such as France and Italy that have cared less about inflation have neither held it down nor stabilized it, but have done a better job of stabilizing real growth. The United States has been extreme in its performance and its indicated preference, seeming to stress a low and stable inflation rate far more (and a high and stable utilization rate far less) than do other countries.

Conclusion

The discussion above leads to the following qualitative conclusions:

1. The government's attitude toward inflation is one determinant of price expectations. A softening of that attitude, revealed in word and deed, is likely to have *some* adverse effect on the tradeoff. Thus, in accepting any given increase in the inflation rate as a price of achieving full employment, the government is likely to find that the actual required increase is somewhat greater than that initially indicated.
2. The variability of inflation over time depends particularly upon the ability and determination of public policy to apply corrective measures when the inflation rate exceeds acceptable limits. Both the historical record of industrial nations and analytical reasoning about the political process suggest that toleration of a higher inflation rate would mean less steady inflation.
3. The same reasoning that would argue for more toleration of inflation in 1971 than in 1965 would point toward acceptance of a still higher

inflation rate the next time a similar unfavorable surprise is encountered. And there are reasons to doubt that the response to a favorable surprise would be symmetrical. Hence, adoption of such a strategy would create *some* presumption of a long-run trend toward accelerating inflation, purely as a result of public policy.

There is no easy solution to the nation's agonizing tradeoff problem. Painless inflation is as much a mirage as painless unemployment. A painless favorable shift of the Phillips curve would also offer only an illusion. But that route deserves a real try through structural reforms, manpower policies, and effective government wage-price policies. The recognition that government policies affect inflationary expectations puts a particular premium on the development of an effective incomes policy in a period of slack demand, for such a policy would demonstrate that the nation will not blithely accept cost-push inflation.

The failure of prices and wages to decelerate in 1970–71 cannot be reconciled with any notion that competitive market forces prevail in determining the price level. Nor would inflation at an unemployment rate of 4 percent be attributable to widespread excess demand in the sense that most firms would refuse to take and fill more orders at existing prices, or would be unable to get more workers at the going wage. If 4 percent unemployment would be accompanied by 5 percent inflation, some strong inflationary biases must contaminate the process of price-wage determination. A fuller understanding of these biases and a determined policy effort to eliminate them would seem to be top priority for the profession and the nation.

Let me say, finally and unequivocally, that I attach no particular virtue to our past attitudes about the tradeoff. If the tradeoff issue were posed on its merits clearly to the American people, it would neither surprise nor pain me if the resulting choice favored a higher, probably more variable, and even possibly accelerating inflation rate accompanied by better, though highly imperfect, cost-of-living protection for their assets and incomes. And I would expect the nation wisely to reject high unemployment, recognizing it as a far greater evil than inflation. But Americans should not be promised a steady and painless inflation, a new mirage offered in place of old myths about the safeguards of balanced budgets and balanced international accounts. The really big issue is the credibility of government, and that issue is at least as important as jobs and prices to the future of our democratic society.

Notes

1. See, for example, the estimates in Paul A. Samuelson and Robert M. Solow, "Analytical Aspects of Anti-Inflation Policy," in American Economic Association, *Papers and Proceedings of the Seventy-second Annual Meeting, 1959* (*American Economic Review*, Vol. 50, May 1960), p. 192.

2. George L. Perry, "Changing Labor Markets and Inflation" (3:1970), pp. 411–41; and Robert J. Gordon, "Inflation in Recession and Recovery" (1:1971), pp. 105–58.

3. Arthur M. Okun, "The Game Plan of Stop and Go," *Business Economics*, Vol. 6 (May 1971), pp. 16–20.

4. See the discussion in *ibid.*

5. James Tobin and Leonard Ross, "Living with Inflation," *New York Review of Books*, Vol. 16 (May 6, 1971), pp. 23–26; and Robert J. Gordon, "Steady Inflation: An Exaggerated Menace," in *The 1971 Midyear Review of the Economy*, Hearings before the Joint Economic Committee, 92 Cong. 1 sess. (1971, forthcoming). Two earlier analytical expressions of this point of view were William S. Vickrey, "Stability through Inflation," in Kenneth K. Kurihara (ed.), *Post-Keynesian Economics* (Rutgers University Press, 1954), pp. 89–122, and Edmund S. Phelps, "Anticipated Inflation and Economic Welfare," *Journal of Political Economy*, Vol. 73 (February 1965), pp. 1–13.

6. See the discussion in Arthur M. Okun, "Inflation: The Problems and Prospects before Us," in Arthur M. Okun and others, *Inflation: The Problems It Creates and the Policies It Requires*, Charles C. Moskowitz Lectures, No. 10 (New York University Press, 1970), pp. 12–25.

7. George Katona, "The Impact of Inflation on Consumer Attitudes and Behavior," *Conference Board Record*, Vol. 8 (March 1971), pp. 48–51.

8. The accelerationist view that steady inflation can do the economy no harm—as well as no good—is developed by Edmund S. Phelps, "Unreasonable Price Stability—The Pyrrhic Victory over Inflation," in Arthur M. Okun (ed.), *The Battle Against Unemployment* (rev. ed., Norton, forthcoming).

9. This qualitative proposition does not imply the existence of any equilibrative mechanism that equates actual and expected rates of price increase. Indeed, in my view, models that invoke such a mechanism do not offer useful insights into the real world.

10. Tobin and Ross, "Living with Inflation."

11. That result would be avoided if cushions against unemployment are improved in parallel so that the relative costs of moving along a given tradeoff locus are unchanged.

12. The correlation coefficient between the two standard deviations is 0.18, while that between the two variables in Figure 1 is 0.78.

The Great Stagflation Swamp

I classify my after-dinner speeches as either indigestion talks or dessert talks. I warn you in advance that this is an indigestion talk. Actually, I much prefer spreading cheer than gloom; and I can be honestly cheerful about the short-term outlook. The slowdown that the economy has been experiencing is probably no more than a slight dent in our growth curve. Consumer spending got ahead of itself during the early months of this year, and it has been marking time more recently; businesses have reacted by slowing the building of their inventories. Meanwhile, the evidence on business spending for fixed investment has brightened considerably; capital spending is now firmly aboard the recovery bandwagon. In my judgment, the expansion still has a good deal of vigor and a substantial life expectancy.

I expect the Carter administration to unveil a program of tax reform and tax reduction that will, on balance, buoy the expectations of investors and consumers in the short run and their incentives and purchasing power in the longer run. In the closing months of 1977, and during the first half of 1978, I expect some renewed reduction in unemployment and a stronger pattern of business activity.

If I spelled out that short-term story in detail for my address tonight, I might even persuade you and send you home happier. But I could do that only by ducking the longer-term outlook, which I regard as distinctly less favorable. The big issue—the $2 trillion question—is whether we are now traveling a road to sustainable prosperity accompanied by reasonable stability of the price level. In my judgment, the current strategy of economic policy probably does *not* lead to a happy ending. And that is why I believe we should not rely on simply more of that same strategy. As I see it, my message is a call for action rather than a forecast of gloom. I have some proposed remedies for the ills, and I will discuss them in detail. But I must warn you that the medicines are not pleasant-tasting, and that they are unconventional and unproven. I hope that my remarks will be thought-provoking and challenging; but, after this initial full disclosure, I shall not be surprised if some of you head for the exits.

Problems and Prospects

In 1977, the United States will record a higher unemployment rate and a higher inflation rate than was experienced in any year between 1952 and 1972. We have not licked either of these two major problems; indeed, they have become intertwined and combined in a way that is historically unprecedented, and, by the verdict of many economics textbooks, theoretically impossible. This nation has had serious inflation problems before; it has had prolonged periods of excess capacity and idle manpower before; but it has never previously faced a serious inflation problem after a prolonged period of slack.

The coexistence of stagnation and inflation or, as it has been dubbed, "stagflation," is a new problem. Yet we are handling it with old policies that are unlikely to solve it. The Carter administration—in this respect, like the Ford administration—is trying through traditional fiscal-monetary measures, to attain both a sustained gradual recovery to full prosperity and a sustained gradual slowdown of inflation.

That strategy is not succeeding. The modest recovery targets have been attained reasonably well over the past two and a half years; the economic expansion has been a rather typical, standard-sized advance. But because the recession that preceded it was double-sized, it has brought us only halfway back to prosperity. Thus, we have paid heavily to keep our recovery moderate, and we have no relief from inflation during the expansion to show for these efforts.

The basic inflation rate has been stuck at 6 percent since the spring of 1975. Nor is there any basis for confidence that relief is forthcoming. Indeed, in my judgment, the inflation rate is more likely to accelerate than decelerate between now and 1979, even with a continuation of a slowly recovering economy. And, once it becomes undeniable that the gradualist anti-inflation strategy has failed, I fear that monetary and fiscal policy will be tightened anew to restrain the growth of the economy, thereby courting the next recession.

In my view, a serious effort to deal with inflation and slack simultaneously must go beyond traditional fiscal-monetary policies. It must invoke specific measures to hold down prices and costs in both the private and public sectors. It must break the wage-price spiral that has so firmly and stubbornly gripped the system. I believe that a number of techniques in pursuit of those objectives deserve serious consideration. Let me state emphatically that the worthy candidates do not include a return to price-wage controls, such as the Nixon administration conducted in 1971–73.

Getting Stuck in the Swamp

As an autobiographical obligation, I must record that the most recent unhappy era of our economic history began late in 1965, while I served as an adviser to President Johnson. That is when the critical decisions were made to finance the Vietnam military buildup in an inappropriate inflationary manner. But the historical record will not support any "original-sin" explanation of inflation that would attribute our ills of a dozen years to that mistake. Every wartime period in U.S. history has been marked by a severe inflation; indeed, the Vietnam episode was the least severe. But the end of every previous war was marked by the end of inflation.

The unique experience of the seventies is that the end of the war was associated with an intensification of inflation. The double-digit inflation of 1973–74 was the product of many new mistakes and misfortunes: excessive monetary and fiscal stimulus in 1972, the devaluation of the dollar, the mismanagement of U.S. grain supplies, and the OPEC shock to energy prices.

Responding to that riproaring inflation, the makers of monetary and fiscal policy adopted extremely restrictive measures that brought on the most severe recession since the late thirties. That recession promptly cut the inflation rate to about 6 percent by the middle of 1975. But there we have been ever since, despite massive excess supplies of idle people, machines, and plants. If our economic institutions responded currently to a slump as they did in 1922 or 1938 or 1949, the recession and prolonged slack would not only have stopped inflation in its tracks but created a wave of falling prices.

In fact, the nature of price- and wage-making has been transformed in the modern era. We live in a world dominated by cost-oriented prices and equity-oriented wages. The standard textbook view of prices adjusting promptly to equate supply and demand applies only to that small sector of the U.S. economy in which products are traded in organized auction markets. And there it works beautifully—the prices of sensitive industrial raw materials *fell* by 15 percent between May 1974 and March 1975.

Elsewhere, however, prices are set by sellers whose principal focus is on maintaining customers and market share for the long run. The pricing policies designed to treat customers reasonably and maintain their loyalty in good times and bad times rely heavily on marking up some standard measure of costs. For most products, prices do not rise faster than standard costs during booms nor do they rise less rapidly than costs during slumps.

Similarly, the long-term interest of skilled workers and employers in maintaining their relationships is the key to wage decisions in both union and nonunion situations. The U.S. labor market does not resemble the Marxist model in which employers point to a long line of applicants ("the reserve army of unemployed") and tell their current workers to take a wage cut or find themselves replaced. Employers have investments in a trained, reliable, and loyal work force. They know that if they curbed wages stringently in a slump, they would pay heavily for that strategy with swollen quit rates during the next period of prosperity. In a few areas, where jobs have high turnover and thus employers and employees have little stake in lasting relationships, wages do respond sensitively to the level of unemployment. But, in most areas, personnel policies are sensibly geared to the long run. Workers seek and generally obtain equitable treatment; and the basic test of equity is that their pay is raised in line with the pay increases of other workers in similar situations. Such a strategy introduces inertia in the rate of wage increase; it creates a pattern of wages following wages.

The customer and career relationships that desensitize prices and wages from the short-run pressure of excess supplies and demands have a genuine social function. They are not creations of evil monopolies but rather adaptations to a complex, interdependent economy in which customers and suppliers, workers and employers benefit greatly from ongoing relationships. In general, the persistence of inflation is not a tale of villainy. By any standard, and by comparison with other industrial countries, American unions have been remarkably self-restrained in recent years. Business, meanwhile, has kept its markups below levels that would be justified by the current cost of capital.

In combination, business and labor have been raising prices about 6 percent a year and increasing hourly compensation (wages, private fringes, and employers' payroll tax costs) by about 8 percent a year. The 8-and-6 combination allows a typical margin of real wage gains in line with the normal trend of productivity. Precisely for that reason, it becomes self-perpetuating. New wage decisions are made against the background of 8-percent advances in other wages and 6-percent increases in prices. And so they tend to center on 8 percent. Then, with hourly labor costs rising by 8 percent, businesses find their labor costs per unit of output up about 6 percent, and so their prices continue to rise by 6 percent.

There is no handle on either the wage side or the price side by which we can pull ourselves out of this stagflation swamp. Nor can any single industry or union provide a handle, except by making an unreasonable sacrifice of its own self-interest. It must do what everybody else is doing in order to protect itself. Analogously, if all the spectators at a parade are standing on tiptoe in an effort to get a better view, no individual can afford to get off his uncomfortable tiptoe stance. Ending the discomfort requires a collective decision.

As a qualification, let me note that my sympathy does not extend to the latest fashion in the wage-price spiral, whereby it is turning into a wage-price-protectionist spiral. In this new variant, a big wage hike is followed by a major price increase and then by a joint pilgrimage of business and labor executives to Washington to demand that the government stop foreign sellers from increasing their share of the American market. Fortunately, the Carter administration has generally resisted such unreasonable demands, instead insisting that business and labor face up to the consequences of their own actions on sales volume and employment.

Production and Jobs

Because prices and wages respond only a little to changes in total spending, production and employment respond a lot. And that is the fundamental limitation of fiscal and monetary restraints as a means of curbing inflation. Those policies clearly can put the lid on total spending for goods and services. The hold down in total spending is then split between a cutback in production and a slowing of inflation. But that "split" is the result of price and wage determination; it is not controlled by Washington. We learned—or should have learned—in the past three years that the split is extremely unfavorable. The reaction to weaker markets is loaded with layoffs, no-help-wanted signs, cutbacks of production schedules, and slashes in capital budgets. It is, at most, sprinkled with hold downs in prices and wages. To save one point on the basic inflation rate through policies that restrain total spending, we lose more than 5 points—easily $100 billion—of our annual real GNP.

The recession and slack of 1974–77 have extracted a toll of $500 billion in lost production of capital goods and consumer goods that could have added to our productivity and our standard of living. That cost should be clearly recognized, although it must be equally recognized that there was, and is, no toll-free route of escape from our problems. In fact, the toll keeps mounting. After thirty months of economic expansion, we have moved only about half the distance from the depths of the recession to a reasonable and feasible level of prosperity or full employment. Serious statistical studies designed to estimate the unemployment rate associated with reasonably balanced—neither slack nor tight—labor markets converge on a range between 5 and 5.5 percent. They demonstrate that, with today's structure of labor markets, full employment certainly cannot be defined as a 4-percent unemployment rate. But neither can it be pegged anywhere near our current 7.1 percent. Since unemployment has come down from 9.0 percent at the worst of the recession to 7.1 percent, we are about halfway to a reasonable cyclical target in the zone of 5 to 5.5 percent.

The excess of nearly 2 percentage points in the unemployment rate is not a structural phenomenon; it is not concentrated in "unemployables," secondary workers, or groups especially affected by government benefit programs. It is instructive to compare the unemployment rates of eminently employable groups today with their 1973–74 average (see table).

Unemployment remains high because production has not grown enough to generate the jobs required to get us back to prosperity. The behavior of the unemployment rate in recent years poses no mystery. Indeed, it has moved remarkably true to form in relation to the growth of production. Between 1973 and 1977, our annual growth rate has been averaging 2 percent, and such a substandard growth performance entails a much increased rate of unemployment. Economists can disagree about whether the nation's "potential growth rate"—the rate of growth of real GNP that maintains a constant unemployment rate—is as low as 3.3 percent or as high as 4 percent, but it surely is not 2 percent. If I use my favorite number, 3.75 percent, for the potential growth rate, the 2-percent average actual growth rate since 1973 would be expected to raise the unemployment rate by 2.3 percentage points, in line with a rule-of-thumb

Unemployment rates of selected groups (August 1977 compared with 1973–74)

	August 1977	1973–74 average
Married men (%)	3.5	2.5
Craftsmen (%)	5.5	4.0
Factory workers (%)	7.0	5.0
"Job losers" (%)	3.4	2.1
Average duration (weeks)	13.5	9.8

In 1973, when the overall unemployment rate was 4.9 percent, labor markets seemed a bit tight, although they contributed very little to the upsurge in inflation. In 1974, at a 5.6 overall rate, they seemed a bit weak on average.

formula that I developed in 1961. That would point to an unemployment rate a little above 7 percent currently, and that is where we are.

The potential growth rate of the economy is influenced by trends in productivity and in labor-force participation. In the seventies, a rising fraction of women and young people have chosen to enter the labor force. That increase in "work ethic" permits the economy to enjoy greater growth without encountering tight labor markets. Indeed, in its absence, the rather disappointing trend in productivity would have significantly lowered our trend of potential growth. To be sure, if women and teenagers stopped hunting for jobs and went back to their knitting and ball-playing respectively, our unemployment figures would be lower. But our labor markets would be tighter, and the potential of the economy would be reduced. The increased labor-force participation of these workers is correctly viewed as an opportunity and not a burden.

At the level required to bring the unemployment rate down to the middle of the 5.0-to-5.5 zone, our real GNP would be about $100 billion—or 5.5 percent—above its present level. The evidence suggests that our plant capacity could accommodate that extra output strain, so long as it was broadly spread across sectors. Such a judgment must rest on estimates of operating rates, which are admittedly imperfect. But they are not likely to be seriously biased, either upward or downward. The estimate of capacity may inappropriately include some outmoded facilities, but is just as likely to omit some rehabilitated facilities.

In short, idle resources and sacrificed output continue to represent an enormous national extravagance. Economists ought to be devoting more of their efforts and ingenuity to correcting that waste and less to talking it away or defining it out of existence.

The Costs of Inflation

Just as 7 percent unemployment is not full employment, so 6 percent inflation is not price stability. For the past two years, inflation has been reasonably steady and relatively well predicted, and yet it remains domestic public enemy number one in the view of a majority of the American people. I find that entirely understandable. In a system that rests on the dollar as a yardstick, a score-keeping device, and a basis for planning and budgeting, the instability of the price level adds enormously to uncertainty and risk.

In our institutional environment, most people cannot hedge their wealth or their incomes against inflation. The single-family home has been the only major asset that has served as an effective inflation hedge during the past decade; and it is obviously not a feasible outlet for gradual maintained flows of saving. Common stocks have been miserable failures as inflation hedges; savings deposits and life insurance offer no effective inflation protection. A small minority of Americans have obtained cost-of-living escalators that protect their real incomes effectively from inflation. But their escalated wages are passed through into prices and thereby destabilize the real incomes of the majority whose earnings are not indexed. Escalators are a means of passing the buck among groups within our society, not of protecting the buck for the whole of society.

Recent professional discussions of inflation-adjusted accounting and inflation-adjusted taxing underline the importance of the dollar yardstick in our institutional structure. Efforts to develop a "real" yardstick as a substitute for the dollar founder on legitimate controversy and unavoidable complexity. Understandably, businessmen typically rely on the dollar. Most continue to set their prices on the basis of known actual costs rather than hypothetical replacement costs for both inventories and capital facilities. And FIFO "pricers" recognize that FIFO accounting tells the true story of their profits, even though it costs extra taxes. But they also know that the dollar is not reliable in an inflationary world. Thus, the gap between actual, historical costs of old plant and equipment and current or predicted costs of new facilities creates agonies in capital budgeting and weakens investment.

This country has not adapted, and is not adapting, to 6-percent inflation. The tolerable rate of inflation in this society is considerably below 6 percent. In the early sixties, 1.5 percent inflation was generally regarded as tolerable; in the early seventies, a 3 percent rate was widely accepted. If we were now to label 6 percent inflation as acceptable, who could believe that such a decision was the final turn of the ratchet? This country needs an effort to restore the reliability of the dollar, not a set of innovations to replace it; it needs an effort to curb inflation, not a program to learn to live with it.

With current prospects and policies, the basic inflation rate is not likely to drop below 6 percent during the remainder of the present economic expansion. To be sure, the inflation rate fluctuates from quarter to quarter, and minor wiggles and jiggles tend to generate vain hopes and groundless fears. Currently, declines in farm prices and a downward blip in mortgage interest rates are generating favorable news. That is genuinely reassuring in proving that the jump in inflation to an 8 percent rate earlier this year was transitory. But the latest figures do not signify any fundamental improvement that is likely to be sustained.

The inflation outlook is a mixed bag. It has favorable elements: the weakness of farm and metal prices, and indeed of world commodity prices in general; the light calendar of union wage bargaining in 1978. But it has unfavorable components as well. Nonunion wages, which have risen much less rapidly than union wages in the last few years, must be expected to accelerate to some degree. A substantial segment of industry will try to widen markups and profit-margins, particularly to narrow the gap between the historical and the current costs of capital facilities. Long before the economy reaches a state of excess demand, a return to to healthier markets would embolden many businessmen to raise their markups.

Finally, our chance for some net relief from inflation has been reduced by a new wave of legislative actions that add to particular costs and prices. Employers' hourly labor costs will be raised by hikes in payroll taxes in January for both social security and unemployment insurance. Further increases in payroll taxes are contemplated to finance proposed reforms of social security. The minimum wage seems slated to move up from $2.30 to $2.65 next year. The first installment of the well-head tax on crude oil is scheduled to take effect in 1978. Government farm programs have reinstituted acreage cutbacks—deliberately reducing the productivity of our agriculture. Many of these cost-raising measures have *some* justification. No one of them spells the difference between price stability and rampant inflation. But, in combination, they may well add 1.5 percent to the inflation rate by late 1978.

This wave of cost-raising measures deserves far more attention and scrutiny than it has received. Reliance on such measures is nothing new, but their total magnitude does set a new record. The Congress may have been tempted to load costs on the budgets of consumers and employers in order to avoid loading more onto the federal budget. In several of these areas, the President initially advanced proposals that were admirably restrained, but then compromised in the face of strong political opposition. (When some of the press welcomes such instances as evidence of the President's education in the ways of Washington, I cannot share the enthusiasm.) Meanwhile, the financial and business community has been so preoccupied with Thursday afternoon reports on M_1 and federal deficit reestimates that it has missed the big new inflationary game in town.

All things considered, my best guess is that, between now and 1979, inflation is more likely to accelerate than to decelerate—and not because of overly rapid growth or excess demand.

With that inflation forecast, a good growth performance in 1979 and 1980 seems unlikely. Bad news on inflation would turn into bad news for prosperity in several ways. First, it would mean higher interest rates. Short-term interest rates cannot be responsibly held below the inflation rate indefinitely. To me, an interest rate on Treasury bills above 7 percent would sound an alarm; it would generate disintermediation and create a mortgage famine that would starve homebuilding. Second, in an environment of stubborn and intensifying inflation, the makers of fiscal policy would be understandably reluctant to provide any stimulus to the investor or consumer that may be needed to sustain growth. Third, bad news on inflation would heighten consumer anxiety and once again weaken discretionary household spending.

The connection between worsening inflation and a subsequent recession is not magic or automatic, but it is genuinely built into the attitudes and expectations of our public and our policy makers. "Inflation backlash" is a reality. Given that reality, we simply cannot take the risk of doing what comes naturally and hoping for good luck.

Thus, my principal message is that we cannot count on our current policies to pull us out of the stagflation swamp. The evidence based on the experience of recent years has accumulated and become overwhelming. "Patience and fortitude" is no longer an acceptable response to our disappointments. The time has come to face the likelihood that we have a losing hand, and to deal a new one.

A Fiscal-Monetary Cure?

Some who accept my grim verdict about current policies call for a new monetary-fiscal strategy. And they point in opposite directions. On one side, the argument takes these lines. If a slack economy is not curing inflation, then why take the high costs of slack? Why not try to grow out of the inflation with stimuli that have reliably spurred growth every time they have been applied in the past—like major permanent tax cuts backed up by a monetary policy committed to low interest rates?

On the other side, the reverse case is made. If inflation is not abating with 5 percent real growth, isn't it clear that we need more restrictive policies to slow the economy down until inflation responds?

These polar-opposite proposals share in common the justified anxiety that our current act of juggling two eggs may lead to both getting broken. But I fear that they have one other thing in common that is less admirable. They are asking us to kid ourselves. The expansionists are right that production and jobs are good things—but not because they alleviate inflation. Any major stimulative strategy—taken alone—will hasten the day when inflation accelerates and inflation backlash sets in. The restrictionists are right that a big enough dose of restraint would curb inflation—but only at the price of some $100 billion of output per point of inflation-reduction.

Some groups in the business and financial community would, no doubt, applaud a hypothetical announcement that the government was cutting its spending by, say, $30 billion and that the Federal Reserve was now setting monetary targets aimed at, say, only 7 percent growth of nominal GNP. But when government contracts were rescinded, when banks began closing loan windows, when cash registers stopped ringing, the responses would be entirely predictable—new waves of layoffs, new slashes in capital budgets, a collapse in productivity, and new demands that the government stop imports, shorten workweeks, and launch programs of makework jobs.

Perhaps the most appealing variant of the restraint prescription is the call for a *very gradual*, but consistently maintained, slowing of monetary growth and reversal of fiscal stimulus. As far as I can see, that strategy—taken alone—offers us a long dull headache instead of a sharp acute one but no smaller total amount of pain. Moreover, its plan to curb demand gently enough to avoid a recession surely sets a new record for fine tuning. It reminds me of the story about the Greek boy who thought he could pick up a full-grown bull if he started with a newborn calf and lifted it every day. The first little trimming of total demand is a mere baby calf. It would not do production and employment much harm (nor would it do our inflation performance much good). But, as time progresses, that calf would grow into a bull—and we cannot count on lifting it.

A Program for Prosperity and Price Stability

We need an anti-inflation program that is not an anti-growth program, and that goes beyond traditional fiscal and monetary measures. In the past three years, I have assembled long menus of measures that might hold down costs and prices without holding down production and employment. Tonight, I offer a specific set of proposals. I do so uncomfortably—I left the business of packaging four-point programs nearly a decade ago, and I prefer to stay out of it. I do so diffidently—because the particular facets of the program have not been polished by staff work or constructive criticism. But I do so enthusiastically because I am convinced that the general approach it embodies represents our best hope for getting out of the stagflation swamp.

No net federal cost-raising. First, the administration should set a target of zero net cost-raising measures for 1978, and should report quarterly to the American people on the achievement of that target. Any new cost-raising governmental action that imposes higher labor costs on employers or higher prices on consumers would have to be neutralized by a federal cost-reducing measure—lightening the burden of some regulation or providing a cost-cutting subsidy. Thus, we would be insured against any encore of the cost-raising actions of 1977.

Sales-tax-cut incentive. Second, the federal government should institute a grant-in-aid program that would defray half the revenue loss of any state or city that reduced or repealed its sales taxes during 1978. Mayors and governors obtaining the federal aid for sales tax cuts would pledge not to increase other cost-raising taxes during the period (but could raise income taxes). An allocation of $6 billion of federal outlays for this program would fund a 1 percentage point cut in the consumer price index. Sales taxes are part of the cost-of-living—both genuinely and statistically. Reductions in them would hold down consumer prices and have anti-inflationary effects on wages that are linked, formally or informally, to the cost of living.

Tax relief for price-wage restraint. Third, a tax-relief incentive should be offered to workers and businessmen who enlist in a cooperative anti-inflationary effort. To qualify for participation, a firm would have to pledge, at the beginning of 1978, to hold the average rate of wage increase of its employees below 6 percent and its average rate of price increase below 4 percent (apart from a dollar-and-cents pass-through of any increases in costs of materials and supplies) during the course of the year. In return for participation, employees of the firm would receive a tax rebate (generally through withholding) equal to 1.5 percent of their wage or salary incomes with a ceiling of $225 per person; and the firm would receive a 5 percent rebate on its income tax liabilities on domestic operating profits.

Any firm covered by a collective bargaining contract would be obliged to consult with union representatives before deciding to participate in the program. Typical workers who were counting on wage increases of 8 percent (before-tax) or less would benefit from participation.

I would hope for strong moral suasion, led by the President himself, to enlist participants in the program. But nonparticipation would be a matter of free choice and would not be subject to any penalty. Each participating firm would file a statement of compliance at the end of the year, which would be subject to audit by the Internal Revenue Service.

The total cost in federal revenues of the cooperative restraint program might approach $15 billion: with the sales tax grants, it could total $20 billion. Tax cuts of that magnitude are being widely espoused in the context of the forthcoming tax reform program. I would postpone the tax cuts in the reform package, with the conviction that a pro-growth, anti-inflation program deserves a more urgent priority on the nation's agenda.

Obviously, the increase in purchasing power and profitability provided by the anti-inflationary tax cuts would stimulate consumption and investment. Indeed, the prospect of a credible attack on inflation could reduce the uncertainty that now constricts capital budgeting. If the program achieves it objective of a mutual and balanced de-escalation of wages and prices, there would be no overhang of "catch-up" wage and price increases in 1979. But opportunities should be held open for renewing the program (or phasing it out more gradually) in an effort to cut inflation once again.

New GNP targets. Fourth and finally, the administration and the Federal Reserve, in cooperation, should set forth revised fiscal and monetary targets designed to ensure full recovery *and* lower inflation. For 1978, those targets should aim for an encore of the increase in *nominal* GNP of 1977—about 10.5 percent—with more real growth and less inflation. For 1979 and 1980, they should aim to bring the growth of nominal GNP progressively into single-digit territory. Thus, they will call for declining federal deficits and slowing money growth (appropriately adjusting for any further significant shifts in velocity). Such a fiscal-monetary strategy should strongly reinforce the credibility of the anti-inflation program and help to ensure that we don't slide back into the swamp.

Still, the first requirement is to get out of the swamp. My program is neither a panacea nor a long-run insurance policy against inflation and stagflation. But its approach offers a good chance of bringing about a mutual de-escalation of prices and wages, and an end to the insidious wave of governmental cost-raising actions. It recognizes that traditional monetary-fiscal policies are powerful tools to promote full recovery and to prevent a resurgence of excess-demand inflation. But it also recognizes realistically that they cannot, by themselves, cure stagflation. That new problem requires the additional help of new remedies, which, of necessity, are unconventional and unproven. Whether the new remedies become politically feasible depends on whether sophisticated Americans, like those in this audience, face up to the reality that we are likely to remain stuck in the stagflation swamp with current policies, and whether they are willing to consider seriously—and to criticize constructively—alternative routes to noninflationary prosperity.

Wage-Price Guideposts—Yes

At the outset, let me state my wholehearted agreement with the following judgments . . . :

1. Although fiscal and monetary policies are our first and most important lines of defense against inflation, they cannot do the whole job of promoting noninflationary prosperity.
2. When marshaled by presidential leadership, the force of public opinion — the "jawbone," if you will—can contribute to improved price-wage behavior in a prosperous economy.

Our fiscal and monetary tools have great power—both for good and for ill. The inflationary problems that concern the Nation today can be traced back to late 1965 and early 1966 when the Federal budget became an engine of inflation during the upsurge in defense spending. After monetary restraint halted the boom late in 1966, we had a period of moderation in inflationary pressures.

But, once again, our stabilization policies veered off course late in 1967, and prices and wages accelerated. Inflation built up momentum and has proved to be stubborn. But it will yield to fiscal and monetary restraint. We have begun to see a significant moderation in the pace of economic activity, and our price performance should begin to improve in the months ahead.

I can be confident that, if maintained long enough and hard enough, fiscal and monetary restraint will cure inflation. But that judgment is not in itself reassuring. For I cannot be confident that, with existing institutions, the cure will be achievable without a major sacrifice of production and growth, jobs and investment opportunities, payrolls and profits.

Current fiscal and monetary policies are testing the terrain and trying to find the minimum sacrifice of output and employment required to cool off the inflationary fever. We should all be thankful for this gradualist approach, though it may sometimes test our patience and our faith.

However, well conceived and wisely executed, no fiscal-monetary strategy can assure both low unemployment and stable prices. We can all hope that a satisfactory compromise is feasible—say, a combination of a 4-percent unemployment rate and a 2-percent rate of price increase. But we cannot be sure that the tradeoff will be even that favorable.

Whether it is will depend not only on the way supplies and demand interact in competitive markets, but also on how discretionary market power is exercised by large firms and unions. Prices and wages reflect both market competition and market power. In many areas, they are not set by an impersonal market mechanism. We accept this as a fact of life in the American economy, even though it complicates our textbooks and our policy strategies.

That fact of life was recognized in the wage-price guideposts, initially formulated by the Council of Economic Advisers under President Kennedy in 1962. These stated the arithmetic principles that (*a*) if hourly wage rates throughout the economy rose in line with the national trend of productivity growth, unit labor costs would remain constant on the average; and (*b*) if prices were geared to unit labor costs in each industry, prices would be stable on the average. After an unpleasant confrontation between President Kennedy and the steel industry in the spring of 1962, no such incident recurred for more than $3\frac{1}{2}$ years. During this period, excessive slack in the economy was surely the main insurance against inflation but, according to a significant body of professional research, guideposts played a constructive role.

When excess demand pulled prices upward in 1966, the guideposts were badly dented. By the beginning of 1967, it was no longer realistic to expect labor to accept increases in money wage rates that merely paralleled the trend-growth of productivity. Such increases, amounting to a little more than 3 percent a year, would have barely matched the 1966 rise in the cost of living, thus providing for no gain in real income. Hence, the Council retreated from the productivity standard in its 1967 report, and stressed as a qualitative interim standard the need for "wage advances . . . substantially less than the productivity trend plus the recent rise in consumer prices." Similarly, in 1968, the heritage of past inflation was recognized in an interim standard which called for settlements "appreciably lower than the $5\frac{1}{2}$-percent average of 1967," and for business firms "to avoid any widening of their gross margins over direct costs and indeed absorb cost increases to the extent feasible."

Neither the guideposts nor the subsequent interim standards could possibly hold up against the tides of overall excess demand. Even so, during that period they helped to moderate prices and wages in many industries, to slow the spiralling of inflation, and to curb inflationary psychology. The need for cooperation and restraint was reiterated by the Council and by President Johnson again and again in meetings with leaders of business and labor. In some instances, regrettable disagreements were aired publicly. But in a great many cases, businessmen quietly and amicably agreed to forgo, delay, or trim price increases which they reported they were planning.

Labor leaders privately took into account the national interest as well as their bargaining power and the needs of their membership. Because of the wage standards, businessmen offered greater resistance to inflationary wage demands. Even in the worst of times for the cause of voluntary cooperation—when excess demand dominated our price performance—the jawbone did ameliorate our price and wage record to a degree.

Now, with fiscal and monetary policy working toward restraint, a program of enlisting voluntary cooperation could be making a particularly large contribution. With the excess demand problem largely behind us but the cost-push problem still with us, there is currently an unusually large range of discretion and judgment in industrial price and wage decisions. The present situation provides a unique opportunity for a new administration to start with a clean slate and capitalize on the experience—indeed, the mistakes—of its predecessors. That opportunity is being squandered. And the resulting costs to the Nation are becoming evident. The price record of gasoline, automobiles, steel, copper, and other metals so far in 1969 is far worse than that of 1968. No one of these areas offers decisive evidence, but together they compel one to conclude that the change in the rules of the game has led to a deterioration in decision making on administered prices.

Let me stress that the inflation of 1969 is not primarily the result of these areas or these decisions. But we are handicapping our efforts to achieve noninflationary prosperity. And we cannot afford even a small handicap in this difficult and vital contest. I am perplexed in interpreting the administration's continued opposition to the exercise of leadership in this area. Is this a case where the risk of failure is deemed to be so great that it has aborted a constructive effort? Is this a rare triumph of ideology over pragmatism in an administration that has been admirably pragmatic in most of its decisions? I must confess my inability to follow the objections to jawboning that have been explained so far.

To be sure, a program of persuasion can conceivably be subjected to abuse. Overenthusiasm about voluntary cooperation could conceivably serve as an excuse for ineffective fiscal and monetary policy. Standards for voluntary cooperation might become a straitjacket if every deviation from them of any size were to be indiscriminately labeled a violation of the public interest. Most serious of all, a system of voluntary cooperation might conceivably get perverted into mandatory wage and price control, but it need not. All of these are arguments for a good system—not arguments against any system.

Many of the arguments against price-wage standards could be equally well formulated as arguments against posted speed limits on highways. Any speed limit has an element of arbitrariness; nobody can be sure that a 50-mile maximum is really superior to 49 or 51. If a 50-mile an hour standard is heeded precisely by every driver, it might result in inefficiency because the passing lane would never be used. Similarly, a passing lane in prices and wages is needed to assure efficiency so that relative shifts can take place over time. That passing lane can be used effectively if the traffic authorities are sensible. Perhaps it is inequitable that not all price-wage decisions that violate the standard are put into the public spotlight; but it is even more inequitable that the traffic patrolman necessarily fails to catch and arrest all the speeders. Despite all their imperfections, highway speed limits serve the Nation well, and so can speed limits on prices and wages.

To shift metaphors, price-wage standards can help us pick the rotten apples out of the barrel, even if they cannot define the ideal apple. They are designed to guide private decision makers to avoid actions which could threaten the national interest in price and cost stability.

Seven years of experience with voluntary standards have taught us much about them. The defects have been the result of an imperfect system administered by imperfect men. And the blemishes stood out particularly in a period when stabilization policy was off course. The right lesson is to build on this experience and to perfect the system of voluntary cooperation—not to scrap it.

A Reward TIP

I am a proponent of a tax-based incomes policy, not because that policy is beautiful, but because it is a lot less ugly than alternative policy strategies. Under present policies, inflation is proceeding at a pace that is unacceptable to the American people; it is not unwinding but rather tending to step up; it is not susceptible to any efficient cure from either fiscal-monetary restraint or price-wage controls.

The Preamble to TIP

Despite persistent excess supplies for more than three years, our economy is suffering from an entrenched price-wage spiral with a 6-percent rate of price increase and an 8-percent rate of pay increase. And although the rate of price increase has been reasonably steady and well-predicted, inflation remains public enemy #1 in the eyes of the overwhelming majority of the American public. Currently inflation seems to be moving a bit above the 6-percent plateau, reflecting an inevitable catch-up of nonunion wages and the consequences of several cost-raising measures taken by the government.

Inflation could be slowed down once more by recession, as it was during 1974–75. But fighting inflation by curbing demand at a time when it is not being caused by excess demand is absurdly inefficient. It is like burning down the house to roast the pig. A wide variety of statistical estimates that I know agree that, under current conditions, a reduction of 1 percent in nominal GNP for 1979 would cost between 0.85 and 0.95 of a percentage point of production and save only between .05 and .15 of a percentage point in inflation. In their discussions on fiscal policy, the Administration and Congress show that they are not willing to pay that price; while in its decisions on monetary policy, the Federal Reserve apparently considers it essential to pay that price. Hence, the nation is facing the serious risk that fiscal policy and monetary policy may be on a collision course. In light of all these unfavorable circumstances, I simply cannot see a realistic happy ending to the present scenario of policy.

The momentum of inflation must be stopped—without another bloodletting of jobs and investment like that of 1974–75 and without a return to the brittle and distorting controls of 1971–72. The same opinion surveys that record the American people's antipathy toward inflation also reveal their basic support for a mutual deescalation of wages and prices. But because this is a decentralized economy, no single group of private decision makers can stop the spiral on its own. On the contrary, firms and unions must run ever faster to protect themselves from higher costs being imposed on them. The spiral can be broken only with the help of a collective, social decision.

Tax-based incomes policy (TIP) is a way of pursuing mutual deescalation. It is not tried and true; but the present scenario has been tried and found sadly wanting. It is not a substitute for lower rates of monetary growth and lower federal deficits as a remedy for inflation, but it is a way to make possible the necessary slowdown of money growth and turnaround of fiscal stimulus without the enormous economic and social costs of recession.

An Outline of a Reward TIP on Wages

I speak as the inventor of the reward TIP; the original, basic-model TIP produced by Henry Wallich and Sidney Weintraub relies on a stick, and I sought to convert it to a carrot. I see some distinct advantages and disadvantages in each of the two approaches. But, most of all, I believe that either of them could work effectively, and that both belong among the options from which the Congress might ultimately select an efficient cure for stagflation.

My thinking about how a reward TIP might best be implemented has evolved during the past six months in light of constructive criticisms and probing inquiries that I have received; and I expect it to change some more. But let me outline my current thoughts on the main features of that program. To begin with, I would like the legislation implementing a reward-TIP for wages to be enacted for a three-year period, with the understanding that the ceiling on the wage increase that qualifies for the reward and the size of the tax credit would be determined annually by the Congress. I would hope to be able to declare victory and let TIP expire after the three-year period, but I would like to hold open the possibility of renewal.

As I envision it, forms would be sent to all employers in the nation on October 1 in the year prior to the initiation of TIP, asking them to enlist in the program. To participate at that time, the firm would have to pledge to limit the *average* pay increase for its workers in the next year to no more than 6 percent. Pay would be defined as wages plus private fringe benefits, and the definition of fringes would be spelled out in detail. The pledge would leave the firm free to grant promotions and merit raises of any size to individual workers so long as its overall average increase in pay was within the limit.

By participating, the firm would qualify all its employees for a tax reduction during the year ahead equal to $1\frac{1}{2}$ percent of their wage and salary income up to some level, say $20,000. For most workers, that tax credit would be the equivalent of a raise a little bigger than 2 percent (before-tax). In other words, the worker would be better off with a 6-percent raise and the tax credit in combination, than with an 8-percent raise and no tax cut. The credit would then be subtracted in calculating the worker's withholding tax, in effect offsetting a portion of the present payroll tax.

The firm would also be asked to state in the initial form how it intended to measure its units of employment for the two consecutive years—for example, as total person-hours or as full-time equivalent employees. It would also be asked to specify how it planned to calculate its average wage increase—for example, simply by using the totality of all pay and all workers, or by weighting increases for distinct occupational groups, plants, subsidiaries, or the like. Once the firm made these decisions, it would be required to stick with them for the next tax year.

I believe that workers would strongly prefer getting the bonus right from the beginning of the year in their take-home paychecks, and that is why I emphasize advance commitments by firms to participate. But some firms may be unable to predict their wage increases in advance or might become unable to keep wages on target under some contingencies they might encounter during the calendar year.

Hence, I think that firms should be given an option to fill out the form, displaying an interest in the program without making a commitment; they would hold open the possibility of qualifying their workers for refunds after the year ends, if they meet the wage limit. In contrast to those firms that delay their decision, any firm that makes an advance commitment must take the responsibility of fulfilling its pledge and must assume the full liability for any subsequent determination that the reduction in withholding taxes from workers was unjustified. For carrying those responsibilities, the firms that sign up in advance (*not* those that only qualify ex post) should receive some reward for themselves—perhaps one-fourth of the amount that is rebated to their workers through withholding.

Thus, the key features of the plan can be summarized as follows:

1. A qualified worker receives an anti-inflationary tax credit equal to $1\frac{1}{2}$ percent of his wage or salary income up to $20,000—equivalent to an extra raise of 2+ percent (before-tax).

2. A worker becomes qualified when his employer either:
A. Pledges in advance that the overall average pay increase for the year will not exceed 6 percent (and then the worker gets the credit in take-home pay through reduced withholding); or
B. Reports on its tax return, ex post, that its average pay increase for the year in fact did not exceed 6 percent (and then the worker gets a tax refund).

3. A firm that enlists in advance (as in 2A above) receives for itself a tax credit equal to one-fourth the total reduction in withholding taxes granted to its workers.

Under present circumstances, I would expect the overwhelming majority of nonunion employers to enlist in the program, with virtually all governmental units and nonprofit institutions leading the parade. Employees would be informed that they would receive tax credits, and, I would expect, most would be assured by firms that, if their relative wage position should fall behind during the course of the program, it would be subsequently restored. I would expect a significant fraction—though probably only a minority—of unionized firms to participate during the initial year of the program. In fact, the size of the pay increases scheduled for the second year and third year of many existing three-year contracts would make participation worthwhile to the workers. Indeed, a substantial fraction of union contracts average less than 8 percent over the life of the contract, even though the average is apparently above 9 percent. As a rough guess, I would expect that about two-thirds of all workers would be enrolled in the program. If the Congress could afford to make the rebate 2 or $2\frac{1}{2}$ percent rather than $1\frac{1}{2}$, that figure might be raised to 80 or 90 percent.

Firms will want to participate in a reward TIP because—and only because—the tax credit to their workers would help them to slow down wages; and that is the basic guarantee that the program would be effectively anti-inflationary. I would expect—and, indeed, I would want—the average wage slowdown to be somewhat smaller than the tax credit so that labor is initially made better off, as well as gaining additional benefits from the subsequent slowdown of prices. I would also expect generally favorable effects from the recognition and the expectation of the deceleration of inflation.

Surely, the slowdown of wages in general will affect union contracts; the influence of relative wages works both ways—from nonunion to union sectors as well as the reverse. Moreover, the deceleration in consumer prices stemming from the slowdown in wages would automatically have further favorable anti-inflationary effects through cost-of-living escalator clauses.

During the second and third years of the program, I would expect an increasing fraction of union workers to be enrolled in it. All participation requires an implicit understanding with employers that, at the end of the program, any group that has fallen behind in relative wages would require some compensatory catch-up. But with broad participation, such adjustments would largely serve to restrain those who did not join up, rather than to compensate those who did.

At the end of each year, employers who qualified their workers for the credit (either by advance pledge or by ex post action) would fill out a supplemental form on their income taxes, totalling wages and all other deducted expenses that are classified as pay, and then dividing that total pay by the number of employment units (say, full-time equivalent workers or total manhours). The calculation would be made for the latest year and for the base year, to show that the 6-percent standard had been met.

There would be no monitoring, investigating, or approval or notification of any wage change during the course of the year. The auditing of tax returns would be the sole technique of enforcement, just as it is now for all provisions of the income tax. In these respects, all types of TIP contrast sharply with controls: no private behavior is prohibited, and no advance approval from the government is required.

If a firm has an acute labor shortage and really needs to raise wages by

12 percent to get the added workers it can profitably use, clearly it should and would stay out of the program. That firm and its workers should then recognize that, in all fairness, they are not entitled to an anti-inflationary tax credit. Analogously, in the case of the investment tax credit, a firm that does not need more equipment is not obliged to invest; but neither does it have any justified complaint about not receiving a tax reward.

Some Features of Alternative Proposals

The advantages and disadvantages of various approaches form an interesting balance sheet:

Revenue costs. The most obvious disadvantage of the reward TIP relative to the penalty TIP is that the reward costs federal revenue, and that is a significant matter.

Scope. Secondly, the reward approach must be *universal*; the tax reductions must be available to employees of the corner grocer and the county sheriff's office as well as to those of major corporations. The penalty approach, on the other hand, can be confined to large firms which may be viewed as the pacesetters in the determination of wages. At a Brookings conference last month that covered this range of subjects, many participants viewed the opportunity for selectivity as a major advantage of the penalty approach, particularly because it avoided the problems of record-keeping, informing, and auditing for very small firms.

In my personal judgment, however, that is not a decisive matter. Small firms are now offered the opportunity of qualifying for the investment tax credit, the employment tax credit, capital gains advantages, deductible travel and entertainment expenses, and all of the other complex tax-minimizing provisions of the income tax. And all of these provisions are enforced solely through the low probability of subsequent audit of returns. But if the Congress should feel that an onerous burden would be placed on tiny firms, then enterprises with, say, less than twenty employees (as well as brand new firms operating in their initial year) could be given a special exemption, enabling them to qualify their workers for the tax credit simply by signing a pledge to adhere to the anti-inflationary spirit of the program. Any sensible employer would convert that into some slowdown of wages.

Special situations. Like any tax incentive program, any newly enacted TIP will run into some special situations that can reasonably be regarded as "inequities." For example, some firm may have granted no pay increases at all in the preceding year, and its workers might well feel that they deserve the elbow room to catch up. Alternatively, another firm might have raised pay by 10 percent on September 1 of the preceding year; that alone would push up the calendar-year average increase of the next year above the 6 percent hurdle, even if no further pay increases were awarded during that calendar year. No manageable set of provisions can "fix up" such special problems. If these are inequities, they are surely far less serious than the inequities imposed by stagflation. The Congress would have to accept some imperfections to ensure an administratively feasible and economically effective program. I suspect that such a course would be more acceptable if the victims of "special situations" are merely deprived of rewards rather than subjected to penalties. In the history of tax legislation, "grandfather clauses" have been typical for newly stiffened rules, but not for new benefits, like the investment or employment tax credits. So this difference is another advantage of the reward approach.

In a somewhat related manner, the reward approach builds in a better incentive for compliance by making employers liable for any unwarranted rebates of taxation to their workers. Firms are much less likely to risk IRS punishment for unjustified claims that benefit workers directly than for minimization or avoidance to shave their own liability for penalties.

Pass-through. In the penalty approach, firms that pay higher taxes because of large wage increases may conceivably pass on the tax penalty to their customers in the form of even higher prices. I do not view the pass-through as an overwhelming problem, but it is avoided by the reward approach.

Fairness to workers. Both the reward and the penalty TIP apply leverage directly to wages rather than to prices. That aspect of TIP needs to be clearly understood. Every TIP proponent knows that labor has *not* been the villain in the present inflation and that wages are *not* out of line on the high side. The reason for focusing on wages is quite different. According to a vast body of statistical evidence, a slowdown in wages is fully and reliably translated, after a reasonably short lag, into a slowdown of prices. The evidence on the conversion of price slowdowns into wage slowdowns is much less clear. Some studies suggest that a 1 percentage point slowdown in prices will slow wages by only 0.2 percentage point, while others give answers as high as 0.9. Mainly, the problem is that economists just don't know. If we were sure that a price slowdown would generate a prompt and substantial wage slowdown, we could break the spiral by a direct attack on consumer prices—for example, a federal program to "buy out" state sales taxes (or to slash federal payroll taxes on employers). I think those steps are well worth taking, but I do not have the faith in their effectiveness to rely entirely on them.

At least in part, wage inflation must be the direct target of any effective TIP. With a reward TIP, I do not see a substantive equity problem: the average take-home pay of workers would probably be increased a little initially, even before they benefit from a slowdown of price inflation.

With the penalty approach, there is a problem of ensuring fairness to workers. They would be better off before long, and would be far better off than they would be if inflation speeds up or if it is curbed by recession. But they are not immediately indemnified for the initial slowdown of wages that is being induced by the tax penalty. As some see a penalty TIP, it requires workers (and only workers) to ante up for the deal, so to speak. Henry Wallich and Sidney Weintraub have been sensitive to such criticisms and have suggested added provisions to achieve equity—like a contingent tax on any shift of income to profits.

Problems of this sort are most relevant in the first year of a penalty TIP, since the statistical evidence warns that it takes a little while for a wage slowdown to be translated fully into a price slowdown. It could help to combine the stick on excessive wage increases with a general carrot for all wage earners in that year—e.g. by enacting an income-tax cut for low and middle income families or, even better, a cut in federal payroll taxes on workers, or, best of all, a federal grant program to induce cuts in state sales taxes.

A Price Restraint Credit?

In the search for still greater evenhandedness, I suggested last fall that a tax reward (perhaps a discount on income taxes) might be offered to those businesses that limited to 4 percent their price increases on a value-added basis (that is, above and beyond increased costs of purchased materials, energy, and supplies). On this proposal, the criticisms that I have received from my professional colleagues have generally been more adverse and, to me, more persuasive than those on the wage reward TIP. I was searching for symmetry, but the economy has a basic asymmetry: it is much harder to measure increases in product prices than increases in wages. New products, quality changes, and widely varied types of output complicate the calculation. I now believe that a price reward can be incorporated into the program *if* the Congress insists that the burden of proof rests on any claimant for such a tax credit—that the firm is responsible to develop the kind of systematic price indexes that would justify its deduction. But my critics would emphasize that such an accounting task would be inherently less difficult for large manufacturing firms, airlines, communications companies, and utilities than for small enterprises.

Frankly, I never expected much additional benefit in slowing inflation from the price reward, but felt that the forging of a social compact would be enhanced by treating wages and prices symmetrically. Now, however, I am concerned that a provision that was intended to reassure workers might turn out to bestow tax cuts arbitrarily on big business. At this point, I would not advocate a tax credit for price restraint.

In summary, TIP requires much more discussion and a major educational effort; and this committee deserves our gratitude for promoting that discussion. Clearly, the basic current controversy is not among alternative forms of TIP. Rather, it is between slowing the wage-price spiral by some form of TIP or other innovative cost-reducing strategy, on the one hand, and the hideous alternatives of letting inflation rip, fighting it by recession, or suppressing it by wage-price controls, on the other. The need to lick stagflation cooperatively and sensibly is the biggest economic challenge facing our nation, and also one of the biggest challenges to our democratic political process.

II IMPLICIT CONTRACTS

Inflation: Its Mechanics and Welfare Costs

Economists continue to be baffled by the mystery of inflationary recession (or stagflation) that has been experienced by industrialized countries during the 1970s. What causes inflation to churn on and on even after excess demand disappears? This whodunit is the latest in a long series that reflects the inadequacy of current theory in explaining the mechanics of how inflation proceeds once it has begun. In this paper, I shall sketch an interpretation of the persistence of inflation based on an interaction of "customer" or "career" markets, in which prices and wages do not equate supply and demand, with "auction" markets, in which prices do reliably clear markets.

Changing Styles in Inflation Theory

The suggested interpretation developed in this paper builds on past theoretical literature, which I shall briefly review as a foundation for the subsequent analysis.

Vintage Keynesianism

Vintage Keynesianism of the World War II period offered a comparative-static view of price-level equilibrium, given an "inflationary gap" and a dynamic view of the approach to that equilibrium.[1] Over a wide range of output from very depressed levels up to full employment, variations in aggregate demand changed output with prices and wages essentially constant. On the other hand, in the inflationary zone above full employment, incremental aggregate demand merely bid up the price level, leaving production unchanged. Thus, the aggregate supply curve relating prices and output had a right angle. And the task of optimum policy was to make aggregate demand intersect supply at the vertex of the right angle—an assignment that could be difficult but that involved no agonizing tradeoff or cruel dilemma.

Given an inflationary gap, equilibrium might be restored at a new higher price level because of a nonaccommodating monetary policy, or the reduced real value of cash and government bonds (the Pigou effect), or automatic stabilizers in the fiscal system. If, however, these equilibrating forces were nonexistent or very weak, hyperinflation might result.

The dynamic determinacy of the price level was attributed to one or both of two basic lags—(1) spending behind income and (2) wages behind prices. In the former, consumers and businessmen formulated dollar budgets for the period ahead, and stuck to them; thus, a sufficient jump in the price level would curb the real volume of spending to the level of full-employment output.[2] The rate of inflation then depended on the size of the inflationary gap and the length of the budgeting lag. In the latter, this period's wage level was set equal to last period's marginal revenue product of labor; real wages thus would be squeezed by inflation and so would real consumer expenditures (even if they did not lag behind income).

Much later, Robert Clower interpreted these lags as imperfections in the process of market recontracting. In the case of the budgeting lag, developments in today's factor markets do not get into today's prices on product markets. In the case of the wage lag, today's developments in product markets cannot get into today's prices on factor markets.[3] These lags produce interesting difference-equation models of the inflationary process.[4] Yet they have not been a fruitful basis for quantification. The lengths of the lags were never estimated with any precision; and no link was established between the rate of inflation and the size of the inflationary gap. Indeed, the very existence of a budgeting lag was never empirically demonstrated. And while wages and prices demonstrably chased each other, the evidence did not establish that real wages were depressed by inflation as the vintage Keynesian wage lag insisted.[5]

Gradually, in response to postwar experience, economists rounded the right angle of the aggregate supply curve, converted full employment into a zone, and developed the concept of a tradeoff. But the early fifties gave them no reason to puzzle over the momentum of rising prices because inflation screeched to a halt in 1951—a development that still stands out in retrospect as an intriguing fortuitous mystery. The events of 1956–57 posed another, unpleasant, mystery: why inflation began so soon at aggregate unemployment and operating rates that apparently did not involve generally excessive demand. Charles Schultze analyzed that puzzle with a refined version of the vintage Keynesian inflation model, stressing sectoral imbalances in demand and asymmetric responses to excess supply and excess demand.[6]

Phillips Approach

The Phillips approach departed fundamentally from vintage Keynesianism by relating a given utilization rate to a given *rate* of inflation rather than an equilibrium *level* of prices, thus positing a continuous tradeoff between inflation and unemployment. As James Tobin put it, "The Phillips curve has been an empirical finding in search of a theory. . . ."[7] Tobin's own rationale rested on a model of "stochastic macro-equilibrium" in which disequilibria in particular markets could maintain some stable positive inflation rate in the presence of some persistent degree of overall labor-market tightness.

Asymmetries and nonlinearities could account for the puzzle of 1960–63—a continuing rate of inflation of 1 or 2 percent in an excess-supply economy. If some prices and most wages are rigid on the down side and if the response of the wages to unemployment is nonlinear, then excess demand in a minority of sectors can produce some upcreep in overall price levels.

Empirically, the Phillips curve looked like a winner for the United States. Annual increases in prices (and wages) relative to unemployment rates for 1954 to 1968 fit a hyperbola like a glove.[8] A few refinements took care of the minor deviations. The persistence of the 1956–57 inflation into 1958 could be explained by some short lags of a vintage Keynesian type; the somewhat better tradeoff performance of the early sixties relative to the fifties could be accounted for by the price-wage guideposts or by "hidden unemployment."[9]

The stubbornness of wage and price inflation in 1970–71 ended the heyday of the Phillips approach. Perry sought to save the Phillips curve by reinterpreting the measure of labor-market tightness to reflect the shifting demographic composition of unemployment.[10] The Perry shift is now generally accepted as a constructive refinement, but it explains only a small part of the "new" inflation of the 1970s. The expansion of unemployment insurance and welfare benefits was also invoked to account for tighter labor markets at a given unemployment rate.

The other major analytical developments stressed expectations. According to one thesis, the economy became more inflation prone because private decisionmakers perceived increased tolerance for inflation and reduced tolerance for unemployment on the part of government. I would not dismiss this hypothesis.[11] But I doubt that it explains much. For one thing, the hypothesis would predict stronger spending behavior—a movement along the Phillips curve, as well as a shift in it. If consumers and firms detect an expansionary bias in stabilization policy, aggregate private demand should be stronger for *given* settings of fiscal and monetary policies; I see no evidence that this has been the case.

Accelerationism

Accelerationism was the most fundamental transformation of the Phillips approach into an expectational format. It hypothesized that inflation will become increasingly rapid in any maintained situation in which unemployment lies below some critical, or "natural," rate. Basically, it argued that the very possibility of getting unemployment below the natural rate depends on a process of fooling people—coaxing out higher employment and higher production with higher prices for the things they sell and then surprising them with higher prices than they expected on the things they buy. Through lags in the perception of inflation, these surprises raise output and employment, but as people learn that they are being fooled, the lags shorten.

When Milton Friedman and Edmund Phelps independently set forth this theory, the Phillips-curve approach seemed to be working very well. Basically, accelerationism was a pessimistic forecast rather than an explanation of experience; whatever else one thinks of the theory, the prophetic accuracy of its pessimism has to be admired.[12] Some of the macroeconomic empirical facts of the early seventies fit the accelerationist theory. Even though the unemployment rate exceeded the natural rate (by anybody's estimate) in 1970–71, people were, according to the accelerationists, still adapting to the inflationary surprises of 1965–69; hence, inflation decelerated very slowly and only after a lag.

More generally, the unemployment-inflation experience of the first half of the 1970s manifestly reveals a far less favorable tradeoff than does that of 1954–68. Clearly, the short-term Phillips curve has shifted upward. In the sense of recognizing that shift, we are all accelerationists now (to reverse Friedman's celebrated concession to Keynes). On the other hand, I believe the inflation-unemployment tradeoff applies to all relevant inflation and unemployment rates and all relevant time horizons. I find particularly incredible the clear (though often ignored) implication of the no-tradeoff view that inflation no longer imposes a cost. If the American public has fully adapted to some anticipated inflation rate like 6 percent, then that inflation cannot do any good in expanding output and employment, but by the same token it cannot do any harm in distorting distribution or allocation. The same public that allegedly adapted to that expected inflation rate still believes that inflation is painful; and so do I.

The microanalytical underpinning of accelerationism is seriously deficient. In part, inflation is supposed to distort temporarily the tradeoff between work and leisure. According to this story, when people observe a rise in money wages, they believe that real wages are rising too. Consequently they take jobs and give up leisure, which they now view as more expensive. Ultimately, however, they find that the cost of living has accelerated too, and the labor supply hence gradually shifts back. But why should people take significantly longer to perceive the movement of the cost of living than that of wages? Even more fundamentally, how can the thesis assume a substantial positive elasticity of the supply of labor with respect to the real wage? While that proposition has been widely accepted (by Keynes, among others), the empirical evidence suggests that the elasticity is close to zero and may not even be positive.[13]

In part, the temporary distortion is supposed to involve the tradeoff between work and search (rather than leisure).[14] According to this variant, because the unemployed do not know the universe of job offers, they interpret a good offer in an improving labor market as a high *relative* wage and take it rather than continuing their search. Thus, the average duration of unemployment and hence the number of unemployed decline. But ultimately job seekers recognize that it is worthwhile to take more time to sort the favorable offers of a strong labor market. As a result, the drop in unemployment must be temporary, lasting only so long as people are fooled.

The facts of the real world do not square with the implications of this work-search hypothesis. First, as Perry has shown, changes in the number of spells as well as in the duration of unemployment account importantly for cyclical fluctuations in unemployment. Second, as Tobin has noted, the quit rate does not lag in an improving labor market. Third, rejections of job offers are less frequent than this theory would imply—except in the trivial sense that every unemployed person has rejected an "offer" to become a self-employed garbage picker.[15]

Some accelerationist models are rooted in product rather than labor markets. In their world, output exceeds its equilibrium level temporarily when expected selling prices are especially high in relation to expected buying prices.[16] I know of no empirical evidence of such cyclically systematic errors in firms' predictions of selling prices relative to buying prices.

Although their explanations are unsatisfactory, I believe that the search of the "search theorists" has not been in vain. They have correctly focused attention on the way wages and employment must adjust through a search process in the absence of a market-clearing mechanism that would adjust wages to keep supply and demand in equilibrium.

The effort to build the analytical base for accelerationism, led by Phelps, has produced constructive research into the "microeconomic foundations" of both employment and inflation theory. The pervasive issue is the relative role of quantity adjustments and of price (wage) adjustments in different types of markets over different time horizons; this tied back into the earlier efforts by Hicks, Tobin, Patinkin, and Leijonhufvud to make sense of the Keynesian theory of involuntary unemployment.[17] And the common theme is that, in markets that lack a clearing mechanism, quantities vary a lot because prices (wages) vary too little and too late. These nonclearing phenomena are the heart of the explanation of both inflationary and recessionary processes.

Purpose of This Paper

I shall now sketch a nonclearing argument that makes sense to me, drawing on various strands of the literature. Because of the absence of market-clearing mechanisms, quantity adjustments carry the burden for many types of product and factor markets, leading to the observed sluggishness and persistence of inflation and of excessive unemployment. While many elements (including some monopoly models, transactions costs, uncertainties, and various sunk costs) can explain the absence of market clearing, I shall stress the cost of information, interpreting it broadly (too broadly, some may feel) to include costs of prediction, of establishing reliability, and the like.[18]

In particular, the costs of information lead to implicitly contractual long-term relationships between employees and employers and between customers and suppliers. These relationships created a zone of indeterminacy for wages and prices and a need for "fair" formulas for the sharing of bilateral monopoly surpluses. By putting price and wage making into a longer-term context, they lengthen the lags and weaken the causal connections between changes in demand and changes in prices or wages.

I shall then explore some implications of the resulting lags in the inflationary process. Prices and wages in "customer markets" will lag behind those in "auction markets." Thus, inflation must affect the allocation of resources and change relative prices. Hence, there can be no uniform "real" interest rate whose constancy might maintain a simple equilibrium of financial markets during inflation.

Customer markets depend heavily on—and in turn enhance—the usefulness of money as a yardstick and as a store of value; that usefulness is impaired in a world of inflation, as are many aspects of buyer-seller relationships that are "efficient" institutions in a complex world. Thus, the welfare costs usually attributed to inflation—haphazard redistributions of income and wealth and socially unproductive economizing of cash balances—should be viewed in a broader context as disturbances to a set of institutions that economize on information, prediction, and transaction costs through continuing buyer-seller relationships. Inflation does fool people, as the accelerationists contend. But it does so, not so much by disappointing their point-estimate expectations as by depriving them of a way of economic life in which they need not depend heavily on the formulation of costly and uncertain point-estimate expectations.

The skeleton I shall sketch below has many missing analytical bones and no empirical flesh. Yet I believe this basic approach has far-reaching implications for both analysis and policy. It reveals weaknesses in proposals for living with inflation by indexation. It explains why most of the American public dislikes inflation so much more intensely than does most of the economics profession. It offers a common approach for product and labor markets, encompassing administered prices and sticky wages. It suggests that the welfare costs of garden-variety, nagging inflation are qualitatively similar to (although far smaller than) the distortions of allocation typically attributed to galloping, acute hyperinflation. It explicitly recognizes the store-of-value function of money and rescues inflation theory from "barter illusion." This approach advances the line of thinking of my 1973 article on upward mobility, but contrasts with views I expressed as recently as 1970 and with most discussions of inflation in the literature.[19] The outstanding exception is John Hicks, whose recent analysis of the welfare costs of inflation delivers the same principal message as does this paper.[20]

Customer Markets

In traditional short-run market analysis, firms are viewed as price takers and quantity makers. In the Marshallian case, the prototype competitive firm has a given quantity of fresh fish or fresh fruit on hand that it dumps onto an auction market to fetch whatever price it will bring.[21] Manifestly, most sellers of products in the real world are quantity takers and price makers; even those with minuscule market shares put price tags on their commodities. In the short run, they are never surprised by the price, and always subject to surprise about the quantities they sell.

If price making meant nothing more than the absence of auction markets, price tags and price lists would introduce only the tiniest lag in the adjustment of prices and trivial fluctuations in quantities. Any firm (competitive or monopolistic) that experienced a surprising rise in demand would tend to raise its prices promptly, and those unfavorably surprised would tend to reduce them. A few other considerations might lengthen that lag a bit: it costs something and takes some time to make and implement the firm's decisions on prices and then to print and distribute the new price lists. But these elements imply an inertia of prices that should last for days or weeks, not years. And they cannot explain movements in the wrong direction—like rising prices in the summer of 1975.

After a shift in demand, competitive producers could, in principle, reach the new equilibrium price after a few rounds of price changes without an auctioneer. Suppose there are many, fairly similar small hotels in a large city, and that the marginal cost of having an additional room occupied is negligible. With no auction (or organized exchange) mechanism to keep occupancy essentially full and stable by varying the price, a downward shift in demand might produce a short interval of depressed occupancy rates; but the restoration of equilibrium would not take very long, *if* the hotels were seriously trying to be do-it-yourself auctioneers. No recession would ensue, in which the hotels accept less occupancy and maintain their room charges while expecting occupancy to continue depressed. Nor would prolonged booms emerge.[22]

The absence of the auctioneer has more important effects. First, it confronts the potential customer for the hotel room with a costly search process (like that of the unemployed worker).[23] Even so, if the potential customer sampled a few hotels randomly every time he contemplated a purchase, the lack of an auctioneer would merely reduce the price elasticity of demand, increasing the effective degree of monopoly within the industry and thus the profit-maximizing price. The real reason that the auctioneer is missed so much and that hotels do not try to be do-it-yourself auctioneers is that the optimizing innkeeper will recognize his ability to influence the search behavior of the customer. Today's occupants have indicated that they regarded the hotel's offer (at least ex ante) as a satisfactory deal. By pledging continuity of that offer, the innkeeper can encourage customers to return to buy, or at least to sample, using yesterday's experience as a guide to today's offerings. A kind of intertemporal comparison shopping develops by which yesterday's offer influences today's demand, as a result of an implied commitment of the seller to maintain his offer.

The customer who counts on that stability believes he knows the terms of his previous supplier's offer without shopping. But he must shop to determine the offers (price, quality, service) of unfamiliar sellers. It is as though that information is recorded on a card that can be purchased for a nontrivial price. In such a situation, maximizing behavior for the customer may resemble satisficing behavior. The expected value of the information card is low when the status quo is satisfactory. Knowing this, the supplier wants to ensure that the customer will not find it worthwhile to buy the information card. He can assume that, if today's offer is maintained, most of today's customers will return. If he also believes that *any* rise in his price will increase discretely the proportion of his customers who will buy information cards, he will tend to leave his price unchanged, even when demand rises.

The Buyer-Seller Relationship

An established customer-supplier relationship introduces a bilateral monopoly surplus that can be split between the cooperating buyers and sellers. In the short run, most customers would pay a slightly higher price to their suppliers without shopping, and most suppliers would, if they had to, sell for a shade less to their customers. This interdependence puts a premium on maintaining the relationship and on limiting conflict over the sharing of the surplus to methods that will not impair its total value.

The supplier obviously cannot promise the customer that he will offer the same deal forevermore. In particular, he may have to raise his price if his costs rise. But he can promise to treat the customer "fairly" on all the dimensions of their transactions, thus offering the customer an implicit contract. It remains implicit because of the high cost of spelling out and negotiating the terms of an explicit, formal contract. The implicit contract may apply to a wide variety of unspecified contingencies extending beyond changes in costs. When the supplier and customer agree on certain rules or conventions of fair play, each offers the other an effective incentive to play by those rules (and a credible threat against the one who breaks them).[24] These implicit contracts serve as efficient substitutes for the costly institutions of formal long-term contracts and organized futures markets.[25]

Empirically, the typical standard of fairness involves cost-oriented pricing with a markup. Apparently, in most industries, the criterion is full rather than variable costs. But it is based on some standard or normal output rather than actual output; thus the customer is not asked to pay for the higher overhead per unit and the lower productivity of recessions. The concept is also apparently historical costs, which are obviously subject to more precise calculation than are replacement costs. The recurrence of transactions between customers and suppliers makes it possible to base the terms of sale on the facts of the past rather than forecasts of the future. Once such cost-based pricing practices become established, the firm can often count on its competitors to set prices in a similar fashion.[26]

It can justify cost-oriented price increases—a desire evident in the dedicated, if fuzzy, statements that firms issue, insisting that higher costs "force" them to raise prices. No supplier can tell his customers: "As a result of stronger demand, I am now in a position to capture a larger share of the surplus from our relationship." This attitude influences price-making behavior as well as public-relations releases. In effect, the supplier firm represents itself to its customers as a kind of procurement agency operating under a brokerage arrangement. The markup onto costs becomes a reasonable way to set a "fair" price for the services of the firm.

More generally, the customer-strategy entrepreneur gears prices to costs because his reliance on customers vastly complicates any fine-tuning of prices to demand for purposes of profit maximization. The price elasticity of demand for his product is relatively low in the short run because of his established clientele (and that of his competitors), but much greater in the long run because information diffuses. Hence, the firm presumably "underprices"—or sacrifices—for the near term if it maximizes the discounted future stream of profits (rather than current-period profits). Thus, a price reduction in response to a temporary weakening of demand would often impose an even greater sacrifice of current profits in order to promote future profits. Moreover, the crucial long-run price elasticities of demand are subject to high degrees of risk or uncertainty, or to estimation only through expensive market research (that is, high information costs). A risk-averse firm may be discouraged thereby from changing prices because it sees high variance in the outcome (à la Brainard) or because it is led to "slant" the probabilities (à la Fellner).[27] In addition, risk-averse investors may like the reduced cyclical volatility of profits that results because firms "underprice" least in periods of weak demand and most (thus, investing most for future demand) in particularly good times.

The Scope of Customer Relations

Customer relationships have some importance to any firm whose demand curve is higher than it would be if the firm were offering its product for sale for the first time—with no clientele, reputation, or record of performance. Those relationships should be most important for heterogeneous products and least important for homogeneous ones, where the price is uncomplicated by a quality dimension. Nonetheless, heterogeneity has many aspects beyond the physical characteristics of the product, including transportation arrangements, credit terms, speed and reliability of delivery. Thus, department stores facilitate the return of merchandise for full refund by regular customers with charge accounts. Wholesalers who have established the reliability of small retailers for trade credit offer financing arrangements to keep them as customers. Similarly, while customer relationships seem less important for professional buyers than for households, even the former cannot assess the long-term reliability of a new supplier, and hence prefer continuing relationships. Thus, in a weak steel market, imported steel may be priced 10 percent or more below the physically identical domestic product. In a strong market, however, the reliable customer of domestic firms is assured of supplies, in amounts geared to his past purchases, at prices below those of imports.

Big-ticket items that are bought infrequently might appear to be least subject to the customer strategy. Yet, repair services on autos and appliances are used to maintain relationships; and firms work to establish brand-name reliability, in effect counting on reputation (a flow of information from one consumer to the next) to substitute for repetition. Finally, oligopolistic market structures that make price competition self-destructive among firms may encourage uniform and sticky "administered prices" accompanied by differentiation of services.[28]

In summary, the prototype of pricing in customer markets is a markup over past costs. But cost changes show up with a lag because prices will be altered only when average costs have changed by some threshold amount or only at specified intervals. As Cagan summarizes the result:

"Empirical studies have long found that short-run shifts in demand have small and often insignificant effects [on prices], and that, instead, costs play a dominant role."[29] This empirical finding of markup rigidity is inconsistent with the classical theory of price determination, in which the strength of demand should alter the ratio of prices to costs.

Cyclical Patterns

By dampening its cyclical price fluctuations, the customer-strategy firm will magnify its cyclical variations in orders and sales. When the firm encounters an unexpected drop in demand, its inventories of finished goods may increase; its utilization of its work force and capital may decline; it may cut its workweek; it may reduce hiring and begin layoffs; or it may speed up deliveries. And these changes in quantities may not be accompanied by changes in price, for the reasons spelled out above.

When demand strengthens after a slump, the same options are thrown into reverse. The firm presumably optimizes so that it is equally costly to meet favorable sales surprises (including successes in attracting new customers) by dipping into inventories, lengthening its workweek, and drawing on its queue of job applicants. Under typical circumstances, the customer-strategy firm is likely to maintain some reserve of capacity in all three forms. The firm may be in disequilibrium throughout and yet make all the adjustments in quantities. The forces inducing changes in prices can be very weak.[30]

Career Labor Markets

Customer-supplier relationships in product markets are paralleled by long-term employer-employee attachments in labor markets; in combination, the two models unify the analysis of quantity-adjusting responses to disequilibrium in labor and product markets.

Actually, the labor-market side of this analysis is better known and more widely accepted, and since I have previously explored it in some detail, I shall treat it only briefly here.[31] Many employers adopt policies to promote long-run attachment by workers. They pursue that strategy because the value of an experienced worker exceeds that of an inexperienced one by a margin greater than the corresponding wage differential. Entering workers impose costs on the firm of screening, hiring, training, and on-the-job learning; yet they cannot be made to bear these costs fully through a lowered entering wage. For one thing, many of these "investments" are valuable to the worker only insofar as he remains an employee of that firm; the nontenured recruit will not pay for them. Second, the relevant interest rate to the worker is likely to be far higher than that to the firm. Third, even the "general" training that improves the worker's marketability to other firms cannot be properly appraised by him, given his information. Finally, the firm will wish to bolster the entering wage in order to ensure a queue of willing applicants that it can sort and screen when it needs to hire new workers.

Thus, the firm really makes an investment in a new worker, spending more to hire, train, and pay him than he is worth in the short run. But it must then amortize that investment by paying wages *below* marginal revenue product to workers who become experienced. Nonetheless, the firm wants to maintain wage rates for experienced workers above those of their next-best opportunity in the labor market in order to hold down quit rates and protect its investment. It will also hold down quit rates by offering its experienced workers regular pay increases and growing seniority privileges in the form of fringe benefits, retirement programs, and provisions for leave and vacation. These arrangements create a bilateral monopoly surplus and a zone of indeterminacy for the wage for an experienced worker. That wage must exceed his perceived best alternative and be less than his current marginal revenue product. Again, because of information costs (and sunk costs), the elasticity with respect to the wage has a time gradient—from low in the short run to high in the long run. These relationships have pervasive empirical consequences—the negative correlation between wage rates and quit rates, the extremely low quit rate of experienced workers in high-paying industries, the countercyclical changes in the size of wage differentials, cyclical patterns of upgrading jobs, the low levels of unfilled vacancies for career jobs even in tight labor markets, and the like.

This long-attachment, or "career," job market is analogous in many features to the customer-product market. But the roles played by buyers and sellers present a set of interesting contrasts. The price (wage rate) is set by the buyer in labor markets (outside of collective bargaining), but by the seller in product markets. The other party then engages in search (or shopping). A seller in product markets and a buyer in labor markets typically make similar transactions with many people on the other side of the market, and they must be price makers, at least in part, to display equitable treatment of the people with whom they deal. Wage discrimination among similar employees of the same firm or price discrimination among its customers would destroy long-term relationships.

Cyclical Responses

Career job arrangements desensitize the wage rate to changes in overall tightness of the labor market. First, because experienced workers earn more than their next-best opportunity wage, strengthening the labor market will increase the quit rate only slightly. Second, the normal queue of applicants allows the firm to hire new workers without raising the entering wage. To be sure, the "marginal effective wage" of the firm may increase.[32] A higher rate of inflow of new workers may push up marginal hiring and training costs and force the firm to hire new workers with poorer credentials. Hence, it may be worthwhile to lengthen the workweek, even at the cost of paying overtime premiums. But the firm has a strong incentive to avoid an unscheduled increase in the entering wage insofar as it would feel obliged to maintain its wage structure by increasing simultaneously the pay of experienced workers.

By making the elasticity of labor supply low in the short run and uncertain in the long run, the nonauction search mechanism creates wage inertia in career labor markets just as it makes prices sticky in customer product markets. Moreover, the quit-rate function may discourage wage changes much as the "information card" decision discourages price changes. That aspect of wage stickiness can be illustrated by the following model. A firm has two classes of workers—experienced and new; their wage differential is fixed by custom or convention. Thus, the firm has a single wage decision; that, in turn, will determine the quit rate of experienced workers, and hence the residual number of them who stick with their jobs. So long as the firm's optimal employment exceeds that level, it will be hiring some new workers out of its queue of applicants, whose quality (innate skill, education, experience) may be assumed to have a distinct and identifiable gradient. For any given wage, the deeper the firm must dip into the queue, the lower will be the productivity (average and marginal) of new workers. Thus, the quality of new workers will depend positively on the wage and negatively on the level of employment.

By setting a higher wage, the firm gains by reducing the quit rate of experienced workers and by raising the quality of its queue. It pays for that, of course, with a bigger payroll. If the supply of new applicants of given quality and the quit rate of experienced workers were both smooth continuous functions of the wage, the optimum wage would turn out to be a continuous increasing function of the level of employment. But the quit rate of experienced workers is likely to be discontinuous—low and fairly insensitive for wages at or above the level that fulfills the firm's implicit long-term obligation to be fair, but jumping discretely for wages below that level. If the discontinuity around the "fair" wage is substantial, that wage may be optimal for a wide range of employment levels.

In the event of a sudden deterioration of the labor market, wage reductions may not play much of a role (even for a nonunion employer). A firm that has sought to establish a prospect of rising wages over the career horizon may destroy its investment by cutting wages. To cut wages and yet avoid a long-term worsening of the quit rate, the firm must prove to the experienced worker that it is "forced" to take such action, which may be possible only if the firm is on the brink of bankruptcy or at least of a shutdown. Otherwise, pay cuts could be interpreted by workers as an "unfair" action by the employer to capture a larger share of the surplus.[33]

When the alternatives are temporary layoffs and wage cuts, the former are likely to be the lesser evil to the firm. To be sure, they are an evil: experienced workers care about steadiness of employment as well as the wage rate, and a laid-off worker may find a better job before he is recalled. In fact, however, wage premiums in many industries are sufficiently large to bring most laid-off workers back when they are recalled.[34] Moreover, as Baily has recently pointed out, layoffs have several partial offsets in the form of transfer income and some value of leisure.[35] Finally, and I believe particularly important, the firm has clean hands in the case of a layoff; since it is not using the worker, it cannot be "taking advantage" of him. All in all, it is easy to understand how the convention that wages are cut only *in extremis* became entrenched in labor markets before unions were significant and before Keynes attached so much weight to the downward rigidity.

For many of the same reasons, a weakening of labor markets may not even substantially reduce the short-run rate of wage increase in career jobs. The big issue in wage setting is a long-run battle over the division of the bilateral monopoly surplus between employers and experienced workers. Each side perceives the short-run elasticity of the other as relatively low, but the long-run elasticity as substantial. Hence, workers do not want to squeeze the firm into gradual extinction; and the firm does not want to press the workers to the point of explosive quit rates. These boundaries, however, may contain a wide area of sharp conflict of interest; and standards of fairness are sought to preserve the surplus available to the two sides combined.

Criteria in Wage Determination

Various groups of employers and workers may opt for different standards of "fairness": gearing wages to other wages or to product prices, or to consumer prices. Any of these standards will weaken the impact of changing labor-market conditions, and strengthen the momentum of a given rate of wage increase.

Wage-wage patterns. One method of achieving "fairness" involves emulating the wages recently set by other firms. The comparability system for compensation of federal employees is the most important example of this practice, but similar methods are used in many private firms. And many smaller industries "pattern" on steel or autos in their collective-bargaining settlements. Such patterning lends inertia to the rate of wage increase in the economy. In particular, overlapping schedules of contracts of long duration may result in a wage settlement that is a moving average of other recent wage settlements that were in turn moving averages of previous moving averages.

Wage-product price patterns. Alternatively, long-attachment wages may follow product prices. Recent price hikes by the employer that widened his profit margin can be legitimately viewed by labor as increasing its marginal revenue product and hence warranting a pay advance. On the other hand, recent rises in the firm's price that merely reflected a pass-through of previous increases in labor or material costs, with an unchanged markup, should make no case for further wage gains.[36]

Wages and consumer prices. Finally, consumer prices may influence wages. Presumably, one of the attractions of a career job is the prospect of a reasonably secure and rising standard of living for the long run. If the cost of living increases sharply relative to wages (or if the real-wage outlook merely becomes far more uncertain), the worker may see less value to his job, perhaps enough less to quit, even with no evidence that his wage has deteriorated relative to the (unknown) alternatives. And if the cost of living would affect quit rates at given wages, it will influence wages—in a way that need not depend on a mythical real-wage effect on leisure.

If the risk of a price-wage squeeze imposes a serious disutility on the worker, unions will seek wage adjustments informally geared to past movements of consumer prices or formal escalator clauses (even though an optimal bargaining strategy would depend on the ability to pay of the employer as well as the ability to consume of the worker).

On reasonable assumptions, the worker should prefer a contract for the next three years that offers certainty about his *real* wage to one with the same expected value that provides a certain nominal wage (and hence an uncertain real wage). On standard assumptions of one-sector inflation models, the employer who must commit himself for three years would also be expected to make the same choice. Surely, the wage escalator should reduce risk for firms in cyclical industries where product demand (and hence the ability to pass increased labor costs into product prices) is typically highly correlated with movements of overall consumer prices. The fact that formal escalators are the exception rather than the rule reveals a defect in the standard theory. Why do employers uniformly resist escalators, even in industry-wide bargaining? In a few conversations I have had with sophisticated businessmen on this issue, their explanations illustrate vividly the importance of certainty about *nominal* future costs in *customer* product markets. Some mention the need to make fixed-price bids or to accept fixed-price orders for production processes of long duration. More generally, they insist on the importance of planning in terms of dollars. They stress vulnerability to interproduct and international competition in a world where escalator clauses are rare. They view their future financial resources as given in nominal, and not constant, dollars. When they have to decide on a purchase of labor-saving machinery, they want to compare its price with some known price for labor over as long a horizon as possible.

Even if, for such reasons, the escalator imposes a net cost on the employer, the firm may recover that cost with an offer of lower expected value if the insurance is worth a lot to the worker. Thus, escalators may be an efficient element in the wage bargain. In fact, they have spread in recent years, although really strong uncapped ones are limited to a few major industries. All in all, consumer prices influence wages through both formal escalators and informal cost-of-living adjustments—ruling out any pure case of a "one-shot" rise in the cost of living.

Inflationary Bias in Wages

Of the various features of a career labor market outlined above, only the downward rigidity of the wage level points to an inflationary bias in wages. Because a wage cut is a qualitatively different and abnormal outcome, it can have sufficiently adverse long-term effects on quit rates to become unprofitable for employers. The qualitative significance of zero as a floor has no parallel for any ceiling. While downward rigidity in this sense can importantly raise the mean wage increase if much of the frequency distribution of wage changes would otherwise lie below zero, it cannot have any influence when the entire frequency distribution lies in the positive range.

Apart from downward rigidity, an inflationary bias might arise from an asymmetry following a regularly scheduled wage increase or a collective-bargaining settlement. The firm still retains the option of "overfulfilling" its pledge, by awarding extra wage increases or Christmas bonuses if labor markets should tighten dramatically. But it cannot underfulfill with negative Christmas bonuses. The resulting phenomenon of upward "wage drift" introduces a long-term bias if any of the temporary bulge becomes permanent (as seems likely, if only because it gets into prices in the interim).

A third possible source of inflationary bias arises because the strike is a recurrent threat that may disrupt any static equilibrium for union wages. Analytical models typically suggest that, while monopoly power of unions may lead to *high* wages, that power, once exercised, should not speed the *rise* of wages over time. But because the strike threat is the enforcement instrument of the union's (bilateral) monopoly power, that standard conclusion is not airtight. In any formal contract, the union makes the concession of disarming itself and burying the strike threat for, say, the three-year duration. When the contract expires, it once again has the opportunity to exercise that threat; *conceivably*, it may seek an additional payment from the firm in return for three more years of disarmament.[37]

In summary, career labor markets make wages less sensitive to labor-market conditions, rigid downward, and subject to a zone of indeterminacy and possibly to an inflationary bias. They also create indeterminacy in the bargaining process, permitting widely varying results in different periods of history and different countries on the extent to which wages follow labor-market tightness, wages, product prices, or consumer prices. Some characteristics of wage behavior are predictable: the rate of wage increase will have momentum; it will ultimately respond to market conditions; it will show downward rigidity. Once adopted, a particular pattern of wage following will persist for some time. But it will change and evolve, and it will defy any general theory with empirical content that is meant to comprehend all labor markets in all countries at all times—as is confirmed by Perry's analysis of worldwide wage experience in this issue.[38]

Inflation in the Mixed Customer-Auction Economy

In the real world, a few products are sold on organized auction markets; a few strictly fit the customer-market model with price tags based on a noncyclical markup over past costs; many lie between these poles; and some may reflect forces that are neither market clearing nor customer oriented. While no labor is marketed in a pure auction exchange, labor markets cover a spectrum of wage flexibility. In this sense as well as in many others, it is a mixed economy.

Figure 1 illustrates the mix in product markets, showing the contrasting behavior of four price indexes in selected periods of varying inflationary pressure. The sensitive industrial materials index, bar D, approximates pure auction prices; it is volatile, often declines, and responds promptly to changes in aggregate demand pressure. A broader group of wholesale industrial materials, whose price changes are shown by bar C, is not quite so volatile, less apt to fall, and less prompt to respond. (The unusual relative behavior of bars C and D over the period 1973:4 to 1974:4 stems from the inclusion of petroleum in C, but not in D.) Wholesale prices for finished products (bar B) are less "auction-like" in behavior than either C or D, while the private nonfarm deflator (bar A) is the least auction-like and most dominated by customer prices.

A Simple Algebraic Model

A simple algebraic model can describe some of the mechanisms of inflation in the mixed economy. For convenience, I shall focus on the auction-customer dichotomy in product markets rather than that in labor markets. I shall assume that customer prices are set by a markup over cost with a one-period lag, while auction prices clear markets. I shall also assume that all the costs of customer products (and none of the costs of auction items) are wages. For simplicity, the supply of auction-priced items is taken as completely inelastic over some significant short period, while the output of customer items can be expanded at constant real costs. Moreover, I shall initially ignore any changes in stocks of auction items (treating them all like fresh fish).

Also for simplicity, income and price elasticities of demand are taken as unity for both types of products, so that each captures a fixed share of

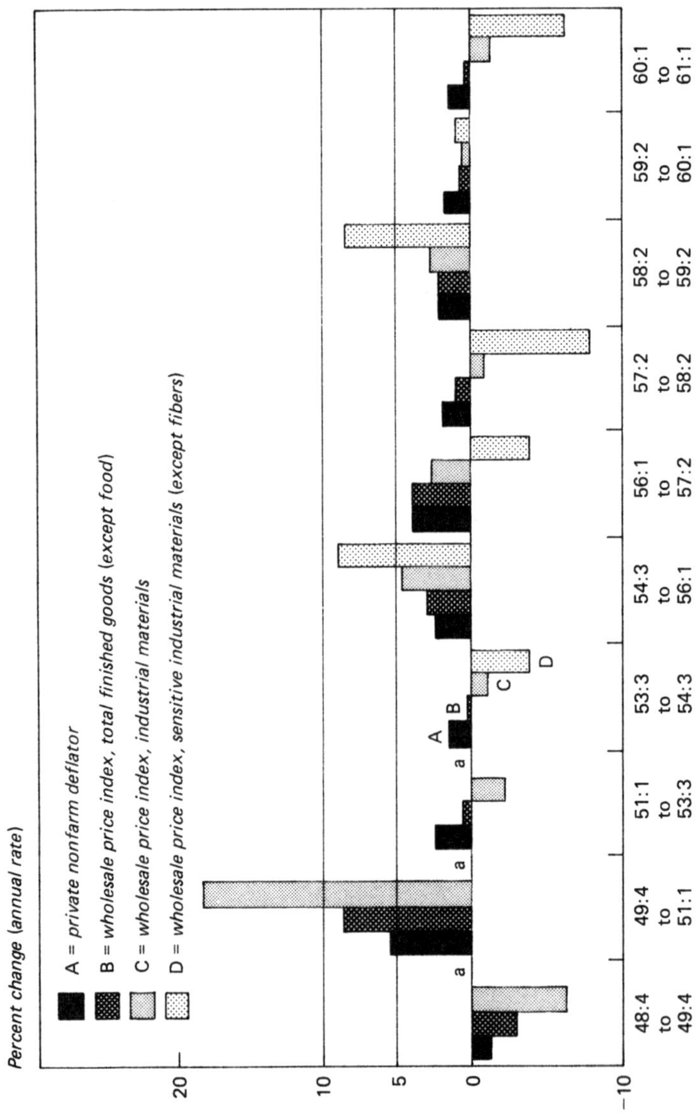
Percent change (annual rate)
A = private nonfarm deflator
B = wholesale price index, total finished goods (except food)
C = wholesale price index, industrial materials
D = wholesale price index, sensitive industrial materials (except fibers)
20
10
5
0
–10
a
a
a
A
B
C
D
48:4 to 49:4
49:4 to 51:1
51:1 to 53:3
53:3 to 54:3
54:3 to 56:1
56:1 to 57:2
57:2 to 58:2
58:2 to 59:2
59:2 to 60:1
60:1 to 61:1

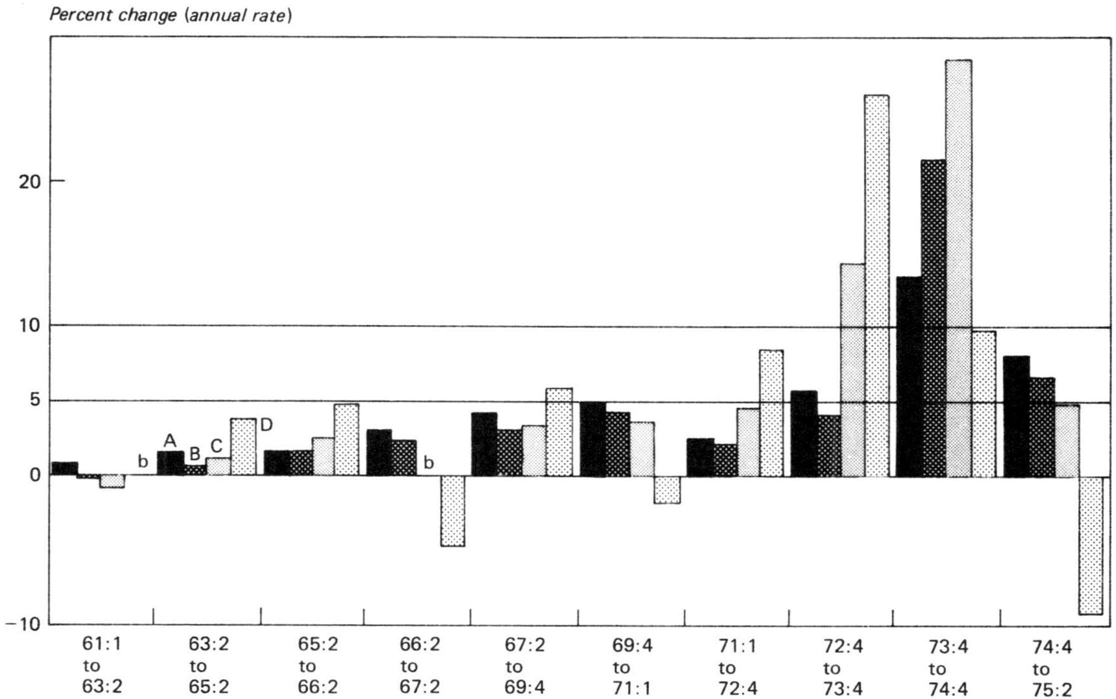

Sources: A—official U.S. Department of Commerce data, from COMETS data bank; B,C,D—unpublished tabulations of special groupings of U.S. Bureau of Labor Statistics wholesale price indexes, compiled by the Board of Governors of the Federal Reserve System.

Figure 1 Inflation rate, selected price measures, over varying intervals, 1948:4 to 1975:2. Key: a—data for this index are not available for years before 1953; b—this change was negligible.

total expenditures. For the moment, I shall note merely that wages, W, may depend upon prices, P, in both sectors, output, Q, in the customer sector (which reflects the strength of demand), and lagged wages, W_{-1}. The model can be represented by the following four equations:

$$P_A \bar{Q}_A = a\bar{Y} \tag{1}$$

$$P_C Q_C = (1-a)\bar{Y} \tag{2}$$

$$P_C = bW_{-1} \tag{3}$$

$$W = f(P_A, P_C, Q_C, W_{-1}), \tag{4}$$

where the A subscript refers to auction items, and the C subscript to customer items; $\bar{Y}$ is nominal income, which (like $\bar{Q}_A$) is taken as exogenous.

Initially, suppose that prices in both sectors are constant and so is income. Now income starts rising persistently at a rate of m percent, perhaps because of stimulative monetary or fiscal policies. The auction-priced items immediately have an inflation rate of m. But the inflation rate of customer items initially is zero, while their output expands at the rate of m.

Developments in subsequent periods depend on the behavior of wages. In the extreme case where wages are absolutely rigid,

$$W = \text{constant}, \tag{4a}$$

the inflation in the auction sector and the expansion of output in the customer's sector would both continue at the same rate of m. The inflation would never spread to the customer sector, and real wage rates would be squeezed although real payrolls would be maintained.

Suppose instead that wages respond promptly but incompletely to output (and hence employment demand) in the customer sector, but not to prices:

$$W/W_{-1} = (Q_C/Q_C^*)^s, \tag{4b}$$

where Q_C is the initial "noninflationary level" and $0 < s < 1$. In this case, P_C starts rising after one period and keeps rising at an increasingly rapid rate that ultimately reaches m and thus matches the rate of increase of P_A. But the ultimate ratio of P_C/P_A is below its initial value by m/s. And the equilibrium value of $\log(Q_C/Q_C^*)$ is also m/s. Finally, the equilibrium value of P_C/W is m below the initial ratio. Thus, real product wages are up and profit margins on customer items are down. Real wages measured in terms of consumer prices may, however, be up or down depending on the weight of auction items in the cost of living. Thus, the initial inflationary phase in which auction prices rise faster than customer prices (and wages) "permanently" changes relative prices.[39]

Finally, suppose wages respond fully and immediately to the cost of living, but not at all to the state of the labor market:

$$W/W_0 = (P_A/P_{A_0})^k (P_C/P_{C_0})^{1-k}, \tag{4c}$$

where k is the weight of auction items in the cost of living. It is convenient to set $P_{A_0} = P_{C_0} = bW_0 = 1$. Remarkably, every single result of this model corresponds to that based on (4b), with the mere substitution of k for s. The (4c) variant does make real wages in terms of consumer prices determinately constant, but the other changes in relative prices that emerge from (4b) apply here as well.

With both (4b) and (4c), ending the growth of nominal income does not halt inflation promptly, although auction prices stop inflating at once. Customer prices still register past wage increases, while wages keep rising as a result of tight labor markets—in (4b)—or of continuing advances in customer prices—in (4c). Thus, inflation damps down only gradually.

Interesting further possibilities can be entertained by relaxing some of the restrictive assumptions made above and thus allowing for more complex lags, partial responses of wages to the cost of living, labor inputs in the auction sector, differential price and income elasticities in the two sectors, auction-priced materials that are embodied in final products, variations in the output of the auction sector, changing real costs of producing customer items, and inertia in wage increases.

Several results appear to be robust for a wide class of such models: (1) the rate of inflation can be viewed as depending on (a) the size of the impact on the auction sector, and (b) the speed of transmission (generally through wages) to the customer sector. (2) A rise in the inflation rate changes relative prices, because the auction prices get out in front and the others do not catch up. (3) The more the output of a sector can rise, the less its price tends to go up. (4) Realized markups are squeezed wherever costs are passed through with a lag. (5) Inflation starts slowly but builds up a momentum that keeps it going even after its initiating source is eliminated.[40]

The implied squeeze on the profit margins of customer firms during inflation raises interesting questions. To be sure, so long as their output is rising rapidly in an inflationary boom, their margins in the real world are buoyed up by a cyclical productivity bonus that does not appear in these models. Yet the implied influence of inflation per se—as distinct from expanding output—in squeezing margins may have some verisimilitude. It clearly applies to public utilities and may apply to customer-strategy industries that are self-regulatory in their passthrough of costs. And since customer-strategy firms account for most U.S. equities, this squeeze could even be one of the reasons why the stock market does not perform well during inflationary times.[41]

Because customer prices lag behind costs in these models, real wages measured in terms of those prices are increased by inflation, regardless of how wage rates themselves are determined. The typical empirical result that real wages deflated by total consumer prices have no distinct cyclical pattern may indeed suggest that they are procyclical in terms of customer prices alone. Of course, this result conflicts sharply with the traditional Keynesian view that employment could increase only with declining real wages. But Keynes' belief in that classical proposition rested on the assumption that firms typically operated with diminishing marginal product of labor, a thesis that has long since been exploded by the facts on cyclical productivity.[42]

Assets and Interest Rates

When inventories of auction items are brought into the analysis, they play a key role, building a bridge to monetary theory. Suppose auction markets are "efficient" in the sense that all worthwhile information is compiled and digested by traders and reflected promptly in market prices. Then the demand for inventories of auction items (like cotton) will be geared to price expectations; cotton (or a futures contract in it) is potentially a portfolio asset for anyone who expects its price to soar. However, for customer items (like dacron), which are extremely illiquid, stock demands are essentially transactions balances of producers, distributors, and ultimate consumers; those stocks are likely to be much less sensitive to inflation and interest rates than are auction stocks. To be sure, cost expectations (for wage rates and the like) can influence sellers, and price expectations can induce intertemporal shifts by buyers (like the bulge in car sales in August 1974), but their scope and magnitude seem sharply limited.

Given an emerging inflation, the responses of asset markets in a mixed world will differ from those of a pure auction world. In the latter (with a sufficient sprinkling of assumptions), a jump in nominal interest rates by the expected rate of inflation will keep portfolios in equilibrium for every asset except non-interest-bearing cash. The induced economizing on money holdings produces the single adverse allocative effect of inflation recognized in standard theory—additional trips to the bank. But those answers cannot apply to the world of two classes of real assets, with the high inflation rate on cotton and the lower (and less relevant) one on dacron. Nominal interest rates cannot rise enough to equilibrate the demand for cotton stocks at the pre-inflationary level without creating an excess supply of loans and dacron stocks.

As a result, the rise in nominal interest rates must leave some expected net return from cotton speculation and thus maintain some additional demand for cotton inventories, limited by the high (and presumably increased) risk of holding these stocks. Sophisticated, wealthy, and risk-neutral (or relatively less risk-averse) investors are handed a windfall by the opportunity for speculation on cotton. Moreover, the buildup of cotton stocks and any possible induced holddown (or buildup) of dacron stocks lengthen the list of real allocative effects of inflation: there are changes in the schedule of trips to lots of suppliers, not just to suppliers of money.

While the expected inflation rate on cotton thus sets an upper limit on the inflation premium in nominal interest rates, I see no compelling reason why the expected inflation rate on dacron should be a lower limit. Surely, nothing guarantees or even suggests that the premium will correspond to the weights of dacron and cotton in any overall price index, or that any general "real" interest rate, however defined, will remain stable, or that the premium thus will offer reasonable insurance to savers who want to hedge against inflation. It is predictable that the structure of interest rates will be altered, because the financial sector is also a mixed auction-customer world. Because thrift institutions borrow short and lend long, they must pursue a customer "pricing" strategy, passing through the sluggish yields on their portfolios in the form of sluggish interest rates to their depositors. The customer strategy has more fundamental causes than the government ceiling on interest, which is really an effort to preserve its viability. In any case, the interest rate received by depositors does not compensate them at all fully for increased inflation.

The role and importance of money and near-moneys become clear in a mixed world. In a hypothetical world of universal, frictionless auction markets, every product is liquid, and a well-diversified portfolio of commodities should dominate over demand deposits. It is precisely because customer items are illiquid assets with sluggish prices that fixed-dollar assets are so attractive to households who may need to spend for automobiles, appendectomies, college tuition, life-insurance premiums, and property-tax bills at uncertain times in the future.[43]

An inflationary world with greater volatility of overall prices and of relative prices reduces the "real" services provided by liquid assets in ways that do not get recorded on balance sheets. The typical household is offered no reliable escape, even if it correctly anticipates inflation. Commodity markets are too risky; equity markets reflect the problems of customer-product firms; borrowing more to accelerate purchases of customer-priced autos and appliances is generally a losing strategy (1974 provided an exception); only homebuying offers hope for salvation, and then only to a limited number of families in those intervals when mortgages are available. Ample reasons emerge for the empirical fact that consumers save more in response to previously unanticipated inflation.[44] The diminished real wealth from nominal assets and the adverse "income effect" associated with greater risk and uncertainty apparently swamp incentives to shift into goods. And households may save particularly in liquid form in order to bolster their dwindling ratio of cash reserves to income and consumption. Thus, in a variety of ways, the new mixed world makes sense of the old story that inflation discriminates against the unsophisticated saver and investor, redistributing wealth from "suckers" to "sharpies."

Inflation may also stimulate investment in plant and equipment by auction industries and depress it in customer industries. The latter may well be confronted with an increased real interest rate (in terms of their product prices). Even if they are not, they may respond negatively to an equal rise in nominal interest rates and inflation rates. A number of businessmen have told me that their firms initially and tentatively evaluate a proposed new plant by estimating how its output (at some "normal" operating rate) would contribute to profits, assuming that the product will be sold, and all inputs bought, at *current* prices. That initial estimate of profitability will be depressed when lenders are getting some inflation premium in nominal interest rates—unless the firm assumes enough inflation of its product price (relative to that of variable inputs) to recoup this inflation premium. As I heard one businessman express his feelings, "I hate to make an investment that can be bailed out only by inflation." In effect, even if his best estimate is that he can push up prices fast enough to recoup the inflation premium, he feels greater uncertainty about profitability and hence greater reluctance to invest.

In summary, inflation has far more pervasive influences on portfolio choices than the traditionally hypothesized shift from nominal assets to real assets. It may push them away from nominal assets, customer items, equities of customer firms, and perhaps even physical capital of customer firms into auction commodities and those few other real assets that are reasonably liquid, like real estate.

Adaptation and Acceleration

The institutions of the customer sector are geared to a basically noninflationary world. And they have to adapt if the world becomes and remains inflationary. Some of these adaptations are taking place today. Customer-strategy firms are trying to widen their markups. They are shortening the intervals at which they pass through cost increases; they change prices more frequently; they are departing from historical cost calculations and trying to anticipate future cost increases. Many firms have begun to think and price LIFO as well as to report LIFO profits; they are focusing anew on the gap between replacement and original costs of capital in setting prices; some have ended the practice of accepting orders with fixed delivery prices, while others are putting future cost increases into those prices; some firms have instituted wage and pension escalators and have shortened labor contract periods. They are searching for new formulas and yardsticks to supplant the dollar yardstick. More and more investors are learning to participate in commodity markets and real-estate ventures. Lenders who need certainty of capital value are increasingly reluctant to make long-term commitments.

Most of these adaptations shorten the lags and increase the intensity of inflation associated with any given level of real economic activity. Thus, they generate an adverse shift of the short-run Phillips curve that reflects the inflationary experience of the past. That shift accords with the prediction of the accelerationist model, although the mechanism of acceleration is very different from that implied by a natural unemployment rate and a particular expected inflation rate. I believe the United States is currently suffering from an acceleration resulting from such adaptations to past inflation, as well as from the momentum of the more normal long lags in customer and career markets.

The gradualness and the costliness of these adaptations reveal the great dependence of customer institutions on the dollar yardstick. The adaptations require new techniques of management control, new—and perhaps inherently less efficient—kinds of customer and employee relationships, and a new breed of accountants. The innovators find themselves out of step and unable to communicate with their customers, suppliers, lenders, and government tax collectors or regulators. And so the economy adapts to inflation at only a tortoise's pace, even though everyone expects inflation to continue at least at a mule's (if not a hare's) pace.

Implications for Welfare and Policy

Customer markets are valuable institutions to society, because information costs are really high. In comparison with a dominantly auction economy, they cut the cost of shopping, and reduce the resources devoted to trading in spot and futures transactions and to the negotiation of formal contracts. They lower job turnover and create reasonably predictable career income profiles; they encourage firms to invest in workers and to build career ladders for them. They economize on resources devoted to point-estimate forecasting of the future. They promote reliance on custom and habit. They allow accounting systems and hence orders, capital budgeting, and financing to be guided by reliable historical costs rather than conjectural future costs. They make money and, more generally, fixed-dollar assets valuable and reasonably reliable claims over a wide range of consumer goods and services that may be desired many years in the future.

Prolonged and intense inflation upsets many habits of economic life, confronting consumers with price increases and price dispersions that send them shopping; making them doubt their ability to maintain their living standards, and downgrade the value of their career jobs and long-term savings; and forcing them to compile more information and to try to predict the future—costly and risky activities that they are poorly qualified to execute and bound to view with anxiety. The recognition by the consumer that economic institutions are gravely disturbed by inflation is an appreciation of reality—not money illusion. The illusion—Walrasian-general-equilibrium illusion or barter illusion—lies in the models of an economy in which inflation does not matter, offering automatic protection to savers through the interest premium on nominal assets and leaving intact the relative prices of cotton and dacron and the relative wages of janitors and professors.

The accelerationist is right that, in some respects, people are fooled by inflation. But the fooling lies, not so much in disappointing predictions of precise outcomes as in undermining the foundations of habit and custom that permit one to live without many point-estimate predictions. And the institutions of the system provide no vehicles of "unfooling" to transport the economy to a no-tradeoff situation of "fully anticipated" inflation and a natural unemployment rate.

I do not know, at this point, how to quantify the benefits of a customer economy or how to assess the fraction of those benefits that would be dissipated by the persistence of rapid and erratic inflation. Clearly, the total benefits are large: consider the welfare loss that would be imposed on a person forbidden ever again to engage in any economic transaction with anyone whom he has voluntarily bought from or sold to in the past—his employer, banker, mechanic, tailor, and the like. The percentage "discount" imposed by intense inflation on these relationships is not enormous, but neither is it trivial, given their dependence on the dollar yardstick. As William Brainard suggested in conversation, estimates of the substantial costs associated with a shift to the metric system may give some clues to the much larger costs of abandoning the dollar yardstick.

However these welfare benefits are evaluated, they must be balanced against the welfare costs of a customer economy—greater volatility of output and employment. In a recessionary world of universal auction markets, price and wage levels would plunge rapidly toward zero, allowing the Keynes effect and the Pigou effect to restore full employment.[45] And rapidly rising prices could similarly halt booms with a brief intense spurt (rather than a long nagging about) of inflation.

Although I cannot prove that the prevalence of customer markets yields a net benefit, subjectively I think the system is worth saving. The ability of the system to limit the waste of idle resources and to contain the inflationary bias in wages looked pretty good in the fifties and sixties, particularly in contrast to the record of the thirties and the forties. Indeed, in that tranquil period, long-run attachments must have paid off well. Infrequent layoffs, low quit rates, good internal ladders served firms and career workers, while sluggish cost-based prices satisfied customers and suppliers. Those successes may well have gradually encouraged more customer and career strategies; and that, in turn, may contribute to the finding that wages and prices have been less responsive in recent years to given cyclical movements of real activity.[46]

Steady Inflation

Some proposed policy strategies with respect to inflation seek an alternative yardstick for the dollar. The proponents of steady inflation—rather than low inflation—would set a target of stability in the first derivative of the value of the dollar rather than in its level. The steadily shrinking dollar may be a reasonable yardstick, but it has to be second best—just as a 5 percent annual decline in the length of a "yard" would be inferior to stability.

I can see two possible arguments for the compromise goal of steady inflation, but I find neither persuasive. First, if the key difficulty of stabilization stemmed from the downward rigidity of the *level* of wages, it could be sensible to aim at a normal inflation rate that kept nearly all wage movements in the positive range—so that absolute cuts in wage rates in significant sectors would not be needed to achieve the desired macro-equilibrium. Second, if the economy were fairly well adapted to some particular inflation rate (like 5 percent), it might not be worth the transitional cost to wring that inflation out of the system. As I have argued above, however, the adaptations are limited adjustments to varying and uncertain inflation (which still leave the system heavily dependent on the dollar yardstick), rather than full adjustments to any particular inflation rate.

The main problem of steady inflation as a goal is its lack of credibility. Targeting on a stable first derivative is admitting failure in the effort to stabilize the level. Why should anyone expect any greater success in stabilizing the rate of change of the price level than in stabilizing the price level? Moreover, in the context of the model of this paper, steady inflation requires such a full adaptation that the same expected inflation rate can pertain to dacron and cotton, and to the wages of professors and janitors. Steady inflation strikes me as even more of a mirage than when I first called it that four years ago.[47]

Indexation

Another proposed strategy for policy would substitute for the dollar yardstick a new cost-of-living unit through indexation of incomes, assets, debts, and taxes. Thus far, explicit cost-of-living adjustments have been enacted for social security and for federal retirement benefits, and both of the formulas written into law involve serious technical defects.[48] Apparently, construction of a substitute yardstick is not a trivial task.

The most far-reaching proposal would promote wage indexation as a general practice. Through indexation, career wages would respond more promptly and more fully to changes in the prices of auction products and in flexible wages. As Robert J. Gordon has convincingly argued, that must be socially undesirable when the changes in auction prices result from changes in supply.[49] But when the price changes are demand induced, presumably indexed wages would more nearly approximate the "shadow equilibrium" wages of an auction labor market.

A program of universal wage escalators would represent an effort to breathe life into the textbook auction model (accompanied by a hope that supply shifts would rarely be the culprit). In the indexed world, like the auction world, the price level would be volatile and would respond rapidly to aggregate demand; hence, a nonaccommodating monetary policy would automatically unleash the Keynes and Pigou effects in the early stages of inflation. Moreover, because the decreased inflation resulting from restrictive discretionary policies would emerge with a much shorter lag behind the reduced output and employment, such policies might become politically more feasible. The thesis is that, if inflation "hangs out" sooner, it will be stopped sooner. I find the argument intriguing, but not persuasive.

The equity case for wage indexation seems even less persuasive. To be sure, escalators make the real wage of an indexed worker less dependent upon such arbitrary elements as the timing of his contract or the effectiveness of his union leader. And they may help to resolve conflict by keeping inflation issues out of the wage bargain. At the same time, by increasing the volatility of price movements, they must exacerbate the uncertainty and variability of real incomes for those who have no escalators. If indexing is less than universal, its equity effects must be uncertain.

And if indexing became universal for wages, contracts for future delivery, claims, and taxes, the market-basket unit would become the yardstick and the numeraire of the economy, and the price level would become highly unstable. Clearly, the price system would go haywire if all the sellers of the items in a comprehensive market basket set "real prices" in market-basket units (only by magic would the prices add up to unity). Now suppose they aim collectively at a real price that exceeds unity, but they have to set price tags in dollars. If everybody's price is geared to full escalation with a short lag, the inconsistency of real aims must result in explosive inflation. The price system can work with gold, peanuts, or dollars as the standard, but it cannot work on an all-inclusive market-basket standard. To put it another way, the money equation would be pushed out of the general-equilibrium system, making that system insoluble.

All things considered, I suspect as good (or as bad) a case can be made for a social effort to discourage the responsiveness of career wages to cost-of-living movements as for one to promote it. If the link could be broken entirely, inflation would be more narrowly confined to auction markets and limited by a different kind of automatic stabilizer—a squeeze on consumer demand due to depressed real labor income. Transitory inflationary shocks might then blow themselves out with much less impact on the price level. The political process might even be improved because inflation would squeeze the majority of voters harder.

Policies for the Auction Sector

If instead of designing alternative yardsticks, policymakers should be aiming to save the dollar yardstick, then they must recognize the special role of the auction sector. While auction items may not be the source of excess demand, they will be the source of major price increases. Speculation on auction-product inventories in a strong cyclical upswing is not a response to any genuine change of relative scarcities, and serves no social function that I can see. Huge price increases of auction items impose macroeconomic welfare costs by transmitting both inflation and, through restrictive fiscal-monetary policies, underutilization to customer and career markets.[50] For these reasons, public stocks of auction items, measures to ensure adequate and reliable domestic supplies, and government disincentives to cyclically speculative stockbuilding all belong in the kit of economic stabilization instruments.

These realities of the mixed auction-customer world have been flagrantly ignored in U.S. agricultural policies of the seventies. Indeed, it is hard to find mistakes in monetary or fiscal policies that can match the macroeconomic damage wreaked by the policies of export promotion (backed by no public stocks) of farm products. Certain policies on the pricing of oil that essentially ignored their macroeconomic inflationary and recessionary effects rate another high place on the horror list.

The especially heavy weight of auction items in U.S. exports and imports has important implications for exchange-rate policies and for the monetary-fiscal mix. The discouragement to imports from a depreciating currency may sacrifice potential anti-inflationary benefits. Thus, the undervaluation of the dollar on trade account in 1974 and 1975 may be significantly impairing U.S. price performance (given the level of economic activity).

The anti-inflationary benefits of a highly valued currency are also an argument—although not necessarily a decisive one—for less monetary stimulus (offset by more fiscal stimulus). With flexible exchange rates, high interest rates that encourage short-term capital inflows may strengthen the currency and help particularly to moderate inflation. Such a shift in the monetary-fiscal mix would also help if domestic inventory holdings of auction commodities are especially sensitive to interest rates. In general, policymakers in the mixed customer-auction world should be critically aware of the possibilities for shifting the inflation-output tradeoff with measures that have their impact primarily on either auction-priced or customer-priced items. Many of those options lie in international economic policies, and some would require negotiation and coordination among trading partners to avoid "inflate-thy-neighbor" strategies.

As has been widely suggested, the worldwide character of the 1973 boom and the 1971–73 devaluations of the dollar contributed to the particular severity of recent inflation in raw materials and other traded commodities.[51] The story of 1966 may have been just the reverse: excess demand in the United States was not shared by its trading partners, and the dollar was increasingly overvalued; as a result, imports poured in, dampening down the inflation rate on commodities. Indeed, commodity inflation was unusually moderate in 1966–69; as shown by figure 1, it did not even match that of the middle and late fifties. That stability in the auction sector may have contributed to the initial complacency of U.S. policy. That experience also contributed in 1972–73 to the serious errors of economic forecasters (including me). We were blindsided by commodity inflation while we focused happily on tranquil labor markets, as though they were the only potential source of serious inflation.

Fiscal Policy

The makers of stabilization policy face a particular problem because customer prices and career wages are lagging indicators. By the time they exhibit a visible acceleration in a cyclical expansion, inflation will have become deeply entrenched. Discretionary policy decisions require the guide of more sensitive indicators that will register excess demand more promptly; quit rates, order backlogs, and the like should be examined carefully for their potential contribution to an early diagnosis.

The reverse problem created by customer and career markets is the need for so much unemployment for so long in order to work off an inflation that has become well entrenched. Under those circumstances, there are overwhelming merits in fiscal devices that would operate directly to hold down prices with less compression of output and employment. The ideal medicine for an economy in which both unemployment and inflation are too high is a value-added subsidy. And the next best is reduction in broad-based excise and sales taxes and payroll taxes. While they would be harmful in excess-demand inflation, these are the only prescriptions that deal directly and efficiently with the disease of stagflation. The one objection I hear again and again in response to my advocacy of such measures concerns their novelty—a disadvantage that would be remedied by their adoption.

Incomes Policy

Finally, a case for price-wage intervention by the government emerges in the customer-auction world. If most wages are heavily influenced by some criterion of fairness (and do not register some precise optimizing intersection of supply and demand), the government can be constructive by promoting a noninflationary criterion (or "guidepost"). In a world where, for good reasons, people care about the stability of the price level, every price or wage that has a zone of indeterminacy imposes an external macroeconomic cost when it is set at the top of the zone and yields a social benefit when it is set at the bottom. To be sure, there are grave difficulties in publicly influencing these private decisions; and misconceived controls can do even more harm to customer and career relationships than inflation does. But the potential social surplus from recognizing the macroeconomic externalities may be large enough to compensate parties that accept some restraints.[52]

The world of mixed customer and auction markets poses serious dilemmas for public policy. It is not the world of costless, fully adjusted inflation or of intractable natural unemployment rates. Its trade-off problem is genuine and genuinely agonizing. The system needs reasonable price stability to preserve its institutional framework: it cannot thrive with a 14 percent or even a 7 percent rate of inflation. And some loss of output and employment is worthwhile and unavoidable in the cure of an entrenched inflation. But because so many prices and wages respond so little to demand in the short run, holding down output and employment is an extremely slow and excruciatingly painful cure for inflation. The prolonged maintenance of unemployment rates of 7 percent or more, and of shortfalls in annual output of $100 billion to $200 billion, is neither a sensible nor a credible strategy. Fortunately, the system offers many opportunities for more efficient policies to dislodge an entrenched inflation. These include measures that counter the destabilizing influence of auction commodities; that use taxes and subsidies to reduce costs without reducing aggregate demand; and that influence wage and price decisions to reflect their macroeconomic externalities.

Notes

I am indebted to Nancy Delaney for her assistance in the research, and to Edward Gramlich and several participants in the Brookings panel for constructive criticism.

1. John Maynard Keynes, *How to Pay for the War* (Harcourt, Brace, 1940). See also, for example, Carl Shoup, Milton Friedman, and Ruth P. Mack, *Taxing to Prevent Inflation* (Columbia University Press, 1943); Ralph Turvey, "Some Aspects of the Theory of Inflation in a Closed Economy," *Economic Journal*, vol. 61 (September 1951), pp. 531–43; and the references in note 4 below.

2. That would not happen, however, if the private decisionmakers formulated their spending plans as shopping lists rather than dollar budgets.

3. Robert Clower, "The Keynesian Counterrevolution: A Theoretical Appraisal," in F. H. Hahn and F. P. R. Brechling, eds., *The Theory of Interest Rates* (St. Martin's, 1965), pp. 112–13, 121–24. The same kind of mechanism underlies the model in Robert J. Barro and Herschel I. Grossman, "A General Disequilibrium Model of Income and Employment," *American Economic Review*, vol. 61 (March 1971), pp. 82–93.

4. For example, see Tjalling Koopmans, "The Dynamics of Inflation," *Review of Economic Statistics*, vol. 24 (May 1942), pp. 53–65; A. Smithies, "The Behavior of Money National Income under Inflationary Conditions," *Quarterly Journal of Economics*, vol. 57 (November 1942), pp. 113–28; and Ralph Turvey, "Period Analysis and Inflation," *Economica*, n.s., vol. 16 (August 1949), pp. 218–27.

5. The frustrations of one young economist with these hypotheses (and his unproductive negative conclusions) are evident in Arthur M. Okun, "The Effects of Open Inflation on Aggregate Consumer Demand" (Ph.D. dissertation, Columbia University, 1956).

6. Charles L. Schultze, *Recent Inflation in the United States*, Study Paper No. 1 of materials prepared in connection with the Study of Employment, Growth, and Price Levels for consideration by the Joint Economic Committee, 86 Cong. 1 sess. (1959), pp. 44–77.

7. James Tobin, "Inflation and Unemployment," *American Economic Review*, vol. 62 (March 1972), p. 9.

8. These gave no reason to suspect that the structure had changed through 1968. In terms of the relationship between prices and the official unemployment rate, the observations for 1966–68 showed, if anything, a slightly more favorable tradeoff than those of 1956–57. See the chart in the *Economic Report of the President together with the Annual Report of the Council of Economic Advisers, January 1969*, p. 95.

9. George L. Perry, "Wages and the Guideposts," *American Economic Review*, vol. 57 (September 1967), pp. 897–904; N. J. Simler and Alfred Tella, "Labor Reserves and the Phillips Curve," *Review of Economics and Statistics*, vol. 50 (February 1968), pp. 32–49.

10. George L. Perry, "Changing Labor Markets and Inflation," *BPEA*, *3:1970*, pp. 411–41.

11. See Arthur M. Okun, "The Mirage of Steady Inflation," *BPEA*, *2:1971*, pp. 485–98, and other contributions to that symposium: William Fellner, "Phillips-type Approach or Acceleration?" pp. 469–83; and Robert J. Gordon, "Steady Anticipated Inflation: Mirage or Oasis?" pp. 499–510.

12. Milton Friedman, "The Role of Monetary Policy," *American Economic Review*, vol. 58 (March 1968), pp. 7–11, and Edmund S. Phelps, "Phillips Curves, Expectations of Inflation and Optimal Unemployment Over Time," *Economica*, n.s., vol. 34 (August 1967), pp. 254–81. Actually, the essential elements of the theory were spelled out much earlier in William Fellner, "Demand Inflation, Cost Inflation, and Collective Bargaining," in Philip D. Bradley, ed., *The Public Stake in Union Power* (University of Virginia Press, 1959).

13. See Robert J. Gordon, "The Welfare Cost of Higher Unemployment," *BPEA*, *1:1973*, table 2, p. 159, and George F. Break. "The Incidence and Economic Effects of Taxation," in Alan S. Blinder and others, *The Economics of Public Finance* (Brookings Institution, 1974), pp. 180–91. Some demographic groups exhibit a positive response to their own wage, but offsetting that are the negative cross-elasticities of the labor supplied by one family member to the wage of other members.

14. Models of work-leisure-search distortions include Dale T. Mortensen, "Job Search, the Duration of Unemployment, and the Phillips Curve," *American Economic Review*, vol. 60 (December 1970), pp. 847–62; Edmund S. Phelps, "Money-Wage Dynamics and Labor-Market Equilibrium," *Journal of Political Economy*, vol. 76 (July/August, 1968), pt. 2, pp. 678–711; and Robert E. Lucas, Jr., and Leonard A. Rapping, "Real Wages, Employment, and Inflation," in Edmund S. Phelps and others, *Microeconomic Foundations of Employment and Inflation Theory* (Norton, 1970).

15. George L. Perry, "Unemployment Flows in the U.S. Labor Market," *BPEA*, *2:1972*, pp. 263–75; Tobin, "Inflation and Unemployment," p. 7; Gordon, "Welfare Cost of Higher Unemployment."

16. See Thomas J. Sargent, "Rational Expectations, the Real Rate of Interest, and the Natural Rate of Unemployment," *BPEA*, *2:1973*, pp. 429–72, especially p. 435.

17. John Hicks, *Capital and Growth* (Oxford University Press, 1965), pp. 74–77; J. R. Hicks, *Value and Capital* (2d ed., London: Oxford University Press, 1946),

pp. 245–72; James Tobin, "Money Wage Rates and Employment," in Seymour E. Harris, ed., *The New Economics* (Knopf, 1947); Don Patinkin, *Money, Interest, and Prices* (2d ed., Harper and Row, 1965), pp. 313–34; Axel Leijonhufvud, *On Keynesian Economics and the Economics of Keynes: A Study in Monetary Theory* (Oxford University Press, 1968), pp. 102–09.

18. I believe my semantics are in the spirit of Kenneth J. Arrow, "Limited Knowledge and Economic Analysis," *American Economic Review*, vol. 64 (March 1974), pp. 1–10. I do not mean that people are ignorant or generally uninformed; I share Michael Wachter's concern (expressed in his comments below) that the terminology may be misleading in that respect.

19. "Upward Mobility in a High-Pressure Economy," *BPEA, 1:1973*, pp. 235–52; and Arthur M. Okun, "Inflation: The Problems and Prospects before Us," in Arthur M. Okun, Henry H. Fowler, and Milton Gilbert, *Inflation: The Problems It Creates and the Policies It Requires* (New York University Press, 1970), pp. 12–22. The best of the "standard" treatments is Robert M. Solow, "The Intelligent Citizen's Guide to Inflation," *Public Interest*, no. 38 (Winter 1975), pp. 39–49.

20. See the concluding portion of *The Crisis in Keynesian Economics* (Basic Books, 1974). Specifically (p. 79): "Any system of prices [and wages] . . . is bound to work more easily if it is allowed to acquire, to some degree, the sanction of custom. . . . This, I believe, is the true reason why inflation is damaging. . . . In conditions of inflation [arrangements] continually need re-fixing, so that issues which had seemed closed have to be reopened."

21. See Alfred Marshall, *Principles of Economics* (8th ed., London: Macmillan, 1947), pp. 369–79, and Hicks, *Capital and Growth*, pp. 49–57.

22. Nor is it conceivable that, despite the shift in demand, each hotel owner believes that the price elasticity of demand at the prevailing price, and hence the profit-maximizing price, is unaffected.

23. See the model presented by Edmund S. Phelps and Sidney G. Winter, Jr., "Optimal Price Policy under Atomistic Competition," in Phelps and others, *Microeconomic Foundations*. I am introducing one new element that is not in their model: relating the customer's search behavior to the supplier's pricing strategy.

24. For a discussion focusing on the labor market that considers a variety of informal methods of dealing with contingencies, see Oliver E. Williamson, Michael L. Wachter, and Jeffrey E. Harris, "Understanding the Employment Relation: The Analysis of Idiosyncratic Exchange," *Bell Journal of Economics*, vol. 6 (Spring 1975), pp. 250–78.

25. For the problems associated with futures markets, see Arrow, "Limited Knowledge."

26. Phillip Cagan, *The Hydra-Headed Monster: The Problem of Inflation in the United States* (American Enterprise Institute, 1974), pp. 21–34.

27. William Brainard, "Uncertainty and the Effectiveness of Policy," *American Economic Review*, vol. 57 (May 1967), pp. 411–25; William Fellner, *Probability and Profit* (Irwin, 1965), pp. 173–80.

28. It is thus understandable that Gardiner Means and John Blair have found and stressed a correlation between industrial-concentration ratios and the kinds of pricing patterns that I attribute to customer markets. See National Resources Committee, *The Structure of the American Economy*, A Report Prepared by the Industrial Section under the Direction of Gardiner C. Means (Government Printing Office, 1939), pt. 1, pp. 138–45; Gardiner C. Means, "Simultaneous Inflation and Unemployment: A Challenge to Theory and Policy," *Challenge*, vol. 18 (September/October 1975), pp. 6–20; and John M. Blair, "Market Power and Inflation: A Short-Run Target Return Model," *Journal of Economic Issues*, vol. 8 (June 1974), pp. 453–78. I do not, however, believe that sticky cost-based prices are unique to oligopoly or could be eliminated by changing market structure.

29. Cagan, *Hydra-Headed Monster*, p. 22; also see the detailed review of empirical findings by William D. Nordhaus, "Recent Developments in Price Dynamics," in Otto Eckstein, ed., *The Econometrics of Price Determination*, A Conference Sponsored by the Board of Governors of the Federal Reserve System and Social Science Research Center (Board of Governors, 1972), pp. 34–43. Moreover, the analytical discussion of short-run pricing by Nordhaus on pp. 21–27 and 31–34 is particularly perceptive. Another valuable discussion is presented by Otto Eckstein, "A Theory of the Wage-Price Process in Modern Industry," *Review of Economic Studies*, vol. 31 (October 1964), pp. 269–71, 281–82. For an analysis of the rationale of fixed pricing intervals, see Stephen A. Ross and Michael L. Wachter, "Pricing and Timing Decisions in Oligopoly Industries," *Quarterly Journal of Economics*, vol. 89 (February 1975), pp. 115–37.

30. In the customer-strategy model, cost decreases are no less likely to be passed through in lower prices than are cost increases of equal magnitude in higher prices. This result is consistent with Tobin's view of the empirical evidence: "This [inflationary] bias cannot be attributed to product pricing, which apparently passes on proportionately the changes in labor costs ... in both directions—down as well as up." See James Tobin, "The Wage-Price Mechanism: Overview of the Conference," in Eckstein, ed., *Econometrics of Price Determination*, p. 10.

31. Okun, "Upward Mobility," pp. 235–44; also, see Stephen A. Ross and Michael L. Wachter, "Wage Determination, Inflation, and the Industrial Structure," *American Economic Review*, vol. 63 (September 1973), pp. 675–92.

32. Robert E. Hall, "The Process of Inflation in the Labor Market," *BPEA*, *2:1974*, pp. 347–60.

33. Some case studies of the extreme conditions that justify pay cuts are presented by Peter Henle, "Reverse Collective Bargaining? A Look at Some Union Concession Situations," *Industrial and Labor Relations Review*, vol. 26 (April 1973), pp. 956–68.

34. Harold L. Sheppard and A. Harvey Belitsky, *The Job Hunt* (Johns Hopkins Press, 1966), pp. 35–37.

35. Martin Neil Baily, "Wages and Employment under Uncertain Demand," *Review of Economic Studies*, vol. 41 (January 1974), pp. 43–47. The psychic cost of unemployment to most breadwinners is an offset to those offsets, however.

36. Many wage equations in the early sixties included the profit margin as an independent variable. See Richard G. Lipsey and M. D. Steuer, "The Relation between Profits and Wage Rates," *Economica*, n.s., vol. 28 (May 1961), pp. 137–55; Otto Eckstein and Thomas A. Wilson, "The Determination of Money Wages in American Industry," *Quarterly Journal of Economics*, vol. 76 (August 1962), pp. 388–401; George L. Perry, *Unemployment, Money Wage Rates, and Inflation* (M.I.T. Press, 1966), pp. 27–29, 48–52. The profit squeeze and wage bulge of subsequent years made the fit deteriorate, so the variable dropped out—but not for analytical reasons. In part, Perry puts it back in his discussion of income shares in the article in this issue.

37. This argument does not imply that the union will capture an ever-larger share of the bilateral surplus in successive rounds of bargaining. For one thing, market conditions do change; for another, firms would ultimately find it worthwhile to resist further wage increases even at the expense of greater risk of a strike.

38. Throughout, some of the phenomena that I view as conventional could be conceptualized as expectational. (The indeterminacy is there in either case.) In part, this choice is a matter of analytical taste. For example, I would describe the current salaries of baseball players as based on last year's performance and argue that this convention rests on the long-term attachment that provides an incentive and a payoff for every year (except the final one in each career). Chicago and Minnesota economists would insist that the pay is an expected value where last year's performance provides the best estimate of this year's. As I see it, the analytical principle of Occam's razor supports my preference, but perhaps an even more ancient principle applies: *de gustibus non est disputandum.*

39. With $P_{C_0} = P_{A_0} = 1$, the solution to the first-order difference equation for P_C is $\log P_{C_t} = mt - m/s + (m/s)(1 - s)^t$; while $\log P_{A_t} = mt$.

40. These models closely resemble one constructed by James Duesenberry way back in 1950. See "The Mechanics of Inflation," *Review of Economics and Statistics*, vol. 32 (May 1950), pp. 144–49. Also, compare the models used by Robert J. Gordon to analyze food inflation in "Alternative Responses of Policy to External Supply Shocks," *BPEA*, *1:1975*, pp. 185–94.

41. Note, however, that FIFO profits are pulled down only to the extent that the cost-passthrough lag is longer than the inventory lag. Several aspects of cyclical movements in profit margins are explored by Charles Schultze in his paper in this issue.

42. See Okun, "Upward Mobility," pp. 211–13.

43. See Leijonhufvud, *On Keynesian Economics*, pp. 80–81; Karl Brunner and Allan H. Meltzer, "The Uses of Money: Money in the Theory of an Exchange Economy," *American Economic Review*, vol. 61 (December 1971), pp. 784–805.

44. George Katona stressed that fact for years to a skeptical profession; see *The Powerful Consumer* (McGraw-Hill, 1960). See also F. Thomas Juster and Paul Wachtel, "Inflation and the Consumer," *BPEA*, *1:1972*, pp. 71–114.

45. To do so, they would have to outweigh any negative impact of deflationary expectations on investment demand and have to escape any liquidity trap. Like

Robert Hall (in his article in this issue), I would expect a high degree of downward wage and price flexibility to restore full employment. But, unlike him, I would attach a large social cost to wage and price volatility.

46. See Cagan, *Hydra-Headed Monster*, pp. 2–8. Tobin points to the declining agricultural share of employment and GNP in the postwar era as another possible contributor. See his "Inflation and Unemployment," p. 14.

47. See "Mirage of Steady Inflation."

48. The defect in social security is discussed in Barry M. Blechman, Edward M. Gramlich, and Robert W. Hartman, *Setting National Priorities: The 1976 Budget* (Brookings Institution, 1975), pp. 175, 182; that in federal retirement introduces a recurrent and compounded rounding error.

49. "Alternative Responses of Policy," pp. 201–02.

50. The macroeconomic externalities can be illustrated by the following arithmetic example. Suppose (1) the price elasticity of U.S. demand for some auction item (say, wheat) is 0.2; (2) in light of the social attitude toward the inflation-unemployment tradeoff, stabilization policy aims at a given *nominal* GNP target. Then the production and domestic sale of one extra bushel, priced at $4, lowers nominal farm GNP by $16 and permits a $16 increase in nominal nonfarm GNP. So the bushel is really worth about $20!

51. See, for example, William Nordhaus and John Shoven, "Inflation 1973: The Year of Infamy," *Challenge*, vol. 17 (May/June 1974), pp. 18–19.

52. See my 1974 proposal for real wage insurance in Arthur Okun, "Incomes Inflation and the Policy Alternatives," in "The Economists' Conference on Inflation: Report," vol. 1 (1974; processed), pp. 369–71.

The Invisible Handshake and the Inflationary Process

Inflation has plagued the American economy and the economics profession throughout the decade of the seventies. Although the prospects for the economy over the near term are grim, I believe that developments within the profession are encouraging, and that they provide significant new insights into the inflationary process.

The New Experience of Chronic Inflation

The economy's problems with persistent inflation date back to the mid-sixties. But economists had no trouble explaining the inflation of the Vietnam period, which was clearly associated with excess demand. That experience fitted all our models, whether we were Keynesian, monetarist, eclectic, or erratic. We explained simply and succinctly that the price level rose because demand in the aggregate exceeded overall supply, just as the price of apples rose when the demand for apples exceeded their supply. The problems for economists emerged in 1970–71 when inflation persisted in the face of excess supply and survived a recession for the first time in the annals of U.S. business-cycle history. And they intensified with a vengeance in 1975–77, when after a severe recession, prices rose at a rate of nearly 6 percent a year while supply in the aggregate exceeded demand by all recognized criteria.

Chronic inflation that persisted in the face of excess supply confronted economists with many problems of interpretation and explanation. Let me focus on one particular puzzle, which I regard as the critical observation of behavior in the inflationary era of the seventies. In millions of instances, we have observed nonunion employers with no contractual obligations granting general pay increases when they had abundant applicants, no vacancies, and negligible quit rates. Profit-seeking employers presumably try to minimize the payroll costs of obtaining the quantity and quality of workers they wish to hire. Why would those employers *raise* pay when their wage and salary scales were already evoking an excess supply of labor? How can that action at such a time make sense—regardless of how employers perceived monetary and fiscal policy or what rates of unemployment or inflation they expected for the future?

I submit that their behavior is sensible. The employers are in fact striving to minimize payroll costs, *reckoned over a substantial time-horizon.* They know that experienced workers deciding whether to stick with or quit their jobs in periods of prosperity evaluate those jobs in terms of the way the employer has treated them during periods of both tight and weak labor markets. Any management that holds down the wages it pays when most wages are rising must expect to be penalized when opportunities for good jobs become abundant. And so the calculations of firms are sensibly focused on quit rates and hiring requirements, not merely for today or tomorrow, but over a longer period, including intervals of prosperity and boom.

The firm finds it worthwhile to make an investment in personnel relationships; it seeks a reputation as a good employer to maintain an experienced and reliable work force for the long run. Thus the employer opts to treat the worker "fairly," invoking standards of relative wages (how other employers are adjusting pay) and real wages (how the cost of living is affecting the purchasing power of workers' incomes). And once the employer adopts and announces such a personnel policy, the workers are led to expect that their pay will reflect those criteria.

Implicit Contracts

This line of reasoning is called the theory of "implicit contracts": firms with no explicit contractual obligations nonetheless act, in the pursuit of long-term profitability, to fulfill certain general commitments to their employees. They are guided by an invisible handshake, as well as by Adam Smith's invisible hand.

This theory, which provides important insights that I will discuss, has had many fathers within the economics profession during the seventies. Had I been asked a decade ago to account for general wage increases in recession, I am not certain exactly how I would have responded. But I am quite certain that my answer would have deserved a failing grade. Of course, all economists recognized that overall pay increases in a very weak economy had occurred in the United States in the mid-thirties and in Brazil on many occasions. But such episodes were explained by special factors rather than by an appeal to sensible strategies of employers and workers.

In retrospect, I can see the theory of implicit contracts foreshadowed in some earlier writings—mainly by labor economists but also by some macroeconomists. But I must confess that I first became impressed with the phenomenon in 1970–71 as a result of some informal conversations with a number of owners and executives of small businesses. I remember one who had experienced declines in sales and profits, had cut back employment, and yet had raised the pay of his workers by 7 percent. He faced no union, saw no threat of unionization, had no need to recruit employees, and was not concerned about current quits. In response to my probing, he explained articulately that, as a conscious policy, he did not "take advantage" of his workers while he had the "upper hand" in the labor market and that he could count on their remembering his actions when the job market tightened. Others echoed the same theme. Some managers mentioned current morale and productivity as well as future labor supply. Whenever I have discussed these issues with business executives, I have been struck by their straightforward, matter-of-fact emphasis on their reputations as employers. Economic theorists have taken a little longer to recognize these considerations. But, after all, we have never met a payroll.

The implicit contract view embraces as a special case the Keynesian assumption of a floor under money wages. Clearly the firm that hires a worker with a career job in mind must lead him to believe that his position will gradually improve, not worsen. Once the firm paints a bright future in order to recruit the worker, any subsequent cut in wages would be a disappointment and a source of antagonism. Hence the firm is inhibited from reducing wages, as Keynes posited. In fact, in an economy where wages normally rise over time, the same inhibitions can also apply to hold-downs or even slowdowns in wages for employees who had been led to expect fairly steady raises.

The same insights also help to resolve puzzles about behavior in many product markets. In periods of boom, many firms that experience excess demand lengthen their backlogs of unfilled orders and some even place their customers on allocation quotas, clearly eschewing price increases that would enhance their current profitability. Their decisions not to exploit fully the potential short-term benefits of tight markets are the understandable result of a longer-run view of their relationships with customers. By foregoing king-size markups in tight markets, the sellers build a clientele and establish a reputation that helps to retain customers when markets ease.

In many industries, firms feel obliged to justify price increases to their customers in terms of cost increases; they want to convince their customers that they are not exploiting a tight market to capture a larger share of the benefits from continuing relationships. And as the mirror image of that behavior in tight markets, these firms adjust prices in line with costs during periods of recession and slack, allowing percentage markups over standard costs to narrow only slightly. During recent recessions, prices in customer markets have not fallen; nor have they even been rigid or sticky. Rather they have kept rising, responding to the push of higher costs but resisting the pull of lower demands.

The cost-oriented pricing in product markets geared to customer relationships offers a dramatic contrast with the behavior of prices for products traded on auction markets. For the latter group, the traditional supply-demand model is confirmed beautifully. The prices of industrial raw materials, which are generally traded in organized commodity markets, fall in periods of recession. For example, they declined on average by 15 percent from a peak in May 1974 to a trough in March 1975. During that same ten-month interval, producers' prices of finished consumer goods other than food and fuel *rose* by 10 percent. Sellers in nonauction and auction markets alike experienced weak demand; they had essentially the same information about their costs and markets; the two groups presumably had similar expectations about the future course of the general price level and economic activity. Their prices behaved differently because they are set differently—one by an impersonal mechanism that equates supply and demand continuously and the other by a managerial strategy oriented strongly toward long-term customer relationships.

The Microeconomic Aspects

The theory of implicit contracts was developed by macroeconomists investigating various aspects of unemployment and inflation in the overall economy. But the theory has important microeconomic aspects, amending many traditional concepts of market efficiency. To be an effective mechanism, an auction market must have a large number of buyers and sellers competing for a standardized product that can be readily defined in terms of quantity and quality. Those requirements are met by products like soybeans, cotton, hides, and lumber, as well as by many financial instruments ranging from common stocks to foreign exchange. And those items are indeed traded through brokers or auctioneers who find the price that equates demand and supply. But that mechanism for making transactions would be abysmally inefficient for neckties, restaurant meals, haircuts, machine tools to produce bicycles, or blue Chevrolets with standard transmission and stereo but without air conditioning. Most important, the labor market cannot rely on an impersonal auction system, because jobs are specialized and the quality of workers cannot be objectively graded. The isolated cases in which hiring decisions are, in effect, made through brokers—for example, for office temporaries and snow shovelers—underline the nearly universal preference for the face-to-face, personalized transaction.

In the absence of the auctioneer, buyers and sellers must make transactions by search and shopping, which are costly activities. Pursuing rational strategies, they will not play at do-it-yourself auctioneering, but will aim to hold down those costs. Because of the high costs of finding a job and of obtaining a productive worker, continuing relationships in career jobs become worthwhile to both workers and employers in most industries. Because sellers in many product markets depend on sales efforts by employees or on shopping by buyers, the firms promote patterns of recurrent purchases, seeking to convert buyers into regular customers by establishing the reliability, predictability, and generally satisfactory character of pricing and services. Even when purchases are not recurrent, sellers strive to build a reputation whereby the satisfied buyer of the past passes a good word along to the potential buyer of the future. While the sellers are serving their own interests with such a strategy, they also improve the efficiency of the economy by reducing transactions costs. These customer and career relationships are efficient adaptations to the realities of a complex, interdependent economy; they should not be interpreted as evidence of some evil monopoly power.

In some cases, the relationships between buyers and sellers are expressed in written formal contracts that specify the obligations of the two participants to each other. But such explicit contracts have a limited scope because of the expenses of negotiating, formulating, and enforcing them, and because of the rigidity that they can impose on the parties. And thus, in many areas, the efficient way to do business is through understandings and conventions involving fair play and good faith. The participants act to facilitate recurrent transactions, but they do not assume legal contractual obligations. Each has an incentive to satisfy the other in order to maintain the relationship that is mutually beneficial.

The arrangements that people make for such continuing relationships take diverse and sometimes contrasting forms, which cannot be precisely predicted or, at this point, fully explained. For example, under the widely recognized implicit contract between large Japanese firms and their employees, the firm is expected to provide a steady job throughout the careers of the workers, regardless of the state of the business cycle. The employers thereby assume the risk of excessive payrolls during recessions but may obtain compensating benefits through greater loyalty or more moderate wage demands by their workers. In contrast, implicit and explicit contracts in the United States give the employer substantially more discretion over the amount of employment, with the result that mass layoffs are a standard feature of our recessions. Much research lies ahead to explain the rationale and the consequences of different types of implicit contracts.

Another challenging area of investigation concerns the issues of equity that implicit contracts bring into the workings of the private marketplace. Implicit contracts can be effective only in a social atmosphere that incorporates a sense of mutual respect and a consensus on principles of fair play and good faith. Equity is thus not an extraneous irritant imposed upon the market by political institutions, but rather a vital lubricant of market processes.

Implicit Contracts and Inflation

The implicit contracts governing wages and prices in many areas are a key reason why any sudden change in total spending has only a small initial impact on inflation and a correspondingly large initial impact on output and employment. Thus an overheated economy initially has a rosy glow from low unemployment rates, ebullient capital formation, and strong productivity growth. For example, during the boom of the late sixties, workers and firms in many sectors gladly supplied more labor input and more output with only moderate deviations of wages and markups above the path regarded as customary and satisfactory. The implicit contracts were in effect shaded, but they were not scrapped. And thus inflation was slow-starting in that prolonged period of excess demand. But for the same reasons, inflation was slow-stopping when demand weakened. In the recession as well as in the boom, output and employment were affected a great deal, but wages and prices only a little.

The slow-starting, slow-stopping nature of inflation has been evident to some degree throughout the era since World War II. Wages and industrial prices responded less sensitively to the business cycle than was the case earlier in our history, reflecting in part the growing role of implicit and explicit contracts. Indeed, the mildness of the postwar business cycle encouraged a longer-run emphasis in wage and markup decisions. During the fifties and sixties, most private behavior was adapted to a modest upward creep in the price level that yielded a secular average inflation rate of 1 or 2 percent, with recurrent cyclical bumps and dents around the trend.

In the seventies, that underlying belief in the long-term stability of the price trend was severely shaken by prolonged experience with rapid inflation. The notion of par-for-the-course on wage increases shifted upward. Thus a pay raise of 4 percent, which seemed decent and fair to a career worker in 1965, was inadequate and insulting in 1970 and has remained so ever since. Similarly, prices in customer markets became depressed relative to prices in auction markets, and have been subject to recurrent upward pressures. Business and labor practices were altered to depend less heavily on the stability of the dollar. Those changes have sped the transmission of cost increases into price increases through the system—with the institution of cost-of-living escalators; the abandonment or shortening of fixed periods for price-setting like the model-year pricing of automobiles; and the erosion of the willingness of sellers to accept orders with guaranteed prices at delivery.

In general, as people adapt to an inflationary world, they make inflation more rapid and more persistent. Any prolonged experience with an inflation rate well above the secular average to which the system has become adapted alters implicit and explicit contracts in ways that make the inflation feed upon itself. And that has been the continuing experience of the seventies in periods of weak demand as well as of strong demand.

Yet even today, Americans continue to depend heavily on the dollar as a yardstick and a standard. Our economy is not adapted to double-digit, or even to 6 percent, rates of increase in prices. If inflation is not brought under control in the near future, the eighties will be marked by even more indexing, further shortening of the lags in transmission of cost increases, and a continuing shift away from dependence on money in implicit and explicit contracts. And such adaptations would further intensify our inflationary woes.

The Costs of Inflation

Implicit contracts introduce new dimensions in the reckoning of the costs of inflation to society. First, even when added inflation stems from a general, economy-wide cause like an excessively stimulative monetary policy and even when it is reasonably predictable, various types of wages and prices respond differently. Auction prices outrun customer prices; escalated wages outpace other wages in career jobs; wages of workers in casual jobs are likely to rise more rapidly than most wages and salaries in career jobs. These changes in relative prices and wages serve no useful function as rewards or market signals; yet they reshuffle income among families. The redistribution is not primarily from rich to poor or from poor to rich; rather it takes the form of a lottery that renders prizes and penalties arbitrarily and inequitably.

Second, because inflation can feed on itself, an acceleration of inflation must increase uncertainty about the future course of inflation. The record over time and across nations makes clear that, when and where the average rate of inflation is higher, the rate for any year is more variable and more volatile. And uncertain inflation generates a crawl away from money. In asset markets, deposits, bonds, and other fixed-dollar assets become less attractive relative to the time-honored inflation hedges like real estate, precious metals, and art objects. Yet these investments are inherently less liquid than monetary assets and subject to large transactions costs for buyers and sellers.

Finally, in job and product markets, the crawl away from money impairs the most important yardstick and means of communication in the economy. A nation that has learned to keep score in dollars on the fairness of implicit contracts, on balance-sheets and income-statements, and in planning for the future, gradually finds that its training has become obsolete. These developments impair significantly the sense of security and well-being of a society, even when they do not show up as a subtraction from real GNP.

The Fiscal-Monetary Arena

This view of the inflationary process highlights the dangers of excessively stimulative fiscal and monetary policies that permit inflation to become established in the system and feed upon itself. Moreover, it suggests the need for a consistent and determined strategy to slow the growth of aggregate spending—that is, the dollar total of GNP. But it also underlines the high cost of a cure for inflation based solely on monetary and budgetary restraint. Unquestionably, such a cure is available: inflation can be halted by a policy of tight money and tight budgets maintained intensively enough and long enough. But the costs are extremely high. Because of implicit (and explicit) contracts, a restrictive policy will, for a considerable period, push down output and employment drastically in an effort to slow prices and wages. According to past experience, the current recession, or a deepening of that recession engineered by restrictive monetary and fiscal policies, will sacrifice roughly $200 billion of production for each point that it reduces the basic inflation rate.

A $1 trillion cure for chronic inflation is unthinkable. It would resurrect the dark days of the thirties and jeopardize the political and social viability of our market institutions. To be sure, some economists argue persuasively that a credible and consistent policy of demand restraint would reduce that cost. But it is impossible to predict with any confidence whether the resulting "discount" from the trillion-dollar figure would be 20 percent or 80 percent. If an anti-inflationary strategy relying solely on demand restraint is adopted on the basis of exceedingly optimistic estimates of its costs, subsequent disappointments could readily discredit and reverse the effort. An undiversified anti-inflationary program is an inefficient, high-risk strategy. Fortunately, there are ample opportunities for diversification.

Prices and the Price Level

In an economy with a significant network of implicit contracts, a jump in the price of any major product raises the price level, and indeed the inflation rate. That connection between particular prices and the price level does not exist in a world of universal auction markets, and that may be the most fundamental difference between the two worlds.

The jump in petroleum prices imposed by the Organization of Petroleum Exporting Countries this year offers a timely example of this distinction. Suppose that the budgetary and monetary dials are controlled in such a way that the dollar total of GNP is not altered by the OPEC action. In an auction world, the consequence of higher fuel prices would then be lower prices for most other things. In particular, the auctioneer in the labor market would ensure that money wages fell enough to keep supply and demand in balance, thus preventing the emergence of unemployment.

It can be true as well in the real world that, if more dollars are spent on petroleum, fewer will be spent on most other items. But the reduced spending on those other items, and particularly on labor, will reduce output and employment—not merely hold down wages and prices. At a given unemployment rate, there is no mechanism to slow wages. Indeed, they will speed up via the chain reaction from fuel prices to the consumer price index to cost-of-living escalators. Given a jump in fuel prices, a policy strategy of stabilizing dollar GNP must put people out of work, waste productive capacity, and discourage investment—including even investment in energy-saving projects and alternative energy sources. It pushes the economy in an inflationary and a recessionary direction at the same time.

The recessionary effects can be avoided if total spending is stimulated by monetary and fiscal policies. But then the inflationary consequences are exacerbated. In addition to the rise in the price level from higher oil prices, the nation is subjected to a prolonged increase in inflation operating through cost-of-living escalation of wages and higher import costs from a likely devaluation of the dollar. The dilemma is genuine. And, incidentally, the more that wages (and other contracts) are indexed to the cost of living, the worse that dilemma is.

The adverse effects of OPEC actions can teach us how to take actions for ourselves with favorable effects. The OPEC price increase is the equivalent of an excise tax imposed on the American consumer, and that quasi-tax can be neutralized by reductions in actual excise taxes—by cuts in state sales taxes or in federal payroll taxes on employers, which act in part as hidden sales taxes on consumers. Although it cannot repeal the higher real cost of oil, that neutralizing strategy can avoid the grim alternatives of accepting a recession or adding to inflation.

The lowering of indirect taxes can also help to counter the inflationary inertia that is now built into our implicit contracts. It can push down on consumer prices and have favorable secondary effects on wages. Various other cost-reducing measures can be used similarly to counter inflation without courting recession. For example, subsidies for low-income workers could substitute for the minimum wage; and acreage controls on farm products could be eliminated. In fact, in recent years, the nation has suffered self-inflicted wounds in the form of higher payroll taxes, much higher minimum wages, and renewed acreage controls. These have inflationary consequences in the real world of the American economy, although not in the hypothetical world of universal auction markets.

The linkage of prices and the price level applies even more broadly. Indeed, the discretionary price and wage decisions made by major American firms (and unions) affect the entire economy. By opting for the top of the relevant range in setting prices or wages, the private decision-maker acts as a mini-OPEC with the same inflationary-recessionary consequence. On the other hand, a decision on the low end of the range bestows upon society the benefit of less inflation and the opportunity for more growth. And so the whole nation is an affected third party when such private decisions are made.

These are macroeconomic examples of what economists have traditionally identified as "externalities"—effects on other parties stemming from a transaction between a buyer and a seller. Wherever important externalities exist, the market can generate an efficient outcome only if the costs or benefits of the bystanders are somehow incorporated into the reckonings of the decision-makers. To reflect the social benefits of certain private actions, we grant tax credits for the purchase of productive machinery and the employment of unskilled workers. The same reasoning establishes the social desirability in principle of tax-based incomes policies, which apply tax penalties or rewards to encourage restraint in wage and price decisions by reflecting the social benefits of such restraint.

Circumstances in the months ahead may provide a neat opportunity to institute a tax-based incentive for price and wage moderation. As one part of a tax reduction, which will probably be appropriate in 1980, investors in plant and equipment are likely to be granted the opportunity to depreciate their assets more rapidly for tax purposes. Such a stimulus to investment would brighten the outlook for productivity growth. But any anti-inflationary benefits it can provide are clearly limited and long delayed. Prompt and substantial anti-inflationary benefits could be obtained by linking major tax benefits of accelerated depreciation to compliance with the price and wage guidelines. Large firms should be required to exercise price and wage restraint as a condition for obtaining the full benefits of the faster writeoffs. The task of enforcing such a provision could be kept simple by imposing the requirement only on firms obtaining a tax reduction in excess of, say, $100,000. These large firms would file certificates of compliance with the Council on Wage and Price Stability, and that agency would be authorized to deny the validity of any certificate, subject to appeal in the courts. Such a measure would test in practice the ability of a tax incentive to help curb inflation, and it would couple the nation's urgent short-term need for price and wage restraint with its longer-term need for strengthened capital formation and improved productivity performance.

The Invisible Handshake

The recognition of the invisible handshake and of its role in the inflationary process highlights the many sources of inflation that go beyond excess demand and the many costs of inflation that go beyond short-term surprises. It reveals the inflationary consequences of value-added and sales taxes, and the dangers of the emerging general trend toward cost-of-living escalators and indexing. It corrects the fundamental errors of economic policy and economic analysis that stem from the assumption of universal auction markets. The hawks and the doves on inflation policy make the same mistake of modeling the American economy as a giant soybean market. The hawks then prove that price stability can be achieved readily by monetary policy alone; and, based on the same "soybean illusion," the doves proclaim the inflation, once it becomes anticipated, is not costly.

Implicit contracts help to explain why inflation is costly and why it is difficult to eliminate once it has become entrenched. But those institutions also create the opportunity for cost-reducing measures and tax-based incomes policies to help curb inflation, along with a consistent fiscal-monetary strategy to slow the growth of total dollar spending. Fundamentally, our economy is more efficient because it is guided by the invisible handshake as well as the invisible hand. And it will work even better when policy-makers and theorists recognize the implications for the cure of chronic inflation—in short, when they choose to act as wise owls rather than fierce hawks or passive doves.

Rational-Expectations-with-Misperceptions as a Theory of the Business Cycle

In my judgment, the theory of rational-expectations-with-misperceptions provides an explanation of the business cycle that: represents a constructive effort to deal with questions that sorely needed to be asked, is logically impeccable and theoretically satisfying in its response to those questions, does not identify in operational terms the specific nature of the cyclical process, and fails to account for the duration and many key features of the actual cycle.

The Micro-Macro Bridge

The centerpiece of microeconomics is the purely competitive auction market in which buyers and sellers participate atomistically as price takers and where supply and demand are equated continuously by variations in price. These individual markets aggregate into a Walrasian general equilibrium model in which aggregate output is supply-determined, changing only when production functions shift, or when stocks of capital and natural resources change, or when the flow of labor offered at a given real wage changes (because of either changes in population or changes in tastes concerning work activity). In that aggregation of perfect markets, shifts in nominal aggregate demand affect only prices and never quantities.

Macroeconomics contrasts sharply with these implications of aggregated microeconomics. It begins with the observation that output and employment display significant deviations around their supply-determined trends that are (a) serially correlated and (b) normally positively correlated with deviations around a medium-run trend of nominal spending. These fluctuations around the trend of real activity are the "business cycle" (a term that is not meant to imply strong periodicity). Clearly, the business cycle could not happen in aggregated classical microeconomics. Thus any macroeconomics that is connected to microeconomics by a solid bridge must explain how it departs from the classical micro model in its conception of the operation of markets.

In fact, Keynes was explicit about the nature of his amendment. He departed from classical microeconomics *only* by modifying the labor supply function to include a wage floor. And, he offered many (indeed too many) explanations for the wage floor. But his bridge was defective; none of the explanations flowed directly from the implications of optimization by economic agents or from a specific institutional constraint. Many of the followers of Keynes operated with no bridge to microeconomics. Instead, they adopted the "fixprice method" (in Hick's terms), explicitly assuming away variations in prices and wages. And then, necessarily, nominal disturbances were found to have—purely and solely—real effects. (Indeed, this tradition began in the pre-Keynesian era, as illustrated by the accelerator theory of investment.)

The fixprice finesse may have helped economists develop a sharper focus and a better understanding of real relationships, like the consumption function, inventory and fixed investment functions, cyclical productivity relationships, and multiplier-accelerator interactions. But it had important costs. One of these was a professionally disturbing gap between macroeconomics and microeconomics. In effect, at the beginning of the macroeconomic semester, students were required to forget what they had learned in microeconomics about the equilibrating function of prices and wages. More seriously, by operating with models that took prices and wages as given for pedagogical purposes, economists tended to think of them as given for general purposes. Thus, the finesse contributed to the long lags in professional progress toward a satisfactory theory of the causes and consequences of inflation.

When the Phillips curve supplanted fixprice in the Keynesian model, it emerged as "an empirical generalization in search of a theory," as Tobin aptly put it. And the entire structure was seriously undermined when that empirical generalization collapsed.

In the last dozen years or so since that collapse, serious professional efforts have been made to construct that sorely needed macro-micro bridge. Those efforts, including the particular ones conducted by the "rational expectations school," are asking the right questions and working to provide illuminating answers.

The Misperceptions View

The particular bridge supplied by the rational expectations school amends the classical model simply and solely by assuming that buyers and sellers in any particular market may have imperfect information about prices in *other* markets. Then, even if each market passes all the standard tests of continuous clearing, complete atomism, and costless transactions, the imperfect information about other markets creates the possibility of a business cycle—of real effects from disturbances in nominal aggregate demand. And there are persuasive reasons why rational agents may have imperfect information about developments in markets in which they are not operating. Some pieces of information have costs that exceed their value. Thus, the theory is firmly grounded in the assumption of rational behavior and optimization.

In response to a generally unexpected jump in nominal aggregate demand, the aggregated classical microeconomics would predict a proportionate rise in all product and factor prices with no changes in quantities. In contrast, the rational expectations theory would envision some initial expansion of quantities resulting from misperception. A seller finding a surprisingly high price in the market for his product may respond by producing and selling a larger volume of output, because he may well not fully recognize the higher replacement costs of his inputs or the higher revenues available from alternative outputs. Some sellers in product markets may be focusing their attention on the markets in which they are operating and thus not become aware of similar price movements in factor markets and other product markets. They may then respond to a higher price for their product as though it was a higher relative price when in fact it may merely parallel the rise in the general price level.

Similarly, following the rise in nominal aggregate demand, workers encountering unexpectedly higher wages in their particular labor market may offer more work. They may respond that way for either or both of two reasons: (1) because they have a positive elasticity of supply of work effort with respect to real wages and fail to recognize the increase in consumer prices occurring in product markets; or (2) because they do not recognize that nominal wages are higher in other labor markets as well, thus raising the return from selling their labor elsewhere.

This model abandons explicitly the assumption (often implicit) of the Walrasian model that all information has zero costs. Information costs to participants in any one market about prices in *other* markets are the grains of sand thrown on the frictionless classical machinery to destroy its conclusion that nominal disturbances have only nominal effects. With that small exception this model preserves the entire apparatus of classical microeconomics. It constructs a logically and theoretically satisfactory bridge. Misperceptions about prices in other markets can account for *some* cycle in real activity.

The Nature of the Missing Information

To begin my critique of the theory, I see no way to assess the role of misperceptions about relative prices in the actually observed cycle until the rational expectations theorists give these misperceptions much more operational content than they have thus far. In general, the proponents stress the rational expectations *despite which* the cycle takes place; I wish they would focus more sharply on the misperceptions or the missing information, which are allegedly the *cause* of the cycle. In the spirit of Howard Baker, I wish to be told what the decision makers don't know, for how long they don't know it, and why they don't find out. Is there any direct empirical evidence that sellers lack timely information about other prices that are relevant to their "true" marginal costs? Are there persuasive a priori reasons why sellers are likely to lack such information in important ways for prolonged periods?

Operating on my own intuition, I find it implausible that important information is sufficiently costly to outweigh its value to rational agents on a timely basis. For one thing, by reading the newspapers, market participants obtain a virtually costless flow of information from the reporting on the monthly indices of consumer and producer prices. Even more significantly, firms and households operate in both product and factor markets at essentially the same time. How much of a communication gap or lag can rationally be maintained between the personnel manager and the sales manager of a given firm? How much of an effort is required within the family to ensure communications between the workers and the shoppers?

How long can a rational agent collect wage offers in various labor markets and still maintain a serious misperception in the face of his actual experience? Any sensible job seeker must be Bayesian. If he samples twenty labor markets and obtains twenty wage offers which all lie below his initial mean expectation of wages, he must revise that expectation downward sharply and quickly—even if he is unable to calculate that the probability of drawing such a sample is slightly less than one in a million.

Is it really plausible, as econometric labor supply functions based on this model imply, that the deviation of "anticipated wages" from actual wages narrows at a rate of only 15 to 36 percent a year?

Let me raise a different question about the nature of the misperceptions and missing information. Any theory that attributes decision-making errors by private agents to missing information implies that there exists, in principle, some set of correct, timely information that would eliminate these errors. That information needs to be identified specifically. Indeed that task may have important implications for public policy. The model seems to point directly to the potential benefit from filling the critical gap of missing information that accounts for decision errors. Clearly, the production of information is subject to huge economies of scale; and, because of laws on disclosure, the government is likely to be the most efficient collector of proprietary information from businesses and households. Within the framework of this model, one must ask whether the Bureau of Labor Statistics holds the key to eliminating the cycle.

The Duration of the Cycle

More evidence about the nature of the missing information might quell my doubts and refute my tentative hypotheses. But if my suspicions are well-founded, misperceptions about relative prices are only a small first step toward accounting for a cycle of the duration and amplitude that are actually observed. And they barely begin to explain prolonged periods, like 1958–63 and 1975–77, when output and employment remained below their equilibrium values (by anyone's measure). How much of the basic profile of such periods should be attributed to consistent, repetitive overestimates by sellers of general inflation (relative to their known selling prices)? Survey data from households and business executives in those periods display no consistent pattern of overestimating inflation, so far as I am aware. Inflation forecasts made by professional economists were remarkably accurate in the early sixties and in 1976–77 as well.

Indeed, the forecasts of real activity made by economists in 1958 and 1975 (and every other recession year) accurately implied that the economy would remain in slack territory for a considerable period of time. Even an unintelligent autocorrelation equation could have rendered that verdict with a high degree of reliability in March 1958 or March 1975. What is going on at such times? When economists predict that rational decision makers will continue to restrict output below a full macroequilibrium, are we really predicting that they will continue to operate with erroneous perceptions of relative prices? And when rational private decision makers hear our voices, how can they keep ignoring valuable free information that identifies their mistake? Because private decision makers are too intelligent to make repetitive, serially correlated errors, misperceptions about relative prices can be only a small part of the story of long slack periods (and equally long boom periods like 1966–69).

When rational expectations theorists explicitly recognize the problem of persistence, they agree—and indeed insist, as an implication of their model—that the forecasting errors of private decision makers on relative prices should be serially uncorrelated over any significant time interval. But then, to account for the persistence of slack and booms, they must graft onto their cycle models lags or adjustment costs (which may be reflected in an accelerator mechanism) that maintain serially correlated movements in output and employment after the initiating relative-price misperception has disappeared. I view this search for a hybrid model as a productive and promising line of inquiry that requires and deserves much further work. It points toward a business cycle theory based on rational expectations with misperceptions and with something else. So far, that something else has been specified much more clearly in terms of the properties of difference and differential equations than in terms of economic behavior. Some of the resulting structures seem to use a Lucas-Sargent snowball to generate a Samuelson-Metzler avalanche. And, in the process, the solid macro-micro bridge of the simple model gets shaky (or at least obscured from my vision). Once misperceptions about relative prices are eliminated, what prevents that prompt restoration of a full-blown Walrasian equilibrium consistent with accurate relative-price information? Is a second type of sand being thrown on the classical machinery in such hybrid models? I look forward to further modeling in this area that should help to answer my questions.

Salient Features of the Cycle

I have raised questions and expressed doubts about the ability of the rational-expectations-with-misperceptions model to account for the duration of the cycle and especially of prolonged periods of slack that are actually observed. I would argue further that many other salient characteristics of the cycle cannot be satisfactorily explained by that model—a Walrasian system modified only by relative-price misperceptions. Obviously, any tractable theory is simplified and cannot explain or predict every feature or characteristic of experience. But it ought to have a fair degree of verisimilitude. In particular, the implications of any model for fiscal and monetary policy can be taken seriously only if its implications for other key features of the cycle stand up under empirical observation. Let me state some stylized cyclical facts which do not seem to be explicable by rational-expectations-with-misperceptions.

Inventory disequilibria. The hallmark of U.S. postwar recessions has been inventory liquidation, following a major buildup of inventories at the peak of the expansion. Standard models that assume price taking and continuous market clearing do not suggest that a disappointment about relative prices will lead traders to liquidate inventories. For example, a sudden drop in the demand for, and hence the price of, wheat that leads farmers to decrease production in the future will generally lead traders to increase stocks initially. (The price tends to fall enough currently relative to its new future expected value to provide traders with that incentive.) Why then, in the business cycle, is the aggregate cutback in production accompanied by a cutback in stocks?

Cyclical productivity patterns. Output per hour worked fluctuates in a procyclical pattern. Extant efforts to explain that phenomenon rest on disequilibria or on transactions and adjustment costs that are non-Walrasian. Can it be explained within the framework of a model that views labor markets and product markets as Walrasian?

Quits and layoffs. Quits have a procyclical pattern and are a coincident indicator at turning points. If workers lack information about wages in *other* labor markets, then they should be less likely to quit when their wages accelerate unexpectedly. According to this model, should not quits be countercyclical or at least display long lags at turning points? Layoffs display a marked countercyclical pattern. Can that (or indeed the very existence of layoffs) be explained by the model? The frequency of help-wanted signs and the volume of help-wanted advertising display strong procyclical variations. Can these be explained in the framework of the classical microeconomics adopted by this model?

Wage differentials. Pay differentials between high-wage and low-wage industries vary countercyclically. And that is the case even though cyclical fluctuations in employment tend to be greatest in the high-wage industries. Can that be explained within the framework of this model?

General pay increases in recession. During recent periods of recession and slack, like 1975–77, many nonunion firms granted general pay increases to their workers when the firms were recruiting *no* new workers at all. Why would sensible employers raise wages under such conditions at those points in time, regardless of how they expected prices or wages to move in the future?

Profits in boom years. Corporate profits (in real terms) are especially high in years of emerging excess demand. If corporations are committing decision-making errors that lead to unduly large output under such circumstances, why do their income statements look so good?

Auction markets. Prices of industrial commodities traded in organized auction markets have fallen in postwar recessions (including 1974–75); most other prices have not fallen (and rose strongly in 1974–75). Can this special behavior of auction markets be explained within the framework of a model that views all markets as auction markets?

OPEC. The record of 1974–79 makes clear that increases in the price of oil add to the price level for a given path of nominal GNP. Should that be viewed as a relative-price misperception? (Some economists invoked rational-expectations arguments to predict erroneously that oil prices could not raise the price level, given nominal GNP.)

Alternative Explanations

In my judgment, rational-expectations-with-misperceptions provides a logically satisfactory but empirically unsatisfactory explanation of the business cycle. I see alternative routes to an explanation that would score much better empirically (in accounting for the duration and the salient features of the cycle) and still have a theoretically satisfactory underpinning, linked to the behavior of individual markets and resting on the rational behavior of economic agents.

I have become convinced that the most promising alternatives drop the assumption of continuous market clearing and recognize price making and wage making. They thus depart farther from the competitive, auction macro model; they are less familiar and may be fundamentally less elegant and less tractable; they show less respect for Walras and Marshall. But none of these features make them untheoretical or unsound. Without propounding my view of the cycle and the inflationary process in any detail, I do want to indicate the possibility that alternative macro views can rest on theoretically sound micro foundations.

Continuous market clearing implies the universality of organized auction markets. But, to be traded on an auction market, a product must be standardized and defined so well (at such low cost) that it can be viewed as homogeneous by a prospective buyer placing orders through a broker.

Soybeans and silver meet that test; while neckties, restaurant meals, and eyeglasses clearly do not. Apparently, they cannot be homogenized or standardized at a cost that would make the auction technique efficient. And apparently from the point of view of employers, skilled workers are heterogeneous or idiosyncratic. Price tags, wage offers, shopping, and search are part of an optimal transactions mechanism for heterogeneous products. It is a tribute to the genuine efficiency of free markets that most products and nearly all types of labor are traded on markets that do not have the price-taking, quantity-making characteristic specified by so-called "efficient-markets theory."

When sellers are price makers, they necessarily act as quantity takers. And then any surprise in demand (even one that is correctly perceived as soon as it happens) must initially alter quantities and leave prices unchanged. Hence, for some very brief period, fixprice results from rational decision making by optimizing agents—and not from an institutional rigidity or from some heroic assumption to disregard market behavior.

That initial very brief period of price fixity or insensitivity is the first of a long chain of implications for optimizing by a price-tag seller. Once a firm sets prices, it must develop a method of price setting. Since that task uses resources, periodic reviews of prices and formulas for price setting can become efficient business practices. Because shopping is costly and hence potential buyers do not monitor prices continuously, sellers have incentives to inform potential buyers about prices. And that communication, to have effective value as information, may commit the seller to sell at the advertised price for a period of some substantial duration.

In general, the seller realizes that buyers extrapolate information obtained from one shopping expedition as a basis for decisions on where to shop next time. Their comparison shopping is necessarily intertemporal. The seller wants satisfied customers to extrapolate their past information and rationally tries to convey a basis for them to believe that his policy on pricing (and service as well) is consistent through time. To promote patterns of recurrent shopping or to convert buyers into regular customers, the seller has incentives to adopt a strategy that sacrifices frequent and transitory price adjustments. In exceptional cases, the seller may even find it worthwhile to assume a contractual obligation to supply his product for months or years in the future at a predetermined price, even while leaving the buyer discretion over the amount to be purchased.

Optimization by the price-tag seller thus does not consist of mimicking the absent auctioneer. Rather it establishes a variety of small and large *commitments* to price tags; and those commitments reduce the speed and magnitude of price changes in response to shifts in demand.

The considerations that lead to wage commitments in labor markets are even more obvious and more important than those that create price commitments in product markets. The costs of finding the most rewarding job are large for a worker; the costs of obtaining the most productive worker are large for the employer; and the benefits of experience on a particular job can be substantial. These considerations promote continuing relationships with substantial bilateral monopoly surpluses. In some cases, they lead to explicit contracts that fix the wage over a substantial interval, even while not fixing the amount of employment. More often, they lead to implicit contracts where the employer and the worker conduct themselves and communicate with each other in ways that help to make the continuation of the relationship worthwhile for both.

These elements can provide a theoretically sound optimization underpinning for Keynes's assumption of a money wage floor, and indeed for a generalization of that assumption. Clearly, the firm that hires a worker with a career job in mind must lead him to believe that his position will gradually improve, and certainly not worsen. Once the firm paints a bright future in order to recruit that worker, any subsequent cut in wages must be a disappointment and a source of antagonism that would jeopardize the firm's investment in that worker. Hence the firm's inhibition about reducing wages has a sound, rational basis. In fact, when money wages normally rise over time, the same inhibitions can also apply to hold-downs or even slowdowns of wages for employees who have been recruited with the expectation of moving upward absolutely and keeping up relatively.

Many so-called "rigidities" in the behavior of wages and prices are genuinely the consequences of optimizing behavior in markets with efficient transactional mechanisms for dealing with heterogeneous products and factors, which involve significant costs of information and transactions. In one sense, I am arguing that the resulting arrangements (price tags, wage offers, search, shopping, customer relations, and career jobs) proliferate the number and accentuate the separateness of "informationally distinct markets," in Lucas's terminology. Every firm becomes, in effect, a distinct labor market. And no worker can readily learn all the relevant information about the opportunities and rewards on the various jobs available elsewhere (that is, in other labor markets). As a result, prolonged and serious misperceptions about relative wages (or prices) become far more plausible in this context than in the Walrasian framework. Yet, I would stress primarily, not the misperceptions, but rather the various commitments to wages and prices that develop in such a world of heterogeneous products and factors. Because rational agents know that full information about other alternatives is costly—in other words, because they recognize their vulnerability to relative-price misperceptions—they establish patterns of behavior to minimize search and shopping costs. And those involve implicit and explicit commitments to wages and prices.

Nominal disturbances then have real effects, even when fully perceived and even when anticipated somewhat ahead of time. These real effects occur because nominal arrangements are real and lasting. Prices and wages are sticky in response to shifts in aggregate demand, basically as the result of efficient transactional mechanisms (rather than of monopoly or of government regulations).

This line of reasoning moves distinctly away from the microeconomics of Marshall and Walras. That is no virtue; but neither is it a sin. I regard it as a necessity in order to understand many macroeconomic observations that otherwise defy explanation. It is needed for fundamental monetary theory as well as for business cycle theory. As others have emphasized, supplying a rationale for money (as anything more than a numeraire) in a Walrasian framework really requires sneaking in some sort of transactions costs. If transactions were genuinely costless, any commodity sold on an auction market should be fully acceptable as a means of payment. Money really matters because the world is different from the classical microeconomic paradigm.

Despite the methodological contributions made by the model of rational-expectations-with-misperceptions, the assumption of universal auction markets has put it into a straitjacket. It offers a logical explanation of how an economy consisting entirely of markets like those observed for soybeans and silver could nonetheless experience some business cycle. The implications of that model strengthen my conviction that a soybean-silver economy would not display a business cycle with the duration or key characteristic actually observed. And I am equally convinced that the resulting guide to macro policymaking in a soybean-silver economy is fundamentally inapplicable to the actual U.S. economy.

III OUTPUT, EMPLOYMENT, AND UNEMPLOYMENT

Potential GNP: Its Measurement and Significance

Potential GNP and Policy

"How much output can the economy produce under conditions of full employment?" The concept and measurement of potential GNP are addressed to this question. It is a question with policy significance because the pursuit of full employment (or "maximum employment" in the language of the Employment Act) is a goal of policy. And a target of full employment of labor needs to be linked to a corresponding target of full employment output, since policy measures designed to influence employment operate by affecting aggregate demand and production. How far we stand from the target of full employment output is important information in formulating fiscal and monetary policy. Thus, quantification of potential output offers one of the guides to stabilization policy and one indicator of its success.

The quantification of potential output—and the accompanying measure of the "gap" between actual and potential—is at best an uncertain estimate and not a firm, precise measure. While there are more precise measures of economic performance, they are not fully substitutable for the concept of potential output. To appraise the vigor of an expanding economy, it is important and enlightening to study customary cyclical measures, such as advance over previous peak levels or advance over recession trough levels. But these measures do not tell us how far we have to go to meet our targets, unless we are prepared to assume that each peak is like any other one and all troughs are likewise uniform. The record of the past decade testifies to the dramatic differences among cyclical peaks in levels of resource utilization.

The evaluation of potential output can also help to point up the enormous social cost of idle resources. If programs to lower unemployment from $5\frac{1}{2}$ to 4 percent of the labor are viewed as attempts to raise the economy's "grade" from $94\frac{1}{2}$ to 96, the case for them may not seem compelling. Focus on the "gap" helps to remind policymakers of the large reward associated with such an improvement.

The Four Percent Unemployment Rate

Potential GNP is a supply concept, a measure of productive capacity. But it is not a measure of how much output could be generated by unlimited amounts of aggregate demand. The nation would probably be most productive in the short-run with inflationary pressure pushing the economy. But the social target of maximum production and employment is constrained by a social desire for price stability and free markets. The full employment goal must be understood as striving for maximum production without inflationary pressure; or, more precisely, as aiming for a point of balance between more output and greater stability, with appropriate regard for the social valuation of these two objectives.

It is interesting and perhaps surprising that there seems to be more agreement that a four percent unemployment rate is a reasonable target under existing labor market conditions than on any of the analytical steps needed to justify such a conclusion. Economists have never developed a clear criterion of tolerable price behavior or any quantitative balancing of conflicting objectives which could be invoked either to support or attack the target of a four percent rate. Indeed, I should expect that many economists who agree on the four percent target would disagree in estimating how prices and wages would behave if we were on target. Nor can the four percent rate be said to meet Beveridge's criterion for full employment—that job vacancies should be equal to the number of unemployed. We simply have no count of job vacancies and could not possibly translate Beveridge's goal into any available measure of unemployment.

Having said what the four percent unemployment rate is not, I shall now state that it is the target rate of labor utilization underlying the calculation of potential GNP in this paper. The statistical and methodological problems would not be altered if a different rate were selected; only the numbers would be changed.

Potential GNP as a Short-Run Concept

In estimating potential GNP, most of the facts about the economy are taken as they exist: technological knowledge, the capital stock, natural resources, the skill and education of the labor force are all data, rather than variables. Potential differs from actual only because the potential concept depends on the assumption—normally contrary to fact—that aggregate demand is exactly at the level that yields a rate of unemployment equal to four percent of the civilian labor force. If, in fact, aggregate demand is lower, part of potential GNP is not produced; there is unrealized potential or a "gap" between actual and potential output.

The failure to use one year's potential fully can influence future potential GNP: to the extent that low utilization rates and accompanying low profits and personal incomes hold down investment in plant, equipment, research, housing, and education, the growth of potential GNP will be retarded. Because today's actual output influences tomorrow's productive capacity, success in the stabilization objective promotes more rapid economic growth.

The Measurement Problem

As it has been defined above, potential output is observed only when the unemployment rate is four percent, and even then must be viewed as subject to stochastic variation. At any other time it must be regarded as a hypothetical magnitude. The observed actual measures of labor utilization tell us by a simple arithmetic calculation how much employment would have to increase, given the labor force, to make the unemployment rate four percent. But they do not offer similar direct information on other matters that might make labor input at full employment different from its observed level:

a. how average hours worked per man would be altered if the level of aggregate demand were consistent with full employment;
b. how participation rates in the labor force—and hence the size of the labor force—would be affected under conditions of full employment.

Nor do the actual data reveal directly what aggregate labor productivity would be under full employment conditions. There are many reasons why productivity might be altered in the aggregate: the added workers, changed average hours, possible alterations in the sectoral distribution of employment, higher utilization rate of capital, and altered efficiency in the use of employees all could make a difference in productivity at full employment.

The Leap from Unemployment to Output

Ideally, the measurement of potential output would appraise the various possible influences of high employment on labor input and productivity and evaluate the influences step-by-step, developing quantitative estimates for each adjustment to produce the desired measure of potential. While I shall discuss the steps individually below, the basic technique I am reporting consists of a leap from the unemployment rate to potential output rather than a series of steps involving the several underlying factors. Strictly speaking, the leap requires the assumption that, whatever the influence of slack economic activity on average hours, labor force participation, and manhour productivity, the magnitudes of all these effects are related to the unemployment rate. With this assumption, the unemployment rate can be viewed as a proxy variable for all the ways in which output is affected by idle resources. The measurement of potential output then is simplified into an estimate of how much output is depressed by unemployment in excess of four percent.

Statistical Estimates

The answer I have to offer is simple and direct. In the postwar period, on the average, each extra percentage point in the unemployment rate above four percent has been associated with about a three percent decrement in real GNP. This result emerged from three methods of relating output to the unemployment rate.

1. *First differences.* In one technique, quarterly changes in the unemployment rate (Y), expressed in percentage points, are related to quarterly percentage changes in real GNP (X). This regression equation, fitted to 55 quarterly observations from 1947-II to 1960-IV, yields:

$$Y = .30 - .30X \qquad (r = .79)$$

According to this estimate, the unemployment rate will rise by 0.3 points from one quarter to the next if real GNP is unchanged, as secular gains in productivity and growth in the labor force push up the unemployment rate. For each extra one percent of GNP, unemployment is 0.3 points lower. At any point in time, taking previous quarters as given, one percentage point more in the unemployment rate means 3.3 percent less GNP.

2. *Trial gaps.* A second method consists of selecting and testing certain exponential paths of potential output, using alternative assumed growth

rates and benchmark levels. The percentage "gaps" implied by these paths are then related to the unemployment rate (U) using a regression equation: $U = a + b$ (gap). The criteria for judging the validity of the assumed potential paths are: (1) goodness of fit; (2) absence of any trend in the residuals; (3) agreement with the principle that potential GNP should equal actual GNP when $U = 4$.

The slope terms in this equation fitted to various paths and different periods consistently ran from .28 up to .38. One such equation was reported in the March 1961 statement of the Council of Economic Advisers to the Joint Economic Committee. It was:

$$U = 3.72 + .36 \quad \text{gap} \qquad (r = .93)$$

where the gap was derived from a $3\frac{1}{2}$ percent trend line through actual real GNP in mid-1955. The equation was fitted to quarterly data for 1953–60. It implies that an increment of unemployment of one percent is associated with an output loss equal to 2.8 percent of potential output—or a somewhat larger percentage of *actual* output when actual is below potential. The estimated unemployment rate associated with a zero gap is 3.72 percent, not too far from the 4.0 percent ideal.

3. *Fitted trend and elasticity.* The first method described above relied on the use of *changes* in GNP and in unemployment. The second method used *levels* but assumed the trend of output-growth at constant unemployment rate. It is also possible to derive the output-unemployment coefficient from data on levels without assuming a trend. The following model permits such a calculation:

a. There is a constant elasticity relationship in the relevant range between the ratio of actual (A) to potential (P) output, on the one hand, and the "employment rate" ($N = 100 - U$) as a fraction of its potential level (N_F):

$$\frac{N}{N_F} = \left(\frac{A}{P}\right)^a$$

b. There is a constant growth rate (r) of potential output starting from some level P_0 such that at any time t:

$$P_t = P_0 e^{rt}$$

By substitution and rearrangement:

$$N_t = \frac{A_t^a \cdot N_F}{P_0^a \cdot e^{art}}$$

Logarithmically:

$$\log N_t = \log \frac{N_F}{P_0^a} + a \log A_t - (ar)t$$

The log of the employment rate is here related to a time-trend and to the log of actual real GNP. When a regression equation is fitted to log N as the dependent variable and log A and t as independent variables: (1) The coefficient of log A is the "output elasticity of the employment rate"; (2) The coefficient of time is the product of that elasticity and the potential growth rate; it therefore yields an estimate of the potential growth rate; and (3) The intercept yields the benchmark (P_0) for any given N_F, here taken as 96.

Fitted to varying sample periods, the estimated elasticity coefficient ran .35 to .40, suggesting that each one percentage point reduction in unemployment means slightly less than a 3 percent increment in output (near the potential level). The trend growth rate, fitted to 1947–60 quarterly data, was 3.9 percent, but it was clear that this was not uniform throughout the period. For the post-Korean period, the estimated trend growth in potential was near $3\frac{1}{2}$ percent, while, for the 1947–53 period, it was near $4\frac{1}{2}$ percent.

The uniformity that emerged from these various techniques was the approximate 3-to-1 link between output and the unemployment rate. My own subjectively weighted average of the relevant coefficients is 3.2, yielding the following estimate of potential:

$$P = A[1 + .032(U - 4)]$$

When the unemployment rate is four percent, potential GNP is estimated as equal to actual; at a five percent rate of unemployment, the estimated "gap" is 3.2 percent of GNP. In the periods from which this relationship was obtained the unemployment rate varied from about 3 to $7\frac{1}{2}$ percent; the relation is not meant to be extrapolated outside this range. I have no reason to expect the 3.2 coefficient to apply if unemployment were either 1 or 15 percent of the labor force.

Smoothing the Potential Path

The dashed line in the accompanying figure shows the implied time-series of potential GNP derived by applying the 3.2 coefficient to excess unemployment for the period 1954 to date. The result is a curve that wiggles from quarter to quarter, even dipping at times. The dips and small increases in estimated potential are concentrated in advanced stages of

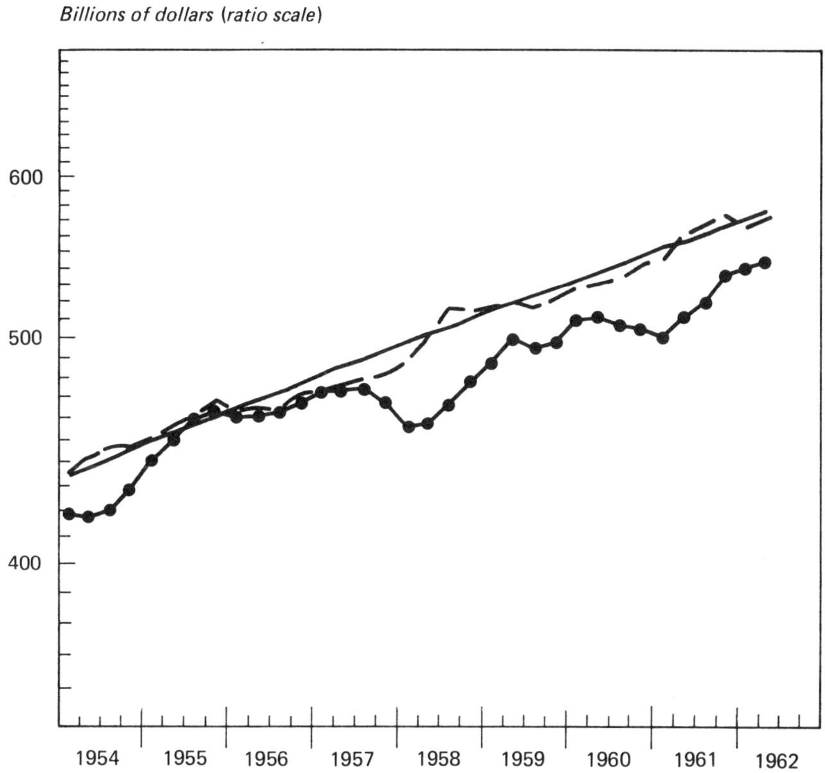

Figure 1 Potential and actual GNP, 1954–1962. The vertical axis is GNP (in 1961 prices), seasonally adjusted annual rates. Key: solid line—$3\frac{1}{2}$% trend line through middle of 1955; dashed line—based on unemployment rate; dotted solid line—actual GNP.

expansion—1956–57, 1959, and early 1962. Quarters of rapid rise in estimated potential output occur in early expansion—1955, 1958, 1961.

The question that arises is whether (1) these wiggles and jiggles should be taken seriously, as indications of irregular or cyclical patterns in the growth of productive capacity or (2) whether they should be attributed to an imperfect correlation of the unemployment rate with unused potential output. In the former case, the irregular path upward shown by the dashed line would be the estimated series of potential GNP. In the latter case, some smoothing of that irregular path would be in order.

One way of smoothing which eliminates all the ripples is to substitute a simple exponential curve that corresponds with the trend and level of the wiggly series. Such a line is obtained by a trend that goes through actual output in mid-1955 as a benchmark and moves upward at a $3\frac{1}{2}$ percent annual rate. The trend measure of potential is shown as the solid line in the figure. It presents an opposite extreme alternative—the view that the upward path of potential GNP has been perfectly smooth in the post-Korean period. On the whole, the two measures agree quite well. A trend line with either a 3 or a 4 percent growth rate—or with a markedly different "benchmark" level—would clearly not fit the dashed line equally well. In general, periods of early expansion—like 1955; 1958-II to 1959-I; and 1961-II to 1961-IV—show larger gaps by the unemployment measure than by the trend technique. The reverse is true for late expansion and recession periods, like 1956-II to 1958-I and 1959-III to 1961-I.

My own inclination is to select the smooth trend measure of potential output for the post-Korean period. I find it difficult to accept the verdict that potential output has actually contracted at times, as the unsmoothed unemployment measure implies. Nor can I believe that the economy's *productive capacity* rises most rapidly in early expansion, even though actual production may be increasing briskly. This is not the period when investment expenditures—much less completed investment projects—are at a peak; nor is it a time of heavy innovations, by an external evidence I know.

The spurts shown in early expansion periods can be accounted for by the hypothesis that unemployment lags somewhat behind the movement of output, and therefore is slow to decline in early recovery. Indeed, in statistical tests of some of the regression equations reported above, it was found that unemployment in the current quarter depends on past as well as current levels of GNP, with a higher level of past output meaning less current unemployment. This implies that decisions on hiring labor for next quarter are strengthened by a high level of current output.

The cyclical ripples in the unemployment measure may also reflect, in part, a lead of the workweek in advance of employment. Total man-hours worked rise more rapidly than employment in early expansion and less rapidly in late expansion. The initial impact of a change in the pace of economic activity is particularly strong on the workweek and is later shifted more fully onto employment. Presumably, this lagged effect might be incorporated into the estimate of potential based on the unemployment rate, in such a way as to smooth that potential curve and bring it closer to the trend estimate of potential. But, for the post-Korean period, there is no obvious shift in the trend of potential; and the $3\frac{1}{2}$ percent trend line, while obviously too smooth a time path, fills the assignment rather well.

The trend estimate of potential for the 1954-62 period still rests on the unemployment-output relationship reviewed above, that an excess of 1 point in the unemployment rate means, on the average, a loss of about 3 percent in output. The trend line, however, suggests that the output loss per point of the unemployment rate exceeds 3 percent in late expansion and in recession and is somewhat less than 3 percent in early expansion.

It should be noted that this trend does not fit the earliest postwar years. If one projected the $3\frac{1}{2}$ percent trend back to 1947, the trend-technique would clearly overestimate potential output. The indicated potential growth of the 1947–53 period is nearer to $4\frac{1}{2}$ percent. The lower potential growth rate of the post-Korean period is associated, in part, with less success in making full use of our potential. The "gaps" between potential and actual have held down the size and held up the average age of our capital stock, thereby lowering the growth of potential.

The Steps

The findings above assert that a reduction in unemployment, measured as a percentage of the labor force, has a much larger than proportionate effect on output. To appraise and evaluate this finding, it is necessary to inspect the steps which were leaped over in the statistical relationships between output and unemployment. Clearly, the simple addition of one percent of a given labor force to the ranks of the employed would increase employment by only slightly more than one percent: $100/(100 - U)$ percent to be exact. If the workweek and productivity were unchanged, the increment to output would be only that 1+ percent. The 3 percent result implies that considerable output gains in a period of rising utilization rates must stem from some or all of the following: induced increases in the size of the labor force; longer average weekly hours; and greater productivity.

Labor Force

Participation in the labor force as we measure it consists of either having a job or seeking actively to work. The resulting measures of labor force are not pure reflections of supply; they are affected by job availability. In a slack labor market, people without a job may give up when they are convinced that job-hunting is a hopeless pursuit. They then may be viewed as having left the labor force though they stand ready and eager to work.

Furthermore, there are secondary or passive members of the labor force who will not actively seek employment but would accept gainful employment if a job came looking for them. This latter group suffers little or no personal hardship in not having work, but the output they would contribute in a fully employed economy is a relevant part of the nation's potential GNP.

There may be induced changes in the labor force in the opposite direction: e.g., the loss of a job by the breadwinner of a family might increase the measured labor force by leading his wife and teen-age children to seek work. The prewar literature debated the probably net effects of these opposing influences on participation rates. However, the postwar record has convincingly delivered the verdict that a weak labor market depresses the size of the labor force. But the magnitude and timing of the effect is not clear.

Even the conceptual problem of defining a potential labor force is difficult—we should not wish to count only the secondary labor force members who would appear for work tomorrow morning; on the other hand, we would not want to include all those who might be attracted by many years of continued job availability. The response of participation rates is likely to be a complicated lagged phenomenon which will not be closely tied to the current unemployment rate. While this aspect of the difference between potential and actual output is hard to quantify, zero is certainly not a satisfactory estimate. At the end of 1960, the Bureau of Labor Statistics estimated the difference between actual and "normal" labor force at 561,000. If this figure is taken as the induced effect of poor opportunities for jobs, it implies that, in those recession conditions, for every 10 people listed as unemployed over and above the 4 percent rate, there were three additional potential workers who were not actively seeking work.

Hours

Taking into account the normal secular decline in hours worked per man, there is a clear relationship between movements in average hours and in output. When output has been rising rapidly, average hours have expanded—or, at least, have not contracted. On the other hand, periods of low growth or decline in GNP mean more rapid declines in average hours per man. The data point toward the concept of a full employment path of average annual hours. But the concept of full employment hours is hard to quantify: e.g., in a rapid rise of output toward full employment, the amount of overtime might well push the workweek above the level consistent with steady full employment. Furthermore, economy-wide data on average hours are notoriously poor. However, using what evidence is available, we find that each one percent difference in output is associated with a difference of 0.14 percent in hours per man, including both overtime and part-time work.

The figure of 0.14 is obtained by fitting a least-squares regression line to annual data for 1947–59. The data are found in the Bureau of Labor Statistics Release (USDL-4155) of June 28, 1960. The variables are percent change in manhours of work per person employed (Y) and percent change in private nonagricultural output (X), restricted to private nonagricultural output and employment; establishment figures are the source of the man-hour estimates. The fitted line is:

$$Y = 0.843 + .142X \qquad (r = .85)$$

When this equation is used to compare average hours for different possible outputs at the same point in time, the 0.142 coefficient reflects the percentage difference in hours per man that accompanies a one percent difference in output.

Returning to the finding that a one percentage point reduction in the unemployment rate means 3.2 percent more GNP, the hours-output estimate above indicates that it will also be accompanied by an increase of nearly one-half of one percent in hours per man, or an addition of about 0.2 of an hour to the workweek. With an allowance for induced gains in labor force, based illustratively on the 1960 estimate cited above, the reduction of one point in the unemployment rate means perhaps a 1.8 percent increase in total labor input measured in man-hours. Then, to get the 3.2 percent increment in output, manhour productivity must rise by about 1.4 percent.

Productivity

The direct checks that could be made on productivity data were consistent with this implication of the output-unemployment relationship. The record clearly shows that manhour productivity is depressed by low levels of utilization, and that periods of movement toward full employment yield considerably above-average productivity gains.

The implications and explanations of this phenomenon are intriguing. Indeed, many *a priori* arguments have been made for the reverse view—that depressed levels of activity will stimulate productivity through pressure on management to cut costs, through a weeding-out of inefficient firms and low quality workers, and through availability of more and higher quality capital per worker for those employees who retain their jobs. If such effects exist, the empirical record demonstrates that they are swamped by other forces working in the opposite direction.

I have little direct evidence to offer on the mechanism by which low levels of utilization depress productivity. I can offer some speculation and try to encourage other researchers to pursue this problem with concrete evidence at a micro-economic level. The positive relationship between output and labor productivity suggests that much of labor input is essentially a fixed cost for fairly substantial periods. Thus high output levels permit the spreading of labor overheads, and low production levels raise unit fixed costs of labor. At times, we may take too seriously our textbook examples which view labor as a variable factor, with only capital costs as fixed. Even the most casual empiricism points to an overhead component in labor costs. There are many reasons why employment may not be easily variable:

1. *Contractual commitments* may tie the hand of management in a downward direction—employees may have guaranteed annual wages, supplementary unemployment compensation, rights to severance pay, etc. as well as actual contracts for a term of employment.
2. *Technological factors*, in a broad sense, may also be important. A firm plans on a division of labor and degree of specialization attuned to "normal" operations. If operations fall below normal, there may be marked indivisibilities which prevent the firm from curtailing its employment of specialists, clerical and sales personnel, and supervisors in parallel with its cutback in output.
3. *Transactions costs* associated with laying off labor and then, in the future, doing new hiring may be another influence retarding the adjustment of labor input to fluctuations in sales and output.
4. *Acquired skills* that existing employees have learned on the job may make them particularly valuable to the firm so that it pays to stockpile underemployed labor rather than run the risk of having to hire untrained men when business conditions improve.
5. *Morale factors* may also make layoffs undesirable.

All of these factors could help explain why slack economic activity is accompanied by "on-the-job underemployment," reflected in depressed levels of manhour productivity. Firms obviously do lay off labor in recession but they do so reluctantly. Their problems may be mitigated, in part, by the presence of voluntary quits which permit a downward adjustment of employment without layoffs. In part, the impact of slack on manhour productivity may be reduced by shortening average hours to spread the work and the wage-bill without a cut in employment. But these appear to be only partial offsets.

To the extent that the productivity losses of recessions are associated with fixity of labor costs, they would not be maintained indefinitely. If the recession was of long duration—or merely was expected to last a long time—firms would adjust their employment more drastically. On this reasoning, in an era when business cycle dips are continually short and mild, one might expect productivity to bear more of the brunt of recession and labor input to be less affected, even relative to the decline in output.

Changes in the level of economic activity are associated with shifts in the composition of employment and output by industry. A slack economy is accompanied by particularly depressed output in durable-goods manufacturing industries, where output per manhour is especially high. My own intuition suggested that this might be an important explanation of the relationship between productivity and the unemployment rate. But calculations on the change in composition from recession to recovery years indicate that, while shifts in industrial composition do influence aggregate productivity in the expected direction, the magnitude of the effect is trivial. There is some significance to the compositional shift between agriculture and nonagricultural industries. Manhour input in agriculture seems to be independent of overall economic activity in the short run, so all variations in labor input can be regarded as occurring in the nonagricultural sector. I assumed illustratively above that a point reduction in the unemployment rate means an increase in total manhours of 1.8 percent. If all of that 1.8 percent goes into nonagriculture, this would add 0.1 percent to economy-wide productivity (for given levels of productivity in each sector). This is still only a minor part of the total productivity gain that accompanies reduced unemployment.

Thus far, I have ignored the dependence of labor productivity on plant and equipment capacity. The entire discussion of potential output in this paper has, in effect, assumed that idle labor is a satisfactory measure of all idle resources. In fact, measures of excess capacity in industrial plant and equipment do show a close relationship to unemployment—idle men are accompanied by idle machines. But the correlation is not perfect and operating rates in industry should be considered along with employment data as an indicator of the gap between potential and actual output. Obviously, if capital were fully employed while there was much unemployed labor, this would hold down the productivity gains that could be obtained through full employment of labor. Robert Solow did use capital stock data together with unemployment data in fitting a production function for 1929 to date (see the *American Economic Review* of May 1962). His estimates of potential output for the post-Korean period agreed remarkably well with those I am reporting.

Still, I shall feel much more satisfied with the estimation of potential output when our data and our analysis have advanced to the point where the estimation can proceed step-by-step and where the capital factor can be explicitly taken into account. Meanwhile, the measure of potential must be used with care. The trend line yields a point-estimate of the "gap," e.g., $31.3 billion for 1962-II. But that specific figure must be understood as the center of a range of plausible estimates. By my personal evaluation of its degree of accuracy, I find potential output useful—and superior to substitute concepts—for many analytical purposes.

Note

My research in this area was done principally while I served on the Staff of the Council of Economic Advisers, and I had the benefit of many helpful comments and suggestions from members of the Council and the Staff.

The Role of Aggregate Demand in Alleviating Unemployment

In our Annual Report this January, the Council of Economic Advisers said "the economy could operate at a 4% unemployment rate today without substantial strains on either labor supplies or plant capacity.... The interim target of a 4% unemployment rate is obtainable, given the required level of demand for goods and services." I should like to discuss today some of the analytical considerations in the choice of a 4% unemployment rate—rather than, say, 5 percent, or no particular rate at all—as the appropriate target for the guidance of current aggregative policies.

Aggregative policies are carried out through fiscal and monetary instruments that influence the level of total demand. Their direct impact is on product markets rather than labor markets and so they influence unemployment indirectly. But economists have long praised the "roundaboutness" in the production process and are neither surprised nor reluctant to rely on measures which are roundabout in the creation of jobs. There has been a strong and striking regularity in the relationship between total production and unemployment. A very simple-minded regression between output and unemployment that I first calculated 4 years ago has estimated unemployment rates consistently within a few tenths of a percentage point for the 1962–64 period. The continued good relationship between unemployment and production gains offers reassurance that the indirect route is reliable.

Aggregate Demand and Other Policies

In dealing with aggregative policies, I am considering only one type of public measure that affects unemployment. Some of our non-aggregative policies affect the human costs of unemployment. Unemployment insurance and the provision of other benefits to the jobless help to pool the risks and costs of unemployment among all members of society and to reduce the burden on the unfortunate individual who is directly affected. There are good reasons for viewing unemployment as a social rather than individual misfortune and for attempting to spread the costs widely, but there are limits on the extent to which society can compensate the affected individual. First, there is a need to leave incentives for the individual to find work, and this requires less than full compensation. Second, the extent of psychic compensation is limited by the fact that joblessness entails a loss of self-respect and an inevitable feeling of inadequacy which cannot be erased by the unemployment benefit check. Most fundamentally, even when the costs are distributed more satisfactorily they are not eliminated—the waste of labor resources still remains.

There are further policy measures—not always conscious or deliberate—which affect the quantitative supply of labor. For example, laws regulating hours of work, child labor, the age of retirement all influence participation in the labor force.

The matching of supplies and demands in our labor markets is influenced by still other Government policies such as those which spread information about available vacancies and which affect geographical and occupational mobility.

Finally and most important of all our non-aggregative policies are those affecting the quality and composition of our labor supply. The whole of public education has a tremendous influence on the skills of the labor force. In addition, adult education and vocational training and retraining are a major responsibility and interest of public policy much more fully recognized now than ever before.

The various policy instruments affecting unemployment have important interrelationships. But they are nonetheless distinct tools and require distinct decisions. Nonaggregative policies on unemployment require Federal outlays and as such become part of the budgetary process. There, they compete with the entire range of Federal programs; and their share of the Budget depends on their costs and benefits. Emphasizing and expanding manpower policies cannot settle the issue of whether fiscal and monetary policies should be expansionary, any more than a decision to turn on head lights determines whether to step on the gas or the brakes. Whatever we decide about appropriate levels of manpower policies, we must still face the puzzles of aggregative policy, and those are the puzzles that I have been asked to discuss.

The Limits of Aggregate Demand

Let me begin with a truism, or at least what ought to be a truism. Sufficient doses of aggregate demand will bring the unemployment rate considerably below 4.0 percent. During World War II, the unemployment rate fell below $1\frac{1}{2}$ percent for 1944. And in the Korean War unemployment rates were around 3% for 3 straight years. It took a wartime experience to produce such results, because only a wartime period generates aggregate demand on such a grand scale.

In peacetime, we have never had a fiscal policy which would have created deficits at rates of resource-utilization even approaching those wartime levels. We simply do not pile on demand to buy butter the way we do to buy guns. But the wartime experiences show what demand can do when unleashed.

Now let me hasten to add the further truism that no one would seriously propose policies to obtain the inflationary heights achieved in these record wartime periods. Demand was clearly too high then; it was overworking and overheating the economy. We must set the speed limit on the economy below the capacity of the engine. It is the risk—or indeed the fact—of inflation, not any absolute limits to the potency of aggregate demand, that sets the restrictions on our unemployment target.

The Trade-Off

The choice of an unemployment target therefore is a typical economic trade-off, which requires balancing the evil of inflation, on the one hand, with lost production and joblessness on the other. Every graduate student knows the formal solution for such a problem: crank in a preference function and an opportunity locus, and grind out an optimal solution. The preference function here obviously involves some weighing of the welfare costs of a little more danger of inflation versus the benefits of a little bit more production. We all recognize the important redistributive and allocative distorting effects that inflation can have at home, and in recent years we have become critically aware of its important costs to our international payments position. But these are painfully hard to quantify and to place in a clear trade-off position with the benefits of increasing production and employment.

Some years ago, Professor Alvin Hansen stated his preferences: he would stop expansionary policies at the point where an added one percent of production began to involve more than a one percent price increase.

The symmetry of this rule has no particular merit, and the preferences are a matter with which one can disagree strongly. Nevertheless, Professor Hansen deserves our applause for laying his preferences on the line. A more candid airing of this welfare issue by the profession and public could be a great aid to the policy-maker.

The opportunity locus relevant to our choice is the price version of the Phillips Curve. We have a name for it, and we even have some estimates of it, but we still know pathetically little about it. We do pick up some clues over time. The record of the past half-dozen years shows consumer prices—as we measure them—rising a little more than 1 percent a year over a fairly wide range of levels of economic activity. A rate of unemployment of 5 percent did not produce a worse record for consumer prices than did a rate of 7 percent.

On the other hand, we all bear in mind the record of the mid-50's when we last enjoyed a 4 percent unemployment rate. Wholesale prices rose by 3 percent a year in 1956 and 1957, while the annual increase in employment costs per man-hour was 6 percent. Lagging slightly behind, consumer prices showed a 3 percent a year rise in 1957 and 1958. Nobody can consider that a satisfactory performance. But there are good reasons to hope and to believe that we would do a good deal better in another shot at the target.

Some Hopeful Signs

First, foreign competition should make an important difference in our price record at high employment. The closer ties of world commodity markets and greater substitution possibilities offered by imports today add to effective competitiveness in product markets, if at the same time they also accentuate the need for price stability.

Second, the composition of demand in product markets seems more favorable. There is good evidence that the effect on prices of excess demand for goods in one market is not fully offset by an equal excess supply in another. As Charles Schultze has lucidly explained, in the mid-50's there was genuine excess demand in selected capital goods industries, which generated inflationary tendencies in the economy in the absence of general excess demand. A better balance of demands and supplies in the various sectors of the economy could mean a much improved price performance with the same over-all rate of utilization. We have a favorable, more balanced distribution of operating rates by industry today, and there is no reason to believe they would have to become unbalanced as they move upward.

Third, we should expect better performance in the price and wage decisions of large firms and unions with market power. The self-defeating character of the cost-push spirals of the mid-1950's should be clear to all. And there is a further harsh lesson in the reaction of aggregative policies, which battled so hard for price stability for years thereafter at very high costs in incomes and employment. To suppose that something was learned in that experience is merely to express some regard for the intelligence of our business and labor leaders. The moral of that lesson is expressed in the Administration's guideposts for wages and prices. The guideposts have clearly heightened the Nation's awareness of the public interest in cost and price stability, and they have the potential to improve our record of price stability at high employment.

Fourth, we have stepped up and initiated manpower policies in the past few years to improve education, training, and job information. These recent developments may well have already improved our Phillips Curve and promise further benefits in the near future.

There are, I believe, several reasons to believe that a 4 percent unemployment rate would be consistent with a satisfactory degree of price stability in the mid-sixties. The Phillips Curve is not immutable. Indeed, the loose fits observed in the aggregate time-series data on price changes and unemployment rates are clear evidence that a variety of institutional and compositional changes shift the relationship around. I cannot expect all to share my judgment that we are not now on the edge of a sharp kink in the Curve. There were skeptics who thought they saw the kink at $5\frac{1}{2}$ percent, and there were additional skeptics about 5 percent; they were wrong, but the 4 percent skeptics and I need further evidence to settle our difference of opinion.

Structural Deterioration Thesis

One important group of skeptics points to the changing structure of labor supply and of private demands for labor as an adverse influence on the Phillips Curve. The question of whether structural deterioration has occurred in labor markets is interesting, and it has fascinated the profession. It has led to many fine papers. It has helped us to understand the heterogeneity and the substitutability among various types of labor. It would be unfortunate, however, if this interest obscured the other critical factors determining the compatibility of full employment and price stability. Issues relating to the welfare costs of risking inflation, and to competitiveness, sectoral demands, and awareness of the public interest in pricing and wage-setting must all be explored to determine whether a given unemployment target makes sense today. A conservative need not embrace the structural deterioration thesis to justify a feeling that 4 percent is too ambitious as an unemployment target. Conversely one might conclude that structural unemployment has become an increasing problem and still argue for an unemployment rate of 4 percent or even lower.

But there can be little doubt that the structural deterioration thesis has been the most popular recent challenge to the further use of expansionary fiscal and monetary policies, and I feel obliged to take up the challenge.

The structure of labor markets is certainly changing, as it has been consistently throughout our history. Major changes in the structure of labor markets and in the composition of the labor force can make an important difference in our ability to reach a given unemployment target. I should think that throughout the twentieth century we have had some persistent forces tending to raise the unemployment rates associated with a given balance of product markets. For example, the self-employed have been a continually declining fraction of the labor force; since they are not subject to significant amounts of unemployment, their lesser importance should tend to raise unemployment rates. Furthermore, women have become an ever-increasing fraction of the labor force, from one-sixth of the labor force in 1890 to more than one-third today. The general shift from rural to urban pursuits should also be unfavorable to our employment record. As far as I can see, the only evident long-term force operating in the favorable direction has been increasing education. Since higher education groups have lower unemployment rates, the persistent trend toward increasing educational attainments helps to achieve lower over-all unemployment rates. Without the trend toward more education, we might well have seen an ever-worsening Phillips Curve dilemma as a secular trend. The education factor has been very much at work in recent years. The composition of the labor force by age-sex groups has moved somewhat unfavorably with a more rapid increase in groups which experience relatively high unemployment rates; meanwhile, however, as the Council pointed out in our 1965 Annual Report, the favorable shift in composition toward higher educational attainments has been quantitatively larger in its effect on the global unemployment rate.

Unemployment and Relative Supplies

Changes in the relative size of a given age, sex, or education group can affect that group's unemployment rate. Substitutability is obviously imperfect between highly educated and poorly educated workers, between young men and older men, between male and female employees. Thus, when one of the groups grows particularly rapidly, the structure of unemployment rates is likely to be affected while the labor market adapts to the change in relative supplies.

A good deal of attention has been recently paid—quite appropriately—to the influence of unemployment on our measured labor supplies, helping us to quantify the influence of changing job opportunities on participation rates. We also need to look at the other side of the coin to see how changing relative supplies affect relative unemployment rates. The relative supply effect must account for one recently observed phenomenon, namely the rising unemployment rates of young people with college degrees. The college diploma is still, of course, a badge of preferred status in the labor force, but less dramatically than formerly because of its increased prevalence. Reflecting this, college education people have experienced very little improvement in their unemployment rate in the past few years, while the global rate was improving considerably. Indeed, for young people, there was actually a notable increase in unemployment: white males under 25 years of age with college degrees had an unemployment rate of 5.0% in March 1962 but a rate of 8.0% in March 1964. Similarly, the unemployment rate for white females under 25 with college diplomas went up from 0.9% to 2.3%. If this occurs with increasing supplies of highly educated workers, it should be no surprise to find higher relative unemployment rates among teenagers and women today in view of their more rapid growth in the labor force.

The relative supply phenomenon is one good reason why a given overall unemployment rate will mean changing unemployment rates for particular demographic or educational groups over time. A return to a 4.0% global unemployment rate would not return all group rates to where they were a decade ago. The unemployment rate among teenagers could not be expected to decline even to its 1956 level of 10.4%. The very high unemployment rate among teenagers is a matter of great social consequence. It argues strongly for careful and thorough exploration of promising manpower policies. But it is also an argument for—and not against—expansionary fiscal-monetary policies. The stability and stubbornness of the teenage rate of recent years reflect a stand-off between upward supply trends and downward demand pressures. Employment opportunities for teenagers have had to rise rapidly just to keep pace with the growth of the teenage labor force.

Teenage employment is highly sensitive to over-all economic conditions, as Professor Bowen's statistical analysis demonstrates and as the time-series data show. In 1962 and again in 1964, teenage employment increased by about a quarter of a million, which was proportionately a much larger increase than that of total employment in these years. In 1963, however, when the over-all employment picture temporarily did not improve, teenage jobs actually declined in number. Teenagers in the labor force are growing rapidly in number. Their job gains tend to be especially small in periods of sluggish over-all increases in employment and particularly large where over-all employment grows rapidly. This means that teenage unemployment is likely to shoot up unless the economy expands briskly. Teenagers are at the back of the hiring line. And it is, therefore, all the more important that the hiring line be shortened sufficiently to bring increasing job gains for them.

The same reasoning about the back of the hiring line also applies to the Negro worker. But since Negroes have not been getting on line at an unusually rapid rate, their unemployment rate has moved quite differently from that of teenagers. There has been a sufficient improvement in over-all employment opportunities to produce some real progress in nonwhite unemployment rates in the past few years. The nonwhite unemployment rate is approximately twice the white rate now, just as it was a year ago and two years ago. This means that it has been coming down twice as fast as the white unemployment rate. To be specific, in the first quarter of 1963 the nonwhite unemployment rate was 12.7 percent compared with a 5.8 percent white rate. The corresponding figures in the first quarter of 1964 were 11.3 percent and 5.5 percent. The first quarter of this year produced a nonwhite rate of 10.1 percent and a white rate of 4.8 percent. Continued performance along this path might mean that the Negro unemployment rate would be above 7 percent with an over-all unemployment rate of 4 percent (and a white rate a little above $3\frac{1}{2}$ percent). The disparity is a distressing commentary on our social structure. It is an argument for cutting down the high Negro unemployment rates at their roots. But it is no reason to sacrifice a further possible decline of 2 percentage points in the Negro rate.

The Search for a Hard-Core

In short, the teenage worker and Negro worker pose a hard problem, but not a hard-core problem. Quite the contrary, their job opportunities are especially sensitive to over-all economic conditions. And if the structural deterioration thesis is intended to imply that there is a kink in the Phillips Curve just ahead, it must point to a hard-core of unemployed who will not fit the demands for labor that are generated by an expanding economy. It must present evidence that the unemployed are in a meaningful sense "unemployable." At a minimum it must show that some deterioration has occurred in the relative "employability" of those people still seeking jobs compared with those at work. Presumably employers are always sorting and choosing between those they hire and those whom they turn down in their attempts to fill vacancies. In some darwinian sense, the unemployed worker is classified as "inferior" to the man who gets a job. But if there is any indication that the difference between the job-holder and the job-seeker is more discrete and wider today than it

Table 1 Changes in unemployment rates and employment, by occupation, 1964 : I to 1965 : I

	Unemployment rate (%)		Change	
Occupation[a]	1964 : I	1965 : I	% points	% of rate
Total	6.2	5.4	−0.8	−13
Nonfarm laborers	15.5	12.7	−2.8	−18
Farm laborers and foremen	10.5	8.2	−2.3	−22
Operatives	8.4	6.6	−1.8	−21
Service workers other than household	7.1	6.6	−.5	−7
Craftsmen and foremen	6.1	5.5	−.6	−10
Private household workers	5.2	4.6	−.6	−12
Clerical workers	4.2	3.7	−.5	−12
Sales workers	3.9	4.1	+.2	+5
Managers, officials, and proprietors	1.8	1.4	−.4	−22
Professional and technical	1.7	1.6	−.1	−6
Farmers and farm managers	.5	.7	+.2	+40

Source: Department of Labor.

a. Ranked by 1964 : I unemployment rate; rates are *not* seasonally adjusted.

was when unemployment rates were higher, that evidence has not been presented.

Let me offer a few pieces of relevant information that emerge when one looks at recent figures in a search for a hard-core of unemployed. Table 1 shows unemployment rates for the 11 recognized occupational categories for the first quarter of 1964 and the first quarter of 1965. The occupational groups are listed in order of their unemployment rate in the first quarter of last year. The third column of that table shows clearly that the groups with the highest unemployment rates have had largest percentage-point improvements in unemployment. Only the three categories at the top of the list have had improvements greater than that in the over-all rate. And the next four categories on the list have had improvements only slightly smaller than the over-all gain of 0.8 percentage points. The last four groups have had considerably smaller improvements (or even deterioration) in their unemployment.

I should consider the percentage-point changes decisive evidence that the occupational groups with high unemployment rates are not a hard-core. But if a stronger rebuke to the hard-core view is called for, the facts will deliver it. The rates at the top of the list have come down even more *relatively speaking* as a percentage of their original level, as shown in the fourth column of the table. The top three categories have improved by about $\frac{1}{5}$ on their original unemployment rate. Only one of the eight categories farther down the list shows an improvement anywhere near that magnitude.

Table 2 tells the story about the duration of unemployment. Perhaps the long-term unemployed would seem to be the most likely candidates for a hard-core group. But, with the over-all improvement in unemployment in the past year, the diminution in unemployment has been progressively greater, the longer the category of duration, ranging from a 6

Table 2 Percentage change in number of persons unemployed by duration, 1964:I to 1965:I

Duration of unemployment	Percentage change in number unemployed
Total	−10.7
Less than 5 weeks	−5.8
5 to 14 weeks	−9.9
15 to 26 weeks	−16.3
27 weeks and over	−22.2

Source: Department of Labor.

percent improvement for under 5 weeks to a 22 percent improvement for 27 weeks and over.

In an attempt to diagnose the true extent of hard-core unemployability, bottlenecks, and wage-price pressures that limit our unemployment target, we should investigate geographical areas that have attained particularly low unemployment rates. It is quite clear why the economy cannot match over-all the best performance among our various labor market areas. The average can never be as good as the best element in it. And the character of the demand for labor in certain cities, for example, Washington, D.C., is particularly favorable to achieving low unemployment. But the potentialities for our society may become most apparent by an analysis of local successes. And we do have some remarkable success stories to analyze in the records of particular major labor market areas over the past 4 years. For example, the Gary, Indiana, major labor market area, which had a 10.1 percent unemployment rate in January 1961, was experiencing a 3.2 percent rate in January 1965. Similarly, Detroit's rate fell from 11.6 percent to 3.5 percent over the same period. Milwaukee, which had a fairly typical level of unemployment at 6.9 percent in January 1961, was down to 3.2 percent in January 1965. I do not claim to know the full explanation of these success stories. But I am suggesting that they deserve investigation to determine whether it takes an unusually favorable composition in the supply of labor to reach truly low unemployment rates.

Conclusion

A wide variety of policies and developments in the economy influence the ability of aggregate demand policies to do their job in improving resource utilization without endangering reasonable price stability. The freedom to pursue fuller prosperity and lower unemployment can be enhanced by improved competitiveness in product markets and labor markets, more enlightened self-interest in price and wage setting, and better structural and sectoral balances of supply and demand in product and labor markets.

It is essential that aggregative policies, manpower policies, and wage-price policies be recognized as complementary tools to achieve noninflationary full employment. Aggregative policies need the backing of manpower policies, not because there has been structural deterioration in labor markets but because we need structural improvement. And manpower policies need job creation through aggregate demand policies unless we are to have what my colleague Otto Eckstein has aptly called "a bitter harvest of trained and educated" people looking for jobs.

The economics profession needs to join forces to get this message across. Improved public understanding of Federal fiscal policy has had an enormous influence on our ability to alleviate unemployment recently. But the battle for full recognition of the potentialities and significance of the Budget remains to be won. In particular, the contribution of fiscal stimulus to unemployment is less obvious to the layman than is its benefit to incomes and profits. To the noneconomist, unemployment is likely to be seen as a problem of particular people in particular occupations in particular cities. Everybody knows that a penicillin shot can cure a sore throat even though it is not injected in the throat. The similar lesson that general economic remedies can flow through the body politic still needs to be taught. And the case for manpower policies needs to be made more effectively, by showing that Federal outlays in this area are a good sound investment of public resources. The case cannot be made by deprecating the role of expansionary aggregative policies.

We have no reason to retreat from our goals in conducting aggregate demand policies. Indeed, we have a fine record of progress in job creation and we should be moving ahead to keep improving it. There is no evidence of structural deterioration in labor markets or from any other source to suggest that we are about to encounter a sharp kink in the Phillips Curve. We must, of course, be aware of the risks. Our brakes must therefore be well-adjusted, but there is a green light ahead and our foot belongs on the accelerator.

Upward Mobility in a High-Pressure Economy

The choice of an aggregate target of resource utilization remains one of the key issues facing policy makers and macroeconomists. Obviously, fuller utilization of labor and capital brings benefits in the form of extra incomes, output, and jobs; at the same time, it clearly imposes costs by increasing inflationary tendencies. Various economists see these benefits and costs very differently. Henry Wallich once suggested that macroeconomists could be classified into advocates of "high pressure" and "low pressure" operation of the economy.[1] At the present time, the controversial range for the target unemployment rate extends from 4 to 5 percent. Generally, high-pressure advocates concede that, with existing labor market institutions, unemployment rates below 4 percent would be associated with unacceptable inflation; while most low-pressure advocates agree that unemployment rates above 5 percent are intolerable.

More than a decade ago, I contributed to this dialogue by estimating the bonus in output associated with a high-pressure economy.[2] I stressed then that unemployment was merely the tip of the iceberg that forms in a cold economy. The difference between unemployment rates of 5 percent and 4 percent extends far beyond the creation of jobs for 1 percent of the labor force. The submerged part of the iceberg includes (a) additional jobs for people who do not actively seek work in a slack labor market but nonetheless take jobs when they become available; (b) a longer workweek reflecting less part-time and more overtime employment; and (c) extra productivity—more output per manhour—from fuller and more efficient use of labor and capital. In light of the findings of other researchers on various aspects of the output-employment relationship, I shall qualify and modify, but basically reaffirm, the three-to-one relationship that I initially estimated between percentage increments in real gross national product (GNP) and percentage-point reductions in the unemployment rate.

That body of research has highlighted several behavioral forces that hold down the addition to unemployment relative to the shortfall of output in a slack economy. Mindful of hiring, training, and recruitment costs, employers hold on to some workers not needed to meet current production schedules. Deterred by search costs, some would-be workers do not hunt for jobs when chances of finding reasonably good ones are poor, and consequently are not counted among the unemployed. Similarly, workers accept cutbacks to part-time employment when full-time jobs are not available.

In addition, I now believe that an important part of the process involves a downgrading of labor in a slack economy—high-quality workers avoiding unemployment by accepting low-quality and less productive jobs. The focus of this paper is on the upgrading of jobs associated with a high-pressure economy. Shifts in the composition of output and employment toward sectors and industries of higher productivity boost aggregate productivity as unemployment declines. Thus the movement to full employment draws on a reserve army of the underemployed as well as of the unemployed. In the main empirical study of this paper, I shall report new evidence concerning the upgrading of workers into more productive jobs in a higher-pressure economy.

The demographic groups experiencing the largest proportionate increases in employment in a higher-pressure economy are secondary workers—teenagers and women—who are typically low paid; on the other hand, the industries with the largest relative increases in employment are those that pay high wages and that normally employ a particularly high fraction of adult male workers. These results reflect a process of ladder climbing: In part, men formerly in poor jobs move into better ones, making way for women and young people in the less well-paid pursuits; in other cases, a disproportionate share of the additional employment in industries that normally hire men is shifted to women and young people.

On a naive view of the allocation of labor by changes in relative wages, the industries generating the largest increases in employment would be expected to experience the largest increases in wage rates on the road to high utilization. And since these are typically high-wage industries, wage differentials among industries would then be expected to widen. Moreover, since low-skill workers experience especially high unemployment rates, the industries that hire them should be less vulnerable to upward pressure on wages. Yet available evidence on relative wage movements points unmistakably in the opposite direction: Skill differentials and industrial wage differentials tend to narrow—not widen—in a high-pressure economy.

Some recent theoretical analyses emphasize nonprice (nonwage) considerations that determine employment in areas where hiring and training costs are substantial and where employers therefore have strong incentives to promote long-run attachments by their workers. Relying on that nonprice allocative mechanism, I shall sketch a model of the labor market that seems consistent with the behavior of relative unemployment rates, relative wage rates, and shifts in industrial composition of employment associated with a high-pressure economy, hoping to explain why the same forces that make for more jobs also make for better jobs and more output per worker. In conclusion, I shall discuss some implications of the findings and analysis for fiscal, manpower, and wage-price policies.

Output and Productivity Dividends

When I first estimated that a 1 percentage point decrement in the unemployment rate was associated with a bonus of output approximating 3 percent, I made the basic calculation by a "leap from unemployment to output." I then interpreted that result by reviewing the shreds of evidence available on the various components: the lengthened average workweek, increased participation in the labor force, and extra productivity. Many economists have since studied the parts carefully and built up the estimate of the gap from the separate pieces.

Increases in Labor Input

One part of the gap calculation is merely a piece of arithmetic. If participation rates, average hours, and manhour productivity are held constant, the extra jobs associated with reducing the unemployment rate from 5.0 to 4.0 percent would add 1/95 to total labor input and, by assumption, that much—1.05 percent—to real output.

Various researchers have obtained similar results in estimating the lengthened workweek—increased overtime and diminished part-time—associated with reduced unemployment. Black and Russell, Thurow and Taylor, Perry, and I, have all found that the increment in total manhours due to the lengthening of the workweek is between 0.35 and 0.5 percent for a drop of a percentage point in the unemployment rate.[3] Taylor and Thurow explicitly recognize the use of overtime as a temporary buffer in periods of rapid growth of output; holding the growth of output constant, they estimate that the workweek expands by 0.4 percent for a 1 percentage decrement in the unemployment rate. Perry's estimate standardizes for differences in average hours among various demographic groups; he finds an increase of 0.35 percent in average hours for a decline of 1 point in the official unemployment rate.

I grasped originally at the straw of a calculation of normal labor force by the Bureau of Labor Statistics and guessed that there might be three "hidden unemployed"—people not seeking work actively who would take jobs in a high-utilization economy—for every ten recorded unemployed in excess of a 4 percent unemployment rate. Other studies have generally produced much larger estimates of the number of hidden unemployed. But some of the largest estimates of the participation response are based on statistical techniques that may create an upward bias, as Jacob Mincer demonstrated.[4] Perry's recent study disaggregates the demographic groups carefully and uses a statistical technique free of bias; on the whole, his estimates tend to be smaller than those of other researchers, partly because he cannot establish a lagged response in annual data. He finds roughly six "hidden unemployed" for every ten recorded unemployed above a 4 percent rate; the increase in participation when the unemployment rate is reduced by 1 percentage point entails an increase in jobs of approximately 0.6 percent.[5]

In light of these other studies, I would now estimate the additional labor input associated with a reduction in unemployment from 5 to 4 percent as follows:

Component	**Percent**
Jobs for the unemployed	1.05
Lengthened workweek	0.40
Increased labor force participation	0.65
Total addition to labor input	2.10

Productivity

The most perplexing component of the output dividend is the productivity bonus that accompanies a higher-pressure economy. Traditional microeconomic theory implies that firms normally operate under conditions where, holding capital constant, a given percentage increase in labor input would add less than proportionately to output. Yet exhaustive empirical research has generally revealed that manhour productivity is boosted by a rise in employment.

The empirical finding becomes comprehensible once it is recognized that, for a substantial period of time, much of labor input is essentially a fixed cost, reflecting contractual commitments, indivisibilities or complementarity with capital, transaction costs of hiring and firing, and the value of skills that workers have acquired on the job. Thus, in periods of recession or slack, the amount of labor kept on the payroll is greater than the amount technologically required to produce the prevailing depressed level of output. Given the initial presence of such on-the-job underemployment, when demand strengthens, output can be expanded without a commensurate expansion in labor input and a spurt of productivity results. But fixity of labor can explain only a temporary—if perhaps quite lengthy—bonus of productivity from higher output and employment.

The remarkable and intriguing puzzle is that most investigators who have studied the output-employment relationship have not been able to make the productivity bonus from higher utilization disappear, even in the long run.[6] Robert M. Solow has commented that "the persistence of what appears to be long-run increasing returns with respect to labor alone [is one of the] two big paradoxes, whose resolution would be a major step toward the unification of long-run and short-run theory."[7]

In light of the work of other researchers, it is clear that both *declining* unemployment and *lower levels* of unemployment stimulate productivity. In an upswing of economic activity, both forces operate, but only the level effect persists. In my initial estimate of the productivity bonus, I did not distinguish between the two sets of forces. The elasticity of output with respect to manhours for the first year of rising utilization can be approximated as 1.5, so that the total increment in output associated with a 2.1 percent addition to manhours exceeds 3 percent. But over a longer horizon—say, three years—the elasticity should be scaled down to about $1\frac{1}{3}$, pointing to a total increment of output of 2.8 percent. These elasticities are consistent with the productivity bonus found by Black and Russell and with the estimate made by Perry, converted into unweighted manhours, from regressing employment on output.[8]

In short, three to one still looks like a good approximation to the relationship between added output and reduction in the unemployment rate. But that estimate represents rounding downward, as I believed initially, only for the first year, and is probably a slight upward rounding for subsequent years. With potential GNP currently approximating $1.3 trillion, the output dividend associated with a choice of a 4 percent rather than a 5 percent unemployment target is between $35 billion and $40 billion a year, over a horizon of perhaps five years.

Over a long-run horizon of decades and generations, no reasonable estimate is possible. To be sure, on theoretical grounds, one can conclude—as Robert J. Gordon does in this issue—that the productivity bonus must *ultimately* disappear and even turn negative, thus reducing the size of the output dividend. But even that contention for the undated ultimate long run is subject to skepticism on two grounds. First, the same theoretical reasoning was once interpreted as demonstrating that productivity moved contracyclically in the short run.[9] Second, it disregards the body to empirical evidence that Solow noted. Fortunately, the horizon relevant to the choices of stabilization policy is not one of decades or generations.

Sectoral Shifts

One important part of the productivity dividend seems to be associated with shifts of resources toward sectors of higher than average productivity. That portion does not pose the analytical mysteries associated with persistently increasing returns to labor within an industry.

The difference between a high-pressure and a low-pressure economy is not simply a proportionate addition of output and employment across all industries and sectors. The exact distribution of the increments would depend on the source of the added aggregate demand, which might be expansionary monetary policy that would particularly stimulate construction and durable goods; or a wartime military buildup that added especially to the federal sector; or tax cuts and increases in transfer payments that boosted consumer goods industries by an extra margin. Despite these possible differences, history reveals a distinct pattern of resource shifts associated with higher utilization; in particular, the sectoral pattern characteristic of a high-pressure economy is favorable to aggregate productivity.

For example, consider the very broad division of GNP by institutional sectors as product originating in nonfarm business, farms, households, the rest of the world, and government. Empirically, the shortfall of output and employment in a slack economy is found to be concentrated in the nonfarm business sector; agriculture, households, and the tiny rest-of-the-world sector show no cyclical sensitivity; and activity in the government sector is properly regarded as exogenous.[10] For 1971, according to published and unpublished estimates of the Department of Commerce, output per manhour in private nonfarm business exceeded output per manhour for the whole GNP by about 20 percent, as shown below:

Sector	**Percent of total output**	**Percent of total manhours**	**Productivity relative**
Total GNP	100.0	100.0	1.00
Private nonfarm business	85.3	71.1	1.20
Nonfinancial corporations	59.2	43.6	1.36
Other private nonfarm	26.1	27.5	0.95

Accordingly, even assuming no productivity gain within private nonfarm business, the shift of resources into that sector would boost aggregate productivity. If in such a case the estimated increase of 2.1 percent in total manhours associated with a difference between a 5 percent and a 4 percent unemployment rate is absorbed by private nonfarm business, real GNP would go up 2.5 percent, reflecting the 20 percent productivity bonus from the sectoral shift.

Disaggregation within private nonfarm business raises the possibility of an even greater boost to aggregate productivity from sectoral shifts. As shown above, the higher than average productivity associated with private nonfarm business stems from the especially high productivity of nonfinancial corporations; output per manhour in the remainder of nonfarm business was actually a shade below the economy-wide average.[11] Nonfinancial corporations also offer high-paying jobs with average hourly compensation about 16 percent higher than the economy-wide average and about 38 percent higher than the average outside that sector. Empirically, the nonfinancial corporate sector accounts for most of the incremental output associated with higher overall utilization. Nonfinancial corporations produce 77.8 percent of the extra output associated with closing the output gap, according to the following equation:

$$\frac{C}{Y_p} = \underset{(14.2)}{-0.2423} + \underset{(34.6)}{0.00091t} + \underset{(43.5)}{0.7784}\frac{Y_a}{Y_p}. \qquad (1)$$

$\bar{R}^2 = 0.983$; Durbin-Watson statistic $= 0.414$; standard error of estimate $= 0.0045$. Here and in subsequent equations the numbers in parentheses are t-statistics. In the equation, fitted to quarterly data for 1954–71,

C is gross product of nonfinancial corporations, Y_p is the official series on potential GNP, and Y_a is actual GNP, all in 1958 prices; and t is time ranging from 1 in 1954:1 to 73 in 1971:4.[12]

If productivity within the nonfinancial corporate sector and within the remainder of private nonfarm business remained constant, while 77.8 percent of extra output associated with reduced unemployment was distributed to the first and 22.2 percent to the second, the productivity on the incremental manhours would be 1.24 times the economy-wide average. Given an increment of manhours of 2.1 percent, the resulting gain in output would be 2.6 percent.

Many interesting questions are raised by the strong sensitivity of corporate output to overall utilization, combined with the above average productivity and wage rates of that sector. In a movement from slack to full employment, what fractions of the extra corporate jobs go to the unemployed and to those previously employed in other sectors? How much of the wage premium enjoyed by the average corporate employee goes to new corporate employees? What demographic groups benefit most from the shift? Unfortunately, these questions cannot be answered because the only available data on employment in nonfinancial corporations consist of annual estimates of total manhours in that sector.[13] At least some answers are possible, however, for industrial sectors, as I shall show below.

The Pattern of Additional Employment

Who would get the extra jobs in an economy with a 4 percent unemployment rate as contrasted with one of 5 percent? Perry has established that the bulk of the extra jobs would go to women and teenagers—secondary workers—with a disproportionately small gain for adult men.[14] On the other hand, most of the extra jobs would be created in industries that typically hire a particularly large fraction of adult males; the seeming inconsistency is resolved by a process of upgrading in the labor market.

Demographic Composition

According to Perry's estimates, in 1970, when the official unemployment rate was 4.9 percent, employment was 1,174,000 below the level that would have been associated with a 4 percent unemployment rate. As a fraction of actual employment, that shortfall or gap in jobs amounted to 1.43 percent. That is consistent with his estimate cited above that, because of the induced drop in labor force participation, a decrement of 1.6 percent

Table 1 Employment, actual, potential, and gap, by demographic group, 1970 (employment in thousands)

Sex and age group	Actual[a]	Potential	Gap between potential and actual	Gap as percentage of actual
Male				
16–19	3,828	4,002	173	4.53
20–24	6,956	7,095	139	2.00
25–64	39,319	39,616	297	0.76
65 and over	2,111	2,134	23	1.08
Female				
16–19	2,766	2,912	146	5.28
20–24	4,545	4,655	110	2.40
25–64	21,610	21,886	276	1.28
65 and over	1,031	1,041	10	0.96
Total	82,166	83,340	1,174	1.43

Sources: Actual—estimates by Edward F. Denison and George L. Perry; potential—Perry estimates associated with an official unemployment rate of 4.0 percent. Total and gaps calculated from unrounded data.
a. Including Armed Forces. Estimates do not agree precisely with official labor force data.

in employment accompanies an extra point in the unemployment rate. Perry's disaggregated estimates, displayed in Table 1, reveal a marked disparity in the percentage employment gaps for the various demographic groups, ranging from less than 1 percent for adult men to about 5 percent for teenagers. Put another way, mature men (25 years and over) accounted for half of total employment in 1970 but for only 27 percent of the job gap. Although the rapid growth of secondary workers in the labor force has accentuated this pattern in recent years, it is not a new development. In 1949, for example, when men 25 and over had 61 percent of total employment, they represented 39 percent of the job gap, according to Perry's estimates.

Secondary workers experience larger relative job gaps both because their participation rates are particularly responsive to levels of economic activity and because their unemployment rates decline by a larger amount when the overall unemployment rate falls. For example, Perry estimated that a decline in the overall rate from 5.0 to 4.0 percent implies a reduction of $2\frac{1}{2}$ to 3 percentage points in the unemployment rate for teenagers, but of only 0.7 or 0.8 percentage points for mature males.[15] Even though the decline for teenagers is a smaller *proportionate* drop in their high unemployment rate, it yields a larger proportionate increase in employment.

Compared with mature men, secondary workers typically earn lower wage rates and work fewer hours per week when employed. Because they account for most of the overall job gap, that gap is smaller when weighted by typical wage rates and hours than when viewed as a count of persons. Perry's concept of weighted employment associates with each demographic group the average hours it works and the average wage rate it earns; for 1970, the weighted employment gap was 1.11 percent of total weighted employment in contrast with the unweighted figure of 1.43 percent. If 1970 had been a year of 4 percent unemployment, the average person who would have gained a job would have earned only 78 percent as much as the average worker, assuming that his "new" job involved the average number of hours and average hourly wage experienced by his demographic group.

Industrial Composition

What kinds of extra jobs are available when the unemployment rate is 4 percent rather than 5 percent? In principle, the distribution of extra jobs could be analyzed in many ways: by institutional sectors (as noted above), or by occupational and skill categories, or by industry. The availability of data—rather than analytical considerations—led me to focus on the pattern of job creation among industries.

To allocate incremental employment by industry, I relied on the employment data by industry published each July in the *Survey of Current Business* as part of the national income accounts. These data are based on reports from establishments (that is, employers), as are the Denison-Perry estimates. The Commerce series differs from the latter by double-counting people who hold two jobs, and by excluding unpaid family workers; they also differ from Perry's estimates (although not Denison's) by including persons under the age of sixteen. The level of total employment in the Commerce series exceeds Perry's, and the proportionate excess has been rising slowly over time: The number of 14- and 15-year-olds at work has increased as a share of total employment, while unpaid family workers have been declining as a share of the total. Yet taking account of the gentle upward trend, the ratio of Commerce employment to Perry employment has been remarkably stable and shows little sensitivity to overall utilization of the economy. For annual data from 1947 to 1970, the relation takes the following form:

$$\log\frac{N_c}{N_p} = \underset{(42.6)}{0.023} + \underset{(23.1)}{0.00093t} - \underset{(1.4)}{0.022\log g}, \qquad (2)$$

$\bar{R}^2 = 0.959$; Durbin-Watson statistic = 0.917; standard error of estimate = 0.00136, where N_c and N_p are total employment measured by Commerce and Perry, respectively; t is time in years (1947 = 1); and g is the ratio of potential to actual employment as estimated by Perry. Thus, $\log g$ is essentially the Perry employment gap as a ratio to actual employment.

The coefficient on $\log g$ implies that total Commerce employment is depressed by 1.02 percent for each 1 percent employment gap in the Perry data; the difference from unity seems so trivial—as well as being statistically insignificant—that I ignored it. I thus attributed the Perry percentage employment gap to the Commerce data, setting the Commerce employment gap in 1970, for example, at the same 1.43 percent measured by Perry. That estimate in turn implies a measure of total potential Commerce employment. I calculated the ratio of actual Commerce employment for each industry (N_i) to total Commerce potential employment, and then sought to determine how that ratio was affected by variations in the overall employment gap.

The initial statistical exploration revealed one problem of reverse causation. Military employment (and even civilian federal employment) was strongly and negatively related to the employment gap. This result reflected the Korean and Vietnam war booms that fiscal-monetary policies permitted at the same time that federal demand for workers was especially strong. The equations reported the influence of the federal sector *on* aggregate employment, rather than the way it was influenced *by* overall employment. Hence, federal employment was taken to be exogenous; total employment for the economy, both actual and potential, was calculated excluding actual employment in the federal sector. As it turned out, this refinement had virtually no influence on the elasticity estimated for any private industry.

For each industry, the log of the ratio of actual industry employment (N_i) to total potential employment—excluding federal—(P) is explained by (1) trend (t) with the year 1947 = 0 and 1970 = 23; (2) the log of the ratio of total actual employment—excluding federal—(A) to P; and (3) the log of the ratio of lagged employment in the industry ($N_{i,-1}$) to P:

$$\log\frac{N_i}{P} = a_0 + a_1 t + a_2 \log\frac{A}{P} + a_3 \log\frac{N_{i,-1}}{P}. \tag{3}$$

The equations of Table 2 were meant to yield a reasonable set of estimates of a_2—the elasticity of industry employment with respect to economy-wide employment. When an employment gap of 1 percent is

Table 2 Parameters of equation (3) for employment by industry, 1948–70[a]

Industry	a_0	a_1	a_2	a_3	$\bar{R}^2$	Standard error	Durbin-Watson statistic
Employees							
Agriculture, forestry, and fisheries	−0.863	−0.0122	−0.965	0.723	0.991	0.0263	2.431
	(3.0)	(3.3)	(3.3)	(7.8)			
Construction and mining	−1.876	−0.0042	1.286	0.331	0.847	0.0223	1.426
	(5.8)	(4.5)	(5.2)	(2.9)			
Nondurable manufacturing	−2.153	−0.0090	1.122	−0.039	0.994	0.0050	1.114
	(17.1)	(16.0)	(18.4)	(0.6)			
Durable manufacturing	−1.417	0.0000	2.651	0.248	0.840	0.0257	0.667
	(7.6)	(0.1)	(9.0)	(2.6)			
Transportation	−2.234	−0.0146	1.692	0.245	0.996	0.0086	1.120
	(13.2)	(11.8)	(16.3)	(4.3)			
Communication and public utilities	−0.923	−0.0004	0.779	0.751	0.805	0.0158	1.083
	(2.3)	(10.7)	(4.5)	(7.2)			
Wholesale trade	−2.237	0.0034	0.680	0.289	0.947	0.0076	1.687
	(6.5)	(7.9)	(8.1)	(2.7)			
Retail trade	−1.709	0.0061	0.993	0.202	0.979	0.0077	1.390
	(9.5)	(11.6)	(10.0)	(2.4)			
Finance, insurance, and real estate	−0.428	0.0020	0.271	0.866	0.994	0.0081	1.606
	(1.8)	(1.8)	(2.9)	(12.3)			
Private household services	−0.177	−0.0034	−0.853	0.935	0.840	0.0443	2.257
	(0.5)	(2.4)	(1.7)	(9.2)			
High-wage services[b]	−3.429	0.0359	0.794	0.223	0.997	0.0155	1.322
	(5.1)	(5.3)	(4.6)	(1.5)			
Other services[c]	−0.613	0.0054	0.208	0.768	0.998	0.0060	1.125
	(2.8)	(3.7)	(3.0)	(9.4)			
State and local governments	−0.734	0.0084	−0.001	0.721	0.996	0.0119	1.225
	(1.6)	(1.8)	(0.0)	(4.4)			

Self-employed workers							
Agriculture, forestry, and fisheries	−1.061	−0.0227	0.089	0.575	0.998	0.0157	1.561
	(2.7)	(2.6)	(0.5)	(3.5)			
Nonagriculture	−0.598	−0.0028	0.076	0.737	0.986	0.0089	1.411
	(2.4)	(2.3)	(0.8)	(6.7)			

Sources: Employees are from *Survey of Current Business*, various July issues, Table 6.3. Self-employed are calculated from *ibid.*, various July issues, Table 6.6 less Table 6.4.

a. The numbers in parentheses are t-statistics.

b. High-wage services are miscellaneous business services, miscellaneous repair services, miscellaneous professional services, and legal services.

c. Other services consist of all the services listed in the source except private households and those enumerated in note *b* above.

Table 3 Aspects of the employment gap, by industry, 1970

Industry	Employment gap, 1970		Employment, 1970[a]		Annual earnings index, 1970[b]	Index of fringe benefits as percentage of wages and salaries, 1971[c]	Men 25 and over as percentage of all employees, 1970[d]
	Number (thousands)	Percentage of allocated employment gap	Number (thousands)	Percentage of total employment			
Employees							
Agriculture, forestry, and fisheries	−21	−2.0	1,389	1.6	46	27	55.8
Construction and mining	81	7.9	4,109	4.8	133	80	78.4
Nondurable manufacturing	141	13.8	8,164	9.5	106	154	51.6
Durable manufacturing	459	44.9	11,250	13.1	125		67.5
Transportation	70	6.8	2,688	3.1	129	94	75.4
Communication and public utilities	22	2.2	1,815	2.1	126	182	57.5
Wholesale trade	40	3.9	3,808	4.4	127	47	64.7
Retail trade	173	16.9	11,299	13.1	70		33.6
Finance, insurance, and real estate	15	1.5	3,673	4.3	105	128	41.5
Private household services	−28	−2.7	2,157	2.5	31	—	6.1
High-wage services[e]	33	3.2	2,686	3.1	108	39	53.0[f]
Other services[e]	27	2.6	8,436	9.8	76		27.2
Government							
State and local	0	0.0	10,111	11.8	94	—	44.1[g]
Federal civilian	—	—	2,932	3.4	142	—	—
Military	—	—	3,096	3.6	90	—	—

Self-employed workers							
Agriculture, forestry, and fisheries	3	0.3	2,043	2.4	—	—	91.7
Nonagriculture	7	0.7	6,261	7.3	—	—	72.5
Rest of the world	—	—	4	—	—	—	—
Total	1,022	100.0	85,921	100.0			

Sources: *Survey of Current Business,* Vol. 52 (July 1972), and unpublished data from the U.S. Department of Commerce and the U.S. Bureau of Labor Statistics. See also notes a through d below. Figures are rounded and may not add to totals.

a. From Tables 6.3 (for employees) and 6.4 minus 6.6 (self-employed), *Survey of Current Business* (July 1972).

b. National average wage and salary workers = 100. Calculated by dividing data in Table 6.2 by corresponding numbers in Table 6.3, *ibid.*

c. Index of all private employee fringe benefits as a percentage of wages and salaries = 100. Based on unpublished Department of Commerce data on "other labor income."

d. Calculated from unpublished Current Population Survey data of the Bureau of the Census.

e. See Table 2, notes b and c.

f. Business and repair employees only.

g. Public administration and education employees only.

closed, log A/P rises from -0.01 to zero; the value of a_2 for any industry describes the percentage gain in industry employment associated with that 1 percent addition to overall employment. Thus, if an industry's a_2 exceeds unity, employment in that industry is increased more than proportionately; if a_2 is zero, industry employment is unaffected; while a negative a_2 implies that industry employment is contracted under those circumstances.

The other variables in the equations serve merely in a pragmatic way to help refine the estimates of the a_2 coefficients. Trend is needed to distinguish secular from cyclical forces; lagged employment reduces (although it does not eliminate) problems of serial correlation. Since P is used to normalize both the dependent and independent variables, lagged industry employment is divided by P (rather than lagged P).

The values of the a_2 elasticity coefficients shown in Table 2 reveal the big differences among industries in cyclical sensitivity. Durable goods manufacturing wins first prize by a wide margin; its employment is estimated to be 2.65 percent higher when overall employment is 1 percent higher in relation to potential.[16] Transportation, construction-mining, and nondurable manufacturing also have more than proportionate responses, as shown by a_2 coefficients exceeding unity. Jobs in retail trade move just about proportionately to total employment. Agricultural and nonagricultural self-employment and employment in state and local governments exhibit remarkable immunity to the gap. Agricultural employees and private household workers showed a decrement of employment at high overall utilization.[17]

In Table 3 the elasticity estimates of Table 2 are used to allocate the employment gap of 1970 by industry. With the federal sector excluded, the percentage gap was 1.54 in 1970; thus the result of multiplying 1.54 times the a_2 for an industry times actual employment in that industry for 1970, is the estimated employment gap of that industry, shown in the first column of Table 3. The importance of durable goods manufacturing in the job gap stands out. Retail trade and nondurable manufacturing also account for substantial parts of the job gap; although their elasticities are not particularly high, they are very large industries. But so are other services and state and local governments, and yet they account for only a trivial part of the job gap. The tendency of poor overall job opportunities to keep workers down on the farm and in domestic service is reflected in negative job gaps for those sectors.

The nature of the equations does not ensure that the total employment gap will be allocated among the industries. In fact, the estimates allocate a little more than 1.0 million jobs to the various industries, rather than the 1.2 million total in the Commerce employment gap.[18]

Key Characteristics In comparison with the demographic composition of the employment gap discussed above, the industrial composition reveals two remarkable divergences:

1. In the industries with high elasticities and large job gaps, men 25 and over typically account for an especially large share of employment. The last column of the table reveals that relationship as well as a few exceptions (agricultural self-employment on the one hand; retail trade on the other). If each industry filled its job gap in 1970 without altering the demographic composition of its work force, men 25 and over would have obtained 61 percent of the extra jobs, in sharp contrast with the 27 percent demographic estimate of the job gap for that group. Teenagers, who also had 27 percent of the demographic job gap, would have obtained only 6 percent of the extra jobs if the demographic composition within industries had been unchanged.
2. The industries with relatively large employment gaps typically offer high-paying jobs. Average compensation for employees in the employment gap weighted by the index of annual earnings by industry (the fifth column of the table) was 16 percent *above* the economy-wide average for all workers, a striking contrast to the 22 percent short fall *below* economy-wide average earnings yielded by the demographic estimates. Again exceptions can be found—such as finance, insurance, and real estate, and retail trade—but the average relationship is strong.

The industrial composition of the job gap is also tilted toward those industries that seem to have stronger attachments between employers and employees. One crude measure of employers' efforts to retain workers over the long run is the volume of fringe benefits (pensions, insurance, and so on). When the job gap by industries is weighted by an index of the proportion of private fringe benefits to wages and salaries among industries (the next to last column of the table), the resulting index of fringes for the jobs in the employment gap is 22 percent above the national average for all private employment.

Finally, the job gap is concentrated in industries with above average output per manhour. In Table 4, Nordhaus' cyclically corrected estimates of productivity relatives among industries for 1971 are shown, after some adjustment to match the industry disaggregation used in Table 2.[19]

Table 4 Employment gap, 1970, and productivity relatives, 1971, by industry

Industry	Percentage of allocated employment gap, 1970	Manhour productivity relatives, 1971
Agriculture, forestry, and fisheries	−1.7	0.66
Construction and mining	8.0	1.04[a]
Nondurable manufacturing	13.8	1.25
Durable manufacturing	44.9	1.23
Transportation	6.8	1.30
Communication and public utilities	2.2	2.74[a]
Wholesale and retail trade	21.1	0.93
Finance, insurance, and real estate	1.5	3.06
Services[b]	3.4	0.56
Government	0.0	0.51
Total	100.0	—

Sources: Employment gap, Table 3, with self-employed allocated among the industry groups; productivity relatives, William D. Nordhaus, "The Recent Productivity Slowdown," *BPEA* (321972), p. 522.
a. Weighted averages of the two industries using 1971 employment data from Table 6.3, *Survey of Current Business* (July 1972).
b. Includes private households, high-wage services, and other services.

Although they refer to manhours of all labor (employees and the self-employed), they should give a rough indication of productivity associated with the employment gap for 1970 identified in Table 3. While there are clear exceptions, most of the added employment would go into industries of above average productivity. The average output per manhour associated with the 1970 employment gap is 21 percent above the economy-wide average.

Obviously, the wage rates, fringes, and productivity of incremental workers in an industry should lie below the average of existing workers in that industry. Yet the available evidence on the earnings of various demographic groups in various industries and occupations suggests that positions that pay high wages pay higher than average wages to each demographic group of workers.[20] Clearly, the earnings (and presumably the productivity) of any worker depend both on his demographic and personal characteristics and on the kind of job he gets. The truth must lie somewhere between the low weights on incremental employment yielded by the demographic characteristics and the high weights associated with the industrial composition. Demographic weighting of incremental employment implies that industrial shifts have no effect—that extra employees earn and produce at average levels associated with their demographic reference groups, regardless of where they are employed. On the other hand, industrial weights imply that pay and productivity are unaffected by the youth and inexperience of the incremental workers. Neither of these extremes is tenable.

Questions about the Longer Run The allocation of the employment gap for 1970 in Table 3 is essentially a short-run estimate. It reflects the impact of the current level of the employment gap on the industrial composition of employment. However, one statistical test demonstrated conclusively that the a_2 coefficients reflect the *level* of the employment gap and not the *change* in the gap. The lagged value of A/P was used as an additional explanatory variable in equation (3), but the coefficients on that term were uniformly trivial (even when lagged industry employment was omitted). If any significant part of the employment patterns I have attributed to high utilization were merely the result of *rising* utilization, then that lagged gap variable should have revealed that influence.

Nonetheless, the immediate impact cannot be sustained indefinitely without some alteration. If the economy shifted permanently from a 5 percent to a 4 percent unemployment rate, stocks of durable goods would ultimately be adjusted upward in balance with the higher levels of income and output, and the especially high elasticity of durable goods employment could not be maintained forever. Some crude calculations suggest to me that the catch-up in stocks could sustain a proportion of employees in durable goods manufacturing of 13.5 rather than 13.1 percent (as implied by Table 3), for roughly six years. Presumably, the share of durable goods would then drop off, but not necessarily to its original level. It is not obvious that, even ultimately, the capital-labor ratio of the high-pressure world would necessarily be precisely that of the low-pressure world. Relative supplies of labor among industries would be different; learning by doing could change productivity relatives; and so forth. In particular, the high-pressure world would mean permanently higher recruitment costs for employers, higher vacancy rates, and higher quit rates. These forces would maintain indefinitely a longer workweek involving more overtime and less involuntary part-time work, and might also keep pushing employers to substitute capital for labor. In any case, the skills accumulated during years of employment in durable goods manufacturing may make workers much more adaptable for good jobs elsewhere.

The gradual growth of stocks of assets in the high-pressure world

Table 5 Implied dynamics of the 1970 industrial employment gap

Industry	Employment gap in year 1		Employment gap in year 2		Employment gap in year 5		Steady-state employment gap	
	Number (thousands) (1)	As percentage of allocated employment gap (2)	Number (thousands) (3)	As percentage of allocated employment gap (4)	Number (thousands) (5)	As percentage of allocated employment gap (6)	Number (thousands) (7)	As percentage of allocated employment gap (8)
Employees								
Agriculture, forestry, and fisheries	−21	−2.0	−36	−2.9	−60	−4.5	−75	−6.7
Construction and mining	81	7.9	108	8.7	121	9.1	122	10.9
Nondurable manufacturing	141	13.8	136	10.9	136	10.2	136	12.1
Durable manufacturing	459	44.9	573	46.1	610	45.9	611	54.6
Transportation	70	6.8	87	7.0	93	7.0	93	8.3
Communication and public utilities	22	2.2	38	3.1	67	5.0	87	7.8
Wholesale trade	40	3.9	51	4.1	56	4.2	56	5.0
Retail trade	173	16.9	208	16.7	216	16.3	217	19.4
Finance, insurance, and real estate	15	1.5	29	2.3	59	4.4	114	10.2
Private household services	−28	−2.7	−55	−4.4	−124	−9.4	−436	−39.0
High-wage services[a]	33	3.2	40	3.2	42	3.2	42	3.8
Other services[a]	27	2.6	48	3.8	85	6.4	116	10.4
State and local governments	0	0.0	0	0.0	0	0.0	−1	0.0

Self-employed workers								
Agriculture, forestry, and fisheries	3	0.3	4	0.4	6	0.5	7	0.6
Nonagriculture	7	0.7	13	1.0	22	1.6	28	2.5
Total	1,022	100.0	1,245	100.0	1,328	100.0	1,118	100.0

Sources: Columns (1) and (2) from Table 3; Columns (3)–(8) generated from equations in Table 2. Detail may not add to totals due to rounding.

a. See Table 2, notes b and c.

would tend to expand employment in finance, insurance, and real estate gradually over a longer-run horizon, far beyond the rather small short-run increment reflected in an a_2 of 0.271. This is the exceptional sector that has above-average earnings, fringes, and productivity yet displays a very low a_2. Finally, in the case of domestic workers and farm workers, a high-pressure economy would mean a permanently lower supply of labor seeking refuge from unemployment in these low-grade jobs; the reduction in supply would alter relative wages and relative prices and induce permanent and perhaps even cumulative contraction.

In principle, the lagged industry employment variable in equation (3) permits an assessment of these longer-run influences. The a_3 coefficient can be viewed as a secondary effect of the employment gap next year through its influence on industry employment this year. However, the lagged employment term also reflects many other forces that persist over time and make the composition of employment less volatile. If one takes this lagged adjustment process seriously as an estimate of the continuing effects of the gap, some of the results seem plausible and some do not. As expected, the response of finance, insurance, and real estate to maintained high pressure builds up very gradually. The exodus of household and farm workers is implied to move at only a snail's pace—perhaps implausibly slowly. Increases in jobs in durable goods manufacturing after several years are estimated to be even larger than those in the initial year or two—contrary to one's strong a priori convictions. I myself would not view the a_3 coefficients as serious estimates of a longer-run adjustment. Indeed, I would have little hope that the essence of such a process could be distilled from the data of a fluctuating economy. But for anyone who might wish to make such an interpretation, I have shown the allocation of the incremental employment that is implied by equation (3), assuming that 4 percent unemployment is maintained for one year, two years, five years, and indefinitely in an economy like the United States in 1970. (See Table 5.)

Regardless of how one interprets these data, they suggest that the resource patterns characteristic of differing utilization rates last long enough to be relevant to the stabilization choices facing the American economy. The upgrading benefits may not be maintained indefinitely in the form of the industrial shifts estimated for the short run; but there is no reason to believe that these benefits, and the accompanying boost to overall productivity, are simply ephemeral.

Demographic Shifts within Industries

According to the findings above, the demographic gap contains too many young people and too few mature men to fill the slots in the industrial gap with unchanged demographic proportions in each industry. Thus the demographic shares of industry employment must be related to the level of the utilization in the economy, at least for some industries.

I was able to investigate cyclical shifts in the demographic composition of employment within industries, through the cooperation of John E. Bregger of the Bureau of Labor Statistics. He supplied unpublished annual data for 1961–72 that cross-classify the employment reported in monthly household surveys by industry and by age-sex group. These data thus estimate the number of teenagers, men, and women employed in construction, trade, and the other industries. I used six demographic categories, separating males and females into three age groups: 16–19, 20–24, and 25 and over.

In principle, these data provided an employment matrix of N_{id} entries where i represents an industry and d a demographic group. Each row total (summing over the six demographic groups for a given industry) should yield total employment for an industry; each column total (summing over industries for a given demographic group) should yield total employment for a demographic group. In fact, estimates of industry employment from the household surveys do not accord precisely with the more reliable reports from establishments. Nor do the employment totals for each demographic group uniformly agree with those estimated by Perry, since he adjusted employment to conform to the establishment-based total.

I assumed that the data from household surveys supply accurate estimates of the composition of workers in any industry among the six demographic groups, without accepting the total employment estimates either for demographic groups or industries. Thus I focused on the values of N_{id}/N_i yielded by the data, in effect assuming that any error in N_i was spread proportionately among the six demographic groups.

I fitted to the annual observations for 1961–72 the following equation:

$$\frac{N_{id}}{N_i} = b_0 + b_1 t + b_2 g, \qquad (4)$$

where the dependent variable is the share of group d in the employment of industry i expressed as a percentage; t is time measured in years from

Table 6 Coefficients (b_2) on percentage employment gap for equation (4), by industry, sex, and age group[a]

	Males			Females		
Industry	16–19	20–24	25 and over	16–19	20–24	25 and over
Private household services	0.144 (3.78)	0.063 (2.59)	0.042 (0.87)	−0.056 (0.45)	0.022 (0.32)	−0.214 (1.66)
Agriculture, forestry, and fisheries	0.125 (3.29)	0.308 (4.32)	−0.380 (3.02)	0.072 (2.54)	0.066 (3.51)	−0.191 (2.64)
Construction and mining	−0.021 (0.45)	0.365 (3.64)	−0.376 (2.60)	−0.013 (2.51)	−0.006 (0.45)	0.051 (1.31)
Durable manufacturing	−0.182 (3.64)	−0.361 (4.30)	0.679 (6.86)	−0.078 (3.06)	−0.102 (2.61)	0.044 (0.63)
Nondurable manufacturing	−0.078 (2.35)	0.067 (2.39)	0.225 (3.57)	−0.082 (3.08)	−0.010 (0.37)	−0.122 (1.69)
Transportation, communication, and public utilities	−0.103 (2.68)	0.000 (0.00)	0.086 (0.44)	−0.178 (4.63)	−0.016 (0.26)	0.211 (3.41)
Wholesale trade	−0.007 (0.27)	0.092 (1.83)	0.028 (0.21)	0.009 (0.20)	−0.068 (2.61)	−0.055 (0.55)
Retail trade	−0.242 (3.90)	0.305 (4.26)	−0.071 (1.19)	0.061 (2.24)	0.118 (6.65)	−0.171 (3.90)
Finance, insurance, and real estate	0.055 (2.41)	0.068 (0.91)	−0.224 (1.77)	−0.033 (0.49)	0.049 (0.51)	0.086 (1.00)
Business and repair services	0.052 (1.10)	0.334 (4.32)	0.140 (1.59)	−0.030 (0.75)	−0.101 (1.32)	−0.396 (3.94)
Education	−0.157 (3.37)	−0.085 (1.70)	0.189 (2.28)	−0.167 (3.32)	−0.181 (3.21)	0.401 (6.57)
Miscellaneous services	−0.086 (4.17)	0.088 (2.82)	0.274 (2.88)	−0.080 (2.06)	−0.072 (2.54)	−0.125 (1.43)
Public administration	−0.110 (2.93)	0.119 (1.69)	0.497 (2.36)	−0.101 (2.18)	−0.242 (3.23)	−0.164 (2.92)

Source: Equation (4), discussed in the text, using unpublished data from U.S. Bureau of the Census, Current Population Surveys, for 1961–72. Other parameters of these equations are available from the author on request.
a. The period of fit is 1961–72. The numbers in parentheses are t-statistics.

1961 = 1; and g is the Perry employment gap expressed as a percentage of total employment (thus, for 1970, $g = +1.43$). For each industry, six equations were fitted, corresponding to the six demographic groups. The equations were specified so that the sum of the b_2 coefficients over the six groups in each industry would be zero, obeying the identity that total industry employment is the sum of its employment over the six demographic groups. The trend term is meant to distinguish secular from cyclical forces. Employment includes the self-employed, since separate data on employees were not available for part of the period. Moreover, since the data did not distinguish between public and private employment in education, the industry categories had to be altered, as detailed in Table 6.

The coefficient b_2 indicates whether the share of a demographic group in the employment of a given industry is responsive to overall labor market pressure. If b_2 equals zero, as it does for males 20–24 in transportation (Table 6), the *share* of transportation jobs that go to male youths is found to be independent of the employment gap; the number of jobs they have in that industry is changed in proportion to the industry total. A positive value of b_2, such as the 0.68 estimate for men 25 and over in durable goods manufacturing, implies that the share of that group in the industry's employment is highest when the employment gap is largest; put conversely, the employment of mature men in durable goods manufacturing rises proportionately less than total employment of that industry when the employment gap is closed. A negative coefficient, like that of women 25 and over in business and repair services, implies that a high-pressure economy increases the group's share of that industry's employment.

Table 7 combines the industry distribution of the 1970 employment gap shown in Table 3 with the demographic shift estimates implied by the b_2 coefficients of Table 6. This is obviously a shotgun marriage: The industry elasticities are based on establishment reports of employment for a sample period from 1948–70; the shift estimates come from household reports for 1961–72. The array of numbers in the table is designed to reveal characteristic patterns rather than to provide point estimates.

The first column of Table 7 takes the job gap estimates by industry from Table 3 with the number of industries slightly condensed for simplification. The remaining columns allocate the incremental employment among the six demographic groups. Each demographic-industrial cell contains three entries. Entry (*a*) is the number of jobs in that industry

Table 7 Demographic-industrial composition of the employment gap, 1970 (thousands of persons)

Industry	Total, males and females		Males 16–19	Males 20–24	Males 25 and over	Females 16–19	Females 20–24	Females 25 and over
Agriculture, forestry, and and fisheries	−18	*a*	−2	−1	−12	0	0	−3
		b	−6	−15	19	−4	−3	9
		c	−8	−16	7	−4	−3	6
Construction and mining	82	*a*	4	8	66	0	1	3
		b	1	−21	22	1	0	−3
		c	5	−13	88	1	1	0
Nondurable manufacturing	141	*a*	5	10	73	3	7	43
		b	9	−8	−26	10	1	14
		c	14	2	47	13	8	57
Durable manufacturing	459	*a*	12	41	311	5	16	75
		b	29	58	−109	12	16	−7
		c	41	99	202	17	32	68
Transportation, communication, and public utilities	92	*a*	2	7	63	2	5	13
		b	7	0	−6	11	1	−14
		c	9	7	57	13	6	−1
Wholesale and retail trade	216	*a*	19	15	92	13	12	65
		b	39	−54	10	−10	−15	31
		c	58	−39	102	3	−3	96
Finance, insurance, and real estate	15	*a*	0	1	7	1	2	5
		b	−3	−4	12	2	−3	−5
		c	−3	−3	19	3	−1	0

Private household services	−28	*a*	−1	0	−2	−5	−1	−18
		b	−4	−2	−1	2	−1	7
		c	−5	−2	−3	−3	−2	−11
High-wage services[a]	34	*a*	2	3	20	1	2	7
		b	−2	−13	−5	1	4	15
		c	0	−10	15	2	6	22
Other services[b] and	29	*a*	1	1	11	1	3	13
government		*b*	31	−10	−80	31	41	−12
		c	32	−9	−69	32	44	1

Sources: Total from Table 3, with self-employed allocated among industries; others computed from U.S. Bureau of the Census, Current Population Surveys, unpublished data.

Entry a = total times age-sex employment as a share of industry employment = the scale effect (see discussion in text). Entry $b = b_2$ coefficients (from Table 6) times 1970 industry employment times −0.0143 (negative of 1970 relative employment gap) = the shift effect. Entry c = the total of entries a and b = the total effect. Details may not add to totals because of rounding.

a. Business and repair shift effect is used for entry *b*. See Table 2, note b, for services included in high-wage services.

b. The sum of education, low-wage services, and public administration shift effects is used for entry *b*. See Table 2, note c, for definition of other services.

that a given demographic group would have obtained if its share of the extra jobs in closing the 1970 employment gap had been the same as its share of actual employment in the industry in 1970. Thus, adult males, who had a little more than half of the jobs in nondurable goods manufacturing in 1970, would, on that basis, have obtained 73,000 additional jobs of the 141,000 created. Entry (*a*) is thus the "scale effect," reflecting the impact of a proportional increase in employment across the demographic groups within any industry. Entry (*b*) is the "shift effect"—the result of any systematic tendency for shares of an industry's employment among groups to change when the employment gap is closed. It is equal to b_2 times industry employment for 1970 times -0.0143 (the negative of the 1970 relative employment gap). Entry (*c*) is then the net estimated increase in employment for a particular demographic group in an industry, summing the scale effect and the shift effect.

The following estimated results from closing the gap seem noteworthy:

1. Men over 25 leave the low-paying sectors of other services and government in substantial number, reflecting a sizable shift effect and a negligible scale effect. Their places are taken largely by young people.
2. In both categories of manufacturing and in transportation, adult men gain a large number of jobs, but fewer than the scale effect alone would generate. Other demographic groups are able to enter these high-paying industries in substantial number. In durables, the primary substitutes for mature men are younger men, while in nondurables women get most of the extra jobs.
3. In construction-mining, employers apparently believe there is nothing like a man, and all the incremental jobs are filled by men over 25.
4. The exodus from agriculture is confined to more mobile young people.
5. Trade is the one low-wage nonfarm sector that holds its share of mature men.
6. All in all, the absolute total of shift effects is substantial—indeed, reaching the same order of magnitude (nearly 1 million) as the scale effects. The shift effects generally can be viewed as movements up the ladder, within demographic groups, from low-wage to higher-wage industries.

The estimated shift effects are distorted by one particular characteristic of the 1961–72 period. For males 20–24, movements into and out of the armed forces dominated the shifts among civilian industries, and were strongly correlated with the overall employment gap. From 1965 to 1966, while the overall employment gap turned negative, military employment for males 20–24 increased 287,000, but their civilian employment rose only 16,000. By contrast, from 1970 to 1971, while the gap was rising sharply, their military employment fell 255,000 and their civilian employment rose 330,000. The elasticity of the civilian employment of this group with respect to aggregate employment is below 0.2 for 1961–72, while that of their total employment (including military) is nearly 1.7 (Perry's estimate is 1.4). Hence, the typical shift effect for that demographic group is unrealistically low (the b_2 is too high) in relation to what would be expected during a peacetime expansion. The puzzling shift of young men out of construction and trade in a high-pressure economy may be primarily a reflection of the Vietnam war.

The opposite side of that coin is that the shift effect does not eliminate enough jobs for men over 25. They get roughly one-third more jobs than the Perry estimates would imply, apparently at least partly because of the reduced availability of younger men in the late 1960s. As a crude judgment, I suspect that a more realistic peacetime pattern would be obtained by removing one-fourth of the net gains of mature men shown in the table, and attributing them to the younger men of 20–24.[21]

The evidence presented above confirms that a high-pressure economy generates not only more jobs than does a slack economy, but also a different pattern of employment. It suggests that, in a weak labor market, a poor job is often the best job available, superior at least to the alternative of no job. A high-pressure economy provides people with a chance to climb ladders to better jobs.

The industry shifts are only one dimension of ladder climbing. Increased upward movements within firms and within industries, and greater geographical flows from lower-income to higher-income regions, are also likely to be significant. Nor is the process confined to age-sex groups. Richard Freeman's paper in this issue demonstrates that black workers benefit especially from upgrading when labor markets are strong.

I have no way of appraising the total value of cyclical upgrading in terms of real wages, or of longer-run career opportunities. I can nonetheless offer one crude calculation of how much the real wage bonus *might* be worth. While the elasticity of real employee compensation with respect to real GNP is well below unity as the economy moves up to higher utilization, it appears to be at least 0.85 over a horizon of three years. Thus, associated with an increment of output of 2.8 percent accompanying a 1 point reduction in the unemployment rate, would be an increment in the real wage bill of about 2.4 percent. With weights for wages and hours based on demographic reference groups, the Perry labor input gap (reflecting increased hours and participation as well as reduced unemployment) is "worth" only 1.7 percent of extra real employee compensation. If the difference between 2.4 and 1.7 results entirely from upgrading, the upgrading bonus is nearly as large as the gain in the real wage bill associated with rescuing 1 percent of the labor force from unemployment and putting them to work at the average wage rates and hours of their demographic reference groups. If, in fact, the unemployed typically have lower average earnings when employed than the averages of their demographic reference groups, as R. J. Gordon suggests in this issue, the bonus attributable to upgrading may be even greater.

Cyclical Facts and Labor Market Theory

Although the cyclical process of upgrading has rarely been discussed in the mainstream of macroeconomic employment theory, it has long been recognized by labor economists. In 1955, Reder stated: "When aggregate labor demand increases sufficiently there will be a tendency for the manual labor force, especially the unskilled, to move toward better jobs and for their places to be filled, if at all, by erstwhile members of the labor reserve. This implies a shift of workers from agriculture to industry, from unskilled to semiskilled jobs, etc."[22]

The facts of cyclical upgrading could be fitted into the traditional framework of labor market theory if wage rates for the usual workers in the high-paid, cyclically sensitive industries rose especially sharply in prosperity, inducing employers to substitute the kinds of workers normally hired in low-paid pursuits. But, as Reder emphasized, the facts do not support that hypothesis, and indeed point in the opposite direction. He showed that differentials among wage rates of more skilled and less skilled occupations have typically (although not universally) tended to narrow in periods of high employment.

The same phenomenon of narrowing wage differentials in prosperity is evident among industries. As Haddy and Tolles reported: "The average wages paid by different industries become more nearly uniform as an economy of the British or American type moves from slack to full employment."[23] Most recently, Michael Wachter has demonstrated very impressively the negative relationship between wage differentials among U.S. two-digit manufacturing industries and the national unemployment rate.

The coefficient of variation among average hourly earnings is about 5 percent lower at 4 percent unemployment than at 5 percent.[24]

The cyclical facts of upward labor mobility cannot be explained in terms of a market-clearing allocation of labor based on relative wage movements. Market queues are an intrinsic part of the story. The nonprice allocation is, in my judgment, best explained in terms of several themes recently stressed in labor market theory: distinctions between employers who aim to establish long-term attachments with their workers, and those who do not; recognition of the fixed and variable costs involved in hiring and training labor; and the analysis of the search process by which the unemployed or new entrants into the labor force acquire jobs.[25]

The Two-Tier Labor Market

Drawing on this literature, I shall sketch a model of labor markets in simple and rather extreme form, using it to explain the various phenomena observed in a higher-pressure economy.[26] Just to use Occam's razor, ignore the existence of unions[27] and assume there are two types of employers: Class A firms are interested in promoting a long-run attachment of workers, while class B firms do not pursue that objective. Obviously, these two classes are a simplified way of describing a spectrum of employment strategies ranging from firms that care least, to those that care most, about worker attachment. Indeed, the same firm may pursue a class A strategy with respect to some types of workers and a class B strategy with respect to others.

Promoting attachments is attractive to many types of employers: (a) firms that can provide specific training that enhances productivity over time; (b) firms that have a production process in which an inefficient worker would be particularly costly (for example, by snarling an integrated assembly line or abusing expensive machinery); (c) firms with ready and inexpensive access to funds for investment in human as well as physical capital; (d) large firms that hire a sizable portion of the workers in their labor markets and could therefore find rapid turnover of labor very costly because of an inadequate pool of potential applicants. In order to promote long-run attachments, class A employers establish a schedule of wage increases at regular intervals, fringe benefits and seniority privileges, and institutionalized provisions for leisure through annual leave and paid vacations.

The wage rates paid by class A employers to a given grade of workers exceed those paid by class B firms. Class A employers provide such a wage premium in order to maintain a reliable work force with a low quit rate and also to ensure a queue of applicants that management can screen before investing in new workers. The evidence is compelling that a significant portion of wage premiums in high-paying industries is aimed at, and succeeds in, holding down quit rates.[28] By providing a wage premium, class A employers are able to select the applicants they want, leaving the remainder either on queue for subsequent class A jobs or else working at lower wage rates for class B firms. In making their selections, class A employers will be influenced by the likelihood that an applicant will stick to his job over the long run. The statistical evidence that young people and women frequently move out of the labor force will influence choices in favor of mature men.

The wage differential between class A and class B workers will be accompanied by a differential in productivity and a differential in unemployment rates. The class A employer of a new worker must expect high productivity, since the marginal revenue product of that worker must cover both the premium over class B wage rates and some amortization of the fixed costs of hiring and training. Once the worker is hired and trained, those investments make his employer less likely to lay him off when markets weaken, for, if he finds a job elsewhere, the firm's capital investment in him would be lost. Therefore, if that capital value is large and the slack period expected by the firm is short, the worker will be retained even if his current marginal revenue product is zero. This "locked in" effect will be smaller (but not absent) if the wage premium offered by the firm is so large that it can lay off workers "without prejudice" and still get most of them back when they are again needed. Thus because the wage premium holds down the quit rate and the sunk training costs hold down the layoff rate, class A workers have less turnover and fewer spells of unemployment.

On the other hand, class B firms hire workers and lay them off without inhibition, depending merely on whether their near-term contributions to marginal revenue product cover their wages. Moreover, the class B workers are likely to have high quit rates because they are tempted to search for a class A job, because they do not have the same opportunities for leisure without quitting that are provided for class A workers, and because they have no lasting stake in their jobs. As a result, class B workers experience higher unemployment rates in any given state of the overall labor market.

In the two-tier labor market, the overall unemployment rate at any sort of equilibrium will thus depend on the proportions of class A and class B workers. Given labor supplies, higher relative demand for labor by class A firms raises the wage premium and lowers the global unemployment rate in any equilibrium. Over the long run, increases in physical capital per worker and in the complexity of technology seem likely to keep pushing personnel strategies toward more class A workers. Rising educational attainment should also promote the class A personnel strategy as workers become more adaptable to specific training. If such forces outweigh any counterforces, the global unemployment rate prevailing in an "equilibrium" of the two-tier labor market would tend to decline over the long run. One obvious counterforce could be a shift in the composition of the labor force toward those demographic groups regarded as less eligible for class A jobs—such as the Perry shift. (Another counterforce in the real world is the secular decline in the number of self-employed, since they are rarely unemployed.)

In the very short run, firms cannot readily shift between class A and B personnel strategies. But some of the responses to innovation, unionization, and minimum wage increases suggest that, with major incentives, firms can and do alter their technologies and personnel strategies rather promptly. Because the "equilibrium" overall unemployment rate changes over time in response to shifts in technology, education, and demography, the concept of a "natural" unemployment rate is likely to be more misleading than instructive.

Finally, wage rates are likely to be more sensitive to easing and tightening of the labor market in class B than in class A firms. The arrangements designed to promote job attachment in class A put wage decisions into a longer-run context, insulating them from cyclical fluctuations. The division of the return from firm-specific human capital between employers and workers may be the big long-term issue for bargaining in class A firms. Because of the typical queue of applicants at their hiring gates, their wage rates need not rise to permit increased employment. Conversely, in a weak labor market, they cannot be cut—perhaps not even readily slowed down—because established workers expect to get "equitable" annual increases in pay.

The Dynamics of an Upswing

Suppose that an economy with a two-tier labor market is initially in equilibrium in the sense that wage rates are, on balance, neither accelerating nor decelerating, and that class A and class B employers have no net incentives to alter the wage differential. Now suppose that equilibrium is disturbed by an increase in the aggregate demand for the output of both class A and class B firms. If the marginal revenue product of class A workers becomes sufficiently high to cover hiring and training costs as well as the wage (including the premium over the class B rate), class A firms will expand employment. If class A firms have some slack in their utilization of physical and human capital, they can expand employment and production in the short run with reduced costs and increased productivity. Under such circumstances, they are likely to respond primarily by expanding production rather than by raising prices.

Because of their wage premium, class A firms can get additional workers merely by hanging up the help-wanted sign, and perhaps by improving the information on the availability of jobs (for example, by spending more on help-wanted advertising). Because marginal hiring and training costs may rise with the rate of inflow of new workers, the firm may adjust initially in large measure by increasing the workweek even at the cost of paying overtime premiums. But class A firms will not need to raise wage rates immediately; moreover, general wage increases (outside of the regular schedule) would be costly since they would have to cover existing workers as well as new employees. Among the efficient adjustments confined to new workers are changes in hiring standards, such as accepting younger and less experienced people, or shifting from "statistical" rules that exclude women or people without diplomas to a more intensive personal screening of applicants.

The upswing affects class B firms quite differently. Workers leave readily to take class A jobs, and competition for workers among class B firms is likely to increase wages promptly. The wage increases, in turn, are likely to push up prices in class B industries, such as low-skill services, which have few opportunities to spread overhead costs if they should expand output. And rising prices will tend to cut their share of real output, even if demands for their output rise as rapidly as those of class A. In fact, the most cyclically sensitive demands for output appear to be concentrated in class A sectors, thus accentuating the relative shift of resources to class A firms, and reinforcing the increase in aggregate productivity. Thus, paradoxical results emerge: The biggest (and earliest) inflationary movements occur in the wage rates of workers with the highest unemployment rates and with the smallest increase in the demand for their typical services, and in the prices of products experiencing the least expansion of demand.

The number of persons employed in the class B areas may rise or fall, depending on the income and price elasticities of the demand for output and on the shrinkage of the supply of labor to class B resulting from the exodus of labor to class A. In extreme cases, such as farm workers and domestic workers, class B industry employment falls; in most cases, however, industry employment rises although its share of aggregate employment falls.

Workers' Responses

Viewed in terms of the behavior of workers, how does the strengthening of labor demand reduce unemployment rates and increase particpation rates? First, the number of spells of unemployment declines because a larger fraction of workers make transitions between jobs without an interventing spell of unemployment,[29] revealing that on-the-job search has some efficiency. Second, the duration of spells falls because a rational job seeker will spend less time searching for a job. Because a larger fraction of firms will be making offers, the job seeker can obtain a reasonable sample in a shorter time. The optimum strategy will lead the job seeker to collect more offers in a firmer labor market but to spend less time between jobs collecting them. For the same reasons, the job seeker is less likely to settle for a class B job when he perceives a better chance of getting class A employment fairly promptly.

A variety of forces operate to encourage some nonparticpants to enter the labor market and search for jobs. The concepts developed by R. J. Gordon in this issue illuminate those forces. Better information about job availability reduces the cost of search, while the value of search activity is raised by the greater probability of getting a reasonable job in a reasonable amount of time. For a woman with children, the setup costs associated with undertaking search activity and making the preparations to accept a job may be very large; the willingness to make that investment quite reasonably depends on the prospective availability of a satisfactory job.

In some early formulations of search theory, the reduced duration of unemployment and increased participation rates of a high-pressure economy emerged as a mystery. To solve that mystery, the deus ex machina of money illusion had to be invoked: People are fooled by higher money wage rates and take jobs too readily on the mistaken view that they offer higher real wages. But those models assumed that firms were always willing to hire new workers at some wage, even in a depression. The mystery dissolves once the market-clearing assumption is relaxed to recognize that class A firms will often not be hiring at all and will not accept an applicant at a substandard wage rate. As Tobin has stressed, explaining the cyclical movement of duration and participation does not require the "inflation illusion story."[30]

Longer-Run Adjustments

If pressure on the labor market is maintained, the inflation originating in class B firms will ultimately spread to class A wages and prices. As queues of applicants shorten, class A employers may begin competing with one another for workers. Meanwhile, the rising prices of class B output reduce the real wages of workers in class A. At the next scheduled adjustment, wage increases by class A firms are likely to be accelerated.

Some forces thus operate to restore the wage differential between class A and class B, but the evidence suggests that they work very slowly.[31] The formal model in the appendix reveals the possibility that such a system has a negatively sloped Phillips curve in which lower unemployment can be achieved at the cost of a higher, but ultimately steady, inflation rate.

The steepness and stability of the Phillips curve depend on the speed and intensity with which class A wages chase class B wages and prices. If class A workers have the determination and the market power (in the real world, through unions) to resist any narrowing of their wage premium over class B, inflationary pressures will be strong, as each rise in the wage rate of class B workers spurs an attempted catch-up in the next class A round. But if class A employees have such power to veto a narrowing of the premium, the economy could not adapt to a rise in the relative supply of class A workers any more than to increased aggregate demand. The possibility of accelerating inflation arises if, over time, the catch-up intervals become shorter and shorter or the game of catch-up is converted into one of leap frog. Although conceivable, such patterns do not seem realistic, in my judgment. In short, the model of a two-tier labor market seems to reinforce the plausibility of the usual empirical finding that the U.S. economy does not exhibit indefinitely accelerating inflation at moderately low unemployment rates.

Some of the forces operating over time are benevolent, and tend to promote a deceleration of inflation at a given unemployment rate. First, the period of high pressure builds up skills and human capital (as well as physical capital) in the class A sector. Entry and exit from class A jobs are asymmetrical; for reasons discussed above, investment in training tends to lock in employers and employees. Even if they should leave their jobs, the new class A workers will have the benefits of some general training and experience that make them more employable in other class A firms. In this way, at least to some extent, the demand for labor creates its own supply.

Second, some employers providing class B jobs may respond to the narrowed wage differential by gradually shifting their personnel strategies and starting to invest in firm-specific human capital—a decision that is likely to be nonreversible. In response to the tight labor market of the late 1960s, some firms adopted more capital-intensive techniques even though capital costs were rising as rapidly as labor costs. A possible interpretation is that increasing capital intensity economizes on personnel costs by shifting toward the more reliable and longer-attachment type of labor. Such a change in the A-B mix generates a favorable shift in the Phillips curve, with less unemployment due to turnover and diminishing inflation at a given unemployment rate. Such a happy ending seems to require that the wage differential between classes A and B remain narrower than initially, although, so long as some productivity bonus persists, class A workers may be able to earn real wages as high as otherwise.

In many respects, the model of a two-tier labor market accords with the facts of inflationary behavior in the excessively high-pressure labor market of the late sixties. It suggests that the loss in the relative wage position of some key unionized industries in 1966–69 may have been more than a mere accident of contract schedules; it explains why areas of labor-intensive services were so inflationary, and why wage rates of low-skill groups like hotel workers rose so strongly. The queues in class A sectors can also account for the mystery that unemployment continued to exceed measured vacancies even in a world of excess demand.

The model also may throw some light on developments in 1970–71, when the economy weakened after a sustained interval of high-pressure operation. The large union settlements during the recession may signify that the "old" class A workers felt cheated and pressed hard for a restoration of their initial wage differentials, even in a very weak labor market. Similarly, after a long period of upgrading, "new" class A workers who were laid off in 1970–71 may have been especially reluctant to return to class B underemployment and hence waited for class A jobs. Such behavior might appear to reflect an increase in "structural" unemployment, and perhaps even suggest to some observers that the nation had developed a work ethic problem.

Some Implications for Policy

The additional jobs available in a high-pressure economy tend to be well-paid jobs, productive jobs, and potentially steady jobs. Such benefits should be valued and cherished in a democratic capitalistic society. The sacrifice of upward mobility must be carefully reckoned as one part of the high cost of accepting slack as an insurance policy against inflation.

Moreover, the social aspects of the loss of upward mobility seem likely to be compounded by other implications of the low-pressure strategy. In particular, a low-pressure economy is bound to mean a much more restrictive fiscal policy. If society decided to shift from a 4 percent to a 5 percent unemployment target, it would be aiming at a level of real GNP $35 billion a year lower than previously. If that reduction of aggregate demand were to be achieved through fiscal policy, the required additional restraint (in real terms) would be about $15 billion per year, in some combination of higher tax rates and curtailed expenditures.[32] It is a fair judgment of our political process that tax rates would not be increased while before-tax incomes were being squeezed. Instead, the major pressure would be exerted on transfer payments for the disadvantaged, manpower programs, and the like, precisely when the increased human costs of a slack economy were being accepted. Meanwhile, society might salve its conscience by concluding that the fault of the unemployed and the underemployed lay in themselves and not in the economic system.

At the same time, this paper should not be read as a clarion call to damn the torpedoes and go full speed ahead. On the contrary, our best hope of achieving 4 percent unemployment with an acceptable price-wage performance rests on our ability to reduce slack more gradually so as to permit smoother and less disruptive shifts of resources, as well as on our willingness to reinforce fiscal-monetary policies with manpower programs and incomes policies.

With the unemployment rate now 5 percent and falling, a major manpower effort to facilitate upgrading seems most promising. The tides are flowing in the direction of upgrading, and government training and information programs may be able to succeed most when they swim with the tide. Barriers to entry into good jobs may be swept away most easily when market forces are making racial and sexual discrimination costly to employers. Now is the time to ask: What incentives can be provided to employers to shift from class B to class A personnel strategies? What kinds of actions can be undertaken to break down barriers of entry that are maintained by discrimination and monopoly power? What kinds of aids to workers now in class B firms can ease the process of movement to good jobs?

This judgment also implies that, in the present situation, manpower programs to aid disadvantaged workers should incorporate a major effort to instill training and the basis for upgrading, rather than merely create more class B jobs. It is tempting to believe that some groups of workers that experience high unemployment rates even in a firm labor market can be aided by the provision of any kind of employment, with little addition to inflationary pressure. But the cyclical record reveals that some groups suffering high unemployment nonetheless have steep Phillips curves. Unless some accurate identification of a true "hard core" is possible, a program providing low-skill, dead-end jobs could be just as inflationary as an equivalent program of raising private demand, and yet jeopardize the upward mobility, the productivity bonus, and the building of skills and job attachments that accompany higher pressure in the labor market. In periods of recession and slack, underemployment may be the only alternative to unemployment, and it is surely a lesser evil. But in periods when the economy can move to prosperity, the creation of more class B jobs may substitute underemployment for class A employment.

The need and rationale for incomes policies become evident in the world of a two-tier labor market. Because nonprice considerations already play an enormous role in allocating jobs, moderate and sensible government intervention that curbs the upward movement of average wage rates need not impair the efficiency of allocation of labor. Incomes policies work to the extent that they influence the attitudes of employers and employees about the size of a reasonable wage increase. With $35 billion a year at stake, ideas for major institutional revision—like the Wallich-Weintraub tax proposals—deserve a more serious hearing than they have yet received. As an alternative to such tax "sticks," it might be preferable to use tax and subsidy "carrots." Some attractive programs to help gain labor's cooperation with an incomes policy might be devised for a fraction of the cost of a slack economy; these could include cost-of-living subsidies or tax credits payable to workers if prices exceed the targets of a wage-price program. Along with the retired and the rentier, senior class A workers may be one of the few groups in the society that gain little directly from a higher-pressure economy. Some way should be found for them to share in the large social dividend of higher utilization.

The need for upward mobility in our society goes far beyond anything that a reasonable full employment policy can provide, as the unemployment rates and the underemployment of black teenagers in the late sixties will testify. But many other policies to promote upward mobility are probably best accomplished in the context of a higher-pressure labor market. The greater diffusion of opportunity and of upward mobility in a full-utilization economy is a vital social benefit; and that benefit helps to explain why the pursuit of full employment is an integral part of a liberal's creed.

Appendix: A Model of the Two-Tier Labor Market

To make the algebra tractable, I assume a very unreal world which has no income from property, no changes in productivity within sectors, and no variation in the labor force. Hence, output can be measured in man-hour units, and prices are the same as wage rates. Thus, for two sectors, respectively:

Output = Manhours	A	B
Price = Wage rate	a	b

Nominal GNP is thus,

$$Y = Aa + Bb. \tag{1}$$

Aggregate demand is determined by a demand-shift parameter, m, such that

$$Y = mY_{-1}. \tag{2}$$

Private demand, monetary policy, and fiscal policy determine m.

Expenditure is divided in fractions, c and $(1 - c)$, between the two sectors so that

$$aA = cmY_{-1} \tag{3}$$

$$bB = (1 - c)mY_{-1}. \tag{3'}$$

In the long-attachment labor market of A, wages are determined by

$$a = a_{-1}W\left[U_{A_{-1}}, \left(\frac{a}{b}\right)_{-1}\right], \tag{4}$$

where U_A = unemployed (also measured in manhours) seeking A jobs. Wages rates are rigid downward, so $W \geqslant 1$. Both high unemployment and a high relative (real) wage for the sector hold down the rate of wage increase, so the partial derivative of W with respect to each argument is negative: $W_1 \leqslant 0$, $W_2 \leqslant 0$.

Through (3) and (4), A and a for any period are predetermined by m, Y_{-1}, $U_{A_{-1}}$, and $(a/b)_{-1}$. Thus, A manhours are absorbed from the fixed total labor force (L); so long as $a > b$ and $A < L$, the sector gets the labor it wants.

The labor force consists of those with jobs and those hunting for jobs in each sector, as reflected by the following identity:

$$A + U_A + B + U_B = L. \tag{5}$$

The labor market in the B sector "clears" in each period, but it is subject to friction and lack of information, which result in unemployment (U_B). For convenience, assume that unemployment is not affected by the state of the labor market and can be taken as proportional to employment in sector B:

$$U_B = fB, \qquad 0 < f < 1. \tag{6}$$

The fraction f is typically much larger than (U_A/A). The decision to be in U_A is a decision to keep hunting for a job in sector A rather than settling for a class B job. Such a decision will depend, first, on the chances of getting jobs promptly in sector A, which in turn will be greater when A is greater; for this reason an added unit of A reduces U_A, ceteris paribus, by $(1 - e)$ (where e is a parameter such that $0 < e < 1$) rather than by a full unit. Secondly, it will depend positively on a/b, the relative wage:

$$U_A = V\left(\frac{a}{b}\right) - A(1 - e), \qquad V' > 0. \tag{7}$$

Now equations (5), (6), and (7) generate a supply of manhours (output) for the B sector:

$$B = \frac{L - V\left(\frac{a}{b}\right) - eA}{1+f}. \tag{8}$$

In conjunction with (3′), the demand curve for B output, (8), determines B and b, given the predetermined values of a and A.

Suppose $m_0 = 1$, and the economy is in equilibrium at A_0, a_0, U_{A_0}, B_0, b_0, U_{B_0}.

Now, in period 1, m rises ($m_1 > 1$). Since a_1 still equals a_0, the entire increase in demand in the A sector (from equation 3) is reflected in more output and employment: $A_1 = m_1 A_0$. Now consider the B sector in period 1; demand (from equation 3′) at a given value of a/b rises by a fraction $m_1 - 1$; but the supply function (equation 8) shifts left. Therefore, $b_1 > b_0$, but the sign of $(B_1 - B_0)$ is indeterminate; clearly, however, $B_1/B_0 < A_1/A_0$. Meanwhile, $U_{A_1} < U_{A_0}$ as a result of both the rise in A and the rise in b.

For subsequent periods, let $m = m_1 > 1$. In period 2, W is pushed up by both its arguments in equation (4), so $a_2 > a_0$. It is not clear whether A_2 will rise further above A_1, fall back, or hold steady.

If in some period t, $A_t = A_{t-1}$, then $a_t = m_1 a_{t-1}$. In turn, equations (8) and (3′) will then ensure that $b_t = m_1 b_{t-1}$ and $B_t = B_{t-1}$; that is, with A the same as in the previous period, B is likewise constant in equations (8) and (3′), so long as a/b is unchanged, both a and b rising at the rate $(m_1 - 1)$. Then in $(t+1)$, W is the same as in t, so $a_{t+1} = a_t m_1$; $A_{t+1} = A_t$; $b_{t+1} = b_t m_1$; and $B_{t+1} = B_t$. Quantities are thus in equilibrium, and prices and wages in both sectors rise henceforth at the rate $(m_1 - 1)$.

I shall not try to show the conditions under which this nonlinear system converges to such an equilibrium of quantities and a steady-state inflation. That depends heavily on the shape of the W function in (4). If the response is very gradual, A will move to its new equilibrium smoothly. If, on the other hand, it is extremely strong and rapid, then the system will overshoot and oscillate divergently. If the system does settle down to an equilibrium set—A^*, B^*, U_A^*, $(a/b)^*$—how will those values compare with the levels of period zero?

In an "equilibrium" situation, with $m > 1$, the function W in equation (4) must exceed its initial value of unity. Hence, *at least* one of the two arguments—U_A^* and $(a/b)^*$—must be below its initial value.

In fact, both must be down, as I shall now demonstrate. From (7) rewrite W in (4) as:

$$W\left\{V\left(\frac{a}{b}\right)^* - A^*(1-e); \left(\frac{a}{b}\right)^*\right\}. \tag{9}$$

If a/b is *not* below its value of period zero, then $A^* > A_0$, so that $U_A^* < U_{A_0}$. But in that event, from (8),

$$V\left(\frac{a}{b}\right)^* = L - (1+f)B^* - eA^* \geqslant V\left(\frac{a}{b}\right)_0. \tag{10}$$

Hence $B^* < B_0$ since $A^* > A_0$; but, by (3).and (3′),

$$\frac{A^*a^*}{B^*b^*} = \frac{c}{1-c} = \frac{A_0 a_0}{B_0 b_0}. \tag{11}$$

This establishes a contradiction since A/B is up, while a/b is assumed *not* down.

Similarly, if U_A is *not* below its initial value while a/b is, then (9) reveals that $A^* < A_0$. But then (10) will show $V(a/b)^* \leqslant V(a/b)_0$, and with A down, $B^* > B_0$. Then both A/B and a/b would be down, contradicting (11).

Hence, any "equilibrium" (for $m_1 > 1$) must entail:

$$\left(\frac{a}{b}\right)^* < \left(\frac{a}{b}\right)_0 \tag{12}$$

—a shift in real (relative) wages unfavorable to those initially working in sector A;

$$U_A^* < U_{A_0} \tag{13}$$

—a drop in unemployment in the A sector;

$$\frac{A^*}{B^*} > \frac{A_0}{B_0} \tag{14}$$

—upgrading and a "productivity bonus" (see 11);

$$A^* > A_0 \tag{15}$$

—an absolute expansion of output and manhours in sector A; this is true because $(1+f)(B/A) = (L/A) - (U_A/A) - 1$, and it must be down while U_A is down; and

$$\frac{a_t}{a_{t-1}} = \frac{b_t}{b_{t-1}} = m_1 - 1 \tag{16}$$

—steady inflation.

As in the case of the impact effect, the ultimate effect on B and U_B is indeterminate in sign (remember the empirical findings on farm workers and service workers). But total unemployment is clearly down; by (6), (7), and (8):

$$U_A + U_B = \frac{f}{1+f}L + \frac{1}{1+f}V\left(\frac{a}{b}\right) - \left(1 - \frac{e}{1+f}\right)A. \tag{17}$$

Both the drop in a/b and the rise in A reduce total unemployment.

In short, if this system converges, it has to be a Phillips curve world. Lower unemployment can be bought "permanently" by accepting some ultimately steady rate of inflation. Each m generates a point on the long-run Phillips curve, and the curve has a negative slope.

The possibilities of accelerating or decelerating inflation—for given low unemployment rates—can be analyzed by amending the model.

Acceleration can be interpreted in terms of wage determination in the A sector, as described by equation (4). As one convenient device, let the time period of the lag in (4) be a variable influenced by the extent and duration of the shortfall in a/b below some normal ("target," "expected," "equitable") level. The lag might shorten as frustration over the depressed level of (a/b) mounts. For example,

$$a = a_{-\theta}W\left[U_{A-\theta}, \left(\frac{a}{b}\right)_{-\theta}\right] \tag{18}$$

$$\frac{1}{\theta_t} = \int_{t-p}^{t} Y\left[\left(\frac{a}{b}\right)_n - \left(\frac{a}{b}\right)_x\right]dx, \tag{19}$$

where θ is the variable lag; n refers to "normal"; p is the relevant length of past calendar time influencing attitudes; and the function Y is positive with $Y' > 0$. So long as (a/b) is held below its normal level, the wage lag in (18) shortens, thus preventing the Phillips result outlined above.

Similarly, incomes policy can be viewed as an effort to reduce the direct influence of a/b in (4)—ideally, to eliminate it. The direct role of a/b in (4) reflects attitudes and expectations as distinct from the indirect effect of a/b on W via (7), which reflects workers' decisions. Eliminating the direct effect would allow a given rise in m and hence in W to cause a larger drop in U_A and (via 7) also in a/b, offset by a larger rise in A. The Phillips curve would then be more favorable, yielding a lower unemployment rate for a given inflation rate, but "old" A workers would then suffer a larger drop in relative (real) wages.

Finally, deceleration of inflation at a given low unemployment rate could work through either of two mechanisms: first, by demand for A labor gradually creating its own supply; or, second, by an induced "secular" contraction of the B sector.

The first route could run as follows: Among workers in U_A in any period, those with some qualifications for or experience in A jobs hold down W more than others. The available stock of experience (X) in U_A is an integral related to the difference between the present level of employment in A and its levels over the relevant past (from $t-q$ to the present, t). Attrition, turnover, friction always result in the presence of some experienced workers in U_A, but they will be fewer when A has risen rapidly from earlier levels and will expand as A tends to reach a stable higher plateau. Thus, (4) is revised to include a third argument, X, in $W(W_x < 0)$; where X is:

$$X = \int_{t-q}^{t} Q(A_h - A_t)\,dh, \tag{20}$$

and $Q \geqslant 0$ and $Q' > 0$.

When A jumps, the "quality" of U_A will be low, intensifying inflationary pressure. But as A approaches an equilibrium value (assuming the system is converging), the quality of U_A reflected in X keeps improving and may push A perpetually upward above the equilibrium that would have otherwise prevailed, with gradually diminishing unemployment at a given inflation rate.

Second, a maintained low a/b may lead some B sector employers to switch strategy and hire A-type workers. The contraction of the B sector can be viewed as proceeding at a time rate, z, which depends on a/b, such that

$$z_t = Z\left(\frac{a}{b}\right)_t, \tag{21}$$

where $z = 0$ for all $a/b \geqslant (a/b)_0$; $z > 0$ for all $a/b < (a/b)_0$; and $Z' \leqslant 0$.

The cumulative shift of output then affects the demand equations (3) and (3′), which must be replaced by

$$A = \frac{cmY_{-1}}{a} + \int_0^t z_j B_j\,dj \tag{22}$$

$$B = \frac{(1-c)mY_{-1}}{b} - \int_0^t z_j B_j\,dj. \tag{23}$$

By shifting jobs and output away from the sector of high frictional unemployment, this process might lower total unemployment gradually over time at a given inflation rate.

Notes

I am indebted to Robert E. Litan and Herbert F. Lowrey, Jr., for their able and extensive assistance in the research, and to George Jaszi and several senior advisers and members of the Brookings Panel on Economic Activity for helpful comments.

1. Henry C. Wallich, "Conservative Economic Policy," *Yale Review*, Vol. 46 (Autumn 1956), p. 68.

2. Arthur M. Okun, "Potential GNP: Its Measurement and Significance," in American Statistical Association, *Proceedings of the Business and Economic Statistics Section* (1962); reprinted in Arthur M. Okun, *The Political Economy of Prosperity* (Brookings Institution, 1970), Appendix, pp. 132–45.

3. See Stanley W. Black and R. Robert Russell, "An Alternative Estimate of Potential GNP," *Review of Economics and Statistics*, Vol. 51 (February 1969), p. 72; Lester C. Thurow and L. D. Taylor, "The Interaction between the Actual and the Potential Rates of Growth," *Review of Economics and Statistics*, Vol. 48 (November 1966), p. 354; George L. Perry, "Labor Force Structure, Potential Output, and Productivity," *Brookings Papers on Economic Activity* (3:1971), pp. 541–42 (these volumes are subsequently referred to as *BPEA*, followed by the date).

4. Jacob Mincer, "Labor-Force Participation and Unemployment: A Review of Recent Evidence," in Robert Aaron Gordon and Margaret S. Gordon (eds.), *Prosperity and Unemployment* (John Wiley, 1966).

5. Perry's estimate of the participation effect is influenced by an important and puzzling data problem. Cyclical spurts and retardations in the growth of employment as reported by firms are substantially more pronounced than those shown in household surveys; for evidence covering 1962–68, see Gloria P. Green, "Comparing Employment Estimates from Household and Payroll Surveys," *Monthly Labor Review*, Vol. 92 (December 1969), pp. 9–20. Perry relies on the employment estimates from firms, judging them distinctly more reliable than those from households, and he allocates the statistical discrepancy to jobs among women and teenagers, implying a pronounced cyclical pattern of misreporting by households of employment increases.

Black and Russell believed that the statistical divergence reflected cyclical fluctuations in moonlighting. However, since direct estimates of moonlighting do not account for the divergence, Edward Denison has interpreted it as a data discrepancy, and Perry followed that practice. Perry's estimate of increased participation closely matches the sum of the two components that Black and Russell attribute to participation and moonlighting.

The statistical divergence was ignored by some earlier investigators such as Thurow and Taylor, and Edwin Kuh, "Measurement of Potential Output," *American Economic Review*, Vol. 56 (September 1966), pp. 758–76. By implicitly accepting the household estimates of employment, while basing their productivity estimates on reports from firms, they introduce a downward bias in the estimate of potential. In my 1962 calculation, because I estimated the productivity bonus residually after allowing for increases in labor input as estimated from household surveys, the cyclical pattern of the statistical divergence was incorrectly reflected as extra productivity rather than as extra labor input.

6. An excellent review of the voluminous literature in this area is presented by Ray C. Fair, *The Short-Run Demand for Workers and Hours* (Amsterdam: North-Holland, 1969). A recent exception to the typical finding is the aggregate equation in William D. Nordhaus, "The Recent Productivity Slowdown," *BPEA* (3:1972), p. 497.

7. Unpublished presidential address to Econometric Society, delivered December 1965. (Solow's other paradox was the inability to find a significant short-run substitution of capital for labor.) In my judgment, Solow's paradox remains unexplained despite some ingenious efforts. See Frank Brechling and Peter O'Brien, "Short-run Employment Functions in Manufacturing Industries: An International Comparison," *Review of Economics and Statistics*, Vol. 49 (August 1967), pp. 277–87; Albert A. Hirsch, "Reconciliation of the Short-Run Employment Function and the Long-Run Production Function" (paper presented at the winter meeting of the Econometric Society, December 1968); Roger Craine, "On the Service Flow from Labour," *Review of Economic Studies*, Vol. 40 (January 1973), pp. 39–46.

8. Perry, "Labor Force Structure," p. 558. Clearly, the estimates are lower when output is regressed on employment. Kuh reported the same phenomenon in "Measurement of Potential Output." The standard lagged adjustment model of labor demand espoused by Brechling and others cited above would call for employment to be the dependent variable; I am unaware of any analytical model that points toward output as the dependent variable. The statistical pitfalls in this area are discussed by Marc Nerlove, "Notes on the Production and Derived Demand Relations Included in Macro-Econometric Models," *International Economic Review*, Vol. 8 (June 1967), pp. 223–42.

9. Most notably: ". . . in general, an increase in employment can only occur to the accompaniment of a decline in the rate of real wages. . . . This is simply the obverse of the familiar proposition that industry is normally working subject to decreasing returns in the short period . . ."—John Maynard Keynes, *The General Theory of Employment, Interest and Money* (Harcourt, Brace, 1936), p. 17.

10. This view is relevant to fiscal decisions in peacetime, even though government product shows some positive relation to overall economic activity historically as a result of wartime booms. Thus a statistical equation relating real gross government product as a share of real potential GNP to time and an activity variable (the ratio of actual real GNP to potential) reveals that government product accounted for 6.4 percent of the output gap on the average over the period 1954–71.

11. Since a tiny fraction of the output of nonfinancial corporations is that of farm corporations, viewing that sector as a component of private nonfarm business is imprecise—but only trivially so.

12. The key coefficient of 0.778 was virtually unaffected by the inclusion of lagged terms. It was even higher when adjusted for autocorrelation.

13. John A. Gorman, "Nonfinancial Corporations: New Measures of Output and Input," *Survey of Current Business*, Vol. 52 (March 1972), p. 26.

14. Perry, "Labor Force Structure."

15. George L. Perry, "Unemployment Flows in the U.S. Labor Market," *BPEA* (2:1972), p. 259.

16. I wondered whether the outstanding elasticity of durable goods employment might reflect, in part, federal arms procurement during the Korean and Vietnam wars. But the errors of the durable goods equation for the war years were not at all unusual, suggesting that the production of durables for the federal government substituted at least in large measure for durable items that would have been acquired by private investors and consumers in a peacetime economy with equally high utilization rates.

17. Because I set 1 million workers as the minimum size of industry to get its own equation, mining was added to construction. I separated and grouped the "high-wage" services—miscellaneous business, miscellaneous repair, miscellaneous professional, and legal—expecting them to show greater cyclical responsiveness than the other services, as they did. That was the only experiment performed to disaggregate industries more finely.

18. When treated like any other industry, military employment had a value of a_2 of 3.6, showing greater cyclical sensitivity than even durable goods manufacturing! Even with the gap redefined to exclude federal workers, part of the difference between the sum of the industry totals and the overall employment gap reflects the excluded military component of more than 150,000 workers in the job gap of 1970.

19. Nordhaus, "Recent Productivity Slowdown," p. 522.

20. For evidence that occupational earnings relatives are similar among male age groups, see U.S. Bureau of the Census, *Current Population Reports*, Series P-60, No. 58, "Year-Round Workers with Low Earnings in 1966" (1969), p. 17. Age-sex occupational earnings relatives were strikingly similar in 1960, according to Bureau of the Census, *U.S. Census of Population, 1960: Occupational Characteristics*, Final Report PC(2)-7A (1963).

Unfortunately, the data by industry are less complete. Earnings by industry are classified by sex in the annual issue of *Current Population Reports* (Series P-60) on income of families and persons, and these suggest that industry earnings relatives are generally comparable between sexes. But the same comparisons cannot be made across age groups from any body of data I know.

21. The entire shift effect was also estimated in the opposite direction—distributing the employment of a given demographic group across industries. For example, employment of male teenagers in retail trade as a fraction of total male teenage employment (N_{id}/N_d) was related to time and the employment gap. That set of equations and equation (4) above provided alternative estimates of each demographic-industrial cell for each year. Although the results were qualitatively similar,

equation (4) gave a better fit, with the grand sum of squared errors over the twelve-year period roughly half as large. The alternative approach would have "solved" the problem of males 20–24 by permitting an allocation of the Perry demographic-gap estimates across industries. But then the industry totals would not have agreed with the industry-gap allocation; in fact, one startling discrepancy emerged—retail trade had virtually no job gap.

22. M. W. Reder, "The Theory of Occupational Wage Differentials," *American Economic Review*, Vol. 45 (December 1955), p. 842.

23. Pamela Haddy and N. Arnold Tolles, "British and American Changes in Interindustry Wage Structure under Full Employment," *Review of Economics and Statistics*, Vol. 39 (November 1957), p. 414.

24. Michael L. Wachter, "Cyclical Variation in the Interindustry Wage Structure," *American Economic Review*, Vol. 60 (March 1970), p. 80.

25. Some of the key contributions in this area are: Robert E. Hall, "Why Is the Unemployment Rate So High at Full Employment?" *BPEA* (3:1970), pp. 369–402, and Hall, "Turnover in the Labor Force," *BPEA* (3:1972), pp. 709–56; Peter B. Doeringer and Michael J. Piore, *Internal Labor Markets and Manpower Analysis* (Heath, 1971); Gary S. Becker, *Human Capital: A Theoretical and Empirical Analysis, with Special Reference to Education* (Columbia University Press for the National Bureau of Economic Research, 1964); Charles C. Holt, "Job Search, Phillips' Wage Relation, and Union Influence: Theory and Evidence," in Edmund S. Phelps and others, *Microeconomic Foundations of Employment and Inflation Theory* (Norton, 1970); Phelps, "Money Wage Dynamics and Labor Market Equilibrium," in *Microeconomic Foundations*; Perry, "Unemployment Flows"; Walter Y. Oi, "Labor as a Quasi-Fixed Factor," *Journal of Political Economy*, Vol. 70 (December 1962), pp. 538–55; James Tobin, "Inflation and Unemployment," *American Economic Review*, Vol. 62 (March 1972), pp. 1–18.

26. See the appendix for a mathematical development.

27. Several aspects of the analysis and discussion that follow are similar to points made by Michael Wachter in three recent articles. The main difference is that he stresses administered price and wage behavior of big firms and unions, while I focus on the long-run attachments between workers and firms. See Wachter, "Cyclical Variation in the Interindustry Wage Structure"; Wachter, "Phase II, Cost-Push Inflation, and Relative Wages," Fels Discussion Paper 23 (University of Pennsylvania, Fels Center of Government, October 1972; processed); Stephen A. Ross and Michael L. Wachter, "Wage Determination, Inflation, and the Industrial Structure," *American Economic Review* (forthcoming). In addition, Donald F. Gordon has offered a similar analysis in a paper, "The Theory of the Phillips Curve," presented to a conference at the University of Rochester, Center for Research in Government Policy and Business (April 1973; processed).

28. For evidence on the strong negative correlation of wage rates and quit rates among industries, see Lloyd Ulman, "Labor Mobility and the Industrial Wage Structure in the Postwar United States," *Quarterly Journal of Economics*, Vol. 79 (February 1965), pp. 81–85; Oi, "Labor as a Quasi-Fixed Factor," pp. 552–53;

and John H. Pencavel, "Wages, Specific Training, and Labor Turnover in U.S. Manufacturing Industries," *International Economic Review*, Vol. 13 (February 1972), pp. 53–64.

29. Perry, "Unemployment Flows."

30. Tobin, "Inflation and Unemployment," pp. 6–7.

31. Wachter, "Cyclical Variation in the Interindustry Wage Structure"; Arnold H. Packer and Seong H. Park, "Distortions in Relative Wages and Shifts in the Phillips Curve," *Review of Economics and Statistics*, Vol. 55 (February 1973), pp. 16–22.

32. Since a lower level of activity would in itself provide a major disincentive to investment for a substantial period, it is unlikely that a rise in real interest rates would be desired or tolerated. Suppose monetary policy aimed at the same real interest rate that had previously prevailed with the high-pressure target, while fiscal policy was used to restrict aggregate demand by $35 billion. In that case, a simple Keynesian multiplier that abstracts from monetary effects would be appropriate. The figure of $15 billion emerges with multipliers between 2 and 2.5 for the relevant fiscal instruments.

Conflicting National Goals

The goal of high employment is important in making national economic policy, but it often conflicts with other objectives and considerations. The first portion of this chapter is devoted to a review of the way the employment goal was conceptualized and implemented in relation to other national economic goals by the Kennedy and Johnson Administrations during the 1960s. I shall not attempt to interpret the goals of the Nixon and Ford Administrations, but I will draw upon the lessons of the 1970s as well as the 1960s in the second part of the chapter to discuss our current employment prospects and policies and their relationship to conflicting goals.

The Conflicts of the 1960s

The basic strategy of employment policies set forth by the Council of Economic Advisers at the start of the 1960s was followed consistently during the Kennedy and Johnson Administrations, although its implementation was initially deferred by political obstacles and subsequently distorted by the Vietnam War. The analytical framework, the basic empirical judgments, and the fundamental social values expressed in 1961 and 1962 held up extremely well during the decade.

When President Kennedy took office early in 1961, the economy was experiencing its third recession in seven years and the unemployment rate was approaching 7 percent. The Kennedy economists saw recession and high unemployment as twin symptoms, in product and labor markets, of the traditional Keynesian disease of inadequate demand. While the Council's analyses stressed the human costs of unemployment as the greatest evil of a weak economy, they also emphasized the huge gap in production—proportionately three times the size of excess unemployment. The short-fall in average weekly hours of the employed, the presence of discouraged jobseekers who were not counted among the unemployed, and the depressed state of productivity in a slack economy all contributed to the size of the GNP gap.

Most of all, the Council sought to rally sentiment in favor of a strong and vigorous expansion, rather than for a mere turnaround from recession. It was in this context that a 4 percent target unemployment rate, which had been accepted at times under President Truman and not at all under President Eisenhower, was adopted by President Kennedy (without a specific target date of fulfillment) in 1961. As Heller reports, that goal was attacked from all sides.[1] In defending itself for not being more ambitious, the Council noted that "the experience of 1955–57 is . . . sobering. . . ."[2] It did stress that the 4 percent goal should be achievable by stabilization policy alone and that other policy measures to improve the functioning of labor markets should "help to reduce the goal attainable in the future below the 4 percent figure."[3]

In implementing its employment strategy during the early 1960s, CEA had to overcome four principal obstacles: budget balancing objectives, price stability concerns, balance-of-payments worries, and the structural challenge.

The Goal of Budget Balancing

The most serious political opposition to the adoption of a vigorous fiscal policy in 1961 stemmed from orthodox budgetary principles through which balanced budgets were viewed as a virtue and deficits as a vice. Although such fiscal orthodoxy is generally linked to worries about the effects of budgetary deficits on inflation and the balance of payments, it transcends those specific concerns and is, in the minds of its exponents, a separate and indeed a prior goal.

After running a $12 billion antirecessionary deficit during fiscal 1959, President Eisenhower unfurled his 1960 balanced budget with the statement, "If we cannot live within our means during such a time of rising prosperity, the hope for fiscal integrity will fade."[4] The issue was integrity—not the price level or the gold stock. President Kennedy did not challenge such principles during the election campaign of 1960; indeed, in response to critics who implied that he would be fiscally irresponsible, he pledged himself to outperform his predecessor. And in 1961 he remained constrained by those campaign promises. However laudable that allegiance may have been on grounds of integrity, it set back the cause of economic rationality. The initial fiscal moves under Kennedy were very timed—calculated to be so small that the deficits of fiscal years 1961 and 1962 could be attributed to the unhappy heritage from Eisenhower rather than to any expansionary actions of the new administration.

Moreover, in January 1962 the President succumbed to the old orthodoxy, submitting a balanced budget even though the unemployment rate remained at 6 percent. It was only when the expansion faltered in the spring of 1962 that Kennedy reached a fork in the road of fiscal philosophy. Speaking at Yale University in June 1962, he "issued his own declaration of economic independence," as Heller has described it.[5] In that speech, the President labeled as a "myth" and an "old and automatic cliche" the proposition that deficits are dangerous and invariably create inflation. In August, Kennedy announced that he would propose a major tax cut in January 1963, which would obviously increase the deficit for the short run. From then until February 1964 "selling" the tax cut—making the case for that unprecedented stimulative measure—was the key assignment of CEA.

Heller and his colleagues had paved the way for the conversion of Kennedy by educating him and the public. One important educational device was the concept of the "full employment budget," which distinguished what the budget did to the economy from what the economy did to the budget.[6] The large surplus in that budget in 1960 and 1961 illustrated both analytical and doctrinal points. First, even though the actual budget was deeply in the red, the full-employment surplus showed that it was relatively restrictive. Second, the large size of the short-fall of tax revenues associated with a slack economy indicated that the best hope for balancing the budget lay in a return to full prosperity. That theme was intended to appeal to budget balancers; a fiscal stimulus would serve their objective, as well as the objectives of higher employment and output. Third, the new fiscal rhetoric implicitly accepted a revised, less dangerous form of fiscal mythology by promising to maintain some surplus in the *full-employment* budget even though Kennedy's economists did not believe that even full-employment deficits were necessarily inflationary under the circumstances.

As Heller reports, both Kennedy and Johnson "recognized that it was necessary to make concessions to popular economic ideology and precepts." In describing the strategy, Heller writes: "Acceptance of the huge tax cut was gained in part by claiming (a) that it was the surest way to achieve a balanced budget in a balanced economy, (b) that the debt would still drop as a proportion of GNP, and (c) that rigid frugality would be practiced in the federal budget." The economists had mixed feelings about "the homage thus paid to balanced budgets and the hostages thus given to the old deficit, debt and spending phobias. . . ."[7] Yet the whole strategy worked and the deficit taboo was basically shattered. In 1970–72 the Nixon Administration stressed full-employment budgeting as a justification for antirecessionary deficits, virtually reading the script that Heller and company had written a decade earlier.

The Inflation-Unemployment Trade-Off

Unlike fiscal orthodoxy, price stability was a major legitimate concern in the eyes of the Kennedy and Johnson economists. Indeed, it is generally recognized as the goal that conflicts most seriously with high employment.

The whole conception of the inflation-unemployment trade-off had changed in the 1940s and 1950s. The original Keynesian formulation of full employment did not pose an agonizing trade-off. It suggested that in a slack economy output would vary with no significant impact on the price level, because wages tended to be rigid. Beyond some point, however, extra doses of aggregate demand would strain the capacity of the economy and hence increase nominal GNP mainly through inflation with no significant further gains in output and employment. In such a world, "full employment" was well-defined. The assignment of fiscal-monetary policy was to locate and achieve the full-employment point—that level of demand that was high enough to maximize output and not so high as to cause inflation. And at that level of demand, unemployment was viewed as an irreducible minimum due to structural and frictional forces. The search for the precise balancing point was recognized as difficult, but not as a head-on confrontation between the objectives of employment and price stability.

The experience of the 1940s and 1950s made clear that such a model was unrealistic. As the unemployment rate plummeted during World War II, reaching an amazingly low 1.2 percent in 1944, it became evident that a sufficiently over-heated economy would melt frictional and structural unemployment. Clearly, if society would accept inflation—either open or else suppressed by controls—the vistas for job creation were boundless. On the other hand, the mid-1950s taught the lesson that inflationary problems could emerge at a time when demand in general was not pressing on capacity and the unemployment rate remained slightly above 4 percent. Inflation rates of 3 and 4 percent in 1956–57 seem mild by today's standards but were terribly disturbing at the time, in part because it was the first inflationary episode in two generations that was not attributable to a war. Moreover, it revealed a sharp political sensitivity to inflation, and that demonstration had a major impact on the attitudes of policy-makers.

That history was vivid in the minds of the Kennedy Administration economists as they formulated their strategy for the 1960s. The Council insisted in 1962: "There is a good reason to believe that upward pressures of this magnitude are not a permanent and systematic feature of our economy when it is operating in the neighborhood of 4 percent unemployment. The 1955–57 boom was concentrated in durable manufactured goods. . . . The uneven nature of the expansion undoubtedly accentuated the wage and price pressures. . . ." In making this argument, the Council was invoking Charles Schultze's "demand shift" explanation for the inflation of the mid-1950s.[8]

The design of the innovative guideposts policy also reflected the CEA diagnosis of that earlier experience, and their determination to prevent an encore. As Heller and his colleagues saw the problem: "Elements of major importance in the 1955–58 episode were thus the existence of relatively high demand, principally in one sector of the economy; the use of market power by management to maintain profit margins despite rising costs; the exercise of market power by labor unions in an effort to capture a substantial share of rising profits for their membership; and the transmission of these developments to other sectors of the economy."[9]

The wage-price guideposts were meant to deal with the second and third elements of that inflationary disease—the battle over income shares "where firms are large or employees well-organized, or both"; and where there is "considerable room for the exercise for private power and a parallel need for the assumption of private responsibility."[10] The guideposts were advanced as a guide to public understanding with the arguments that an informed public "can help to create an atmosphere in which the parties to such decisions will exercise their powers responsibly."[11] The guideposts themselves were a piece of arithmetic that spelled out sufficient conditions for price stability. If the rate of increase in wages (including fringes) in each industry equalled the trend of overall productivity increase for the entire economy, then labor costs per unit of output for the economy as a whole would be stable; if, moreover, prices moved in parallel with unit costs everywhere, then over-all prices would be stable, although some would rise and others decline.[12]

Just a few months after the guideposts had been promulgated, a sharp confrontation emerged between President Kennedy and the steel industry; it culminated in a roll-back of an announced price increase for steel and a victory for the administration.[13] From that point until the end of 1965, no further battles between business and the administration took place. The main deviation from guidepost performance on the part of corporations was a sin of omission—prices were not reduced in line with the guidepost criterion in some areas where productivity growth was especially rapid. Organized labor, on the other hand, consistently opposed the guidepost principle; indeed, it strongly resented the implicit acceptance of the existing distribution of income between employers and workers. Nevertheless, labor made no concerted "guidepost-busting" effort; the wage guidepost affected collective bargaining mainly by stiffening the backbone of business. It made productivity trend growth, a figure of roughly 3 percent, a wage limit that management could defend with patriotic fervor and made any price increases that would follow larger wage settlements harder to justify.

In fact, prices rose only slightly more than 1 percent per year from 1962 to 1965, and economy-wide wage increases averaged roughly 4 percent per year. To be sure, that was not guidepost perfection; indeed, by some standards, it remains puzzling that an economy with clear excess supplies (at least in 1962 and 1963) did not display a decelerating inflationary trend. Still the price performance was satisfactory and it dispelled the inflationary fears widely expressed at the outset of the decade. While it is impossible to know precisely how much the guideposts contributed to the good performance, there is substantial evidence that they did help some.[14]

The guidepost strategy was reinforced by other measures designed to reconcile the goals of high employment and price stability—that is, to shift the Phillips Curve in a more favorable direction. The planning for expansion sought a balanced advance of the various sectors of the economy—consumption, business investment, and housing—in an effort to avoid bottlenecks and pockets of excess demand. Within the administration the Kennedy and Johnson economists fought for a variety of microeconomic measures to improve the competitive functioning of markets, including liberal policy toward imports to insure their favorable price-competitive effects, reformed regulation of transportation and public utilities industries, the elimination of federal price "floors" on agricultural prices, resale price maintenance agreements, and various labor arrangements. Political obstacles to such structural reforms remained intense, and, outside the area of international free trade, the efforts were not very successful. As discussed below, manpower policies were also increasingly stressed as important tools for improving the trade-off.

With an expansion that operated within reasonable speed limits and with the aid of guideposts and other ancillary policies, the economy remained basically noninflationary as the unemployment rate moved down to 4.5 percent in mid-1965. Defense outlays for Vietnam first became a significant economic influence in July 1965, and they produced a major spurt in the economy during the second half of that year and into 1966. The war boom ended the era of price stability and initiated an era of inflation. Much of the inflation of the late 1960s is clearly attributable to the fiscal stimulus of the war and to the way the politics of limited war vetoed the recommendations of Johnson's economists to finance the war out of higher taxes. The balance of the expansion was disturbed by the big jump in demand for durable manufactures, and the reasonable speed limits were exceeded just as the economy neared the 4 percent unemployment target.[15]

If one abstracts from Vietnam—as I would love to do, for many reasons—it is nonetheless clear that the inflation problem would have intensified to some extent. By mid-1965, the absolute stability of wholesale prices that had marked the early years of the 1960s had given way to a modest upward trend. Some price pressures due to demand were beginning to appear. In my judgment, the 4.5 percent unemployment rate that had been reached by mid-1965 was on the outer edge of the danger zone. I would guess that even a moderately paced move downward to 4 percent unemployment through aggregate demand policies would have entailed a rising inflation rate—perhaps up to 3 percent. And I further suspect that such a rate would not have been acceptable to the nation. In short, I believe that the 4 percent unemployment target of aggregate demand policies adopted by the Council in 1961, though close to the mark, was probably a shade on the over-ambitious side.

When the economy became engulfed by excess demand during the

Vietnam boom, the guideposts were badly battered. The first major outburst of inflation took place outside the province of big labor and big business—in food and services, and in wages of low-skilled workers. With nonunion wages accelerating and consumer prices rising 3 percent during 1966, it became patently unrealistic for the Johnson Administration to insist that collective bargaining settlements be limited to the 3 percent trend growth of productivity. The Council backed away from its numerical wage guideposts in 1967 and 1968, stressing the need for less than full escalation of wages, but offering no specific quantitative standard for a partial offset to increases in the cost-of-living. Jawboning efforts to curb price increases were stepped up, and informal campaigns were conducted to talk down wages in some specific settlements.[16]

The experience of 1969, when these efforts were disbanded by the Nixon Administration, indicated that the 1966–68 suasion had had some success.[17] But voluntary restraint had never been meant to hold back the tides of excess demand, and it did not. Some historical studies of the period imply that a more determined and better coordinated administration effort on specific wage settlements, like the airline mechanics in 1966, might have made the differences.[18] As I see it, with excess demand driving up prices and wages outside the big labor and big business sectors, the guidepost dike was fundamentally undermined. The particular wage negotiation that shattered the dike might have been altered; but its ultimate collapse was inevitable and could not have been prevented simply by better jawboning. With unemployment at 3.5 percent and industrial operating rates above 90 percent, demand was too strong to avoid inflation.

The Balance of Payments

Defending the dollar—or, more accurately, the convertibility of the dollar for gold at the stated price of $35 per ounce—was a major goal of policy in the 1960s, and it conflicted with the targets for domestic prosperity and high employment. The Bretton Woods system was predicated on the dollar's role as a reserve currency, which in turn was linked to its convertibility with gold. Maintenance of that role for the dollar was conceived as a part of U.S. world leadership and national security, and thus its perceived value to the United States transcended any objective economic calculation. After major U.S. payments deficits and gold losses in the late 1950s, the commitment of the Kennedy Administration to $35 gold convertibility was an issue of worldwide suspicion in 1961. To restore confidence, President Kennedy made such convertibility an article of faith and honor. President Johnson renewed those pledges with equal vigor and vehemence when he took office. Thus, in order to help maintain the exchange rate, our presidents gave hostages against any subsequent devaluation. The presidential commitments delighted many Treasury officials and most private bankers; but pained most economists—in and out of government.

Attempting to reconcile the objective of international payments equilibrium at a fixed exchange rate with domestic full employment was a challenging assignment for economic policy-makers. Clearly, higher levels of domestic demand entailed higher demands for imports (and also some discouragement to the supply of exports), which worsened the payments deficit. The Kennedy economists argued however that the U.S. trade surplus would improve despite a return to full employment so long as U.S. prices remained stable. That prediction was borne out during the first half of the 1960s. Until the Vietnam inflation, the progress in the U.S. trade account exceeded even the most optimistic estimates at the beginning of the decade. In fact, relative prices improved as the United States, unlike many of our major trading partners, maintained price stability.

The reconciling strategy of the Kennedy economists also included other elements. One was the role of supply capabilities in influencing the trade account: "Advances in productivity and improvements in technology will also enable U.S. goods to compete more effectively with foreign products. . . ."[19] Competitiveness of foreign trade thus became a key argument for the investment tax credit, as well as for accelerated depreciation and for a cut in corporate rates. Another element was "operation twist," an effort to influence the structure of interest rates "so as to hold down the cost of long-term funds for investment in new plant and equipment while raising short-term rates to minimize the outflows of volatile funds to other countries."[20] Aid-tying, domestic procurement, and similar measures were also used to save foreign exchange, but these policies often pained the economists, who saw them as distorting allocation.

The Kennedy economists believed that, by providing more incentives to invest at home, prosperity would curtail foreign investments, which were a key outflow in the overall deficit.[21] That argument was logical and plausible, and even had bipartisan support.[22] Nevertheless, it turned out to be wrong—virtually alone among the many analytical principles and predictions made by the original Kennedy Council. Domestic prosperity did indeed encourage investment at home, but not at the expense of investment abroad; instead, it seemed to whet the appetite of the business community for more capital spending everywhere. Early in 1965, the Johnson Administration launched a voluntary cooperation program to hold down direct investment abroad by U.S. companies and foreign borrowings from U.S. banks. In 1968, these direct controls on capital outflows were made mandatory. Kennedy and Johnson economists had to grit their teeth repeatedly about these specific interferences with the international flow of capital; but they saw them as lesser evils than policies that would have destroyed jobs at home in order to attain payments balance. Flexible exchange rates (or devaluation) remained "unthinkable" alternatives throughout the 1960s, and CEA had to accept that fact of life. In retrospect, one can merely sigh with relief that the reconciling strategy kept us from doing even more foolish things than we did to "defend the dollar." It is more comic than tragic now that a valuation of the dollar, established at a time when Western Europe and Japan were in shambles, became a prime article of national prestige. It probably is no accident that it took a Republican administration to cut the link to gold (just as to forge a link to China!).

The Structural Challenge

The final major obstacle to the implementation of the CEA strategy for full employment in the early 1960s was the alternative diagnosis of high unemployment as "structural" rather than macroeconomic. Emphasizing that even at the peak of expansion in 1960, the unemployment rate remained at 5 percent, and that unemployment was very uneven among demographic groups, occupations, industries, and regions, some insisted that the unusually high rate of unemployment in 1961 was far more than a cyclical phenomenon and that it lay beyond the reach of fiscal-monetary stimulation. They contended that the economy had experienced a structural deterioration in labor markets. Some linked this thesis to automation; for example, Robert Theobald predicted without qualification: "Unemployment rates must therefore be expected to rise in the sixties. . . . No conceivable rate of economic growth will avoid this result."[23]

It was an unfortunate historical accident that structural efforts to improve labor markets were presented to the government and the public largely as substitutes rather than complements for aggregate demand policies. To be sure, some eclectic economists thought that manpower programs deserved a greater emphasis right from the start and yet were prepared to support CEA's macroeconomic fiscal-monetary strategy. But the main emphasis on the structural side came from those who expounded a structural deterioration thesis that was inconsistent with demand stimulation. This group included some strange bedfellows. Its conservatives felt that structural deterioration made it necessary to do nothing and simply accept higher unemployment rates. A less conservative and less conventional splinter group advocated shorter work weeks, earlier retirement, and "make-work" projects of low productivity. Still another group advocated manpower training and labor market placement and information as ways to make the square pegs fit into the round holes of the labor market.[24]

At every step of its efforts to promote a more stimulative fiscal policy in 1961–63, the Council was challenged by the structural deterioration thesis. In the first major public presentation of its strategy in 1961, CEA offered a 13-page supplement that lined up the numbers to demonstrate that unemployment was not hardcore and that the "high overall rate of unemployment comes from higher unemployment rates group by group category by category, throughout the labor force."[25] The Council was supported by a JEC staff study later in 1961.[26] In promoting the tax cut in 1963, CEA was again battling the same enemy.[27] And as late as May 1965, I was involved in the old debate.[28] When the returns were in, it became clear that, as the CEA had predicted, the overall reduction in unemployment had strongly benefited those who had been at the back of the hiring line and viewed by the structuralists as "hardcore." Unemployment fell most among black adults, the less educated, the low-skilled and those in depressed regions.

Table 1 shows unemployment rates for various demographic, occupational, industrial, and educational groups for five years in the past generation: three prosperous ones in which the unemployment rate ran between four and five percent—1956, 1965, 1973—and two particularly bad years—1961 and 1975. By any reasonable standard, I believe the most significant message of the table is the stability of the structure of unemployment rates over time. If one adds roughly a quarter to each group's unemployment rate in 1961, a remarkably good estimate of its unemployment in 1975 is obtained (just as the overall rate rose by roughly one-fourth from 6.7 to 8.5).

There have been some detectable shifts over the period, nonetheless. Between 1956 and 1965, unemployment grew worse for teenagers, especially for nonwhite teenagers. Adult males, both white and nonwhite,

Table 1 Unemployment rates for selected groups, 1956, 1961, 1965, 1973 and 1975[a]

	1956[b]	1961[b]	1965	1973	1975
Total, all civilian workers	4.1	6.7	4.5	4.9	8.5
By demographic group					
Nonwhites, 16 to 19	18.1	27.7	26.5	30.3	36.9
Whites, 16 to 19	10.1	15.3	13.4	12.6	17.9
Nonwhite males, 20 and over	7.4	11.7	6.0	5.7	11.7
Nonwhite females, 20 and over	7.8	10.6	7.5	8.2	11.5
White females, 20 and over	3.7	5.7	4.0	4.3	7.5
White males, 20 and over	3.0	5.1	2.9	2.9	6.2
By occupation					
Blue-collar	n.a.	9.2	5.3	5.3	11.7
Service	n.a.	7.2	5.3	5.7	8.6
White-collar	n.a.	3.3	2.3	2.9	4.7
By industry[c]					
Manufacturing	4.7	7.8	4.0	4.3	10.9
Wholesale and retail trade	4.5	7.3	5.0	5.6	8.7
Finance and services	4.0	5.5	4.1	4.3	6.6
Government	1.7	2.5	1.9	2.7	4.0
By duration of employment					
15 weeks and over	0.8	2.2	1.0	0.9	2.7
By educational attainment[d]					
Less than 8 years[e]	7.1	8.8	6.8	5.6	12.4
8 years	4.7	7.2	5.0	6.7	11.3
12 years	3.0	5.1	4.1	4.6	9.1
13 to 15 years	2.9	3.7	3.3	4.0	6.9
16 years or more	0.7	1.4	1.4	2.1	2.9

Source: U.S. Department of Labor.

a. The subgroups within each group are ordered according to the rank, from high to low, of their 1961 unemployment rate.

b. Unemployment rates by educational attainment are not available for 1956 and 1961. The rates shown are for 1957 and 1962.

c. These data are for all wage and salary workers rather than all civilian workers.

d. For 1957, 1962 and 1965, the data are for persons aged 18 and over. In 1973 and 1975, they are for persons aged 16 and over.

e. This group includes persons reporting no school years completed.

have experienced a favorable shift over time, although a change in the unemployment questionnaire in 1967 was one contributor to this development. On the other hand, some particularly favored groups—white collar workers, government workers, and people with college diplomas—seem to have lost a bit of their sheltered position over time.

All in all, the one significant shift in the structure of unemployment has been the relative rise among teenagers. Their share of the labor force has increased enormously, reflecting the baby boom of the late 1940s and the 1950s, and their unemployment rates stayed high. I conceded that one point (and no more) to the structuralists back in 1965, but reiterated the importance of prosperity even for that group: "The stability and stubbornness of the teenage rate of recent years reflect a standoff between upward supply trends and downward demand pressures.... Their job gains tend to be especially small in periods of sluggish overall increases of employment.... Teenagers are at the back of the hiring line. And it is, therefore, all the more important that the hiring line be shortened sufficiently to bring increasing job gains for them."[29]

CEA spokesmen had emphasized repeatedly that structural unemployment was a problem, although not worse than it had been in the 1950s. In March 1961. Heller and his colleagues had insisted: "It is no part of our intention to cry down structural unemployment or explain it away. The problems of younger and older workers, of nonwhite members of the labor force, of the technologically displaced, and of the distressed need to be attacked at the source."[30]

The 1962 Report strongly endorsed employment services and training programs as ways of ultimately facilitating an even more ambitious unemployment target.[31] To the Council, success in training programs required an expansion of overall labor demands; thus Otto Eckstein warned against the danger of a "bitter harvest of trained and educated" jobseekers if labor markets were allowed to weaken as training was stepped up.

Consistent with that view, CEA enthusiasm for manpower policies increased during the latter 1960s when aggregate demand policies had accomplished (indeed, overaccomplished) their objectives. Gardner Ackley sounded a strong appeal for manpower activities in October 1966.[32] Both the 1967 and 1969 CEA Reports devoted substantial sections to ways in which frictional and structural unemployment might be reduced, including on the menu, relocation assistance, general education subsidies, programs to reduce seasonality, and direct training.[33] In the

1969 Report, the swansong of the Kennedy-Johnson era, the Council felt emboldened to express its concerns about "negative" manpower policies such as overly restrictive occupational licensing and excessively rapid rises in minimum wages.[34]

In retrospect, manpower programs had to compete with many other techniques by which Johnson's Great Society sought to advance social conditions at the same time that a war was being fought. Those programs experienced a major expansion, but, in my judgment, did not get as high a priority as they deserved. I suspect that the initial push for manpower policies by some of their advocates as substitutes rather than complements for macroeconomic policies harmed the cause of those programs throughout the debate.

In retrospect the basic Council strategy worked amazingly well and achieved full utilization of resources on a macroeconomic basis. While it lasted, full employment meant a great deal to the country. It restored confidence in the vigor and vitality of the American economy that had been seriously in question at the outset of the decade—when Khrushchev was threatening to bury us economically and Gunnar Myrdal was identifying the weakness of the American economy as the world's most serious economic problem. In combination with various new and expanded social programs, it helped to accomplish the remarkable 40 percent reduction in people under the poverty income-line during the 1960s, facilitated the mobility of workers that narrowed geographical income disparities, and widened employment opportunities for women and black men. It defused the political pressures for protectionism, make-work, and labor supply restrictions. Indeed, full employment did everything that could reasonably have been expected of it, and nearly everything CEA had predicted—with the exceptions of foreign investment and teenage unemployment. But the overfull employment of the Vietnam period did one thing that was unexpected and unpredicted at the outset; it created a torrent of inflation.

Challenge of the Late 1970s

The Johnson legacy to the Nixon Administration included the boon of prosperity and the bane of inflation. From 1969 to 1976, prosperity disappeared (except for a brief interval in 1972–73), but inflation was preserved and seriously intensified (except during 1972). Apart from the resort to comprehensive and stringent price and wage controls in 1971–

72, the primary instrument for fighting inflation since 1969 was fiscal-monetary restraint: and it lowered growth and raised unemployment. But, as it turned out, high levels of unemployment have proved to be rather ineffective curbs on inflation. Thus, the nation has had the worst of both worlds. Macroeconomic strategies that required high unemployment were socially mitigated by extension of unemployment insurance, a major growth in food stamps, and other palliatives that reduced the human costs imposed on the victims of unemployment. While such measures have made unemployment somewhat more tolerable and less inhumane, it remains costly to its victims and to the nation.

The unemployment rates of virtually all groups in 1976 exceeded those of fifteen years before at the outset of the Kennedy Administration. Unquestionably, the medicine of macroeconomic stimulation—tax cuts, increased federal spending, accommodative monetary policies—that generated the unemployment reductions of the early 1960s have ability to repeat the cure in the late 1970s. Again, the limitations arise from conflicting goals. But it is now a single conflict—not a fourfold set of obstacles. Although budgetary orthodoxy has occasionally reared its irrational head in the Ford Administration—as in the speeches of John Simon, Secretary of the Treasury—it does not have much force. In that respect, the 1960s accomplished a lasting improvement in fiscal policy-making. The system (or nonsystem) of flexible exchange rates has clearly removed the balance-of-payments constraint as a symbol of pride or prestige and a do-or-die issue. The more valid parts and proposals of the structural challenge have been gradually blended into a synthesis with macroeconomic policies. Three of the four major obstacles that stood in the way of full employment policies in the early 1960s have been chopped down if not fully rooted out. But the remaining obstacle—concern with inflation—looms far larger today than it did then. We have dispelled myths; we have changed institutions: but we have lost ground persistently on the inflation-unemployment trade-off.

In this environment, the creation of jobs threatens the creation of inflation in the minds of the American public and their elected representatives in Washington. And that is why the prospects for employment during the remainder of the decade look so bleak.

The last bright spot in our economic annals was a period in 1972 when inflation was reduced to a 3 percent rate, while the economy gained momentum and unemployment declined. Although the abatement of inflation was enhanced by the price and wage controls in effect at the time, these controls clearly were not conflicting seriously with market forces during the course of 1972. The explosion of inflation that began early in 1973 is still hard to explain or comprehend in full. Labor markets were not tight, and wages did not accelerate for quite a while; the unemployment rate of 4.9 percent in 1973 was not accompanied by shortages of labor or indications that employment was overfull. Nor were industrial operating rates in the aggregate particularly high. The evidence does suggest, however, that excess demand became acute in certain world-traded commodities and in some key materials and materials-processing industries at home. Starting in the fall of 1971, the economy was spurred by highly stimulative fiscal-monetary policies, and it is clear in retrospect (but to me—and to nearly all economists—*only* in retrospect) that these policies should have been tightened sometime during 1972. Nonetheless, most of the explosion of consumer price inflation to a 9 percent rate during 1973 and a 12 percent rate by the end of 1974 cannot be attributed to fiscal and monetary policy by any stretch of the imagination. In my judgment, mismanagement of domestic food supplies added more to inflation in 1973 than did all the monetary and fiscal errors combined; from December 1972 to September 1973, the acceleration of food accounted for five-sixths of the total acceleration in prices. The devaluation engineered at the beginning of 1973 impaired price stability far more than had initially been recognized. By the end of the year, OPEC made fuel the key factor in the inflation that continued and intensified during 1974, even as the economy slumped into recession.

As a result of repeated decisions to use monetary and fiscal policy to fight the inflation rather than the recession, the economy experienced its most severe recession since the 1930s.[35] The decline in real GNP from late 1973 to early 1975 was twice the size of our deepest previous postwar recession. Unemployment averaged 8.5 percent during 1975, far above the previous postwar annual high of 6.8 percent for 1958. Inflation moderated roughly to a 6 percent rate early in 1975 but displayed little further deceleration during the course of the year.

Forecasts for 1976, including those of the Ford Administration, pointed to a continuation of 6 percent inflation. Indeed, the Administration predicted essentially the same figure for 1977.[36] In longer range projections that are carefully distinguished from best-estimate forecast, the Administration showed unemployment rates remaining high—6.9 percent in 1977, 6.4 percent in 1978, and 5.8 percent in 1979. This moderate but sustained recovery should ultimately, according to these projections, bring the inflation rate down to 1 percent at the end of the decade.[37] The assessment paints a bleak picture, both of our prospects for employment gains and of the effectiveness of high unemployment as a remedy for inflation. The pessimism on the latter count should be regarded as candid realism. Among the many statistical estimates made by economists, even the more optimistic ones suggest that about 2 extra points of unemployment for a year—a loss of roughly $100 billion in real GNP—are needed to yield a 1 point deceleration in the rate of wage (or price) increase.

The Seriousness of the Inflation Conflict

The Administration's strategy thus envisioned a large sacrifice of employment and output and only a modest further deceleration of inflation. Some who supported their aim of a moderate sustained recovery hope for greater gains on the inflation front. Those optimists argue that expectations of rapid inflation are a key influence on actual inflation, and that a sufficiently restrictive government policy can break the back of those expectations, producing a prompter and larger move to price stability for given cost in unemployment. On the other hand, one can be properly skeptical of even as much deceleration as the Administration projects. The experiences of 1933–37 and of 1959–63 call seriously into question the view that the inflation rate will keep decelerating during the recovery so long as the economy has a lot of slack. A decline in the inflation rate during the course of a recovery (with no controls) has never occurred in our modern history—although the high inflation rate that prevails at the start of this recovery is also unprecedented.

Obviously, the cost of the Administration's strategy is prolonged high unemployment. If, in the years after 1976, real GNP should grow at a rate of 8 percent rather than the 6 percent envisioned by the Administration, the unemployment rate would fall about twice as fast, reaching about 5.2 percent in 1978 rather than in 1980, as projected by the Administration. On a reasonable bet, I believe that the 8 percent growth path would probably not *accelerate* inflation during 1976–78; but I believe that it would foreclose any likely prospect for a deceleration below the 6 percent inflation rate. If unaccompanied by other policies, the rapid recovery scenario basically should be viewed as an acceptance of 6 percent inflation, a willingness to live with it, and a determination to stabilize it near the present rate.

Moreover, as I read the evidence, pushing the unemployment rate down below 5 percent through sole reliance on aggregate demand measures would make an *acceleration* of inflation likely. Indeed, allowing for the serious possibility that bottleneck factors creating excess demand inflation will again emerge from capacity limitations of specific industries (rather than from labor market tightness), unemployment rates below 5.5 percent must be viewed as getting into the danger zone. Obviously, economists will learn some more about the inflationary acceleration threshold of the economy as the recovery progresses. Conceivably, for once, we may be pleasantly surprised to find more elbow room for employment and production than we did in the disheartening experiences of the recent past. But if the nation insists on relying solely on aggregate demand policies and is committed to avoid a new acceleration of inflation, then I would reluctantly conclude that the lowest prudent, realistic target for the unemployment rate at the end of the decade is 5.5 percent.

Moreover, I do not believe that a mere levelling-off of the inflation rate at 6 percent was a credible or acceptable target under the circumstances. By the standards of any year prior to 1973–75, 6 percent is an extremely high inflation rate; it means that the purchasing power of money is cut in half in twelve years. As I see it, our economic institutions are not adapted to such intense inflation as a steady diet. If inflation does not decelerate, I would expect a drastic movement away from the current reliance on the dollar as a yardstick of measurement and a basis for calculating prices and costs.[38] The indexing of wages and salaries to the cost of living would become widespread, extending to areas where compensation has remained sticky (perhaps even including the pay of the Federal Judiciary). That could be a dramatic change since only 2 or 3 percent of all employees now have uncapped escalator clauses. The substantial fraction of private business that still do cost accounting on a FIFO inventory basis, that gear prices to original costs, and that accept fixed-price orders for future deliveries would be bound to alter those practices. Conventional limits to one price change per year in some industries would continue to disappear. The concept of replacement cost depreciation would be adopted into pricing practices to a much greater extent. Public utility and transport regulation would have to depart from the long established historical cost basis for price setting. Interest rates on thrift accounts could not remain at levels that give small savers negative real yields. Property tax assessments and specific excise taxes would be further reformed. Most of the adaptations in this process would tend to intensify inflation and thus to reduce the likelihood that the inflation rate could, in fact, be stabilized at 6 percent.

Against the background of history, I would expect that any acceptance of a 6 percent inflation rate in 1976 would lead to the acceptance of still higher inflation rates in the future, and I would expect most informed observers to reach the same conclusion and to behave accordingly. In the 1950s and most of the 1960s, 1 percent was regarded as the "normal" inflation rate of the United States, while 3 or 4 percent was viewed as the rate experienced in unusually inflationary years. By the early 1970s, 3 or 4 percent came to be regarded as the normal inflation rate, with 6 percent reserved for the really bad years. If, in the late 1970s, 6 percent is taken as the normal inflation rate, I do not believe that this will be the last turn of the ratchet. The inflation rate cannot be kept steady at 6 percent (or at zero or at any other rate); sometime in the future inflation will accelerate and society is again unlikely to take the steps necessary to lower it to its previous point: the ratchet will thus turn once more. In short, I am convinced that 6 percent inflation is not a credible target for policy.[39] It really reveals a willingness to accept any acceleration that comes along.

Any job-creating strategy that leads to accelerating inflation would, in my view, gain more employment now only at the expense of much less employment later. It would entail another recession whose job losses would swamp the job gains accomplished in the interim. Inflation breeds recession, not through any mechanistic economic process, but through the democratic political process. Because the public will not accept rising inflation, the policy-makers will respond to their wishes and attempt to stop it; and for that reason, they will resort to restrictive fiscal and monetary policies that will destroy jobs and spawn recession.

I believe that the public's antipathy to inflation is rational and sensible, not a figment of their imagination or a symptom of money illusion. But regardless of why the public hates inflation, the evidence that it does is incontrovertible. In October 1975, with unemployment at 8.5 percent and the inflation rate receding into the 6–7 percent range, 57 percent of respondents in a Gallup survey identified the nation's most important problem as inflation while 21 percent pointed to unemployment. A year earlier, with inflation at 12 percent and unemployment at 6 percent, Public Enemy No. 1 was inflation for 79 percent and unemployment for a mere 3 percent.[40] The fact that these attitudes are reflected in the political process offers testimony that democracy really works.

In that sense, if aggregate demand policies were the only available tools, the Administration strategy of slow growth and prolonged high unemployment would not be unreasonable. What is unreasonable is its narrow focus on aggregate demand policies alone.

The Potential Contribution of Other Policies

There are important potentialities in a variety of measures that go beyond fiscal-monetary policies in ameliorating the bitter conflict between inflation and unemployment. The basic criterion for a successful policy of this type is not whether it creates jobs but whether it provides some elbow room for creating jobs without creating inflation. Even a humble economist can proclaim with confidence that we know how to create jobs; the problem is how we can put that knowledge to use without colliding with the goal of avoiding inflation. I shall discuss five types of policies, offering quite different verdicts on their promise and potential for the future. These include: (1) pinpointed job creation: (2) manpower training and related efforts; (3) policies to promote competition: (4) direct price-reducing measures; and (5) wage-price restraints.

Pinpointed job creation. Some efforts, like the current public service employment program, seek to fund certain job slots and establish eligibility requirements to ensure that they are filled by people who are unemployed or otherwise in need of a job. These programs do not purport to build careers or to train workers, and they are typically structured to be of a temporary character.

Such measures may be valuable, in my opinion, at a time of severe recession or early recovery in producing an employment gain more rapidly than tax cuts or transfer programs might accomplish, in redistributing the burden of unemployment somewhat less inequitably, and perhaps in permitting more of a job gain to be accomplished within the constraint of a maximum budget deficit. But I see no reason to believe that the programs presently in operation or even proposed offer any improvement in the inflation-unemployment trade-off. To the extent that they remove unemployed people from the ranks of applicants for private jobs, they must sacrifice downward pressure on the rate of wage inflation, just as any stimulative measure does. In principle, it would appear that some kinds of people in the ranks of the jobless may exert less of an antiinflationary effect on wages than do others, and if pinpointed job creation can fill slots with those people who make particularly small antiinflationary contributions by standing and waiting for jobs, the strategy could genuinely accomplish a greater reduction in unemployment for a given inflation performance than could general fiscal stimulation. On the basis of the evidence I know, however, the feasibility of such a refined selection from the ranks of the unemployed is virtually nonexistent. It is wrong to assume that unskilled workers represent such a group. Their wages are particularly responsive to labor market conditions; even though their unemployment rates are high, lowering those rates may reduce the antiinflationary pressure on labor markets as much as, or even more than, measures that put skilled people to work.

Much of the enthusiasm for pinpointed job creation rests on a much less sophisticated view that I have called the penicillin-in-the-throat fallacy.[41] Many political decision-makers, who trust their doctors' judgment that a penicillin shot administered in the rear will indeed cure laryngitis, do not trust the equally well-supported judgment of economists that fiscal and monetary injections into the spending stream will cure unemployment. Hence they prefer programs that directly and visibly create jobs without relying on the circulation of any medicines through the economic system.

Such naive views are even more blatantly apparent in proposals to deal with the unemployment problem by encouraging early retirement, shortening work weeks, and introducing greater protection against imports. By any reasonable standard, these are thoroughly counterproductive measures, representing the least efficient way to bring down the unemployment rate. They have to mean less production and more inflation than macroeconomic alternatives. Even if a shorter work week, for example, is not offset by higher hourly pay, it would lower unemployment merely by redistributing the existing amount of work with no extra production: and the resulting reduction in the unemployed standing in the lines of willing applicants must impose as much of a loss of antiinflationary pressure as would a stimulative program that created the same number of added jobs with more production and more payrolls. The continuing popularity of such proposals reflects the basic misconception that it is difficult to create jobs, when, in fact, it is difficult only to create jobs without creating inflation. Such pinpointing offers no way to solve the problem of job creation without inflation creation.

Manpower training. In addition to their potential for equalizing employment opportunity, for augmenting human capital, and thus for raising the quality of jobs, manpower training efforts offer an opportunity to achieve lower unemployment rates for a given inflation rate. One way they can improve the trade-off is by reducing mismatches between the demands and supplies of various types of workers. To the extent that training can be channeled to expand the supply of workers for occupations or industries that have particularly strong demands, it can prevent bottlenecks in the labor market. Since pockets of excess demand for labor have greater inflationary effects on wages than the corresponding deflationary effects of excess-supply pockets of equal size, any improvement in the match is a bonus on the trade-off. In a sense, training is also a technique of pinpointing, but it aims at categories of jobs rather than of workers, and hence seems far more promising to me.

Another way in which training can provide such a bonus is by qualifying more people for the kinds of jobs that involve long-term attachments between employees and employers. Unskilled jobs typically have very high turnover rates—both quits and layoffs. As a result it takes a large pool of unemployed simply to balance the demands and supplies for such types of labor. On the other hand, in more skilled occupations, workers have a stake in their job and employers a stake in their workers. The turnover is thus much lower, and the required pool of unemployed needed to fill slots as they arise without creating inflationary pressures is much smaller.

In general, recent evidence about the workings of labor markets for teenagers and disadvantaged adults suggest that, in conditions of prosperity, their problems are primarily in finding good and lasting jobs rather than merely in finding jobs. The demographic and occupational groups that are most prone to unemployment have *fairly* short durations of unemployment in prosperity; they do find jobs, but they do not find jobs that are worth keeping nor employers who are interested in keeping them. The best promise for a major inroad on structural unemployment in periods of prosperity thus lies in the creation of good jobs and career jobs—with quality more important than quantity. In these efforts, proposals for government subsidies to employers and young workers who stick together for some specified period seem intriguing as a way to reinforce the benefits of formal training programs.

In general, much needs to be done to evaluate alternative manpower programs and to appraise their potential. It is not true that manpower training has been tried and has failed: some options have not been seriously tried, some have not been seriously evaluated, and some seem to have had a fair measure of success. As Eli Ginzberg concluded in a brief survey of these efforts: "Our option, the critics notwithstanding, is not to discard manpower programming, but to strengthen and enlarge the existing manpower structure."[42]

Promoting competition. In a variety of ways, government regulations shelter various prices from competition and establish price floors without price ceilings. Nearly all the economists participating in President Ford's domestic "Summit" in the fall of 1974 signed a petition backing a program to slaughter these "sacred cows," whose existence has been popularized by Hendrik Houthakker.[43] They listed many anticompetitive regulations, including acreage controls that remain on rice and a few other farm products, milk marketing orders, shipping regulations that prevent competition, resale price maintenance (since repealed), and federally endorsed union apprenticeship restrictions. A wide consensus within the economics profession opposes such measures because they worsen the inflationary bias of the economy. But there is extremely strong political inflationary bias of the economy. But there is extremely strong political support for these measures; every sacred cow is the special pet of some producer's interest group.

In contrast, there is no consensus among economists about the role of monopoly and oligopoly in the inflationary process. The evidence is compelling that prices in highly concentrated industries do not respond promptly to excess supply pressures during recession and slack periods. On the other hand, these prices also are sluggish upward in a period of accelerating inflation, and it is not clear that they add significantly to inflation on balance over an entire cycle. Much the same can be said of collective bargaining arrangements, which appear to lag and display inertia both on the upside and the downside. In my personal judgment, specific reforms of anticompetitive practices in both product and labor markets can help to improve the trade-off, but I do not see much potential gain from a general trust-busting or union-busting campaign.

Price-reducing measures. The government influences many prices and costs directly through the tax system, stockpile programs, and international commodity and exchange-rate policies. Constructive and innovative use of these tools could provide a much more efficient and humane way of cutting down the momentum effect of past high inflation rates than that offered by the high-unemployment strategy. Particularly attractive are opportunities for restructuring taxes in recognition of the fact that excise and payroll taxes are passed through into prices and costs far more than are income taxes. If, for example, the $20 billion of tax cuts enacted in 1975 had been used to reduce state and local general sales taxes rather than federal income taxes, the increase in the cost of living in 1975 would have been 2 percentage points lower than it was in fact. In that event, wage prospects for 1976 would be more favorable, reflecting the impact of past cost-of-living rises on wages through both formal and informal arrangements.

On another front, much of the disastrous food price experience of recent years can be attributed directly to federal policies of export promotion and to the absence of any public stocks of major farm commodities. A reassessment of these agricultural and commodity policies that pays proper attention to their inflationary costs could brighten the prospects for the future. More generally, the current undervaluation of the dollar in foreign exchange markets is benefiting our trade surplus, but clearly harming our price performance. A higher exchange rate for the dollar would, to be sure, cost some jobs in export industries, but could well enhance the disciplinary effect of foreign competition on domestic prices and thus provide the needed elbow room for pursuing more ambitious overall employment goals. Judging from the experience of 1973–74 when devaluation permitted U.S. firms to widen their profit margins because they had so much less to fear from foreign competitors, net exports may be the most inflationary component of our GNP.

Wage-price restraints. Despite enormous slack in product and labor markets, prices and wages are rising rapidly in 1976 because they have been rising in the past. It is the heritage of past inflation that keeps inflation churning. Under these circumstances, both business and labor are on a treadmill that they cannot get off through their own initiative. Every group of workers must try to protect itself with larger wage increases, and every business firm must act in self-defense and try to pass its cost increases on to its customers. Yet, if there were some way by which all workers and all firms could agree to raise all prices and wages, say, 3 percentage points less than they otherwise would, everybody would be better off—with less inflation, more jobs, and more real income and output. This is a classical type of situation that cries out for cooperative collective action. It is like the guntoting Western frontier town, where no one could afford to disarm unilaterally, but where the collective political process provided a means to achieve personal security—a sacrifice of the freedom to tote guns in return for the reduced risk of getting shot. The inflationary firearms toted by American businessmen and workers in recent years have caused a lot of accidental bloodshed, and bilateral disarmament could serve their mutual interests.

Ideally, a government wage-price policy would achieve a parallel reduction in prices and wages below what they would otherwise be, thus not distorting the structure of relative prices and wages or the basic distribution of income. Obviously, such a perfectly "neutral" wage-price policy is not feasible. The record of Phase III and Phase IV mandatory controls in 1973 and early 1974 reduced the political acceptability of all types of wage-price measures. In retrospect, the Nixon controls were overly ambitious, overly rigid, and badly administered. But they do demonstrate the inherent difficulties of comprehensive price controls, which were fully recognized during the 1960s and which explained Ackley's and my opposition to controls even during the Vietnam War. The recent lessons underline the attractiveness of more informal and more flexible policies of government-business-labor cooperation, like the Kennedy-Johnson guideposts.

Under the circumstances which prevailed in 1976, a guidepost approach could be particularly effective. Suppose that after full consultation (although not necessarily full agreement) with business and labor, the President and the Congress established on a bipartisan basis a 6.5 percent guidepost for wage increases in 1976, along with a price guidepost that limited price increases to the pass-through of costs, with no margin widening. Even without any mandatory or statutory provisions behind these standards, the 6.5 percent wage guidepost would in my judgment, become an effective ceiling in the current labor market, just as a 5.5 percent standard under Phase II required virtually no enforcement in 1972.

In 1976 employers are raising wages rapidly mainly because other employers are also doing so; they feel obliged to treat their workers "equitably" to maintain morale and productivity and to hold down quit rates in the next period of prosperity. Once the government standard ensures that other employers will be limiting their wage increases, each individual employer is taken off the hook and happy to enforce the standard in a weak labor market. Moreover, every acceleration and deceleration in wages reliably shows up in a commensurate movement of prices after a very short lag. That statistical finding has stood up consistently through time in contrast with the reverse finding that what happens to prices is not reflected in wages on a one-for-one basis. Hence, if the standard forecast for 1976 of 8.5 percent for wage increases and

6 percent for price increases is correct, the hypothetical guidepost program could be expected to bring the inflation rate down to 4 percent by the end of 1976—not by the end of the decade after years of enormous slack, as the Ford Administration projects. Moreover, in the hypothetical world, if that program were successful during 1976, it could be repeated during 1977 with the targets lowered to perhaps 5 percent for wage increases and no more than 2.5 percent for inflation.

Clearly, the wage-guidepost side of this program would have more teeth through employer enforcement than would the price guidepost through any actions of the government. Understandably, political decision makers might be concerned that, despite the econometrician's conviction that labor costs show up one-for-one in prices, such a program might redistribute income away from workers and toward employers. I have previously suggested that such a concern could be appropriately met by contingent tax legislation that essentially provided "real wage insurance."[44] That legislation would provide that, if the consumer price index rises more than the target rate (say, 4 percent) during 1976, a tax credit on 1976 income payments would be activated for any worker with income under (say) $15,000, with the rate of tax credit set at the excess of any increases in the consumer price index above 4 percent. That tax credit would appear on tax returns for 1976 to be filed early in 1977; it would apply to the whole of wage and salary income up to the ceiling and not just to the part subjected to the income tax. For example, if the consumer price index rose 6 percent (rather than 4) during 1976, a $10,000 income worker would get back $200 through the tax credit.

With such a commitment from the government, workers could have confidence that the Executive Branch would do its utmost to meet the target, both to avoid the large drain on the Treasury that would accompany failure, and to pave the way for renewal of the program at an even lower inflation target for 1977. Meanwhile, the prospect of a significant deceleration in inflation would enable us to raise our sights on the vigor of the recovery and on manpower training and other routes to job creation.

Guideposts and real wage insurance are examples of the many items on the menu for a social compact to attain wage and price restraint equitably. As I see it, a happy ending to the stagflation story *must* involve some incomes-policy or social-compact arrangement. The experience of the last decade has demonstrated that our price and wage making institutions are prone to inflation, and our public is strongly adverse to it. The realistic alternative to wage-price restraint is prolonged high unemployment where long lines of applicants for jobs supply a costly and unreliable insurance policy against accelerating inflation. As I stated earlier in this paper, with no new arrangements to improve the price and wage performance of this economy, I would regard an unemployment target below 5.5 percent as unrealistic and imprudent. But if we can eliminate our inflationary bias and background, we can raise our sights. With the development of an effective wage-price policy, and with the support of measures to improve manpower training, promote competition, and take proper account of the direct price effects of a variety of public measures, I would be far more optimistic. I would personally bet that an unemployment target of 4 percent could be made feasible by 1980—although I would urge any public official not to commit himself to such an ambitious target until the policies are tested by experience.

Notes

1. Walter W. Heller, *New Dimensions of Political Economy* (Harvard University Press, 1966), p. 64.

2. *Economic Report of the President* together with the *Annual Report of the Council of Economic Advisers, January 1962*, p. 47. Hereafter these documents are referred to either as *Economic Report* or *CEA Annual Report* followed by the year.

3. *Ibid.*, p. 48.

4. *Public Papers of the President of the United States: Dwight D. Eisenhower, 1959* (1960), p. 12.

5. Heller, *New Dimensions*, p. 33.

6. *CEA Annual Report, 1962*, pp. 78–84.

7. Heller, *New Dimensions*, pp. 38–39.

8. See Charles L. Schultze, *Recent Inflation in the United States*, Study Paper No. 1 of materials prepared in connection with the Study of Employment, Growth, and Price Levels for consideration by the Joint Economic Committee, 86th Congress, 1st session (1969), pp. 44–77. The quote is from *CEA Annual Report, 1962*, p. 47.

9. *Ibid.*, p. 171.

10. *Ibid.*, p. 185.

11. *Ibid.*

12. *Ibid.*, p. 189.

13. See William J. Barber, "The Kennedy Years: Purposeful Pedagogy" in Craufurd D. Goodwin, ed., *Exhortation and Controls* (Brookings Institution, 1974), pp. 135–91.

14. See, for example, John Sheahan, *The Wage-Price Guideposts* (Brookings Institution, 1967), esp. pp. 79–95; George L. Perry, "Wages and the Guideposts,"

American Economic Review, vol. 57 (September 1967), pp. 897–904; comments by Paul S. Anderson, Michael L. Wachter, and Adrian W. Throop, and reply by Perry, *American Economic Review*, vol. 59 (June 1969), pp. 351–70; Otto Eckstein, "Money Wage Determination Revisited," *Review of Economic Studies*, vol. 35 (April 1968), 133–43; and Robert M. Solow, "The Wage-Price Issue and the Guideposts," in Frederick H. Harbison and Joseph D. Mooney, eds., *Critical Issues in Employment Policy*, A Report of the Princeton Manpower Symposium, May 12–13, 1966 (Princeton University, 1966), pp. 57–73.

15. See Arthur M. Okun, *The Political Economy of Prosperity* (Brookings Institution, 1970), pp. 62–99.

16. See James L. Cochrane, "The Johnson Administration: Moral Suasion Goes to War" in *Exhortation and Controls*, pp. 193–298.

17. See Arthur M. Okun, "Inflation: The Problems and Prospects before Us," in Arthur M. Okun, Henry H. Fowler, and Milton Gilbert, *Inflation: The Problems It Creates and the Policies It Requires* (New York University Press, 1970), pp. 43–53.

18. W. W. Rostow, *The Diffusion of Power* (Macmillan, 1972), pp. 321–323.

19. *CEA Annual Report, 1962*, p. 162.

20. Heller, *New Dimensions*, p. 75.

21. Walter S. Salant and others, *The United States Balance of Payments in 1968*, materials presented by the Brookings Institution to the Joint Economic Committee for consideration in connection with its Study of the United States Balance of Payments, 88th Congress, 1st Session (1963), pp. 21–23.

22. See Paul W. McCracken, "The U.S. Balance of Payments Problem and Domestic Prosperity," in Paul W. McCracken and Emile Benoit, *The Balance of Payments and Domestic Prosperity*, Michigan International Business Studies, 1 (University of Michigan, 1963).

23. Robert Theobold, "Abundance: Threat or Promise?" *The Nation*, May 11, 1963, p. 394.

24. See Charles C. Killingsworth, "The Bottleneck in Labor Skills," in Arthur M. Okun, ed., *The Battle against Unemployment* (Norton, 1965).

25. Council of Economic Advisers, "The American Economy in 1961: Problems and Policies," in *January 1961 Economic Report of the President and the Economic Situation and Outlook*, Hearings before the Joint Economic Committee, 87th Congress, 1st session (1961), Supplement B, p. 378.

26. Joint Economic Committee, Subcommittee on Economic Statistics, *Higher Unemployment Rates, 1957–60: Structural Transformation or Inadequate Demands*, 87th Congress, 1st session (1961).

27. *CEA Annual Report, 1964*, Appendix A.

28. Arthur M. Okun, "The Role of Aggregate Demand in Alleviating Unemployment," in William G. Bowen and Frederick H. Harbison, eds., *Unemployment in a Prosperous Economy*, A Report of the Princeton Manpower Symposium May 13–14, 1965 (Princeton University, 1965).

29. *Ibid.*, pp. 75–76.

30. Council of Economic Advisers, "American Economy in 1961," p. 382.

31. *CEA Annual Report, 1962*, pp. 92–95.

32. Gardner Ackley, "Vandeveer Memorial Lecture," delivered at Southern Illinois University, Carbondale, Illinois, October 26, 1966 (processed).

33. *CEA Annual Report, 1967*, pp. 100–13; and *1969*, pp. 98–106.

34. *CEA Annual Report, 1969*, pp. 102–3.

35. For a more detailed discussion of the 1973–74 period, see Arthur M. Okun, "What's Wrong with the U.S. Economy? Diagnosis and Prescription," *Quarterly Review of Economics and Business*, vol. 15 (Summer 1975), pp. 21–34 (Brookings General Series, Reprint 305).

36. *The Budget of the United States Government: Fiscal Year 1977*, p. 25.

37. *Ibid.*, p. 26.

38. See Arthur M. Okun, "Inflation: Its Mechanics and Welfare Costs," *Brookings Papers on Economic Activity*, 1975, no. 2, pp. 351–90.

39. For a fuller treatment of this issue, see the views expressed in Arthur M. Okun, "The Mirage of Steady Inflation," *Brookings Papers on Economic Activity*, 1971, no. 2, pp. 485–98, and other contributions to that symposium: William Fellner, "Phillips-Type Approach or Acceleration?" pp. 469–83; and Robert J. Gordon, "Steady Anticipated Inflation: Mirage or Oasis?" pp. 499–510.

40. *Gallup Opinion Index*, Report No. 125 (November-December 1975), p. 93.

41. Okun, "Role of Aggregate Demand," p. 80.

42. "Manpower Training: Boon, Not Boondoggle," *Challenge*, vol. 16 (September/October 1973), p. 56.

43. For a description of the proposed changes in government regulations, see Thomas G. Moore, "A Program to Ease Price Pressure," in "The Economists' Conference on Inflation: Report," vol. 1 (1974; processed), pp. 325–335. A listing of the economists who endorsed the proposals appears in *Ibid.*, pp. 11–13.

44. Arthur M. Okun, "Incomes Inflation and the Policy Alternatives," in *Ibid.*, pp. 369–70.

IV FISCAL AND MONETARY POLICY

Monetary Policy, Debt Management and Interest Rates: A Quantitative Appraisal

Introduction

Discussions appraising the effectiveness of monetary policy in recent years have been frequent, intense, and illuminating; but they have rarely been quantitative. It is the purpose of this paper to advance quantitative measures of the effect of monetary and debt-management actions on interest rates. The numerical estimates advanced below are necessarily speculative and highly tentative. They are drawn from time-series data of the United States postwar economy and they are subject to all the limitations of statistical manipulation on highly intercorrelated and auto-correlated time-series variables. They do, however, represent a possible partial answer to the needs of monetary economists for a more specific assessment of the potentialities of monetary and debt-management instruments. Theoretical discussions can help to tell us whether curves should be drawn steep or flat: and the exponents and disparagers of the central bank's role can debate such matters to the benefit of the profession and the policy-maker. But the issues are quantitative—an appraisal of the effectiveness of monetary policy should estimate the changes in macroeconomic variables that will be achieved by central bank actions. Quantitative measures of effectiveness offer something to debate, discuss, and refine; qualitative appraisals of effectiveness may depend heavily on preferences about the definitions of the word "effective."

Monetary Policy in Keynesian Theory

The Keynesian model of short-run income determination provides a clear specification of the way in which central bank instruments affect the level of output. A change in the volume of money alters the rate of interest so as to equate the demand for cash with the supply: the change in interest affects the level of investment: the change in investment has a multiplied effect on equilibrium income. The present paper is an empirical study of the first link in this chain of effects, i.e., the relationship between money and interest. In the Keynesian model, the central bank is assumed to fix the supply of money, while the public's demand for money depends on income and interest, as expressed in the liquidity preference function. In the world of the model, a single homogeneous earning asset is available to the public as an alternative to cash. The yield required to induce the appropriate demand for the earning asset relative to zero-yielding cash depends on the supply of money relative to income. Thus, when the central bank alters the volume of money, it affects the rate of interest.

The liquidity preference function is expected to display a negative relationship between the demand for money and the rate of interest. In the *General Theory*, this negative slope is explained primarily by inelastic expectations regarding interest rates.[1] The public allegedly feels that, when bond prices are low relative to their historical averages, they are more likely to rise and less likely to fall farther. Thus, when bond yields are high, the chance that interest returns will be canceled by capital losses appears smaller, and bonds are more attractive. Tobin has shown that aversion to capital-value risk is sufficient to account for a negatively-sloped liquidity preference function, even if there are no expected capital gains or losses.[2] A higher yield on bonds compensates the investor for taking greater risk in holding an expanded volume of bonds. The rate of interest on a financial claim equates the attractiveness, on the margin, of safe zero-yield cash and the risky earning asset as portfolio components. When monetary policy alters the relative supplies of the earning asset and of cash, the equilibrium yield on the earning asset is changed. Furthermore, when income rises while the supply of cash is constant, more money is demanded for transactions purposes, and the interest rate must increase to maintain the required demand for earning assets.

This theoretical world supplies an instructive approximation to reality, and it is amenable to empirical verification. The rate of interest, according to liquidity preference theory, should be positively related to the level of income and negatively related to the supply of money. These hypotheses have been tested statistically any number of times and they have been confirmed.[3] There is no need for a further test of the qualitative relationships: if one found opposite results at this stage, suspicion would be cast on his empirical procedures rather than on the theory. The quantification of the relationships, however, deserves much additional study. For this purpose, the simple theoretical world is not so easily translated into operational terms. It must be adapted in a number of ways to yield estimates of relevant magnitudes.

Federal Reserve and Treasury Actions

In the first place, the institutional factors governing public control of the monetary system must be duly recognized. In the theoretical world, the central bank simply and directly controls the supply of money. In reality, public control over the volume of money is imperfect and indirect. The Federal Reserve System and the Treasury have particular instruments of monetary and debt policy at their disposal. These actions have complex effects on balance sheets. A review of these actions can assist the construction of an appropriate empirical framework for the evaluation of monetary policy instruments as determinants of interest rates.

When the Federal Reserve System purchases Government securities on the open market, it reduces the volume of interest-bearing federal debt held by the private sector and increases the volume of zero-yielding demand obligations (deposits in the Federal Reserve and currency) of the government. This exchange of demand obligations for marketable term securities will normally increase the volume of money in the community. The maximum potential increase in money is easily calculated as the amount of the open-market purchase divided by the percentage reserve requirement on the demand deposits of member banks. But the actual increase may differ substantially from the maximum potential: any induced rise in currency holdings of the public, any increase in excess reserves of commercial banks, any induced reduction in member bank borrowing from the Federal Reserve will make the actual fall short of the maximum. The resulting increase in money is the outcome of private actions and is not subject directly to control by public authority.

Another important instrument of Federal Reserve policy is the setting of the required reserve ratio for deposits of member banks. Changes in reserve requirements have no direct impact on the balance sheets of economic units. They alter the volume of demand deposit liabilities that can be supported by a given quantity of member bank reserves. When the Federal Reserve lowers reserve requirements, there is a determinate possible maximum increase in the supply of money. As in the case of open-market transactions, the actual expansion is likely to differ from the potential, as banks and their customers make choices which are not directly subject to Federal Reserve control.

The discount rate is the cost to member banks of borrowing from the Federal Reserve. Changes in the discount rate induce movements in the volume of member bank reserves to the extent that the amount of borrowing changes. Again, the commercial banks, rather than the central bank, determine the resulting alteration in the stock of money.

The Federal Reserve may also alter the composition of its security-holdings by selling Government obligations of a given maturity and simultaneously purchasing an equal volume of bonds of a different maturity. In this case, there is a change in the term structure of the federal debt held in the private sector. Investors are induced to trade one type of Government obligation for another.

The debt-management actions of the Treasury have effects on balance sheets which are identical to the pair of Federal Reserve open-market transactions described above. When the Treasury retires one type of outstanding security at maturity and issues a new security in equal volume, it lengthens the term structure of the federal debt. The private sector holds an unchanged volume of federal interest-bearing obligations, but the disappearance of the old issue and the sale of the new one alters relative supplies of debt of different lengths. The mere passage of time shortens the debt in the absence of Treasury action.

The concept of debt management is usually applied to the handling of the maturity structure (and other characteristics) of a public debt of given size. It is thus distinguished from fiscal policy which may involve a change in the magnitude of the public debt over time through surplus or deficit operations. Fiscal actions do have distinct balance-sheet effects which are relevant to the determination of interest rates. If the Treasury markets additional new securities to the private sector with the intention of financing a deficit, the sale immediately raises private holdings of federal interest-bearing securities. It simultaneously lowers, by an equal amount, private holdings of federal demand obligations, since payment for the bonds reduces the volume of Federal Reserve deposits of member banks and currency. As the Treasury spends the proceeds of the borrowings the volume of member bank deposits and currency is restored. Treasury deficit-financing, like a Federal Reserve open-market sale, expands the volume of interest-bearing obligations held by the public. But while the Federal Reserve trades bonds for money, the Treasury, in effect, makes payments to the public with bonds, thus increasing the volume of government liabilities to the private sector. Treasury surplus-financing has opposite effects.

The open-market operations of the Federal Reserve and the debt management operations of the Treasury alter the composition of federal debts to the public. In principle, actions undertaken which have the same balance-sheet effects on the private sector can be viewed as identical whether they are carried out by the Treasury or by the Federal Reserve. The market has little reason to care whether a billion dollars of extra bonds are being offered by the Treasury or the central bank. The market does have every reason to try to anticipate future moves of the Treasury and the Federal Reserve. For this reason, there may be instances where a relatively small move by either agency could be given great significance as a harbinger of future actions. The quantitative effect of any transaction on interest rates may be ultimately dependent on how much it surprises the market and how it alters expectations. However, the effects on expectations are likely to be complicated and to depend on the specific circumstances surrounding each policy decision: they cannot be adequately handled by lumping actions of the Federal Reserve together and separately combining all actions undertaken by the Treasury. Consolidation of the Federal Reserve and the Treasury appears to be the optimal strategy for evaluating monetary and debt policy.

The combined debts of the Federal Reserve and the Treasury to the public consist of non-interest-bearing demand obligations and interest-bearing dated obligations. The former category consists of cash assets: the components are Treasury and Federal Reserve currency held outside the federal government, and deposits of member banks and others (excluding the Treasury) in Federal Reserve banks. These cash obligations of the government are designated as federal demand debt. Federal demand debt is the foundation of the money supply—the currency items are themselves money, while the deposits in the Federal Reserve are the basis for the creation of demand deposits by the commercial banks. Open-market operations change the supply of demand debt and the supply of interest-bearing debt in opposite directions by equal amounts. Changes in reserve requirements may be viewed as shifting commercial bank demand functions for federal demand debt. Changes in the discount rate alter the price at which commercial banks can directly acquire federal demand debt by borrowing from the Federal Reserve. Treasury debt actions (and Federal Reserve open-market "swaps") alter the maturity composition of federal interest-bearing debt. Treasury surplus or deficit financing acts to alter the volume of federal interest-bearing debt.

The monetary authorities have direct control over the volume of private holdings of interest-bearing federal debt; because of member bank borrowing, they have less complete control over the quantity of demand debt; they have only imperfect and indirect control over the volume of money. The indirect route by which policy actions affect the money supply raises a problem of strategy in the explanation of how these actions influence interest rates. A quantitative explanation of interest rates that employs components of private balance sheets as independent variables does not provide a direct estimate of the way interest rates are affected by particular policy actions. Another quantitative link is needed to relate the private balance sheet items to the variables under policy control. E.g., suppose the reduction in interest per billion dollar increase in the money supply is known; then the determination of the effect on interest of open-market purchase of $1 billion requires the further knowledge of how large an increase in the stock of money is induced by the purchase. A two-stage explanation emerges, running from policy action to private liquidity and then from private asset-holdings to interest rates. An alternative approach would seek to consolidate the two steps and relate interest rates to variables directly under public control, ignoring the money supply and other balance sheet items that are not completely controlled by public authority. The choice between these approaches will be discussed below.

The Multiplicity of Financial Assets

The existence of a large variety of heterogeneous earning assets constitutes another important difference in reality from the world of the simple Keynesian model. All of the yields reported on the financial pages of the press are candidates for explanation. Presumably their yields are all interdependent and dependent on the supplies of each type of asset. In principle, this difficulty can be met. The liquidity preference function can be generalized into a set of demand curves for financial assets. Cash, bonds of various types, and equities compete for their shares in the portfolios of investors. Some pairs of these alternative securities are clearly close substitutes, and one would expect a change in the supply of one type to have substantial cross-effects on the yield of the other. In general, the demand for any type of asset can be expressed as a function of: (a) Income; (b) Wealth; (c) Its own yield; and (d) The yield of related assets. From such a system, one could determine the yield of each asset from formation on the supplies of all assets and the level of income. Similarly, for given changes in the supply of any asset, changes in yields could be estimated for all assets.

While the procedure can be readily described, the empirical formulation and estimation of such a general equilibrium system of financial markets is a huge task. It is far beyond the scope of this paper. Certainly, everything depends on everything else in financial markets. However, progress can be made by focussing on a small set of key variables. Yields on marketable obligations of the federal government stand out as worthy of particular attention. In dollar volume, federal debt is far greater than any other single type of marketable claim in the postwar American economy. Furthermore, monetary policy deals in federal debts to achieve its objectives. All federal security issues share the exclusive property of being absolutely free of default risk; since the United States Government can print money, it can always meet its legal obligations to redeem matured securities for currency. Interest-bearing marketable claims on the Treasury differ among themselves only by having individual maturity dates. The interest rates on three-month Treasury bills and on long-term federal bonds stand at extreme ends of the maturity spectrum for Governments. The principal emphasis of this paper will be on these two interest rates.

Claims against private borrowers differ in degree of default risk from one another and from Governments. The differential in yield between any one of them and a Government obligation of equal maturity will vary as the compensation required for assuming default risk is consistently revalued in financial markets. Despite the varying differentials, it will be shown below that the explanation of government yields accounts for the major portion of the variation in private yields as well.

The simple Keynesian theoretical model suggests that the yields on Governments should be related to the stock of money and the level of income. The general equilibrium view of financial markets suggests that the stocks of all other financial assets should be considered as possible determinants of the interest rates on federal debt. The approach adopted here is an intermediate one. There are strong *a priori* reasons for believing that the size and composition of the federal debt will have considerable influence on Treasury bond and bill yields; these supplies are therefore used as explanatory variables for the selected interest rates. On the other hand, the magnitudes outstanding of particular types of private obligations are excluded. These are potential substitutes for Governments and may well affect the government rate: an autonomous change which doubled the supply of corporate AAA bonds would be expected to raise government long-term yields. However, the volume of private assets is considered in this paper only by the inclusion of total private wealth as a possible explanatory variable. Thus, income, the supply of money, the volume and composition of federal debt, and total wealth are the tentative explanatory variables for government interest rates. Other possible influences will be discussed subsequently.

Interest Rates and Maturity

The dependence of long and short rates on the term structure of the federal debt follows from theoretical reasoning. Only if bills and bonds could be viewed as perfect substitutes would their yields be independent of their relative supplies. In a world of perfect foresight, no investment costs, and complete shiftability, the long rate would be purely an average of future short-term rates;[4] arbitrage would guarantee that the two rates could not be affected by changes in the term structure of the public debt. Any modification of these extreme assumptions will, however, provide a role to the composition of debt.

Suppose that foresight is not perfect but that investors are risk-neutral and thus act purely to maximize expected return. Then each investor chooses between long and short securities by balancing the expected return on long bonds against the expected return on bills. If the relevant period is taken as the three-month lifetime of bills, the expected short yield is certain: it is simply the market interest rate on bills. The expected return on bonds, however, differs from the market interest rate by any expected capital gain on bonds over the three-month interval. People anticipating a rise in the long rate must deduct an expected capital loss in their estimates of the return from long securities. On the other hand, those investors who anticipate a decline in long rates will have expected returns greater than the current market long rate. The equilibrium market differential will then, in general, depend on the relative supplies of longs and shorts. On Chart 1, investors are ordered according to the size of their expected capital gain (or loss) on bonds, expressed as a percentage per year. Those with the largest expected capital gain are farthest to the left; each investor is weighted by the magnitude of his demand for longs and shorts combined. The horizontal axis is scaled as fractions of the

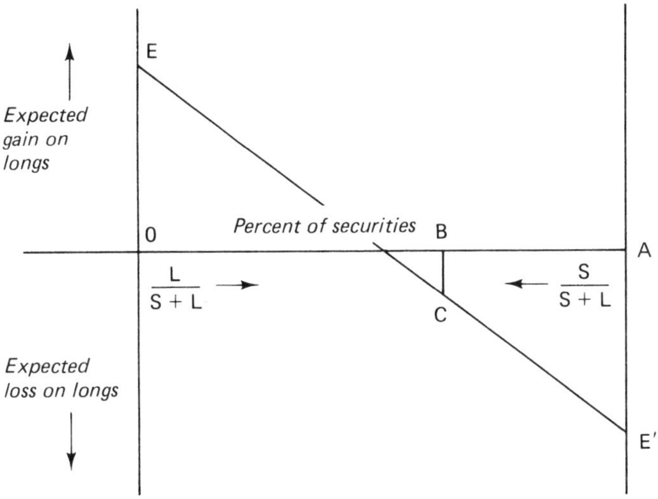

Chart 1

total outstanding supply of long plus short securities with the distance *OA* representing 100 percent. Given the expected gain curve *EE′*, if the outstanding securities are split into *OB* percent of longs and *BA* percent of shorts, the equilibrium market long rate must exceed the short rate by *BC*, just enough to offset the expected capital loss of the marginal long investor. People on the *EC* portion of the expectation curve will hold longs while those along *CE′* hold shorts. If the long-term fraction of the total security supply exceeded *OB* while the *EE′* curve was unchanged, a larger rate differential would be required. A smaller relative supply of longs would be associated with a smaller excess of the long rate over the short rate. The slope of the *EE′* curve depends on the extent to which investors differ in their estimates of future long rates. The greater the unanimity of opinion, the smaller the influence of relative supplies on the rate structure. So long as there are different views, even in the world of no risk-aversion and no investment costs, relative supplies do matter.

Once attitudes towards risk and costs of transactions are considered, additional reasons are found for the dependence of rates on relative supplies. At equal expected returns, longs and shorts would not be equally attractive to every investor; furthermore, individual investors might well choose to mix longs and shorts in their portfolios. Because a bill is always close to its maturity date, the price of a short security is unlikely to vary substantially; the bill offers little danger of capital loss and slight hope of capital gain. Capital-value risk is thus small for a bill but large for a long security. To a risk-averting investor, this would be a feature favoring the holding of short-term securities. On the other hand, an investor who continually held short securities would incur large transactions costs as he was forced to reinvest his proceeds each time his short holdings matured; the economy of investment costs favors the holding of long-term securities. Furthermore, each time the investor acquired a new crop of shorts, he would be subject to the whims of the market. At any point in time, he would be assured of the level of his interest income for only a brief interval in the future. The short portfolio has substantial *income risk*.[5] The holder of longs gains assurance of a steady flow of interest income over the long run by sacrificing safety on the market value of his portfolio in the near future. The security-holder who is able to stay with his holdings for a long period is thus encouraged to go into bonds. Hence, long-term securities typically are preponderant in the portfolios of universities and insurance companies. Because of their many differing features, short and long securities should be viewed as imperfect though close substitutes like tea and coffee; they are not well conceived of as perfect substitutes like nickels and dimes. Theoretical reasoning suggests that relative supplies will affect relative yields; only quantitative empirical research can determine how much of an effect will exist.

The Empirical Framework

The following decisions of strategy emerge from the discussion above:

1. The market yields of Treasury bills and of long-term Government bonds are the two key dependent variables to be investigated.
2. The balance sheets of the Treasury and the Federal Reserve System are to be consolidated; all other economic units are aggregated into a single private sector.
3. The volume and composition of the interest-bearing federal debt should be treated as possible determinants of the yields on Governments.
4. Measures of income and wealth will also be included as potential explanatory variables.
5. Some measure of money supply is required as an explanatory variable. If the traditional notion of demand deposits plus currency is employed,

a further link is needed to relate money to policy variables. Alternatively, use could be made of some measure of money supply directly controlled by public authorities.

Certain of these decisions require further implementation. The volume of federal interest-bearing debt is taken as the dollar maturity value of marketable issues held outside of government agencies and the Federal Reserve. (Savings bonds are thus omitted.) This total is divided into three categories:

S Issues maturing within one year
I Issues maturing in one to five years
L Issues maturing in five years or more

The classification depends only on the distance of a security to its maturity date at the particular point in time considered. It does not consider the original length-to-maturity of an existing issue. A bond may have a fifteen-year term when it is originally sold by the Treasury, but fourteen years later it is a short-term one-year obligation and presumably will be so evaluated in the market. Call provisions are uniformly ignored: the procedure which takes the term of an issue to run only to its call date when its price exceeds par is rejected because it makes maturity dependent on bond prices.

The principal limitation to this (or any other) categorization procedure is that it produces abrupt changes in the classes at discrete points in time. The aging of bonds is continuous: a bond changes character gradually when it moves toward its maturity date from 61 months away to 60 months and then to 59 months. But these two movements are reflected very differently in the data. As a 60-month issue, the security remains in the long category; at 59 months, it shifts into the intermediate class. A mean maturity variable (T) for the long category is introduced to mitigate this problem. The T variable expresses the mean length to maturity of all obligations with maturity dates 60 or more months away. Thus, when a security falls into the intermediate class with the passage of time, the reduced volume of the L group is potentially offset by the rise in T. Obviously, the mean maturity of the long category is increased by the disappearance of a 60-month issue from that class.

The income variable is designed to reflect private transactions demand for liquidity. Since government needs for cash balances should not be included, there is an argument for omitting government outlays from

Gross National Product. However, government purchases from business require transactions balances in the private sector. For this reason, the income variable selected is Gross Private Product (GNP less compensation of government employees). Since state and local governments are part of the "private sector," the logic would argue that only federal compensation to employees should be deducted, but the quarterly data do not permit this distinction to be made.

The wealth variable is Net Private Wealth. It differs from National Wealth by including all government liabilities and excluding all assets of the government. This is the same wealth variable relevant to the Pigou effect; it is sometimes designated Patinkin wealth.[6]

The data employed are quarterly observations for the period 1946–59. All stocks are measured at the end of the quarter. The Bill Rate is taken as the yield on newly-issued Treasury three-month bills during the last month of the quarter; the long rate is the average yield to maturity for the last month of the quarter on a group of long-term Government bonds due in more than ten years. The bonds included in the long-term rate index change occasionally, and the maturity length of the sample covered is not held constant; however, since all the components of the sample are very long issues, the variation in maturity does not seem important.

The functional forms by which interest rates are explained are all linear. There are strong reasons to believe that non-linearities will exist; the Keynesian liquidity preference function is usually drawn convex to the origin. It seemed that the most convenient way to introduce non-linearity was to transform the dependent variable from r to the reciprocal of r or to $(r + \text{constant})^{-1}$. The independent variables would then remain in linear form. However, experimentation with such transformations of the interest variables produced discouraging results and led to the decision to restrict the regression equations to linear forms. Thus, the equations explaining the long rate (r) and the bill rate (b) take the following form:

$$r(\text{or } b) = a_0 + a_1 \cdot \text{Money} + a_2 \cdot S + a_3 I + a_4 L + a_5 T + a_6 Y + a_7 W \tag{1}$$

An alternative approach assumes that interest rates are homogeneous of degree zero in all stocks and income: a doubling of income, wealth, all types of federal debt, and money would be expected to leave rates unaffected. This hypothesis leads to equations of the following type:

$$r(\text{or } b) = c_0 + c_1 \frac{\text{Money}}{Y} + c_2 \frac{S}{Y} + c_3 \frac{I}{Y} + c_4 \frac{L}{Y} + c_5 T + c_6 \frac{W}{Y} \quad (2)$$

The variables S, I, L are the three categories of federal debt, while T is the maturity variable: Y and W represent income and wealth, as defined above. The money variable has not yet been defined. An obvious choice is the conventional definition of money, namely demand deposits adjusted plus currency outside of banks. An alternative choice was suggested by Gurley's study of liquidity in the postwar period.[7] There, Gurley explains interest rates by the volume of all liquid assets, appropriately weighted, in relationship to income. He argues that the demand for money may be reduced by expansion of the supply of non-monetary liquid assets; therefore the traditional liquidity preference function should be generalized to include money-substitutes. Interest rates are determined by the supply of liquidity relative to income, as in the original Keynesian view; but, according to Gurley, liquidity must be measured as a weighted total of all liquid assets, not merely media of exchange. The resulting view of the liquidity function is that the rate of interest depends on the volume of all liquid assets, appropriately weighted in relation to the level of income.

Liquid assets are defined as "claims held by nonfinancial sectors of the economy that are ... fixed in price and redeemable into money on demand."[8] Gurley adopts a weight for all non-monetary liquid assets (N) equal to one-half the weight for money (M'), where money is given its usual meaning of adjusted demand deposits plus currency. The measure of aggregate liquidity is thus $Q = M' + (N/2)$, and the aggregate liquidity-income ratio is taken as the ratio of Q to Gross National Product (Y_g). Gurley's empirical support for his thesis rests on the close negative relationship found between Q/Y_g and the interest rate in annual postwar United States data. The relationship holds for both the yield on corporate BAA bonds and the prime commercial paper rate.

Empirical explorations with the Gurley liquidity ratio were disappointing, however. In the quarterly data for 1946–59, the ratio of money to income (M'/Y_g) provides a better explanation of both the long government rate and the Bill Rate than the ratio Q/Y_g. The addition of one-half the volume of non-monetary liquid assets worsens the fit. Calculated results for the long rate are:

$$r = -5.3Q/Y_g + 6.4; \qquad R^2 = .56 \quad (3)$$

$$r = -7.4M'/Y_g + 5.5; \qquad R^2 = .66 \tag{4}$$

For the short rate, the findings are:

$$b = -9.6Q/Y_g + 8.3; \qquad R^2 = .60 \tag{5}$$

$$b = -12.7M'/Y_g + 6.4; \qquad R^2 = .62 \tag{6}$$

When the ratio of non-monetary liquid assets to income (N/Y_g) is used as a second independent variable with M'/Y_g to explain r and b, positive coefficients surprisingly emerge for N/Y_g: the implication is that, for any given M'/Y_g, interest rates will be higher for higher N/Y_g. There is no obvious reason why an expansion of non-monetary liquid assets should raise interest rates. It could mean that N responds to the strength of demand for money—money-substitutes increase in volume when liquidity preference is particularly strong. Alternatively, it might be a spurious result: the positive coefficient is statistically significant only in the equation for r. In any case, these data give no support to the view that the rapid postwar growth of non-monetary liquid assets has held down interest rates. On these grounds, the volume of non-monetary liquid assets was discarded as a potential explanatory variable.

In addition to the conventional definition of money, consideration was given to other candidates for the money variable that are more directly controlled by public policy. The discussion above enumerated the various possible slippages between a central bank action and the resulting change in the supply of money. There is only one open link in the Federal Reserve's control over the volume of demand debt; that lies in possible changes in member bank borrowing from the Federal Reserve. Subject to its ability to offset autonomous fluctuations in borrowings, the monetary authority can regulate the volume of federal demand debt. On these grounds, one can take the volume of demand debt (M) in relation to the required reserve ratio (R) as a measure of the money supply permitted by the central bank. If there were no currency and no excess reserves and if all demand debt were utilized to back demand deposits of the private sector, the money supply would be M/R. This volume of money is a *maximum maximorum* relative to the government balance sheet. The actual supply will never reach M/R, but that magnitude can serve as one measure of potential money. Furthermore, if given fractions of demand debt were absorbed by excess reserves, currency, foreign deposits in the Federal Reserve, and backing against time deposits, it could still be argued that fluctuations in M/R were associated with proportionate changes in the volume of demand deposits. The M/R variable would be a good gauge of the conditions under which the monetary authority allowed commercial banks to create demand deposits for their customers.

The data suggests that currency has absorbed a variable proportion of demand debt over time in the postwar period. On these grounds, it may be preferable to view the demand for currency as exogenous, and to treat $(M - C)/R$ as potential demand deposits. Here, the actual volume of currency (rather than a zero volume) is taken as a benchmark; and potential demand deposits are viewed as the portion of demand debt which is not absorbed in currency divided by the required reserve ratio. The concept of potential money which then emerges is the sum of potential demand deposits plus actual currency or $[(M - C)/R] + C$. Here, currency includes holdings of commercial banks since these absorb federal demand debt. In measuring M', currency in commercial banks is excluded.

Results are reported below with the money variable defined in three ways:

1. Currency plus demand deposits, i.e., the actual stock of money;
2. Demand debt divided by the required reserve ratio, i.e., maximum potential money;
3. Potential deposits plus actual currency, where potential deposits equal demand debt exclusive of currency divided by the required reserve ratio.

It was pointed out above that income could reasonably be treated as a separate independent variable, as in equation (1); or as a divisor of all the stock variables, as in equation (2). Empirical findings strongly suggest the use of the separate treatment. When the divided-through form was used, the reciprocal of income was highly significant statistically as an additional variable, carrying a negative coefficient. This led to the rejection of the homogeneity hypothesis. It implies that a doubling of income and of all stocks will affect interest rates; they are raised by this event. It is not clear why this should be the case—if anything, economies of scale in the handling of cash-balances lead to the possibility that rates would be reduced by an equiproportionate increase in income and all assets. The empirical results here imply the opposite behavior of interest rates. The assumption of homogeneity does not stand up empirically, and equation (2) is therefore the form adopted. An alternative possibility involves using the divided form, as in equation (1), with the addition of another independent variable, $1/Y$. While this form differs from equation (2) only slightly, it does not fit so well.

Further empirical experimentation showed that the wealth variable produced insignificant results. It was expected that the coefficient of wealth would be negative: larger wealth totals for given supplies of money and Government securities mean that claims on the federal government are a smaller fraction of private net worth. As such, a lower yield should be required to induce the holding of this volume of government debt. In general, the expanded size of portfolios has a wealth effect which should raise the demand for Governments and thus reduce their yield. The wealth variable, however, offered no assistance whatsoever in explaining the long rate. It did consistently have a negative coefficient in various formulations explaining the Bill Rate, but the coefficient was never as large as twice its standard error. Because it could not meet conventional criteria for statistical significance, the wealth variable was dropped. Theoretically, it is a relevant variable. Its failure may be attributable to a number of factors. Wealth is highly correlated with income, for one thing. Secondly, the empirical formulation does not consider the changing composition of wealth, which may overshadow the growth of the total.

The three-way categorization of federal interest-bearing marketable debt (S, I, and L) also ran into difficulties. The coefficient of I (one- to five-year intermediate-term issues) proved quite unstable with respect to the choices of functional form and auxiliary variables. In certain cases, it exceeded substantially the coefficients of both S and L: in others, it was the smallest of the three by far. Much more reasonable and more stable results were obtained when I was combined with S to form just two categories of federal debt: $(S + I)$ represents those issues maturing within five years, and L is the category of those having five or more years to run. The judgment was therefore made to present all results in terms of this two-way classification.

Because of varying seasonal demands for liquidity combined with stock variables that are not seasonally adjusted, suspicion arose that a seasonal factor would distort the regression equations. Tests showed that this suspicion was well-founded in the case of the Bill Rate, but not for the long rate. Consequently, a quarterly seasonal dummy variable was inserted into all equations explaining the Bill Rate. In effect, there is a separate intercept for each quarter of the year. In the first quarter, $Q_1 = 1$ while Q_2 and Q_3 are set equal to zero. In the second quarter, Q_2 alone has

Table 1 Alternative equations explaining bond and bill yields

	Dependent variable	Type of money variable	Coefficients										
			"Money"	$S+I$	L	T	Y	Constant	Q_1	Q_2	Q_3	R^2	σ_u
(7)	r	M'	−.0072	+.0159	+.0138	+.0047	+.0091	−1.92	—	—	—		
			(.0084)	(.0040)	(.0023)	(.0028)	(.0016)	(1.14)				.929	.158
(8)	r	M/R	−.0066	+.0219	+.0197	+.0046	+.0105	−2.21	—	—	—		
			(.0021)	(.0042)	(.0029)	(.0023)	(.0014)	(.69)				.935	.152
(9)	r	$\frac{M-C}{R}+C$	−.0127	+.0168	+.0141	+.0045	+.0096	−1.31	—	—	—		
			(.0058)	(.0037)	(.0022)	(.0024)	(.0014)	(.95)				.929	.158
(10)	b	M'	−.0976	+.0217	+.0139	—	+.0252	−3.93	−.83	−.76	−.49		
			(.0483)	(.0115)	(.0070)		(.0068)	(5.49)	(.34)	(.31)	(.28)	.819	.459
(11)	b	M/R	−.0370	+.0576	+.0410	—	+.0227	−1.57	−.62	−.47	−.21		
			(.0051)	(.0074)	(.0068)		(.0025)	(.65)	(.14)	(.13)	(.13)	.899	.340
(12)	b	$\frac{M-C}{R}+C$	−.1067	+.0287	+.0128	—	+.0241	+6.37	−.80	−.72	−.35		
			(.0139)	(.0066)	(.0045)		(.0025)	(1.31)	(.15)	(.14)	(.13)	.904	.331

a unity value. In the fourth quarter, Q_1, Q_2 and Q_3 are all equal to zero.

It was repeatedly found that T, the mean maturity of long debt, was not significant in explaining b although it was typically a significant explanatory variable for r. It is not surprising that a change in the age composition of long-term Government bonds will affect the yield of a given long-term issue but will not noticeably influence the Bill Rate. On these grounds, T was retained in the r equations but dropped from the b equations.

Empirical Results

At last, fitted equations are given in Table 1; there are three pairs, using the alternative "money" variables. The actual money supply (M') is the least successful in explaining the Bill Rate by a wide margin. The coefficient of determination in equation (10) is .819, in contrast with .899 and .904 for equations (11) and (12), respectively. M' is not significant in explaining r, even though equation (7) nearly matches (8) and (9) in terms of R^2. The goodness of fit criterion offers no grounds for choosing between the two potential money variables: maximum potential money is superior by a slight margin in explaining the long rate, while potential demand deposits plus actual currency wins by an equally small margin in the Bill Rate equation. The standard errors of estimate (σ_u) are about one-third of 1 percentage point for the Bill Rate and only half as large for the long-term interest rate. The coefficient of determination is higher for the long rate; the variance of r is smaller and a larger percentage of that variance is explained by the selected independent variables.

As expected, the coefficients of $(S + I)$, L, T, and Y are positive, and each of the money variables has a negative coefficient. The quarterly dummy variables in the b equations indicate that the Bill Rate would rise substantially in the third and fourth quarters if additional cash was not provided to meet seasonal demands for greater liquidity. This is reasonable, and corresponds with the adjustment factors used to eliminate seasonality from official time-series for currency.

Surprisingly, the coefficient of $(S + I)$ exceeds that of L in each of the r equations: this means that an increase in the supply of long-term debt would raise the long rate by less than an equal increase in the supply of bills or other short-term securities. The difference between these coefficients is trivial—both by statistical criteria and in terms of the magnitudes of economic effects. An increase of one billion dollars in the supply of long-term securities (with average maturity for the L category) coupled with a decrease of one billion dollars of shorts produces an estimated decline of .002 or .003 percentage points in the yield on long-term bonds. The calculated effect is miniscule and its direction cannot be taken seriously. The result is further qualified by the positive coefficient on the maturity variable, T: a lengthening of the federal debt is estimated to increase the long rate insofar as it raises the mean maturity of issues with more than five years to run. Thus, a sale of 10-year bonds by the Federal Reserve coupled with a purchase of an equal volume of 20-year bonds has an estimated positive influence on r. If this is the case, surely a sale of bills accompanied by a purchase of 10-year bonds should have a similar effect. Perhaps, in retrospect, the inclusion of a mean maturity variable for short and intermediate securities would have helped to isolate this effect. Despite all these necessary qualifications, a principal conclusion of this study is that the long rate is relatively insensitive to changes in the maturity composition of the public debt. This finding, discussed in detail below, emerged consistently with a variety of functional forms and alternative sets of independent variables that were used to explain bond yields.

Standard errors of the coefficients in Table 1 are shown in parentheses below the estimated coefficients; as presented, most of the estimates differ significantly from zero at the 1 percent level. However, many possible variables—like wealth—were discarded when they did not pass standard tests of statistical significance. Since statistical significance was one of the criteria employed in the selection of explanatory variables, it is hardly surprising that most of the survivors passed this test. The "mining" of the data through experimentation detracts from the statistical evaluation of the results. This is no catastrophe, however, since the study is designed to develop optimal point estimates rather than to test hypotheses.

Further attempts were made to refine the results shown in Table 1. A number of lagged stock variables and first differences in stocks were tested as possible additional explanatory variables. The use of end-of-quarter stocks in the equations of Table 1 implies that the bond market adjusts immediately and completely to the supplies which are offered to the public. On the other hand, in most qualitative discussions of the behavior of interest rates, the bond market is viewed as imperfect by financial experts.

References to the "thinness" of the bond market imply that a large increase in the supplies of securities will raise yields sharply in the process of being absorbed by bond-holders. An "overshoot" theory of interest rate determination emerges: a given new issue will raise yields initially by more than will be maintained when the issue is safely committed to portfolios. Indeed, if investors are exceedingly reluctant to trade securities and concentrate mainly on the allocation of new cash-inflow in their investment decisions, the flow of net new issues—rather than the total existing stock—would be the principal determinant of interest rates. To the extent that there is general reluctance to review portfolios or to engage in trading because of transactions costs, net new issues would be expected to influence yields.

In this event, changes in stocks of securities should bear positive coefficients when they are inserted into the equations of Table 1 as additional independent variables. In fact, quarterly changes in the volume of federal long debt (ΔL) and other debt ($\Delta[S + I]$) are not significant in explaining either r or b. These are not ideal variables: they record changes in $(S + I)$ and L due to certain issues crossing the 60-month dividing line between maturity categories as equivalent to changes attributable to open-market operations, Treasury new issues, and maturing securities. As an alternative, gross new issues of Governments by the Treasury was tried with a similar lack of success. Nor did the inclusion of new corporate issues with the new Governments improve the results. Gross new issues also is a faulty variable: it omits open-market actions and ignores the volume of maturing securities. Still, the consistency of negative findings with the various flow variables is striking.

It would be most rash to conclude that the bond market is and has been sufficiently perfect in the postwar era to make "thinness" a myth. A more reasonable view is that the imperfection of the market is not evident in the data because the monetary authorities have confined themselves to rather modest quarterly flows of net new issues and net acquisitions in the open market. The Federal Reserve and the Treasury have kept their net transactions in any quarterly period small relative to the size of the outstanding public debt. Partly because the monetary authorities subscribe to an overshoot theory of the bond market, no large sudden shifts are observed in the volume of federal debt. If larger shifts occurred, perhaps evidence of thinness would emerge. In private discussion of these findings, my colleague Henry Wallich suggested the following analogy. The monetary authorities have consistently viewed the bond market as thin ice and they have therefore skated with great care. According to the data, they have never fallen through the ice. Yet, it cannot be justifiably concluded that the ice is solid and the caution gratuitous.

Pressing the skating analogy a bit further, one does not even find evidence that the ice cracked or showed any warning signs in the postwar period. Perhaps, therefore, the skaters could afford to display more boldness while watching carefully for indications of danger. If, however, the ice of the bond market would suddenly break under the rash skater with no warning, any counsel of relaxed caution would be misguided.

Other experiments with the equations of Table 1 were directed toward the incorporation of cyclical influences. Suppose that the levels of Gross Private Product were identical in two quarters five years apart and that the combined Treasury-Federal Reserve balance sheets were also identical for these two periods. Each of the equations presented in Table 1 would estimate identical values of r (or, of b) for these two quarters. Obviously, however, the later period would be marked by depressed economic activity and widespread unemployment. With continued secular advances in productivity and the labor force, constant output would be associated with increasing slack over time. On *a priori* grounds, one might well believe that interest rates on Government securities would be lower in the later, depressed period because unfavorable expectations and slump psychology would raise demands for relatively safe assets. Such a possible effect could be investigated if secular and cyclical changes in income are distinguished.

This distinction was most successfully accomplished by the inclusion of a variable reflecting the full-employment level of output in addition to the actual output variable. If full-employment is taken to mean a 4 percent rate of unemployment, the potential level of GNP at full utilization can be estimated through an adjustment of actual GNP for any excess or shortfall of the unemployment rate from 4 percent. Each percentage point difference in unemployment is associated with a much more than proportionate difference in GNP because hours worked per man, the size of the labor force, and man-hour productivity all vary with the level of resource utilization. Statistical analysis, recently conducted by the Council of Economic Advisers, suggests that on the average, a 3.2 percent increment in GNP accompanies a 1 percentage point decrement in the unemployment rate.[9] This yields the following estimate of potential GNP (P):

$$P = \text{Actual GNP} \cdot (1 + .032\,[\text{Actual Unemployment Percentage} - 4])$$

When both actual and potential output variables are included, the potential variable reflects secular forces, leaving the actual variable free to register cyclical factors. For any given potential output, actual Gross Private Product shows the strength of private demand in the economy.[10]

Table 2 Alternative equations explaining bond and bill yields with inclusion of potential GNP

Rate		Money variable	Coefficients "Money"	$S+I$	L	T	Y	P	Constant	Q_1	Q_2	Q_3	R^2	σ_u
(13)	r	M/R	−.0051	+.0223	+.0192	+.0046	+.0119	−.0018	−2.41	—	—	—	.936	.152
			(.0027)	(.0042)	(.0030)	(.0023)	(.0022)	(.0021)	(.73)					
(14)	r	$\frac{M-C}{R}+C$	−.0080	+.0195	+.0153	+.0045	+.0125	−.0032	−1.99	—	—	—	.933	.155
			(.0064)	(.0040)	(.0023)	(.0024)	(.0022)	(.0019)	(1.02)					
(15)	b	M/R	−.0218	+.0601	+.0342	—	+.0345	−.0161	−3.65	−.43	−.31	−.09	.916	.313
			(.0064)	(.0069)	(.0066)		(.0042)	(.0048)	(.85)	(.14)	(.13)	(.13)		
(16)	b	$\frac{M-C}{R}+C$	−.0705	+.0431	+.0181	—	+.0363	−.0160	+1.69	−.58	−.50	−.21	.928	.289
			(.0152)	(.0064)	(.0041)		(.0038)	(.0040)	(1.65)	(.14)	(.14)	(.12)		

Table 2 shows the results obtained when P is added to the independent variables of equations (8), (9), (11), and (12). These were the equations of Table 1 that used M/R and $[(M - C)/R] + C$ as money variables. The coefficients of P are all negative as hypothesized; for given Y, the more slack in the economy, the lower interest rates will be. In equations (15) and (16), P is significantly negative. The coefficient of determination of .916 in (15) may be compared with the .899 for equation (11), which is identical in all respects except for the inclusion of P. The R^2 of .928 for equation (16) similarly corresponds to a value of .904 for equation (12). The explanation of b is substantially improved by the inclusion of P.

The explanation of r is, in contrast, assisted only slightly by the P variable. The estimated coefficients of P in equations (13) and (14) do not differ significantly from zero, although the decision is a close one in equation (14). The rise in R^2 over the corresponding equations of Table 1 is trivial. On empirical grounds, P has fully earned a place in the b equations but not in the r equations. Yet, from analytical reasoning, the cyclical effect should emerge in long as well as short yields.

The coefficient of Y is increased by the inclusion of P. This is a plausible finding: a rise in Y now represents purely a cyclical increase at a point in time with a greater impact on expectations. However, the estimated coefficients of the money variables are uniformly lowered in absolute value by the inclusion of P and this is a less plausible finding. In particular, the money coefficients in both r equations are no longer statistically significant, in contrast with the results in Table 1. No analytical support can be invoked to explain why the inclusion of P should reduce the estimated effect of a change in demand debt on the long rate.

These considerations leave doubt as to whether the equations of Table 1 or those of Table 2 should be accepted as the basic estimates. My judgment calls for a sacrifice of symmetry in following the empirical results by employing equations (15) and (16), which include P, for b, and using equations (8) and (9), excluding P, for r.

The cyclical-secular distinction was also aimed at eliminating the significantly positive serial correlation of residuals that occurred for the equations of Table 1. That objective was not achieved: positive autocorrelation remains in the equations of Table 2. If r (or b) is above the value estimated by the equation in one quarter, it is likely to exceed its calculated value again in the next quarter. The serial correlation coefficients run in the neighborhood of one-half. Also, there is positive

Table 3 Changes in interest rates for selected periods: actual and estimated

	Actual change	Estimated change	Estimated changes attributed to: "Money" $\left(\frac{M-C}{R}+C\right)$	Publicly held marketable debt (S, I, L, T)	Aggregate economic activity (Y, P)
Recession periods					
Short rates (b)					
53-II to 54-II	−1.58	−1.55	−.54	−.19	−.82
57-II to 58-II	−2.43	−1.94	−.98	−.02	−.94
Long rates (r)					
53-II to 54-II	−.58	−.29	−.10	−.09	−.10
57-II to 58-II	−.39	−.25	−.18	+.03	−.10
Expansion periods					
Short rates (b)					
54-II to 55-II	+.88	+.98	−.05	+.14	+.89
54-II to 57-II	+2.69	+2.20	−.22	+.69	+1.73
58-II to 59-II	+2.37	+2.58	+.49	+.79	+1.30
Long rates (r)					
54-II to 55-II	+.27	+.39	−.01	+.09	+.31
54-II to 57-II	+1.03	+.92	−.04	+.21	+.75
58-II to 59-II	+.90	+.79	+.09	+.24	+.46

covariance of the r and b residuals: when the long rate is above its estimated value, the Bill Rate also tends to have a positive error.

Nevertheless, the equations trace the cyclical patterns of interest rates quite well over the period of observation. Table 3 shows the actual and estimated movements during selected period of recession and expansion. The estimated changes are based on equations (9) and (16), which use $[(M - C)/R] + C$ as the money variable. The estimated changes are divided into three categories: those resulting from changes in the money variable; those attributable to changes in the volume and structure of publicly-held marketable debt; and those stemming from changes in actual output and, for the case of b, in potential output. The only weak spot in these estimates is the underestimate of the decline in r during recessions, and, even there, the order of magnitude is not out of line.[11]

In the two periods of recession, income changes accounted for roughly half the estimated decline in rates. The other half is attributable to changes in the money variable and in the structure and volume of marketable debt—in this sense, policy accomplished about half of the estimated reductions in yields. Most of the increase in rates during the 1954–57 expansion is attributable to the rise in aggregate activity, but changes in money and public debt also pushed rates upward, especially after mid-1955. In 1958–59, the money and debt variables subject to policy control accounted for a substantial part of the rise in rates. In this sense, policy was actively—not just passively—tight.

Estimated Effects of Policy

The equations set forth above provide estimates of the effects on interest rates of hypothetical policy actions that might be undertaken by the monetary authorities. Table 4 presents these estimates for six actions and for a change in Y. For certain of the actions, the estimated changes in rates depend on the initial values of some of the variables. Therefore, a benchmark period must be adopted for specific calculations. The fourth quarter of 1959 was selected, and values of the relevant variables in that quarter are show in the table. The effects are estimated with the assumptions that income, currency-holdings in the private sector, and member-bank borrowings are constant, i.e., that they are not altered by the policy action. These restrictions will be relaxed subsequently. In the last example, the change in Y is supposed to occur instantaneously and to be independent of any action of the Treasury or Federal Reserve.

Two sets of estimates for each rate are shown in Table 3, corresponding to the two money variables M/R and $[(M - C)/R] + C$. The estimates for r are based on equations (8) and (9) of Table 1; those for b rely on equations (15) and (16) of Table 2, including the potential GNP variable. Open-market sales or "swaps" can also be interpreted as Treasury new issues or refundings. Changes in reserve requirements are shown separately for increases and decreases, since the legal reserve ratio enters the equations non-linearly. In all other cases, a reversal of the action (e.g., from sale to purchase) simply changes the sign of the estimated effect without altering its magnitude.

A sample calculation is offered herewith for any reader who might wish to roll his own. Consider the effect on b of a \$1 billion open-market sale of shorts, as estimated by equation (16). The sale raises outstanding $(S + I)$ by \$1 billion and lowers M by \$1 billion. The estimated effect of the $\Delta(S + I)$ is .0431 percentage points, applying the coefficient of $(S + I)$. The ΔM must be divided by the required reserve ratio, .154, to get the decline in $[(M - C)/R] + C$. Then that figure, -6.494, multiplied by the relevant coefficient, $-.0705$, has a product of $+.4578$. The .501 figure shown in the table is the sum of .0431 and .4578.

Table 4 Estimated effects on r and b of hypothetical policy actions (percentage-point change)[a]

Example	Estimated change: In r — Equation (8) (M/R)	Equation (9) $\left(\frac{M-C}{R}+C\right)$	In b — Equation (15) (M/R)	Equation (16) $\left(\frac{M-C}{R}+C\right)$
A An open market sale of $1 billion of bills, notes, or other short-term issues	+.064	+.099	+.202	+.501
B An open market sale of $1 billion of 20-year bonds	+.073	+.106	+.176	+.476
C A rise in reserve requirements by one percentage point	+.135	+.096	+.447	+.537
D A decline in reserve requirements by one percentage point	−.154	−.110	−.509	−.610
E Retirement of $1 billion of 5-year bonds and simultaneous issue of $1 billion of 20-year bonds	+.020	+.019	0	0
F Retirement of $1 billion of bills or certificates and simultaneous issue of $1 billion of 20-year bonds	+.010	+.007	−.026	−.026
G A rise in Y of $1 billion	+.010	+.010	+.034	+.036

a. Variables in 1959–4: $M = 51.8$; $C = 32.6$; $R = .154$; $L = 42.3$; $T = 150.5$.

One obvious matter of interest is the consistency of the two sets of estimates for each rate, based on the alternative money variables. These are distressingly far apart for the effects of open-market actions on the Bill Rate. A sale of \$1 billion of bills (Example A) is expected to raise the bill yield by 20 basis points according to equation (15), while 50 basis points is the estimate from equation (16). On the other hand, the two estimates of the effects on r resulting from open-market sales are fairly close together and so are the pairs of estimated effects due to changes in reserve requirements.

Intuitive feelings about the magnitude of effects on rates are so rare and so weak that it is difficult to get a subjective judgment on the plausibility of these estimates. A few economists have told me that the estimated effects of monetary actions on the long rate seem surprisingly small to them.[12] To achieve a decline in r of 1 percentage point, the Federal Reserve would have to buy an estimated \$9 billion of bonds according to equation (9), and nearly \$14 billion according to equation (8). Alternatively, reserve requirements would have to be cut by some 6 percentage points to attain the same objective. The estimated elasticity of r with respect to potential demand deposits and currency (as of the end of 1959) was under 1/2, which does seem small. In contrast, the estimated elasticity of r with respect to Y was slightly greater than unity.

The much greater volatility of short-term rates is clearly reflected in the estimates. Changes in reserve requirements and open-market sales are expected to have three to five times as much effect on bill yields as on long-term yields. The short rate can be altered by 1 percentage point through a 2 point change in reserve requirements, for example. According to equation (16), the elasticity of b with respect to the money variable was more than two, while its income-elasticity exceeded three.

Comparison of Examples A and B reveals that an open-market sale of very long securities has an estimated effect on r only about 10 percent greater than an equal sale of bills. Similarly, sales of shorts affect b only slightly more than do equal sales of bonds. As a result, the estimated changes in the cases of trades (Examples E and F) are uniformly small. Since T was not included in the b equations, a change in the maturity composition of the long category has a zero estimated effect on the Bill Rate. A comparison of Examples E and F for the long rate reveals incredible results, which occur because the coefficients of $(S + I)$ were slightly greater than those of L in the r equations. Certainly no one can believe that the long rate is increased to a greater extent when very long securities are sold to acquire five-year bonds than when the very longs are traded in exchange for bills. The important conclusion is that both examples have small effects. Example G shows that income changes lead to an estimated Δb that is over three times the corresponding Δr. When A and F are compared, it appears that an open-market purchase of bills of \$100 to \$160 million is required to hold r constant when Y rises \$1 billion. The corresponding estimates for holding b constant in that event is \$70 to \$170 million.

The results of Table 4 reveal the limitations of a linear function. Since the estimated effect of an open-market purchase of bills is simply proportional to the volume of the purchase, large purchases could have estimated effects which would turn rates negative.

Interest rates influence the level of income and yet here Y is treated as an exogenous variable. As a result, the estimated regression coefficients are biased. To remove the bias would require the construction and estimation of a complete aggregative econometric model, a task which is obviously beyond the scope of this paper.

Thus, far, member bank borrowings have been taken as constant regardless of monetary policy. However, suppose the Bill Rate rises as a result of sales of securities by the monetary authorities. If the discount rate was unchanged, there would be increased incentive for borrowing by member banks. Any increase in borrowing would raise federal demand debt and thereby modify the increase in rates. The net effect of a sale on demand debt would then be less than the amount of the sale. The quarterly data for 1946–59 confirm the hypothesis that member bank borrowings (B) are positively related to the Bill Rate and negatively related to the discount rate (d):

$$\begin{aligned} B = .188 + &.487b - .306d; \qquad R^2 = .535 \\ (.118)\ \ &(.120)\quad (.152); \qquad \sigma_u = .249 \end{aligned} \tag{17}$$

Borrowings rise by an estimated \$487 million for each percentage point increase in b, with d constant.

This result can be used to adjust the estimates shown in Table 4. Since additions to B are increases in M, the amount by which b is altered by a unit change in M (denoted as a_M) is also the effect on b of a unit change in B. So Δb^* (adjusted for changes in B) will differ from Δb, as shown in Table 4, by $a_M \Delta B$: $\Delta b^* = \Delta b + a_M \Delta B$. In turn, from (17), ΔB is estimated as .487 times the true (or adjusted) Δb^*. Therefore,

$$\Delta b^* \frac{\Delta b}{1 - .487a_M} \tag{18}$$

With the legal reserve ratio equal to .154, the value of a_M derived from equation (15) is $-.142$ (or $-.0218/.154$), while equation (16) gives a value of a_M of $-.458$. The final conclusion is that, for estimates based on equation (15), $\Delta b^* = .935\Delta b$; while, for those derived from equation (16), $\Delta b^* = .818\Delta b$. Induced borrowing by member banks acts as a stabilizer on interest rates. According to the equation which uses $[(M - C)/R] + C$ as the money variable, they are a rather important influence, curtailing changes in the Bill Rate by nearly one-fifth. The M/R equation attributes much less influence to the induced change in borrowings.

By the same reasoning, a correction for the estimates of Δr is required. Even though borrowings are assumed to depend solely on short rates, any change in B affects r. The adjusted change in r (Δr^*) from any event is:

$$\Delta r^* = \Delta r + .487\ a'_M \Delta b^* \tag{19}$$

where Δr is the estimate made on the assumption of constant B; a'_M is the estimated effect of a unit ΔM on r; and Δb^* is the adjusted change in the Bill Rate due to the event in question. The estimated adjustment from equation (8) is:

$$\Delta r^* = \Delta r - .021\Delta b^* \tag{19a}$$

The adjustment from equation (9) is:

$$\Delta r^* = \Delta r - .040\Delta b^* \tag{19b}$$

One further adjustment is in order for the estimated effects of a change in Y from equations employing $[(M - C)/R] + C$ as the money variable. To the extent that the demand for currency may be viewed as a pure transactions demand, it is reasonable to take C as independent of interest rates, but it cannot be independent of Y. By raising transactions demand for money, an increase in Y should expand C. In fact, the data confirm this hypothesis:

$$\underset{(4.40)}{C = 23.68} + \underset{(.0014)}{.0185Y}; \qquad R^2 = .774; \qquad \sigma_u = .753 \tag{20}$$

The expansion in C, in turn, has a multiplied effect in reducing potential demand deposits and therefore lowers $[(M - C)/R] + C$ for given M. It should reinforce the effect of an increase of Y in raising interest rates.

Table 5 Estimated effects on r and b of hypothetical policy actions—adjusted for estimated changes in borrowings and currency (percentage-point change)

	Estimated change			
	In r		In b	
Example	Equation (8)	Equation (9)	Equation (15)	Equation (16)
A An open market sale of $1 billion of bills, notes, or other short-term issues	+.060	+.083	+.189	+.410
B An open market sale of $1 billion of 20-year bonds	+.070	+.090	+.165	+.389
C A rise in reserve requirements by one percentage point	+.126	+.088	+.418	+.439
D A decline in reserve requirements by one percentage point	−.144	−.090	−.476	−.499
E Retirement of $1 billion of 5-year bonds and simultaneous issue of $1 billion of 20-year bonds	+.020	+.019	0	0
F Retirement of $1 billion of bills or certificates and simultaneous issue of $1 billion of 20-year bonds	+.010	+.007	−.024	−.021
G A rise in Y of $1 billion	+.010	+.010	+.032	+.030
H A rise in the discount rate by one percentage point	+.013	+.025	+.043	+.140

However, the income-effect on C, while highly significant in statistical terms, is very small—less than \$20 million per \$1 billion increase in Y. Hence, this adjustment makes very little difference in the estimated effect of a change in Y.

Table 5 repeats the examples of Table 4 with the estimates adjusted for changes in borrowings and currency. Except for reducing somewhat the wide gap between the alternative estimates of Δb in a few cases, the adjustment does not alter the results of Table 4 markedly. Table 5 also includes estimated effects of a change in the discount rate. According to equation (17), a rise in the discount rate of 1 percentage point will reduce B and hence M by \$306 million. The table shows the resulting changes estimated for b and r. Again, the two estimates are far apart quantatively, but they agree in attributing little potency to the discount rate as an instrument of monetary policy. An open-market sale of \$250 million has about as large an estimated influence as an increase of 1 percentage point in the discount rate. Of course, the discount rate may have an important influence on expectations by signaling the attitude of the Federal Reserve System. Such effects would not be reflected in the estimates shown. Furthermore, the Federal Reserve reacts to rates and the level of borrowings in deciding whether to change the discount rate. If the observations reflect high values of d that result from high levels of B, the true deterrent effect of the discount rate on borrowing would be underestimated by the regression equation. It is precisely because d has frequently followed b rather than leading it, that the discount rate was not employed as an explanatory variable for b. The Federal Reserve System obviously controls the discount rate but it has apparently used this instrument at times to follow the bill market. As a result, it is particularly difficult to quantify the causal influence of the discount rate on the bill market.

Interest Rates on Private Assets

The monetary authorities are dealers in federal debt, but their actions influence yields of private assets. In fact, monetary policy affects aggregate demand for output by altering the cost and availability of funds to private borrowers. The relative importance of changing rates and changing availability need not be evaluated here. Even if availability was all important, changes in interest rates on marketable securities would be an unfailing symptom of variations in the tightness of financial markets. Hence, regardless of the mechanism by which monetary actions ultimately influence the demand for output, the effect of policy on private interest rates is a matter of importance.

Interest rates on key private assets are related to one another and to government yields in Table 6. No attempt is made here to explain these other yields by their basic stock and flow determinants. Table 6 is designed to show the extent to which various rates have moved together in the postwar years. Fourteen interest rates are considered, and those make up both the rows and columns of the table. Entered in the table are the simple correlation coefficients among various pairs of yields for 55 quarterly observations from 1946 through the third quarter of 1959. Since each rate is, of necessity, perfectly correlated with itself, all the diagonal elements of the matrix are unity. Because the correlation of y with x is identical to the correlation of x with y, only half of the off-diagonal elements need to be filled.

The concept of an interest rate structure gets support from the close relationships among corporate bonds, municipal bonds, prime commercial paper, larger bank loans, and Governments. Generally, the correlation coefficients between pairs of these yields exceed .8. On the other hand, both dividend and earnings yields on common stocks typically show nega-

Table 6 Simple correlations among various interest rates (based on 55 quarterly observations from 1946-1 to 1959-3)[a]

	(1)	(2)	(3)	(4)	(5)	(6)	(7)	(8)	(9)	(10)	(11)	(12)	(13)	(14)
1	1	.855	.714	.556	.220	−.501	.852	.213	.641	.743	.816	.955	.841	−.463
2		1	.938	.824	.476	−.604	.863	.486	.829	.880	.910	.868	.930	−.631
3			1	.959	.732	−.470	.887	.731	.913	.901	.877	.736	.815	−.584
4				1	.826	−.315	.812	.823	.896	.847	.790	.589	.705	−.482
5					1	.090	.654	.948	.757	.631	.511	.223	.265	−.175
6						1	−.358	−.025	−.364	−.447	−.521	−.544	−.621	.825
7							1	.658	.882	.895	.890	.847	.723	−.498
8								1	.839	.716	.598	.262	.257	−.329
9									1	.978	.936	.694	.673	−.583
10										1	.983	.792	.764	−.624
11											1	.861	.825	−.649
12												1	.851	−.520
13													1	−.531
14														1

a. Data sources given in Appendix Table A1: 1, Treasury bills; 2, Long-term U.S. bonds; 3, Corporate Aaa bonds; 4, Corporate Baa bonds; 5, Dividend yields-preferred; 6, Dividend yields-common; 7, Prime commercial paper; 8, Bank loan rate \$1–10 Th; 9, Bank loan rate \$10–100 Th; 10, Bank loan rate \$100–200 Th; 11, Bank loan rate \$200 and up; 12, Discount rate; 13, High grade municipals; 14, Earnings/price ratio-common stocks.

tive correlations with the yields of debt issues. Yields on preferred stock and the rate on small bank loans ($1,000–$10,000) display relatively low correlations with most other rates but a surprisingly close relationship to each other.

Table 6 also points to the rate on long-term Governments as the pivotal yield in the interest structure. Every one of the eleven private yields is more closely related to the long rate than to the Bill Rate. This would have been expected for corporate and municipal bonds, but it seems surprising for short-term private debts like bank loans. Even the prime commercial paper rate maintains the unanimity, although by an insignificant margin. And the negative relationship with common stock yields is close for the long rate. These findings suggest that, if monetary policy influences the long rate in the ways indicated in earlier sections of this paper, it will also alter yields on private assets. This conclusion gives a causal interpretation to the correlations of Table 6, implying that other yields have moved because of changes in the government yield. The data, of course, show only association and not causation. It could be argued that common forces have typically acted in the same direction on yields of both government and private debt, but that concerted monetary policy actions to alter government yields would not be transmitted to private securities. This argument requires an answer: for example, the negative correlation between equity returns and the government rate is clearly not causal. The usual *a priori* view is that a tightening of monetary policy depresses equity prices, thus raising their yield just as it raises the yield on Governments. The data are, however, dominated by the fact that cyclical forces change the relative demands for equities as opposed to claims. When profits and the price level seem headed upwards, investors will accept lower current returns on common stock and will demand higher compensation for holding bonds. But the Federal Reserve would not promote bullishness on Wall Street by making a large open-market sale of Governments.

While a non-causal interpretation must be supplied for the negative correlation between equity and debt yields, that does not discredit the positive relationship among yields of debt issues. Marked changes in the relative preferences of investors among claims are far less likely to occur. If they did happen during the postwar period, the positive correlations shown in Table 6 are smaller than those that would emerge solely from autonomous changes in supplies. It seems reasonable to use the high positive correlations to approximate the effects of a change in the government yield attributable to public policy. Then, the slopes of simple regressions

Table 7 Estimated slopes of regressions of various interest rates on long-term U.S. bond yield[a]

Yield	Slope on r
Corporate Aaa	.961
Corporate Baa	1.018
Dividend yields—preferred	.470
Prime commercial paper	1.577
Bank loan rate $1–10 thousand	.692
Bank loan rate $10–100 thousand	1.124
Bank loan rate $100–200 thousand	1.398
Bank loan rate $200 + thousand	1.567
High grade municipals	1.240

a. 55 quarterly observations from 1946-1 to 1959-3.

of various private yields on Governments can be used to estimate the change in other interest rates accompanying a given change in r.

These slopes are shown in Table 7. In each case, the long-government rate is the independent variable and a private rate is dependent. The coefficients in the table show the estimated change in the private rate accompanying a change in r of 1 percentage point. The estimated changes for corporate and municipal bonds are about equal to Δr: those for large bank loans and commercial paper are about one and a half times as large. Only for small bank loans and yields on preferred stock is the slope much below unity. These results suggest that changes effected in the yield of long-term Governments will be transmitted without diminution to private rates.

Conclusions: Summary of Empirical Findings

1. The interest rates on long-term Government bonds (r) and Treasury bills (b) are both positively related to the following independent variables:

$(S + I)$ The volume of federal debt with maturity of less than five years held outside government agencies and the Federal Reserve System

L The volume of federal debt with maturity of five years or more held outside government agencies and the Federal Reserve System

Y Gross Private Product, i.e., GNP minus government payrolls

In addition, r is positively related to the mean maturity (T) of long debt. Quarterly dummy variables affect b significantly, reflecting a seasonal pattern, but they do not influence r. The Bill Rate is negatively affected by deficiencies in aggregate demand as reflected by a potential GNP variable used in conjunction with actual output; the same effect was expected but could not be empirically established for the long rate.

Two alternative "money" variables are negatively related to both r and b. One of these consists of federal demand debt divided by the legal revenue ratio (M/R): it represents the hypothetical maximum volume of money that could exist with the given combined balance-sheets of the Treasury and Federal Reserve System in the absence of currency, time-deposits, and excess reserves. The other "money" variable takes the actual volume of currency outside the Treasury and Federal Reserve and adds to that the remainder of demand debt divided by the legal reserve ratio. The resulting variable is the sum of actual currency plus potential demand deposits, where the potential would be reached only if time deposits and excess reserves were both zero.

2. Both of the hypothetical money variables are more successful in explaining interest rates than is the actual volume of money. Furthermore, the addition of private near-monies to the money supply does not aid the explanation of rates. The hypothetical variables reflect the conditions established by the monetary authorities under which commercial banks can create demand deposits. There is little ground for choice between M/R and $[(M - C)/R] + C$ on either analytical grounds or criteria of empirical success.

3. The resulting equations account for 92 to 93 percent of the variance of b and r in 56 quarterly observations covering 1946 to 1959. The residuals of the equations, however, display significantly positive autocorrelation of residuals.

4. Net private wealth was expected to influence rates negatively, but the data did not confirm this hypothesis.

5. Changes in stocks of the public debt and flows of new securities could not be established as influences on b and r. This finding undoubtedly depends on the relatively small magnitudes of quarterly changes in the postwar period. Nevertheless, extreme views—or extreme fears—that attribute great imperfection to the Government bond market get no support from the evidence.

6. As expected, the Bill Rate is much more sensitive than the long rate to given changes in federal debt and in the level of income.

7. Open-market purchases and sales and changes in reserve requirements have very substantial estimated effects on b. The long rate is much less sensitive, but it can be altered significantly by major actions of monetary policy. In a few cases, the effect of a given action estimated from the M/R equation differs substantially from the estimate relying on $[(M - C)/R] + C$. It is obviously important whether an open-market sale of $1 billion is likely to raise b by 20 or 40 basis points. Yet, neither estimate can be

rejected on the grounds of subjective implausibility. If 20 and 40 seem equally sensible to monetary economists, one must conclude that the profession has done very little quantitative thinking in this area. Much more needs to be done to refine the highly tentative and speculative estimates advanced above.

8. The estimated effects of open-market actions are very similar, whether they are conducted by means of bills or of long bonds. The sale of very long bonds will produce an estimated increment in r only about ten percent higher than that associated with an equal sale of bills. Similarly, a bill sale has only a slightly larger estimated influence on b than an equal sale of bonds.

9. The effects of changes in the discount rate can be evaluated only insofar as they alter the volume of member bank borrowings. The discount rate appears to be a rather weak instrument of monetary policy in contrast with changes in reserve requirements or with open-market sales and purchases. The estimate does not reflect any impact of the discount rate on expectations. Still, there is no apparent reason why a movement in the discount rate should be a more dramatic signal to investors than altered reserve requirements or large open-market actions.

10. It is estimated that changes effected in the yield of long-term U.S. bonds are transmitted without diminution and without any substantial time-lag to corporate bonds, municipal bonds, and most bank loan rates.

Conclusions: Implications for Theory and Policy

According to the empirical findings of this study, the long rate, the short rate, and the differential between them are all determined principally by the balance sheet of the monetary authorities, the legal reserve ratio, and the level of income. When the demand debt of the federal government is large relative to interest-bearing government debt and to the level of income, financial markets reflect the ease of monetary policy in low rates of interest for both short-term and long-term Government securities and in a large excess of the long rate over the short rate. A smaller volume of demand debt, more interest-bearing debt or higher income raises the yields of all Government securities, but has a particularly strong effect on the short rate. Thus, greater tightness reduces the excess of r over b. The rate differential fluctuates widely; it depends principally on the over-all tightness of financial markets. This is shown schematically in Chart 2.

The greater sensitivity of b to the degree of tightness makes $(r - b)$ dependent on the over-all state of financial markets. If monetary con-

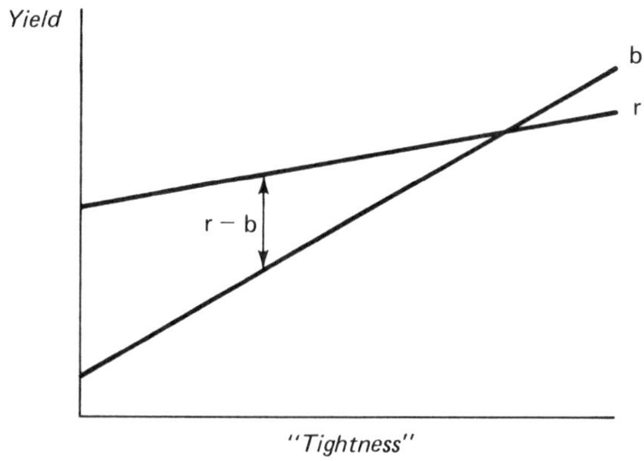

Chart 2

ditions are sufficiently stringent, the Bill Rate is estimated to lie above the long rate. To account for the much greater volatility and sensitivity of the short rate, one must invoke inelastic expectations concerning future rates. If any change in the short rate altered expected future short rates by an equal amount, there could scarcely be a consistently smaller change in the long rate. The expected returns from longs and shorts would be kept in equilibrium only by an equally large change in the long rate. If, however, there are inelastic expectations, expected short rates through the future are altered by only a fraction of the current change in the short rate, and then the long rate should display a smaller change. Yet the *a priori* case for inelastic expectations is not compelling.[13] Nor is there any means of obtaining direct evidence on this score. All one can say is that inelastic expectations would account satisfactorily for the greater volatility of the short rate and they are the only basis of an adequate explanation. Culbertson has advanced an interesting alternative non-expectational explanation.[14] He argues that short rates may be more volatile because the volume of outstanding private short-term debt declines by a far greater proportion in a recession than does long-term debt. Hence, if many investors have strong preferences for holding short-term claims, they will accept much smaller returns on those short assets which are available. Because no adequate quarterly series of private debts by maturity category could be assembled, no direct test of the Culbertson thesis was made in this study. But Culbertson's emphasis on relative supplies of long and short private debt seems inconsistent with the small significance that relative supplies of long and short public debt had in my results. Furthermore, Culbertson's explanation would not account for the finding that b is much more sensitive than r to given changes in the volume of federal demand debt. In my judgment, the explanation must rest on inelastic expectations of future interest rates.

The insensitivity of the rate differential to relative supplies of longs and shorts suggests that the expectation curve shown back in Chart 1 should be drawn flat. Investors cannot differ greatly in their best guesses about future long rates, for, if they did, relative supplies would play a greater role. Furthermore, one can infer that, to a substantial group of investors, bills and bonds are very close substitutes. This group presumably does not have a strong intrinsic preference for shorts versus longs and is willing to alter the maturity composition of portfolios in response to small changes in the yield differential, given the state of market expectations. I cannot identify this important group of arbitragers. This is one of the many areas where my results need to be investigated and appraised at a microeconomic level.

The slight significance attributed to relative supplies suggests that changes in the maturity structure of federal debt will not have dramatic effects on the rate structure. The managers of the debt will reduce $(r - b)$ if they retire long bonds and issue bills, but the magnitude of the estimated effects is small. By the same reasoning, these findings imply that controversy over recent monetary policy has vastly exaggerated the importance of "bills only" as a determinant of the structure of interest rates. If the results of this paper are anywhere near the mark, *how much* the Federal Reserve buys (or sells) is far and away more important than *what* issue it chooses to deal in. This does not mean that "bills only" was wise policy, or that it was foolish policy. It does imply that it was not a policy of overwhelming significance. The furor over whether the Federal Reserve tied one hand behind its back in adopting "bills only" has obscured the crucial issue of how it used the hand that was unquestionably free.

Monetary policy can alter both long and short rates. While the redirection of a given open-market action between longs and shorts will not accomplish much, large purchases (or sales) and changes in reserve requirements can have decisive effects. The long rate is not easily moved, however. To alter the long rate substantially as an aid to stabilization policy, the Federal Reserve System must be prepared to take strong measures in varying the magnitude of its security holdings and the legal reserve ratio. Vigor is indispensable in the conduct of effective monetary policy.

Appendix

Table A1 Yields On financial assets

Yr.	Qtr.	Short-term U.S. bills (%) (1)	Long-term U.S. bonds (%) (2)	High grade municipal bonds (%) (3)	Corporate AAA bonds (%) (4)	Corporate BAA bonds (%) (5)	Dividend Yields: Preferred stock (6)	Dividend Yields: Common stock (7)	Discount rate (%) (8)
1946	1	.375	2.09	1.49	2.47	2.94	3.45	3.42	.50
	2	.375	2.16	1.55	2.49	3.03	3.46	3.41	1.00
	3	.375	2.28	1.75	2.58	3.10	3.57	4.24	1.00
	4	.375	2.24	1.97	2.61	3.17	3.76	4.41	1.00
1947	1	.376	2.19	2.02	2.55	3.15	3.72	4.80	1.00
	2	.376	2.22	1.92	2.55	3.21	3.76	5.09	1.00
	3	.791	2.24	1.92	2.61	3.23	3.72	5.21	1.00
	4	.948	2.39	2.35	2.86	3.52	4.07	5.41	1.00
1948	1	.997	2.44	2.52	2.83	3.53	4.12	5.58	1.25
	2	.998	2.41	2.26	2.76	3.34	4.04	5.30	1.25
	3	1.087	2.45	2.46	2.84	3.45	4.20	6.06	1.50
	4	1.153	2.44	2.26	2.79	3.53	4.15	6.78	1.50
1949	1	1.162	2.38	2.21	2.70	3.47	4.07	6.88	1.50
	2	1.158	2.38	2.28	2.71	3.47	3.98	7.22	1.50
	3	1.061	2.22	2.22	2.60	3.37	3.85	6.39	1.50
	4	1.102	2.19	2.13	2.58	3.31	3.88	6.58	1.50
1950	1	1.138	2.27	2.07	2.58	3.24	3.81	6.40	1.50
	2	1.174	2.33	2.09	2.62	3.28	3.85	6.35	1.50
	3	1.315	2.36	1.88	2.64	3.21	3.85	6.45	1.75
	4	1.367	2.39	1.77	2.67	3.20	3.89	6.89	1.75
1951	1	1.422	2.47	1.87	2.78	3.23	4.00	6.66	1.75
	2	1.499	2.65	2.22	2.94	3.49	4.17	6.79	1.75
	3	1.646	2.56	2.05	2.84	3.46	4.16	6.03	1.75
	4	1.731	2.70	2.10	3.01	3.61	4.28	5.56	1.75
1952	1	1.658	2.70	2.07	2.96	3.51	4.16	5.54	1.75
	2	1.700	2.61	2.10	2.94	3.50	4.04	5.48	1.75
	3	1.786	2.71	2.33	2.95	3.52	4.12	5.63	1.75
	4	2.126	2.75	2.40	2.97	3.51	4.11	5.14	1.75
1953	1	2.082	2.89	2.61	3.12	3.57	4.23	5.36	2.00
	2	2.231	3.13	2.99	3.40	3.86	4.47	5.60	2.00
	3	1.876	3.01	2.88	3.29	3.88	4.30	5.76	2.00
	4	1.630	2.79	2.59	3.13	3.74	4.20	5.54	2.00
1954	1	1.053	2.53	2.38	2.86	3.51	4.04	5.07	1.75
	2	.650	2.55	2.48	2.90	3.49	4.05	4.74	1.50
	3	1.007	2.52	2.29	2.89	3.47	3.98	4.31	1.50
	4	1.174	2.59	2.33	2.90	3.45	3.93	4.09	1.50
1955	1	1.335	2.78	2.45	3.02	3.48	4.01	4.18	1.50
	2	1.432	2.82	2.48	3.05	3.51	3.98	3.71	1.75
	3	2.086	2.92	2.63	3.13	3.59	4.06	3.76	2.25
	4	2.564	2.91	2.71	3.15	3.62	4.05	3.92	2.50
1956	1	2.310	2.93	2.69	3.10	3.60	4.01	3.68	2.50
	2	2.527	2.93	2.75	3.27	3.75	4.17	3.82	2.75
	3	2.850	3.21	3.07	3.56	4.07	4.39	4.04	3.00
	4	3.230	3.40	3.44	3.75	4.37	4.63	3.90	3.00
1957	1	3.140	3.26	3.32	3.66	4.43	4.46	4.16	3.00
	2	3.316	3.58	3.75	3.91	4.63	4.69	3.79	3.00
	3	3.578	3.66	3.90	4.12	4.93	4.79	4.27	3.50
	4	3.102	3.30	3.47	3.81	5.03	4.49	4.58	3.00
1958	1	1.354	3.25	3.45	3.63	4.68	4.42	4.35	2.25
	2	.881	3.19	3.26	3.57	4.55	4.28	3.98	1.75
	3	2.484	3.75	3.96	4.09	4.87	4.58	3.54	2.00
	4	2.814	3.80	3.84	4.08	4.85	4.63	3.17	2.50
1959	1	2.852	3.92	3.76	4.13	4.85	4.48	3.28	3.00
	2	3.247	4.09	4.04	4.46	5.04	4.79	3.09	3.50
	3	3.998	4.26	4.13	4.52	5.18	4.80	3.13	4.00
	4	4.572	4.27						4.00

Table A1 (continued)

Yr.	Qtr.	Prime commercial papers (%) (9)	Bank rates (19 cities): size of loan (thousands of dollars) 1–10 (%) (10)	10–100 (%) (11)	100–200 (%) (12)	200+ (%) (13)	Common Stock Price per share ($) (14)	Earnings per share ($) (15)	Earnings price ratio (%) (16)
1946	1	.75	4.10	3.10	2.30	1.70	52.00	1.32	2.54
	2	.75	4.20	3.10	2.20	1.70	53.70	3.22	6.00
	3	.81	4.00	3.10	2.10	1.70	44.38	3.97	8.95
	4	1.00	4.40	3.20	2.10	1.80	46.03	5.61	12.19
1947	1	1.00	4.30	3.10	2.50	1.80	45.67	4.74	10.38
	2	1.00	4.10	3.10	2.60	1.80	45.93	4.93	10.73
	3	1.06	4.10	3.10	2.40	1.80	45.85	5.39	11.76
	4	1.19	4.10	3.20	2.50	1.80	47.34	6.22	13.13
1948	1	1.38	4.20	3.30	2.50	2.10	46.60	6.35	13.63
	2	1.38	4.49	3.47	2.70	2.16	50.77	6.85	13.49
	3	1.56	4.53	3.58	2.92	2.29	46.87	7.25	15.47
	4	1.56	4.50	3.58	2.97	2.34	46.33	7.65	16.51
1949	1	1.56	4.62	3.64	2.89	2.42	46.21	6.60	14.28
	2	1.56	4.63	3.70	3.04	2.44	43.48	6.00	13.80
	3	1.38	4.62	3.64	2.98	2.31	48.18	6.75	14.01
	4	1.33	4.53	3.61	2.98	2.35	52.28	7.05	13.49
1950	1	1.31	4.45	3.54	2.94	2.31	53.76	6.59	12.26
	2	1.31	4.50	3.65	2.94	2.39	55.56	8.66	15.59
	3	1.66	4.51	3.63	2.95	2.34	61.27	9.44	15.41
	4	1.72	4.60	3.37	3.10	2.57	64.46	9.08	14.09
1951	1	2.04	4.68	3.88	3.27	2.76	67.40	7.62	11.31
	2	2.31	4.73	3.93	3.32	2.81	66.75	7.42	11.12
	3	2.19	4.74	3.99	3.36	2.78	74.09	6.36	8.58
	4	2.30	4.78	4.05	3.49	3.03	74.24	8.09	10.90
1952	1	2.38	4.85	4.16	3.66	3.24	75.63	6.79	8.98
	2	2.31	4.90	4.21	3.72	3.29	77.01	6.61	8.58
	3	2.31	4.91	4.22	3.74	3.27	74.58	6.76	9.06
	4	2.31	4.88	4.21	3.77	3.29	80.89	8.54	10.56
1953	1	2.36	4.89	4.25	3.75	3.32	77.64	7.26	9.35
	2	2.75	4.98	4.38	3.91	3.53	74.28	7.76	10.45
	3	2.74	5.01	4.40	3.93	3.54	72.09	7.76	10.76
	4	2.25	4.98	4.39	3.96	3.57	77.06	8.08	10.48
1954	1	2.00	4.99	4.37	3.94	3.52	85.53	7.97	9.32
	2	1.56	4.97	4.35	3.89	3.37	94.34	8.49	9.00
	3	1.31	4.99	4.32	3.82	3.32	102.88	7.63	7.42
	4	1.31	4.92	4.29	3.84	3.31	115.64	9.43	8.15
1955	1	1.69	4.93	4.29	3.83	3.30	117.61	9.70	8.25
	2	2.00	4.92	4.29	3.83	3.30	133.41	10.80	8.10
	3	2.54	4.98	4.44	3.99	3.56	138.21	9.94	7.19
	4	2.99	5.01	4.52	4.14	3.75	145.67	11.60	7.96
1956	1	3.00	5.05	4.55	4.13	3.74	155.90	10.75	6.90
	2	3.38	5.18	4.69	4.34	3.97	151.11	10.50	6.95
	3	3.50	5.30	4.86	4.52	4.19	145.06	8.70	6.00
	4	3.63	5.32	4.90	4.63	4.20	150.74	11.45	7.60
1957	1	3.63	5.38	4.94	4.59	4.21	141.98	11.12	7.83
	2	3.79	5.37	4.94	4.61	4.23	155.23	10.65	6.86
	3	4.00	5.67	5.29	5.01	4.69	138.73	9.40	6.78
	4	3.81	5.66	5.29	5.01	4.71	128.38	9.90	7.71
1958	1	2.33	5.55	5.10	4.75	4.29	134.17	7.35	5.48
	2	1.54	5.45	4.88	4.40	3.95	144.74	7.30	5.04
	3	2.93	5.45	4.90	4.47	4.00	161.34	8.10	5.02
	4	3.33	5.49	5.06	4.68	4.33	177.75	10.70	6.02
1959	1	3.35	5.53	5.09	4.74	4.32	174.47	10.30	5.90
	2	3.83	5.68	5.33	5.06	4.72	187.48	11.60	6.19
	3	4.63	5.91	5.65	5.43	5.15	184.64	8.00	4.33
	4								

Notes to Table A1: based on descriptions of series in *Business Statistics*, 1959 ed., U.S. Department of Commerce.
Col. (1) Yield on short-term U.S. Government bills.
Source: *Federal Reserve Bulletin*
Yield on 3 month bills. Data for 1946 represent average rates on issues announced within the period; thereafter, on new bills issued within the period. Data are for last month of quarter.
Col. (2) Yield on long-term U.S. Government bonds.
Source: *Federal Reserve Bulletin*
The data are averages of daily figures computed, beginning with April 1953, on the basis of the closing bid quotations on the over-the-counter market; prior thereto, on the basis of the mean of the closing bid and asked quotations. The series includes bonds as follows: Beginning April 1953, fully taxable marketable bonds due or callable in 10 years and over; from April 1952 through March 1953, fully taxable marketable bonds due or first callable after 12 years; prior thereto, bonds due or first callable after 15 years. Data are for the last month of quarter.
Col. (3) Yield on High Grade Municipal Bonds.
Source: Standard and Poor's Corporation
The series is an arithmetic average of yields to maturity of 15 high-grade domestic municipal bonds. The yields are based on Wednesday closing prices and the monthly figures are averages of the four or five weekly figures for the month. Data are for the last month of the quarter.
Cols. (4) and (5) Yields on Corporate AAA and Corporate BAA Bonds.
Source: Moody's Investors Service
These averages were set up in 1928 to include 10 bonds of each rating for each group (railroad, public utility, and industrial). There has not uniformly been a full set of 10 bonds in some rating classifications because of the limited number of suitable issues. On September 1, 1958 there were 6 AAA and 10 BAA bonds in the railroad group; 10 AAA and 10 BAA bonds in the public utility group; and 7 AAA and 10 BAA bonds in the industrial group.

Occasional substitutions in the bond list have been made. Suitable adjustments (usually small) which are gradually amortized, are introduced to prevent such substitution from impairing the comparability of the series. No convertible or other unusual issues are included. The average maturity on September 1, 1958 was 25 years.

Averages are computed as follows: A daily yield based on the closing price for each individual bond is first computed and then unweighted arithmetic averages of these yields are compiled for the different rating classifications. The monthly series are averages of daily figures. Data are for the last month of the quarter.
Col. (6) Dividend Yields on Preferred Stocks.
Source: Standard and Poor's Corporation
Yields are computed for each of 14 high-grade non-callable issues (15 prior to April 1948), including public utility as well as industrial preferred stocks. The group yield is currently determined from the average of the 8 median yields (formerly 9). The indexes are based on one price weekly (as of Wednesday's close) with the monthly index computed from the average of the four or five weekly indexes of the month. Data are for last month of the quarter.
Cols. (7), (14), and (15) Dividend Yields, Price per Share and Earnings per Share 125 industrial common stocks.
Source: Moody's Investors Service
Dividends are at annual rates (without adjustment for seasonal variation) and are determined at the end of each month on the basis of each company's most recent declaration. These dividends are multiplied by the number of each company's common shares outstanding and the products are added to obtain aggregate values which are divided by the total number of shares outstanding, free from the effects of stock splits and stock dividends, to obtain per share figures.

Individual stock prices at the end of each month are used as a basis for deriving per-share prices. Earnings are net after taxes and contingencies less preferred dividend requirements (whether actually paid or not). Data represent quarterly earnings—partly estimated—at annual rates. There is no adjustment for seasonal variation. The method of computing price per share is similar to method of computing dividends per share described above.

Yields are obtained by dividing per-share dividends by per-share prices.

Yield and price data are for the last month of the quarter. Earnings data are quarterly totals at annual rates.

Col. (8) Discount rate.
Source: *Federal Reserve Bulletin*
Data are discount rate in effect on last day of quarter.

Col. (9) Interest Rate on Prime Commercial Paper 4–6 Months.
Source: *Federal Reserve Bulletin*
Beginning with 1951, the data represent averages of daily quotations; prior thereto the figures are averages of weekly prevailing rates.

Data are for the last month of the quarter.

Cols. (10), (11), (12), and (13) Bank Rates on Short-term Business Loans in 19 Large Cities.
Source: *Federal Reserve Bulletin*
Data represent averages of rates charged on loans maturing in 1 year or less to business in the specified cities.

Since June 1948 data were reported on forms that call for the amount of the loans and the interest rate actually charged for each new loan or renewal made in the first half of March, June, September and December by a selected sample of banks (mainly large ones) in 19 leading cities.

Col. (16) Col. 15 ÷ Col. 14.

Table A2 Money supply

Yr.	Qtr.	Member bank reserves (1)	Other deposits (2)	Currency outside gov't. (3)	Federal demand debt (4)	Required reserve ratio (5)	Excess reserves (6)	Member bank borrowings (7)	Currency outside banks (8)	Demand deposits adjusted (9)
1945	4	15,915	1,308	28,515	45,738	.183	1,364	334	26.5	75.9
1946	1	14,853	1,212	27,879	43,944	.183	971	683	26.1	75.0
	2	16,123	1,250	28,245	45,618	.183	867	119	26.5	79.5
	3	15,910	1,069	28,507	45,486	.183	824	141	26.5	81.4
	4	16,139	822	28,952	45,913	.183	872	193	26.7	83.3
1947	1	15,264	971	28,230	44,465	.183	739	153	26.1	80.4
	2	16,112	881	28,297	45,290	.183	741	114	26.0	82.5
	3	16,784	842	28,567	46,193	.183	884	98	26.3	84.1
	4	17,899	961	28,868	47,728	.183	939	262	26.5	87.1
1948	1	16,639	1,000	27,781	45,420	.190	732	304	25.6	81.5
	2	17,389	859	27,903	46,151	.196	765	97	25.6	82.7
	3	19,986	843	28,118	48,947	.216	768	328	25.7	83.9
	4	20,479	1,189	28,224	49,892	.216	782	139	25.7	85.8
1949	1	19,118	1,154	27,439	47,711	.216	579	208	25.1	81.1
	2	17,867	940	27,493	46,300	.202	616	130	25.0	82.2
	3	15,947	1,050	27,412	44,409	.176	685	192	24.9	83.1
	4	16,568	1,517	27,600	45,685	.176	773	52	25.0	86.7
1950	1	15,657	1,133	27,042	43,832	.176	600	253	24.6	83.2
	2	15,934	1,431	27,156	44,521	.176	640	51	24.6	85.4
	3	16,709	1,374	27,161	45,244	.176	603	140	24.5	88.0
	4	17,681	1,460	27,741	46,882	.176	851	283	25.0	93.2

Table A2 (continued)

Yr.	Qtr.	Member bank reserves (1)	Other deposits (2)	Currency outside gov't. (3)	Federal demand debt (4)	Required reserve ratio (5)	Excess reserves (6)	Member bank borrowings (7)	Currency outside banks (8)	Demand deposits adjusted (9)
1951	1	19,014	1,323	27,119	47,456	.196	524	374	24.4	89.0
	2	19,020	1,261	27,809	48,090	.196	561	211	25.0	89.5
	3	19,391	1,127	28,288	48,806	.196	669	195	25.4	92.0
	4	20,056	889	29,206	50,151	.196	815	551	26.3	98.1
1952	1	19,733	845	28,473	49,051	.196	1,130	138	25.7	94.8
	2	19,381	845	29,026	49,252	.196	700	189	26.0	95.8
	3	20,066	881	29,419	50,366	.196	1,094	282	26.6	96.4
	4	19,950	1,005	30,433	51,388	.196	858	1,703	27.5	101.5
1953	1	19,322	878	29,754	49,954	.196	605	924	26.9	97.4
	2	19,561	703	30,125	50,389	.196	1,154	281	27.1	97.2
	3	19,309	864	30,275	50,448	.183	564	318	27.5	97.7
	4	20,160	916	30,781	51,857	.183	813	211	27.8	103.3
1954	1	19,194	857	29,707	49,758	.183	732	175	26.9	96.7
	2	19,011	922	29,922	49,855	.180	839	138	27.1	98.1
	3	18,676	883	29,985	49,544	.170	588	78	26.9	101.2
	4	18,876	871	30,509	50,256	.170	621	243	27.4	106.7
1955	1	18,283	798	29,800	48,881	.170	490	652	26.7	102.4
	2	18,066	822	30,229	49,117	.170	490	402	27.1	103.2
	3	18,423	764	30,422	49,609	.170	483	888	27.2	104.9
	4	19,005	956	31,158	51,119	.170	683	753	27.9	109.8
1956	1	18,799	748	30,339	49,886	.170	572	1,196	27.2	104.4
	2	18,443	977	30,715	50,135	.170	595	756	27.5	105.0
	3	18,831	610	30,768	50,209	.170	503	705	27.4	105.4
	4	19,059	758	31,790	51,607	.170	704	641	28.5	110.8

1957	1	18,629	615	30,585	49,829	.170	609	819	27.4	105.2
	2	18,399	757	31,082	50,238	.170	546	1,003	27.8	105.6
	3	19,034	598	31,073	50,705	.170	547	1,100	27.8	105.5
	4	18,532	602	31,834	50,968	.170	652	781	28.9	109.1
1958	1	18,532	644	30,666	49,842	.163	688	164	27.4	104.6
	2	18,784	689	31,172	50,645	.154	668	99	27.8	105.7
	3	18,147	653	31,245	50,045	.154	593	433	27.9	108.1
	4	18,504	663	32,193	51,360	.154	656	790	28.7	115.5
1959	1	18,192	695	31,250	50,137	.154	458	600	27.9	110.3
	2	17,640	657	31,914	50,211	.154	457	876	28.3	110.7
	3	17,760	760	31,848	50,368	.154	220	721	28.5	111.4
	4	18,174	1,039	32,591	51,804	.154	464	928	29.4	115.4

Notes to Table A2: Source: All data are taken from the *Federal Reserve Bulletin.*
Col. (1) Member bank reserves (millions of dollars):
"Statement of Condition of the Federal Reserve Banks." Data as of the end of the quarter.
Col. (2) Other deposits in Federal Reserve Banks (millions of dollars): Sum of "Foreign deposits" and "Other deposits."
Col. (3) Currency outside the government (millions of dollars):
Currency in circulation outside the Treasury and Federal Reserve Banks. Data as of the end of the quarter.
Col. (4) Federal Demand Debt (millions of dollars):
Sum of Cols. (1) + (2) + (3).
Col. (5) Reserve requirements index:
Weighted average of reserve requirements for central reserve city banks, reserve city banks, and country banks on net demand deposits at the end of the quarter. The weights are .32 (central reserve city banks), .40 (reserve city banks) and .28 (country banks).
Col. (6) Excess reserves (millions of dollars):
Excess reserves of all member banks, average of daily figures for last week of the quarter.
Col. (7) Borrowings (millions of dollars):
Borrowings at Federal Reserve banks of all member banks, average of daily figures for last week in last month of the quarter. Figures for the fourth quarter of 1945 is monthly average.
Col. (8) Currency outside banks (billions of dollars, not seasonally adjusted):
Data as of last Wednesday of quarter.
Col. (9) Demand deposits adjusted (billions of dollars, not seasonally adjusted):
Data as of last Wednesday of quarter.

Table A3 Federal debt, income, and wealth

Yr.	Qtr.	S (1)	I (2)	$S+I$ (3)	L (4)	T (5)	Y_g (6)	Gov't. pay-rolls (7)	Y (8)	Net national wealth (9)	W (10)
1946	1	46,077	16,259	62,336	104,975	191.6	198.0	24.9	173.1	584.4	740.1
	2	39,187	18,320	57,507	101,413	189.8	206.3	20.2	186.1	598.3	749.3
	3	38,025	12,604	50,629	103,037	188.3	217.1	18.8	198.3	649.8	796.1
	4	31,715	16,635	48,350	98,496	187.8	221.2	18.5	202.7	700.9	842.4
1947	1	28,277	18,591	46,868	96,528	187.2	226.0	17.9	208.1	736.4	872.8
	2	28,295	15,557	43,852	97,441	184.2	230.0	17.4	212.6	758.9	890.2
	3	30,958	17,689	48,647	92,456	188.9	235.6	16.9	218.7	807.7	933.9
	4	27,886	21,615	49,501	88,310	187.5	245.1	17.4	227.7	843.5	964.5
1948	1	33,701	15,667	49,368	85,392	184.5	249.5	17.7	231.8	867.4	985.1
	2	32,981	14,995	47,976	85,474	181.5	257.7	18.1	239.6	888.3	1002.7
	3	28,935	25,255	54,190	75,108	189.4	264.0	19.2	244.8	914.8	1025.9
	4	30,382	27,340	57,722	70,825	190.7	265.9	20.0	245.9	928.4	1036.3
1949	1	28,215	29,170	57,385	70,826	189.3	259.8	20.1	239.7	935.7	1044.9
	2	32,860	31,499	64,359	65,945	198.6	256.4	20.3	236.1	934.1	1044.7
	3	35,747	30,450	66,197	65,938	195.6	258.8	20.6	238.2	923.5	1035.4
	4	36,709	36,669	73,378	57,608	209.6	257.0	21.0	236.0	932.0	1045.3
1950	1	32,792	40,323	73,115	58,263	206.6	265.8	21.0	244.8	957.4	1067.6
	2	25,362	49,207	74,569	56,937	208.5	274.4	21.2	253.2	981.9	1089.0
	3	33,940	37,668	71,608	57,106	207.2	293.2	22.4	270.8	1034.8	1138.8
	4	30,379	40,420	70,799	55,568	205.4	304.3	24.3	280.0	1067.1	1168.1
1951	1	27,348	41,358	68,706	53,743	202.4	317.8	26.4	291.4	1105.7	1204.8
	2	29,387	40,407	69,794	44,462	186.2	326.4	28.2	298.2	1133.6	1230.7
	3	30,592	39,667	70,259	44,437	183.2	333.8	30.2	303.6	1147.4	1242.6
	4	33,692	38,563	72,255	44,381	180.2	338.1	30.8	307.3	1164.6	1257.8

1952	1	33,985	37,640	71,625	44,870	175.5	341.0	32.1	308.9	1184.5	1277.1
	2	33,339	37,649	70,988	44,085	171.2	341.3	32.9	308.4	1199.6	1291.6
	3	39,108	30,450	69,558	48,125	160.3	347.0	33.4	313.6	1204.6	1296.0
	4	42,071	30,479	72,550	48,052	157.2	358.6	33.6	325.0	1214.1	1305.0
1953	1	44,035	27,532	71,567	47,177	155.8	364.5	33.7	330.8	1227.6	1319.7
	2	48,921	25,726	74,647	44,482	167.2	368.8	34.0	334.8	1242.6	1335.9
	3	50,735	28,864	79,599	44,462	164.2	367.1	33.9	333.2	1253.6	1348.1
	4	56,088	23,020	79,108	46,056	159.5	361.0	33.9	327.1	1259.3	1355.1
1954	1	48,392	16,902	65,294	56,519	146.3	360.0	34.0	326.0	1267.8	1363.5
	2	43,736	21,453	65,189	56,583	143.3	358.9	34.3	324.6	1280.8	1376.4
	3	44,829	25,783	70,612	55,603	142.4	362.0	34.6	327.4	1291.2	1386.7
	4	43,342	26,382	69,724	59,694	138.8	370.8	34.8	336.0	1306.3	1401.7
1955	1	34,399	30,182	64,581	61,464	145.6	384.3	35.1	349.2	1325.9	1419.7
	2	32,224	34,216	66,440	61,436	142.6	393.0	36.1	356.9	1349.7	1441.9
	3	39,335	30,382	69,717	62,175	143.5	403.4	36.2	367.2	1371.9	1462.5
	4	39,467	36,320	75,787	58,443	145.4	408.9	36.6	372.3	1401.9	1491.0
1956	1	37,329	35,481	72,810	58,450	142.4	410.6	37.1	373.5	1432.4	1517.5
	2	37,545	30,410	67,955	58,349	139.4	415.0	37.7	377.3	1464.3	1545.4
	3	42,814	28,874	71,688	56,111	139.2	421.0	38.5	382.5	1488.2	1565.3
	4	45,516	39,940	85,456	44,998	153.3	430.0	38.9	391.1	1518.2	1591.3
1957	1	45,700	40,875	86,575	44,975	150.3	437.7	39.4	398.3	1546.5	1617.0
	2	49,649	37,293	87,942	40,237	157.4	442.4	39.9	402.5	1584.0	1651.9
	3	50,395	41,843	92,238	40,211	154.1	447.8	40.7	407.1	1610.3	1675.6
	4	51,705	43,334	95,039	38,576	159.0	442.3	40.7	401.6	1629.6	1692.3
1958	1	50,045	38,276	88,321	44,420	155.7	431.0	41.8	389.2	1639.6	1702.5
	2	43,873	38,492	82,365	52,226	148.0	434.5	42.9	391.6	1658.3	1721.4
	3	45,584	45,482	91,066	45,016	157.4	444.0	44.0	400.0	1667.1	1730.4
	4	50,900	46,741	97,641	44,977	154.4	457.1	44.3	412.8	1702.3	1765.9

Table A3 (continued)

Yr.	Qtr.	S (1)	I (2)	$S+I$ (3)	L (4)	T (5)	Y_g (6)	Gov't. pay-rolls (7)	Y (8)	Net national wealth (9)	W (10)
1959	1	47,168	54,920	102,088	41,843	160.6	470.4	44.6	425.8	1734.4	1798.6
	2	51,341	51,253	102,594	42,389	157.2	484.8	45.4	439.4	1766.1	1830.9
	3	54,194	52,917	107,111	42,345	157.2	478.6	46.1	432.5	1782.6	1848.0
	4	58,765	53,176	111,941	42,285	150.5	483.5	46.7	436.8	1793.8	1859.9

Notes to Table A3
Cols. (1) and (4) U.S. Government Debt (millions of dollars).
All marketable direct public securities, excluding those held by federal agencies and trust funds and the Federal Reserve Banks. Classified according to maturity.
Sources: *Treasury Bulletin* 1946 through first quarter of 1953; *Federal Reserve Bulletin* second quarter of 1953 through fourth quarter of 1959. Beginning with the September 1953 issue of the *Federal Reserve Bulletin*, the basis for classifying bonds with optional call dates was changed from a first call to a final maturity date.
Col. (1) Short-term U.S. Government Debt-securities maturing within one year.
Col. (2) Intermediate-term U.S. Government Debt-securities maturing from one to five years.
Col. (3) Sum of Cols. (1) and (2).
Col. (4) Long-term U.S. Government Debt-securities maturing in five years or more.
Col. (5) Maturity of U.S. Government Debt due in five years or more (in months).
Source: Calculations from *Federal Reserve Bulletin.*
Maturity is a weighted average of the maturity of marketable direct public securities outstanding at the end of each quarter which are due in five years or more.
Col. (6) Gross National Product, seasonally adjusted quarterly totals at annual rates, current prices (billions of dollars).
Source: *U.S. Income and Output* (1946–1955) *Survey of Current Business*, July 1959 and May 1960 (1956–1959).
Col. (7) Government Civilian and Military Salaries and Wages, seasonally adjusted quarterly totals at annual rates, current prices (billions of dollars).
Source: *Ibid.*
Col. (8) Gross Private Product: Col. (6) less Col. (7).
Col. (9) U.S. Net National Wealth (Goldsmith), current prices (billions of dollars).

The quarterly series was constructed by interpolating a quarterly series on net private domestic investment derived from U.S. Department of Commerce data into annual estimates of total national wealth excluding military wealth constructed by Goldsmith. Goldsmith's estimates of wealth from 1945 to 1958 were taken from an unpublished table. The estimates pertain to the end of the year. The figures for wealth in 1959 were extrapolated according to a formula given below.

The first step in the interpolation was to compute quarterly net private domestic investment in constant dollars. To do this, it was necessary to construct a constant dollars depreciation series to deduct from gross private domestic investment in constant dollars. The depreciation series was constructed by deflating capital consumption allowances by a weighted average of the new construction and producers durable equipment implicit price deflators. A weight of .6 was assigned to the new construction deflator, and a weight of .4 was assigned to the producers durable equipment deflator.

The second step was to express net investment in each quarter as a percent of net investment during the year; e.g., investment in the first quarter of 1947 was divided by net investment in 1947.

The third step was to apply the percentage of annual investment per quarter to Goldsmith's estimates of the annual increment to wealth in constant dollars. For example, Commerce data shows that 25 percent of net investment in 1947 occurred in the first quarter. Therefore it is estimated that 25 percent of the increment in real Goldsmith wealth between December 1946 and December 1947 occurred in the first quarter of 1947.

The final step was to convert the quarterly wealth series from constant dollars to current dollars. To do this it was necessary to construct a quarterly wealth deflator. This was done by taking the first difference of the capital consumption allowance deflator; expressing the first difference as a percent of the change in the deflator over one year; computing a Goldsmith wealth deflator (wealth in current dollars divided by wealth in constant dollars); taking the first difference of the Goldsmith wealth deflator (annual increment in the price of wealth); and applying the percentage of annual increase in the capital consumption allowance deflator per quarter to the annual increase in the Goldsmith wealth deflator. For 1959 the Goldsmith wealth deflator was carried forward by the percentage change—quarter to quarter—of the capital consumption allowance deflator.

Col. (10) U.S. Net Private Wealth in current prices (billions of dollars).

Private wealth is defined as national wealth minus the net worth of the public sector. The quarterly series on private wealth was constructed by computing an annual (fourth quarter) series and making a straight line interpolation of annual increments in the net worth of the public sector.

Net worth of the public sector is equal to: U.S. deposits in Federal Reserve and commercial banks plus Public assets less Net public debt less Gold certificates less Treasury currency.

Sources: Net public debt; *Survey of Current Business*, July 1960. Gold certificates and Treasury currency, *Federal Reserve Bulletin*. U.S. deposits, *President's Economic Report for 1960*, Table D-40. Public Assets, Goldsmith, unpublished table; sum of public civilian structures, public producers durables, public land and monetary metals.

Notes

This paper was prepared for and financed by the Commission on Money and Credit. The research was done at the Cowles Foundation for Research in Economics at Yale University. I wish to thank Mrs. Charlotte Phelps, Mrs. Karen Hester, and Mrs. Wilma Heston for their able assistance with the empirical work presented below. I am currently on academic leave from Yale as a member of the staff of the Council of Economic Advisers.

1. John Maynard Keynes, *The General Theory of Employment, Interest and Money* (New York: Harcourt Brace, 1936), pp. 201–202.

2. James Tobin, "Liquidity Preference as Behavior Towards Risk," *Review of Economic Studies*, XXV (February 1958), pp. 65–86.

3. See the following: A. J. Brown, "Interest, Prices, and the Demand Schedule for Idle Money," *Oxford Economic Papers* (May 1939), pp. 46–69; M. Kalecki, "The Short-Term Rate of Interest and the Velocity of Cash Circulation," *Review of Economics and Statistics*, XXIII (May 1941), pp. 97–99; James Tobin, "Liquidity Preference and Monetary Policy," *Review of Economics and Statistics*, XXIX (May 1947), pp. 124–131; A. M. Khusro, "Investigation of Liquidity Preference," *Yorkshire Bulletin of Economic and Social Research*, IV (January 1952), pp. 1–20; Henry Allen Latané, "Cash Balances and the Interest Rate—A Pragmatic Result," *Review of Economics and Statistics*, XXXVI (November 1954), pp. 456–460; Andrew C. Stedry, "A Note on Interest Ratés and the Demand for Money," *Review of Economics and Statistics*, XLI (August 1959), pp. 303–307; Martin Bronfenbrenner and Thomas Mayer, "Liquidity Functions in the American Economy," *Econometrica*, XXVIII (October 1960), pp. 810–834.

4. Friedrich A. Lutz, "The Structure of Interest Rates," *Readings in the Theory of Income Distribution* (Philadelphia: Blakiston, 1946), pp. 499–504; J. R. Hicks, *Value and Capital*, Second Ed. (Oxford: Clarendon, 1953), pp. 141–145; Joseph W. Conard, *An Introduction to the Theory of Interest* (Berkeley: University of California, 1959), pp. 290–301.

5. Joan Robinson, "The Rate of Interest," *The Rate of Interest and Other Essays* (London: Macmillan, 1952), pp. 5–10.

6. James Tobin, "Asset Holdings and Spending Decisions," *American Economic Review*, XLII (May 1952), pp. 110–120.

7. John G. Gurley, "Liquidity and Financial Institutions in the Postwar Economy," *Study of Employment, Growth, and the Price Levels*, prepared for the U.S. Congress, Joint Economic Committee (Washington: U.S. Government Printing Office, 1960).

8. *Ibid.*, p. 3.

9. Council of Economic Advisers, "The American Economy in 1961: Problems and Policies," *Hearings on the January 1961 Economic Report of the President*, Joint Economic Committee (Washington: U.S. Government Printing Office, 1961), pp. 327–329, 373–377.

10. There is a possible objection to the inclusion of government payrolls in the potential variable when it is excluded from actual *Y*, but the alternative of constructing a concept of potential Gross Private Product seemed even less appealing.

11. A few sample calculations suggest that the equations were much less successful in tracing the cyclical movements of rates during 1960 and 1961.

12. Arthur Broida of the Board of Governors of the Federal Reserve System offered helpful comments and criticisms on these matters.

13. See Hicks, *op. cit.*, pp. 262, 281.

14. John M. Culbertson, "The Term Structure of Interest Rates," *Quarterly Journal of Economics*, LXXI (November 1957), pp. 485–517.

The Full Employment Surplus Revisited

The current effort of fiscal and monetary policy makers to achieve disinflation without recession has put the spotlight of public attention once again on the federal budget—as well as on monetary policy and the state of private demand. Some of the discussion of the budgetary impact on the economy has focused on the recent and prospective disappearance of the federal surplus. The surplus of the federal sector in the national accounts, which was $13.5 billion (annual rate) in the second quarter of 1969, virtually vanishes in the first half of 1970. Moreover, some who have predicted that the President's budgetary program for fiscal 1971 will actually turn out in deficit have interpreted such an outcome as a shift toward stimulus in fiscal policy.

In a period of slowdown in economic activity, the movement of the actual surplus or deficit in the federal budget must be carefully interpreted. If a shift to deficit merely reflects a slower growth of federal revenues associated with a weakening of economic activity, that shift is an automatic stabilizer bolstering demand rather than a stimulus propelling the economy.

Economists have long been concerned with the inadequacy of the actual surplus (or deficit) as a measure of fiscal impact. It fails to distinguish the budget's influence on the economy from the economy's influence on the budget. The actual surplus (or deficit)[1] is the composite result of the budget program, as defined in terms of expenditures and tax rates, and the strength of aggregate demand. To remedy the basic defect of the actual surplus as a fiscal indicator, the concept of the full employment surplus was developed. The full employment surplus is an estimate of what the federal surplus would be if the economy were operating along the path of its potential gross national product (GNP). It is thus not affected by fluctuations in economic activity that shrink or swell the revenue base relative to that associated with the path of potential growth. The full employment surplus is thus a way to focus on the policy actions that determine expenditure programs and tax rates, and to separate them from a consideration of the autonomous strength of private demand and of the posture of monetary policy.

Uses of the Concept

Although it has roots in the 1930s, the concept can be directly dated back to a proposal made in 1947 by the Committee for Economic Development (CED) that the budget be designed to "yield a moderate surplus at high-employment national income."[2] The full employment surplus was applied by E. Cary Brown in an historical analysis of the thirties, which demonstrated that the federal deficits of the period were primarily the result of automatic stabilization rather than of active stimulation.[3]

The concept was used by several economists analyzing the sluggish economic situation and outlook in 1960 and early 1961—David Lusher, James Knowles, Herbert Stein, and Charles Schultze.[4] They stressed the large shortfall of federal revenues associated with the shortfall of the economy below high employment, pointing out that fiscal policy was considerably more restrictive than was evident in the actual federal accounts.

The full employment surplus was explained in detail in the *Annual Report of the Council of Economic Advisers* for 1962. The 1964 and 1965 *Annual Reports* analyzed the President's budget program prospectively in terms of movements of the full employment surplus, and the 1966 *Report* showed it in a chart. But the concept retreated into the background thereafter, when fiscal policy became excessively stimulative during the Vietnam buildup. Because the difference between actual and potential real GNP did not exceed 1.8 percent between mid-1965 and the end of 1969, the full employment and actual surpluses told very similar stories. Actual deficits of about $12 billion in 1967 made clear the highly stimulative character of fiscal policy. The major shift to restraint was likewise clearly reflected in substantial actual surpluses during 1969.

During this period, the Federal Reserve Bank of St. Louis kept the quantitative concept before the public with its quarterly release, "Federal

Budget Trends." The President's Commission on Budget Concepts endorsed the "basic ideas embodied in this measure."[5] The Committee for Economic Development also continued to nurture its child, most recently in recommending a full employment surplus of $6 billion to $9 billion for calendar year 1970 and fiscal 1971.[6] The *Annual Report of the Council of Economic Advisers* for 1970 mentions the high employment surplus (page 67) and discusses its longer-run implications (pages 82–83), although no quantitative estimates of its current size are presented.

The full employment surplus has been a useful tool for clarifying various messages, lessons, and issues concerning stabilization policy.

Indicator of Changes in Fiscal Policy

A higher full employment surplus is an indicator of a more restrictive fiscal policy. The concept can be used in comparing two alternative fiscal programs that might be applied in a given forthcoming period, or to compare the degree of fiscal restraint in two different periods. For appropriate comparisons over a considerable time interval, the full employment surplus should be viewed as a percentage of potential GNP in order to take account of the growing size of the economy. Most often, the comparison is made from one year to the next, showing whether the net shift of fiscal policy is toward restriction or stimulus. The desirability of such a shift should be appraised in terms of the current and target levels of economic activity, current and planned monetary policy, and expected changes in the strength of private demand. The full employment surplus helps to keep the analytic eye on the ball.

Guardian against Perverse Fiscal Policy

From the time of the 1947 CED statement to the present, economists have felt the need to warn policy makers not to set a target for an actual surplus independent of the level of economic activity. Such a strategy would have perverse economic effects, leading, for example, to added outlays (or tax cuts) if revenues are swollen by a boom. It is not hard to imagine now that, if revenues for fiscal 1971 should have to be revised downward from the administration's estimates because the economy is weaker than anticipated, some would propose to preserve the projected actual surplus and hence to reduce expenditures, thus further weakening the economy. In effect, putting the focus on the full employment surplus guards the automatic stabilizers in the political decision process.

Standard for Long-Term Fiscal Posture

The mirror image of the full employment surplus is the excess of private investment over private saving (including the surplus of the state and local sectors) required to achieve equilibrium at full employment. Economists have some rough notion of how private investment would normally compare with private saving for an assumed monetary policy. Most longer-term projections of a desirable and feasible pattern of economic activity provide for some moderate positive full employment surplus to avoid excess demand and tight money. On the other hand, nobody would prescribe, as a normal diet, full employment surpluses amounting to 2 percent of GNP, such as prevailed in 1960 and 1961. The full employment surplus tends to keep discussions of long-run fiscal strategy within a reasonable range. In the early sixties, those who valued the balancing of the budget as a fiscal discipline could be assured that, even with a big tax cut, the budget would still come into the black at full employment. Today, legislators can be reminded to leave room for some full employment surplus in their long-run plans.

Criterion for Long-Run Monetary Policy

How much private investment demand exceeds private saving at full employment depends critically on the character of monetary policy. Thus the appropriate size of the full employment surplus must be evaluated with regard to the desired or probable posture of monetary policy. For any given utilization target, the choice of a larger average surplus over the long run requires a more expansionary monetary policy and implies a desire to shift resources into homebuilding and other investment through the mechanisms of private markets.

Delineator of Fiscal Dividend and Drag

The increases in annual revenue associated with economic growth provide a useful benchmark in fiscal planning. In the early sixties, it was important to stress in public discussion that, because of this annual fiscal dividend, the budget becomes tighter if expenditures and tax laws stand still. If allowed to operate, fiscal drag would tend to hold the economy below its potential growth. Today the fiscal drag message lingers only in nostalgia. The relevant current lesson is that no more than the annual fiscal dividend can be added to spending (or given away in tax cuts) without making fiscal policy more stimulative. And a further caveat is required—that much of the dividend has been committed in advance through built-in increases in expenditures or already enacted tax cuts. Although the lesson has changed, the same concept helps to teach it.

Quantifying the Concept

Most of these uses require a quantification of the full employment surplus in a consistent time series. The standard calculations have been based on an assumed level of real output equal to "potential output," which in turn is the estimated trend line of production consistent with an average unemployment rate of 4 percent of the civilian labor force.[7]

The implicit price deflator for the GNP, as reported in the national income accounts, is used to convert potential GNP into current dollars. Then income shares—such as personal income and corporate profits—are estimated on the basis of potential GNP in current dollars; and full employment estimates of federal revenues are then derived in terms of the tax laws applicable to the period in question.

Full employment expenditures differ from those actually reported in the national accounts only through the adjustment of unemployment compensation benefits to reflect differences of the actual unemployment rate from the target of 4 percent. In point of fact, some other types of federal expenditures, such as social security benefits and farm support payments, may be influenced by the level of economic activity. But that relationship is not readily quantified or very dependable. Furthermore, at any given point in time, many—perhaps most—federal expenditures are not subject to control, having become built in as a result of previously enacted legislation and previous executive action. Yet these outlays are properly viewed as discretionary, rather than automatic, in the sense that they are not dependent on the current level of economic activity.

The full employment surplus is simply the difference between full employment revenues and full employment expenditures. The difference between the full employment and actual surpluses for any period measures the automatic stabilization of the fiscal system—the impact on revenues (and unemployment benefits) resulting from deviations of actual economic activity from the path of potential. The change in the full employment surplus from period to period is equal to:

a. the increase of federal revenues, with unchanged tax rates and base, associated with economic growth along the potential path,

plus

b. the dollar value at full employment of net changes in tax rates taking effect in that time interval,

minus

c. the increase in adjusted expenditures.

The full employment surplus is linked to the federal sector of the national income accounts. This concept of the budget is convenient because it fits with the rest of the national accounting system. Two major conceptual differences between the federal sector and the recently adopted unified budget affect the surplus in the two measures. First, some receipts and expenditures in the federal sector are on an accrual basis, while the unified budget is entirely on a cash basis. Second, the federal sector excludes all lending. Federal lending clearly has economic significance, but it should be viewed in the context of monetary and debt management policy rather than fiscal policy.

Thus defined and thus calculated, the full employment surplus has been a useful tool for the presentation and public discussion of some key issues in stabilization policy. It offers a simple, one-parameter description of the macroeconomic effects of fiscal policy of presidents, legislators, journalists, and concerned citizens. In particular, it offers them a clearly superior alternative to the actual surplus.

It is not, and was never meant to be, a precise measure of fiscal impact for use by the expert. Indeed, the expert has no dire need for a single, publicly available summary number. The internal development of a budget program by government fiscal experts can and should be based on more sophisticated concepts and computations. The research economist specializing in fiscal policy is free to exercise his own options. He will not summarize fiscal policy if he chooses to develop a structural econometric model; instead, he will apply many fiscal variables and many income-expenditure relationships to spell out the impact of the budget on the economy. If he pursues a shortcut technique relying on a single independent variable to characterize fiscal policy, he can and will concoct his own, using whatever sophisticated refinements, weights, and transformations he considers useful.

At the current stage of knowledge of fiscal policy and of income-expenditure relationships, the specialists do not agree on the best recipe. Awaiting the development of firm scientific knowledge and of professional consensus on the precise measurement of fiscal impact would sacrifice the opportunity to provide a useful quantified concept for informed public discussion.

In short, the aim should not be to solve all the problems of aggregate demand analysis in the calculation of the full employment surplus, but rather to achieve professional agreement on the procedures for defining and estimating the full employment surplus as a useful and standardized quantitative indicator of fiscal impact. As refinements are established and agreed upon, they can be incorporated into the measure to increase its accuracy. Most economic time series are used as indicators rather than precise measures—the unemployment rate as an indicator of the tightness of labor markets, published series on operating rates as indicators of excess capacity in industry.

Professional users should be fully aware of the many limitations and problems associated with the full employment surplus. Some of these will now be discussed—weighting, timing, price adjustment, the target path, and hypothetical revenue estimation. Updated historical estimates of the full employment surplus are then presented, and the President's 1971 budget is quantified and discussed in terms of the full employment surplus.

Weighting Components

Like the actual surplus, the full employment surplus implies that all federal outlays have equal bang for a buck and that all federal revenues have an equal and opposite impact on demand. No one would seriously defend that proposition. Suggestions for weighting the various components have been made by Gramlich and Musgrave.[8]

On the expenditure side, a weighting scheme can begin by conventionally assigning a coefficient of unity to a dollar of government purchases of goods and services. Of course, that is not an estimate of the total ultimate impact on real GNP. In an underemployed economy with an accommodative monetary policy, the spending multiplier provides that estimate.

Because the marginal propensity to consume of individuals is less than unity, government transfers to persons would receive a coefficient reflecting that fact—perhaps 0.9. The appropriate weight for federal grants to states and localities raises more significant empirical issues. The weight should be less than unity to the extent that grants tend to increase state and local surpluses, reduce pressure on these governments to raise their taxes, or generate extra transfer payments rather than added direct purchases. On the other hand, given the matching provisions of some federal grant programs, the grants might actually magnify purchases made by states and localities and even shift their budgets toward deficit. Federal sudsidies and payments of net interest probably exert less stimulus per dollar than the outlays mentioned above.

On the revenue side, the weight on personal taxes should be somewhat less than unity to reflect the marginal propensity to save of taxpaying households. In terms of the impact on national product in money—rather than real—terms, the coefficient of restraint on indirect taxes perhaps might be somewhat smaller than that on personal taxes, given the evidence that excises are shifted forward into prices.

The treatment of the corporate tax is the most difficult problem. The correct coefficient depends on the shifting of the corporate tax, the restraining effect of the unshifted portion on corporate investment spending, and the impact on consumption through induced changes in dividend payments and in the valuation of equities. These issues are subjects of major professional controversy and no clearcut answer can be given. The considerations do point, however, toward a somewhat smaller coefficient of restraint on corporate than on personal taxes.

The estimates of the full employment surplus since mid-1955 (shown in Table 2 near the end of this paper) have been recalculated with several weighting systems. The following set of weights seems reasonable:

Expenditures		**Revenues**	
Purchases of goods and services	1.0	Personal taxes	−0.9
Transfer payments to persons	0.9	Corporate taxes	−0.75
Grants to state and local governments	0.9	Indirect taxes	−0.9
Interest	0.7	Payroll taxes	−0.9
All other	0.7		

This (or any similar) weighting system illustrates the point of the balanced budget multiplier theorem: A dollar's worth of federal purchases is not completely offset by a dollar's worth of tax revenue. As in most plausible sets of weights, the average coefficient of restraint applied to the revenue side is smaller than the average coefficient of stimulus from expenditures. As a result, the level of the weighted full employment surplus is lower than that of the unweighted one. For the period between mid-1955 and the end of 1969, the average unweighted full employment surplus as a percentage of potential GNP amounts to 0.75 percent. On the other hand, the weighted scheme yields an average full employment *deficit* of 0.63 percent of potential GNP for that period.

But if the difference between the two were consistently 1.38 percent of potential GNP, the weighting scheme would be of little consequence. The level of the measure is of no particular interest. The importance of weighting hinges on whether changes in the composition of the budget or in the size of the budget relative to GNP are sufficiently large to produce a different profile of movements in the weighted and unweighted full employment surplus. In fact, for the past decade and a half, the profiles have been exceedingly similar. In quarter-to-quarter changes of the two series, the biggest disparity shows up in the movement from the fourth quarter of 1968 to the first quarter of 1969: The weighted figure shifts toward restraint by $9.4 billion while the unweighted one shifts in that direction by $10.7 billion, a disparity of $1.3 billion, or about 0.15 percent of GNP. Another disparity in quarterly movements amounting to 0.15 percent of potential GNP occurs from the fourth quarter of 1967 to the first quarter of 1968. Between mid-1955 and 1967, no quarterly disparity is as large as $1 billion.

On an annual basis, the biggest disparities in movement are from 1967 to 1968 and from 1968 to 1969; in each case the unweighted series shows a slightly more than $2 billion greater shift toward restraint than the weighted series. Over the two years combined, the unweighted figure shifts to restraint by $21.6 billion while the weighted one shifts by $17.3 billion. No other annual disparity exceeds $800 million. The most restrictive period by both measures is the year 1960, with the first quarter taking the prize as the most restrictive of all. Both measures reveal the period from the beginning of 1967 to mid-1968 as clearly the most stimulative. Nor is the long-term trend different: 1956 and 1969 are years of somewhat above average fiscal restrictiveness by both measures. In short, any interesting statement about fiscal policy that would emerge from one of these series could be made with the support of the other.

Although future budget plans point to a fairly significant drop in purchases as a fraction of total federal outlays, they also confirm the relative insignificance of weighting. The shift in the composition of expenditures between calendar 1969 and 1970 is equivalent to a restraining action of about $800 million. The shift projected between 1969 and 1975, according to the *Annual Report of the Council of Economic Advisers* for 1970, is equivalent to about $1 billion of restraint.

It is reassuring that the full employment surplus consistently tells the same story whether it is unweighted or weighted by the illustrative scheme, for disagreement within the profession on the appropriate weights creates a serious obstacle to the weighting of components in a time series designed for broad use and discussion. For example, in contrast to the weights selected as most reasonable above, Musgrave has expressed his preference for coefficients of 1 on grants and subsidies, 0.3 on net interest, and -0.5 on corporate taxes.[9]

It is surely more practical to agree not to weight—and to remember that omission—than to negotiate the coefficients. As indicated above, the omission is generally not serious.

If there were to be a major upheaval in the composition or size of the budget, weighting would have to be borne in mind. Moreover, major issues occasionally arise concerning the appropriate weighting of a specific fiscal action. For example, according to a number of studies, the investment tax credit had a particularly large impact per dollar. And a temporary suspension of that measure—such as occurred during 1966 and 1967—might have been expected to have an especially magnified effect. On the other hand, theoretical reasoning suggests that a temporary corporate income tax imposes relatively little restraint. Some discount on the restrictiveness of the individual income tax surcharge was also called for in light of its temporary character, although the relevant empirical studies generally show only a small difference between the marginal propensities to consume out of small windfalls and out of regular income.

These are significant issues, but their resolution cannot be built into a standard weighting system. Rather they should be handled as reminders and footnotes to be analyzed specifically when they become relevant. The use of the full employment surplus as an indicator of fiscal impact should not blind us to these other considerations.

Timing Issues

In some respects, the full employment surplus is a static concept. It describes how much fiscal policy is pushing the economy in a given period—it does not spell out the expected timing of the resulting movement of economic activity. Some dynamic multiplier process is implied, but not specified; the time phasing of the subsequent impact is left to be investigated by econometric studies. Indeed, the time shape is likely to vary for different types of fiscal actions. The multiplier impact flowing from grants to states and localities may be less rapid than that associated with an increase in transfer payments to persons, even if both have ultimately equal stimulative effects per dollar.

Sometimes, however, the choices in timing become issues of kind rather than merely of degree. In the case of changes in the corporate tax base or rates, the national accounts annualize the impact over a calendar year. Thus a legislative action that affects liabilities during the year it is taken is reflected in subsequent data as a fiscal stimulus or sedative for periods in advance of its enactment. Starting with the first quarter of 1962, the federal sector of the national accounts reflects the reform of depreciation regulations that was made in July 1962 and the investment credit that was enacted in October 1962. Similarly, the corporate tax surcharge, which was not enacted until June 1968, shows up at the start of that calendar year.

A related problem arises in the case of increases in the payroll ceiling for social security taxes. In point of fact, such increases have negligible effects on aggregate take-home pay until late in the calendar year, since the worker pays social security contributions at an undiminished rate during the year until he reaches the ceiling for that calendar year. Yet, starting with the first quarter, the seasonally adjusted national accounts reflect the full impact of any rise in the payroll tax base. Surely, these oddities of annualizing need to be recognized and taken into account. This can be done either by footnoting the amounts at issue in the relevant quarters or by adjusting full employment revenues differently from actual revenues. We prefer the former route in order to avoid another wedge between actual and full employment revenues.[10]

The annualizing problem is probably minor compared with other uncertainties about the timing of the fiscal impact of tax changes. Most major tax actions hang in the legislative balance for a considerable time before enactment and, during that period, private decision makers try to predict the ultimate outcome. Tax proposals can have impacts before they are enacted into law and, indeed, even if they are ultimately rejected. Moreover, when tax provisions are legislated far in advance (as in the 1969 law), they can influence private demand before they have any direct impact on after-tax incomes.

The timing problem on the expenditure side of the accounts has been given special and detailed attention by Murray Weidenbaum.[11] He has stressed that decisions to increase procurement may stimulate economic activity before they actually affect federal purchases. In particular, they would show up as private inventories of purchased materials and goods-in-process before delivery to the federal government. The Office of Business Economics of the Department of Commerce has estimated on an annual basis the inventory investment associated with the step-up of defense procurement since 1965. Obviously, these calculations are of a highly tentative and tenuous character. They show the following rates, in billions of dollars, of inventory investment attributable to defense activity:

1965	0.4
1966	2.6
1967	2.1
1968	1.3
1969	1.2

From 1965 to 1966, the rise of $2.2 billion in the rate of inventory investment represents an added fiscal stimulus of some significance, although it is not so large as Weidenbaum and Galper and Gramlich have suggested. This is another fiscal consideration that must be borne in mind as an addendum to the full employment surplus. It clearly cannot be built into any quarterly time series nor can it be reliably predicted, given present data and knowledge.[12]

Adjustment for Prices

Standard calculations of full employment revenues have been based on a concept of potential GNP in current prices in which real potential GNP is multiplied by the *actual* price level (GNP deflator) of that period. Because actual prices are thus incorporated into historical estimates of the full employment surplus, no allowance is made for automatic stabilizing revenue gains due to the price acceleration of excess demand inflation.[13]

The President's Commission on Budget Concepts spoke out strongly on this issue:

> . . . If the high employment surplus is to be used as a measure of budget impact in a period when demand is strong and prices rising more than normally, some allowance for the effect of rising prices on budget revenues should be made to avoid understating the stimulative impact of the budget.[14]

The understatement of fiscal stimulus referred to by the commission arises in the following way: When actual output exceeds potential output and prices accelerate, actual federal revenues are swollen by both the added real incomes and the inflation. Yet, while the revenues associated with extra real output are reflected as an automatic stabilizing element in the budget, the added revenues due to acceleration of prices are built into full employment revenues. The impact of higher prices on federal expenditures is neither as prompt nor as automatic as that on revenues. Thus excess demand inflation can make the fiscal program look more restrictive ex post than ex ante, merely because autonomous private demand or monetary policy shifted into higher gear or because the budget itself was inappropriately expansionary. Some adjustment for inflation is hence appropriate, but it is not clear what specific adjustment will do the job.

The bulge in output and the bulge in prices are treated asymmetrically in the calculation of full employment revenues. But the problem cannot be solved by a consistent symmetrical treatment over a period of years, because the two bulges do not behave symmetrically over the longer run. Suppose the economy starts at potential with output growing 4 percent a year and prices creeping up at a "normal" rate. A boom then pulls both output and prices above their respective trend paths. If the boom ends and output returns to potential, the old path should essentially still be a reasonable measure of potential output. But empirically the price level works on a ratchet; although the rate of increase in prices may come back down to normal, the level of prices will not roll back just because excess demand is eliminated—it will stay above the old path.

This fact of life is reflected in economic policy. A rollback of the price level is not considered by any government to be a desirable or feasible objective, once inflation has been experienced. The aim is to restore a tolerable rate of price increase rather than to return to any particular target price path. Thus it would not be satisfactory to draw a "normal path" of prices and to stick to that path for calculating full employment revenues regardless of what happens. At some point, bygones on the price level must be treated as bygones. Unlike the path for potential output, the future normal path for prices is subject to major revision in light of past deviations from that path.

With due apologies, the reader is asked to plow through the following example. Suppose real output exactly matches potential at $500 billion in year zero; meanwhile, prices creep upward at a "normal" rate of 2 percent a year. Revenues, let us say, are always 20 percent of GNP. In year zero, the actual budget is balanced, with revenues and expenditures both equal to $100 billion. The full employment surplus, like the actual surplus, is clearly zero, as shown in Table 1. So far, everything is fine.

Now consider year one. Suppose expenditures are set at $106 billion. If real output continued to match potential, it would grow 4 percent, and

Table 1 Illustrative calculation of full employment revenues in inflation

Year	Expenditures	Revenues	Surplus	GNP	Deflator
Ex ante					
0	100	100	0	500	100
1	106	106	0	530	102
2	112	112	0	560	104
Actual					
0	100	100	0	500	100
1	106	111	5	555	104
2	112	114	2	570	106
Full employment calculation (current practice)					
0	100	100	0	500	100
1	106	108	2	540	104
2	112	114	2	570	106

prices would rise another 2 percent. Revenues would then also be $106 billion. Prospectively, the full employment surplus is zero once again.

Suppose, however, that private demand surges in year one. Real output grows 7 percent while prices rise 4 percent, yielding a GNP of about $555 billion. Actual revenues then rise to $111 billion. Meanwhile, suppose expenditures are unaffected by the boom and go to $106 billion as anticipated. The actual surplus is thus $5 billion. The $5 billion bulge in revenues due to the boom is, in effect, the sum of a $3 billion bonus resulting from the 3 percent rise in real output, and a $2 billion increment due to the extra 2 percent jump in prices. The former portion is eliminated from the full employment calculation; but the latter gets folded into the estimate of the full employment surplus when full employment revenues are calculated in terms of the actual deflator of 104 for year one. Clearly, the ex ante zero estimate of the full employment surplus was a better measure of fiscal impact than the ex post estimate of $2 billion. The apparent lesson is: Don't use actual prices of year one; stick with the normal deflator of 102 and calculate full employment revenues from a money potential GNP based on that deflator. The solution looks easy.

It is not. Problems appear when year two is considered. One possibility is to stick to your guns. If the normal price level was 102 in year one and if 2 percent is still the estimated rate of price rise at potential for the long run, the normal deflator for year two might conceivably be taken as 104. In that event, full employment revenues for year two would be taken ex ante as $112 billion. Suppose, for a moment, that expenditures are also set at that level. Suppose further that real output grows only 1 percent and thus returns to the real potential path; nonetheless, prices are still going to rise. Even if they rise by only a normal 2 percent, the deflator for year two will be 106 and GNP will be about $570 billion. The realization of potential output will thus bring in $114 billion of actual revenues and an actual surplus of $2 billion. Private investment has to exceed private saving for full employment to be achieved, even though the full employment surplus is supposed to be zero.

If this paradox seems tolerable for a year, try it for longer. Suppose the inflationary boom continues for four years, with prices rising steadily at 4 percent a year and a bulge in the actual price level above the assumed normal level amounting to 8 percent. If actual output finally slowed down to match potential in year five and prices slowed down to their normal rate, the actual surplus might be $8 billion when the full employment surplus was allegedly zero. With the old normal price path as the basis for a calculated full employment surplus of zero in year five, one would be saying: At a deflator of 110, private investment would merely have to match private saving at high employment. That is not an illuminating proposition in a world where the price deflator is at least 118. The budget really has become a lot more restrictive.

The introduction of one further note of realism into this example will reduce the problem, but not eliminate it. In point of fact, some government expenditures will, after a lag, respond more or less automatically to inflation. For example, a formula that gears pay increases for federal workers to the movement of private wage rates has that effect. If full employment expenditures are adjusted downward to exclude such inflation-induced outlays, the resulting estimate of the full employment surplus will be a less unrealistic measure of fiscal impact. But there is no reason to believe that the automatic price elasticity of expenditures is large enough to cure the problem.

Clearly, at some point, the ratchet in the price level of the real world must be reflected in the calculation of the full employment budget. The key issue is when and how bygones should be accepted as bygones. In the absence of any evident "right answer," all one can do is legislate a statute of limitations. The annual character of the budget-planning process makes a one-year period appealing. For a period of this length, federal expenditures can be reasonably regarded as not automatically responsive to concurrent price increases—an assumption that would be unrealistic over the longer run. If the price path for the calculation of full employment revenues can be set forth a year in advance, the calculation is made independent of economic activity (both predicted and realized) for that period, and the worst offenses of current practice are eliminated. In a boom year, added actual revenues resulting from extra output and those due to extra price increases are both treated as automatic stabilizers that make the actual surplus exceed the full employment surplus.

If a price adjustment is to be made, it requires a rule or convention under which the potential GNP in money terms for a year is independent of the actual (or predicted) price behavior during that year. Can any rule of reason be devised?

Here another fact of economic life rears its ugly head. In addition to its ratchet behavior, the price level also displays momentum in its pace of advance. After excess demand is eliminated, the *rate of increase* in prices continues to be above normal for some time. This momentum would not be allowed for in a rule that defined normal prices of the current year as last year's actual prices marked up by the long-run normal rate of upward creep in prices. On the other hand, if the calculation of full employment revenues is based on a continuation of the past year's inflationary rate of price increase, it assumes no slowdown of prices.

The first rule—back to the normal rate of price increase immediately—seems to produce too low a result, while the second rule—assume continuation of recent rates of inflation—seems to yield an implausibly high deflator. The compelling conclusion emerges that one should average and get something in the middle. A compromise rule is that the price level associated with the calculation of full employment revenues should allow for disinflation over a year's period that brings the trend of price increases halfway back to the normal rate. If prices rose 4 percent last year and if 2 percent is the normal rate, this year's potential price level should be taken as 3 percent above last year's actual price level.

The resulting formula for calculating the relevant potential price (P^*) path is:

$$P_T^* = \frac{P_{T-1}}{2}\left[1.02 + \left(\frac{P_{T-1}}{P_{T-2}}\right)\right].$$

On a quarterly basis, the formula can be modified to the following:

$$P_t^* = \frac{P_{t-4}}{2}\left[1.02 + \left(\frac{P_{t-4}}{P_{t-5}}\right)^4\right].$$

The proposed rule is intended only as a convention that yields results that are not unreasonable, that accepts bygones as bygones in a systematic way, and that responds to the recommendation of the President's Commission on Budget Concepts. It is not meant to forecast how prices would behave if output returned to potential. It is surely not intended to describe or prescribe the ideal transitional process of price deceleration once excess demand inflation has occurred.

The formula given above applies to cases of unusually low rates of price increase as well as to inflation. And in principle it should be symmetrical. If prices advance at a subnormal rate in a slack economy, actual revenues are depressed by the departure below the normal price path as well as by the gap in real output. Both types of revenue shortfall should be classified as automatic stabilizers.

Empirically, however, the issue is not quantitatively significant during periods of slack. The old rule of using actual prices as potential prices is quite adequate. The biggest *positive* difference since mid-1955 between the price deflator yielded by this formula and the actual deflator occurs in 1961 and amounts to 0.7 percent. This would increase the estimate of full employment revenues by approximately three-quarters of a billion dollars.

The 2 percent figure for the normal upward trend of prices at 4 percent unemployment was meant to be illustrative throughout. Nobody knows what the correct number is or will be, or how it might be influenced by policy measures to improve the trade-off. Probably, few members of the profession believe it is as low as 2 percent. But the very fact that 2 percent is not a down-the-middle empirical forecast may make it a more acceptable standard for a conventional calculation.

Unanticipated inflation need not result solely from excess demand. In principle, the full employment surplus calculation should treat such price surprises differently. Returning to the illustration, suppose that money GNP in year one had risen 6 percent, just as targeted ex ante. But suppose the trade-off proved more unfavorable than had been anticipated and the 6 percent rise in money GNP reflected a 3 percent increase in prices and a growth of real output of only 3 percent. The actual budget might be balanced, just as projected. But the 1 percent shortfall in real GNP below potential testifies to the fact that the full employment surplus was positive; if potential output had been realized, revenues would have exceeded expenditures. If 3 percent a year must be accepted as an irreducible normal trend of prices at potential output, then society must reconsider its targets, deciding either to accept a higher normal rate of price increase or else a higher unemployment target (and thus a lower path of potential output).

On the other hand, when output is below potential, prices may increase rapidly as a result of transitional frictions associated with a very rapid rate of growth or a major shift in the composition of demand. The extra revenues collected from the added price increases during such a period would help to moderate the climb, and can be regarded as automatic fiscal stabilizers that work when reasonable speed limits are exceeded.

These issues become empirically relevant in interpreting the behavior of prices and output during 1956–57. At that time, actual output did not exceed estimated potential, nor did the unemployment rate fall below 4 percent. Yet prices accelerated markedly. One might argue that the normal price path should not be taken as lower than actual prices since output did not exceed potential. On the other hand, the adjustment can be defended on the grounds that the price rise was "abnormal," reflecting an excessive speed of advance in 1955, sectoral bottlenecks, or other special factors. If the price adjustment is made, it lowers full employment revenues for fiscal 1957 by about $1\frac{1}{2}$ percent, or a little more than $1 billion.

Actual output has typically exceeded potential during the inflation since 1966. The formula set forth above calls for an adjustment below the actual GNP deflator throughout the period since the second quarter of 1966 by amounts varying up to 1.9 percent, or nearly $4 billion of full employment revenues (see Table 3 in the concluding section).

In summary, the problem of price adjustment in the calculation of full employment revenues is a thorny conceptual issue that has no self-evident satisfactory solution. The rule proposed here is awkward, inelegant, and arbitrary. Yet it avoids some pitfalls and paradoxes in existing practice. Until somebody has a better solution, the alternatives facing the profession are to live with a conventional rule or to live with no adjustment for inflation—remembering what we are doing in either case.

The Target Path

Price instability is just one possible source of problems in estimating the level or growth of full employment revenues. Some of the others are as large or larger in quantitative importance.

One problem of a conceptual nature arises when the unemployment rate does not bear its usual relationship to actual and potential output. The year 1969 provides an egregious example (so did 1956 and the first half of 1957). In 1968, actual output exceeded estimated potential output by 1.1 percent and the unemployment rate was 3.6 percent of the civilian labor force. The distance of the unemployment rate below 4 percent—0.4 percentage point—was consistent with the 1.1 percent overshoot of output, on the basis of past experience. In 1969, however, output just matched potential and the unemployment rate "should" have come back up to 4 percent. In fact, it fell a bit further to 3.5 percent. Longer-run estimates of the path of real potential output are not being revised down on the basis of this reading; rather the experience is attributed to transitory developments such as labor hoarding, or to a normal lag of employment demand behind shifts in demand for output.

The calculations of full employment revenues are geared to potential output as estimated from longer-term trends of the labor force, productivity, and hours worked. They are linked only indirectly to the unemployment rate. The quantitatively less important difference between potential and actual payments of unemployment compensation benefits will, however, directly reflect the current unemployment rate.

One could conceivably argue that the 4 percent unemployment target path should take priority over the trend path of potential GNP when the two disagree. In effect, an interim potential GNP that matched 4 percent unemployment would be drawn below the trend potential path, and the associated estimate of full employment revenues would be marked down correspondingly. In 1969, that downward adjustment would be substantial, perhaps $4 billion or $5 billion. The issue is whether the calculation should tell what the budget would be doing at a GNP that yielded 4 percent unemployment (accepting the past history of actual output and employment), or whether it should be linked to a steady path of output that would be "basically" consistent with 4 percent unemployment. The choice of the former alternative would open up a Pandora's box of dynamic and transitional problems. And there is less compelling reason to confront these problems than those associated with price fluctuations. In this instance, using the trend of potential output seems quite tolerable and does no violence to the concept. Obviously, if experience suggested that estimates of potential GNP were out of line for a considerable period, some adjustment would have to be made.

We just have to remember what we are doing. Lags and wiggles in the relationship of unemployment to output create inescapable problems in the formulation of fiscal and monetary policy. The kind of phenomenon experienced in 1969 may point to the need for especially restrictive policies on the aggregate demand for output if demand pressures on the labor market are to be eased promptly. But that is an argument for a *higher* full employment surplus (given the stance of monetary policy) rather than for a redefinition of the measure.

Revenue Estimation for a Hypothetical World

The estimation of full employment revenues from a given potential money GNP involves all the problems of forecasting federal revenues on a given economic projection, and a few additional ones. Just as the standard revenue-estimating problem of translating a given personal income into the level of personal income tax payments requires assumptions about such issues as the magnitude of taxable capital gains, the amount of nontaxable income, and the size distribution of income, so these same questions must be answered in some explicit or implicit way in the full employment estimate of personal tax revenues. An estimate of "normal" growth in revenue derives a tax base from a given money potential GNP and assumes some "normal" full employment trend of capital gains, income distribution, and the like. The revenue estimator dealing with the real world gets one annual observation per year to check the accuracy of his techniques, but the estimator of full employment revenues gets directly relevant observations only when the economy is close to the full employment path.

For a given money GNP, the biggest source of uncertainty in the revenue estimation for the real world concerns the magnitude of corporate profits. Because the tax rate on corporate profits is much higher than typical rates on personal income, a shift of one dollar from personal income to corporate profits (out of a given dollar total of GNP) adds more than twenty-five cents to federal revenues.[15] The uncertainty about the magnitude of corporate profits is an even more critical problem to the estimator of full employment revenues. Directly or indirectly, it is usually the largest source of difference among estimates of the full employment surplus for a given budget program.

In fact, however, the most serious problems involving corporate profits taxes in the calculation of the full employment surplus are conceptual issues rather than uncertainties of estimation. Even if profits were readily predictable for any given actual GNP and potential GNP, the calculation of corporate tax revenues at full employment would require some difficult decisions about what is to be reflected in the difference between actual and full employment revenues.

The basic guide for such decisions is that the full employment surplus should not be affected by shifts in the autonomous strength of private demand and in monetary policy; yet it should take into account secular and structural changes in the economy. Any long-term changes in the composition of demand between corporate and noncorporate output, in the relative returns to capital and labor, and so on, should influence the estimate of full employment profits and the accompanying taxes. But shifts in aggregate private demand and accompanying cyclical changes in price-cost relationships and in productivity should not, in principle, affect the full employment estimate.

This guide provides a clear answer to the quantitatively important issue of handling the inventory valuation adjustment. Although capital gains on business inventories are excluded from the national income accountant's concept of profits, they are included to a large extent in the tax base, given the accounting systems used by most corporations. Although some small "normal" negative inventory valuation adjustment would accompany the upward price trend on a full employment path, the absolute size of the inventory valuation adjustment will be much larger than normal when prices are rising rapidly, thereby swelling the actual total of corporate profits taxes. Deviations from normal in the inventory valuation adjustment are primarily attributable to shifts in aggregate economic activity. Thus they should show up as part of the automatic stabilizing gap between actual and full employment federal revenues. And they do when the full employment estimate of corporate tax revenues reflects the normal—rather than actual—level of the inventory valuation adjustment. That is the appropriate treatment of the windfall in corporate tax revenues resulting from rapidly rising prices.

The basic guide also suggests the proper handling of another troublesome feature of corporate profit behavior. It is empirically true that the level of profits depends on the rate of increase of GNP as well as on its level and its relation to potential. Corporate costs lag behind revenues both when activity rises sharply and when it turns sluggish; thus any major change of pace in the demand for corporate product has a much bigger impact on corporate profits immediately than after a couple of quarters.

The calculation of full employment revenues should be based on an estimated full employment level of profits that abstracts from this influence of spurts and sags in economic activity. It should express what the level of corporate profits would be at full employment if the economy had been traveling along a full employment path for at least a couple of quarters. The difference between actual and full employment revenues will then depend on the current and very recent speed of economic advance as well as on the size of the gap between actual and potential GNP. This is quite satisfactory. Automatic fiscal stabilization does depend on the speed—as well as the level—of the economy. If profits drop when the economy slows down, the resulting dent in actual revenues reflects the automatic operation of the tax system to bolster a sagging trend of economic activity.

The working of these elements could be seen in 1969. Although actual and potential output were essentially identical, corporate profits (including the inventory valuation adjustment) for this year of slow real growth amounted to only 9.5 percent of GNP, about 1 percentage point below the typical estimate of the normal full employment ratio. Although this dent in profits depressed actual revenues, the totals of full employment and actual revenues were nearly identical (abstracting from the price adjustment set forth above). The main offsetting factor was the very large (negative) size of the inventory valuation adjustment, which contributed an extra $\$1\frac{1}{2}$ billion to actual revenues. Another offset came from extra personal and social security taxes, reflecting the fact that individuals received the incomes that corporations did not get.

This serendipitous situation has developed before. As Levy showed,[16] the "surplus gap"—that is, the calculated full employment surplus minus the actual surplus—has generally borne a close relationship to the gap between potential and actual GNP. Indeed, Knowles used that approach in his 1961 study.[17] Instead of estimating revenues for full employment levels of income, he calculated a marginal federal fiscal coefficient that was to be multiplied by the GNP gap to give a measure of the surplus gap. Some modest variation in the coefficient is called for when tax rates change, but such an adjustment presents no major problem. The surplus gap technique is a handy computational shortcut. But if an abnormally large inventory valuation adjustment and a large rate-of-change influence on profits (or an unusual magnitude of capital gains on long-term assets) reinforced—rather than offset—each other, the surplus gap computation could differ significantly from estimates based on levels. And the latter is conceptually superior.

The cost of exercising that preference, however, is the task of estimating full employment profits. For the period 1955–61, it was quite satisfactory to apply a simple rule that allocated to full employment profits before taxes $11\frac{1}{4}$ percent of potential GNP. Beginning in 1962, the proportion was lowered to $10\frac{2}{3}$ percent to adjust for the depreciation reform of that year. Since 1962, this ratio might translate into about 10.4 percent for profits in the national income sense, including the "normal" negative inventory valuation adjustment at high employment. With output rising rapidly and exceeding potential during most of 1968, the actual share of profits (including the inventory valuation adjustment) would have been expected to exceed 10.4 percent. But it did not. And, in 1969, as noted above, it was only 9.5 percent. It is a major task, beyond the scope of this paper, to determine whether the latest readings reflect a structural long-run shift to a lower profits share at full employment. At this point, however, most of the dent can be tenably attributed to transitory factors. The relationship of costs to corporate revenues seems to be most seriously affected by the slowdown in productivity—which may well be temporary—rather than by any unusual movement of hourly labor compensation in relation to prices, which might have longer-run implications. Nor does the capital goods boom explain the rises in costs; corporate capital consumption allowances have not risen as a share of corporate gross product in recent years.

One recent development in the structure of corporate costs will, however, have continuing implications, even if the economy moves back to full employment promptly. That is the shift in net interest payments by the corporate sector. Until recent years, financial and nonfinancial corporations, taken as a group, were net lenders to the noncorporate economy. Between 1955 and 1965, the net interest received by the corporate sector and reflected in corporate profits varied between $2 billion and $3 billion a year or between 0.3 and 0.5 percent of potential GNP. Since 1965, corporations have moved steadily into a net debtor position, and, in 1969, they *paid* $1.6 billion in net interest. Clearly a shift by corporations to debt financing through borrowing from the noncorporate sector should be reflected in relatively lower profits, as the result of higher interest payments. The trend is a reflection of aggregate demand and monetary policy, but it is bound to be long lived, unlike the productivity slowdown. This shift of about one-half of 1 percent of GNP could reasonably be built into the estimate of full employment profits for the late sixties and early seventies.

Omitting transitory influences on corporate profits from the calculation of the full employment surplus does not rule them out of consideration in the formulation of fiscal policy. If, because of transitory or cyclical factors, especially high or low profits in any year are foreseeable, a more or less restrictive policy may be in order. A shift away from profits will add to total after-tax private incomes because of the higher marginal tax rate applied to corporate profits. The differential in tax rates would then result in an expansionary influence on aggregate demand, even if the marginal propensities to spend out of corporate after-tax income and out of personal disposable income were identical. But the differential in tax rates is not the only reason that fiscal policy might need to take account of the distribution of income between the corporate and non-corporate sector. Since dividends move sluggishly and investment does not respond dramatically to moderate changes in profits after tax, the marginal propensity to spend out of corporate income may be appreciably lower in the short run than the marginal propensity to spend out of personal disposable income. For that reason alone, a redistribution of income away from corporations would tend to have a net expansionary effect even if tax rates on the two types of income were identical. If such a shift is predictable, then the consequences for aggregate demand should be recognized in the formulation of stabilization policy. Here is another consideration relevant to fiscal policy that cannot be appropriately reflected in the full employment surplus—any more than it can reflect a strong plant and equipment survey or a weak survey of consumer buying intentions and attitudes.

The Estimates

Table 2 shows estimates of full employment revenues, expenditures, and surplus from mid-1955 through 1969. Expenditures are adjusted for that portion of unemployment compensation benefits attributable to departures from an unemployment rate of 4 percent. The actual surplus is shown for comparison with the full employment surplus. Also, to facilitate appropriate comparisons over considerable periods of time, the full employment surplus is shown as a percentage of potential GNP. The basic technique for these calculations has been set forth previously.[18] The profit share is taken as $10\frac{2}{3}$ percent of GNP from 1962 to the present and 11.2 percent prior to the reform of depreciation guidelines in 1962. These calculations do not incorporate the adjustments set forth above for price inflation or for the shift in corporate financial structure.

The profile of fiscal policy over the past decade and a half as described by this table might be briefly summarized as follows:

The full employment surplus rose to a little more than 1 percent of potential GNP during 1956. If, however, the figures for 1956 and the first half of 1957 were adjusted for price acceleration, the surplus as a percentage of GNP would remain on a plateau from mid-1955 through mid-1957.

Fiscal policy actually tightened a bit during the 1957–58 recession, but then moved significantly in the direction of stimulus when the recovery

Table 2 Full employment revenues, expenditures, and surplus, third quarter 1955 through fourth quarter 1969 (seasonally adjusted annual rates; dollar amounts in billions)

Year and quarter		Personal taxes ($)	Corporate taxes ($)	Indirect taxes ($)	Social security taxes ($)	Total revenues ($)	Total expenditures ($)	Full employment surplus ($)	Actual surplus ($)	FES as percent of potential GNP (%)
1955	3	31.8	19.4	10.6	9.5	71.3	68.3	3.0	5.0	0.7
	4	32.5	19.7	10.8	9.7	72.6	69.0	3.6	6.0	0.9
1956	1	33.2	20.0	11.0	10.3	74.5	69.3	5.2	6.3	1.3
	2	33.9	20.4	11.2	10.5	76.0	71.8	4.2	5.5	1.0
	3	34.8	20.8	11.5	10.7	77.9	72.3	5.6	4.9	1.3
	4	35.6	21.2	11.7	10.9	79.4	74.1	5.3	6.0	1.2
Year		34.4	20.6	11.4	10.6	76.9	71.9	5.1	5.7	1.2
1957	1	36.3	21.6	12.0	12.3	82.2	78.1	4.1	4.3	0.9
	2	37.1	21.9	12.2	12.5	83.7	79.7	4.0	2.5	0.9
	3	37.9	22.3	12.4	12.7	85.3	79.4	5.9	2.6	1.3
	4	38.6	22.6	12.6	12.9	86.7	79.8	6.9	−1.5	1.5
Year		37.5	22.1	12.3	12.6	84.5	79.3	5.2	2.1	1.1
1958	1	39.4	23.0	12.8	13.1	88.3	82.2	6.1	−8.1	1.3
	2	40.1	23.3	12.9	13.3	89.6	86.1	3.5	−12.4	0.7
	3	40.8	23.6	13.1	13.4	90.9	88.0	2.9	−10.8	0.6
	4	41.5	23.9	12.7	13.6	91.8	91.2	0.6	−9.8	0.1
Year		40.5	23.5	12.9	13.4	90.1	86.9	3.3	−10.2	0.7
1959	1	42.2	24.3	12.9	15.5[a]	94.8	90.5	4.3	−4.2	0.9
	2	42.9	24.6	13.0	15.6	96.1	89.6	6.5	0.8	1.3
	3	43.6	24.9	13.2	15.8	97.5	90.2	7.3	−1.0	1.4
	4	44.3	25.1	13.9	16.0	99.4	90.4	9.0	−0.6	1.7
Year		43.3	24.7	13.3	15.7	96.9	90.2	6.8	−1.2	1.3
1960	1	45.0	25.5	14.1	18.5	103.1	89.3	13.8	7.1	2.6
	2	45.8	25.8	14.3	18.7	104.6	91.2	13.4	5.6	2.5
	3	46.6	26.1	14.2	19.0	105.8	93.4	12.4	1.5	2.3
	4	47.4	26.5	14.3	19.2	107.4	94.1	13.3	−0.6	2.4

Year		46.2	26.0	14.2	18.8	105.2	92.0	13.2	3.5	2.5
1961	1	48.1	26.8	14.5	19.4	108.8	97.0	11.8	−4.9	2.1
	2	48.8	27.1	14.7	19.6	110.2	99.8	10.4	−4.5	1.9
	3	49.4	27.3	14.8	19.8	111.4	101.5	9.9	−3.8	1.7
	4	50.4	27.7	15.1	20.1	113.3	103.3	10.0	−1.9	1.7
Year		49.2	27.2	14.8	19.7	110.9	100.4	10.5	−3.8	1.9
1962	1	50.7	25.6[b]	15.1	21.6	113.0	107.7	5.3	−5.0	0.9
	2	51.4	25.8	15.3	21.8	114.3	109.7	4.6	−4.5	0.8
	3	52.2	26.1	15.5	22.0	115.7	109.1	6.6	−2.6	1.1
	4	53.1	26.4	15.5	22.3	117.3	111.1	6.2	−3.2	1.0
Year		51.9	26.0	15.4	21.9	115.1	109.4	5.7	−3.8	1.0
1963	1	53.9	26.8	15.7	24.2	120.6	112.5	8.1	−2.4	1.3
	2	54.8	27.1	15.9	24.5	122.3	111.3	11.0	1.8	1.8
	3	55.6	27.4	16.1	24.7	123.8	113.4	10.4	1.2	1.7
	4	56.7	27.8	16.3	25.1	126.0	114.3	11.7	2.1	1.8
Year		55.3	27.3	16.0	24.6	123.2	112.9	10.3	0.7	1.7
1964	1	52.7	27.0	16.5	25.4	121.7	117.1	4.6	−2.5	0.7
	2	48.0	27.4	16.7	25.7	117.8	117.9	−0.1	−6.3	0.0
	3	49.7	27.8	17.0	26.1	120.6	117.6	3.0	−2.7	0.5
	4	51.3	28.1	17.2	26.5	123.2	117.3	5.9	−0.6	0.9
Year		50.4	27.6	16.9	25.9	120.8	117.5	3.3	−3.0	0.5
1965	1	54.4	27.4	17.5	26.9	126.1	118.3	7.8	4.4	1.2
	2	55.4	27.7	17.1	27.3	127.4	119.9	7.5	4.7	1.1
	3	53.7	28.1	15.8	27.6	125.1	126.3	−1.2	−3.1	−0.2
	4	54.3	28.5	16.0	28.0	126.7	128.5	−1.8	−1.1	−0.3
Year		54.5	27.9	16.6	27.4	126.3	123.3	3.1	1.2	0.5
1966	1	56.9	29.0	14.8	32.1[a]	132.8	135.1	−2.3	1.4	−0.3
	2	60.5	29.5	15.5	32.7	138.3	138.5	−0.2	3.0	0.0
	3	62.1	30.1	15.4	33.4	140.9	146.6	−5.7	−1.2	−0.8
	4	64.2	30.6	15.6	34.0	144.4	151.2	−6.8	−4.1	−0.9

Table 2 (continued)

Year and quarter		Personal taxes ($)	Corporate taxes ($)	Indirect taxes ($)	Social security taxes ($)	Total revenues ($)	Total expenditures ($)	Full employment surplus ($)	Actual surplus ($)	FES as percent of potential GNP (%)
Year		60.9	29.8	15.3	33.0	139.1	142.9	−3.7	−0.2	−0.5
1967	1	65.4	31.1	15.9	35.7	148.1	159.6	−11.5	−12.0	−1.5
	2	64.9	31.6	16.1	36.3	149.0	161.4	−12.4	−13.2	−1.6
	3	67.9	32.3	16.5	37.0	153.7	165.3	−11.6	−13.4	−1.5
	4	69.7	33.0	16.8	37.8	157.3	168.8	−11.5	−12.3	−1.4
Year		67.0	32.0	16.3	36.7	152.0	163.8	−11.8	−12.7	−1.5
1968	1	71.2	37.2[b]	17.1	38.7[a]	164.3	174.2	−9.9	−8.4	−1.2
	2	73.6	38.0	17.5	39.5	168.6	180.5	−11.9	−9.5	−1.4
	3	82.2	38.7	17.8	40.3	179.1	184.4	−5.3	−2.8	−0.6
	4	85.8	39.5	18.2	41.1	184.6	187.8	−3.2	−0.1	−0.4
Year		78.2	38.4	17.7	39.9	174.1	181.7	−7.6	−5.2	−0.9
1969	1	92.2	41.2	18.6	44.4	196.4	188.9	7.5	10.1	0.8
	2	95.2	42.2	19.0	45.4	201.7	189.6	12.1	13.5	1.3
	3	93.5	43.2	19.5	46.4	202.5	193.9	8.6	7.7	0.9
	4	96.5	44.1	19.9	47.4	207.9	197.0	10.9	6.7	1.1
Year		94.4	42.7	19.2	45.9	202.1	192.4	9.8	9.5	1.0

Sources: Authors' estimates except for actual surplus figures, which are from *Survey of Current Business,* various issues, for third quarter 1955 through 1968 and from *Economic Indicators,* March 1970, for 1969. Figures are rounded and may not add to totals.

a. Reflects increases in wage ceiling.

b. Reflects retroactive changes in tax rates.

began in the spring of 1958. The fiscal program was most expansionary at the end of 1958; it then moved sharply in the direction of restraint through 1959 and into the first half of 1960. Some relaxation of that restraint took place during 1961, but the full employment surplus was still about 2 percent of potential GNP. The low level of the full employment surplus shown in the first half of 1962 is partly the result of the retroactive accounting treatment of depreciation reform and the investment tax credit. In any case, the budget moved back to a more restrictive position in 1963.

As a result of the tax cut of early 1964, the full employment surplus declined sharply; but it headed upward later in the year and into the first half of 1965. At that point, the full employment surplus was back above 1 percent of GNP. The full employment budget then swung into deficit and remained deeply in the red during the Vietnam period until the enactment of the surcharge in 1968. Even during the second half of 1968, the full employment budget was still significantly in deficit. In 1969, the surplus was restored to about 1 percent of GNP.

From 1966 through 1969, the full employment surplus would be lowered if the two adjustments set forth above—for inflation and corporate interest—were built into the estimate. Obviously, if these two revisions became accepted procedure, they would be directly incorporated into the estimates of full employment revenues rather than handled as separate adjustments. As adjusted in Table 3, the full employment surplus underlines the fact that fiscal policy remained unusually expansionary even after enactment of the surcharge in the second half of 1968. It also records the 1969 fiscal position as somewhat less restrictive than does the unadjusted full employment surplus.

A Forward Look at Fiscal Impact

The 1971 budget program set forth by the administration in February projected surpluses in the federal sector of the national accounts amounting to \$3.6 billion in fiscal 1970 and \$1.6 billion in fiscal 1971. The economic forecast underlying that budget assumes that real GNP will grow less rapidly than potential from fiscal 1970 to fiscal 1971 and that its level will be below potential output throughout fiscal 1971.[19] To evaluate the fiscal impact of the 1971 budget, it is necessary to consider the surpluses that would emerge if the economy moved along the potential path instead of dropping below it.

A movement toward smaller actual surpluses has already occurred,

Table 3 Full employment surplus adjusted for inflation and shift in corporate financial structure, first quarter 1966 through fourth quarter 1969 (dollar amounts in billions of current dollars)

		Adjustment for inflation		Corporate financial structure		
Year and quarter		Normal prices minus actual prices as percent of actual[a](%)	Adjustment to full employment revenue for inflation[b]($)	Shift in corporate interest[c]($)	Adjustment to full employment revenue for shift in interest[d]($)	Adjusted full employment surplus[e]($)
1966	1	0.11	+0.1	0.8	−0.2	−2.4
	2	−0.60	−0.8	1.0	−0.3	−1.3
	3	−1.56	−2.2	1.4	−0.4	−8.3
	4	−1.54	−2.2	1.8	−0.5	−9.5
Year		−0.90	−1.3	1.2	−0.3	−5.3
1967	1	−0.72	−1.1	2.0	−0.5	−13.1
	2	−0.01	0.0	2.2	−0.6	−13.0
	3	−0.35	−0.5	2.8	−0.8	−12.9
	4	−0.85	−1.3	3.0	−0.8	−13.6
Year		−0.48	−0.7	2.5	−0.7	−13.2
1968	1	−1.25	−2.1	3.4	−1.0	−13.0
	2	−1.82	−3.1	3.6	−1.1	−16.1
	3	−0.94	−1.7	3.9	−1.1	−8.1
	4	−0.75	−1.4	4.0	−1.2	−5.7
Year		−1.19	−2.1	3.8	−1.1	−10.8
1969	1	−1.39	−2.7	4.2	−1.2	3.6
	2	−1.51	−3.0	4.4	−1.3	7.8
	3	−1.87	−3.8	4.5	−1.3	3.5
	4	−1.83	−3.8	4.7	−1.4	5.7
Year		−1.65	−3.3	4.4	−1.3	5.2

a. Computed from quarterly formula for price adjustment.
b. Column 1 applied to full employment revenues as shown in Table 2. (Proportionality of revenues to price level is assumed for simplification.)
c. Difference between actual corporate payments of net interest and −0.3 percent potential GNP (the 1965 level of interest). Actual net interest is from *Survey of Current Business,* various issues.
d. Excess of tax rate on corporate income over tax rate on personal income (which ranges from 25 to 30 percent) applied to column 3.
e. Sum of columns 2 and 4 and full employment surplus in Table 2.

with the rate of nearly $12 billion in the first half of calendar 1969 tapering down to $7 billion in the second half. The administration's estimates for the fiscal 1970 totals implied that the actual surplus would be in the neighborhood of zero for the first half of calendar 1970, extending the marked downward trend of the second half of 1969.[20]

The Federal Reserve Bank of St. Louis has presented estimates for the second half of calendar 1970 intended to be consistent with the administration's program; these place actual revenues and expenditures essentially on a plateau during the two halves of the year. The budget is expected to edge into deficit in the second half. In that event, a return to a moderate rate of actual surplus—roughly approaching $5 billion—would be implied for the first half of calendar 1971, to be consistent with the published estimates for the whole of fiscal 1971.

Table 4 records estimates of the full employment budget by half-year intervals over the recent and prospective period. The projected expenditure figures are based on the St. Louis Bank's half-yearly phasing of outlays; the projected "actuals" are adjusted downward slightly to allow for induced unemployment compensation benefits associated with an unemployment rate a little above 4 percent.

Full employment revenues are based on an estimate of money potential GNP intended to be consistent with the CEA projection of price developments. The GNP deflator rises at annual rates of 4.2 percent in the first half of 1970 and 3.7 percent in the second half. This path would yield the 4.3 percent year-to-year increase in the deflator projected by CEA. A further slowdown to an annual rate of 3.3 percent is built into the estimate for the first half of 1971.

The important impact on full employment revenues of recent changes in tax laws is shown separately in the calculation of full employment revenues.[21] These tax changes markedly reduce the growth of full employment revenues during 1970. Nevertheless, because expenditures grow so little, the sum of expansionary fiscal actions—tax cuts and rises in outlays combined—is close to the fiscal dividend of $16 billion during 1970.[22] Although the full employment surplus moved down a little in the first half and up somewhat in the second, it does not stray far from a $10 billion level, about 1 percent of potential GNP. Compared with the record since mid-1955, this represents a slightly above average degree of fiscal braking.

For the first half of 1971, however, the full employment surplus rises markedly. The big difference in this period comes from the sharp reversal in the impact of tax changes. Instead of absorbing a major share of the

Table 4 Federal fiscal impact, by selected periods, 1969–71 (seasonally adjusted annual rates in billions of dollars)

	Calendar years							Fiscal years	
	1969		1970		1971				
Description	First half	Second half	First half	Second half	First half	1969	1970	1970	1971
Full employment revenues									
Basic revenues[a]	178.3	186.5	194.3	202.5	210.9	182.3	198.5	190.5	206.7
Surcharge	14.2	12.0	5.4	1.2	0	13.1	3.3	8.7	0.6
Tax reform and relief	0.5	0.5	3.7	1.9	−0.5	0.5	2.8	2.1	0.7
Social security taxes	5.7	5.8	6.1	6.4	12.4[b]	5.8	6.2	5.9	8.4[b]
Other	0.4	0.4	0.4	1.1	1.1	0.4	0.7	0.4	1.1
Total revenues	199.1	205.2	209.9	213.1	223.9	202.1	211.5	207.6	217.5
Full employment expenditures									
Actual expenditures	188.9	195.2	201.3	202.0	205.6	192.0	201.6	198.2	203.8
Unemployment compensation adjustment	0.3	0.3	−0.2	−0.3	−0.4	0.3	−0.2	*	−0.3
Total expenditures	189.2	195.5	201.1	201.7	205.2	192.3	201.4	198.2	203.5
Full employment surplus	9.9	9.7	8.8	11.4	18.7[b]	9.8	10.1	9.4	14.0[b]
Addenda									
Price adjustment	−2.9	−3.8	−2.3	−0.9	−1.2	−3.4	−1.6	−3.1	−1.0
Corporate financial adjustment	−1.3	−1.3	−1.4	−1.5	−1.6	−1.3	−1.4	−1.4	−1.6
Adjusted full employment surplus	5.7	4.6	5.1	9.0	15.9[b]	5.1	7.1	4.9	11.4[b]

Source: Authors' estimates.
a. Tax rates of 1967.
b. The first half of 1971 shows the $2\frac{1}{2}$ billion increase at seasonally adjusted annual rates from the rise in the social security wage ceiling; the fiscal year total includes only $200 million for the effect of the change.
* Less than $0.05 billion.

fiscal dividend as previously, they now reinforce restraint, because of the rise in social security taxes. Part of that tax increase (about $2½ billion at annual rates) is a rise in the maximum ceiling of the payroll base; for most wage earners that portion will have merely a "seasonally adjusted" impact on take-home pay during the first half of calendar 1971.[23] Even allowing for this factor, fiscal restraint clearly increases in that period.

Table 4 also shows the full employment surplus adjusted for inflation and for the shift in corporate financial structure in the manner described above. The adjustments lower the indicated level of the full employment surplus throughout; by this standard, 1970 (like 1969) should be characterized as a year of *about* average (rather than *above* average) fiscal restraint by comparison with the adjusted record since mid-1955. The price adjustment has an interesting effect on the profile during the period. As inflation becomes less intense on the projected path, the adjustment for automatic anti-inflationary fiscal stabilization properly shrinks. Hence, the increase in fiscal restraint from the first to the second half of calendar 1970 is larger according to the adjusted measure than to the unadjusted one.

With either measure, these are the two key conclusions: (1) For calendar 1970, the President's budget program involves no significant change in fiscal restraint from that of calendar 1969; by historical standards, it is at least of average restrictiveness. (2) The fiscal program is markedly more restrictive in the first half of calendar 1971 than in 1969–70 and also considerably more restrictive than average historical experience.

Different verdicts have been delivered on the basis of other benchmarks of fiscal policy. This fact demonstrates both the usefulness of a well-defined measure of fiscal impact and the need for professional dialogue to standardize the procedure for deriving such a measure.

Notes

1. The paper is not going to be sprinkled with this reminder. From here on, a surplus can be positive or negative. When negative, it is a deficit. Also, "full employment," "high employment," and "potential" are used synonymously throughout the paper.

2. Committee for Economic Development, *Taxes and the Budget: A Program for Prosperity in a Free Economy* (CED, November 1947), pp. 22–25.

3. E. Cary Brown, "Fiscal Policy in the Thirties: A Reappraisal," *American Economic Review*, Vol. 46 (December 1956), pp. 857–79.

4. David W. Lusher, "Some Key Economic Variables in the 1960's," in J. A. Stockfisch (ed.), *Planning and Forecasting in the Defense Industries* (Wadsworth, 1962),

pp. 33–50; James W. Knowles, "Staff Memorandum on the Relationship of the Federal Budget to Unemployment and to Economic Growth," in *1961 Joint Economic Report*, Report of the Joint Economic Committee on the January 1961 Economic Report of the President. H. Rept. 328, 87 Cong. 1 sess. (1961), pp. 119–25; statement by Herbert Stein and following discussion, *January 1961 Economic Report of the President and the Economic Situation and Outlook*, Hearings before the Joint Economic Committee, 87 Cong. 1 sess. (1961), pp. 209–25; statement by Charles L. Schultze and following discussion, *Current Economic Situation and Short-Run Outlook*, Hearings before the Joint Economic Committee, 86 Cong. 2 sess. (1961), pp. 114–39.

5. *Report of the President's Commission on Budget Concepts* (October 1967), p. 20.

6. Committee for Economic Development, *A Stabilizing Fiscal and Monetary Policy for 1970* (CED, December 1969), p. 10.

7. Nancy H. Teeters, "Estimates of the Full-Employment Surplus, 1955–1964," *Review of Economics and Statistics*, Vol. 47 (August 1965), pp. 309–21; Federal Reserve Bank of St. Louis, *Review*, Vol. 49 (June 1967).

8. Edward M. Gramlich, "The Behavior and Adequacy of the United States Federal Budget, 1952–1964," *Yale Economic Essays*, Vol. 6 (Spring 1966), pp. 134–35; Richard A. Musgrave, "On Measuring Fiscal Performance," *Review of Economics and Statistics*, Vol. 46 (May 1964), p. 213.

9. Even so, the application of Musgrave's weights does not significantly change the profile of movements shown by the unweighted full employment surplus. Prior to 1967, only two quarterly movements disagree by as much as $1 billion. The most noticeable difference is that fiscal policy is nearly as stimulative in 1968 as in 1967 by the Musgrave weights, reflecting the lower coefficient on the corporate surcharge. But by the end of 1969, the two measures are back in step.

10. It may be possible to develop a new seasonal pattern. We would insist that quarterly figures jibe with annual ones. If there were a good alternative, the national income accountants would not be following their current practice in the calculation of actual revenues.

11. Murray L. Weidenbaum, "Impact of Vietnam War on American Economy," in *Economic Effect of Vietnam Spending*, Hearings before the Joint Economic Committee, 90 Cong. 1 sess. (1967), p. 199. See also Harvey Galper and Edward Gramlich, "A Technique for Forecasting Defense Expenditures," *Review of Economics and Statistics*, Vol. 50 (May 1968), pp. 152–54.

12. This issue is not unique to the federal sector. Private orders for machinery and equipment and contracts for private construction also generate inventory investment before they are registered as fixed investment.

13. This issue was recognized in the pioneering 1947 statement of the Committee for Economic Development and was raised anew by Herbert Stein in private correspondence during 1966. Edward M. Gramlich discussed this problem in some detail in 1967; see "Measures of the Aggregate Demand Impact of the Federal Budget," in President's Commission on Budget Concepts, *Staff Papers and Other Materials*

Reviewed by the President's Commission (1967), pp. 431–45. In fact, the taxation of capital gains on inventories and other assets does introduce some automatic stabilizing revenue gains while prices are rising rapidly.

14. *Report of the President's Commission on Budget Concepts*, p. 21.

15. There are other revenue effects beyond this primary one. Social security taxes would tend to be somewhat lower if there is a shift toward profits and away from wages. Changes in dividends should also be taken into account.

16. Michael E. Levy, *Fiscal Policy, Cycles and Growth* (National Industrial Conference Board, 1963), pp. 23–24.

17. Knowles, "Staff Memorandum on the Relationship of the Federal Budget to Unemployment and to Economic Growth."

18. Teeters, "Estimates of the Full-Employment Surplus."

19. *The Economic Report of the President together with the Annual Report of the Council of Economic Advisers, 1970*, p. 85.

20. Official revisions of budget estimates released in May imply a significant deficit in the federal sector of the national accounts for both halves of calendar 1970.

21. See the discussion in Charles A. Waite and Joseph C. Wakefield, "Federal Programs for Fiscal 1971," *Survey of Current Business*, Vol. 50 (February 1970), pp. 12–18.

22. Revised official estimates of the fiscal 1971 budget, released on May 19, would raise the annual rate of expenditures in the second half of 1970 by approximately \$4½ billion above the estimates in the budget document. This is partially offset by a \$1.6 billion increase in revenues from a proposed tax on lead used in the manufacture of gasoline. The full employment surplus, therefore, would be approximately \$3 billion (annual rate) lower in the second half of 1970 than is shown in Table 4. In the first half of 1971, expenditures would be approximately \$3½ billion larger than shown in the table; but this increase is more than offset by the continuing added revenue from the proposed gasoline tax and the temporary increase in revenues (\$3.0 billion at annual rates) resulting from the proposal to accelerate collections of estate and gift taxes. Thus the full employment surplus for the first half of calendar 1971 shown in the table remains approximately correct in light of the May 19 revision.

23. That is why the full employment surplus for fiscal year 1971 is \$1 billion less than the average of the seasonally adjusted annual rates for the two half-year periods.

The Personal Tax Surcharge and Consumer Demand, 1968–70

The Revenue and Expenditure Control Act of 1968 was the key measure responsible for a large fiscal swing toward restraint from a full employment deficit of roughly $10 billion in the first half of 1968 to a full employment surplus of about the same size in the first half of 1969.[1] That fiscal restraint was intended to halt the boom and thereby to curb inflation. As everyone knows, it did not stop inflation—nor has any of the host of other economic policy actions undertaken in the United States since 1967. The linkage between halting a boom and curbing inflation has turned out to be a much more difficult and less reliable process than the profession judged three years ago.

An even more serious criticism of the 1968 act is that it did not halt the boom as promptly or decisively as had been predicted by its proponents. Actual output exceeded estimated potential for a year after the tax surcharge and the expenditure hold-downs were instituted. Yet the record does show a marked deceleration in the pace of economic activity starting in mid-1968. Whereas real GNP had grown at a $6\frac{1}{2}$ percent annual rate during the first two quarters of 1968, it decelerated progressively to a rate of $3\frac{1}{2}$ percent in the latter two quarters of 1968 and $2\frac{1}{2}$ percent in the first two quarters of 1969.

Thus the fiscal restraint program failed to achieve its objective with respect to prices and did not even fully realize the desired prompt slowdown of aggregate activity. In this sense, the surcharge period offers a dramatic contrast to the experience that followed the tax cut of 1964, when economic activity accelerated markedly, just as the proponents had promised. Discussing that earlier experience in a paper completed in September 1965, I began with the statement, "The best known fact about the Revenue Act of 1964 is that, in the year and a half since it took effect, economic activity has expanded briskly."[2] Basically, I am obliged to begin the current discussion of the Revenue Act of 1968 by pointing out that the best-known fact about it is that inflation has continued unchecked since its enactment.

The second sentence of my paper on the 1964 tax cut, however, said: "But such *post hoc, propter hoc* reasoning will never do." That statement remains true in 1971. The fact that the fiscal restraint program of 1968 didn't do all it was supposed to do doesn't prove it did nothing. To what extent was it responsible for the significant deceleration in activity that followed it? To what extent did it curb demand ceteris paribus, only to be swamped by a strengthening of private demand that would have occurred quite independently of the fiscal restraint? To what extent did it have restraining effects that were offset by a shift toward ease in monetary policy?

These questions deserve answers.[3] In this paper I will focus on only a single aspect of these questions by reviewing one element of the program of fiscal restraint—the 10 percent surcharge on personal income taxes. To estimate the extent to which consumption was directly curbed by the added personal income taxes, I shall first describe the nature of the change in the tax law; next discuss some theoretical positions that might generate different expectations about the probable effectiveness of the surcharge; and finally examine the empirical evidence on consumer demand in 1968–70, as interpreted by the consumption equations of four well-known econometric models.

The Nature of the Surcharge

The Revenue and Expenditure Control Act of 1968 was signed into law by the President on June 28. Its enactment was the culmination of a bitter legislative battle that lasted for more than ten months after President Johnson proposed a 10 percent surcharge on corporate and individual income taxes on August 3, 1967.

The act provided for a surcharge of 10 percent on federal corporate income taxes, retroactive to January 1, 1968. As it was subsequently extended, the corporate surcharge continued at the 10 percent rate through calendar year 1969; it then dropped to a 5 percent rate for the first half of 1970, statutorily translated into a $2\frac{1}{2}$ percent rate on profits for calendar year 1970.

The limitations on federal budget outlays contained in the act called for expenditures to be reduced by \$6 billion below levels set forth in the January 1968 budget document for fiscal year 1969, but the act exempted outlays on Vietnam, interest on the public debt, veterans' benefits and services, and social security benefits.

The personal tax surcharge, which is the focus of this paper, was enacted at a 10 percent rate, retroactive to April 1, 1968 and continuing to June 30, 1969. At an annual rate, it added about \$8 billion to aggregate liabilities for personal income taxes. The law exempted low-income taxpayers, such as families of four with incomes of less than \$5,000; but this relief provision amounted to only \$300 million per year in the aggregate. For a typical family of four with a \$10,000 annual income, the surcharge added \$111 to tax liabilities on a full-year basis; at a \$25,000 income, it was worth \$441.

Specifically, the 1968 law provided for a $7\frac{1}{2}$ percent increase in the liabilities of covered taxpayers for the calendar year 1968 (reflecting a 10 percent surcharge for three-quarters of the year), and 5 percent for 1969 (a 10 percent surcharge for half the year). The withholding rate of personal income taxes was raised on July 15, 1968, to take account of the surcharge. Because of its retroactive feature, the surcharge provision reduced refunds and increased final tax payments on 1968 liabilities in the spring of 1969. Subsequently, in 1969, the surcharge was extended at a 10 percent rate for the second half of the calendar year, and at a 5 percent rate for the first half of calendar 1970. It expired in effect on June 30, 1970, although the law provided for a $2\frac{1}{2}$ percent increase in liabilities for the 1970 calendar year.

The payment of federal income taxes is recorded in the national income accounts at the time the taxpayer actually parts with cash, either through withholding or through payment of estimated or final installments. From the liability rates and the withholding rates that prevailed before and after the enactment of the surcharge, the incremental federal personal income taxes attributable to the surcharge (for given before-tax incomes) can be estimated in a fairly straightforward manner. The resulting estimates, recorded in Table 1, were provided by Charles Waite of the Department of Commerce.[4] The series begins in 1968:3 and then takes a temporary jump in the first half of 1969, reflecting the retroactive feature; it steps down at the beginning of 1970 when the surcharge rate fell to 5 percent; and it finally drops to a negligible figure after mid-1970.

Table 1 Impact of tax surcharge on federal personal income tax payments, 1968–70 (billions of dollars, seasonally adjusted annual rates)

Year and quarter	Current dollars			1958 dollars[a]
	Withheld	Nonwithheld	Total	Total
1968:3	5.3	0.8	6.1	5.1
4	6.3	0.8	7.1	5.9
1969:1	6.5	4.2	10.7	8.8
2	6.7	4.2	10.9	8.9
3	6.9	0.2	7.1	5.7
4	7.1	0.2	7.3	5.8
1970:1	3.6	1.4	5.0	3.9
2	3.6	1.4	5.0	3.9
3	0.0	0.4	0.4	0.3

Source: Tabulation by Charles Waite, U.S. Department of Commerce, Office of Business Economics, December 23, 1970.
a. Deflated by implicit deflator for personal consumption expenditures.

The Link to Consumption

The question of how the consumer responded to the income tax surcharge merely asks to what extent the resulting cutback in disposable income held down consumption outlays and to what extent it held down personal saving. An arithmetic identity ensures that any change in income must be allocated between a change in consumption and a change in saving.[5] According to the historical record of aggregate quarterly data on household income and its disposition, most changes in disposable income are primarily reflected in altered consumption, at least after a lag of a few quarters. On the margin as well as on the average, the largest portion of disposable income is consumed. The record provides evidence on how much and how fast a typical change in disposable income is translated into a change in consumption. The same historical record, however, warns us that disposable income is not the only determinant of consumption outlays. Such variables as stocks of consumer goods, wealth, liquid assets, and credit conditions have been found (by at least some investigators) to influence consumption significantly. And even with all the determining factors that can be quantified, economists cannot explain perfectly the allocation of income between consumption and saving. The behavior of the consumer does not precisely follow statistical predictions and at times departs widely from such relationships.

Ever since economists have become interested in fiscal policy, they have operated generally on the fundamental premise that changes in after-tax income resulting from a change in personal tax rates are basically equivalent in their influence on consumption to changes in income arising from other sources. In fact, there is not much direct empirical evidence to validate (or refute) this fundamental premise. Following the big tax cut in 1964, consumer outlays corresponded very well with the assumption that the tax cut would affect consumer spending about as much and as rapidly as any other addition of equal size to spendable income. But most of the support for the fundamental premise is analytical. So long as a tax increase has no special effects on consumer expectations, asset values, or income distribution, and so long as it does not result in additional public services that were previously purchased in the private market, a tax increase of one dollar "ought" to offset a before-tax income gain of one dollar. In a sense, the premise is an implication of the more fundamental postulate that consumers behave rationally with respect to their budget constraints. After-tax income sets the constraint on the sum of consumption and saving; it is the income available for allocation by the household. If, by coincidence, a family were to experience a sudden but sustained rise in income before taxes at the same time and by the same amount that tax rates were increased, the household would be neither better off nor worse off; there would be no clear reason to expect it to raise or lower its standard of living (or thus to alter its rate of saving). A family's spending is not expected to depend significantly upon whether it is paid in check or in cash, or whether payday is Friday or Monday; by the same reasoning, its consumption is not expected to depend merely on the way its disposable income is made up of before-tax income and subtractions for income taxes.

Reservations and Qualifications

Although the fundamental premise is intuitively appealing, it is merely suggestive, rather than conclusive. A tax change could have special effects on expectations and on other subjective determinants of consumption. In any particular episode, it is easy to offer reasons that might make the consumer respond differently and uniquely. In the case of the surcharge, several such reasons have been suggested. The most important of these hypotheses is related to the permanent income view of consumer demand; it will be explored in detail below. But first, several other hypotheses deserve a brief analytical review.

The triviality argument. Many laymen seem puzzled that economists ever expect a significant effect on consumer expenditures from a change in after-tax income that amounts to only a dollar or two a week for middle-income families. Why, they ask, should that change anybody's standard of living? It seems too trivial to matter.

Such arguments have never carried much weight within the profession, however. Although the economist can imagine income changes that may be too trivial to matter, he can't decide whether they would be too trivial to affect consumption or too trivial to affect saving, and they have to affect at least one of the two. The rhetorical question can be turned on its head: Why should a small change in income affect people's decisions on the desirable rate of increasing their wealth? The implication of that question is that any small increment (or decrement) in income will be matched by a change in consumption and have no effect on saving.

Moreover, discontinuities at the household level could still be consistent with continuity in the behavior of aggregates. Even if every family were prepared to hold its consumption constant unless and until its income changed enough to cross some threshold, some families would be close to their threshold at any one time and could be pushed into a substantial change of consumption by a tiny change in income. Perhaps it is merely a professional bias, but the economic analyst relies on continuity of aggregate responses to all sorts of small changes in the economy, and rarely does he find empirical evidence that contradicts this assumption.

The ratchet argument. Nearly a generation ago, James Duesenberry and Franco Modigliani provided good analytical and empirical evidence of an asymmetrical response of consumption to increases and decreases in income. Generally, consumption declines less when income falls below a previous peak than it rises in response to an equal increase in income to a new peak.[6] There is a ratchet effect and a resistance to belt-tightening when income declines.

But the ratchet argument seems to have little relevance to the tax surcharge experience. Of course, most American workers experienced a slight dip, of roughly 1 percent, in their take-home pay at the moment the surcharge withholding rates took effect. But, for most families, changes in before-tax income must have swamped this effect within a short interval. From 1968:2 to 1968:3, per capita disposable income actually rose in real as well as nominal terms. The ratchet argument would have important implications for aggregate consumption only if an extraordinary fraction of American families experienced income declines or remained below their previous peak incomes for a sustained period. And there is no evidence to suggest that such was the case.

The variability of income for individual households is enormous. As an earlier study showed, seven-eights of all families reported that some event between January 1964 and May 1965 had changed their income by 10 percent or more. Two-thirds reported that some event had *decreased* their income by such an amount during this period, although most of these families also experienced events resulting in even larger income increases. Only about half of all families had incomes in 1964 that were within 10 percent of their 1963 incomes.[7] As these data suggest, only an infinitesimal fraction of families have exactly the same before-tax incomes two years in a row. It is hard to believe that a significant fraction of total income belonged to the group of families that was pushed from no change (or a minuscule rise) in income into the minus zone as a result of the surcharge. The ratchet argument applies to absolute declines in (real or money) income, and the surcharge itself was rarely responsible for absolute declines.

Interaction with inflation and inflationary expectations. Since the impact of recent or expected price increases on consumer demand is uncharted, it attracts conjecture and speculation. If consumption seems unusually weak while prices are rising strongly (as in 1968:2 or 1970:3), one tends to suspect that the consumer is resisting inflation or adjusting to a reduction in the real value of his liquid assets. On the other hand, when consumer demand seems particularly strong in an inflationary period (like 1966:1), one wonders whether inflationary expectations are encouraging consumers to buy now in order to beat subsequent price increases. And indeed both conjectures may conceivably be right.

Putting the tax surcharge into the picture permits endless variations, in either direction, on the causal arguments. To sample one line of conjecture: When people feel squeezed by inflation, they want to rationalize actions to maintain consumption and trim saving. The tax surcharge gave them an excuse for saving less, and they grabbed it, especially since they were fairly liquid and found it easy to borrow. Another conjecture invokes a self-denying prophecy: People felt uncertain because of the inflation, and they thought the government was stopping inflation when the tax surcharge was passed; therefore they might have spent more of their income and stimulated the inflation.

Advance perception of the tax increase. The long legislative debate over the tax surcharge gave the consumer an opportunity to anticipate its impact. He may accordingly have reduced consumption before the enactment of the surcharge, particularly on durable goods involving installment charges. Indeed, in advance, many people seemed to overestimate the impact of the tax surcharge on their incomes, even interpreting it as an added liability amounting to 10 percent of their *income* rather than 10 percent of their *taxes*. Thus, the anticipation might have been worse than the realization.

Such highly subjective, ad hoc conjectures defy systematic verification, but they cannot be dismissed.

The Permanent Income Hypothesis

Among all the conceivable reasons that the surcharge could have had a significantly different impact from other cutbacks in the growth of disposable income, the most serious and most challenging is the permanent income hypothesis—the proposition that consumption is altered much less in response to changes in income that are viewed as transitory than in response to those viewed as permanent. As stated strongly by Robert Eisner:

> The basic economic error of those who saw in the 10 percent income tax surcharge an adequate measure against inflation may be charged to failure to take into account the implications of the permanent income hypothesis.... Dealing in terms of equilibrium or permanent income, an increase in tax withdrawals of some ten or eleven billion dollars per year may be expected to have a very substantial depressant effect on aggregate demand.... But the tax increase legislated in the surcharge did not represent a corresponding reduction in *permanent* after-tax income.[8]

Permanent Income and Temporary Tax Changes

The analysis of a temporary tax change in light of the permanent income hypothesis raises a number of important theoretical and empirical issues.

Among the assumptions and implications of the permanent income hypothesis, the one that makes it relevant to the tax surcharge is the view that households gear their standards of living, not to measured income in a single calendar quarter or year, but to their longer-run income expectations or "permanent income." When a family experiences a change in current income that it expects to be sustained through time, the response of consumption is full and reasonably prompt. However, when the change in current income is viewed as transitory and does not alter expected future income, the household tends to spread the transitory or windfall component over a long horizon, allowing only a small portion to alter consumption in the current year.[9]

In its loosest qualitative terms, the hypothesis has overwhelming appeal. Anybody who does any saving reveals that his relevant time horizon for planning is longer than the current period. Unless wealth accumulation is his primary and ultimate goal, he must be concerned about fitting consumption to his needs over a longer time horizon. If a family gets substantial income receipts that it views as windfalls, the impact on current consumption is bound to be smaller than would be the case from an equal addition to income that is expected to be recurrent and permanent. The controversial issue is how much difference this makes: What types of income items do consumers identify as purely transitory and under what circumstances? What is the length of the horizon they focus on in their consumption decisions?

Even between the principal pioneers of the permanent income view, the judgments are far apart: Friedman uses a three-year horizon, assessing the marginal propensity to consume out of windfalls at roughly one-third, while Modigliani–Brumberg take a lifetime horizon, implying an annual impact as small as 0.04. These authors agree, however, in limiting the scope of the permanent income hypothesis to consumer expenditures on nondurables and services. They distinguish between the purchase of durable goods and the enjoyment of a flow of services from durables; both analyses view the acquisition of additional durable goods as one of the many ways in which transitory income may be added to wealth.

Empirical Tests

The response of consumers to windfalls can be investigated directly only through the few surveys of household budgets in which sources of income have been identified in sufficient detail that presumptive windfalls can be isolated. Several tests have been performed by Ronald Bodkin and others on a 1950 U.S. survey that isolated windfall income consisting largely of National Service Life Insurance dividends. Both in his initial report and in subsequent investigations, Bodkin found no evidence that the marginal propensity to consume was less from windfall income than from other income. Indeed, Bodkin ran into the problem that his data tended to prove too much: The marginal propensities to consume from windfall income generally exceeded those from regular income. This curious result lent some plausibility to Friedman's conjecture that the amount of the life insurance dividend might have been indirectly related to the permanent income of the household.[10]

Another group of studies investigated Israeli data in which the prime source of windfall income was restitution payments to German refugees. There the authors found a resounding difference between spending propensities, just as would be implied by the permanent income hypothesis. According to Mordechai Kreinin, the marginal propensity to consume out of windfalls was about one-fourth that out of other income, as revealed in the Israeli data.[11]

A persuasive reconciliation of the Bodkin and Kreinin findings was presented by Michael Lansberger.[12] The windfalls in the Kreinin study were large, of roughly the same order of magnitude as the regular income of the recipients. In contrast, the windfalls in the 1950 U.S. data averaged about 7 percent of the total income of recipients. Lansberger showed further that the marginal propensity to consume out of windfalls was, in the Israeli data, very strongly negatively related to the size of the windfall in relation to other income. This pattern suggested that households segregate large windfalls from regular income and treat them specially as capital account items, but that families typically lump small windfalls with regular income. The same results were suggested by a survey of Colorado families analyzed by Conrad Doenges.[13]

Indeed, no empirical study suggests that a negative windfall as small as the surcharge's dent of 1 percent of disposable income would be treated any differently from a permanent reduction in income of the same size. In short, the windfall view of the surcharge gets no support from the direct empirical tests.

That view is also subject to other reservations. First, influenced in part by the history of the Korean war "temporary" taxation, American citizens typically were skeptical that the tax surcharge would actually expire in a short time. Secondly, the very nature of the wartime inflationary economy of 1966–68 must have created enormous uncertainties about long-run prospects for both before-tax and after-tax real incomes. Some workers in defense plants must have doubted the viability of long-term careers in their Vietnam-related jobs. Other manufacturing workers who had unusual opportunities to work overtime must have questioned whether the phenomenon was temporary or the hallmark of a new age of perennial full (or overfull) employment. Married women must have asked the same questions about the ready availability of jobs for them. The new experience with inflation after almost a decade of abeyance must have raised important questions about the longer-run horizon among both people who were hurt by price increases and those who reaped gains. In that environment, a great many elements may have created a gap between current income and permanent income, as perceived by consumers. Any and all of these could have influenced consumer demand. So could anything that altered the degree of confidence people felt about the long run, given the precautionary character of some saving. The surcharge may have been one of the special factors, but it hardly seems reasonable to believe that it was a key element in the transitory components of household incomes.

Just as a matter of autobiographical fact, I wondered and guessed about these issues in 1967–68; as I reported in 1969: "Viewing the surcharge in advance, I felt that some discount on its restraining effect should be taken for its temporary character. There was no certainty about the right size of the discount, but 20 or 25 percent seemed to be in the ballpark." [14]

The Tax Reform Act of 1969 raises another issue about the interpretation of temporary and permanent income tax rates. That act provides for a cut in personal taxes of $9.5 billion a year, with the reductions scheduled to take effect in stages lasting until January 1973. Thus, Congress adopted lower permanent tax rates but essentially enacted a temporary measure delaying their effective date. On a logical interpretation of Modigliani–Brumberg and (to a somewhat lesser degree) Friedman, the reduction in permanent tax rates should have been a major determinant of consumer outlays in 1970 and should have generated an unusually high rate of consumption in relation to current income. Recent consumption-income patterns do not confirm this view, nor has any permanent income exponent followed the logic of his theory to argue this case. Of course, many consumers may not even be aware of these forthcoming changes in the tax base and rates; but that in itself is relevant to the issue. To take the long horizon view of consumer budgeting seriously, one must believe that families are careful forecasters of their own financial future and energetic collectors of relevant information. A man who does not read news reports on such matters as changes in tax rates and in social security benefits is simply not a Modigliani–Brumberg man.

The Nature of the Experiment

Any theoretical position that dismisses or strongly discounts the consumption impact of the tax surcharge would point to higher levels of consumer spending during the surcharge period than those implied by the alternative view that the surcharge was effective in curbing consumption.

According to the windfall view of the surcharge, the expected differences would be concentrated in outlays for nondurable goods and services. These differences permit empirical tests of the alternative views.

Statistical relationships that use officially measured disposable personal income as the income variable in explaining consumption implicitly count on the surcharge to be as effective as any other cutback in spendable income, with no discount necessary to allow for the transitory income effect or for any other reason. This may be called the *full-effect* view of the surcharge. Of course, the standard equations allow for lags in the response of consumption to income; any income change results at first in a relatively small change in estimated consumer spending, with the effects building up over time. If, during the surcharge period, consumption equations based on the full-effect view predicted consumer outlays with errors that were not unusually large and that averaged close to zero, the full-effect view would be confirmed.

The full-effect view may be contrasted with a *zero-effect* view that the surcharge had no influence on consumption (that is, its total impact was on saving). According to the zero-effect view, the relevant concept of income for predicting consumer expenditures during the surcharge period should be disposable personal income (as officially measured) *plus* the amount of extra personal taxes imposed by the surcharge. If predictions of consumption during the surcharge period based on this adjusted income concept yielded satisfactory results with errors symmetrically distributed around zero, the zero-effect view would be confirmed.[15]

A Schematic Presentation

These alternative hypotheses are shown schematically in Figure 1. The level of officially measured disposable income for any quarter in the surcharge period, consistent with the full-effect view, is designated by Y. The adjusted income concept based on the zero-effect view is Y', which is

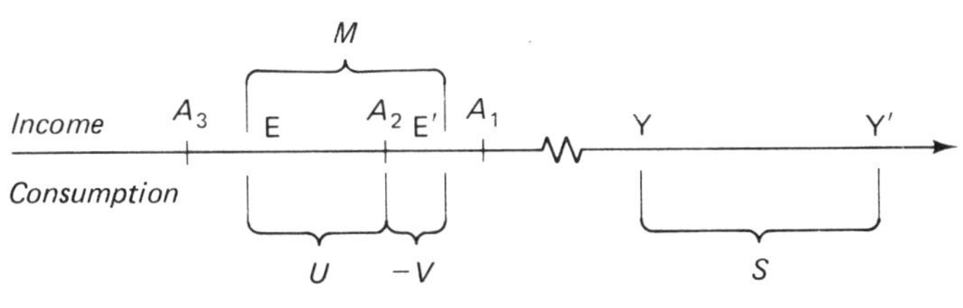

Figure 1 Schematic diagram of full-effect and zero-effect views of surcharge.

higher than Y by S, the dollar amount of the surcharge. Now assume that there is an agreed set of "best" statistical relationships for estimating consumer demand, given the relevant concept of income. There will then be two alternative estimates of consumption, designated E and E', based on the two income concepts, Y and Y', respectively. Of course, because it assumes a higher value of relevant income, E' exceeds E. The distance between E and E' is the expected direct impact (M) of the surcharge on consumer spending, as interpreted by the full-effect view.

Now suppose that the actual value of consumption for a given quarter is observed, and that it turns out to be A_2 in the diagram. Then the prediction error based on the full-effect view is $(A_2 - E)$; in accord with the convention that the error is measured as actual value minus predicted value, the underprediction yields a positive error designated as U. The prediction error based on the zero-effect view is $(A_2 - E')$, in this case a negative number designated as V. In general, $M = U - V$.

The basic empirical test to discriminate between the full-effect and zero-effect hypotheses consists of comparing the size (in absolute terms, independent of sign) of the typical U and typical V. If A_2 (between E and E') were the typical observation throughout the surcharge period, the results would point to a partial effect of the surcharge: U would be positive (reflecting underprediction by the full-effect view) and V would be negative (reflecting overprediction by the zero-effect view). In particular, if, as predicted, A_2 is somewhat closer to E' than to E, U is larger in absolute size than V, revealing the full-effect view as less accurate than the zero-effect view. In that event, however, an hypothesis of less than half of the full effect would be more accurate than either the zero- or full-effect view. If the typical consumption observation was A_1 (greater than E'), U would be larger (absolutely) than V and the zero-effect view would be the more accurate by far. However, in that case, with actual consumption higher than the estimate based on the zero-effect view, it would have to be inferred that some other stimulative factor was operative, even with the surcharge having zero effect. Similarly, if actual consumption ran consistently below E, as illustrated by A_3, then the full-effect view would be superior, but something besides the tax surcharge must have been working to hold consumption down.

Such an interpretation begins essentially with the hypothesis that the only forces consistently and significantly pushing consumption upward or downward during the surcharge period were the variables specified in the consumption equations and the surcharge. If actual consumption outlays remain, on average, between E and E', this hypothesis is maintained. If, however, they lie outside that range, it becomes necessary to discard the hypothesis that other forces averaged out.

To the extent that the surcharge had any direct impact on consumption, it also would have had subsequent multiplier effects curbing the growth of before-tax income and accelerator effects dampening business investment. It might also have led to a change in monetary policy. None of these second-round or subsequent effects is reflected in M. That measure of direct impact simply records the first-round impact based on the full-effect view, when all other relevant variables are known, including the components of personal income, the relevant monetary and credit factors, the level of employment, and so on.

The Need for Dynamic Simulation

Since the empirical test focuses on the direct impact of the surcharge and not on multiplier effects, it is perfectly satisfactory to review consumer behavior during the surcharge period using *actual* values of disposable income (as interpreted by either the zero- or full-effect view), prices, money variables, and unemployment. A serious problem arises, however, because many of the consumption equations include as explanatory variables the past value of the consumption component that is being predicted. The proposition that expenditures for gasoline (for example) this quarter depend, in part, on previous expenditures for gasoline obviously does not imply a causal relationship. Rather, lagged expenditure is designed to reflect habit formation and persistence of consumer tastes through time. But the lagged terms also are useful for predictive purposes because they correct recent errors in the causal explanation of that component of consumption and because they may capture autocorrelated measurement errors in the data. Basically, in attributing substantial weight to past expenditures, the computer is telling the investigator: When consumption is higher than expected in one quarter, history teaches us that it is also likely to be somewhat higher than would otherwise be expected in the next quarter.

The lagged expenditure term thus permits predictions based on an incorrect theoretical view of consumption to be mechanically corrected and to approach the predictions based on the valid analytical view. It may become impossible to tell who is right and who is wrong if errors are mechanically corrected quarter after quarter. If the full-effect view of the surcharge is all wrong, the investigator may observe at the start of the surcharge period that consumption is higher than he anticipated; if he then uses these higher actual values to raise his predictions for subsequent quarters, he may fuzz up the distinction between the zero-effect and full-effect views. Static simulation, the formal term for this quarter-by-quarter technique, will thus not produce efficient discrimination. As a result, one must turn to another technique known as dynamic simulation. In this experiment, the investigator is asked to "forecast" consumption for the surcharge period, knowing all the relevant determining variables *except* the actual values of consumption during that period. Whenever his statistical relationships say that current consumption depends in part on previous consumption, the investigator must rely on the values of previous consumption that he himself predicted.

The choice of the technique of dynamic simulation requires the further choice of a starting point. When should the experimenter be required to stop looking at the consumption data? There is good reason to blindfold him well before the surcharge period begins because the influence of the state of demand in the last known quarter diminishes over time; this practice makes the results during the surcharge period less sensitive to the particular conditions of demand in the last known quarter.[16] I selected 1967:2 as the last known quarter before seeing any of the simulations. I liked it because it was the quarter immediately preceding the surcharge proposal, because consumer expenditure was not behaving very abnormally in relation to income at that time, and because a head start of five quarters prior to the surcharge period is enough to dilute much of the influence of the jump-off point.

Thus, the experiment consists of "predicting" consumer spending during the surcharge period of 1968:3 to 1970:3 on the two extreme assumptions of full effect and zero effect. The ex post predictions are made with full information on actual economic activity prior to mid-1967 and on all relevant matters after mid-1967 *except* actual values of consumer expenditures.

The Models

The consumption equations of four well-known econometric models were applied to this experiment: Data Resources, Inc. (DRI); Michigan's DHL-III; Office of Business Economics (OBE); and Wharton.[17] The consumption components in DRI are expressed in current dollars while those in the other three models are expressed in 1958 dollars; for purposes of comparison, all errors and predictions of each equation of the DRI model have been converted into 1958 dollars in the tables and discussion below.

The sample periods for the statistical estimates also differed among the models: They were 1954:1 to 1970:2 for DRI; 1954:3 to 1967:4 for Michigan; 1953:2 to 1968:4 for OBE; and 1953:3 to 1970:1 for Wharton. Ideally, the equations employed for this experiment should have used sample periods terminating before the onset of the surcharge in 1968:3. Since the official disposable income series used in the equations reflects the full-effect view of the surcharge, the inclusion of quarters after 1968:2 might tend to pull the estimated coefficients in the direction of that view. Only the Michigan model meets the criterion of purity; the OBE sample period is nearly pure. Wharton and DRI, on the other hand, include most of the surcharge period in their samples. Still, the surcharge period represented only about one-eighth of the total sample period, and none of the results below casts suspicion on this particular feature of the test.

The models vary in their degree of disaggregation of consumption expenditures, with three equations for Michigan; four for Wharton; five for OBE; and eleven for DRI. (A detailed listing of these equations is available on request from the author.) Nondurable goods and services outlays combined are explained in a single equation by the Michigan model. That relationship has three explanatory variables: the level of spending on nondurables and services in the preceding quarter (with a coefficient of 0.945), disposable income in the current quarter, and disposable income in the preceding quarter.

At the other extreme of disaggregation is the DRI model, which identifies and explains eight separate components of nondurables and services. Each of these equations relies on disposable income for the current quarter as the single income variable. Most of the equations contain a relative price variable, and some also include population or a time trend. In addition, each includes a weighted average rate of consumption of the item in question over the preceding four quarters, whose predetermined weights range downward, counting from the preceding quarter, from 0.4 to 0.1. The coefficients on this lagged spending term are roughly 0.5 for most of the nondurable goods categories, but for gasoline and oil and for the services they run between 0.78 and 0.92. Coefficients of this magnitude ruled out a meaningful static simulation.

The OBE approach employs a single equation for nondurables and two for services. The nondurables equation includes average expenditures on nondurables for the preceding four quarters as one explanatory variable. It also has the special feature of distinguishing transfer payments from other components of disposable income; the estimated impact of transfer payments on consumption of nondurables is about one and one-half times as large as that of other disposable income, presumably reflecting the tendencies of transfer recipients, such as social insurance pensioners, to devote more of their incomes to nondurables and less to autos and saving. The two service components, housing and other services, are explained on a per capita basis, both with a term to correct for last period's error. The housing equation is unique in having no direct income variable; instead it uses the sum of expenditures on nondurables and services in the preceding four quarters, presumably as an indicator of how much is available for expenditure on housing.

The Wharton model devotes one equation each to nondurables and services: Current disposable income appears in both equations, as does the expenditure in question with a one-quarter lag. The coefficients on the two lagged expenditure terms differ widely: 0.98 for services and 0.37 for nondurables. In addition, the nondurables equation has a relative price term. A noteworthy "non-Keynesian" feature of these two Wharton equations is a money-stock term, which attributes to recent increases in broadly defined money (currency, demand deposits, and time deposits) a modestly stimulative influence on consumer outlays for nondurables and services.

Consumer expenditures on durable goods, excluding autos and parts, are explained in a single equation by three of the models. Michigan uses three variables: disposable income in the current quarter and in the immediately preceding quarter, and expenditures on nonauto durables in the preceding quarter. The 0.87 coefficient on the lagged expenditure term shows strong persistence of demand patterns.[18] The OBE model accounts for nonauto durables with two explanatory variables: disposable income of the current quarter, and a liquid asset measure. In the Wharton model, the explanatory variables are disposable income of the current quarter, a relative price measure, the growth of the broadly defined money supply over the last four quarters, the unemployment rate and its change over the past four quarters, and residential construction activity.

In the DRI model, consumer expenditures on nonauto durables are divided into two categories with furniture and appliances separated from all other items. Disposable income and the unemployment rate of the current quarter are explanatory variables in both equations. In addition, the demand for furniture is taken to be positively related to recent housing starts and negatively related to current expenditures on automobiles and parts.[19]

Each of the models has an equation explaining consumer demand for automobiles. All include a "dummy" to allow for strike effects. In addition, DRI uses the following variables: current disposable income net of transfer payments, unemployment, the stock market, and an income change variable. In the Michigan model the explanatory variables are disposable income lagged one and two quarters; the unemployment rate for males of age twenty and over, lagged one and two quarters; a relative price variable; and lagged expenditures on automobiles of the preceding quarter. In OBE, the variables are disposable income net of transfers, the manufacturing work week, the stock of automobiles, relative prices, and a correction for the prediction error of the preceding quarter. Wharton's equation includes current disposable income net of transfers, a relative price variable, the unemployment rate, a consumer credit dummy, and a variable reflecting the interest rate structure. Both OBE and Wharton explain automobiles and parts net of expenditures on mobile homes, although the latter are included in the auto component of the official statistics.

The Empirical Findings

In discussing the results, I will follow the least common denominator of disaggregation among the models and thus divide the discussion into (1) nondurable goods and services, (2) nonautomobile durables, and (3) automobiles.

Nondurables and Services

Despite the differences in the explanatory variables of the statistical relationships and in the degree of disaggregation, the four models yield remarkably similar estimates of the direct impact that the tax surcharge should have had on consumer spending for nondurables and services on the assumption of full effectiveness. They imply that the first-round impact of the surcharge should have curbed consumer expenditures on nondurables and services by between \$1.2 billion and \$1.6 billion at annual rates in the second half of 1968 and by between \$2.5 billion and \$2.6 billion in 1969 (see the impact column in Table 2). The impact estimates fan out a little in 1970, reflecting the varying importance attributed to longer-lagged effects; the largest estimated impact during the first three

Table 2 Impact and prediction errors of selected models assuming full effect and zero effect of personal tax surcharge on consumption, 1968:3–1970:3 (billions of 1958 dollars, seasonally adjusted annual rates)

	Data Resources, Inc.			Michigan			Office of Business Economics			Wharton		
Year and quarter	Impact	Full-effect error	Zero-effect error	Impact	Full-effect error	Zero-effect error	Impact	Full-effect error	Zero-effect error	Impact	Full-effect error	Zero-effect error
Nondurable goods and services												
1968:3	1.0	0.8	−0.2	1.5	−0.1	−1.6	1.2	−2.0	−3.3	1.1	−1.2	−2.3
4	1.5	−0.9	−2.4	1.8	−1.8	−3.6	1.6	−3.9	−5.5	1.7	−3.2	−4.8
1969:1	2.4	0.2	−2.2	2.8	−0.5	−3.3	2.5	−3.0	−5.5	2.5	−2.2	−4.8
2	2.8	1.0	−1.8	3.0	−0.3	−3.3	2.9	−2.6	−5.4	2.9	−1.5	−4.4
3	2.6	0.8	−1.8	2.3	−1.4	−3.7	2.5	−3.3	−5.8	2.5	−1.6	−4.0
4	2.8	0.6	−2.2	2.4	−1.8	−4.3	2.7	−3.6	−6.3	2.3	−1.6	−4.0
1970:1	2.6	2.2	−0.3	2.0	−0.6	−2.6	2.4	−2.3	−4.6	1.9	−0.1	−2.0
2	2.6	0.6	−2.0	2.0	−3.4	−5.4	2.3	−5.2	−7.5	1.8	−2.7	−4.5
3	1.8	0.5	−1.3	1.0	−3.3	−4.4	1.4	−5.1	−6.5	1.0	−3.8	−4.8
Nonautomobile durables												
1968:3	0.4	0.6	0.2	0.6	0.5	−0.2	0.6	1.4	0.8	0.5	0.4	−0.1
4	0.2	−0.3	−0.5	0.7	0.2	−0.5	0.7	1.0	0.3	0.6	−0.2	−0.8
1969:1	0.7	0.4	−0.4	1.1	0.9	−0.2	1.0	1.9	0.9	0.9	0.7	−0.2
2	0.6	0.4	−0.2	1.1	1.5	0.4	1.0	3.1	2.1	0.9	1.2	0.3
3	0.5	−1.4	−1.9	0.7	−1.2	−1.9	0.6	1.3	0.7	0.6	−0.8	−1.4
4	0.7	−1.1	−1.8	0.7	−1.3	−2.0	0.6	2.0	1.4	0.6	−0.9	−1.5
1970:1	0.3	−0.1	−0.5	0.5	−0.5	−1.0	0.4	3.4	3.0	0.4	0.4	*
2	0.5	0.4	*	0.8	−1.3	−2.1	0.4	4.0	3.6	0.4	0.3	−0.1
3	*	−0.3	−0.3	0.4	−1.9	−2.2	*	3.7	3.7	*	−0.6	−0.6
Automobiles												
1968:3	0.4	2.2	1.9	0.0	3.7	3.7	0.4	5.1	4.7	0.4	2.5	2.1
4	1.4	1.9	0.5	1.0	3.5	2.6	0.4	3.4	3.0	0.5	1.0	0.5

1969:1	0.8	2.3	1.5	0.7	4.2	3.5	0.6	4.0	3.4	0.7	1.4	0.7
2	1.3	2.7	1.4	1.0	4.4	3.4	0.6	4.2	3.6	0.7	1.5	0.8
3	0.5	1.3	0.9	0.7	4.1	3.5	0.4	3.1	2.7	0.4	0.7	0.3
4	−0.1	0.6	0.8	*	3.6	3.7	0.4	3.4	3.1	0.4	0.7	0.3
1970:1	0.3	−1.5	−1.8	0.2	0.2	*	0.2	0.2	*	0.3	−2.5	−2.8
2	−0.1	−0.3	−0.2	−0.1	1.9	2.0	0.2	2.3	2.1	0.3	−0.2	−0.5
3	*	−0.4	−0.4	0.1	0.8	0.7	*	1.6	1.6	*	−0.9	−0.9
Total consumption except for autos												
1968:3	1.5	1.5	*	2.1	0.4	−1.8	1.8	−0.6	−2.5	1.6	−0.8	−2.4
4	1.7	−1.2	−2.9	2.6	−1.6	−4.2	2.3	−2.9	−5.2	2.3	−3.4	−5.7
1969:1	3.1	0.6	−2.5	3.9	0.4	−3.5	3.5	−1.0	−4.6	3.4	−1.6	−5.0
2	3.4	1.5	−2.0	4.1	1.2	−2.9	3.9	0.5	−3.3	3.8	−0.2	−4.1
3	3.1	−0.6	−3.7	3.0	−2.6	−5.6	3.1	−2.0	−5.1	3.0	−2.4	−5.4
4	3.5	−0.5	−4.0	3.2	−3.1	−6.3	3.3	−1.6	−4.9	2.9	−2.6	−5.5
1970:1	2.9	2.1	−0.8	2.5	−1.2	−3.6	2.8	1.2	−1.6	2.3	0.3	−2.0
2	3.0	1.0	−2.0	2.9	−4.6	−7.5	2.8	−1.2	−3.9	2.2	−2.4	−4.6
3	1.8	0.2	−1.7	1.4	−5.2	−6.6	1.4	−1.4	−2.8	1.0	−4.4	−5.4
Total consumption												
1968:3	1.9	3.7	1.9	2.1	4.1	1.9	2.2	4.4	2.2	2.0	1.7	−0.3
4	3.1	0.7	−2.4	3.5	1.9	−1.6	2.7	0.5	−2.2	2.7	−2.4	−5.1
1969:1	3.9	2.8	−1.1	4.6	4.6	*	4.1	3.0	−1.2	4.1	−0.2	−4.3
2	4.7	4.1	−0.5	5.1	5.6	0.4	4.5	4.7	0.3	4.5	1.2	−3.3
3	3.5	0.7	−2.9	3.7	1.6	−2.1	3.5	1.1	−2.4	3.4	−1.7	−5.1
4	3.3	0.1	−3.2	3.1	0.6	−2.6	3.7	1.8	−1.8	3.4	−1.8	−5.2
1970:1	3.2	0.6	−2.6	2.7	−0.9	−3.6	3.0	1.4	−1.7	2.6	−2.2	−4.8
2	2.9	0.7	−2.2	2.8	−2.7	−5.5	3.0	1.1	−1.9	2.5	−2.6	−5.1
3	1.9	−0.2	−2.0	1.5	−4.3	−5.9	1.4	0.2	−1.2	1.0	−5.2	−6.3

Sources: Derived from data provided by Data Resources, Inc., the University of Michigan's Research Seminar in Quantitative Economics, the Office of Business Economics of the U.S. Department of Commerce, and the University of Pennsylvania's Economic Research Unit. Figures are rounded and may not add to totals.

* Less than $0.05 billion in absolute value.

quarters is $2.3 billion (annual rate) for DRI and the smallest is $1.6 billion for Wharton. (All dollar figures throughout are in 1958 prices.)

The lags in the models allow for a considerable buildup period before changes in income have a nearly proportional effect on outlays for nondurables and services. In the first half-year of the surcharge, only about one-fourth of the $5.5 billion rate of the surcharge is expected to show up as a decline in outlays for nondurables and services. Even during 1969, the expected impact is approximately 35 percent of the $7.3 billion withdrawal from income accounted for by the surcharge. On the average, however, nondurable goods and services account for about three-fourths of total disposable income. If a change in income were sustained for an indefinite period, the ultimate impact on nondurables and services would be roughly three-fourths in both the Michigan and Wharton models. In the case of OBE, it would be about a half, whereas in the DRI model, it approaches 0.9. Thus, standard econometric models reflect the evidence that sudden changes in income—whether permanent or temporary—have gradually increasing effects on consumption. The estimated impacts for 1970, which linger on after the surcharge expires, also reflect the diffusion of the effects over time.

The errors on nondurable goods and services in the experimental predictions are clearcut (see Table 2). For every single quarter in all four models, the zero-effect view of the surcharge overpredicts expenditure on these items. However, in three of the models (DRI is the exception), the full-effect view also overpredicts the level of expenditures on nondurables and services in every single quarter, although these errors are substantially smaller in absolute size. In the case of DRI, the full-effect view tends to underpredict a little—on the average, $0.6 billion in contrast with the $1.6 billion average overprediction of the zero-effect view. By a more refined statistic described in the appendix and shown in Table 3, the DRI verdict is that the tax surcharge was 69 percent as effective as a standard change in disposable income in curbing consumer expenditures on nondurables and services. By the other three verdicts, however, the surcharge was (at least!) 100 percent as effective as a standard change in income on these components of consumption.

Three of the four models produce errors on nondurables and services during the surcharge period that must be regarded as biased: They clearly do not lie symmetrically around zero. But the errors based on the full-effect view are not large in magnitude. OBE is the only model that ever makes an error as large as 1 percent of the total of consumer outlays on nondurables

Table 3 Degree of effectiveness of the 1968 tax surcharge on consumption, 1968:3–1970:3, according to selected models

Type of expenditure	Data Resources, Inc.	Michigan	Office of Business Economics	Wharton
Nondurable goods and services	0.69	1.58	2.46	1.86
Nonauto durables	1.29	1.11	−2.05	0.69
Autos	−0.86	−3.62	−6.85	−0.69
Total nonauto consumption				
Without constraint	0.82	1.48	1.31	1.62
With 0,1 constraint[a]	0.74	1.00	0.78	0.93
Total consumption				
Without constraint	0.53	0.47	0.34	1.33
With 0,1 constraint[a]	0.63	0.88	0.70	0.80
With auto adjustment[a]	0.59	0.88	0.70	0.80

Source: Based on methods set forth in text of appendix; effectiveness is computed over the period 1968:3–1970:3 using tabulations set forth in Table 2.
a. For explanation of constraints and adjustments, see text.

and services. While there is no standard statistical measure of par for such dynamic simulations, the root-mean-square errors for nondurables and services (Table 4) must be regarded as quite respectable.[20] The errors of the zero-effect view are nearly twice as large as those of the full-effect view. Static errors for nondurables and services (available from the author on request) tend to correct the overpredictions as time goes on; but all except DRI still contain a mean overprediction based on the full-effect view and, of course, larger overpredictions on the zero-effect view. Although they blur the distinctions, the static residuals are consistent with the general verdict in favor of the full-effect view for expenditures on nondurables and services during the surcharge period. They also indicate that the results cannot be attributed to any peculiarity of the dynamic simulation nor specifically to the choice of 1967:2 as the last known quarter. (Further evidence on this issue is presented in the appendix.)

Still, it is puzzling that three of the four models overpredicted nondurables and services consistently during the surcharge period. There is no evident built-in tendency for the models to "run uphill" on these components. I have some suspicion that the difference between DRI and the other models may be related to the use of current-dollar variables by DRI. As a percentage of disposable income, outlays on nondurables and services for 1968:3–1970:3 were about the same in current dollars as in the period 1965:1–1968:2; but they were about 0.7 percentage point lower in con-

Table 4 Root-mean-square errors of full-effect and zero-effect simulations (billions of 1958 dollars)

Type of expenditure	Data Resources, Inc.		Michigan		Office of Business Economics		Wharton	
	Full effect	Zero effect	Full effect	Zero effect	Full effect	Zero effect	Full effect	Zero effect
Nondurable goods and services	1.0	1.8	1.9	3.7	3.6	5.7	2.2	4.1
Nonauto durables	0.7	0.9	1.1	1.4	2.7	2.2	0.7	0.8
Autos	1.7	1.2	3.3	2.9	3.3	3.0	1.5	1.3
Total consumption except autos	1.2	2.5	2.8	5.0	1.5	4.0	2.4	4.6

Source: Computed for the period 1968:3 through 1970:3 from data in Table 2.

stant dollars. Price variables could in principle take care of this difference, but it is not obvious that they would.

Three of the four consumption models suggest that any puzzle about consumer spending on nondurables and services during the surcharge period is why it was so *low*. The surcharge is one element that was supposed to hold consumption down, and it does not look at all suspect from this point of view. The models do not reveal what else could be accounting for the extra downward tug on consumption, and they necessarily leave open the possibility that the surcharge may have been ineffective but made to look good by other forces that exerted very large downward pulls on consumer demand. In summary, the data provide no reason for questioning the effectiveness of the surcharge on those components of consumption where the basic challenge of the permanent income hypothesis was focused.

Nonauto Durables

As recorded in Table 2, the expected impact of the surcharge on nonauto durables expenditure is quite similar among the models, with the 1969 impact ranging from a low of \$0.6 billion for DRI to a high of \$0.9 billion for Michigan. For the first half of 1970, the expected impact ranges from \$0.4 billion to \$0.6 billion. Lags are short for this component; and, on the full-effect view, the surcharge is expected to curb these outlays a little more than proportionately.

The OBE model consistently underpredicts nonauto durables in every quarter for both the full-effect and the zero-effect versions.[21] The other three models hand down a quite different verdict, however; they consistently overpredict on the basis of the zero-effect view (see Table 2). Of the nine quarters of observations, overpredictions occur in eight cases each for DRI and Michigan and seven for Wharton. On the other hand, in these three models, the full-effect view gives results that are essentially unbiased: The signs of the errors are split 5 to 4 consistently, and the mean error over the nine quarters ranges between a negative \$0.3 billion for Michigan to a positive amount of less than \$0.1 billion for Wharton. As shown in Table 4, the root-mean-square errors for the models other than OBE are not far larger than the roughly \$0.5 billion standard errors of the sample period; moreover, they are uniformly smaller for the full-effect than for the zero-effect view, although not by a wide margin. The measured degree of effectiveness (Table 3) in these three models is close to unity, again consistent with the full-effect view.

Automobiles

According to the full-effect view as interpreted by the four models, the surcharge should have had a prompt and marked impact on automobile demand, curbing outlays by between $0.5 billion and $0.6 billion in 1969. But there is no evidence whatsoever that it had any impact. Indeed, even the zero-effect view consistently underpredicts automobile outlays during the second half of 1968 and every quarter of 1969. Only in 1970 do any overpredictions appear in any of the four models: DRI and Wharton then overpredict on both bases, while OBE and Michigan continue to underpredict. But by 1970, the expected impact of the surcharge on autos, on the full-effect view, is negligible—even in a few cases, paradoxically stimulative because of auto stock or income-change effects.

As shown in Table 2, the underpredictions of OBE and Michigan are consistently in the range of $3 billion to $5 billion for the second half of 1968 and throughout 1969. For the entire surcharge period, Michigan's and OBE's root-mean-square errors (Table 4) are three times the size of the $1 billion standard error during the sample period. Wharton and DRI have much smaller root-mean-square errors. They also underestimate during the first six quarters of the surcharge period, but by a considerably smaller average: $1.8 billion for DRI and $1.3 billion for Wharton.

In neither the Wharton nor the DRI equation does the size of the automobile stock have a significant effect on current demand for autos; that is probably one reason for their smaller underpredictions. The rapid buildup of the stock in 1964–68 tends to generate low estimates of demand for 1968 and 1969 in the OBE and Michigan models.[22] The stock market variable of DRI and the interest rate structure variable of Wharton may also help; neither Michigan nor OBE has any credit or financial variable in the auto equation. Finally, the inclusion of much of this period in the sample period for Wharton and DRI may have improved their estimates. It is beyond the scope of this paper to explore more fully the possibilities that might have accounted for the consistent underprediction of automobile demand in the second half of 1968 and in 1969. On the basis of the test of this paper, I find absolutely no evidence that automobile demand was held down by the surcharge.

Summary of Empirical Findings

The four models agree remarkably on the amount that the surcharge "should" have curbed consumption in accord with the full-effect view.

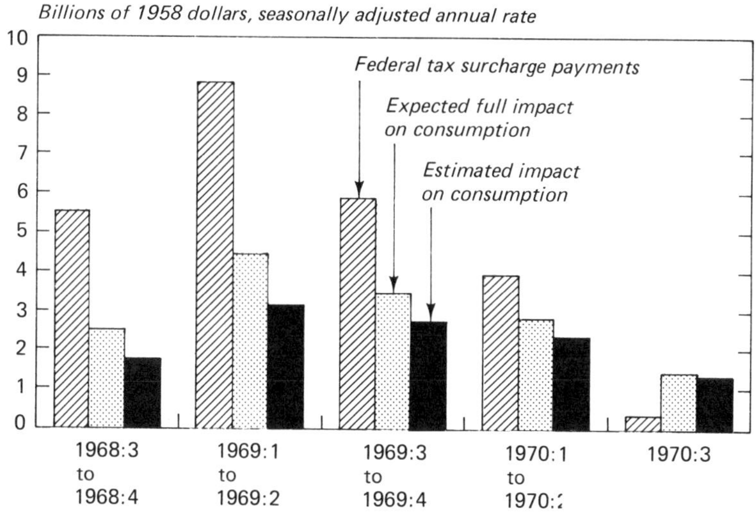

Source: Author's estimates; see text.

Figure 2 Direct impact of tax surcharge.

The direct impact on real consumer outlays was expected to be about $2.5 billion (annual rate, as always in 1958 prices) in the second half of 1968, $4 billion in 1969, and between $2.5 billion and $3 billion (annual rate) in the first half of 1970. During the entire interval, a little more than half of the surcharge's drain on disposable income was expected to be reflected in consumer outlays, with a prolonged small effect continuing after the expiration of the surcharge. The expected full-effect impact, averaged for the four models, is shown in Figure 2.

The divergence between the results on automobile outlays and those on other consumption complicates the task of drawing conclusions about the actual effectiveness of the surcharge. On the average, about 14 percent of the expected direct impact was supposed to fall on automobiles, but no evidence was uncovered that automobile demand was, in fact, held down by the surcharge. On the other hand, when consumption of nondurables and services during the surcharge period is interpreted in light of the full-effect view, demand appears to be fairly weak rather than strong. Hence the evidence offers no reason to doubt the effectiveness of the surcharge in that broad area. According to three of the four models, the surcharge was (at least) 100 percent effective on nondurable goods and services in the sense that it had as much impact per dollar as would have been expected from the loss of an equal amount of other income. However, in the fourth model (DRI), the surcharge is estimated as 69 percent effective on nondurable goods and services. The clear verdict on nondurables and services is of particular interest, because the transitory income view of the surcharge points to a low degree of effectiveness for these components.

For nonauto durables, the verdict is essentially the same. Three of the models show a degree of effectiveness ranging between 0.7 and 1.3, while OBE shows no restraint. I find it reasonable to sum up these results by imposing theoretical restrictions on the estimated effectiveness of each component. On analytical grounds, I am unwilling to believe that the surcharge could have had greater than full effectiveness (that is, more impact per dollar than a loss of other income) in curbing consumption excluding automobiles. But neither can I believe that the surcharge actually had a *stimulative* effect on automobile demand. In line with these theoretical beliefs, I take as the summary measure of overall effectiveness a weighted average of the estimated impact on nondurables and services, on nonauto durables, and on autos, but do not allow the estimate for any component to exceed 100 percent or to be less than zero.[23] Then, the estimated effectiveness on nondurables and services is taken as unity for the Michigan, OBE, and Wharton models, and at 0.69 for DRI. The estimated effectiveness for nonauto durables is then zero for OBE, unity for DRI and Michigan, and 0.69 for Wharton. The estimated effectiveness for autos is zero in all four models. The appropriate weight of autos in the average is the expected direct impact on that component as a fraction of the total direct impact on consumption over the period; it is 16 percent for DRI, 12 percent for Michigan, 12 percent for OBE, and 14 percent for Wharton. Allowing for this dilution, and some dilution on nonauto outlays, the effectiveness of the surcharge on total consumption is found to be 63 percent for DRI, 88 percent for Michigan, 70 percent for OBE, and 80 percent for Wharton.

If no constraints are placed on the results for the components, then one is obliged to argue that the surcharge had a stimulative effect on automobile demand. Indeed, the result would interpret each dollar of surcharge as equivalent to a *rise* in disposable income of between 69 cents (Wharton) and $6.85 (OBE) in its impact on auto demand. By the same token, one has to defend Michigan, OBE, and Wharton verdicts that the surcharge was 148, 131, and 162 percent, respectively, effective in curbing nonauto consumption. I find such an interpretation absurd. For example, that approach would have ruled the surcharge 100 percent effective if it had zero indicated effectiveness on nonauto consumption and a coefficient of 800 percent effectiveness on autos. For the same reason that such a result could not be taken seriously, neither can the negative coefficient actually found for autos. Just for the record, nonetheless, the no-constraint approach yields coefficients of overall effectiveness of 34 percent for OBE, 47 percent for Michigan, 53 percent for DRI, and 133 percent for Wharton.

While the extraordinarily strong demand for automobiles cannot reasonably be interpreted as a result of the surcharge, the weakness of demand for other consumption categories might conceivably have been, to some degree, a mirror image of the intensity of automobile demand. Consumers may have held down other expenditures in order to fulfill their desire to spend more on cars. In that event, the strength of automobile demand would have worked along with the surcharge to curb outlays for other components of consumption.

In fact, DRI has investigated the relationship between errors on automobile demand and other components and has found that unexpectedly high expenditures on automobiles are normally associated with especially low outlays on nonauto durables. According to their results, an extra dollar spent on cars above normal rates is associated with 30 cents less spending on nonauto durables and 70 cents less saving. If this adjustment is made during the surcharge period to the estimated demand for nonauto durables, the coefficient of overall effectiveness is reduced from 63 to 59 percent. But the adjustment actually worsens the predictions of nonauto durables within the surcharge period, raising the root-mean-square error from $0.7 billion to $0.9 billion.

One implication of the mirror image hypothesis would be that the quarters during the surcharge period when automobile demand was especially strong should have been the quarters in which nonauto consumption demand was especially weak. For Michigan, the reverse was true: Errors in autos and errors in nonauto consumption were positively related. For Wharton, there was no relationship between the two sets of errors. However, DRI and OBE both displayed a modest negative relationship. The DRI result was consistent with the adjustment made above. The OBE result for the surcharge period suggests that of an extra dollar of auto outlays, 77 cents comes out of saving and 23 cents out of nonauto consumption. If this information is used to generate a new series of OBE predictions for nonauto consumption, assuming that automobile demand is known in advance, the OBE coefficient of effectiveness for nondurables and services remains above 100 percent. The results on the surcharge are thus quite firm, although the behavior of automobile demand remains enshrouded in mystery. The estimated effectiveness based on the auto adjustment line of Table 3 was translated into dollars and averaged for the four models; it is shown in Figure 2, and is close to the expected impact.

In conclusion, the evidence of the surcharge period as interpreted by four econometric models indicates that the surcharge curbed consumption nearly as much as was expected in the models, and that any shortcomings in its effectiveness have no evident connection to the permanent income hypothesis.

Perspective on the Results

These detailed statistical findings stand in marked contrast to some intuitive conclusions that the surcharge was ineffective in curbing consumer outlays.[24] In part, that widespread impression may stem from the unusual strength of automobile demand during much of the surcharge period. Secondly, the reputation may be attributable to the extreme weakness of consumer demand in the spring of 1968, the quarter immediately preceding the initiation of the surcharge. From the second to the third quarter, consumer outlays of all types rose unusually sharply. But the second quarter had been an especially dismal period for soft goods. All the models overpredicted the sum of nondurables and services substantially in that quarter: DRI by $1.3 billion; Wharton by $2.4 billion; Michigan by $2.7 billion, and OBE by $3.8 billion. During the spring of 1968, the press reported the disappointing performance of retail sales, attributing it in part to the assassination of Martin Luther King and subsequent civil disturbances in several urban areas. Nonetheless, these data were fresh in people's minds during the summer of 1968, and the large rises from those presurcharge benchmarks seemed distressing. In retrospect, it is clear that the abnormality of that period with respect to nonauto consumption was not that the third quarter was unusually strong but that the second quarter was especially weak.

Furthermore, the reputation of the personal tax surcharge may have been sullied by unreasonable expectations rather than inadequate accomplishments. And I am personally obliged to concede that unreasonable expectations may have stemmed in part from a possible overselling of the measure by officials of the Johnson administration who had to convince a reluctant, recalcitrant Congress and skeptical public of the need for fiscal restraint. It may have also stemmed from overly eager journalists who dissected retail sales reports during the summer of 1968 in an effort to reach a verdict on the success of the surcharge. The expected direct impact of the surcharge in that quarter was so small that it could not have been visible in monthly retail sales data.[25]

Another source of intuitive disappointment may be the tendency to focus on the saving rate—the ratio of personal saving to disposable personal income—as the key indicator of the strength of consumer demand. This practice implicitly translates changes in income into expected changes in consumption immediately, unlike the time-consuming process that is embodied in the econometric models. In the models, any change in income has gradually increasing effects on nondurables and services; a year after an income change has begun, only 50 to 60 percent of it is expected to show up in consumption.[26] The models teach the important general lesson that it takes time for tax changes—whether permanent or temporary—to build up to their complete direct impact on consumption.

By the verdict of the models, however, the personal tax surcharge was no placebo. In curbing consumption directly by most of the expected $4 billion (1958 prices) in 1969, the surcharge also must have triggered off important multiplier and accelerator effects, and must have had significant induced effects on prices by dampening demand. It can easily be credited with curbing the growth of money GNP by at least 1 percent during its initial year of operation.

Nonetheless, both real and money GNP continued to exceed policy targets until late in 1969. As discussed above, automobile demand displayed surprising strength. Business investment rose sharply, defying all forecasts. Homebuilding meanwhile proved to be resistant to rises in interest rates. Two weak monthly reports on housing starts for May and June 1968 (which subsequently turned out to be erratic) contributed substantially to the misassessment of the true strength of private demand and to the mistakes in monetary policy in the summer of 1968. Later on, when the boom was finally halted by a combination of fiscal and monetary restraint, inflation proved to be remarkably immune to market forces.

All of this history merely documents a misdiagnosis of the economic situation. But it is important to recognize the nature of the errors in economic diagnosis and prescription. According to the evidence cited above, the medicine of the personal tax surcharge did lower the patient's fever. To be sure, the patient was more feverish than the doctors recognized and consequently their antifever prescription was inadequate. But don't blame the medicine; it did most of what it should reasonably have been expected to do. In short, the evidence of the surcharge period provides further confirmation of the general efficacy and continued desirability of flexible changes in personal income tax rates—upward or downward, permanent or temporary.

Appendix

This appendix contains two parts. The first explains the derivation of the coefficient of effectiveness statistic shown in Table 3 and used in the text. The second part discusses the significance of the use of 1967:2 as the last known quarter in the dynamic simulation. A supplementary appendix, available upon request, gives the prediction errors resulting from static simulations of the four econometric models for the surcharge period and lists their equations of the consumption sector.

Measurement of Degree of Effectiveness

Suppose the surcharge had some impact per dollar in curbing consumption but only a fraction a $(0 < a < 1)$ as much as a dollar loss of income from other sources. The "proper" income variable is then neither official disposable income (Y), which is the choice of the full-effect view, nor the zero-effect concept that adds back the surcharge (S) to get ($Y + S$), but something in between: $Y + (1 - a)S$. If M, the impact calculated according to the full-effect view, is linear and homogeneous in current and lagged S, then the impact attributed to the surcharge in the partial-effect view is aM. The predicted value of consumption in the partial-effect view will be below that of the zero-effect view by aM, and the residual (W) will exceed the zero-effect residual (V) by aM:

$$W = V + aM. \tag{1}$$

Over the period of observations, the sum of squared errors of predictions based on the partial-effect view is

$$\sum W^2 = \sum V^2 + 2a \sum MV + a^2 \sum M^2. \tag{2}$$

To determine a^*, that value of a most consistent with the evidence, one should minimize the sum of squared errors in (2). First differentiate (2) with respect to a:

This appendix was prepared by Richard H. Mullins.

$$\frac{d(\sum W^2)}{da} = 2\sum MV + 2a\sum M^2. \tag{3}$$

Assuming the existence of an extremum (necessarily a minimum), set (3) equal to zero and solve for a^*:

$$a^* = \frac{-\sum MV}{\sum M^2}. \tag{4}$$

Figures in the text and in Table 3 referring to the "degree of effectiveness" are values of a^*.

The OBE, Wharton, and Michigan models are in accord with the assumption that M is linear and homogeneous in S; DRI departs from it in only one trivial respect, through its percentage income-change variable in the auto equation.

The calculated a^* is not constrained to lie between zero and unity. If the Vs tend to be positive (that is, if even the zero-effect view underestimates consumption), then the calculated degree of effectiveness will be negative: $a^* < 0$. On the other hand, if the Vs are negative and tend to be larger in absolute value than M, so that even the full-effect view generally overestimates consumption, a^* will turn out to be greater than unity.

Choice of the Last Known Quarter

As discussed in the main body of the paper, the technique of dynamic simulation requires that the investigator be "blindfolded" with respect to information on actual consumption expenditures after some point. From that point on, he is compelled to use his own predicted values of consumption whenever lagged consumption is an explanatory variable in an equation. It was decided in advance to use 1967:2 as the last quarter for which actual consumer spending was to be known. After the simulations were completed, a check was made on the Michigan and Wharton models to see how other choices for the last known quarter would have altered the results.

Whenever lagged consumption is an explanatory variable, the strength of demand (relative to that predicted by the equation) in the last known quarter affects the subsequent track of predicted values. If consumer outlays are especially strong in that quarter, then the predicted value for the next quarter is higher because it includes some positive coefficient multiplied by the expenditure of that last known quarter. If the coefficient on lagged consumption expenditure is far below unity, the effect of strength in the last known quarter will decay rapidly. But if it is as high as 0.9, as it is in some of the equations for nondurable goods and services, then the residual of the last known quarter exerts a substantial impact on the track of predicted values for a considerable period.

None of the four models used in this study was very far from the mark on nondurables and services in 1967:2, although all four overpredicted: Wharton by $0.4 billion, DRI by $0.7 billion, Michigan by $1.1 billion, and OBE by $1.7 billion. In the case of nonauto durables, Michigan is the only model in which lagged expenditure enters significantly as an explanatory variable; the Michigan model predicted nonauto durables exactly in 1967:2. In the case of autos, lagged expenditure is included in the Michigan and OBE models in a significant way; both underpredicted this component in 1967:2, Michigan by $0.9 billion and OBN by $2.1 billion.

The use of every quarter from 1966:1 to 1968:2 as the last known quarter was explored for Michigan. In the case of automobiles, the choice turns out to have no significance at all: Every one of the ten hypothetical jumping-off points leads to exactly the same errors to the nearest tenth of a billion dollars after 1969:1; at the start of the surcharge period in 1968:3 the biggest difference of any simulation from that employed in this paper is only $0.3 billion. This result reflects the fact that the coefficient on lagged automobile expenditure is 0.34, small enough to decay rapidly. In the case of nonauto durables, the highest track of predicted values would have been obtained with 1966:3 as the last known quarter. In 1968:3, that track is $0.4 billion above the one actually employed with the 1967:2 jumping-off point; but the difference diminishes to only $0.2 billion in 1969:3, and is down to $0.1 billion by 1970:3. On the other extreme, the lowest track of predicted values would have been obtained with 1967:3 as the jumping-off point, and that track differs from the one actually used by $0.2 billion in 1968:3 and only $0.1 billion in 1970:3. None of these alternative choices would have made a qualitative difference in the findings.

In the case of nondurable goods and services, the various tracks of predicted values differ substantially and remain far apart throughout the surcharge period. The choice of 1966:1, 1966:2, 1966:3, and 1967:1 as the last known quarter would have yielded an even higher track of predicted values than did that actually employed and thus would have resulted consistently in even larger overpredictions of actual spending on nondurables and services. The choice of 1968:1 as the last known quarter would have yielded a track essentially indistinguishable from that of

1967:2. On the other hand, the choice as the last known quarter of weaker quarters of consumer spending on nondurables and services, such as 1966:4, 1967:3, 1967:4, and 1968:2, would have resulted in lower tracks of predicted values than did that actually employed in the dynamic simulation.

The only jumping-off point that would have changed Michigan's basic conclusions on nondurables and services would have been 1968:2. Reflecting the extreme weakness of consumer demand for these items during that quarter, the subsequent track of predicted values for the full-effect view would have been enough lower to produce an average *underprediction* of consumer spending on nondurables and services during the surcharge period. Quite apart from the extreme weakness of consumer demand during that quarter, any economist planning such an experiment in advance would have decided not to use the quarter immediately preceding the surcharge as the last known quarter for dynamic simulation just because it would emphasize whatever errors or shocks occurred in that quarter. The rationale of any dynamic simulation argues for getting a head start several quarters before the surcharge period. The next lowest track of the ten possibilities explored took 1967:4 as the last known quarter; on the full-effect view, it would have shown nearly unbiased results with an average underprediction of $0.2 billion a quarter during the surcharge period. Every other possible jumping-off point that was explored yielded substantial average overpredictions, as did the one actually employed.

The Wharton model has a coefficient of 0.37 on lagged expenditures for nondurables, and this effect decays rapidly; no jumping-off point between 1966:1 and 1968:2 produces differences amounting to more than $0.3 billion in any observed quarter after 1968:3. In the case of services, which have a coefficient on lagged expenditures of 0.98 in the Wharton model, a few of the tracks are considerably different from the one actually employed with the 1967:2 jumping-off point. The highest track of predicted values is that employing 1966:1 as the last known quarter: At the start of the surcharge period in 1968:3, it is $0.6 billion above the track actually employed, and at the end of the surcharge period in 1970:3 it is still $0.5 billion higher than the track used above. The lowest track of predicted values takes 1968:2 as the last known quarter; it runs consistently about $1.2 billion below the track that was actually employed. But even that lowest track of the ten yields an average overprediction of service outlays on the full-effect view, overpredicting in six of the nine quarters of the surcharge period.

Notes

Richard Mullins assisted in the research. This paper was made possible by the generous contribution of time (human and computer) and effort by Otto Eckstein, Charles Warden, and Fred Bamber of Data Resources, Inc.; Harold Shapiro of the University of Michigan; Maurice Liebenberg and George Green of the U.S. Department of Commerce, Office of Business Economics; and Lawrence Klein of the University of Pennsylvania. Constructive comments on an earlier draft were received from George Jaszi and Robert Eisner, as well as from several participants in the Brookings Panel on Economic Activity.

1. Nancy H. Teeters, "Budgetary Outlook at Mid-Year 1970," *Brookings Papers on Economic Activity* (2:1970), p. 304; and *Economic Report of the President together with the Annual Report of the Council of Economic Advisers, February 1971*, pp. 24 and 73.

2. Arthur M. Okun, "Measuring the Impact of the 1964 Tax Reduction," in Walter W. Heller (ed.), *Perspectives on Economic Growth* (Random House, 1968), p. 28.

3. Interesting answers are suggested by Lawrence R. Klein in "An Econometric Analysis of the Revenue and Expenditure Control Act of 1968–69" (paper prepared as a contribution to the forthcoming Musgrave Festschrift).

4. The estimates are expressed in terms of seasonally adjusted annual rates. Seasonal adjustment of the nonwithheld portion is not a straightforward matter, unfortunately.

5. It seems safe to ignore the possibility that the tax increase led to a quantitatively significant change in the remaining minor component of disposable income, personal transfer payments; these consist of payments of interest on personal debt to businesses, and gifts to persons overseas. Personal transfers amounted to 2.6 percent of disposable income throughout the period.

6. James S. Duesenberry, *Income, Saving, and the Theory of Consumer Behavior* (Harvard University Press, 1949); and Franco Modigliani, "Fluctuations in the Saving-Income Ratio: A Problem in Economic Forecasting," in *Studies in Income and Wealth*, Vol. 11, *Conference on Research in Income and Wealth* (National Bureau of Economic Research, 1949).

7. George Katona and Eva Mueller, *Consumer Response to Income Increase* (Brookings Institution, 1968), pp. 54–67.

8. Robert Eisner, "Fiscal and Monetary Policy Reconsidered," *American Economic Review*, Vol. 59 (December 1969), p. 898. Eisner also argues that investment could not have been curbed to any significant degree by the temporary corporate surcharge, and I find his argument on that issue more persuasive.

9. Milton Friedman, *A Theory of the Consumption Function* (Princeton University Press for the National Bureau of Economic Research, 1957); and Franco Modigliani and Richard Brumberg, "Utility Analysis and the Consumption Function: An Interpretation of Cross-Section Data," in Kenneth K. Kurihara (ed.), *Post Keynesian Economics* (Rutgers University Press, 1954).

10. Ronald Bodkin, "Windfall Income and Consumption," *American Economic Review*, Vol. 49 (September 1959), pp. 602–14; Margaret G. Reid, "Consumption, Savings and Windfall Gains," *American Economic Review*, Vol. 52 (September 1962), pp. 728–37; Roger C. Bird and Ronald G. Bodkin. "The National Service Life-Insurance Dividend of 1950 and Consumption: A Further Test of the 'Strict' Permanent-Income Hypothesis," *Journal of Political Economy*, Vol. 73 (October 1965), pp. 499–515; and Milton Friedman, "Comments," in Irwin Friend and Robert Jones (ed.), *Proceedings of the Conference on Consumption and Saving* (University of Pennsylvania Press, 1960), Vol. 2, pp. 197–98.

11. Mordechai E. Kreinin, "Windfall Income and Consumption—Additional Evidence," *American Economic Review*, Vol. 51 (June 1961), pp. 388–90.

12. Michael Lansberger, "Windfall Income and Consumption: Comment," *American Economic Review*, Vol. 56 (June 1966), pp. 534–40.

13. R. Conrad Doenges, "Transitory Income Size and Savings," *Southern Economic Journal*, Vol. 33 (October 1966), pp. 258–63.

14. Arthur M. Okun, *The Political Economy of Prosperity* (Brookings Institution, 1970), p. 96.

15. Neither the transitory-income view of the surcharge nor any of the other skeptical views cited above necessarily implies that the surcharge would have no effect whatsoever; the zero-effect view is simply a convenient benchmark of extreme skepticism.

16. The persistence of the effect depends on the coefficient of the lagged expenditure term. It decays exponentially through time at a rate depending on its distance from unity. A coefficient of 0.5 gets down to 0.06 of the initial error in four quarters, while one of 0.9 is still 0.66 at that point.

17. The most recent published descriptions of these models are Data Resources, Inc., *The Data Resources Econometric Forecasting System: A Preliminary Account* (DRI, November 1970); Saul H. Hymans and Harold T. Shapiro, "The DHL-III Quarterly Econometric Model of the U.S. Economy," in *The Outlook for 1970*, Seventeenth Annual Conference on the Economic Outlook at the University of Michigan, November 20–21, 1969 (1970); Maurice Liebenberg, Albert A. Hirsch, and Joel Popkin, "A Quarterly Econometric Model of the United States: A Progress Report," *Survey of Current Business*, Vol. 46 (May 1966), pp. 13–39; Michael K. Evans and Lawrence R. Klein, programmed by George R. Schink, *The Wharton Econometric Forecasting Model* (University of Pennsylvania, 1967). The OBE and Wharton models have been revised extensively, and new publications on both are forthcoming. In addition, some or all of the equations in the Data Resources and Michigan DHL-III models have been updated.

18. This is the mirror image of a relatively slow quarterly rate of adjustment ($0.13 = 1 - 0.87$) to the discrepancy between actual and equilibrium stocks of nonauto durables. See the discussion of this point in Hymans and Shapiro, "The DHL-III Quarterly Econometric Model."

19. In the simulations, *predicted* values of autos and parts are used.

20. "Root-mean-square error" is a standard statistical concept of average error that

gives extra weight to particularly large deviations. The errors are squared, and the square root of the average squared error is taken. In a dynamic simulation over a considerable period, the root-mean-square error is expected to be larger than the standard error over the sample period, because the dynamic simulation does not get the benefit of correction from actual lagged expenditure. Standard errors during the sample period for nondurables and services are in the neighborhood of $1.2 billion to $1.5 billion. The root-mean-square errors during the simulation period for the full-effect view in three of the models are roughly one to one and one-half times that size—surely as good as should be expected.

21. Curiously, the errors for nondurables and services and those for nonauto durables in the OBE model are strongly offsetting. The combined OBE estimates (covering consumption excluding autos) are remarkably accurate on the full-effect view, as Table 4 reveals.

22. See the discussion of this point by Saul H. Hymans, "Consumer Durable Spending: Explanation and Prediction," *Brookings Papers on Economic Activity* (2:1970), pp. 191–92.

23. Imposing these constraints on each of the three components involves some danger of biasing results. If the surcharge were, in fact, 100 percent effective, purely random errors would result in the estimated effectiveness for some components exceeding 100 percent and others lying below 100 percent. If no figure above 100 percent were accepted, the result would be biased downward. Similarly, if the true degree of effectiveness were zero, ignoring negative values for some components while accepting positive ones would bias the result upward.

24. On the other hand, for two professional views consistent with the findings of this study, see Paul W. McCracken, Statement before the House Ways and Means Committee, May 20, 1969, and Murray L. Weidenbaum, "Fiscal Policy for a Period of Transition," *Federal Reserve Bank of St. Louis Review*, Vol. 52 (November 1970), pp. 14–17.

25. On September 18, 1968, I said: "My statistical estimates would project [the surcharge's] impact on GNP during the third quarter at $2 billion. . . . There is no evidence yet visible—even in the CEA microscope—that the surcharge has moderated the pace of consumer spending. But there was never any reason to believe that there should be evidence of this nature by now." Arthur M. Okun, "Perspectives on Business in 1969," *Conference Board Record*, Vol. 5 (November 1968), p. 22.

26. The single aggregate consumption equation I employed in my 1965 paper on the tax cut worked somewhat faster than these models; it implied that, four quarters after an income change was initiated, consumption was affected by 80 percent of the change in income. I am not totally convinced that the lag structure of these models is accurate; indeed, too slow a process could be one source of the overpredictions of nondurables and services during the surcharge period.

Rules and Roles for Fiscal and Monetary Policy

When economists write text books or teach introductory students or lecture to laymen, they happily extol the virtues of two lovely handmaidens of aggregate economic stabilization—fiscal policy and monetary policy. But when they write for learned journals or assemble for professional meetings, they often insist on staging a beauty contest between the two. And each judge feels somehow obliged to decide that one of the two entries is just an ugly beast. My remarks tonight are in the spirit of bigamous devotion rather than invidious comparison. Fiscal policy and monetary policy are both beautiful; we need them both and we should treat them both lovingly.

The General Eclectic Case

In particular, both fiscal and monetary policy are capable of providing some extra push upward or downward on GNP. In fact, if aggregate stimulus or restraint were all that mattered, either one of the two tools could generally do the job, and the second—whichever one chose to be second—would be redundant. The basic general eclectic principle that ought to guide us, as a first approximation, is that either fiscal or monetary policy can administer a required sedative or stimulus to economic activity. As every introductory student knows, however, fiscal and monetary tools operate in very different ways. Monetary policy initially makes people more liquid without adding directly to their incomes or wealth; fiscal policy enhances their incomes and wealth without increasing their liquidity.

In a stimulative monetary action, the people who initially acquire money are not simply given the money; they must part with government securities to get it. But once their portfolios become more liquid, they presumably use the cash proceeds to acquire alternative earning assets, and in so doing they bid up the prices of those assets, or equivalently, reduce the yields. Thus prospective borrowers find it easier and less expensive to issue securities and to get loans; and investors who would otherwise be acquiring securities may be induced instead to purchase real assets such as capital goods. Also, because market values of securities are raised, people become wealthier, if in an indirect way, and may hence increase their purchases of goods and services. Thus many channels run from the easing of financial markets to the quickening of real economic activity.[1]

A stimulative fiscal action is appropriately undertaken when resources are unemployed; in that situation, an action such as expanded government purchases, whether for good things like hospitals or less good things like military weapons, puts resources to work and rewards them with income. The additional cash received by some people is matched by reduced cash holdings of those who bought government securities to finance the outlay. But the securities buyers have no income loss to make them tighten their belts; they voluntarily traded money for near money. In contrast, the income recipients become willing to spend more, and thus trigger a multiplier process on production and income. So, while fiscal and monetary routes differ, the ultimate destination—the effect on national product—is the same, in principle.

Indeed, the conditions under which either fiscal tools or monetary tools, taken separately, have zero effect on GNP are merely textbook curiosities rather than meaningful possibilities in the modern U.S. economic environment. For stimulative monetary policy to be nothing more than a push on a string, either interest rates would have to be just as low as they could possibly go, or investment and consumption would have to show zero response to any further reduction in interest rates. The former possibility is the famous Keynesian liquidity trap, which made lots of sense in describing 1936, but has no relevance to 1971. With prime corporations paying 8 percent on long-term bonds, interest rates are still higher than at any time in my lifetime prior to 1969.[2] There is plenty of room for them to decline, and, in turn, for states and localities, home-buyers and consumer installment credit users, as well as business investors, to be encouraged to spend more by lower costs of credit.

The opposite extreme, impotent fiscal policy, is equally remote. Fiscal policy must exert some stimulative effect on economic activity (even when the monetary policy makers do not accommodate the fiscal action at all) unless the velocity of money is completely inflexible so that no economizing on cash balances occurs. Though the money supply does not rise in a pure fiscal action, spending will tend to rise unless people are totally unable or unwilling to speed up the turnover of cash. And money holders do economize on cash to a varying degree—they do so seasonally and cyclically, and they do so dependably in response to changes in the opportunity cost of holding money. The holder of zero-yielding cash is sacrificing the opportunity to receive the going interest rates of earning assets. The higher interest rates are, the more he sacrifices; and hence, economic theory tells us, the more he will economize on his holdings of cash.

And the facts confirm the theory. The negative relationship between the demand for money and the rate of interest is one of the most firmly established empirical propositions in macroeconomics.[3] So a pure fiscal stimulus produces a speedup in the turnover of money and higher interest rates, and more GNP.

The fact that people do economize on cash balances in response to rises in interest rates demonstrates the efficacy of fiscal policy. Anybody who reports that he can't find a trace of fiscal impact in the aggregate data is unreasonably claiming an absolutely inflexible velocity of money—a vertical liquidity preference function[4]—or else he is revealing the limitations of his research techniques rather than those of fiscal policy.

A few other artful dodges, I submit, make even less sense. Try to defend fiscal impotence on grounds of a horizontal marginal efficiency schedule —that means investment is so sensitive to return that even the slightest interest variation will unleash unlimited changes in investment demand. Or make the case that people subjectively assume the public debt as personal debt and feel commensurately worse off whenever the budget is in deficit. Or contend that businessmen are so frightened by fiscal stimulation that their increased demand for cash and reduced investment spoils its influence.[5] Or use the argument that Say's law operates even when the unemployment rate is 6 percent.[6] It's a battle between ingenuity and credulity!

The eclectic principle is terribly important, not because it answers any questions, but because it rules out nonsense questions and points to sensible ones. It warns us not to get bogged down in such metaphysical issues as whether it is really the Fed that creates inflation during wartime. Every wartime period has been marked by enormous fiscal stimulus, and yet that fiscal fuel-injection could have been neutralized by some huge amount of pressure on the monetary brakes. In that sense, the Fed could have been sufficiently restrictive to offset the stimulus of military expenditures. Anyone who chooses to blame the resulting inflation on not slamming on the monetary brakes, rather than on pumping the fiscal accelerator, can feel free to exercise that curious preference. Take another example: Did the expansion following the tax cut in 1964–65 result from monetary policy? Of course it did, the eclectic principle tells us. If the Fed had wished to nullify the expansionary influence of the tax cut, surely some monetary policy would have been sufficiently restrictive to do so. There is no unique way of allocating credit or blame in a world where both tools can do the stabilization job.

Side Effects as the Central Issue

So long as both tools are capable of speeding up or slowing down demand, the decisions on how to use them and how to combine them must be made on the basis of criteria other than their simple ability to stimulate or restrain. Nor do we typically get any help by considering *how much* work monetary or fiscal tools do, because usually the right answer is, "as much as needed," providing the shift in policy is large enough. In more formal terms, two instruments and one target produce an indeterminate system.

Of course, there are two basic targets of stabilization policy: price stability and maximum production. But the two tools will not serve to implement those two goals simultaneously. A pen and a pencil are one more tool than is needed to write a letter, but the second tool can't be used to mow the lawn. In the same way, fiscal and monetary policy can both push up aggregate demand or push down aggregate demand, but neither can solve the Phillips curve problem. Subject to minor qualifications,[7] the fiscal route to a given unemployment rate is neither less nor more inflationary than the monetary route to that same unemployment rate.

We can have the GNP path we want equally well with a tight fiscal policy and an easier monetary policy, or the reverse, within fairly broad limits. The real basis for choice lies in the many subsidiary economic targets, beside real GNP and inflation, that are differentially affected by fiscal and monetary policies. Sometimes these are labeled "side effects." I submit that they are the main issue in determining the fiscal-monetary mix, and they belong in the center ring.

Composition of output. One of the subsidiary targets involves the composition of output among sectors. General monetary policy tools, as they are actually employed, bear down very unevenly on the various sectors of the economy. Homebuilding and state and local capital projects are principal victims of monetary restraint. Although the evidence isn't entirely conclusive, it suggests that monetary restraint discriminates particularly against small business. In the field of taxation, we agonize about incidence and equity. The same intense concern is appropriate in the case of monetary restraint and, in fact, increasing concern is being registered in the political arena. In the 1969–70 period of tight money, many efforts (such as Home Loan Bank and Fannie Mae operations) were made to insulate housing from the brunt of the attack. But the impact on homebuilding was still heavy. Moreover, there is considerable basis for suspicion that these actions defused—as well as diffused—the impact of monetary restraint. A more restrictive monetary policy, as measured in terms of either monetary aggregates or interest rates, is required to accomplish the same dampening effect on GNP if the sectors most vulnerable to credit restraint are shielded from its blows.

The concern about uneven impact may be accentuated because, in 1966 and again in 1969–70, monetary restraint hit sectors that rated particularly high social priorities. But that is not the whole story. Any unusual departure of monetary policy from a "middle-of-the-road" position may lead to allocations that do not accord with the nation's sense of equity and efficiency. For example, in the early sixties, it was feared that a very easy monetary policy might encourage speculative excesses in building because some financial institutions would be pressured to find mortgage loans in order to earn a return on their assets.

In the last few years, some economists—most notably, Franco Modigliani—have argued that monetary policy may have a significant impact on consumption through its influence on the market value of equity securities and bonds[8] in addition to its more direct impact through the cost and availability of installment credit. In my view, the jury is still out on this issue. On the one hand, it's easy to believe that a huge change, say, \$100 billion, in the net worth of the American public, such as stock market fluctuations can generate, could alter consumer spending in relation to income by a significant amount like \$3 billion, even though that change in wealth is concentrated in a small group at the very top of the income and wealth distribution. On the other hand, previous empirical work on this issue came up with a nearly unanimous negative verdict.[9] In 1966 and 1969, however, the timing of stock market declines and the sluggishness in consumer demand seemed to fit fairly well with the hypothesis.

One would like to believe the wealth hypothesis because it would suggest that monetary policy has broad and sizable effects on consumption, especially on that of high-income consumers; monetary restraint would then be revealed as less uneven and less inequitable. But before embracing that judgment, one should wait for more decisive evidence.

Interest rates and asset values. Another major consideration in monetary policy is its effects on interest rates and balance sheets. Some economists may argue that the only function of interest rates is to clear the market and the only sense in which rates can be too high or too low is in failing to establish that equilibrium. Every Congressman knows better! Interest rates are a social target. That is the revealed preference of the American public, reflected in the letters it writes to Washington and the answers it gives to opinion polls. And this is no optical illusion on the part of the citizenry. They have the same good reasons to dislike rising interest rates that apply to rising prices—the haphazard, redistributive effects. And they are concerned about *nominal* interest rates just as they are concerned about prices. It is not clear that such major groups as businessmen or workers are particularly hurt or particularly helped by tight money (or by inflation), but the impacts are quite haphazard in both cases. The resulting lottery in real incomes strikes most Americans as unjust.

The largest redistributive effect of tight money, like that of inflation, falls on balance sheets rather than income statements. People care about their paper wealth and feel worse off when bond and equity prices nose dive. Even though society is not deprived of real resources when security prices drop, it is hard to find gainers to match the losers. Although Alvin Hansen stressed the social costs of distorted, fluctuating balance sheets in the 1950's,[10] this issue gets little attention from economists. But it never escapes the broader and keener vision of the American public.

Financial dislocation. A restrictive monetary policy may also have important, dislocating effects on the financial system. The key function of a financial system is to offer people opportunities to invest without saving and to save without investing. If people want risky assets, they can acquire them beyond the extent of their net worth; if they wish to avoid risk, they can earn a moderate return and stay liquid. The trade of funds between lovers of liquidity and lovers of real assets produces gains to all. "Crunch" and "liquidity crisis" are names for a breakdown in the functioning of the financial system. Such a breakdown deprives people of important options and may permanently impair their willingness to take risks and to hold certain types of assets. To the extent that very tight money curbs an inflationary boom by putting boulders in the financial stream, a considerable price is paid. And to the extent that extremely easy money stimulates a weak economy by opening the flood gates of speculation, that too may be costly.

Balance of payments. The pursuit of a monetary policy focused single-mindedly on stabilization goals would have further "side effects" on the balance of payments, to the extent that it changes international interest rate differentials and hence influences capital flows. There are strong arguments for fundamental reforms of the international monetary system—especially more flexible exchange rates—that would greatly reduce this concern. But those reforms are not on the immediate horizon; nor is the United States prepared to be consistently passive about international payments.[11] Meanwhile, the external deficit casts a shadow that cannot be ignored in the formulation of fiscal-monetary policies.

Growth. A final consideration in the mix of stabilization tools is the long-run influence of monetary policy on the rate of growth of our supply capabilities. An average posture of relatively easy money (and low interest rates) combined with tight fiscal policy (designed especially to put a damper on private consumption) is most likely to produce high investment and rapid growth of potential. That becomes relevant in the short-run because the long-run posture of monetary policy is an average of its short-run swings. If, for example, the nation relies most heavily on monetary policy for restraint and on fiscal policy for stimulus, it will unintentionally slip to a lower growth path. The contribution of extra investment to growth and the value of the extra growth to a society that is already affluent in the aggregate are further vital issues. Recently, enthusiasm for growth-oriented policies has been dampened by the concern about the social fallout of rapid growth and by the shame of poverty, which calls for higher current consumption at the low end of the income scale. Nonetheless, the growth implications of decisions about the fiscal-monetary mix should be recognized.

In the light of these considerations, there are good reasons to avoid extreme tightness or extreme ease in monetary policy—even if it produces an ideal path of real output. Tight money can be bad medicine for a boom even if it cures the disease, just as amputation of the hand is a bad remedy for eczema. The experience of 1966 provides an object lesson. Judged by its performance in getting GNP on track, the Federal Reserve in 1966 put on *the* virtuoso performance in the history of stabilization policy. It was the greatest tight-rope walking and balancing act ever performed by either fiscal or monetary policy. Single-handedly the Fed curbed a boom generated by a vastly stimulative fiscal policy that was paralyzed by politics and distorted by war. And, in stopping the boom, it avoided a recession. To be sure, real GNP dipped for a single quarter, but the unemployment rate did not rise significantly above 4 percent; the 1967 pause was as different from the five postwar recessions, including 1970, as a cold is different from pneumonia. Moreover, inflation slowed markedly in the closing months of 1966 and the first half of 1967. What more could anyone want? Yet, you won't find the 1966 Fed team in the hall of fame for stabilization policy. In the view of most Americans, the collapse of homebuilding, the disruption of financial markets, and the escalation of interest rates were evils that outweighed the benefits of the nonrecessionary halting of inflation. The Fed itself reacted by refusing to give an encore in 1967–68, accepting renewed inflation as a lesser evil than renewed tight money.

All of this leads up to my first rule for stabilization policy: *Keep monetary conditions close to the middle of the road.* Let me explain that, no matter how monetary policy affects GNP, the rule must be interpreted in terms of interest rates and credit conditions, and not in terms of monetary aggregates. Suppose, for a moment, that the monetary impact on GNP is so powerful and the growth rate of the money supply is so critical that a growth rate of money only a little bit below normal will offset the aggregate demand impact of a huge fiscal stimulus (just for example, a $25 billion Vietnam expenditure add-on). The results would still be very tight money in terms of credit conditions, interest rates, and the impact on the composition of output. The shift in financial conditions required to "crowd out" $25 billion of private expenditures can hardly be trivial—even if the needed shift in monetary growth were trivial.

The "middle of the road" is deliberately a vague concept, relying on the existence of some general long-run notion of appropriate and normal interest rates and liquidity ratios. To be sure, it is hard to tell when we are in the middle of the road, but it is easy to tell when we are far away from it.

The Implications for Fiscal Policy

My second rule follows immediately from the first: *Operate fiscal policy to avoid forcing monetary policy off the middle of the road.* If fiscal policy is inappropriately stimulative or restrictive, a conscientious and (at least somewhat) independent monetary authority will be obliged to shoulder most of the burden for stabilizing the economy. In historical perspective, it is important to recognize that this sense of responsibility has not always prevailed. In World War II and again in the initial stages of the Korean War, the Federal Reserve reacted to an inflationary fiscal policy simply by pegging interest rates and creating all the liquidity demanded in an inflationary boom. Through these actions, the Federal Reserve not only passed the buck right back to fiscal policy but became an active accomplice in the inflation, intensifying excess demand by holding nominal interest rates constant as prices accelerated. It was technically feasible for the Federal Reserve to behave similarly during the Vietnam war. The fact that it picked up the ball after the fiscal fumble of 1966 demonstrated a new and greater sense of responsibility by the central bank for overall stabilization. So long as both fiscal and monetary policy makers feel that responsibility, as they appropriately should, and inappropriate fiscal policy is bound to push monetary policy off the middle of the road. Obviously, fiscal buck passing can also occur in a situation when stimulus is in order. In 1971, a rather neutral fiscal program accompanied by ambitious targets for recovery threatens to overburden the Federal Reserve with the responsibility for stimulus.

Fiscal Tools and Composition

To avoid pushing monetary policy off the middle of the road, fiscal policy must itself depart from the middle of the road—turning markedly more stimulative or more restrictive than its normal long-run posture—when private demand is especially weak or especially strong. But such swings in fiscal policy must also be made in light of compositional constraints that apply to federal expenditures, and especially to federal purchases of goods and services. Our preferences about the composition of output imply some notion of appropriate levels of civilian public programs. No one would wish to double or halve the size of the Census Bureau or the Forest Service in order to accord with the cyclical position of the economy. Moreover, these limitations based on principle are reinforced by limitations of a practical character. First, federal civilian expenditures on goods and services involve a mere $2\frac{1}{2}$ percent of GNP and thus afford very little leverage for stabilization. Second, most federal programs involving purchases of goods and services have long start-up and shut-off periods that make it extremely difficult to vary timing greatly without impairing efficiency.

Popular discussions of fiscal stabilization tend to stress expenditure variation despite these clear constraints. Why are the lessons ignored? Could any informed person have seriously regarded a curb on civilian public programs during the Vietnam build-up period as a meaningful antidote to the stimulus of increasing military expenditures? Could anybody familiar with the history of the lags in public spending support a public works program as a way to create jobs and strengthen recovery in 1971 or 1972?[12] The evidence suggests that people with strong views on the desirable size of the public sector tend to invoke the cause of stabilization as a rationalization for their social preferences. To an advocate of additional government spending, a recession provides a useful additional talking point: to a crusader for cutbacks in government spending, excess demand inflation offers an excellent excuse.

Federal "transfer" programs, such as social security, unemployment compensation, and veterans' benefits, are not subject to serious implementation lags, but their room for maneuver is limited by the principle of intertemporal equity. The aged, the poor, or the unemployed cannot justifiably be treated better in a recession than in prosperity or in a boom. The unfortunate people who are jobless when the unemployment rate is low deserve no less generous benefits than those who are unemployed when the rate is high; indeed, if misery loves company, those unemployed in prosperity may suffer psychically because they have less of it.

Some significant elbow room nevertheless appears for varying such transfer programs. Society's agenda always contains some new initiative or additional step to strengthen transfer programs in a growing economy with growing overall income; and the next step can be timed to come a little sooner or a little later, depending on the economy's cyclical position. In the present context, the administration's family assistance program provides a good example. The proposed initial date for benefits is July 1, 1972, but the program could be made effective six months earlier. Similarly, there is some opportunity for varying the timing of benefit liberalization and of payroll tax increases with respect to the social security program. Congress displayed wisdom early in 1971 by deferring for a year the proposed increase in the maximum earnings base of the payroll tax.

While this pure timing flexibility is important, it may not provide enough leeway for a flexible fiscal policy to respond to the needs of a very slack or very taut economy. Beyond it, the most attractive fiscal tool is variation in personal income tax rates. In principle, significant and indeed frequent changes in these rates are acceptable. Because they affect the huge consumption sector most directly and because their impact is spread over Americans throughout the middle- and upper-income groups, personal taxes are an ideal instrument for flexibility. While the income tax is specifically aimed to redistribute income in a more egalitarian way, the basic function of taxation is simply to restrain demand, given the socially desired level of public expenditures. A prima facie case exists for suspending or repealing any tax (or tax rate) that is not essential for the purpose of restraining demand sufficiently to avoid both inflation and monetary restraint. Moreover, according to compelling historical evidence, changes in personal tax rates—upward or downward, permanent or temporary—have reasonably reliable effects on consumer spending and hence on GNP.[13]

Political implementation is the one troublesome problem with changes in personal tax rates. Obviously, unlike shifts in monetary policy, any change in tax rates requires legislative action. And the record of congressional response to presidential requests for such changes has left much to be desired. Many constructive proposals have been made to improve that story. In 1961, the Commission on Money and Credit asked Congress to delegate authority for tax changes to the President subject to congressional veto; others have urged Congress to enact rules that would commit it to fast action—favorable or unfavorable—in response to a presidential request. Presidents Kennedy and Johnson made proposals for speeding the legislative process in their Economic Reports of 1962 and 1969, respectively. Herbert Stein presented a constructive proposal along similar lines in 1968. Even the Joint Economic Committee of the Congress expressed its concern in its 1966 report, "Tax Changes for Shortrun Stabilization."[14] But the Congress has generally ignored these proposals, jealously guarding its prerogatives over taxation, and refusing to bind its own hands with respect to procedures.

Under the present rules of the game, the President must ask Congress to do what seems best for the country and must count on presenting the case persuasively. The discussion and debates of recent years have put Congress on its mettle to respond promptly and pragmatically to any presidential request for tax changes designed for short-run stabilization purposes. Moreover, the 1963 and 1967 stalemates reflected special factors that seem obsolete—budget orthodoxy in the earlier case and Vietnam strategy in the later one. Our traditional procedures deserve another try.

These thoughts on the uses of alternative fiscal tools can be summarized as my third rule: *When additional fiscal stimulus or restraint is needed, opportunities for varying the timing of new initiatives in federal spending or tax programs should be the first line of attack: if these are inadequate to achieve the desired swing in fiscal policy, a change in personal tax rates should be sought.* We must keep urging and prodding the Congress to respond more promptly when tax changes are proposed. And we must not give up, for it will heed this message eventually.

Full Employment Surplus

The problems of executive-legislative coordination apply to expenditures as well as taxes. The fractionated process by which appropriations are made on Capitol Hill leads to frightful difficulties in the overall control of federal spending. As I have suggested elsewhere, one path to improvement might involve the following procedures: The President would make explicit the fiscal decision underlying his budget; and the Congress would then focus on that decision, approving or modifying it; and it would then commit itself to undertake an iterative review of appropriations and tax legislation during the course of the year to assure that the budget stayed within the bounds.[15]

I believe that the concept of the full employment surplus can be extremely useful as the focus of the fiscal plan and review. It is a simple enough summary number of the budget's impact on the economy to be understood by the participants, and it is a good enough summary to serve the purpose. It permits the stimulus or restraint in the budget to be compared with that of the previous year and other relevant previous periods.[15a] While administration officials cannot hope to provide a scientific demonstration that the budget has the proper amount of stimulus or restraint, they can generate an informed discussion and enlightened decision process by explaining their forecast of the strength of private demand, the proper role for monetary policy, and the likely response of the economy to proposed fiscal changes.

The main function of the full employment surplus in policy discussion is to correct the misleading impression generated by the actual budget surplus or deficit when the economy is off course. In a weak economy, revenues automatically fall far below their full employment level and the budget is hence pushed into deficit. That automatic or passive deficit may be misread as evidence that the budget is strongly stimulating the economy and hence that further expansionary action is inappropriate. By the same token, a boom resulting from a surge in private demand or an easing of monetary policy would automatically swell federal revenues, thereby tending to produce a surplus in the budget. These automatic shifts in federal revenues are important and significant; such built-in stabilizers help to cushion cumulative declines and dampen cumulative upsurges, but they should be properly recognized as shock absorbers rather than either accelerators or brakes.

I believe the focus on the full employment budget by the administration this year has helped to raise the level of fiscal debate. It reveals that the big deficits of fiscal years 1971 and 1972 are symptoms of a weak economy, rather than of a strong budget.

Guide vs. rule. The full employment budget shows where the fiscal dials are set; but it cannot say where the dials *ought* to be set. It is an aid to safe driving much like a speedometer, but it cannot prescribe the optimum speed. That depends on road conditions. A maintained target for the full employment surplus represents a decision to drive by the dashboard and to stop watching the road. Road conditions do change significantly from time to time in our dynamic economy. The evidence of the postwar era suggests that zero is too low a full employment surplus for a period of prosperity and too high a full employment surplus for a period of slack and slump. From long-term saving-investment patterns, one might guess that a full employment surplus of one-half of one percent of GNP would be about right on the average to accompany a middle-of-the-road monetary policy. But even that judgment would be highly speculative; and it would not tell us how to identify the rare case of an average year or how to quantify the departure of any particular year from the average. Economists have no right to be presumptuous about their ability to forecast in either the short-run or the long-run; and it is far more presumptuous to claim that the proper size of the full employment surplus can be determined for the long-run than to believe that it can be nudged in the correct direction in any particular year on the basis of the evidence then at hand.

Adoption of a fixed full employment surplus implies a firm determination by fiscal policy makers to counteract any major surprises that arise *within* the federal budget. If Congress rejects the President's proposals for major expenditure programs such as revenue sharing or family assistance, the advocate of a fixed full employment surplus is committed to propose alternatives for those stimulative actions. Similarly, if uncontrollable expenditures spurt, some compensatory action is required to keep the overall full employment budget close to its original position.

At the same time, however, the advocate of the fixed full employment surplus is determined *not* to act in response to surprises in private demand or monetary policy, no matter how large or how definite these may be. The resulting decision rule is illogical and indefensible. Once it is recognized that some surprises within the federal budget are large enough to call for offsetting fiscal action, it must be conceded that some surprises in consumer spending, plant and equipment outlays, or Federal Reserve decisions might also point to shifts in the fiscal course.

In fact, the Nixon administration has not adopted a fixed full employment surplus, but rather a rule that the full employment budget shall be *at least* in balance on the unified basis of budget accounting. The doctrine of balancing the full employment budget has obvious antecedents in the less sophisticated orthodoxy of balancing the actual budget. The new rule is far less harmful than its predecessor, but it is equally arbitrary. Its arbitrariness is perhaps illustrated by the fact that zero on the unified basis for the 1972 fiscal year turns out to be $7 billion on the national income accounts basis, which is the way Herbert Stein[16] first unveiled the concept and the way every economics student has learned full employment budgeting for a generation.

Statics vs. dynamics. The rule really reflects the administration's concern about overdoing fiscal stimulus, and that concern has a valid basis. There is genuine danger that stimulative fiscal action appropriate to today's slack and sluggish economy could commit the nation to stimulative budgets in future years when they would be markedly inappropriate. We might then be obliged to offset that stimulus by relying on monetary restraint or by seeking tax increases or cutbacks in expenditure programs once the economy approached full employment. Reliance on monetary restraint as an antidote to excessive budgetary stimulus violates rules one and two above. And to count on subsequent neutralizing measures of fiscal restraint is to ignore the serious doubts about the political feasibility of such legislative action. Congress is particularly unlikely to raise tax rates for the purpose of bailing out an overly enthusiastic anti-slump program that added mightily to federal spending. It would see such action as an open invitation to continued upward ratcheting of federal expenditures through time—with major expenditure initiatives in slumps and offsetting tax increases in booms. Whatever one's views on the appropriate size of the public sector, a cyclical ratchet is not a proper tool for decision making in the democratic process.

All of this argues for making stimulative fiscal policy with one eye on preserving our fiscal fitness for the next period of full employment. And that does require a rule, or at least some form of discipline that guards against excessive long-term commitments of revenue or expenditure. Hence, my fourth rule: *Stimulative fiscal programs should be temporary and self-terminating so that they don't jeopardize our future budgetary position.* The rule reminds us that the key issue is not whether full employment balance is maintained when the economy needs fiscal stimulus, but whether the budget remains in a flexible position from which it can be moved back readily into full employment surplus when restraint once again becomes appropriate.[16a] It cautions against permanent changes in the levels of taxation or expenditure programs for stabilization purposes; it puts a time-dimension on the third rule, which identifies the types of fiscal variation consistent with compositional objectives. Both rules argue against public works as a tool for stabilization. They also cast doubt on the recent liberalization of depreciation allowances as a stabilization device; that measure sacrificed $4 billion of revenue annually on a permanent basis in order to get $2 billion into the economy in 1971.

The Dependence on Forecasting

The rule for relying on quick-starting and self-terminating fiscal measures is designed to ensure flexibility and thus to limit the time horizon over which the forecasting of aggregate demand is essential to policy decisions. But that time period remains substantial and the success of policy remains dependent on the accuracy of economic forecasting. Tax cuts, for example, add cumulatively to aggregate demand for a considerable period after enactment. Thus, while they deliver some prompt stimulus to aggregate demand, they also involve a package of future add-ons to demand. The only way to lift the economy this quarter is through a tie-in sale that lifts the economy further for several subsequent quarters.

If any fiscal or monetary tool exerted its full impact instantaneously, stabilization policy making would be a different ball game. Indeed, this difference has been highlighted by the Laffer model, which finds that the effects of a shift in the money supply on aggregate demand are concentrated in the very quarter of the policy action.[17] While GNP is determined by the money supply in the Laffer model, the implication for policy strategy is diametrically opposite to that of previous monetarist views. Because of its instantaneous total effects, the Laffer model issues an unequivocal mandate in favor of monetary fine tuning. Monetary policy makers are encouraged to take all the action appropriate to hit their economic targets today; and they should then wait for tomorrow and correct any errors by twisting the dials again. Unlike more traditional views about the timing impact of economic policies, the Laffer model finds no tie-in sale or longer-term commitment that would caution against large and abrupt changes in policy.

Because Keynesians and most monetarists agree that the time stream of economic impact following a policy action begins virtually at once but continues into the more distant future, they seat the forecaster at the right hand of the policy maker. When policy decisions necessarily affect the future, they must be made in light of uncertain forecasts of the future and not solely on the basis of the facts of the present. To act otherwise is to adopt implicitly the naive forecast that the future is going to be merely a continuation of the present. The historical record of economic forecasting in the past two decades demonstrates that professional forecasting, despite its limitations, is more accurate than such naive models.[18] Moreover, even the naive model that tomorrow will be like today is far more accurate than the super-naive or agnostic model that tomorrow's aggregate demand is just as likely to be below the social target as above it regardless of where today's aggregate demand stands. That agnostic model is the extreme point in the decision analysis set forth by Milton Friedman and William Brainard.[19] If forecasts could not beat the agnostic model, it would be important to do nothing. The stabilization policy maker should simply stay home, for action by him would be just as likely to push the economy in the wrong direction as in the right direction and it could push the economy off the proper course when it would otherwise be there.

In fact, the professional forecaster can beat the agnostic model by a wide margin. I can think of only two years in the past twenty—1955 and 1965—when the January consensus prediction of economic forecasters would have led policy makers to administer stimulants when they were inappropriate and no cases when the consensus forecast would have pointed toward sedatives when stimulants were really appropriate.

A Propensity to Overreact?

Nonetheless, the fact that forecasters can guide policy makers to the right choice as between sedatives and stimulants is not necessarily decisive. Even if some sedative medicine would help a patient, he may be better off with nothing than with a massive overdose of sedation. And it is sometimes claimed that policy makers tend to prescribe overdoses.[20] According to this claim, because their medicines operate only with a lag and because neither the time shape of that lag nor the total impact of the policy is readily determined in advance, the policy makers become impatient; hence they continue to take more and more action until they have done too much of a good thing, which may be worse than nothing.

This intuitive argument has a certain appeal as a description of a human foible. We have probably all behaved in much this way in taking a shower. When the water is too cold, we turn up the hot faucet; and, if we are still cold ten seconds later, we may turn up the faucet some more, assuming that the first twist was inadequate. As a result of our first impatience, we may find ourselves scalded. And even after one or two experiences of this sort, we repeat that behavior and indeed find it difficult to discipline ourselves completely. If, indeed, fiscal-monetary policy makers have the same proclivities as the man in the shower, rules or discipline may help them to resist their impulses to overreact. But whether the Federal Reserve Open Market Committee or the Troika overtwist the faucets in their respective showers is an empirical issue, a proposition about their behavior that ought to be supportable or refutable by evidence. And I have yet to see evidence to support the proposition.

In the case of fiscal policy, I believe the record shows that policy makers generally have not behaved like the man in the shower. Below is a list of the major changes in fiscal policy during the past fifteen years, as defined by shifts in the full employment surplus,[21] and a capsule evaluation based on hindsight.

1. During 1958, the full employment surplus was reduced from more than 1 percent of GNP to near zero.	Stimulative direction proper; inadequate size, and timing delayed.
2. In 1959–60, fiscal policy was sharply reversed toward restraint with the full employment surplus reaching $2\frac{1}{2}$ percent of GNP in 1960.	Inappropriate restraint.
3. During 1961–62, that surplus was gradually trimmed.	Stimulative direction proper; inadequate size and timing delayed.

4. After backsliding during 1963, fiscal policy became considerably more stimulative with the enactment of the tax cut at the beginning of 1964.	Appropriate stimulus.
5. From the second half of 1965 to the end of 1968, the full employment budget was in deficit, reflecting the buildup of Vietnam expenditures.	Inappropriate stimulus.
6. In 1969, as the result of the tax surcharge and expenditure cutbacks, a full employment surplus of 1 percent of GNP was restored.	Appropriate restraint; much delayed timing.
7. In 1970 and the first half of 1971, fiscal policy was relaxed a bit with the full employment surplus roughly cut in half.	Relaxation proper; inadequate size.

Items 1, 3, 6, and 7 all depart from the ideal in the direction of too little and too late rather than too much and too soon. In each of these cases moves that were larger or earlier or both would have produced better stabilization results. Item 5—the inappropriate fiscal stimulus of the Vietnam period—was not the overreaction of the man in the shower. The hot water was turned up, but not because anyone believed that the economy needed warming.

Item 2—the shift to restraint in 1959—can be viewed, in a sense, as a premature and excessive cooling of economic expansion. But that policy simply was not keyed to the general economic diagnosis or forecast, which saw the temperature as remaining extremely mild, but rather to a non-economic budgetary orthodoxy. The full employment surplus was jacked up enough to balance the actual budget, as an end in itself rather than as a means to curb any present or prospective boom.

By any standard, the preponderant balance of mistakes in fiscal policy is revealed as errors of omission rather than commission—errors of doing too little too late, rather than too much too soon. Our fiscal man in the shower, in fact, tends to wait too long to ascertain that the water is really staying cold before he decides to turn it up. When he finally does turn the faucet, he acts timidly and hesitantly. When the water is hot, he also hesitates too long and moves indecisively. To shift metaphors, he is not trigger happy, but, rather, slow on the draw. And so I come to my fifth rule: *Face the fact that policies must be made on the basis of a forecast, and don't be slow on the draw!*

My rules for fiscal discretionary judgment will work well only if stabilization policy is guided by the professional expertise of economists. Obviously, that has not always been the case; and when politics vetoed economics, serious fiscal destabilization resulted. Indeed, in the past generation, the economy has been more severely disrupted by government actions obviously inconsistent with the objective of economic stabilization than by autonomous shifts in private demand. The 1950–51 Korean inflation, the 1953–54 post-Korean recession, the 1960–61 recession, and the Vietnam inflation were all government-induced fluctuations, in which the budget departed from any and all professional prescriptions for stabilization. In three of the four cases, swings in military expenditures created the problem; in the remaining case, it was caused by attachment to a taboo of budgetary balance. In light of these instances, one might well find that a fixed, moderate full employment surplus in peace and war, even years and odd years, would have yielded better overall results than those obtained from the actual fiscal process. But this is no argument for fixed parameters! The proposal to control political officials with a nondiscretionary rule reminds me of the suggestion to catch birds by pouring salt on their tails. Neither the political officials nor the birds will cooperate. If every economist in the nation had sworn (falsely) to Lyndon Johnson and Wilbur Mills that any deviation of the full employment surplus from 0.5 percent of GNP was a mortal sin, that wouldn't have changed fiscal policy in 1965–68. Why not tell our statesmen the truth and try to convince them to heed professional advice on fiscal policy? As unpalatable as that message might be, it has more chance of convincing elected public officials than the rule of maintaining a fixed and rigid full employment surplus for all time. And so I offer my sixth rule: *Presidents should listen to the advice of their economists on fiscal policy and so should the Congress.*

Signals for the Monetary Authorities

Under the circumstances I envision, the tasks of the Federal Reserve would depend upon how well the fiscal rules operate. If the budget no longer generates disruptive shifts in aggregate demand and if it offsets, to some degree, any major autonomous shift in private demand, then the monetary policy makers may be able to hold money and credit conditions close to the middle of the road without much difficulty. Under those best of all possible circumstances, economists might begin to wonder what all the shouting was about in the debate on the relative importance of aggregate quantities and interest rates as guides to monetary policy. In 1962–65, a monetary policy that was oriented toward interest rate targets did not produce large or abrupt shifts in the growth of the money stock, simply because the demand for money did not undergo enormous fluctuation. Presumably, if monetary policy had been pursued with respect to quantity rather than rate targets, those quantity guides would have left interest rates reasonably stable. If the demand for goods and the demand for money stay on course, then it makes little difference whether the directives to the trading desk are couched in terms of maintaining a given set of interest rates in the money markets or a given growth of the money supply.

It is not safe, however, to count on the world becoming that tranquil. Surprises will occur, and the policy makers will be forced to decide on the emphasis they wish to give to interest rates and aggregate quantities relative to one another. And it is a matter of degree—of relative emphasis. Anyone interested in diagnosing or influencing financial markets would obviously pay attention to both prices and quantities, just as he would in looking at any other market. Nobody has ever improved on Paul Samuelson's summary that Federal Reserve governors were given two eyes so that they could watch both yields and quantities.[22] In a more serious vein, James Duesenberry has recently sketched how the monetary authorities might appropriately be guided by both quantities and interest rates.[23] At a theoretical level, William Poole has shown the conditions for preferring rate-oriented, quantity-oriented, or mixed monetary strategies.[24]

Quite apart from the issue of appropriate guides, the chief problem facing the monetary authority is likely to be when and how much to depart from a "normal" or average posture in order to provide additional stimulus or restraint to economic activity. Monetary policy can and should find some elbow room without major deviations from the middle of the road. For one thing, monetary policy is light on its feet; the short implementation lag in Federal Reserve decisions provides an enviable contrast with the long lags in the legislative process for altering fiscal policy. In nudging economic activity to offset modest surprises, the speed of implementation makes monetary policy particularly useful.

Second, there is a case for a belt and suspenders strategy of making fiscal and monetary changes in the same direction when stimulus or restraint is desired. The quantitative effect of specific fiscal and monetary changes on GNP is uncertain. Errors in the estimates of these effects are likely to be negatively related or at worst unrelated—if the economy's response to monetary changes is larger than expected, the response to fiscal swings seems likely to be less than our estimates. How extensive the monetary swings should be and at what point the benefits in aggregate stabilization are outweighed by the costs of the side effects discussed above, are issues that require careful judgment and the best use of discretion.

Any recommendation for discretionary monetary policy runs into the contention that the Federal Reserve also shares a propensity to overreact; I find it more difficult to interpret that contention than the one regarding fiscal policy; but, as I read the evidence, it is also untrue. Whether judged in terms of interest rates or of aggregate quantities, I cannot see that the Federal Reserve has behaved like the man in the shower. It was not overly expansionary during most recessions and early recoveries. If the monetary policies of 1957–58, 1960–62, or 1970 could be replayed with the aid of perfect hindsight, monetary policy would surely be more expansionary than it was in fact. The only example of such a period that might stand on the opposite side is late 1954, when in retrospect the Fed seems to have been excessively generous.

Nor in periods of strong economic advance has the Fed generally applied the brakes too strongly or too soon. It may have done so in the case of 1959, but it clearly stayed off the brakes too long in 1965 and probably in 1955. Most clearly, the Federal Reserve has revealed the propensity to underreact to economic chill in late expansions and early stages of recession: with perfect hindsight, it is clear restriction was maintained too long in 1953 and again in 1957. In my judgment, the error in the 1969 performance should also be interpreted as unduly prolonged restraint—staying on the brakes too long and too hard late in the year—although others might argue that the restraint was applied too vigorously early in the year. There have been other mistakes in monetary policy, like the misdiagnosis of 1968, but they have little to do with either overreaction or underreaction, so far as I can see. Nor does the basic decision of 1967, which gave side effects priority over aggregate stabilization targets, reveal a propensity to overreact.

Thus I come to my final rule: *The makers of monetary policy should be guided by both aggregate quantities and interest rates and by the present and prospective state of aggregate demand; they will serve the nation best by using fully their capability to make small and prompt adjustments in light of the best current evidence and analysis.*

The Lessons of 1969–71

My rules aren't nearly so elegant nor so definitive nor as capable of making a high school boy a qualified CEA or Federal Reserve Chairman as the rules for maintaining fixed growth of the money supply and fixed full employment surpluses. The only thing in favor of the rules I am offering is that they happen to be better rules. We can do far better by using our intelligence in diagnosing, forecasting, and prescribing than by adopting rigid formulas that ignore the state of economic activity, the outlook for private demand, and the "side effects" of policies.

My kind of rules calls for an activist economic policy. Events since early 1969 strengthen my conviction that the optimum amount of activism is a lot of it. This debate easily degenerates into a semantic game. The opposition scoffs at "fine tuning"; I call it "sensible steering." Some people warn against going overboard; I worry about napping at the wheel. Trying diligently to avoid loaded words, I state as fact that, for better or for worse, the Nixon administration has been much more reluctant than its predecessors to alter fiscal-monetary policies on the basis of discretionary judgment. Apart from the issue of wage-price or "incomes" policy, this has been the biggest difference in economic policy since early 1969. (And the incomes policy difference may also be related to the preference for less activism.)

Along with a messy economic situation, the Nixon administration inherited a reasonably appropriate fiscal policy and an appropriate target of achieving disinflation without recession. The fiscal policy was not altered much within the course of 1969 and it was not controversial. While opinion differed about the extension of the tax surcharge, the repeal of the investment credit, and the desirability of the revenue-losing "tax reforms" of 1969, the controversies reflected primarily preferences for more or less public expenditure rather than for more or less fiscal restraint. Now did the fiscal 1971 budget program presented in January 1970 seem surprising or unreasonable. What was highly questionable, as I saw it then and see it now, was the emphasis on achieving an *actual* surplus in fiscal 1971 with no explicit contingency for the obvious risk of an economic slump that would make the surplus inappropriate. Although the father of the full employment surplus concept was a member of the Council of Economic Advisers, and one of the most ardent and effective exponents of the concept was the CEA Chairman, the lesson of the full employment surplus was essentially ignored in the initial Nixon budget. Instead, it unveiled a new, very short-lived budget concept known as the "credible surplus."

By May 1970, actual economic developments were clearly far more recessionary than had been predicted by the administration (and by me!) at the beginning of the year. Nonetheless, when the administration re-estimated the budget on May 19, it stuck to a tight fiscal program which called for a $10 billion full employment surplus (on the national accounts basis) in the face of a recession. And it advanced two new proposals to increase tax revenues—a speedup of estate and gift taxes and a tax on leaded gasoline. The economic situation had changed enormously between January and May 1970, but the fiscal posture was not changed. After fifteen months during which fiscal policy had been basically bipartisan, it became strongly controversial at that point.

On July 18, 1970, the President adopted the principle of full employment budgeting, but he did not alter the posture of the fiscal 1971 program. Indeed in August, he vetoed appropriations for education and for housing, endorsing those programs on social grounds but insisting that additional expenditures on them would be excessively stimulative.

After the economy sank far below the target path, the administration set an ambitious goal for rapid economic recovery in 1971, but the fiscal program continued to propose a full employment surplus on a national income accounts basis of about $7 billion, virtually unchanged from the level of 1970. The cautious fiscal program has failed to achieve the bold targets for output and employment growth, but the fiscal program has been reaffirmed. It is hard to understand the midyear decision to stand pat. Does the jack-in-the-box view of private demand linger on? Has the rule of full employment balance on the unified budget paralyzed fiscal policy? Does the rapid monetary growth of the first half of 1971 convince some administration economists that rapid expansion is just around the corner? Perhaps all of these contribute, but I would emphasize still another factor—the propensity to underreact.

Monetary policy in 1969–71 has also differed from the prescriptions that were being offered by outside observers of the Keynesian "new economics" school. Unlike the monetarists, most of us applauded extreme monetary restraint through the spring and summer of 1969 as necessary medicine to halt the investment boom and curb excess demand. In the fall, however, the Keynesians joined the monetarists in calling for less restraint. We heard the economy yelling "Uncle," but the Federal Reserve did not. Thus, extreme monetary restraint was maintained until 1970 began; again the error was in underreacting.

During the first half of 1970, attachment to consistency and a desire for a steady pace of monetary growth inhibited the Federal Reserve from making a full contribution to the end of recession and the start of the recovery. Since the fall of 1970, the Federal Reserve has had a difficult problem of interpreting divergent signals coming from money growth, on the one hand, and interest rates, on the other. From September 1970 to January 1971, credit conditions eased dramatically and interest rates fell sharply, but demands for active cash balances were weak and the money supply grew very slowly despite a high rate of growth of overall bank reserves. For reasons that are not clear, the demand for active balances rose sharply between January and June 1971—more than enough to provide a catch-up for the period of sluggish growth. Meanwhile, interest rates turned up spectacularly. Balance-of-payments problems added further complications. The Federal Reserve has seemed to compromise on these goals: it wishes to strengthen an evidently sluggish recovery, but it wants to avoid a massive outflow of short-term funds and big numbers on money growth. The Federal Reserve official directives focus on money supply targets, while the actions have been much more eclectic and pragmatic. The seeming inconsistency of word and deed had confused the Fed watchers in the financial markets and thereby added to the instability of interest rates and to the demand for liquidity. I strongly suspect that a policy of holding the Treasury bill rate close to some moderate level—like 4 percent—through the first half of 1971 would have produced much lower long-term interest rates *and* slower monetary growth.

At times during the early months of 1971, spokesmen for the administration and the Federal Reserve made no secret of their preference for a more stimulative stabilization policy than was in fact being pursued. The administration's fiscal policy makers emphasized the possibility for additional monetary stimulus while Federal Reserve spokesmen pointed toward additional fiscal stimulus. Anyone familiar with the problems of the bureaucratic division of labor in Washington can understand, sympathize with, and agonize about the tendency to "let George do it." It is only natural that the Federal Reserve would prefer to "let George [Schultz] do it" while the administration would wish the Board to do it. The picture has been disturbing, nonetheless, in raising doubts about the effectiveness of monetary-fiscal coordination between the independent

Federal Reserve and the administration. Proper coordination ought to guarantee that the fiscal-monetary mix has approximately the overall degree of stimulus or restraint that seems appropriate to both fiscal and monetary policy makers. Disagreements on the appropriate amount of stimulus may be inevitable, but when both sides agree that more stimulus is necessary, that should be forthcoming. It is much less important how much George does and how much the Board does, than that somebody act with determination to promote the solid recovery the administration wants and the nation needs. The eclectic principle reminds us that both can and should contribute.

Notes

1. There is general agreement between Keynesians and monetarists regarding the mechanism for transmitting monetary changes. See Milton Friedman and Anna J. Schwartz, "Money and Business Cycles," in Friedman. *The Optimum Quantity of Money and Other Essays* (Aldine, 1969), pp. 229–34. Reprinted from *Review of Economics and Statistics*, Vol. 45 supplement (February 1963), pp. 59–63.

2. Even when any reasonable allowance is made for inflation, it is hard to view today's *real* rates as low by historical standards.

3. See Okun, *The Political Economy of Prosperity* (Brookings Institution, 1970), p. 58, and the bibliography on pp. 146–47 for a list of articles reporting empirical results confirming this relationship.

4. For discussion of a model implying the existence of a vertical liquidity preference function, see Leonall C. Andersen and Jerry L. Jordan, "Monetary and Fiscal Actions: A Test of Their Relative Importance in Economic Stabilization." Federal Reserve Bank of St. Louis, *Monthly Review* (November 1968).

5. See Roger W. Spencer and William P. Yohe, "The 'Crowding Out' of Private Expenditures by Fiscal Policy Actions," in Federal Reserve Bank of St. Louis, *Monthly Review*, Vol. 52, No. 10 (October 1970), pp. 17–24.

6. See "Interest Rates and the Demand for Money," Chapter 7 in Milton Friedman, *The Optimum Quantity of Money*. Reprinted from *The Journal of Law and Economics*. Vol. 9 (October 1966), pp. 71–85. So far as I can see, Friedman is invoking Say's Law.

7. An unbalanced composition of demand among regions and industries means more inflationary pressure at a given overall utilization rate. Thus, particularly concentrated excess demands (e.g. for defense goods or for new homes) may harm the cause of price stability. But the degree of balance cannot be uniquely linked to fiscal-monetary choices.

8. See Franco Modigliani, "Monetary Policy and Consumption—The Linkages via Interest Rate and Wealth Effects in the Federal Reserve-MIT-Penn Model" (paper prepared for the Federal Reserve Bank of Boston Conference at Nantucket, Massa-

chusetts, June 1971; offset), esp. part I.3. For earlier discussions of the effects of monetary policy as it operates in the Federal Reserve-MIT-Penn Model, see the following: Robert H. Rasche and Harold L. Shapiro, "The FRB-MIT Econometric Model: Its Special Features," in American Economic Association, *Papers and Proceedings of the Eightieth Annual Meeting, 1967* (*American Economic Review*, Vol. 58, May 1968), pp. 123–49; Albert Ando and Franco Modigliani, "Econometric Analysis of Stabilization Policies," in American Economic Association, *Papers and Proceedings of the Eighty-First Annual Meeting, 1968* (*American Economic Review*, Vol. 59, May 1969), pp. 296–314; Frank de Leeuw and Edward Gramlich, "The Federal Reserve-MIT Econometric Model," *Federal Reserve Bulletin*, Vol. 54 (January 1968), pp. 11–40; de Leeuw and Gramlich, "The Channels of Monetary Policy," *Federal Reserve Bulletin*, Vol. 55 (June 1969), pp. 472–91.

9. See John J. Arena, "The Wealth Effect and Consumption: A Statistical Inquiry," *Yale Economic Essays*, Vol. 3 (Fall 1963), esp. pp. 273–84 and "Postwar Stock Market Changes and Consumer Spending," *Review of Economics and Statistics*, Vol. 47 (November 1965), pp. 379–91; Saul H. Hymans, "Consumption: New Data and Old Puzzles," *Brookings Papers on Economic Activity* (1:1970), pp. 121–26.

10. See, for example, *The American Economy* (McGraw-Hill, 1957), pp. 53–55.

11. On the question of a passive stance, see Lawrence B. Krause, "A Passive Balance-of-Payments Strategy for the United States," *Brookings Papers on Economic Activity* (3:1970), pp. 339–60; and Gottfried Haberler and Thomas D. Willett, *A Strategy for U.S. Balance of Payments Policy* (American Enterprise Institute, February 1971).

12. For a brief documentation of the disappointing results of the 1962 public works program, see Nancy H. Teeters, "The 1972 Budget: Where It Stands and Where It Might Go," *Brookings Papers on Economic Activity* (1:1971), pp. 232–33.

13. See my papers, "Measuring the Impact of the 1964 Tax Reduction," in Walter W. Heller (ed.) *Perspectives on Economic Growth* (Random House, 1968); and "The Personal Tax Surcharge and Consumer Demand, 1968–70," *Brookings Papers on Economic Activity* (1:1971), pp. 167–204.

14. Report of the Commission on Money and Credit, *Money and Credit—Their Influence on Jobs, Prices and Growth* (Prentice-Hall, 1961), pp. 133–37; *Economic Report of the President together with the Annual Report of the Council of Economic Advisers, January 1962*, pp. 17–19, and *Economic Report*, January 1969, pp. 12–13; Herbert Stein, "Unemployment, Inflation, and Economic Stability," in Kermit Gordon (ed.), *Agenda for the Nation* (Brookings Institution, 1968), pp. 292–93; *Tax Changes for Shortrun Stabilization*, A Report of the Subcommittee on Fiscal Policy of the Joint Economic Committee, 89 Cong, 2 sess. (1966), p. 16.

15. See Okun, *The Political Economy of Prosperity*, pp. 121–22.

15a. Arthur M. Okun and Nancy H. Teeters, "The Full Employment Surplus Revisited," *Brookings Papers on Economic Activity* (1:1970), pp. 77–81.

16. Committee for Economic Development, *Taxes and the Budget: A Program for Prosperity in a Free Economy* (CED, November 1947), pp. 22–25; and Herbert Stein, *The Fiscal Revolution in America* (University of Chicago Press, 1969), esp. pp. 220–232.

16a. See Frank Schiff's development of this point in "Control of Inflation and Recession" (speech delivered before the Seventy-fifth Annual Meeting of The American Academy of Political and Social Science, Philadelphia, April 1971; processed), pp. 12–16.

17. Arthur B. Laffer and R. David Ranson, "A Formal Model of the Economy" (paper prepared for the Office of Management and Budget, 1971; offset), pp. 25–27.

18. See Victor Zarnowitz, *An Appraisal of Short-Term Economic Forecasts* (National Bureau of Economic Research, 1967), esp. pp. 6, 14–19, and 83–120; Geoffrey H. Moore, "Forecasting Short-Term Economic Change," *Journal of the American Statistical Association*, Vol. 64 (March 1969), esp. pp. 3–4 and 15; and Victor Zarnowitz, "Forecasting Economic Conditions: The Record and the Prospect" (paper prepared for the National Bureau of Economic Research's Colloquium on Business Cycles, September 24, 1970; offset).

19. "The Effects of a Full-Employment Policy on Economic Stability: A Formal Analysis," in Milton Friedman, *Essays in Positive Economics* (University of Chicago Press, 1953), pp. 117–132; and William Brainard, "Uncertainty and the Effectiveness of Policy," in American Economic Association, *Papers and Proceedings of the Seventy-Ninth Annual Meeting, 1966* (*American Economic Review*, Vol. 57, May 1967), pp. 411–25.

20. See "The Role of Monetary Policy," Chapter 5 (esp. p. 109), in Friedman, *The Optimum Quantity of Money*. Reprinted from *American Economic Review*, Vol. 58 (March 1968), pp. 1–17.

21. Okun and Teeters, "The Full-Employment Surplus Revisited," pp. 102–103; Teeters, "Budgetary Outlook at Mid-Year 1970," *Brookings Papers on Economic Activity* (2:1970), p. 304; and Teeters, "The 1972 Budget: Where It Stands and Where It Might Go," p. 228.

22. "Money, Interest Rates and Economic Activity: Their Interrelationship in a Market Economy," in American Bankers Association, *Proceedings of a Symposium on Money, Interest Rates and Economic Activity* (ABA, 1967), p. 44.

23. "Tactics and Targets of Monetary Policy," in Federal Reserve Bank of Boston, *Controlling Monetary Aggregates*, Proceedings of the Monetary Conference, Nantucket Island, June 8–10, 1969 (FRB of Boston, 1969).

24. "Optimal Choice of Monetary Instruments in a Simple Stochastic Macro Model," *Quarterly Journal of Economics*, Vol. 84 (May 1970); pp. 197–216.

V

ECONOMIC PERFORMANCE, 1960–1980

Measuring the Impact of the 1964 Tax Reduction

Author's Note—June 1967

This paper was written during the summer of 1965. It reported on the way the Revenue Act of 1964 had served as a major stimulus to economic activity in the preceding year and a half. Just about the time that this paper was completed, we entered a new chapter in our economic history in which the key fiscal impact on the economy came from the extra defense expenditures required to fulfill our commitments in Southeast Asia. Any analysis of fiscal impact that covered the more recent period could no longer treat monetary policy as a passive supporting force, nor could it continue to ignore the influence of higher levels of aggregate demand on prices. Moreover, an updated version of this paper would revise the quantitative estimates associated with the tax reduction. Both revisions in earlier data and more recent experience would influence the point estimates. But neither the consideration of the most recent period nor the statistical refinement would change the basic conclusion that the tax cut of 1964 carried us a giant step toward full employment.

In the process of doing so, it also had important consequences for economic growth, which justify the inclusion of this topic in a volume of essays dealing with the subject of growth. To be sure, the Revenue Act of 1964 was aimed at the demand, rather than the supply, side of the nation's economy. Its objective and achievement was primarily to put productive capacity to work by raising private demand. Effects on the productive capability of the nation were largely incidental but nonetheless important.

By promoting fuller use of capacity, the tax cut created powerful incentives for growth-oriented activity by business. This was most apparent in the subsequent investment boom with its important widening, deepening, and updating of our capital stock. Fuller employment of labor, meanwhile, encouraged greater efforts in the private training of manpower and improved the mobility and upgrading of our human resources.

Finally, the tax cut set the stage for a heightened interest in public policy to stimulate growth. When the nation was failing to make full use of its existing productive capacity, there were good reasons for policy-makers to be unenthusiastic about measures that promised an accelerated growth of supply capabilities. Indeed, there was even a powerful attraction to proposals that sought deliberately to curtail growth, such as by enforcing artificially a marked shortening of the workweek or earlier retirement of senior workers. The realization of full employment was a prerequisite for the serious consideration of policies to stimulate economic growth. Once we can enjoy an environment of peacetime prosperity, growth policy will come to the fore. And it will owe much to the demonstration through the 1964 Revenue Act that we can make full use of rapidly growing productive capacity.

Introduction

The best-known fact about the Revenue Act of 1964 is that, in the year and a half since it took effect, economic activity has expanded briskly. But such *post hoc, propter hoc* reasoning will never do. Many things happened early in 1964, and by reference only to the course of events, one could attribute the buoyant performance of the economy to Illinois' victory in the Rose Bowl or to Goldwater's decision to stand in the New Hampshire primary. *Post hoc, propter hoc* somehow always seems to be on the other guy's side. If the economy had slipped into recession in 1964, it would have been viewed as a refutation of the efficacy of the tax cut. It would have been awfully difficult to get a serious discussion of whether an even worse setback might have occurred if not for the tax cut. At least now one can attract an audience to consider more analytical types of reasoning.

The analytical principles of macro-economics argue that rises in the incomes of individuals stimulate their consumer spending, while some combination of profit rates, cash flow, and sales is important as a determinant of business investment. The Revenue Act of 1964 affected these variables directly by adding to personal disposable income and to corporate profits after taxes. To the extent that the tax cut raised spending by consumers and businessmen through this direct route, it should also be credited with additional effects through the familiar multiplier process, whereby the spending of one individual or firm adds to the incomes and hence to the spending of others.

In the area of consumer spending, just a casual observation of the recent aggregative data suggests that there must be some validity to this story. By the second quarter of 1965, consumption expenditures had registered a remarkable rise of $45 billion from their rate in the last quarter of 1963—the quarter immediately preceding the tax cut. Such an increase over six quarters is unmatched in our peacetime history. If one ignores the tax cut, that surge is an insoluble mystery. On the other hand, the expansion of consumer purchases is easily accounted for by the income gains associated with the tax cut and the hypothesis that consumers have treated the increase in take-home pay from the tax reduction in the same way they treat increases in take-home pay from other sources.

By definition, individuals do something with income gains—they cannot ignore them and, according to the principles of utility maximization, they will not throw income away. Hence, the issue is how they allocate the proceeds between consumption and saving.[1] Both on the average and on the margin, the bulk of disposable income is consumed. If tax-cut gains are treated like other increases in income, most will be consumed and only a little will be added to saving.

The premise that tax-cut dollars are treated like other dollars of additional income is the foundation of the analysis. It is only fair to give warning that once this premise is accepted, the rest of the story follows readily. For our historical time-series data yield consumption-income relationships in which the marginal propensity to consume is very close to the average. Similarly, the quantitative record on investment tells us statistically that profits and sales have substantial effects on capital outlays. Indeed, this fundamental premise is the reason that so many economists expected so much from the 1964 Revenue Act. This premise can be subjected to some empirical check, although it cannot be supported by any refined verification from aggregative time-series data. If relationships established in the past hold up reasonably well after the tax cut, when tax-cut gains are added to other dollars of income, that supports the premise. But the real appeal is analytical: It is hard to see why people should want to segregate tax-cut dollars and treat them or think of them differently from other gains in their pay-checks or their corporate tills.

Given the fundamental premise, the analysis of the effects of the tax cut is an exercise in the dynamics of income-expenditure relationships. But that does not mean it is a simple exercise. Virtually every issue in aggregative econometrics bears on the result. The answer ought to be based on a fully articulated set of economic relationships that takes proper account of all the ways that everything depends on everything else in the economy. You will not be surprised to learn that the estimates developed below do not rest on such a complete analysis of the economy. Instead, they depend on a few key estimated functions and a liberal sprinkling of assumptions (which I note along the way) that other possible effects can be ignored.

In fact, I will temporarily assume that the only effects that need to be considered are those on consumption and personal disposable income. This gives us the familiar case of the pure consumption multiplier, where any and all effects on investment are ignored, and where the increment in Gross National Product is taken to consist entirely of consumption. The consumption gain can be divided into two parts. One reflects the direct result of tax reduction in raising personal disposable income, and the second stems from the extra incomes generated by additions to consumer spending. The first of these is logically prior to the second. Nevertheless, because consumers do not adjust spending fully and immediately to the increases in their incomes, the two parts will overlap chronologically, and both will contribute to the growing increment in GNP over time.

To pure consumption case is interesting and instructive, and its dynamics are challenging. But it is certainly misleading. Nobody can really believe that a surge in consumer spending and a major rise in corporate profits and sales would have no impact on outlays for plant, equipment, and additional inventory. We must move on into the world of the accelerator or supermultiplier, as difficult as it is to quantify that world. Hence, I will emphasize quantitative estimates of the effects of tax reduction when both consumption and investment outlays are taken into account. But first I must back up and start at the beginning.

The Size of the Tax Cut

The first question in evaluating the impact of the 1964 tax cut is how big was it? And the answer is not as easy as one would wish. We can estimate that the tax reduction for individuals lowered liabilities on Federal individual income taxes by \$6.7 billion for 1964 and by \$11.5 billion for 1965.

But the reduced liability is not the way the tax cut shows up in personal disposable income.

Our national income accounting takes the view that the spending of individuals (unlike that of corporations) is influenced by income taxes when these are paid rather than when the liabilities accrue. Actual payments were affected when the withholding rate declined from 18 percent to 14 percent in March 1964. The corresponding reduction in withheld taxes during 1964 amounted to a good deal more than $6.7 billion; indeed, it was above $8 billion. During the year, people were getting increases in take-home pay that exceeded the reductions in their tax liabilities. In part, this was associated with a reduced claim on the Federal Government for tax refunds early in 1965—any nontaxable dollar to which withholding had been applied generated a fourteen-cent refund rather than the eighteen-cent refund associated with the old withholding rate. Moreover, it was no secret that the 14 percent rate applied to ten months of the year would leave many people on less of a pay-as-you-go basis than they had been under the previous regime. In principle, anyone who changed his withholding voluntarily to maintain his degree of "pay-as-you-go" should have this adjustment subtracted from the dollar value of the tax cut for 1964.

There obviously were some such adjustments of withholding on a voluntary basis. Quantitatively, however, the best guess today is that they did not amount to much. Similarly, some of the self-employed reduced their estimated tax payments in June and September of 1964 in light of the lower tax rates. But, again, the adjustment does not seem to have been quantitatively significant and it would have operated in the other direction. Hence, we get a good approximation to the effect of the tax cut on disposable income through 1964 if we take actual withheld taxes after March, collected at a 14 percent rate, and apply a 2/7 ratio to them, so as to allow for the decline of four percentage points. For the first half of 1965, we must allow for the reduced refunds and the somewhat larger "clean-up payments" on the 1964 liabilities, which reduce the magnitude of the tax cut.

In principle, we should calculate the dollar value of the tax cut by applying the lower rates to incomes as they would have been in the absence of the tax cut and not to incomes as they actually turned out. But this difference is minor, and there are enough big problems to justify compromises on the little ones. I have rounded down the dollar estimates to make a rough allowance for this difference. The resulting estimates in billion of dollars (seasonally adjusted at annual rates) run as follows:

1964-I	3.2
-II	10.0
-III	10.0
-IV	10.0
1965-I	9.0
-II	9.5
-III	10.0
-IV	10.0

For corporations, the calculation is easier, simply because we treat taxes on a liability basis. The two-point reduction in the corporate tax rate for 1964, augmented by a switch between normal and surtax rates and by a liberalization of the investment credit, added up to $1.8 billion for the year. Another rate cut of two points took effect in 1965, and brought the 1965 total to $3 billion. The really important question about the corporate tax cut is whether it was shifted (either forward to consumers or backward to workers) or whether its benefits remained in the corporate sector. Without great conviction, I assume that there was no shifting in the short-run period covered by this paper.

The Pure Consumption Multiplier

The case of the pure consumption multiplier assumes away many of the difficult issues. To deal with it, all we need to know is (a) how much the tax cuts adds directly to disposable income, (b) how much each dollar increase in disposable income adds to consumption, and (c) how much a dollar of additional consumption, in turn, adds further to disposable income.

The basic ingredient is the consumption-disposable income relationship. This is the most famous of all quantitative economic relationships, and it has appeared in all shapes, sizes, degrees of disaggregation, and other variations on the Keynesian theme. I shall use a simple form which treats consumer spending as a single total. It makes aggregate consumption in the current quarter depend only on aggregate consumption of the preceding quarter and on the personal disposable income of the current quarter. The presence of lagged consumption does, however, introduce a cumulative influence of the whole history of consumption and income on current consumption. The lagged consumption variable implies the

Table 1 Incremental consumption associated with a maintained \$1 increase in disposable income

Quarter	Incremental consumption
0	0
1	.371
2	.597
3	.735
4	.819
5	.870
6	.901
.	.
.	.
.	.
∞	.949

$C_t = -1.40 + .371 Y_t + .609 C_{t-1}$
(billions of current dollars; fitted to period from 1954-I to 1964-IV)*
$\bar{R}^2 = .999$ $\bar{S}_E = 1.71$

* A homogeneous form $C_t/Y_t = .343 + .635 C_{t-1}/Y_t$ gives virtually identical results.

presence of habit persistence or inertia in living standards. The equation has a respectable genealogy, going back (at least) to an article by T. M. Brown in *Econometrica* of July 1952.

The equation is spelled out in Table 1, as are its implications. According to it, an additional dollar of disposable income in the current quarter raises current consumption by 37.1 cents. If the income gain is maintained, consumption in the next period will be above its base level by 59.7 cents—the sum of 37.1 cents and .609 of 37.1 cents. Ultimately, the effect on consumption reaches 94.9 cents, as can be seen by solving the equation for $C_t = C_{t-1}$.

The intercept of this equation is a small negative number, surprisingly suggesting that the marginal propensity to consume is larger than the average propensity. But the difference is very small and has no economic significance despite the statistical significance of the intercept. If the consumption function is forced through the origin and fitted homogeneously, one obtains a very similar equation which yield essentially the same results over time. These equations were also fitted with lagged income as well as lagged consumption, but the results were not improved. Asset variables deserve an opportunity to help explain consumption,

Table 2 Marginal shares of receipts from a maintained $1 increase in Gross National Product

		Quarter				
		0	1	2	3	... 6
1.	*Gross National Product*	0	1.000	1.000	1.000	1.000
2.	Corporate Profits before Taxes	0	.667	.340	.340	.340
3.	Corporate Taxes	0	.264	.134	.134	.134
3a.	Federal	0	.248	.127	.127	.127
3b.	State and Local	0	.015	.008	.008	.008
4.	Corporate Profits after Taxes	0	.404	.206	.206	.206
5.	Corporate Dividend Payments	0	.020	.029	.037	.058
6.	Undistributed Corporate Profits	0	.384	.177	.169	.148
7.	Indirect Business Taxes	0	.056	.056	.056	.056
7a.	Federal	0	.023	.023	.023	.023
7b.	State and Local	0	.033	.033	.033	.033
8.	Social Insurance Taxes	0	.011	.025	.025	.026
8a.	Federal	0	.009	.021	.021	.022
8b.	State and Local	0	.002	.004	.004	.004
9.	Transfer Payments	0	−.035	−.035	−.035	−.035
9a.	Federal	0	−.035	−.035	−.035	−.035
9b.	State and Local	0	0	0	0	0
10.	*Personal Income*	0	.251	.572	.580	.600
11.	Personal Taxes	0	.036	.082	.083	.086
11a.	Federal	0	.030	.068	.068	.071
11b.	State and Local	0	.006	.015	.015	.015
12.	*Disposable Personal Income*	0	.215	.490	.497	.514
Addendum: Net Government						
Receipts		0	.402	.333	.334	.338
Federal		0	.345	.273	.274	.277
State and Local		0	.057	.060	.060	.061

Details may not add to totals due to rounding.

(10) = (1) − (3) − (6) − (7) − (8) + (9)

(12) = (10) − (11)

Corporate profits were estimated marginally from:

$(P + CCA)_t = -6.4229 + .1686Y_t + .3267\Delta Y_t - .5502X_t$

$\bar{R}^2 = .961 \qquad \bar{S}_E = 1.403 \qquad \text{d.w.} = .846$

where $(P + CCA)$ is Corporate Profits before Taxes including Inventory Valuation Adjustment plus Corporate Capital Consumption Allowances, Y is Gross National Product and X is a measure of excess capacity associated with unemployment.

$(U - .0400) \times$ GNP, where U is the unemployment rate.

The equation was fitted to quarterly data (seasonally adjusted at annual rates) for the period 1954-I to 1964-IV, and variables were measured in billions of current dollars.

but they did not get their chance in this analysis. Nor was there any attempt to disaggregate consumption, such as by separating out expenditures for durable goods.

The consumption function alone would enable us to estimate the consumption gains associated with the direct income gains of the tax cut. But those direct income gains do not account for the full increase in personal disposable income. Part of the gain in disposable income results from the addition to consumption. Hence, we need to know how much each extra dollar of consumption (or, equivalently, of GNP) adds to disposable income. The best way I know to deal with the marginal share of disposable income in GNP is to subtract the other leakages that do not go into disposable income. It turns out that the marginal share of disposable income in GNP is considerably less than the average ratio of disposable income to GNP.[2] One major reason for this is that, in the short run, when GNP increases, Government transfer payments do not keep pace; in fact they are actually reduced through a decline in unemployment insurance benefits. The other and even more important reason is that corporate profits get a very large marginal share of GNP, particularly when the increase is sudden. Since dividends adjust very slowly through time, the bulk of the marginal share of profits is a withdrawal from disposable income.

As noted in Table 2, I have explained the sum of profits and corporate capital consumption allowances, using as independent variables the level of GNP, the change in GNP from the preceding quarter, and a utilization variable which multiplies GNP by the excess of the unemployment rate

Table 2 (notes continued)

The incremental calculation estimates that the unemployment rate is reduced by one percentage point by a 3.2 percent increment in GNP.

Throughout, capital consumption allowances are taken to be unaffected by changes in GNP.

Dividend payments were determined quarterly on the margin from:

$D_t = .92D_{t-1} + .05AP_t$

where AP is Corporate Profits after Taxes.

Corporate profits taxes were estimated at 39.5 percent of corporate profits.

Other taxes were estimated by taking the actual 1964 ratio to either GNP (Y) or Personal Income (Y_p), as appropriate, and using the following elasticities:

Federal Indirect Taxes	0.9	on	Y
State and Local Indirect Taxes	0.5	on	Y
Federal Social Insurance Taxes	0.75	on	Y_p
State and Local Insurance Taxes	0.75	on	Y_p
Federal Personal Taxes	1.2	on	Y_p
State and Local Personal Taxes	1.2	on	Y_p

over 4 percent. On the basis of this equation, the marginal corporate share is a strikingly large 67 percent when GNP rises in a quarter, and it remains at 34 percent in succeeding quarters if the gain in GNP is maintained. The importance of fixed costs supplies good analytical reasons for a large marginal corporate share. Still, the quantitative estimates of the marginal share derived from equations are always surprisingly large to me. After investigating the effect of alternative variables on the magnitude of the corporate marginal share, I bow to the persistence of the empirical results.

The other leakages in Table 2 are based on elasticity estimates which have a variety of underpinnings. They are nowhere nearly so troublesome as profits in the probable error they introduce in the marginal disposable income calculation. Taking account of the various leakages, we conclude that a dollar increase in GNP raises disposable income in the current quarter by 21.5 cents; if the GNP gain is maintained, the disposable income gain reaches about 50 cents in the second quarter. It keeps creeping up slightly because dividends keep rising very gradually in response to

Table 3 Sources of gains in disposable income (pure consumption multiplier) (in billions of current dollars)

	1964				1965	
	I	II	III	IV	I	II
Direct gain from personal tax reduction	3.2	10.0	10.0	10.0	9.0	9.5
Dividends attributable to corporate tax reduction	0.1	0.2	0.3	0.3	0.4	0.6
Induced gains						
a. Due to GNP gain of preceding quarter	—	0.8	2.6	4.1	5.3	6.0
b. Due to additional GNP gain in current quarter	0.3	0.7	0.6	0.5	0.3	0.3
Total increment in personal disposable income	3.6	11.7	13.5	14.9	15.1	16.4

Details may not add to total because of rounding.

The results of Table 2 are used here in a simplified form, which assumes that the marginal share of disposable income is constant at .505 after a lag of one quarter. The simultaneous share is taken at .215 as shown in Table 2. Accordingly, the *induced* gain in disposable income consists of:

a. .505 of the preceding quarter's gain for GNP plus
b. .215 of the *increase* in the GNP gain in the current quarter.

The induced gains in disposable income shows here are calculated from the bottom line of Table 4. "Gain" or "increment" for a given quarter refers to the amount over and above the hypothetical no-tax-cut situation; it does not denote the quarter-to-quarter change.

the increase in corporate profits. The whole process can be simplified and summarized adequately by assuming that, in the second and succeeding quarters, the marginal share of disposable income in GNP levels off at .505. In the pure consumption case, there is one further influence to take into account: The corporate tax reduction generates extra dividends through time. Quantitatively, this does not amount to much; but it is registered in the results shown in Table 3.

Now we have, in effect, a two-equation system. The marginal consumption tells us how much added consumption is generated by extra disposable incomes; while the marginal disposable income-GNP relationship tells us what further gains in disposal income are produced by added consumption. Tables 3 and 4 show the numerical solutions of this system. By the fourth quarter of 1964, through the pure consumption route, disposable income is estimated to have been \$15.1 billion higher as a result of the tax cut and consumption to have been \$10.5 billion higher. These gains continue to expand in the first half of 1965 but at a slower rate. In part, the leveling off reflects the downward bump in the size of the tax cut for the first half of 1965; in part, it suggests that the process was, by that time, beginning to approach its full effects.

Table 4 Consumption and GNP gains related to disposable income gains (pure consumption multiplier)

Quarter	Gain in disposable income	Resulting gain in consumption in					
		1964-I	1964-II	1964-III	1964-IV	1965-I	1965-II
1964							
I	3.6	1.3	0.8	0.5	0.3	0.2	0.1
II	11.7		4.3	2.6	1.6	1.0	0.6
III	13.5			5.0	3.0	1.9	1.1
IV	14.9				5.6	3.4	2.1
1965							
I	15.1					5.6	3.4
II	16.4						6.1
Total consumption (or GNP) gain in given quarter		1.3	5.1	8.1	10.5	12.0	13.4

Details may not add to totals because of rounding.

The cells above show the "phasing-out" of income gains into consumption gains in accordance with the consumption equation set forth in Table 1. That consumption equation and the disposable income relationship summarized in the note to Table 3 form a two-equation system in consumption and disposable income.

In the "pure consumption multiplier" case, the GNP gain is set equal to the consumption gain.

But the ultimate full effect is considerably larger than the $13.4 billion gain in consumption shown for the second quarter of 1965. Holding the personal tax cut at $10 billion and the corporate reduction at $3 billion, we would ultimately reach a consumption gain of more than $21.2 billion.

The corporate tax reduction would be credited with a $3 billion contribution to consumption after the very long wait required for dividends to be fully adjusted. This is not a great performance as a consumption stimulus, but corporate tax cuts have never been expected to star in that respect.

The bulk of the ultimate consumption gain—$18.2 billion—would be attributable to the personal tax reduction. Based on a .949 marginal propensity to consume and a .505 marginal share of disposable income, the steady-state multiplier is 1.82. Given the nature of this calculation, "close to two" remains a good familiar approximation to the pure consumption multiplier for a tax cut.

Induced Investment

Now I move to the more difficult but more realistic situation in which induced investment is recognized. We will continue to assume that neither net exports nor residential construction is affected by the tax cut or by the subsequent increases in incomes. These simplifying assumptions are not likely to be quantitatively important and at least they are offsetting in direction: Net exports would be lowered by higher GNP, while residential construction would be favorably affected, given the state of credit conditions. The induced effects we deal with are those on business fixed investment and inventory investment.

The choice of an equation for explaining business fixed investment is exceedingly difficult. Here, we cannot take advantage of the survey data and other barometric indicators that are so helpful in forecasting plant and equipment. Sales, utilization measures, and cash flow variables all have excellent claims for appearing in the equation. But when all of these are allowed to compete in equations fitted from time-series data, chaos results. The coefficients are highly unstable with respect to the choice of lags and the specification of variables. I trust that the econometric conflict between cash flow and accelerator models will be settled some day, but I am convinced that the decisive battle will not be fought with aggregative time-series data.

Many time-series equations with a few lags and a few variables perform about equally well. A cash flow equation with four quarterly lags in that

Table 5 Increments in business fixed and inventory investment from a maintained $1 increase in final sales of GNP

Quarter	Business fixed investment	Inventory investment
0	0	0
1	0	.041
2	.118	.163
3	.134	.207
4	.163	.197
5	.176	.157
6	.154	.105

Business fixed investment was calculated marginally from:

$I_t = 9.02 + .293F_{t-1} + .182F_{t-2} + .162F_{t-2} + .110F_{t-4}$

$\bar{R}^2 = .968 \quad \bar{S}_E = 1.30 \quad \text{d.w.} = .609$

F is corporate cash flow (corporate profits after tax, including inventory valuation adjustment, plus corporate capital consumption allowances).

The equation is fitted to quarterly data for 1954-I through 1964-IV and all variables are quarterly totals at seasonally adjusted annual rates expressed in billions of current dollars.

F was estimated marginally using the profits function set forth in Table 2 and an estimated profits tax share of 39.5 percent, as noted in Table 2.

Inventory investment was calculated from:

$V_t = -45.56 - .1715H_{t-1} + .5842V_{t-1} + .0428S_t + .1099S_{t-1}$

$\bar{R}^2 = .733 \quad \bar{S}_E = 1.908 \quad \text{d.w.} = 1.886$

where V is the change in Business Inventories; H is V cumulated from 1947-I; and S is GNP Final Sales.

Variables are quarterly totals, seasonally adjusted at annual rates in billions of 1958 dollars. The equation was fitted to 1954-I to 1964-IV but omitting the period from 1959-II to 1960-I.

single variable gave good results and reasonable coefficients. That is what I am using, as shown in Table 5. To the extent that cash flow really serves here as a proxy for other influences, such as sales and utilization, this should not be disturbing. The reliance on cash flow does credit the corporate tax cut with direct influence, but the omission of after-tax profits in the investment equation would assume that it had no direct effect. According to this equation, a dollar of extra after-tax corporate profits ultimately raises investment by seventy-five cents, working out its effects over the succeeding four quarters, as shown in Table 5.

The results of the inventory equation are also shown in Table 5. Inventory investment is explained using lagged stocks, lagged inventory investment, and current and last quarter's final sales of GNP. This equation and other inventory equations was a terrible estimator for the period from the second quarter of 1959 to the first quarter of 1960, when inventory investment was dominated by first the expectation, then the realization, and finally the recovery from the steel strike. Nevertheless, other periods of steel-dominated inventory activity did not show unreasonable results. Hence, the four misbehaving quarters were thrown out of the sample from which the equation was calculated. Because of the presence of the stock variable, there is no ultimate maintained level of inventory investment. As Table 5 shows, the induced inventory investment associated with a $1 maintained increase in GNP begins to decline after three quarters. It would eventually turn negative and oscillate, ultimately converging to zero.

The fixed investment and inventory equations do not include any monetary variables. In principle, they belong here. I would certainly expect a significant change in the costs or availability of credit to have an important influence on business investment. In practice, dealing with the period from early 1964 through mid-1965, I cannot believe that the omission of monetary variables can make a serious difference. By any measure of interest rates or credit conditions I know, there were no significant monetary changes that would have either stimulated or restrained investment to a major degree. Obviously, the rising incomes and investment of this period generated increased demands for financial assets and for loans. In this environment, the maintenance of stable interest rates and stable credit conditions required action by the monetary authorities to expand the reserve base more rapidly so as to accommodate expansion.

In this sense, monetary policies made a major contribution to the advance, but that contribution can be appropriately viewed as permissive rather than causal. The monetary authorities supplied a good sound set of tires for the economy to roll on, but they did not contribute the engine. That came from fiscal policies. If monetary policy had been the driving force, that would have shown up—at least initially—in a decline of interest rates and a relaxation of credit conditions.

It is reasonable to ask now much slower the overall economic advance might have been and how much less expansionary the tax cut would have been if monetary policy had not been accommodating. One could hypothesize an alternative monetary policy which held down the growth of bank reserves or the money supply (or other liquidity variables) to some stated degree. And one could then try to assess what difference this tighter monetary policy would have made in the pace of economic advance. That would be an interesting statistical exercise. It just does not

Table 6 GNP gains by components allowing for induced investment (in billions of current dollars)

	1964				1965	
Gains in	I	II	III	IV	I	II
Corporate Cash Flow	2.4	4.1	5.2	6.1	8.0	8.8
Direct from profits tax reduction	1.8	1.8	1.8	1.8	3.0	3.0
Induced profits before tax	1.0	3.8	5.6	7.2	8.3	9.6
Less: Induced profits taxes	−0.4	−1.5	−2.2	−2.8	−3.3	−3.8
Disposable Income	3.6	11.9	14.5	17.1	18.5	21.2
Direct from personal tax reduction	3.2	10.0	10.0	10.0	9.0	9.5
Dividends attributed to corporate tax reduction	0.1	0.1	0.2	0.3	0.4	0.5
Induced	0.3	1.8	4.2	6.8	9.1	11.2
Consumption	1.3	5.2	8.6	11.6	13.9	16.3
Business Fixed Investment	—	0.7	1.6	2.6	3.7	4.8
Inventory Investment	0.1	0.4	1.2	2.1	2.8	3.2
Total GNP	1.4	6.3	11.4	16.3	20.5	24.4

happen to be the particular statistical exercise which this paper attempts to perform.

We can now put the whole process in motion, using the inventory and the investment equations along with the disposable income relationship and the consumption function discussed earlier. The results are shown in Table 6. The gains in GNP are, of course, larger than those estimated in the pure consumption case. Indeed, consumption itself rises more strongly because of the greater induced gains in disposable income. And, after a slow start, the investment components are contributing about one-third of the estimated total gain in GNP after the fourth quarter of 1964. The total gain in GNP reaches $17.1 billion in the final quarter of 1964 and goes on to $24.4 billion in the second quarter of 1965. If we continue the process for another two quarters, the GNP increase would exceed $30 billion in the fourth quarter of 1965.

And it will be rising. With a $10 billion personal tax cut and a $3 billion corporate reduction, the GNP gain would ultimately be $36.2 billion, $7.8 billion in business fixed investment and $28.4 billion in consumption. In this final situation, inventory investment would no longer contribute to the gain.

Of this "final" $36.2 billion gain in GNP, $25.9 billion results from the personal tax reduction and $10.3 billion from the corporate tax cut. The "steady state" multiplier for personal taxes is 2.59. The ultimate multiplier for the corporate tax cut is estimated at 3.4. But the corporate cut takes a much longer time to approach its full effects, because dividends creep up so slowly and gradually. Throughout the first two years following a tax cut, the estimated impact per dollar of the personal tax reduction is substantially greater than that of the cut for corporations. Moreover, we should recognize the possibility that the cash flow character of the investment equation may be too generous to the corporate tax cut.

According to these results, the Federal Government received $7 billion of extra net receipts in the second quarter of 1965 (on a national income accounts basis) as a result of the gains attributable to the tax cut. By this Federal budgetary criterion, the tax cut had paid for more than half of itself by then, and the fraction was rising. In addition, state and local governments were the beneficiaries of an estimated $1.5 billion increase in net receipts in the second quarter. In the ultimate situation, the induced gain in Federal net receipts would be $10 billion, and the state and local gain $2.2 billion, adding to a total that nearly matches the $13 billion of tax reduction.

Conclusion

This is not the first quantitative estimate that has been made for the Revenue Act of 1964; and it will not be the last. I trust also that it will not be the best. At the Council of Economic Advisers, we hope to improve the tools needed in this analysis and to remedy some of the limitations I have noted above.

Nevertheless, the results shown in Table 6 looks sensible and plausible to me. One way of viewing the conclusions is to consider what they imply about the hypothetical world in which no tax reduction had taken place. The hypothetical no-tax-cut world is constructed by subtracting from actual national accounts variables the estimated gains from the tax cut over the six quarters from the beginning of 1964 to mid-1965. Instead of a rapid growth in GNP of more than $10 billion a quarter in that period, the world without a tax cut has an average quarterly increase of $6.3 billion, as shown in the accompanying chart. When the same thing is done for the other key variables, the results form a consistent pattern—slow growth in disposable income, small advances in consumption, and a leveling off in fixed investment in the first half of 1965 following some slippage in corporate profits during 1964. This no-tax-cut world would have shown rising unemployment and sagging operating rates.

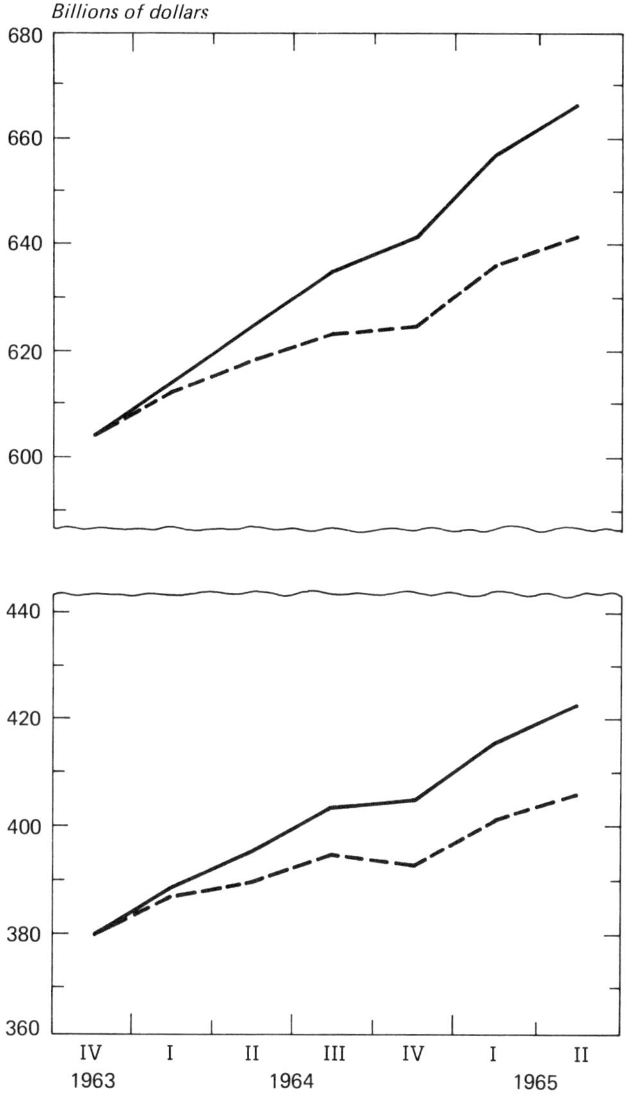

Chart GNP (top) and consumption (bottom)—actual (solid lines) and hypothetical (dashes lines)—"no tax cut" (seasonally adjusted annual rates).

I suggested at the outset one possible check on the fundamental premise that tax cut dollars are treated like other dollars: It consists of looking at empirical relationships established in the past to see whether they went haywire in the period following the tax cut. I can report that the equations held up quite well. Of course, they do not fit perfectly during the last year and a half, but neither did they fit perfectly in the years prior to the tax cut.

In the consumption function, there were sizable errors for two quarters, a $4.5 billion overestimate in the fourth quarter of 1964 and an offsetting $3.5 billion underestimate in the first quarter of 1965. In view of the slow deliveries of new cars during the auto strikes of the autumn of 1964 and the subsequent extraordinary catch-up, this pattern seems perfectly sensible. The profits equation fits unusually well during 1964 and the first half of 1965. Its largest error is in the second quarter of 1965, when it understates the level of profits by $1.7 billion; during the sample period, its standard error of estimate was $1.4 billion. The root-mean-square error in the inventory equation for the six quarters was identical to its $1.9 billion standard error of estimate over the sample period. Fixed investment is exceedingly well estimated for the first half of 1964; but it is underestimated consistently thereafter by amounts ranging from $1.2 to $3.5 billion and averaging $2 billion per quarter. There are grounds for suspicion that the investment equation we have used may have been conservative in its estimate of the induced effects stemming from personal tax reduction.

According to the estimates cited above, the tax cuts of 1964 are credited with a $25 billion contribution to our GNP by mid-1965, a $30 billion effect by the end of 1965, and an ultimate $36 billion increment. I have mentioned many reasons why these point estimates should be viewed as the center of a sizable range. Even with all the appropriate qualifications, these results provide important analytical confirmation that the Revenue Act of 1964 lived up to the intentions and expectations of its advocates, and that it has delivered a powerful stimulus to economic expansion.

Notes

This paper was made possible by the able assistance of Allen Lerman.

1. The Department of Commerce's recently amended conceptual framework introduces a new third option for consumers. They are now free to engage in personal transfers to businesses or to foreigners by paying interest on personal debt or making

gifts to persons overseas. All empirical work in this paper is based on the revised national accounts data shown in the *Survey of Current Business*, August 1965.

2. I have discussed this elsewhere. See "Short-Term Forecasting by the President's Council of Economic Advisers" in O.E.C.D., *Techniques of Economic Forecasting*, Paris, 1965, pp. 163–65.

Achieving Sustained Prosperity

One of the most pleasant assignments of the Council of Economic Advisers under President Johnson was the responsibility for keeping straight the arithmetic on the duration of the nation's economic expansion. By January 1969, we were able to report that the economy had advanced for ninety-five months since the last recession ended early in 1961. Nobody asks me for that statistic any longer; but I still enjoy keeping score. As of this writing (November 1969), the nation is in its one-hundred-and-fifth month of unparalleled, unprecedented, and uninterrupted economic expansion.

Obsolescence of the Business Cycle Pattern

The persistence of prosperity has been the outstanding fact of American economic history of the 1960s. The absence of recession for nearly nine years marks a discrete and dramatic departure from the traditional performance of the American economy. Our long-term record of economic progress has been a series of two steps forward followed by one step back. Over the past century, periods of economic expansion have averaged about two and one-half years in length, ending in recession or depression. Before 1961, the longest expansion was an eighty-month period largely during the Second World War, and the holder of second place was the fifty-month extended but incomplete recovery from the Great Depression during the 1930s. The three expansions between 1948 and 1960 lasted forty-five, thirty-five, and twenty-five months.[1] Reflecting in part the built-in stabilizers of our fiscal and financial system, the postwar recessions were brief and mild as compared with the prewar record. But, until 1961, recessions were not significantly less frequent than previously.

Western European nations managed to make prosperity last during the fifties, but the United States did not share this success.

According to the historical record, once the American economy pulled out of a recession, there was a safe period of approximately eighteen months during which a rebound in inventory investment virtually assured the expansion of overall activity. Once that safe period passed, it was about an even bet that an expansion would last another ten months and this estimated life expectancy applied regardless of whether the expansion had already lasted eighteen or thirty-eight months.[2]

Thus, on the basis of previous performance, the odds in February 1961 against the new expansion surviving one hundred and five months were about 400 to 1. For one hundred and eight months, the chance would have been 1/512—the compound probability of getting through nine ten-month periods after the initial safe interval, equivalent to the likelihood of a fair coin coming up heads nine times in a row.

When recessions were a regular feature of the economic environment, they were often viewed as inevitable. Indeed, the Doctor Panglosses saw them as contributors to the health of our best of all possible economies, correcting for the excesses of the boom, purging the poisons out of our productive and financial systems, and restoring vigor for new advances. And the latter-day Machiavellis saw potentially great political significance in the timing of turning points. They spun out fantasies, suggesting or suspecting—depending upon whether their party was in or out of office—that the business cycle would be controlled so that the inevitable recession would come between elections and would be replaced by a vigorous economic recovery during the campaign period.

Professional thinking about overall economic performance was also deeply rooted in the business cycle approach. It focused on our position in terms of the stage of the business cycle, attempted to diagnose how long an expansion could continue, and considered what might be done when a recession took place. Policy was often geared to the simple judgment that sustainable expansion was the good and recession was the bad in the economic tides of the nation. Economic forecasts were concentrated on finding the next turning point—the time when the economy would shift from expansion to contraction or the reverse.

The experience of the sixties has made a marked and lasting change in business cycle mentality. Since November 1968, the monthly Bureau of the Census publication of economic data carries a new title. *Business Conditions Digest*, instead of *Business Cycle Developments*. It continues to be known as BCD, but, as a sign of the times, the "Business Cycle" has disappeared. Today few research economists regard the business cycle as a particularly useful organizing framework for the overall analysis of current economic activity, and few teachers see "business cycles" as an appropriate title for a course to be offered to their students. Now virtually no one espouses the fiscal formula that was most popular with thinking conservatives just a decade ago—that of balancing the federal budget over the course of a business cycle.

In 1965 President Johnson was making a controversial statement when he said: "I do not believe recessions are inevitable."[3] That statement is no longer controversial. Recessions are now generally considered to be fundamentally preventable, like airplane crashes and unlike hurricanes. But we have not banished air crashes from the land, and it is not clear that we have the wisdom or the ability to eliminate recessions. The danger has not disappeared. The forces that produced recurrent recessions are still in the wings, merely waiting for their cue.

Recessions did not just happen; they reflected the vulnerability of an industrial economy to cumulative movements upward and downward. While they have diverse specific causes, cyclical fluctuations can usually be viewed as the result of imbalances between the growth of productive capacity and the growth of final demands for its output. During periods of prosperity, a significant part of the nation's output is used to increase productive capacity through investment in plant and equipment and in business inventories. If the growth of final demand by consumers and government keeps pace and hence sales expand, the increase in fixed and working capital normally turns out to be profitable. The expansionary decisions of businessmen are thus validated, and further expansion is encouraged. The advance then generally keeps rolling along, although it might be deterred by tight credit or unfavorable cost-price developments.

If, on the other hand, final demand fails to grow sufficiently to make use of growing capacity, businessmen have an incentive to slow down the expansion of the stocks of plant, equipment, and inventories. Even if these capital stocks continue to grow, the mere decline in the rate of expansion of capacity can mean an absolute cutback in the demand for capital goods and for output to be added to inventories. Payrolls and other incomes are thus reduced in some areas; in turn, these income declines lead to more widespread reductions in spending and may generate a decline in total demand. Thus a slowdown in economic activity may be converted into an absolute downturn—a recession or depression.

The balance between final buying and stock building can be upset on either side. Overbuilding of inventories apparently played a key role in the first postwar downturn in 1948. A sharp decline in the government's final demand for defense products precipitated the second postwar recession in 1953. In 1956–57, final demand grew very slowly while productive capacity was expanding rapidly in a major boom for capital goods. In 1959–60, when fiscal and monetary policies were very restrictive, final demand grew too slowly to support even the moderate expansion of capacity that was taking place. Various imbalances have also developed at times in the 1960s, but they have never become so large or so widespread as to turn the economy down. The nature of economic fluctuations has not changed; policies to contain them have made the difference.

The record of economic advance in the sixties has been impressive in strength as well as length. As we caught up and kept up with our productive capacity in eight and one-half years of expansion, our real output grew 51 percent, or 5.0 percent a year, in contrast with our long-term annual average of 3 percent. Real disposable income per capita—our best price-corrected measure of the purchasing power of the average consumer—rose one-third, as much of a gain as in the preceding nineteen years. Corporate profits doubled. The number of civilian jobs increased more than 12 million, enough to match the growth of the labor force and to reduce unemployment by more than 2 million persons.[4]

The record presents a striking contrast to the sluggish growth and recurrent recessions of the late fifties. From 1953 to 1960, the growth of industrial production in the United States averaged only 2.5 percent a year, below the pace of every other industrial nation. Between 1956 and 1961, real gross national product (GNP) rose at an average rate of 2.1 percent, so far below the 6.4 percent estimated rate of the Soviet Union[5] that it made credible Khrushchev's threat to "bury" us economically. In June 1962. Gunnar Myrdal identified as "the world's greatest problem" neither peace nor race relations, but "economic stagnation" in America.[6]

As the economy entered the sixties staggering rather than soaring, observers drew cosmic implications from its unsatisfactory performance. Some saw it as hopelessly stagnant, arguing that automation and technical progress had altered labor requirements so much as to make high employment an impossibility. We heard dire forecasts raising the specter of automation, the threat of the "triple revolution,"[7] the prospect of persistent structural deterioration of labor markets. Thus Robert Theobald predicted:

Unemployment rates must therefore be expected to rise in the sixties. This unemployment will be concentrated among the unskilled, the older worker and the youngster entering the labor force. Minority groups will also be hard hit. No conceivable rate of economic growth will avoid this result.[8]

In fact, of course, unemployment has fallen sharply during the 1960s. As shown in Figure 1, unemployment rates in the spring of 1969 were not only dramatically lower than in the first quarter of 1961 but also well below those of the spring of 1959, one of the most prosperous quarters of the late fifties. Although teenagers remained victims of high unemployment rates, particularly impressive gains were made by adults who had been at the back of the hiring line.

The attitudes of the early sixties seem dim today. This is proof *par excellence* that at least some controversies in economics get resolved. It also reveals the dangers of cosmic generalizations based on a limited period of experience. Predictions of a chronic dollar shortage, chronic stagnation, chronic secular deterioration in labor markets, and the like have all been sounded in the past generation. And all have been refuted by subsequent developments. Yet the lessons seem to go unheeded. We now see the start of a new wave of cosmic generalizations centering on perpetual inflation, perpetual strength of investment demand, and perpetual credit scarcity. This new wave may already have influenced policy by serving as an intellectual justification for the permanent repeal of the investment tax credit. It will be surprising if the new generalizations hold up much better than their predecessors.

The New Strategy of Economic Policy

More vigorous and more consistent application of the tools of economic policy contributed to the obsolescence of the business cycle pattern and the refutation of the stagnation myths. The reformed strategy of economic policy did not rest on any new theory: Ever since Keynes, economists had recognized that the federal government could stimulate economic activity by increasing the injection of federal expenditures into the income stream or by reducing the withdrawal of federal tax receipts. For generations they had noted the influence of the cost and availability of credit on expenditures financed with borrowed funds.

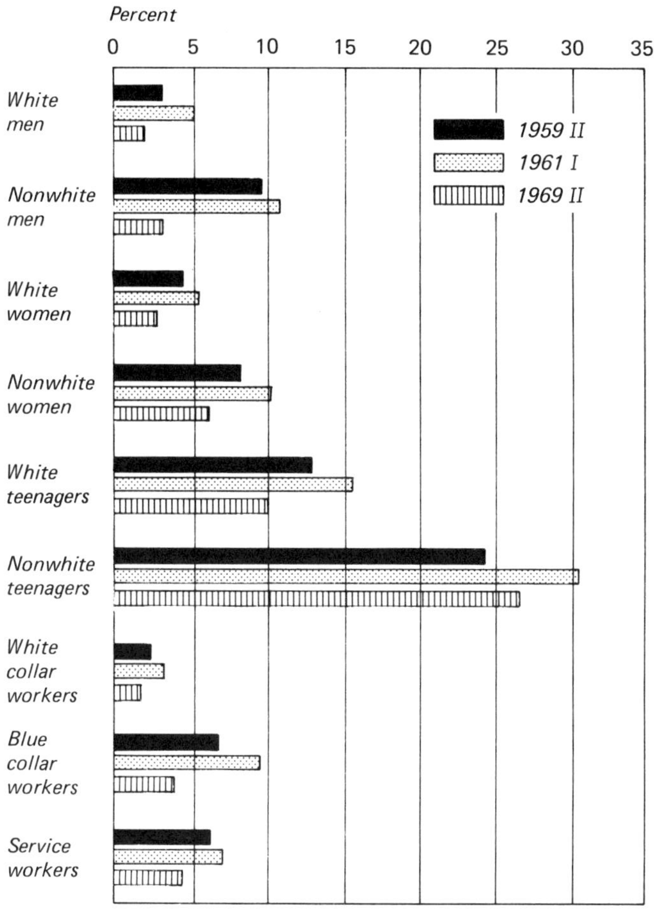

Source: U.S. Department of Labor.

Figure 1 Unemployment rates for selected groups, spring 1959, winter 1961, and spring 1969. Data for men and women are for persons 20 years old and over; data for teenagers are for persons 16 to 19 years old.

Nor were the tools of policy new and different. Some stimulative fiscal actions had been taken under the aegis of the New Deal in the 1930s. The Employment Act of 1946 declared the federal government's continuing responsibility to promote "maximum employment, production, and purchasing power,"[9] relying mainly on fiscal and monetary devices. During each of the four postwar recessions, some countercyclical fiscal and monetary measures had been adopted; and each period of inflationary boom had been met with some counteracting policies of economic restraint.[10]

Until the 1960s, however, the use of the federal budget for purposes of economic stabilization often followed a fire-fighting strategy. Deliberate stimulus or restraint through budget deficits or substantial surpluses was applied only when the alarm sounded. At other times, the orthodox rule of balancing the budget seemed to dominate. And because the deliberate application of fiscal policy was widely viewed as an emergency measure, there were considerable inhibitions about initiating a policy program. Any time the President proposed budgetary measures designed to serve economic objectives, he was conceding that the economy was in an emergency and needed the fire department for a rescue operation. That inhibition contributed to delays in the adoption of appropriate antirecessionary measures in each of the four postwar slumps. Similarly, there was eagerness to return to business-as-usual once the recession emergency ended.

These attitudes were particularly pronounced in the late 1950s. Thus, with the unemployment rate near 6 percent, President Eisenhower said in his State of the Union Message of January 1959. "If we cannot live within our means during such a time of rising prosperity, the hope for fiscal integrity will fade."[11] In recalling a decision of the Eisenhower administration not to reverse its restrictive fiscal program early in 1960, Richard Nixon reported, ". . . There was strong sentiment against using the spending and credit powers of the Federal Government to affect the economy, unless and until conditions clearly indicated a major recession in prospect."[12] As Mr. Nixon's summary makes clear, the restrictive fiscal policy of 1959–60 should not be construed as a conscious and deliberate effort to stop growth in order to eliminate inflationary expectations.[13] Surely, the 1960–61 recession was not intentionally planned by the Eisenhower administration. Nor was a 5 percent rate of unemployment regarded as a minimum for the nation. To be sure, risks were consciously taken on the side of excessive restraint, but these corresponded to the preference for orthodox budgetary principles that largely ignored the economic impact of fiscal policy. The basic strategy was to stick with orthodox principles unless the fire alarm of recession tolled loud and clear. This ruled out the use of stimulative—or even supportive—fiscal policies during periods of expansion.

In the late forties and early fifties, the possible need for stimulative policies even during expansionary periods was widely discussed.[14] But events did not put this strategy to the test during the first postwar decade. Spurred by the Korean buildup in 1950, the economy rose swiftly to—and beyond—full employment in its recovery from the first postwar recession. Again in 1954–55, the rebound from recession was strong and prompt, carrying the nation to essentially full utilization by the close of 1955. From that point on, however, expansion and full utilization did not go hand in hand. The growth of output was very sluggish during the last year and a half of the 1954–57 expansion. Even at its peak in the spring of 1960, the recovery from the 1957–58 recession left the economy far short of full employment. These experiences highlighted the distinction between high employment and cyclical expansion.

Against this background, the strategy of economic policy was reformulated in the sixties. The revised strategy emphasized, as the standard for judging economic performance, whether the economy was living up to its potential rather than merely whether it was advancing. Ideally, total demand should be in balance with the nation's supply capabilities. When the balance is achieved, there is neither the waste of idle resources nor the strain of inflationary pressure. The nation is then actually producing its potential output. The concept of potential output was imprecise and so was its quantification. Yet it helped to deliver and dramatize the verdict that idle resources were a major national extravagance in the late fifties and early sixties. And the quantification, which had been heatedly debated in 1961,[15] held up surprisingly well during the sixties, as Figure 2 indicates.

The shift of emphasis from the achievement of expansion to the realization of potential had a number of important corollaries. First, by establishing a moving target for economic performance, it stressed the growth of the economy. The supply capabilities of the United States economy advance continually, reflecting both our expanding labor force and the improving productivity that results from advancing technology and investment in human and physical resources. In the late fifties, the growth of potential had amounted to about $3\frac{1}{2}$ percent per year; the

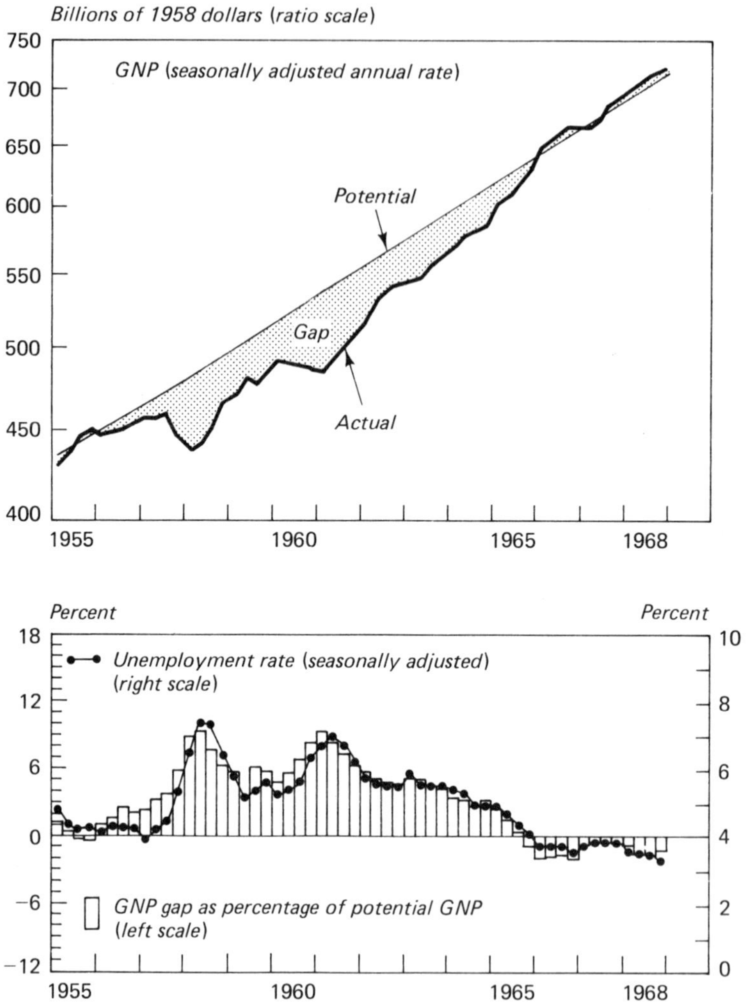

Sources: U.S. Department of Commerce, U.S. Department of Labor, and Council of Economic Advisers.

Figure 2 GNP, actual and potential, and unemployment rates, 1955–68.

shortfall of actual performance below that pace showed up in rising unemployment. The actual growth performance was unsatisfactory because it failed to take full advantage of our growing supply capabilities, even though new record highs in income and employment were achieved.

Second, the focus on the gap between potential and actual output provided a new scale for the evaluation of economic performance, replacing the dichotomized business cycle standard which viewed expansion as satisfactory and recession as unsatisfactory. This new scale of evaluation, in turn, led to greater activism in economic policy: As long as the economy was not realizing its potential, improvement was needed and government had a responsibility to promote it.

Finally, the promotion of expansion along the path of potential was viewed as the best defense against recession. Two recessions emerged in the 1957–60 period because expansions had not had enough vigor to be self-sustaining. The slow advance failed to make full use of existing capital; hence, incentives to invest deteriorated and the economy turned down. In light of the conclusion that anemic recoveries are likely to die young, the emphasis was shifted from curative to preventive measures. The objective was to promote brisk advance in order to make prosperity durable and self-sustaining.

All of this added up to a coherent view of stabilization policy. Something here was new and different. Arthur Burns has summarized it perceptively:

> The central doctrine of this school is that the stage of the business cycle has little relevance to sound economic policy; that policy should be growth-oriented instead of cycle-oriented; that the vital matter is whether a gap exists between actual and potential output; that fiscal deficits and monetary tools need to be used to promote expansion when a gap exists; and that the stimuli should be sufficient to close the gap—provided significant inflationary pressures are not whipped up in the process.[16]

The adoption of these principles led to a more active stabilization policy. The activist strategy was the key that unlocked the door to sustained expansion in the 1960s. The record of economic performance shows serious blemishes, particularly the inflation since 1966. To some degree, these reflect errors of analysis and prediction by economists; to a larger degree, however, they reflect errors of omission in failing to implement the activist strategy.

The expansion can be divided into two distinct parts, which are discussed in some detail below. The remainder of this chapter is devoted to the period from early 1961 until mid-1965, when the main task was to invigorate the economy. The major problem could be simply and clearly diagnosed as inadequate total demand, and the equally simple remedy was stimulative fiscal and monetary policy. By mid-1965, that diagnosis had become accepted and much of the remedy had been applied.

Thereafter, the assignment was to hold to a course of noninflationary prosperity, a problem for which the economist does not have a simple and satisfactory solution. It is inherently a much more difficult task, and it was made ever so much more difficult by large increases in defense spending. The record after mid-1965 is reviewed in Chapter 3.

Onward and Upward

As Walter Heller has said: "In 1961, with over five million unemployed and a production gap of nearly $50 billion, the problem of the economic adviser was not what to say, but how to get people to listen."[17] The appropriate remedy required—at least for a time—budgetary deficits and increases in the national debt. There was widespread professional agreement on this prescription. In Herbert Stein's judgment, "If [President Kennedy] had chosen six American economists at random the odds were high that he would have obtained five with the ideas on fiscal policy which his advisers actually had, because those ideas were shared by almost all economists in 1960."[18]

Outside the profession, however, antipathy toward such unorthodox federal budgeting was deeply entrenched; it had been strongly nurtured during the fifties, and remained an obstacle to rational action in 1961. John F. Kennedy had not challenged the orthodox principles during the 1960 election campaign; indeed, he had criticized President Eisenhower's $12 billion budgetary deficit of fiscal 1959.[19] President Kennedy bent but did not break the traditional rules in taking steps to invigorate recovery during 1961 and in heeding the advice of his economists that the Berlin defense buildup did not call for higher taxes. Then the President bowed to the orthodox rules in January 1962, proposing a balanced budget at a time when 6 percent of the labor force was unemployed.[20]

It was only when the expansion faltered in the spring of 1962 that Kennedy reached a fork in the fiscal road. In a memorable commencement address at Yale University in June 1962, he spoke out clearly and strongly against budgetary orthodoxy:

The myth persists that Federal deficits create inflation and budget surpluses prevent it. . . . Obviously deficits are sometimes dangerous—and so are surpluses. But honest assessment plainly requires a more sophisticated view than the old and automatic cliché that deficits automatically bring inflation. . . .

. . . What we need is not labels and clichés but more basic discussion of the sophisticated and technical questions involved in keeping a great economic machine moving ahead.[21]

Once President Kennedy called this play, Walter Heller carried the ball and brought the "sophisticated and technical questions" before the public. The press served as the textbook for the biggest course in elementary macroeconomics ever presented. In fact, Professor Heller captured his millions of students with new labels in place of old. The "full employment surplus," "constructive deficit," "fiscal dividend and fiscal drag," and "output gap" were drummed home in repeated lessons. The message was effectively conveyed to the business and financial community and to the nation's legislators by the Secretary of the Treasury, C. Douglas Dillon, and then Under Secretary Henry H. Fowler.

The administrative reform of depreciation guidelines and the enactment of the investment tax credit in 1962 were two new policy initiatives which directly stimulated business investment and made their largest direct contribution to business incomes. It was probably no coincidence that the first installment of the expansionary strategy worked to benefit directly the groups that seemed particularly hostile to a heterodox, deficit-prone fiscal policy. Remarkably, the proposed investment tax credit was initially viewed as a Grecian gift by many businessmen; their support was enlisted through a major educational effort led by Under Secretary Fowler.

The next stage was bigger, bolder, and more progressive in its distributive impact. Facing up to legislative realities, President Kennedy decided not to ask for an immediate general tax reduction in the summer of 1962. But in August he publicly announced that he would propose a substantial tax reduction in January 1963.

The tax-cut proposal was designed by economists and promoted by economists on economic grounds. As Heller has explained, the size of the proposed tax reduction was based on careful and quantitative professional judgment—although hardly a scientific determination—of that amount of fiscal stimulus appropriate to close the remaining gap between the potential and actual output.[22] With the envisioned shift in fiscal policy, the federal budget would come into approximate balance when the nation attained its potential output, but it would no longer dampen demand with large surpluses at full employment. In addition to the rate reductions, the tax package included many proposals for significant reform of the tax structure to improve equity and efficiency. These reform proposals undoubtedly contributed to the long delay in the enactment of the tax reduction; but, more generally, there was no political consensus during 1963 in favor of the new strategy of relaxing fiscal restraint. While tax reduction was rarely opposed in principle, support for it was sometimes linked to sharp cutbacks in federal outlays that would have vitiated the intent to provide significant fiscal stimulus.

When the tax cut was finally enacted under President Johnson's leadership in February 1964, it was unprecedented in many respects. It was the largest stimulative fiscal action ever undertaken by the federal government in peacetime, cutting individual income tax liabilities by almost one-fifth and corporate tax bills by one-tenth. In combination with the two 1962 tax actions, the new measure reduced the effective rate of corporate taxes by one-fifth compared with its 1961 level. The 1964 tax cut was progressive in its distributive effects. In part, this was the result of the only two significant reforms that were enacted—the minimum standard deduction and the repeal of the dividend credit. In part, it resulted from the slash in the lowest tax rate from 20 to 14 percent, associated with the splitting of the bottom bracket into four segments.[23]

The big tax cut was the first major stimulative measure adopted in the postwar era at a time when the economy was neither in, nor threatened imminently by, recession. And, unlike U.S. tax reductions in the 1920s, late 1940s, and 1954, the 1964 action was taken in a budgetary situation marked by the twin facts that the federal budget was in deficit and federal expenditures were rising.

The tax cut added to demand by leaving more purchasing power in the hands of consumers and businesses. Consumers responded by spending most of that extra income for added goods and services. For businessmen investment became both more profitable and easier to finance out of internal funds. The direct stimulus of the tax cut was multiplied over time. The extra spending it generated meant more jobs and hence more incomes for many families; it strengthened markets and thus encouraged greater investment to expand capacity.

The stimulus of tax reduction dominated the economic scene in 1964 and the first half of 1965. The unemployment rate, which had been fluctuating aimlessly in the range between $5\frac{1}{2}$ and 6 percent all during 1962 and 1963, fell to 5 percent during the course of 1964 and declined further to 4.7 percent during the spring of 1965. The time series on consumer spending registered a sharp take-off early in 1964. According to my estimates, the tax cut added $24 billion (annual rate) to our GNP by the second quarter of 1965, and ultimately provided a lift of $36 billion.[24]

The Revenue Act of 1964 provided for two stages of tax reduction: The first was effective in 1964 and the second took place at the beginning of 1965. Beyond the second-stage tax cut, the January 1965 budget program shifted into neutral gear. A major phased reduction of excise taxes was slated to begin at mid-year, and a stimulative liberalization of social security benefits was also envisioned. But other federal budgetary expenditures were expected to grow very little, and defense spending was scheduled to continue downward. Indeed, according to the budget plan, fiscal policy was to shift moderately toward restraint in the first half of 1966 when social security taxes were to rise. There was no new net injection of economic stimulus, and no further downward trend in the budgetary surplus as measured at full employment. As stated by the Council in January 1965: ". . . The rate of economic advance in the next eighteen months will reflect, to an increasing degree, the strength of private demand. The record of this period should test the economy's ability to advance in high gear with a small, but no longer declining, full-employment surplus."[25]

The economy seemed to be passing the initial stage of that test with flying colors in the first half of 1965. Private demand was somewhat more vigorous than had been anticipated, although not so strong as to cause serious concern. Both consumer spending and business investment forged ahead, and unemployment moved down. Revenue gains from higher personal and corporate incomes flowed into the Treasury, and brought the federal budget into surplus (on a national accounts basis) during the first half of the year. Meanwhile, in May 1965, the duration of economic expansion toppled the previous peacetime record of fifty months.

The nation's balance-of-payments deficit remained a nagging problem, and the quality of some types of credit gave cause for uneasiness. There was also concern lest complacency develop about the economy; this was expressed by the Chairman of the Federal Reserve when he reminded us of "disquieting similarities" between the existing economic scene and that of the late 1920s.[26] Nonetheless, any danger of complacency reflected the exceedingly desirable state of economic activity. After tolerating a high cost of wasted resources and lost output during 1962–63, the nation had finally unleashed the private economy.

The price-cost record of the economy was also generally reassuring, although it was flashing some caution signs by mid-1965. The average of wholesale industrial prices was within 1 percent of its level at the beginning of 1961. It had risen 0.5 percent during the course of 1964, mostly because of nonferrous metals prices, which were pushed up by world supply problems. During the first half of 1965, industrial wholesale prices rose 0.6 percent, with increases more widely dispersed. In manufacturing industries with rapidly rising productivity, price declines, which had previously been common, were going out of style. Yet very few large firms with market power were raising prices to widen profit margins; and there had been no further confrontation between business and government like that in April 1962 when President Kennedy had strongly condemned an increase in steel prices.

Labor costs were remarkably stable in both organized and unorganized areas. In the spring of 1965, unit labor costs in both the total nonfinancial corporate sector of the economy and in manufacturing were *below* their levels of a year earlier. Productivity advanced briskly and wage rates rose only modestly; thus unit labor costs behaved very well, even though the amount of work paid for at premium overtime rates had expanded significantly. Consumer prices were rising moderately by about $1\frac{1}{2}$ percent per year—only a trifle more than in 1960–63—and the price deflator for overall gross national product was advancing at a $1\frac{3}{4}$ percent rate.

To be sure, the price record of 1964 and the first half of 1965 was distinctly different from that of earlier years. But it had been recognized all along that the achievement of a high-employment economy would necessarily involve some retreat from the exceptional price stability of the early sixties. When the slack in resource utilization was taken up, it was no surprise to find a departure from the virtually absolute stability of industrial wholesale prices that had ruled in earlier years. The deterioration in our price performance seemed relatively small and readily tolerable. This was not inflation by any definition I know.[27]

The 1964–65 price record generally confirmed the judgment that the Council had made way back in 1961 that an unemployment rate of 4 percent was an appropriate interim target for full utilization of manpower, consistent with the maintenance of a reasonable degree of price stability. It was felt that the achievement of a 4 percent unemployment rate along a smooth path of advance might be accompanied by a 2 percent rate of overall price increase. Such a rate would not be dramatically more rapid than the 1960–63 performance; it seemed likely to be acceptable to the nation and would not be so large as to feed on itself and accelerate through time. Thus in the spring of 1965, the President's Troika—the fiscal advisory group consisting of officials of the Treasury, the Budget Bureau, and the Council of Economic Advisers—was looking ahead to fiscal year 1967 and shaping a program to promote a continuing advance in real output that would bring the unemployment rate gradually down to the 4 percent target.

The prospects for achieving noninflationary high employment had to be viewed in many dimensions. Excise tax cuts were a particularly appropriate form of fiscal stimulus since they countered upward cost pressures. The advance in plant and equipment outlays seemed likely to strengthen our productivity performance. Several newly launched manpower programs were expected to help avoid bottlenecks in labor markets. Moreover, as labor markets began to firm, private business management intensified its own efforts to upgrade and train manpower in ways that would effectively increase both the quality and quantity of our labor supply over the long run. The vigor of foreign competition was another encouraging anti-inflationary sign.

Finally, as one element of the total program, public education on the need for price and wage restraint in areas of market power—the administration's guidepost policy—seemed to be having a favorable influence on decisions by big business and big labor.

The guideposts, first formulated by the Council of Economic Advisers in 1962, were meant to help avoid repetition of the experience in 1956–57 when price-cost stability deteriorated badly in areas of market power. They stressed the arithmetic truth that price stability could be maintained only insofar as gains in money income per unit of input remained within the bounds of advances in national productivity. This formula pointed toward increases of a little more than 3 percent a year in wage rates, paralleling the trend growth of productivity, and toward pricing policies that were geared to unit costs. The guideposts were intended to influence the decisions of large corporations and large unions by enlisting the force of public opinion against the discretionary use of market power to promote inflation. It is impossible to tell just how much influence they had in 1962–65, but there is considerable evidence that they deserve some credit.[28]

The Recipe for Fiscal Stimulus

The heavy reliance on tax cuts, rather than expenditure increases, in providing fiscal stimulus was a particularly interesting feature of the period. For the first time in history, an expansionary fiscal strategy was pursued without enlarging the relative size of federal expenditures in our economy. From the fourth quarter of 1960 to the second quarter of 1965, the federal sector was the slowest growing major area of the economy. While our gross national product rose 34 percent, total federal outlays—purchases, transfer payments, and so forth—increased 26 percent, or $25 billion. Federal purchases of goods and services were up 20 percent. National defense purchases rose only 7 percent.

Changes in tax laws contributed a net total of $12 billion to the annual rate of private purchasing power by the spring of 1965. Even after increases in social security taxes are netted out, tax cuts provided a third of the total gross stimulative actions undertaken during the four-and-one-half-year period. They accounted for two-thirds of the gross stimulus during the initial one and one-half years of the Johnson presidency, as total federal outlays rose only $5 billion from the last quarter of 1963 to the second quarter of 1965.

This heavy reliance on tax reduction reflected neither an economic judgment on the relative efficacy of the two types of fiscal stimuli nor the administration's assessment of national priorities, but rather the political constraints of the day. A deficit budget might be tolerated by the nation if it stressed tax reduction; it would be much less popular if it featured rapid increases in government spending. Moreover, a crusade for enlarged social programs seemed to have no prospect of success. Indeed, it could not have been launched by simply requesting additional appropriations for existing programs; most of the key authorizing legislation underlying current major social efforts in education, housing, manpower, and health was not yet on the statute books in 1963. The makers of fiscal policy believed that additional federal outlays could add equally well to total demand, but they did not regard this as a realistic alternative. The real choice was between tax cuts and no fiscal stimulus at all.

The Fiscal-Monetary Partnership

The stimulus to the economy also reflected a unique partnership between fiscal and monetary policy. Basically, monetary policy was accommodative while fiscal policy was the active partner. The Federal Reserve

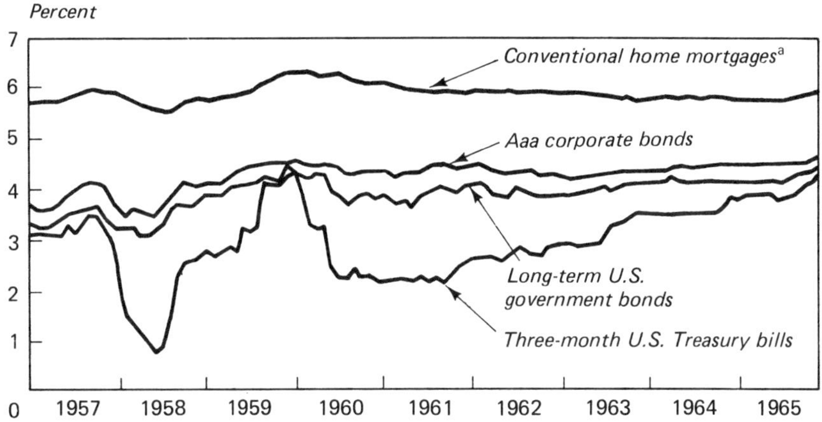

Sources: Federal Reserve Board, U.S. Treasury Department, and Federal Housing Administration.

Figure 3 Selected interest rates, 1957–65. Key: a—before April 1960, new and existing homes; after that date, new homes only.

allowed the demands for liquidity and credit generated by a rapidly expanding economy to be met at stable interest rates. The stability was neither perfect nor complete because of the concern that very low short-term interest rates would worsen our balance-of-payments performance. Hence short rates, such as those on Treasury bills, were nudged upward whenever additional capital outflows seemed to be encouraged by a widening gap between domestic and foreign yields in money markets. Remarkably, this proved to be possible without a major upward impact on the longer-term interest rates that seem to be most important to domestic spending. As Figure 3 indicates, long-term yields were far more stable in the early sixties than in the late fifties. While the Federal Reserve obviously did not "peg" bond yields, it did aim to stabilize long-term interest rates. The resulting increases in the quantity of money, bank credit, business loans, and total borrowing all reflected shifts in demands for funds with an essentially passive response on the supply side.

This rate-oriented posture was a major departure from tradition. In previous periods of significant economic expansion, the Federal Reserve had not allowed the supply of credit to expand in pace with growing demands, and interest rates had tended to rise. Monetary policy had thus acted to moderate and contain expansions. But the Fed did not "lean against the wind" during 1961–65. As long as the economy continued to operate below its potential and prices remained stable, the Fed was prepared to provide the liquidity to sustain the advance.

Milton Friedman has attributed to monetary policy the chief causal role in stimulating the expansion of that period. Indeed, he argues:

> . . . So far as I know, there has been no empirical demonstration that that tax cut [the 1964 reduction] had any effect on the total flow of income in the U.S. There has been no demonstration that if monetary policies had been maintained unchanged . . . the tax cut would have been really expansionary on nominal income. . . .
>
> What Okun did [in an analysis of the tax cut] was to assume away the whole problem because he looked only at the effect of fiscal policy without asking what role monetary policy played during that period.[29]

Friedman's critique raises, first of all, a conceptual issue of whether my study of the impact of the tax cut did "assume away the whole problem." In trying to provide a meaningful answer to the common sense question of what impact the tax cut had on economic activity, one has to make some assumptions about what monetary policy would have been if the tax cut had not been enacted. Monetary conditions are merely one of the many assumptions that must be specified in assessing the impact of the tax bill. It is also necessary, for example, to assume what would have happened to federal expenditures if the tax reduction had not taken place. In my paper, I assumed that they would have been exactly what they were in fact. This, of course, is an arbitrary assumption, but it is a reasonable way to focus on the impact of the tax cut.

The assumptions about monetary factors seem equally reasonable. It is factually clear that the Federal Reserve had conducted an accommodative monetary policy before the tax cut, and that it continued to pursue an accommodative monetary policy for a year and a half afterwards. Both preceding and following the enactment of the tax cut, monetary strategy was geared to provide the reserves needed to stabilize interest rates and the availability of credit. In that sense, monetary policy was unchanged by the tax cut, and I assumed it would have been unchanged if there had been no tax cut. Since interest rates remained remarkably stable during the entire period, it seems reasonable to assume that, in the absence of the tax cut, they would also have been kept stable by an accommodative, rate-oriented monetary policy.

Of course, because of the tax cut, the unchanged rate-oriented monetary policy accommodated a more rapid growth of demand for funds and, hence, provided more growth of the money supply, bank credit, and other related financial flows than would have taken place without the tax cut. An interesting and perfectly reasonable statistical exercise could explore what would have happened after the tax cut if the Federal Reserve had shifted strategy and decided not to accommodate the extra demands for funds. But that exercise is not the way to assess the impact of the tax cut of 1964.

Perhaps this analogy will help. During the early sixties, the Federal Reserve took the position of a ticket seller ready to sell tickets at a fixed price to anyone on line. Given this policy, sales of tickets were determined by the number of people who got on line. One cannot explain adequately why more people saw a show by saying that the ticket seller sold more tickets (at a given price). It doesn't make any more sense to say that the economic stimulus in 1964–65 came from a change in monetary policy. The tax cut does explain why more people got in line; given the willingness of the ticket seller to expand his sales, activity increased. I was concerned with estimating the magnitude of that expansion and, hence, had no reason to ask what would have happened if the ticket seller had refused to sell more tickets.

All of this relates entirely to the issue of whether my study of the tax cut asked the right question, not whether it gave the proper answer to the question it asked. In any comparison of two situations, both involving an accommodative, rate-oriented monetary policy but one with a tax cut and one without it, Friedman would not disagree, to the best of my knowledge, that the tax cut situation would be associated with a higher gross national product.[30]

There are a number of other empirical judgments in comparing hypothetical situations on which "new economists" and "monetarists" can agree. For one thing, I believe that the success of the fiscal strategy depended on the monetary response. If, when the tax cut was enacted, our ticket seller had been reluctant to issue more tickets, interest rates would have risen rather than remaining stable, and credit availability would have been restricted; GNP would then have moved along a lower path than the one that actually resulted. Surely the Fed could have imposed a sufficiently restrictive monetary policy to nullify entirely the expansionary effects of the tax cut.

Moreover, I have no reason to doubt that, in principle, there existed a monetary route to high employment as an alternative to the fiscal route that was traveled. As much additional demand as resulted from the tax cut could have been generated, without fiscal support, by a sufficiently aggressive Federal Reserve policy to increase liquidity and reduce interest rates. The monetary route would have involved significantly lower interest rates. As a political judgment, I am confident that the route would not have been traveled, given the constraints of the balance of payments on lowering interest rates as they were viewed—rightly or wrongly—by the administration and the Federal Reserve. But that is a political judgment.

One can get a debate on empirical economic issues between a monetarist and a new economist by asking whether the monetary route to full employment without the tax cut would have involved the *same* growth of the money supply that in fact took place along the fiscal route. While both would agree that the no-tax-cut situation would have involved lower interest rates, the monetarist would deny that it would have required a larger money supply than was actually experienced. According to the monetarist, we got the GNP we did because of the size of the money supply; and *that* level of total spending for output would have come from *that* money supply regardless of interest rates.

I do not regard this as a very exciting question, but I do have great confidence that the monetarist's answer is wrong. It is one of the best-established empirical propositions in economics that, for a given level of spending, the amount of money people are willing to hold is greater the lower the interest rate.

After reviewing the research in that field, David Laidler reports:

> Of the many experiments that have been performed, only one failed to find a relationship between the demand for money and the rate of interest, and that was carried out by Friedman for the period 1869–1957. . . .
>
> . . . There is an overwhelming body of evidence in favor of the proposition that the demand for money is stably and negatively related to the rate of interest. Of all the issues in monetary economics, this is the one that appears to have been settled most decisively.[31]

This checks with both theory and common sense. The interest return on nonmonetary liquid assets—like thrift accounts and marketable securities—is what people and firms sacrifice in holding money, which yields no interest. Thus lower interest rates provide a reduced incentive to economize on cash balances. Since interest rates would have had to be lower to get the same GNP without the tax cut, a larger money supply would have been necessary to do the job. More generally, because of the link between the demand for money and interest, the relationship between money and income cannot be unique. When the tax cut raised take-home pay, people could and would have spent somewhat more even if the Fed had not provided extra cash balances. In that event, interest rates would have had to rise enough to hold the demand for money down to the available supply.

The ticket analogy to money has to be modified in this case. People need cash tickets to buy goods and services, but they hold an inventory of tickets and can make the tickets turn over faster even if the ticket seller refuses to increase his sales. To be sure, the rise in interest rates resulting from the increased scarcity of money would have curtailed—but not eliminated—the economic expansion generated by the tax cut.

In short, the strong economic expansion of 1964–65 would not have taken place in the face of a highly restrictive monetary strategy. Moreover, the job could in principle have been accomplished by a very expansionary monetary strategy without a stimulative fiscal policy. But the rate-oriented monetary policy that was actually pursued would not in itself have quickened the pace of the economy. It supplied a good set of tires for the economy to move on, but fiscal policy was the engine.

The Problems of High Employment

The high-water mark of the economist's prestige in Washington was probably reached late in 1965. At that point, for a brief moment, even congressmen were using the appellation "professor" as a term of respect and approval. There could be no greater tribute to the success of the expansionary policy strategy.

Even under the best of circumstances, with no defense buildup, the attainment of full utilization would have ushered in a new environment with new challenges to economic policy making. In the first place, the growth of output and real incomes was bound to slow down. A significant part of the growth in the 1961–65 period represented a reduction in the initial \$50 billion gap between actual and potential output. We were catching up as well as keeping up with productive capacity. Once that catchup was completed, the growth rate could no longer persistently exceed that of potential—about 4 percent per year. A slowdown in growth from a $5\frac{1}{2}$ to a 4 percent rate had to involve some strain and disappointment. With the extra margin in the rapid $5\frac{1}{2}$ percent advance, the national pie was growing so fast that there was unusually little displeasure about the distribution of the pie among labor and business and other groups. Squabbling about fair shares was bound to intensify once the growth rate slowed down. To paraphrase the travel slogan, half the fun of a full-employment economy is getting there.

Second, once full utilization was attained, the range of tolerance for policy error would have to shrink. Because there had been little risk of excessive demand in the early sixties, any growth performance between 4 and 6 percent could be viewed as qualitatively successful: It would be fast enough to reduce unemployment and not so rapid as to jeopardize essential price stability. Once the economy is close to target, however, there are necessarily dangers from both inadequate and excessive demand. In the earlier period, economists knew what to prescribe, and the medicine worked once the patient was persuaded to take it. But in a healthy, prosperous economy, there was no sure tonic. Like physicians, we can cure pneumonia and look great, but we can't keep our patient from catching cold.

Third, in a world of full utilization, the problem of keeping the economy close to a chosen course is compounded by the uncertainties in choosing the course. The ideal rate of utilization is necessarily a difficult compromise between the objective of maximum production and employment, on the one hand, and the objective of price stability, on the other. We have had little experience historically in confronting that hard choice because the nation has so rarely remained on a reasonably satisfactory growth path. Except during wartime inflations, we have not been at full employment long enough to test, under these circumstances, the supply capabilities of the economy, its price-cost performance, or public attitudes toward price increases of various rates.

In 1965 the nation was entering essentially uncharted territory. The economists in government were ready to meet the welcome problems of prosperity. But they recognized that they could not provide a good encore to their success in achieving high-level employment. As Gardner Ackley put the problem in a talk delivered during December 1965:

> . . . The plain fact is that economists simply don't know as much as we would like to know about the terms of trade between price increases and employment gains. We would all like the economy to tread the narrow path of a balanced, parallel growth of demand and capacity—at as high a level of capacity utilization as is consistent with reasonable price stability, and without creating imbalances that would make continuing advance unsustainable. But the macroeconomics of a high employment economy is insufficiently known to allow us to map that path with a high degree of reliability. . . .
> . . . It is easy to prescribe expansionary policies in a period of slack.

Managing high-level prosperity is a vastly more difficult business and requires vastly superior knowledge. The prestige that our profession has built up in the Government and around the country in recent years could suffer if economists give incorrect policy advice based on inadequate knowledge. We need to improve that knowledge.[32]

Notes

1. For the chronology of business cycles, see *Business Conditions Digest*.

2. Arthur M. Okun, "On the Appraisal of Cyclical Turning-Point Predictors," *Journal of Business*, Vol. 33 (April 1960), pp. 101–20.

3. *Economic Report of the President together with the Annual Report of the Council of Economic Advisers, January 1965*, p. 10. Hereafter, this document will be referred to as *Economic Report* or *Annual Report of the CEA*, followed by the year.

4. Figures on aggregate economic activity are official government statistics, generally produced by either the Department of Commerce or the Department of Labor, and will not be individually footnoted.

5. *Soviet Economic Performance: 1966–67*, Materials Prepared for the Subcommittee on Foreign Economic Policy of the Joint Economic Committee, 90 Cong. 2 sess. (1968), p. 12.

6. *Washington Post*, June 9, 1962.

7. *New York Times*, March 23, 1964. The triple revolution entails cybernation, weaponry, and human rights.

8. Robert Theobald, "Abundance: Threat or Promise?" *The Nation*, May 11, 1963, p. 394.

9. 60 Stat. 23.

10. For a detailed, scholarly treatment of the history of fiscal policy, see Herbert Stein, *The Fiscal Revolution in America* (University of Chicago Press, 1969).

11. *Public Papers of the Presidents of the United States: Dwight D. Eisenhower, 1959* (1960), p. 12.

12. Richard M. Nixon, *Six Crises* (Doubleday, 1962), p. 310.

13. In *Fiscal Revolution*, Herbert Stein notes this hypothesis, quoting Samuelson's reference to the "investment in sadism by the second Eisenhower Administration" (p. 506). But Samuelson made clear his judgment that the "investment" stemmed from "inactivism and errors of omission" rather than a deliberate choice to abort economic growth. Arthur F. Burns and Paul A. Samuelson, *Full Employment, Guideposts and Economic Stability* (Washington: American Enterprise Institute for Public Policy Research, 1967), p. 87.

14. See, for example, *Economic Report, 1953*, esp. pp. 14–24; Gerhard Colm, "The Federal Budget and the National Economy," in National Planning Association, *The Need for Further Budget Reform*, Planning Pamphlets, 90 (Washington: NPA, 1955), esp. pp. 55–59; Leon H. Keyserling, "The Council of Economic Advisers'

Tasks in the Next Decade," in Gerhard Colm (ed.), *The Employment Act, Past and Future—A Tenth Anniversary Symposium*, Special Report 41 (Washington: National Planning Association, 1956), pp. 67–73.

15. See, for example, the statement of the Council of Economic Advisers, "The American Economy in 1961: Problems and Policies," and testimony of Walter W. Heller, Chairman, in *January 1961 Economic Report of the President and the Economic Situation and Outlook*, Hearings before the Joint Economic Committee, 87 Cong. 1 sess. (1961), pp. 290–419; Arthur M. Okun, "Potential GNP: Its Measurement and Significance," in American Statistical Association, *Proceedings of the Business and Economic Statistics Section* (1962), pp. 98–104, reprinted in the Appendix; and exchange of Arthur Burns with the Council of Economic Advisers: Arthur F. Burns, "Examining the New 'Stagnation' Theory," reply by the Council of Economic Advisers, "The Council's View," and rebuttal by Burns, "A Second Look at the Council's Economic Theory," published in *Morgan Guaranty Survey*, May 1961, pp. 1–7, and August 1961, pp. 1–6 and 6–15, respectively.

16. Burns, in a dialogue with Samuelson, *Full Employment, Guideposts and Economic Stability*, pp. 31–32.

17. Walter W. Heller, *New Dimensions of Political Economy* (Harvard University Press, 1966: W. W. Norton, 1967), p. 27.

18. Stein, *Fiscal Revolution*, p. 380.

19. See, for example, *Freedom of Communications*, Pt. 1: *The Speeches, Remarks, Press Conferences, and Statements of Senator John F. Kennedy, August 1 through November 7, 1960*, Final Report of the Senate Committee on Commerce, Prepared by its Subcommittee of the Subcommittee on Communications. S. Rept. 994, 87 Cong. 1 sess. (1961), p. 1077.

20. For an interesting account of this period, see James L. Sundquist, *Politics and Policy: The Eisenhower, Kennedy, and Johnson Years* (Brookings Institution, 1968), pp. 34–46.

21. *Public Papers of the Presidents of the United States: John F. Kennedy, 1962* (1963), pp. 472–73.

22. Heller, *New Dimensions*, p. 72.

23. Joseph A. Pechman, "Individual Income Tax Provisions of the Revenue Act of 1964," *Journal of Finance*, Vol. 20 (May 1965), pp. 247–72 (Brookings Reprint 96).

24. Arthur M. Okun, "Measuring the Impact of the 1964 Tax Reduction," in Walter W. Heller (ed.), *Perspectives on Economic Growth* (Random House, 1968).

25. *Annual Report of the CEA, 1965*, p. 100.

26. William McChesney Martin, Jr., "Monetary History and International Policy," *Columbia University Forum*, Vol. 8 (Summer 1965), pp. 4–9.

27. For a contrasting view on this issue, see Arthur F. Burns, "The Perils of Inflation," in Arthur F. Burns, *The Business Cycle in a Changing World* (Columbia University Press for the National Bureau of Economic Research, 1969). Burns concluded, "Clearly, inflation had already taken hold and become widespread many

months before Vietnam began adding appreciably to aggregate monetary demand" (pp. 287–88). Burns stresses the 3 percent rise in overall wholesale prices between June 1964 and June 1965. A temporary jump in farm prices was the main element in that result, however.

28. See John Sheahan, *The Wage-Price Guideposts* (Brookings Institution, 1967), esp. pp. 79–95; George L. Perry, "Wages and the Guideposts," *American Economic Review,* Vol. 57 (September 1967), pp. 897–904, comments by Paul S. Anderson, Michael L. Wachter, and Adrian W. Throop, and reply by Perry, *American Economic Review,* Vol. 59 (June 1969), pp. 351–70: Otto Eckstein, "Money Wage Determination Revisited," *Review of Economic Studies,* Vol. 35 (April 1968), pp. 133–43; and Robert M. Solow, "The Wage-Price Issue and the Guideposts," in Frederick H. Harbison and Joseph D. Mooney (eds.), *Critical Issues in Employment Policy,* A Report of the Princeton Manpower Symposium, May 12–13, 1966 (Princeton University, 1966), pp. 57–73.

29. Milton Friedman and Walter W. Heller, *Monetary vs. Fiscal Policy* (W. W. Norton, 1969), p. 55. Friedman refers to my paper, "Measuring the Impact of the 1964 Tax Reduction."

30. For the professional technicians in the house, these points can be most readily discussed in terms of the Hicksian apparatus of the IS and LM curves. An accommodative or rate-oriented monetary policy fixes the interest rate and makes the LM curve horizontal in the relevant range. There is no dispute among economists that a permanent tax cut (or an increase in most types of government expenditures) shifts the IS curve. Given a horizontal LM curve, a shift in the IS curve necessarily changes the level of income. The income elasticity of the demand for money then determines the associated change in the money supply. The elasticity of the marginal efficiency of capital and the elasticity of the demand for money with respect to the rate of interest cannot affect income or interest when the LM curve is horizontal. Whether the Fed *should* pursue a rate-oriented policy that produces a horizontal LM curve is not the issue. The fact is that it *did* in 1963, 1964, and the first half of 1965.

31. David E. W. Laidler, *The Demand for Money: Theories and Evidence* (Scranton, Pa.: International Textbook Company, 1969), pp. 96–97. Because these findings disprove the quantity theory of money, a list of the references in the literature is given in the Selected Bibliography on Money and Interest, starting on p. 146.

32. Gardner Ackley, "The Contribution of Economists to Policy Formation," *Journal of Finance,* Vol. 21 (May 1966), pp. 174 and 176.

Political Economy: Some Lessons of Recent Experience

The period from the start of the Nixon Administration, on January 20, 1969, to the President's adoption of a new economic policy on August 15, 1971, marks a distinct chapter in macroeconomic policymaking in the United States. The latter half of that chapter, beginning early in 1970, must be regarded, along with 1958–60 and 1965–66, as one of the unsatisfactory episodes in stabilization policy since the passage of the Employment Act of 1946.

I should like to present my views of this experience and its lessons for the future. I offer personal observations rather than definitive history. I speak entirely as a spectator; I have watched the plays carefully during this period, but I do not know what went on in the huddles. As a former player, I know how rough the game is, and how much easier it is to sound smart when one is sitting in the comfortable seat on the fifty-yard line that I now occupy. But I have done penance by putting my true confessions of the mistakes and problems of 1965–68 on the record,[1] and I shall take the liberty of being candidly critical of developments in the 1969–71 period.

I. The Game Plan

The hallmark of the policy strategy during the period from January 20, 1969, to August 15, 1971, was the attachment to a "game plan" or steady course of fiscal-monetary policies, or, to put it negatively, an aversion to "fine tuning." As Paul McCracken put it back in 1968, "The most

Reprinted by permission from *Journal of Money, Credit, & Banking* 4(February 1972, Part 1), 23–34.

fundamental requirement for orderly movement along the full employment growth path is that fiscal and monetary policies themselves pursue a more steadfast course. It is here that the greatest gains are to be had.... If we can keep expenditures in reasonably close balance with revenues that the tax system will generate at full employment and if the course of monetary expansion also moves more steadily along the full employment growth path, we can reasonably expect that the economy will come even closer to ... 'maximum employment, production, and purchasing power.'"[2]

This theme was repeated again and again through the period. In his *1970 Economic Report* (p. 10), President Nixon stated, "We must achieve a steadier and more evenhanded management of our economic policies. Business and labor cannot plan and consumers and homebuyers cannot effectively manage their affairs when Government alternates between keeping first the accelerator and then the brake pedal to the floor."

The dedication to a steady course of policy reflected in part the conviction that the basic policy mistakes of the 1965–68 period had been that of over-reacting to changes in the economic situation. The Nixon economists viewed the fiscal stimulation of 1965–66 as an unwarranted and excessive follow-up to the full employment program.[3] They saw the monetary squeeze of 1966 as an excessive though belated reaction to the inflationary boom, and the subsequent easing of money as an overly dramatic shift in response to the economic pause of late 1966 and early 1967. They also pointed to such fiscal actions as the temporary suspension and subsequent restoration of the investment credit within six months as further examples of oversteering. They argued that the frequency and magnitude of changes in discretionary economic policies had been pretentious and had created unreasonable expectations that the economy could be held on a precise narrow track.[4] More generally, the "game plan" approach to economic policy fitted in with the concept of a "low-profile" administration that President Nixon stressed.

In identifying the steady course as the hallmark of vintage Nixon stabilization policy, I disagree with some critics who stress other dimensions—and suggest that the administration favored the interests of the wealthy or of business, that it gave much greater weight to price stability than to unemployment, or that it put top priority on holding down the size of the public sector. To be sure, Republican and Democratic attitudes differ to some degree on all these matters. But these alleged differences do not illuminate the intrinsic nature of the Nixon stabilization policies or their main distinctions from the policies of Johnson and Kennedy nearly so well as the "game plan" characteristic.

The three main tenets of the game plan were steadiness in the budget posture, steady growth of the money supply, and consistent nonintervention on the wageprice front. I should like to review the experience in each of these three areas.

II. The Fiscal Record

President Nixon inherited a feverish economy, but he also inherited a reasonably appropriate restrictive fiscal policy, which was in surplus on both the actual and full employment bases for all concepts. That policy was not particularly controversial and it was not altered much within the course of calendar 1969. Of course, there were strong differences of opinion in the nation about the desirability of the extension of the 10 percent income tax surcharge, the repeal of the investment tax credit (a Nixon initiative inconsistent with the thesis of pro-business bias), and the revenue-losing "tax reforms" of 1969. But these controversial issues focused mainly on the proper structure of taxation and the proper size of the public sector rather than on the proper amount of fiscal restraint.

By the end of 1969, the boom was no longer a threat, and additional policy restraint to slow down economic growth was no longer in order. The main argument in favor of maintaining a reasonably restrictive fiscal policy was to leave room for a marked relaxation of monetary policy, which had become extremely restrictive in 1969. From that point of view, the fiscal 1971 budget program, which was presented by the Nixon administration in February, 1970, maintained a degree of restraint that seemed justifiable and reasonable to me.

As I noted then, however, some of the rhetoric accompanying the budget seemed unreasonable.[5] It emphasized the need to achieve an actual surplus in both fiscal 1970 and 1971, and ignored the risk of an economic slump that would make an actual budget surplus undesirable and inappropriate. The first lesson of fiscal economics is to distinguish between what the budget does to the economy and what the economy does to the budget. The concept of the full employment surplus is one way to highlight this distinction, and to remind officials and the public that a surplus in a weak economy represents a much more restrictive fiscal policy than the same surplus in a strong economy: Herbert Stein is the father of the full employment surplus concept, and Paul McCracken has been one of its most ardent and effective exponents through the years.

Yet the basic lesson of the full employment surplus was essentially ignored in the initial Nixon budget. Instead, it unveiled a new and short-lived fiscal concept known as the "credible surplus." Conceptually, the fiscal argumentation marked an abrupt return to the era of the 1950s when a target for actual budget balance was vested with economic significance of its own. A little black ink in the budget was treated implicitly as a necessary and sufficient guarantee against inflation regardless of whether private demand continued to weaken or whether it stepped up again.

That particular policy posture is very hard to understand. Did administration politicians feel that actual budget balance had a strong symbolic value? Was it felt that the public's inflationary expectations would be alleviated to a greater extent if the fiscal position was framed in terms of an actual rather than a full employment surplus? Or was the full employment surplus regarded as too subtle a concept for the Federal Reserve Board, which the administration wished to induce to easing monetary policy? Perhaps some day these questions will be answered by people who were in the huddle.

In any case, actual economic developments pursued a far more recessionary course than had been predicted by the administration (*and* by me) at the beginning of 1970. Nonetheless, when the administration reestimated the budget on May 19, it stuck to a tight fiscal program which called for a large full employment surplus (on the national accounts basis) of $10 billion in the face of a recession.[6] And it advanced two new proposals to increase tax revenues—a speedup of estate and gift taxes and a tax on leaded gasoline. The economic situation had changed enormously between January and May, 1970, but the fiscal posture was not changed. The earlier rhetoric had surely reduced the flexibility of fiscal policy. The steady attachment to the game plan was not shaken by the unsteadiness of economic activity. At that point, fiscal policy became strongly controversial after fifteen months in which it had been basically bipartisan.

On July 18, 1970, the administration altered its fiscal rhetoric. In conceding that he could not balance the actual budget, the President pointed out that he was balancing the full employment budget and that the resulting actual deficits should not be regarded as inflationary. At that time, he endorsed the principle of full employment budgeting, but established a principle against deficits on the full employment basis. Even with this change in posture, the fiscal 1971 budgetary program was not altered. Indeed, in August, the President vetoed appropriations for education and for housing, calling it "painful" on social grounds to hold down those programs but insisting that the additional funds Congress had provided would be excessively stimulative and inflationary. The unemployment rate had crossed 5 percent by that point, but apparently in the administration's view it was cresting. In fact, the rate reached 6 percent late in 1970 and remained essentially there throughout 1971.

At the beginning of 1971, the administration set an ambitious goal for rapid economic recovery, and stressed that the budget called for bare balance at full employment on the unified basis. Yet that fiscal program was not strongly stimulative. It involved a $7 billion full employment surplus (virtually unchanged from the outcome, as modified by Congress, for calendar 1970) on the national accounts basis, which is the way Herbert Stein had unveiled the concept and the way economics students had learned to measure the full employment surplus for a generation.

III. The Monetary Record

In the closing months of 1968, private demand displayed more strength and tenacity than had been expected by the economists of the Johnson administration and the Federal Reserve. Additional fiscal-monetary restraint was clearly in order and the extra ingredient had to consist of monetary tightening. In light of developments, the easing of monetary policy undertaken in the spring of 1968 was revealed as a mistake. The views in the Federal Reserve, among outgoing officials, and outside economists, were thus all congenial to the new administration's desire for a more restrictive monetary policy to be reflected in a slower growth of the money stock. By that criterion and every other indicator, monetary policy became restrictive in 1969. Indeed, as measured by the aggregates, it became extremely tight in the second half of 1969, with demand deposits on a plateau and time deposits falling sharply.[7] This was not the slow and steady path that monetarists had recommended, and outside monetarists became sharply critical of the Federal Reserve during the summer for overdoing restraint. It is not clear whether some (or even all) of the Nixon economists shared that concern at that time. During the spring and summer, most Keynesians (including me) viewed Federal Reserve policy as appropriate—though potent—medicine to halt the investment boom and curb excess demand. In the early autumn, however, we joined the monetarists in calling for less restraint, as the task of halting the boom was clearly being accomplished. In retrospect, I would reaffirm the subjective judgment that the error of monetary policy in 1969 was in keeping the brakes on hard late in the year rather than in jamming them on early in the year,[8] but this is a debatable issue. In any case, extreme monetary restraint—rather than adherence to the "game plan" of steady growth—was maintained until the Federal Open Market Committee meeting of January 15, 1970, two months after the nation's fifth postwar recession had begun.

Early in 1970, the Federal Reserve explicitly adopted its game plan with primary focus on the narrowly defined money supply. Initially, the target value for money growth was apparently 4 percent; but, partly because preliminary data understated the growth, the money supply expanded at a 6 percent rate through the first three quarters of 1970. Although month-to-month variations were larger than they had been in periods when steadiness of money growth was not explicitly sought, the Federal Reserve achieved its target of steadiness in money growth on a quarterly basis during that period.[9] This was "game plan" monetary policy. However, through the first half of the year, long-term interest rates failed to decline and basic private short-term rates were very sticky; some traditional indicators of money market conditions—like net free reserves—also showed little easing. By living with the game plan of steady money growth, the Federal Reserve may well have contributed less to the end of the recession than would have been the case if a traditional antirecession policy of easing money market conditions had been pursued.

Between September, 1970, and January, 1971, divergent signals came from the growth of the money stock, on the one hand, and interest rates and time deposits, on the other. The Federal Reserve maintained a high rate of growth of overall bank reserves; credit conditions eased dramatically; and interest rates fell sharply. The rapid expansion of reserves, however, was reflected in a surge of time deposits while growth of the money stock slowed. Obviously, the Fed could have stuck to the game plan and pushed the growth of money during that interval, but with other indicators easing, it saved its ammunition.

It subsequently used the ammunition during the period from January, through July, 1971, when the money stock was allowed to expand at a rate of 12 percent. Even so, the Federal Reserve did not accommodate the full upsurge in monetary demand during the first half of 1971; indeed, it permitted a marked rebound in the Treasury bill rate and in short-term private interest rates. From July, to September, 1971, money growth was exceedingly slow once again, while interest rates have moved down sharply. As in the closing months of 1970, the Federal Reserve seemed to be saving its ammunition for when it was needed. From September 1970 to September 1971, the record of the various interest rate and quantity indicators would suggest that the Federal Reserve focused eclectically on several criteria and indicators. Money supply growth was 7.0 percent—close to target—but large variations were permitted over substantial intervals in order to cushion interest rate movements. Meanwhile, the published Federal Reserve official directives have seemed to stress the money stock target. Whenever extremely high or low rates of money growth emerged in the statistics, the Federal Reserve has appeared apologetic. I suspect that if it had been possible to provide additional reserves in a way that would not enter the statistics, the Federal Reserve would have been more generous during the first half of 1971.

In retrospect, the surge in demand for money during the first half of 1971 probably reflected (a) a lagged response to the 1970 drop in interest rates; (b) the general syndrome of caution by the American consumer; and (c) international uncertainties. Apparently, circumstantial evidence from data on the distribution of demand deposits points to a spurt in the personal checking accounts of individuals. The same uncertainties that led households to save at an unusually rapid rate also may have led them to stockpile savings in liquid form—including even demand deposits—rather than in equities or other high-risk assets. According to these possible explanations, the surge in the demand for money reflected a lagged response and/or an upward shift of liquidity preference—a sign of weakness rather than of strength in aggregate demand. If that is the correct interpretation, the spurt in money demand should have been fully accommodated; nonetheless, the Federal Reserve deserves a good grade for accommodating as much of it as it did.

It is perhaps an historical accident that this first major upsurge of money demand under a policy geared to monetary aggregates consisted of a strengthening of liquidity preference rather than an expansion of transactions demand. Perversely, the last upsurge, during the summer of 1968, under a monetary policy geared to interest rates represented an increased desire for money to spend rather than for money to hold.

All in all, the game plan of steady money growth clearly influenced Federal Reserve policy in 1970–71, but did not entirely determine the actions of the monetary authority. In terms of the performance of the economy, I cannot see how a case could be made that deviations from the game plan during that period represented serious errors of policy.

On the contrary, the mistakes seem to lie in the attachment in word to the steady course and in the hesitation in deed about departing from it.

IV. The Wage-Price Posture

A corollary of the reliance on the fundamentals of fiscal and monetary policy to influence inflation and economic activity was the policy of nonintervention on business and labor decisions with respect to prices and wages. On January 27, 1969, in his first postinaugural news conference, President Nixon stated, "I do not go along with the suggestion that inflation can be effectively controlled by exhorting labor and management and industry to follow certain guidelines.... The leaders of labor and the leaders of management, much as they might personally want to do what is in the best interests of the nation, have to be guided by the interests of the organizations that they represent."

The President's unequivocal statement was widely read as an invitation to business and labor to eschew self-restraint. Price increases accelerated most for those industries that had cooperated with the Johnson administration in response to "jawboning" activities during 1966–68. For nineteen industries that had been responsive to the Johnson administration's request for restraint, prices rose 6 percent during the course of 1969 in sharp contrast with the average 1.7 percent increase during the preceding three years. For the remainder of industrial wholesale prices, the acceleration from 1966–68 to 1969 was much more moderate—from 2.3 to 3.5 percent. These nineteen industries represented roughly a quarter of the industrial wholesale price index, and their extraordinary spurt relative to the rest of the index added somewhere between a half a percent and a full percent to the 1969 increase, as I calculated at the time.[10] The experience of 1969 made me feel a good deal more confident that the ad hoc efforts to talk down prices and wages during 1966–68 had had a distinct and beneficial effect. But administration economists did not read the evidence this way, and my calculations were criticized in detail by George Shultz.[11]

The administration maintained its noninterventionist posture consistently with only a few deviations. In one instance, the President indicated that he was not enthusiastic about a huge increase in the price of steel, and he did impose a tripartite organization for wage restraint on the construction industry in the spring of 1971. Economists within the administration were not unanimous on the issue of nonintervention. Arthur Burns was reported to have advocated an incomes policy in 1969 while still a White House adviser to the President; and as chairman of the Federal Reserve he subsequently became a public advocate of a wage-price policy. Indeed, he was roundly criticized by some administration spokesmen during the early summer of 1971 when he strongly and publicly urged action to restrain wages and prices. Murray Weidenbaum, Assistant Secretary of the Treasury, and Maurice Mann, Assistant Budget Director, seemed to share that view, but they returned to private life before it triumphed within the administration. As late as August 4, the President's attachment to nonintervention in wages and prices seemed unswerving.

V. Obituary of the Game Plan

In my judgment, the seeds of destruction of the game plan were planted by the ambitious goal for rapid economic recovery set by the administration at the start of 1971 and epitomized in the forecast of a GNP of $1,065 billion. That figure startled and puzzled the profession. It was not clear whether the administration was taking an exceedingly optimistic jack-in-the-box view of private demand or, alternatively, whether it was handing a large and open-ended assignment to the Federal Reserve to do whatever was necessary to create a rapid rebound. No economist I know outside the administration had a GNP forecast higher than $1,057 billion, and only a few monetarists significantly topped $1,050 billion. Experts who covered a broad ideological and methodological spectrum had numbers just below $1,050 billion. There was basic agreement on the outlook among economists as wide apart in their orientation as Alan Greenspan and Otto Eckstein, Walter Hoadley and Walter Heller. 1971 happened to be a year in which the standard economic forecast turned out to be remarkably correct. As generally predicted, output grew at a rate below 3 percent and prices rose at a rate above 4 percent. The annual rate of real GNP as 1971 drew to a close ran about 3 percent below the administration forecast.

I cannot hope to explain why the world looked so different to the economists in the Executive Office Building from the way it did to their professional fraternity brothers elsewhere. The Laffer model probably contributed somewhat to that bullish economic forecast, particularly by helping to convince Budget Director Shultz of the feasibility of a rapid recovery. Mechanical extrapolations of previous patterns of business cycle recoveries also probably led some officials astray.

Quite apart from how they arrived at the $1,065 billion figure, administration economists could not have lived with a forecast of $1,050 billion because it represented an unsatisfactory outcome. After suffering through a recession in 1970, they could not publicly envision—or, I would suggest, privately let themselves believe that 1971 would record the most sluggish recovery from recession in postwar history. They wanted a more vigorous recovery than that, and yet they were unwilling or unable to provide a sufficiently stimulative policy to convert that desire into a realistic prospect. The modest character of the policy stimulus may have reflected the constraint of the principle of a balanced full employment budget, the fear of unleashing inflationary expectations by an active display of government stimulation, or, perhaps, the verdict of political officials.

Despite its failure as a forecast, the "1065 episode" had extremely important beneficial effects on subsequent policy. It offered a long, loud cheer for brisk economic expansion and, although it expressed the hope and bet that nature would do the job, it implicitly pledged support for nature if that should prove necessary. The majority of the bond and banking community and part of the economics profession would have favored a year of slow growth as "convalescence" from inflation before the renewal of strong expansion. The administration's explicit dissent from that view was significant: its preferences on the unemployment-inflation tradeoff gave more weight to unemployment.

As I interpreted the official position in February 1971,

> That forecast represents a binding commitment to get the economy moving again toward full employment.... Administration economists really do want a vigorous recovery and a reduction in unemployment during 1971, and they will be disappointed if that doesn't happen. They will react to convincing evidence of an inadequate and weak recovery with further stimulative policy measures. In the mid-year environment of say a second quarter GNP of $1,040 billion, Federal Reserve policy simply has to be easy.... Fiscal policy will also have to supply additional fuel for the economic engine.... Some mid-year little budget is bound to emerge from our scenario.[12]

Against the background of these expectations, I was surprised by Secretary Connally's statement at mid-year that the game plan would not be altered in 1971. The nation was told that the administration was now doing nothing decisively rather than indecisively; no actions or recommendations were forthcoming for tax reductions, expenditure increases, or wage-price policies. Secretary Connally underlined an optimistic assessment of the outlook, although he did not quantify his views. The adverse reaction of informed business, financial, and political opinion was fortunately torrential. Opinion surveys registered new lows of confidence by the American public in the President and in the Republican Party for the management of prosperity. Significantly, twelve Republican senators, before leaving for home at the recess early in August, issued a manifesto explicitly disassociating themselves from the economic policies of the administration. The plea for patience and fortitude was no longer credible. There was no sign of strengthening in the recovery; deceleration in prices and wages was visible only under a microscope; and overly optimistic forecasts and diagnoses of developments had outworn any usefulness in placating public opinion. When the inaction decision on the economy was followed by the initiative on China, some political observers inferred that the President had adopted a strategy of stressing foreign policy issues and downplaying the domestic scene. One financial executive summarized these concerns privately, "The President is too busy reading the thoughts of Chairman Mao to pay any attention to the economic mess at home."

VI. The Big Bold Initiative

When Secretary Connally's mid-year plea for patience and fortitude fell on wisely unreceptive ears, the game plan had to be changed. International pressures on the dollar undoubtedly catalyzed the decision and made it come on August 15th, rather than later, such as perhaps when Congress reassembled after Labor Day. Given the decision to do something, the President had the option of presenting a modest program, including such fiscal measures as he did in fact propose, and the appointment of a wage-price review board accompanied by a plea for voluntary restraint in private decision-making. Such domestic measures could have been advanced as evidence that the United States would correct the fundamental problems plaguing our international accounts, and they probably would have bought time and sympathy from our trading partners. But—whether it would have been better or worse substantively—a moderate and limited program would probably have been regarded by public opinion as a shabby retreat from the game plan; and the President could have anticipated such a reaction. Given the alternative of a shabby retreat, a big, bold, new initiative was clearly more attractive to a wise and pragmatic political official.

The strong and lasting attachment to do nothing thus led directly to exceedingly dramatic action once it was decided that something had to be done. A crisis was convenient, even necessary. The bigger and bolder the package, the more likely it was to capture public support as a brand new initiative, a comprehensive attack on fundamental problems, and a display of leadership. The President had locked himself into a position from which he could escape only by breaking down the door. And he did!

Although defense cutbacks, international speculators, and unfair trade practices abroad were mentioned as sources of our economic problems, it is remarkable how little effort was devoted to defending the old policy or to explaining its failure. Indeed, some officials stressed that this was the biggest economic policy package in nearly forty years—as though that was a triumph rather than a declaration of bankruptcy. It seems revealing that the previous "biggest economic program" was unveiled when Roosevelt took over from Hoover.

As a political strategy, the President's decision scored a victory. The public responded warmly to the display of leadership and initiative and apparently took in stride the confession of error. To the political official, a dramatic and effective goal-line stand may be even better than a defense that keeps the opponent from crossing mid-field. The trouble is that the analogy with football is not consistently applicable. In the football game, nothing may be lost if the opponents are kept from scoring, while in public policy a delay in correcting economic ills necessarily imposes a very large cost.

In short, political officials get rewarded or penalized for results. They are bound to be pragmatic and to change course at some point when their policies are not producing results. In contrast, the academic economist—including the academic economist temporarily occupying public office—is paid for being right, for proving that he is right, and for being right for the right reasons. And so he is bound to be extremely reluctant to change his mind while any shred of possibility remains that events will confirm the validity of his original thinking. The economists who had gone out on the limb insisting that inflation could be cured by fundamentals without recourse to wage and price policies had everything to lose and nothing to gain personally and professionally from the adoption of controls.

The economic profession was sharply divided about the desirability of wage-price efforts by the government in 1969, and it remains divided today. Indeed, I know of no economist who has changed his mind in either direction during that period. Both advocates and opponents of incomes policy were represented among the advisers to the President and undoubtedly gave him conflicting advice throughout the period.

Similar persistence was displayed in appraisals of the outlook for 1971. Those who had held the jack-in-the-box view early in the year dug in their heels. As late as July, the St. Louis Federal Reserve Bank was forecasting a GNP of $1,061 billion and the First National City Bank was issuing warnings about the impending boom. As in the wage-price case, various economists within the administration must have been offering the President differing views about the desirability of additional fiscal stimulus to pep up the lagging expansion. The same kind of battle occurred in 1961–62 when the economic and financial advisers to President Kennedy differed, some insisting that more stimulus was necessary and others warning that it would be inflationary. After a disappointing slowdown in the pace of recovery during 1962. President Kennedy cast his lot with those who advocated additional fiscal stimulus. Again, none of the experts changed his mind, but the President did and ultimately came down on the right side.

By the time any expert professional adviser reaches a position close to the ear of the President, he has developed a professional reputation, a respected record for making correct analyses and predictions, and a point of view. That point of view—indeed, that element of dogmatism—makes him useful to the President. But it makes him useful as an adviser rather than as a decision maker.

The American people are well served by having a democracy rather than a technocracy. Presidents need professional advisers who battle for their minds, but the American public needs a president who understands how to make decisions and how to choose among divergent considerations and conflicting pieces of advice. When I have met economists who have not served a hitch in Washington, the question I have been most often asked is how much economics President Johnson "really understands." The question itself reveals much about the expert professional mind. For the answer is not a significant indicator of the qualifications of a president or his likelihood of success in the field of economic policy. The far more important question is whether he understands how to listen to experts and how to make his own decisions in light of the information and advice that they give him.

VII. Some Lessons for the Future

The fact that President Nixon did break down the door on August 15, 1971, is a tribute to his pragmatism. The fact that he got locked into a position for so long raises questions about how our economic policymaking institutions and procedures can be made more conducive to small and more continuous adjustments of policy. The most important lesson is to avoid placing a premium on decisive inaction. That means eschewing policy positions that are dignified as game plans and elevated into false principles, like the non-negative full employment surplus, the steady growth of the money supply, or total nonintervention in the wage-price process. The way to ensure that policy need not lurch is to make sure that it can move gently and smoothly.

International

The best example of a policy-making institution that impedes rational political economy by putting a premium on decisive inaction is the system of pegged exchange rates. Under that system, whenever a currency showed a tendency to weaken, it became incumbent on the Chief Executive to discourage speculation by insisting that the basic strength of his nation's currency had never been greater and that devaluation was inconceivable under any set of circumstances. The system made honest men compromise their integrity to promote the immediate welfare goal of avoiding a currency crisis. The British have developed a rather neat device for minimizing the evil consequences of this arrangement. The Prime Minister subcontracts the task of boasting and vowing to the Chancellor of the Exchequer so that the latter can be the scapegoat whenever devaluation becomes required.

The need for flexibility of exchange rates should be a prime consideration in the construction of the new international monetary system. Since most countries still seem determined to maintain some form of pegged exchange rates, I suppose, realistically but regretfully, that the resolution of the current international financial crisis will involve the adoption of some set of tentatively pegged rates. The only confident forecast I can make about those rates is that they will turn out to be wrong. They will not maintain equilibrium in 1972 or 1973 or any other year. Further adjustments will be required. The success of the new system will depend heavily upon whether it introduces some degree of automaticity, some mechanism for smoother and smaller realignments of exchange rates that prevents any currency from getting as far from equilibrium as the U.S. dollar did in recent years.

Price-Wage Policies

Although the total price-wage-rent freeze President Nixon adopted on

August 15, went far beyond any measures that I would have recommended, I am convinced that some direct action was required on the price-wage front. First, if a policy of substantial fiscal-monetary stimulus had been undertaken without some restraint on prices and wages, it would have been read by the private sector as compelling evidence that the government had given up any effort to curb inflation; the initiative would have intensified inflationary habits, attitudes, and expectations.

Second, the price-wage record remained a miserable disappointment as of August 15. On a careful and comprehensive look at our various price and wage indices, one must agree with Arthur Burns' judgment of July that substantial progress had not been made in checking inflation.[13] The deceleration of rises in the consumer price index from a 6 percent annual rate during 1969–70 to 4.5 percent by mid-1971 greatly overstates the fundamental improvement. Nearly 1 point of the 1.5 point swing in that index reflects the 10 percent rise in mortgage interest rates during 1969–70 and their subsequent sharp decline of 11 percent by mid-1971. Commodities excluding food did not slow down; their 4.0 percent rate of increase between mid-1970 and mid-1971 essentially repeated the 4.1 percent advance from 1969 to 1970. The rise in the deflator for the consumption component of GNP (which excludes interest rates) edged down merely from 4.8 percent in 1969–70 to 4.4 percent from spring 1970 to spring 1971; food prices accounted for most of that total slowdown. Consumer services in the GNP actually accelerated as did the prices of consumer durable goods. The wholesale price index, which had registered a 3.7 percent increase from 1969 to 1970, continued to move up at a 3.5 percent rate from mid-1970 to mid-1971. The best comprehensive index of quarterly price movements, in my judgment, is the chain price index for gross private product: Its 4.8 percent annual rate of increase during the second quarter of 1971 was actually a shade higher than the rise during 1969 and 1970.

Nor did wages slow down perceptibly: The year-over-year increase in compensation per man hour for both the private economy and the nonfarm sector was 7.5 percent in the second quarter, one of the highest figures attained in the current inflation. In adjusted hourly earnings for the private nonfarm sector, a 7.4 percent increase over a year earlier similarly set a new high for that measure in the second quarter.

I cannot fully explain the puzzling stubbornness of wage and price inflation in the face of recession and a maintained 6 percent rate of unemployment. I know that it cannot be explained as the result of a competitive determination of wages and prices by the balance of supply and demand. That view of the economy cannot account for wages continuing to rise rapidly—much less for their continuing to accelerate—when the omnipresence of excess supplies was reflected in every indicator of labor market conditions. I suspect, although I cannot prove, that large and highly visible wage settlements that made newspaper headlines contributed to norms or habits of wage inflation that pervaded the atomistic sectors of the economy.[14] Small, unorganized employers want the good will of their workers for the long run, and they felt obliged to provide equitable wage increases (that is, to approach the big visible union settlements) even when there was no danger that existing workers would quit or that additional workers would need to be recruited.

I also suspect, although I cannot prove, that "target-profit" pricing rules in large firms kept the spiral in orbit. In the years of inflationary boom, the profits of industrial giants were doing well, and they felt no urgency to increase prices at a rapid rate. When profits fell sharply during the slowdown and recession, pressures mounted to pass on cost increases with a markup in order to keep profit margins from dropping way below target. That supposition is consistent with the seemingly inexorable recent prefreeze of prices in durable goods industries, which are dominated by large firms with market power.

My conjectural diagnosis would not support the prescription of a comprehensive system of wage and price controls. It would suggest that the nation would be much better off if the Nixon administration had tiptoed into the wage-price area back in 1969 with an informal and unenforced program, focused on the key price-wage decision-makers who do not respond passively to the will of the marketplace and who do set the visible norms for much of the economy. By tiptoeing into this sensitive area, the government might have determined how far it was necessary and feasible to go, whether any legal sanctions seemed necessary and appropriate, how an influence on the average increase of wages and prices could be consistent with efficient allocation of resources and with the maintenance of a basic social consensus among interest groups. A strategy of tiptoeing in early rather than plunging in late could have avoided the spectacle of high government officials occupied in fixing the compensation of professional football players and drawing dividing lines between pickles and cucumbers. It would have avoided other difficult problems that confront us today when a thaw on controls is in order. The maintenance of comprehensive federal controls on rents and retail prices would be a nightmare, in my judgment; yet it may be extremely difficult politically to decontrol rents after the freeze, and it may be impossible to convince the housewife that the typical retailer is merely the bearer of sad tidings on prices and not the cause of the inflation that she experiences.

Nonetheless, I am hopeful that Phase Two price and wage restraints will not be unduly severe, that they will hold together, and that they will make some contribution to breaking the momentum of the wage-price spiral. Phase Two can and should move us 90 percent of the distance from freeze to free markets. And a further movement in that direction should be made during 1972. But there should remain a mechanism for incomes policy in the federal government. I cannot imagine any president in my lifetime again declaring that wage and price decisions are of no interest to the federal government, exposing himself to the risk of another big turnaround. Rather, I should expect us to move to a situation like that of 1962–65, in which the government expresses a point of view and uses its influence to break inflationary habits in the private sector—but without frequent confrontations or widespread legal sanctions.

In my view, institutions such as the Price Commission and the Pay Board should be maintained for the long run. I believe they can be a useful forum for discussing and influencing key aspects of the wage and price process that may contribute to the inflationary biases so evident in our economy's performance throughout the postwar period. If they have no serious problems, the members can make speeches heralding the success of the nation in reconciling price stability and prosperity. With such an institutional mechanism, we can gradually create a means for the federal government to express the public interest in wage and price restraint in ways consistent with the market system.

Fiscal Policy

As I read the lessons of recent experience, they stress the need for institutional changes and policy strategies that facilitate small and frequent adjustments in fiscal policy as a matter of routine. One important improvement could be made simply by having the executive cease and desist its practice of acting as cheerleader in interpreting economic news. In the early postwar years, the Truman and Eisenhower administrations reacted on occasion to soggy economic news by denying its significance and insisting that no recession was imminent. When it became clear that a recession had begun, the previous statements of reassurance made it harder for the administration to take antirecessionary measures. The official interpretations of unemployment figures and price statistics during 1970–71 reveal that federal candor has not improved much over the past generation.

The task of implementing changes in fiscal policy through our legislative process must be eased in the years ahead. Presidents will not make proposals that have no chance of enactment. And if they will not ask for change, they will feel obliged to insist no change is needed. Again, bad institutions encourage public officials to dig in their heels and compromise their integrity in order to promote the public welfare.

Finally, we must avoid entrenched doctrines and locked-in positions that inhibit needed adjustments. The only proper game plan for fiscal policy is to adjust the budget to the state of the economy. The steadiness of the policy instruments is no criterion of success or failure in stabilization policy. The meaningful goal and meaningful test is the stability of the growth performance of the economy. The profession knows enough to contribute to greater stability of that performance. For all the limitations of economists, our professional judgment beats the agnosticism of nondiscretionary rules.[15]

If every fiscal program of the President has a distinct, definite, and warranted change in its full employment surplus from that of the previous budget, no big deal will be made of it. Small variations should be accepted and implemented as a matter of course. In contrast to the rule for steady full employment surpluses, I would argue that almost never will two consecutive years call for exactly the same fiscal policy. In particular, the amount of fiscal shove needed to get our economy out of the mud will surely be excessive once the economy gets rolling. I believe we are about to begin a long, slow movement back to prosperity. Our prospects for restoring full prosperity in a reasonably short period of, say, two years are inhibited by the fear of overdoing stimulus. And there is a genuine danger that providing strong fiscal and monetary stimulation now will lead to excess demand inflation later. That danger argues most strongly for temporary and self-liquidating fiscal measures—like temporary tax cuts—rather than in favor of timidity. It argues for a readiness and a willingness to moderate the amount of fiscal stimulation once the economy gets rolling. If we are willing to turn the wheel routinely and adjust to the existing situation and the reasonably predictable near-term future, we can hope to avoid another round of stop and go.

Monetary Policy

Recent years have given us a diversity of experience on the money and credit front. At times, aggregate quantities and interest rates have moved in remarkably divergent ways; at times, growth rates of the various aggregates have been spectacularly far apart; at times, the money supply has been a good predictor of economic activity, and during 1971 it was a terrible predictor of activity. These experiences should shake the conviction of any mortal man that he has a reliable formula or a trustworthy guide for action by the Federal Reserve. To me, the experience argues in favor of small, flexible, and unpresumptuous adjustments of monetary policy. The Federal Reserve must face reality by asking itself why interest rates move as they do, and why the money demand curve shifts at a particular time. Sometimes, it will give the wrong answers and make mistakes, but it is more likely to be right than wrong on a careful, dispassionate analysis of these issues. And it is more likely to support and promote our social goals by taking some risks and making its judgments than by following rigid rules. During 1970–1971 in particular, the Federal Reserve has acted best when its deeds have deviated from its game-plan words.

VIII. Conclusion

In short, the only way to get the activism we need when we need it is to avoid making a virtue out of an inactive and entrenched policy strategy. This is a key argument in favor of what some people denounce as fine tuning and what I endorse as sensible steering. The flexibility I recommend will surely not keep us on a precise and narrow path, but it should help keep us from getting very far off track and it will avoid occasional enormous shifts in government policy. Those who favor complete inactivism and a thoroughgoing self-denial of discretionary economic policy have lost the battle in the democratic process. The events of 1971 demonstrate that the American people want and expect their government to deal with important national problems, and that the government will be responsive, sooner or later.

The relevant choice is between acting sooner and acting later—between small flexible adjustments made promptly and frequently, and enormous lurching shifts made belatedly and infrequently. The dangers of the latter course are enormous: the costs of delay, the loss of predictability and confidence in government, the likelihood of overdoing the correction in a crisis atmosphere. Academic economists have long been trying to convince international bankers that the costs of small day-to-day fluctuations in exchange rates on currencies would be trivial, far smaller than the uncertainties associated with the threat of enormous financial crisis and occasional huge shifts in parities. That same argument applies to domestic economic policy. The case in favor of a steady course argues against crisis economics. And the only genuine alternative to crisis economics is flexible, sensible-steering economics that develops institutions and procedures conducive to small and timely adjustments. That is the way to buy insurance against the need for another massive program. If we learn our lessons well, the Nixon package of August 15, 1971, will retain its championship as the biggest and boldest economic program for the rest of the century, and political economy will have taken a major step forward.

Notes

1. Arthur M. Okun, *Political Economy of Prosperity* (Washington: Brookings Institution, 1971), Chapter 3.

2. Paul McCracken, "Economic Policy and the Lessons of Experience," in Melvin Laird (ed.) *Republican Papers,* New York: Anchor Books-Doubleday, 1968, pp. 389–90.

3. See, for example, Arthur F. Burns, "The Perils of Inflation," *The Business Cycle in a Changing World* (Columbia University Press for the National Bureau of Economic Research, 1969).

4. For some "outside" views along these lines, see Charles B. Reeder, "Business Economists and National Economic Policy," *Business Economics,* 3 (Fall, 1967), 7–10; Beryl W. Sprinkel, "The 'New Economics'—Limitations and Alternatives," a speech presented at the annual meeting of the Illinois Chamber of Commerce Oct. 27, 1967; George Terborgh, *The New Economics* (Washington: Machinery and Allied Products Institute and Council for Technological Advancement, 1968), pp. 166–72. My disagreements with these interpretations are spelled out in *The Political Economy of Prosperity,* pp. 109–15.

5. See statement of Arthur M. Okun in *The 1970 Economic Report of the President*, hearings before the Joint Economic Committee. 91st Congress, Second Session, 1970, Pt. 2, p. 424.

6. See Nancy H. Teeters, "Budgetary Outlook at Mid-Year 1970," *Brookings Papers on Economic Activity* (2: 1970), p. 306.

7. See John H. Kareken, "Monetary Policy in 1969," *Brookings Papers on Economic Activity* (1: 1970), pp. 152–61.

8. One shred of evidence in support of this view is the character of "money path B" in William Poole, "Gradualism: A Mid-Course View," *Brookings Papers on Economic Activity* (2: 1970), pp. 280–82.

9. See John H. Kareken, "FOMC Policy: 1970 and Beyond," *Brookings Papers on Economic Activity* (3: 1970), pp. 476–81.

10. Arthur M. Okun, "Inflation: The Problems and Prospects before Us," in Arthur M. Okun, Henry H. Fowler, and Milton Gilbert, *Inflation: The Problems It Creates and Policies It Requires* (New York: New York University Press, 1970), pp. 43–53.

11. George P. Shultz, in the National Bureau's Fiftieth Anniversary Dinner: Transcript of Proceedings, pp. 11–20 (Supplement to National Bureau Report #6, 1970); and George P. Shultz, statement before the Joint Economic Committee, *The 1970 Economic Report of the President,* Hearings, Pt. 1, pp. 263–69.

12. Arthur M. Okun, "The Game Plan of Stop and Go," *Business Economics* (May, 1971), pp. 16–17.

13. See Arthur F. Burns, "Statement" before Joint Economic Committee (July, 1971).

14. See the discussion, George L. Perry, "After the Freeze," *Brookings Papers on Economic Activity* (2: 1971), pp. 445–49.

15. See the discussion in Arthur M. Okun, "Rules and Roles for Fiscal and Monetary Policy," in James J. Diamond (ed.), *Issues in Fiscal and Monetary Policy: The Eclectic Economist Views the Controversy* (DePaul University, 1971), pp. 65–69.

The Conduct of Monetary Policy

In attempting to offer this distinguished committee some advice on the conduct of monetary policy, I am much more confident about the right questions than about the right answers. At the same time, I believe that a focus on the right questions about monetary policy can make an important contribution to the search for the right answers. As I see them, the key questions relevant to your deliberations are:

1. What is a desirable and acceptable path of economic recovery during the second half of this year and 1976?
2. What course of money-market interest rates controllable by the Federal Reserve is most likely to help promote the achievement of that recovery path?

In labelling these the key questions, I am obviously conveying the judgment that projections of the growth of M1, M2, bank reserves, and other monetary aggregates are ancillary questions.

The Profile of a Desirable Recovery Path

Prospects

Today's unemployment rate of 9 percent and inflation rate of 6 percent are both intolerably high. The present level of unemployment—unprecedented in the history of the Employment Act—involves a loss of output and incomes of Americans of $200 billion (annual rate) compared to what would be produced with a more normal unemployment rate of 5 percent. Idle men and idle machines are an intolerable national waste. The losses extend far beyond those who are counted in the ranks of the unemployed: the workweek is down 3 percent (equivalent to a loss of $2\frac{1}{2}$ million jobs); the quality of jobs has been downgraded; discouraged jobseekers have left the labor force; the loss of markets for business has brought real investment in plant and equipment at least 20 percent below prosperity levels.

Meanwhile, in the depths of recession, today's inflation rate exceeds that of any year between 1952 and 1972. Any acceleration of inflation from present rates would be, and should be, unacceptable to the American public. Indeed, if inflation does not abate further after so severe a recession, the perception that 6 percent inflation is as low as we can go would have far-reaching consequences in weakening our economic and financial institutions that rest on the reasonable stability of the dollar.

The inflation outlook has one encouraging aspect. In an economy marked by pervasive slack, the pressures of excess supply should continue to operate gradually and with a lag to bring down the inflation rate in every reasonably competitive sector of our economy. If the past is any guide, disinflation does not end when the recession ends; history would point to a continued deceleration of inflation over the next year. That hopeful outlook could be upset by external forces such as a major price increase in energy products, a deficiency of food available for domestic consumers, or, conceivably, an end of the self-restraint that has been practiced by U.S. labor unions, or by the initiation of anti-competitive pricing practices by U.S. business. These uncertainties restrain my optimism, and they have some clear implications for federal policy, but they cannot be remedied by the pursuit of restrictive fiscal-monetary policies.

I also see grounds for encouragement in the outlook for production and employment. In my judgment, the forces of private demand are poised for a vigorous recovery. The major drag on production currently exerted by inventory liquidation will gradually be lifted during the months ahead. Between mid-1975 and mid-1976, the swing in inventories alone should contribute 3 percentage points to the growth of real GNP. The wise stimulative fiscal measures that you enacted early this year will continue to strengthen consumer markets for the next few quarters. The renewed growth of real household incomes has begun to bolster automobile sales. Finally, homebuilding has begun to recover, although haltingly and erratically.

In offering my assessment of the vigor of private demand (which is one of the more optimistic among professional economists), I should emphasize that the *level* of economic activity will remain dismal and depressed for a long time, even as it records gratifying *gains*. We have experienced virtually a double-sized recession. The decline of 8 percent in real GNP, the duration of a year and a half, the jump in the unemployment rate by over 4 percentage points all roughly double the average setback in previous postwar recessions. The bottom from which we start is a woefully sore bottom. But the feasible rate of improvement seems to me to be as great as in previous upturns.

Targets

In the initial four quarters of recovery following the last three inventory recessions, the growth rate of real GNP averaged more than 8 percent.[1] I believe that a par-for-the-course rate of economic recovery between mid-1975 and mid-1976 is desirable as well as feasible. On the present outlook, in my judgment, the achievement of such a path is not likely to require a major further push from monetary and fiscal policy. But it cannot be attained with a big drag from changes in taxes, expenditures, interest rates, or energy prices.

I realize the strong case that could be made for an above-average rate of economic recovery after a double-size recession. But the seriousness of the inflation is an important reason to buy insurance on a sustainable noninflationary recovery. There is no quick fix for unemployment now any more than there was a quick fix for inflation last year. And another attempt to apply a quick fix could be just as costly as last year's effort in the opposite direction. We know we can grow this fast without unleashing demand forces that would worsen inflation anytime during 1976. With an 8 percent rate of growth of real GNP, sustained through 1976, the unemployment rate should fall nearly 2 percentage points by the end of next year. That will still leave unemployment around 7 percent, higher than it has been at the trough of most previous recessions. And industrial operating rates would also resemble those previously experienced at the very bottom of recessions. Still, we would be on the road to economic health and about half way back to prosperity at the end of 1976.

The Secretary of the Treasury has mentioned 6 percent growth as his target for the initial phase of recovery. I appreciate his forthrightness in discussing this key issue, even though I disagree with his verdict. The difference between a 6 and an 8 percent rate of growth is enormous, because it takes 4 percent growth merely to prevent further deterioration of unemployment and operating rates. It is only the *extra* margin above 4 percent real growth that puts idle jobseekers and idle machines back to work. Thus, a 6 percent growth rate means a half-speed recovery from a double-size recession. Real GNP would not even cross its previous peak of 1973:IV until 1976:IV. That snail's pace of progress would impose a significant human and economic toll and provide only trivial additional insurance for disinflation. The unemployment rate would most probably remain above 8 percent throughout 1976. (See figure 1.) That weak recovery would prolong the customer shortage that has depressed business investment and erase any realistic prospect of a significant rebound in plant and equipment. If sustained through 1977, the loss of production and income imposed by a 6 percent rather than 8 percent recovery rate would total about $100 billion or over $1,500 for the average American family.

In discussing targets for recovery, I must emphasize that our aim is faulty. If we do all the sensible things that economists and public officials know how to do in order to hit any target, we still have to count on a substantial margin of error. In aiming at a par-for-the-course recovery of 8 percent real growth, I would expect realistically to achieve a result above 6 percent and below 10 percent. But the diligent pursuit of a growth target of 6 percent runs a risk of producing results as low as 4 percent—and that entails no reduction in unemployment whatsoever.

When any economist—or any noneconomist—in or out of government offers you his views on the desirable course of recovery, all he can give is a personal preference. Professional economists can assess the virtues, the risks, and the costs involved in alternative strategies. But that is all we can do. There is no right answer to this difficult issue. The decision cannot be technical; it must be political, in the best sense of the democratic process. It must safeguard the interests of your constituents in a sustainable recovery—and those would be jeopardized by pulling out all the stops to lower the unemployment rate as rapidly as possible in the short run. But it must also safeguard their interests in jobs and incomes—and those would be sacrificed by a snail's pace of recovery.

Apart from the possibility of mistakes in fiscal and monetary policy, the largest single cloud on the economic horizon is the possibility of an encore of the 1974 oil shock. In combination, a significant rise in oil prices by OPEC and an unfortunate U.S. legislative stalemate resulting in abrupt decontrol of all oil prices at the end of August would gravely weaken the prospects for an adequate economic recovery and for further slowing of inflation. My colleague, Charles Schultze, discussed these dangers in testimony before the Joint Economic Committee last week.

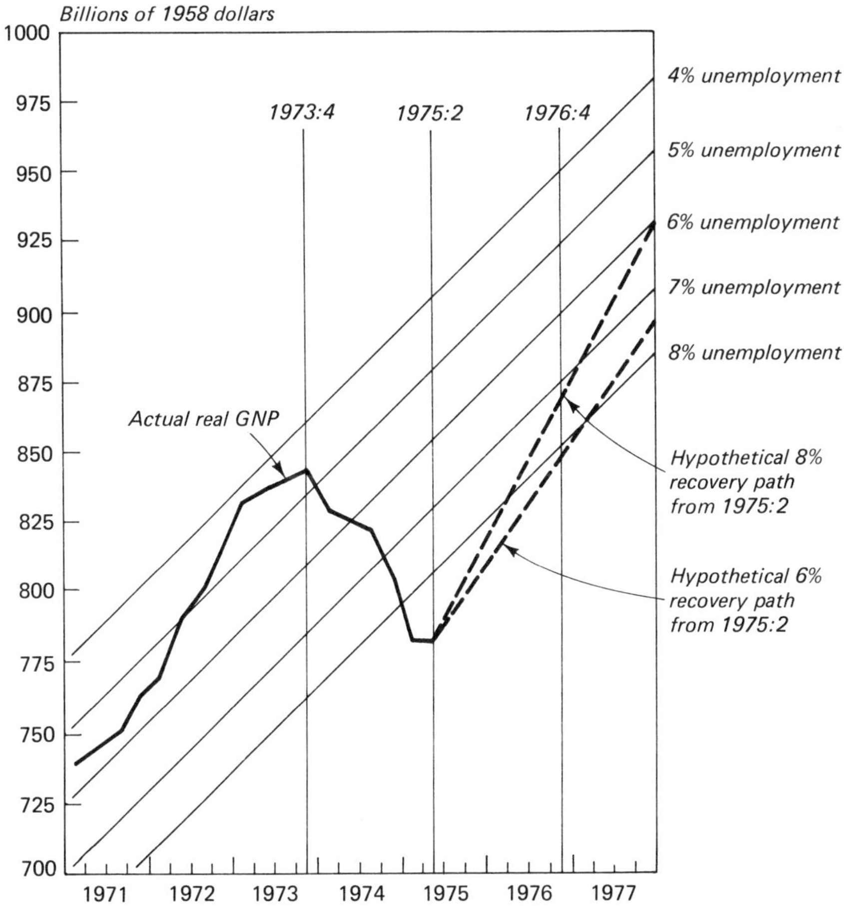

Figure 1 Alternative recovery paths for real GNP and their implications for unemployment.

erely reiterate his central conclusion: "It is absolutely impera-he loss of consumer purchasing power from whatever oil price increases do occur be offset by appropriate fiscal actions." Oil price increases also have important implications for monetary policy, as I shall note below.

The Role of Monetary Policy

The vigor of this recovery will depend crucially on the cost and availability of credit to businessmen, buyers of consumer durable goods, and potential buyers of homes. If interest costs reach levels that force businessmen to reassess plans for capital spending and that impair their renewed willingness to accumulate inventories as sales expand; if they put a drag on the potential recovery of consumer purchases of automobiles and appliances; and (most seriously in the near term) if they sap the supply of mortgage funds by attracting deposits away from thrift institutions, then I see little hope for achieving a desirable path of recovery. The Congress could seek to offset such monetary restraint with more tax cuts, housing aids, and other spending programs; indeed, it would have a clear obligation to try. But tight money is a powerful force, as we have all learned in recent years, and could severely frustrate even your best dedicated efforts.

In my judgment, an interest rate on three-month Treasury bills above 7 percent (along with other rates that would normally accompany it) would jeopardize my hopes for a par-for-the-course recovery. At such levels of short-term interest rates, deposit inflows into thrift institutions would be distinctly dampened, and the willingness of mortgage lenders to make commitments would rapidly wane. The rise in Treasury bill rate from 5.0 to 6.0 percent in just the past four weeks is disturbing news. That rise occurred because the Federal Reserve increased markedly the interest rate on federal funds late in June, bringing it up distinctly above the narrow range around $5\frac{1}{2}$ percent that it had maintained all spring. In itself, that action is not of overwhelming significance; I trust it is not a harbinger of a long hot summer of rising interest rates. But it does leave us uncomfortably close to the point where rising interest rates would begin to sap the vigor of the recovery.

Let me set forth a basic precept for the desirable conduct of monetary policy for the remainder of this year, and then discuss its rationale in some detail. In the infancy of this economic recovery, *monetary policy should aim to stabilize the interest rate on federal funds, raising it only for the purpose of checking an excessively rapid recovery.* In particular, it should hold that interest rate at levels that would not diminish thrift inflows unless a slowdown in the housing recovery is desired in order to keep the pace of overall recovery in check.

The test of whether a monetary policy that stabilizes the federal funds rate (preferably in the zone pursued from March to June) is excessively stimulative is whether it is permitting and promoting an excessively rapid economic recovery. Many elements should enter into any discussion and decision on the desirability of curbing the speed of recovery. Obviously, that decision should depend upon the target adopted for the pace of recovery. It should draw on evidence about the strength of private demand and the course of fiscal policy.

It should also carefully monitor the course of money and other monetary aggregates as indicators of the economic outlook. If an upsurge in monetary aggregates suggested a burgeoning of private credit demand or an accumulation of liquidity that was likely to trigger a sudden surge of spending, then it would point to the need for a rise in interest rates. Thus, the course of the money stock (and other aggregates) would serve as one of several key guides in determining whether stability of the interest rate on federal funds seemed consistent with a desirable, but not excessive, pace of recovery. Through this process, the Federal Reserve would concentrate on what it can do to facilitate appropriate growth of the *economy*, rather than on what it can do to produce some particular growth path for the money stock.

I offer this recommendation for a change in strategy in light of the historical lessons of monetary experience in the past five years. From the end of 1969 until the middle of 1974, the Federal Reserve made the money stock (M1) rise at a remarkably steady rate of $6\frac{1}{2}$ percent per year. (See figure 2.) That $6\frac{1}{2}$ percent trend may well have been too high. Perhaps if it had been 2 percentage points lower, the inflation rate experienced in 1973–75 might have been as much as 2 percentage points lower than it was in fact. But the variation around that $6\frac{1}{2}$ percent trend—the degree of unsteadiness of the money stock—was far smaller than in previous periods; indeed, it could not have had any significant influence on either inflation or unemployment. With the benefit of hindsight, one can applaud the Federal Reserve for the slight deviation of M1 above trend in the first half of 1971 when the recovery was lagging, and for the slowdown of M1 late that year and early in 1972 when recovery strengthened and interest rates nonetheless fell. Again, with the important

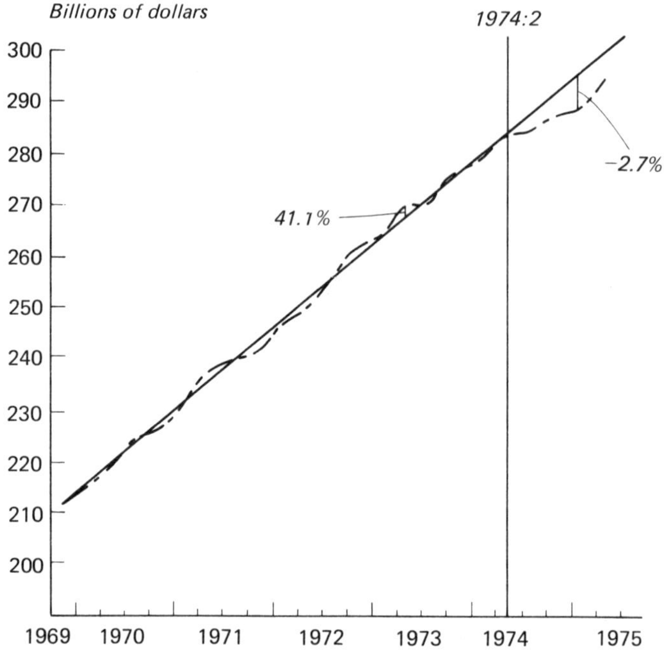

Figure 2 Money stock (M1), actual and trend, 1969 : IV to 1975 : II. The solid line represents a trend growth of 6.58 percent, drawn to connect the actual values of 1969 : IV and 1974 : II. The dashed line is actual M1 as reported by the Federal Reserve Board of Governors.

benefit of hindsight, one can judge as unwise the rise of the money stock above the track late in 1972 and early in 1973. But right or wrong, these were microscopic departures from the track. The maximum deviation of the money stock above its trend path was a mere 1.1 percent (in 1973 : II). By anybody's economic theory, that could not have influenced the inflation rate for 1973–75 by more than a fraction of one percent.

The most serious error of monetary policy in recent years was made in the first half of 1974, when the Federal Reserve stayed right on that money growth track, refusing to finance any part of the enlarged needs for cash associated with the oil price explosion. The resulting surge of short-term interest rates into double-digits made inevitable the collapse of housing that greatly intensified the recent recession.

As far as steadiness of the money stock is concerned, the policy actually pursued by the Federal Reserve during the period from the end of 1969 to the middle of 1974 would have been ex ante a monetarist's dream.

Ex post, however, it has been everyone's nightmare. Stability of the money stock did not stabilize the growth rate of nominal GNP, the inflation rate, the unemployment rate, interest rates, or any other magnitude that anyone should care about. In short, the monetarist experiment of stabilizing the path of the money stock has been tried and failed.

The Federal Reserve abandoned the monetarist strategy after the middle of 1974. Whatever the intentions of the Federal Open Market Committee, the result of open market policies was a steady decline of the federal funds rate in virtually a straight line from $13\frac{1}{2}$ percent early last July to $5\frac{1}{2}$ percent early this March. During this period, the Federal Reserve effectively aimed at, and achieved, a steady gradual decline in short-term interest rates. Keeping that decline gradual in the face of a collapse in private credit demands meant accepting a dramatic slowdown in the growth of M1 and the whole array of monetary aggregates.

Between March and June, by holding the federal funds rate in a narrow range, the Federal Reserve achieved stability in short-term interest rates at moderate levels. After mid-June, the federal funds rate was raised 100 basis points in two weeks. That action by the Federal Reserve followed a period of six weeks in which the money supply rose rapidly, partly—perhaps wholly—because of tax cuts and large out-payments by the Treasury. To me, the interesting question is the basis on which the Federal Reserve decided to make that limited, but distinct, move toward restraint. Did it see in the bulge of money growth some potential danger of a sudden recovery explosion? Or was it reacting primarily to the prospect of reporting that the money stock grew at an 18 percent annual rate in June? And if it did see some danger of an economic spurt in that monetary bulge, was it planning to bring the federal funds rate back down if and when that bulge disappeared?

Let me stress that I see good (as well as bad) reasons for creating fluctuations in interest rates. And in recommending that the Federal Reserve focus on that interest rate which is directly under its control—namely, the rate on federal funds, I should explicitly insist that other interest rates must be freely determined in the marketplace. Lastly, in recommending a provisional target of stability in the federal funds rate over a six-month period, I have no sympathy for freezing interest rates over the longer run, or trying to peg them at recession levels.

Today, we face the pervasive fact of economic life that what is appropriate as a long-term norm would be totally inappropriate in the near term when economy is so abnormal. Even those economists who are most strongly dedicated to balanced budgets as a long-term norm recognize that such a fiscal policy would wreck the economy today. Monetary policies based on long-term norms could be equally harmful. A par-for-the-course economic recovery might require a growth of nominal GNP of 14 percent, far greater than any acceptable long-term average. If such an above-average growth of nominal GNP is accompanied by only an average growth of the money stock, significant increases in interest rates are likely (although far from certain); in that event, a renewed wave of disintermediation would pull the economy below a desirable recovery path. Thus, facilitating a par-for-the-course recovery with reasonably stable short-term interest rates may well entail temporarily a growth of the money stock that is substantially above normal.[2] But if money growth does not make the economy's growth excessive, then that money growth is acceptable. And any money growth that, through higher interest rates, makes the economy's growth inadequate, is excessively restrictive.

The important uncertainty concerning the future of oil prices provides a further temporary advantage of a monetary strategy that aims at stability of interest rates rather than of the money stock. Higher oil prices raise the amount of cash needed to finance a given level of real economic activity. With a strategy of fixed money growth, the increased demands for money lead to higher interest rates, so that the nation fights oil inflation by building fewer houses and fewer machines. The record of 1974 demonstrates the futility of such a response. With a basic strategy of stabilizing the federal funds rate, the additional cash requirements would be forthcoming without depressing the entire economy.

In conclusion, I should again like to focus on the right questions. For the remainder of 1975 and for 1976, what rate(s) of expansion of real GNP should be regarded as an appropriate pace of recovery? If the recovery threatens to exceed such reasonable speed limits, would not an increase in short-term interest rates be desirable? In a recovery that is *not* exceeding a desirable path of economic activity, would a rise in short-term interest rates be warranted in order to prevent the growth of the money stock from exceeding $7\frac{1}{2}$ percent (or any fixed target)? Under similar conditions, would a big rise in oil prices call for an increase in interest rates? A debate on these issues would focus on the important problems that lie ahead of us in achieving a vigorous but noninflationary recovery.

Notes

1. The periods included and the corresponding growth rates are: 1954:III–1955:III, 8.6 percent; 1958:II–1959:II, 9.2 percent; and 1961:I–1962:I, 7.6 percent. In each of these cases, real final sales grew about 6 percent, with the swing from inventory liquidation to accumulation providing the additional growth. I omit 1970–71 because the recession involved no inventory liquidation.

2. In the current issue of *Brookings Papers on Economic Activity*, James Pierce reports some relevant calculations (pp. 103–4) from an econometric model. Assuming a 12.3 percent rate of nominal GNP growth for the second half of 1975, it takes a growth rate of M1 above 9 percent to make stability of short-term interest rates an even bet. (With 14 percent growth of nominal GNP, I suppose the estimate of required M1 growth from the model would be close to 11 percent.) Also of importance is the finding by Franco Modigliani and Lucas Papademos in that issue (p. 162) that "a rate of growth of money well above 10 percent for the next few quarters is perfectly consistent with decreasing inflation. . . ."

A Postmortem of the 1974 Recession

The decline of 2.1 percent in real gross national product from 1973 to 1974 was the fourth annual dip since the mid-forties (the others occurred in 1954, 1958, and 1970) and by far the largest. With the benefit of hindsight, I shall, in this brief paper, discuss what happened to the economy and to the economic forecasters in that bleak year. In the comments addressed to forecasting. I shall not allocate blame or praise; my purpose rather is to raise some questions and infer some lessons that may be relevant for future research and application.

What Happened

In combination, the decline in real consumption and in residential construction activity from 1973 to 1974 accounted for more than the total decline in real GNP (table 1). These were also the main areas of disappointment relative to the expectations of forecasters.

Consumption

The 2.3 percent decline in real consumption in 1974 is attributable mainly to the 2.7 percent decline in real disposable income, although, by historical standards, aggregate consumption was weak relative to income. The personal saving rate of 1974 was 7.9 percent, virtually unchanged from the 7.8 percent average of the first three quarters of 1973, before automobile demand plummeted. Moreover, the saving rate of 1974 essentially matched the 7.8 percent average of 1970–73; in all years of the 1970s thus far, except 1972, the personal saving rate has been higher than in any year of the 1950s or 1960s.

The share of disposable income devoted to nondurable goods and ser-

Table 1 Levels of gross national product and selected components, and quarterly changes, 1973–74 (amounts in billions of 1958 dollars)

	Level		Change									
			1973 to 1974		1973:4 to 1974:1		1974:1 to 1974:2		1974:2 to 1974:3		1974:3 to 1974:4	
Component	1973	1974	Amount	Percent	Amount	Percent	Amount	Percent	Amount	Percent	Amount	Percent
Gross national product	839.2	821.2	−18.0	−2.1	−15.2	−1.8	−3.4	−0.4	−4.0	−0.5	−19.1	−2.3
Final sales	828.4	812.5	−15.9	−1.9	−5.8	−0.7	−1.0	−0.1	−0.8	−0.1	−25.0	−3.1
Personal consumption expenditures	552.1	539.5	−12.6	−2.3	−6.6	−1.2	3.0	0.6	4.5	0.8	−19.0	−3.5
Nondurable goods and services	438.5	436.3	−2.2	−0.5	−4.6	−1.0	1.3	0.3	3.7	0.8	−4.0	−0.9
Durable goods	113.6	103.1	−10.5	−9.2	−2.0	−1.9	1.6	1.5	1.0	0.9	−15.0	−13.9
New automobiles[a]	38.3	31.0	−7.3	−19.1	−2.1	−6.3	0.8	2.6	3.1	9.7	−9.8	−27.8
Residential structures	32.9	24.0	−8.9	−27.1	−3.4	−11.4	−0.7	−2.7	−2.1	−8.2	−3.2	−13.6
Nonresidential fixed investment	94.4	94.0	−0.4	−0.4	0.3	0.3	0.2	0.2	−2.4	−2.5	−4.9	−5.2
Disposable personal income	619.5	602.9	−16.6	−2.7	−12.6	−2.0	−6.8	−1.1	−0.6	−0.1	−8.1	−1.3
GNP deflator	—	—	—	10.3	—	2.9	—	2.3	—	2.8	—	3.4

Sources: *Survey of Current Business*, vol. 55 (March 1975), tables 1, 2, 5, 17; *Business Conditions Digest* (April 1975), table A-2.
a. The personal consumption expenditures component of gross auto product.

Table 2 Shares of selected components of disposable personal income during peak and recession years, and change, selected years, 1957–74

Period	Nondurable goods and services	Total durable goods	New automoblies[a]	Personal consumption expenditures	Saving
Level (percent)					
1957	78.0	13.2	5.1	91.2	6.7
1958	79.1	11.9	4.0	91.0	7.0
1960	80.0	12.9	4.9	92.9	4.9
1961	79.9	12.1	4.2	92.0	5.8
1969	77.0	14.3	5.0	91.3	6.0
1970[b]	76.0	13.5	4.3	89.5	8.0
1973	74.7	14.4	4.8	89.1	8.2
1974	76.5	13.0	3.8	89.5	7.9
1973, first three quarters	74.8	14.8	5.1	89.6	7.8
Change (percentage points)					
1957–58	1.1	−1.3	−1.1	−0.2	0.3
1960–61	−0.1	−0.8	−0.7	−0.9	0.9
1969–70	−1.0	−0.8	−0.7	−1.8	2.0
1973–74	1.8	−1.4	−1.0	0.4	−0.3
1973, first three quarters-1974	1.7	−1.8	−1.3	−0.1	0.1

Sources: U.S. Department of Commerce, *The National Income and Product Accounts of the United States, 1929–1965: Statistical Tables* (1966), pp. 26, 33, 41, and Department of Commerce, *U.S. National Income and Product Accounts, 1964–69* (1973), pp. 48, 51, 52; *Survey of Current Business*, vol. 54 (July 1974), pp. 19, 22, 23, and vol. 55 (March 1975), pp. 8, 9.

a. The personal consumption expenditures component of gross auto product.

b. Fourth quarter excluded because of auto strike.

vices (in current dollars) rose from 74.7 percent in 1973 to 76.5 percent in 1974, the biggest one-year jump in the past generation. But the share spent on durables fell from 14.4 percent in 1973 to 13.0 percent in 1974, the biggest one-year drop in the past generation. Autos, of course, led the plunge: the share of disposable income spent on new cars fell to a post-Korean annual low of 3.8 percent from 4.8 percent in 1973 (5.1 percent in the first three quarters). But the decline in new cars generally eclipses that of all other consumer goods in recessions, quite apart from an energy crisis: their share dropped between 0.7 point and 1.1 points in the three previous recession years (table 2).[1] In short, the auto collapse in 1974 should be attributed more to a shortage of real income than to a shortage of gasoline, given income.

Of course, in line with standard theoretical reasoning and empirical evidence, a dip (or even slowdown) of real income does not normally have an immediate proportionate effect on consumer expenditure. Hence, a drop in the saving rate is to be expected when income sags. In that sense, the unchanged (as well as historically high) saving rate of 1974 is a mark of unusual weakness in consumer demand. But, in fact, the saving rate has not displayed any distinct countercyclical pattern during recessions in the postwar era. The share of disposable income spent on nondurables and services has typically risen (as it did in 1974); but the share spent on durables has invariably declined, sometimes dominating the aggregate consumption-income ratio.

In retrospect, it is not at all difficult to account for historically low consumption in relation to disposable income during 1974. In line with past experience, accelerating (unanticipated) inflation may have depressed consumer demand.[2] Another contributor may have been the sharp decline in real household financial wealth (33 percent during 1973–74), reflecting inflation and falling stock and bond prices. Indeed, consumer expenditures held up far better in 1974 than would have been implied by some estimates of the size and speed of the impact of changes in wealth (or in real cash balances).

To be sure, the bumpy quarterly pattern of consumer demand during 1974 can be explained only in terms of special and transitory influences like the unavailability of gasoline in the first quarter, the way the announcement of major price increases slated for the 1975 automobile models helped to sell 1974 cars during the third quarter, and the way that temporary rebound in automobile demand itself weakened the fourth-quarter performance. Nonetheless, for the year as a whole, the behavior of consumption was not much of a mystery, given the decline in real disposable income.

Disposable Income

Thus, the basic question about consumption in 1974 is, what made real disposable income so weak? And weak it was! It registered its first annual decline of the postwar era, and its drop (2.7 percent) even exceeded that of real GNP. The average of past postwar performances would have suggested that a 2.1 percent drop in real GNP would be associated with approximately zero change in real disposable personal income.

By that standard, 1974 produced an unusual income squeeze, exceeding $2\frac{1}{2}$ percent. Relative price movements account for about half of that squeeze. The implicit deflator for personal consumption expenditures rose 11.4 percent from 1973 to 1974; whereas it typically increases a bit less than the GNP deflator, it advanced by 1.1 percentage points more in 1974. Imported oil was the key item that pushed up consumer prices relative to the GNP deflator.

The other half of the unusual dent in disposable income stemmed mainly from fiscal impacts. Most significantly, the built-in flexibility of the personal income tax did not play its usual role of cushioning a recession. Because the value of personal exemptions and the width of tax brackets are set in nominal rather than real terms, the progressivity of the tax system operated with respect to gains in nominal income even though real income was falling. As a share of "earned personal income" (personal income minus transfer payments), federal personal taxes rose from 12.2 percent in 1973 to 13.0 percent in 1974. That rise squeezed disposable personal income by 0.8 percent ($8 billion). In fact, with no change in income tax laws, the federal tax share of earned income would normally be expected to fall in recession.[3] For example, from 1957 to 1958, it declined 0.4 percentage point. A second and smaller fiscal squeeze, exceeding $2 billion, stemmed from the increase in personal contributions for social insurance resulting from a rise in the maximum earnings base. Transfer payments did provide some cushion, rising about 19 percent in nominal terms, but the additional buying power provided by incremental transfers was eroded by inflation. The real increase amounted to $6\frac{1}{2}$ percent, far smaller than in previous recession years.

In nominal terms, earned personal income rose at the same rate as GNP. But that reflected the net effect of many contrary forces: a drop in farm income, a sharp rise in personal interest income, remarkable strength of employment in the face of declining output, and a weak gain in hourly compensation relative to prices of private nonfarm output.[4]

Residential Construction

While many forces influenced the level of homebuilding, its decline during 1973–74 can be linked closely to the movement of short-term interest rates. With a remarkably brief lag, these seemed to affect deposit inflows into thrift institutions, which in turn altered the supply of mortgages and then homebuilding in a prompt chain reaction. Short-term interest rates soared in the spring and summer of 1973, reaching levels far above yields on thrift deposits. Monthly deposit inflows into thrift institutions, which had averaged $3.6 billion throughout 1972 and $2.6 billion in the first half of 1973, shrank to $1.3 billion for the period June–

October 1973; housing starts fell sharply in the second half of 1973.

Late in that year and early in the next, short-term rates eased off and net thrift inflows rebounded, averaging $2.1 billion a month from October 1973 to April 1974. But, as interest rates turned up sharply, monthly thrift inflows averaged less than $1 billion in the period from April through October 1974. Housing starts, which had averaged about 1.6 million units (annual rate) from December 1973 to June 1974, plunged to less than a million by the end of 1974. In this period of tight money, unlike others, expenditures on mobile homes were hit hard too; they fell from $4.1 billion (annual rate) in 1974:2 to $2.3 billion in 1974:4.

The high and rising pattern of interest rates during most of 1973 is readily understandable: nominal GNP was growing at a rate of 12 percent while the money stock was kept close to the $6\frac{1}{2}$ percent growth track that characterized the entire period from the end of 1969 to the middle of 1974.[5] Why the emerging slowdown of late 1973 was enough to turn interest rates down for a while, and why they then soared in the spring and summer (when the growth rate of nominal GNP averaged 9 percent), is not clear. The turnaround was associated with a surge of business loan demand that the Federal Reserve, holding M_1 right on track during the spring quarter, did not accommodate.

The spurt in short-term interest rates from March to July made inevitable the second-half plunge in homebuilding and mobile homes. After midyear, the Federal Reserve shifted from a quantity-oriented monetary policy to a rate-oriented strategy, and allowed the money stock to sag below the previous track, as credit demands waned. While it had tolerated an abrupt rise in interest rates during the spring, it cushioned the decline in rates during the fall and winter. If the Federal Reserve had maintained its quantity-oriented policy after midyear, it might have sped the turnaround in the credit-sensitive areas by several months, but it could no longer have prevented the housing collapse of the second half.

While the impact of high interest rates on residential construction and mobile homes is obvious, any major prompt influence of those rates on other components of expenditure (consumer durables other than mobile homes, inventory investment, and plant and equipment) is not visible to the naked eye—at least not to mine.

Business Investment

As currently estimated by the Department of Commerce, inventory investment held up unusually well during 1974 in relation to final sales.

During the first three quarters of 1974, real final sales ran nearly 2 percent below their peak rate of 1973:3, almost matching in that early stage the maximum peak-to-trough decline of any previous postwar recession. Yet accumulation of inventories continued at a rapid rate all year long. Never before in the postwar period had inventory investment remained positive when real final sales stayed below their peak for more than two quarters.

Clearly, most of the accumulation over that prolonged period of five quarters of submerged real final sales must have been voluntary; otherwise, production would have been slashed sooner. And it is understandable that business wanted additional stocks. First, the rapid advance of final sales in 1972 and early 1973 must have left many firms with inventories below desired levels late in 1973. Second, the shortages, delivery delays, and rising prices that marked 1973 and much of 1974 must have led many businessmen to raise their targets on desired inventories in relation to sales.

Business fixed investment also remained strong during much of 1974, barely dropping in real terms until the fourth quarter. Plant and equipment outlays anticipated by businessmen early in 1974, unlike those in previous recession years, were not scaled down sharply during the course of the year. Actual outlays for the year corresponded closely to the anticipations reported in February 1974 ($112.4 billion actual vs. $112.7 billion projected). Of course, since prices of capital goods rose more sharply than businessmen had anticipated, fulfilling their dollar capital budgets meant acquiring less physical capital than had been expected.

The same pattern of business resistance to declining final sales evident in inventory and fixed investment also was displayed in the demand for labor. As I have argued previously,[6] the expansive personnel policies seem attributable to (1) the momentum of forces and attitudes that developed during the 1973 boom; (2) an overly optimistic interpretation of weak final sales early in 1974 as merely an embargo-induced "energy spasm"; and (3) "FIFO illusion," a tendency to take seriously the favorable profits bloated by inflationary inventory gains. For those reasons, firms felt no strong incentive to retrench on employment, or inventories, or fixed capital.

In summary, the consumer was clobbered by U.S. fiscal policy and the "oil tax" during 1974; and homebuilding was battered by monetary policy. For much of the year, business spending and hiring supported the economy and resisted the downward pull of the declining sectors. It is not clear why so many businessmen seemed to realize so suddenly around August that they were holding up the economy merely by selling goods to one another and retaining workers they did not need. In any case, business finally lost the tug-of-war, and then the whole economy plunged in the closing months of 1974. The trimming of personnel and production that might have been accomplished gradually earlier in the year then took place abruptly and frenetically in 1974:4 and 1975:1.

What Was Expected

While the typical forecast of real economic activity for 1974 was revised downward periodically, it remained overly optimistic throughout.

Pre-Embargo

The first round of forecasts for 1974, prior to the imposition of the oil embargo in October, revealed a broad consensus that the year would experience moderate increase in real output (2 to 3 percent), some modest uptrend in unemployment, and a distinct slowing of inflation (to roughly 5 percent). (The median forecast of a sizable sample that reports quarterly is shown in table 3.) As James Duesenberry characterized this consensus

Table 3 Median predictions of changes in real gross national product and in the GNP deflator, 1974 over 1973, and actual changes (percent)

	Date of prediction					
Prediction period	August 1973	December 1973	February 1974	May 1974	August 1974	Actual
Real GNP						
1974 over 1973	2.6	1.1	0.6	−0.3	−1.2	−2.1
1974:1 over 1973:4	0.6	−0.1	−0.6	−1.5[a]	−1.8[a]	−1.8
1974:2 over 1973:4	1.2	0.1	−0.7	−1.6	−2.1[a]	−2.2
1974:3 over 1973:4	1.7	0.4	−0.1	−1.1	−2.1	−2.7
1974:4 over 1973:4	2.8	1.0	0.8	−0.2	−1.7	−4.9
GNP deflator						
1974 over 1973	4.6	5.9	7.0	8.4	9.4	10.3
1974:1 over 1973:4	1.0	1.5	1.8	2.6[a]	2.9[a]	2.9
1974:2 over 1973:4	2.0	2.7	3.5	4.7	5.2[a]	5.3
1974:3 over 1973:4	3.1	4.1	5.0	6.4	7.4	8.3
1974:4 over 1973:4	4.0	5.2	6.5	7.9	9.4	12.0

Sources: American Statistical Association and National Bureau of Economic Research, "Third Quarter 1974 Survey of the Economic Outlook" (September 1974: processed), and preceding relevant issues, table 1; *Survey of Current Business*, vol. 54 (May 1974) and vol. 55 (March 1975), tables 1, 17.
a. Actual value based on Commerce Department estimate at that date.

in September 1973: "Most forecasters see a 'welcome slowdown'.... projecting growth rates below the rate of expansion of potential output, but still positive.... The strength comes from plant and equipment and inventory investment, while the weakness lies in homebuilding and a projected rise in personal saving rates."[7] The predicted slowdown in inflation stemmed from an expected leveling-off of the prices of farm products and other raw materials.

With the embargo and explosion in oil prices, the basic premises of that initial forecast suddenly became obsolete. From the point of view of a macroeconomist, an event like the quadrupling of oil prices by the cartel is fundamentally exogenous. If improvements are to be made in appraising the likelihood of such major disturbances, the assignment will have to be undertaken by foreign policy and commodity experts, rather than mere GNP-men. Even in the absence of the oil crisis, overall prices in 1974 would probably have risen distinctly more and output somewhat less than in the pattern envisioned by the forecasters. Nonetheless, their basic scenario of a nonrecessionary slowdown might well have been realized had it not been for the oil shock.

Turn of the Year

The forecasts made at the turn of the year cranked in some impact from the petroleum developments and some lessons from continued bad news on inflation. The consensus remained fairly broad as it shifted toward more inflation and less real growth. The typical January–February forecast for 1974 had the following characteristics:

1. Nominal GNP was expected to grow by about $100 billion, or nearly 8 percent.
2. Real GNP was expected to rise only a fraction of 1 percent, and prices were marked up some 7 percent.
3. The expected quarterly pattern of real GNP was in the shape of a saucer, with the first quarter generally pegged down, and the final quarter up; disagreements on the sign of movements focused on the two middle quarters, but they were expected to register only small changes, whether plus or minus.

The true magnitude and significance of the increases in oil prices were still not apparent. In January, the price of imported oil was not expected to exceed $8 a barrel; it ultimately rose above $12. The Council of Economic Advisers noted that the price rise through December 1973, when applied to the volume of imports of 1973, would amount to "less than 1 percent" of GNP, and labeled this calculation as "probably an outside estimate of the costs in 1974."[8]

The weakened demand for automobiles had become apparent, and was the key element in the accurate forecast of a decline in real output for 1974:1. A few forecasters expected major losses in the nation's productive capability as a result of the scarcity of oil, but the majority correctly anticipated no serious supply impact from the embargo. Generally, some explicit assumption—most often, "near midyear"—was made about the termination of the embargo. That event was expected to aid the rebound in the second half, particularly by promoting recovery of automobile demand. A few economists called attention to the drain that the "oil tax" inflicted on real consumer income, quite apart from the embargo, but many ignored it. Continuing strength in plant and equipment spending and a rebound in housing were expected regardless of the oil situation.

The expected rebound in housing was linked to a dip of interest rates to levels that would restore thrift inflows. Interest rates were, in fact, falling at the turn of the year; but, as Tobin pointed out,[9] it was hard to reconcile the prediction of continued declines with the prevailing expectations of 8 percent growth of nominal GNP, on the one hand, and $5\frac{1}{2}$ or 6 percent growth of the money stock, on the other.

Another bullish element was the expected strength of inventory investment. That prediction was seriously biased upward by the original Commerce Department underestimate of inventory investment in 1973. Initially, inventory investment for 1973:4 was pegged at $15.9 billion (annual rate), in contrast to the current estimate of $28.9 billion for the period; that for the entire year 1973 was initially put at $7.4 billion, in contrast to the present $15.4 billion. The forecasters were told that the shelves were bare, and expected them to be restocked.

The forecasters were also misled about the prospects for federal expenditures in the first half of 1974. Actual expenditures on the national income and product basic during fiscal 1974 ran $7 billion below the projection in the budget document of February 1974. While $2 billion of that total reflected an accounting change (involving a complex transaction with India), the remaining $5 billion—$10 billion at annual rates during the first half of 1974—did make a substantial difference.

Because the large errors on the price level and output were offsetting, the prediction of nominal GNP turned out to be accurate. In fact, the GNP deflator rose 10.3 percent while output fell 2.1 percent, yielding the same 8 percent gain in nominal GNP implied by the projected 7 + 1 pattern. Indeed, CEA predicted a rise in nominal GNP of $102 billion, the increase now shown by the Commerce estimates. But the significance of the actual $102 billion was drastically different from what had been envisioned.

In both 1969 and 1973, when price inflation had been substantially underestimated by the profession, real GNP was forecast quite accurately and the projection of nominal GNP was far too low. In 1969, prices and wages were underestimated by about equal amounts and thus the error in the inflation forecast per se made no big difference in the estimates of real disposable income. In 1973, an unexpected squeeze on real wage income emerged, but the bonus went to farmers, thus maintaining real disposable income. Moreover, with an unexpected $10 billion rise in net exports, foreigners helped to buoy up real GNP (as well as to intensify inflation) in 1973. For 1974, however, the price predictions were much further below the mark than the wage forecasts, and the emerging squeeze on real disposable income was not anticipated.[10]

After the End of the Embargo

By spring, the forecasters had to digest disappointing news on both prices and output for the first quarter. On the other hand, as of March 18, the lifting of the embargo became a fact and not merely a working assumption. Moreover, after a weak interval in January and February, industrial production and private employment leveled off. While the forecasters scaled down projected levels of real activity throughout 1974 and in May the median forecast called for a tiny decline of real GNP from 1973 to 1974, a cumulative decline in economic activity seemed to most a less serious threat than it had at the turn of the year. The predicted annual increase in the deflator was marked up into the 8 to 9 percent range, but inflation as well as output was expected to look better in the second half. The script was much the same as at the beginning of the year: continued gains in plant and equipment spending, a recovery in housing, a rebound in consumer durables (which played a larger role than it had in the turn-of-the-year forecasts), and less inflation in commodities (including oil).

Summer

In July, the forecasters got a new view of the inventory situation from the Department of Commerce. That revision raised a few doubts—but only a few—about the outlook for continuing strength in inventory investment.

Although short-term interest rates were now soaring to unprecedented levels, the median expectation on housing starts in the ASA-NBER survey of forecasters in August was a plateau of 1.5 million units during the second half. At that point, most gave up on a second-half rebound of real GNP, projecting instead an essentially flat pattern. Still, they were prepared to bet 2 to 1 against a decline in real GNP in the fourth quarter and nearly 3 to 1 against such a decline for the first quarter of 1975. Again, they expected imminent improvement in inflation (in part, counting on good crops and hence falling farm prices) and an emerging recovery in the market for consumer durables (perhaps extrapolating the higher rate of car sales in the summer).

In light of subsequent developments in the economy and in fiscal policy, the administration's restrictive fiscal program of October 8 must be rated as the most misconceived stabilization package of the past generation. But at least by some tastes on the output-inflation tradeoff, it was not unreasonable against the background of the typical forecast then prevailing.

The Lessons of 1974

The serious errors in appraising the 1974 outlook cannot be tied to any particularly defective forecasting theory or technique. Indeed, the striking fact is the basic agreement of most of the quantitative forecasters, whether Keynesians or monetarists, builders of large econometric models, devotees of leading indicators, or gazers into crystal balls. The tendency toward agreement may reflect the incentive system operating on forecasters: the costs in income and status of being wrong when alone must be far higher than the costs of being wrong in good company.

It is as easy to be wise in retrospect as it is difficult to be right in prospect. Yet a number of clues that became evident along the way pointed to a different assessment of the outlook and indeed were so interpreted by a few observers.

First, by January or February, some economists appraised the impact of the oil crisis fairly accurately and adjusted their projections of real consumption downward to reflect the dent of the "oil tax" on real disposable income. Unfortunately, in the minds of many forecasters, the embargo apparently "excused" the setbacks in the early months of 1974 and thus masked the basic weakness of the economy. In addition, only a few forecasters expressed concern that unanticipated inflation might depress consumer demand.

Second, at least by midyear, there were good reasons to expect some weakening of employment demand in relation to output. The minority who foresaw layoffs and rising unemployment expressed doubts about the belief—maintained so wrongly by so many for so long—that the consumer would come back to market.

Third, by spring, a few economists were raising questions about the impact on inflation of the end of wage and price controls on April 30. And the less optimistic forecasts of inflation were accompanied by greater concern about tight money and adverse consumer attitudes.

Fourth, by late spring, when interest rates were soaring and funds once again began to flow out of thrift institutions, an imminent decline in homebuilding should have been foreseen. At least, the widespread belief in a "floor" on starts of 1.5 million units should have been subjected to closer scrutiny.

Fifth, a few—but very few—monetarists viewed the declining real money stock in the first half of 1974 as a danger to real activity. If M_1 had been growing at a zero rate with inflation at 4 percent, monetarists would generally have been very bearish about real GNP. It is not clear why 6 percent M_1 growth and 10 percent inflation did not make them equivalently bearish.

Sixth, the growing excess of inventories should have been diagnosed as final sales remained (and were expected to remain) far below their previous peak. The forecasters were betting against a regularity of postwar history in expecting no inventory liquidation. Particularly after the July statistical revisions, major markdowns of projected inventory investment were in order. Although such markdowns would have worsened the accuracy of inventory forecasts for the second half (when stocks piled up involuntarily), they would have dramatically improved the forecasts of real GNP.

Even the possibility of a traditional, typical inventory (and employment) cycle was widely dismissed until it roared into reality at the end of 1974. Many forecasters seemed to regard the business cycle as obsolete. For fourteen years, they economy had escaped liquidation of inventories and significant reduction of work forces. The samples of data incorporated in equations and memories alike were heavily weighted with observations from a period of unusual stability in real economic activity. In this connection, what many of the forecasters missed was not something new but something old: multiplier-accelerator interactions and other cumulative cyclical processes. In days of yore, these were deeply imprinted in the profession's thinking—from the experience of the fifties; the time-series analysis of Arthur Burns, Wesley Mitchell, and others at the National

Bureau of Economic Research; the inventory-cycle models of Lloyd Metzler; and the general multiplier-accelerator analysis of Paul Samuelson. Those old tracts could have helped to keep the forecasters on the right track.

Notes

I want to thank Nancy Delaney for her assistance in the research.

1. The auto share held up rather well in the early stages of the 1957–58 and 1960–61 recessions, unlike 1974. It then recovered very slowly later in 1958 and 1961, after the economy turned up.

2. F. Thomas Juster and Paul Wachtel, "Inflation and the Consumer," *BPEA* (1:1972), pp. 71–72.

3. Joseph A. Pechman, "Responsiveness of the Federal Individual Income Tax to Changes in Income," *BPEA* (2:1973), pp. 403–05.

4. The movement of the "statistical discrepancy" in the national accounts from −\$5.0 billion in 1973 to −\$0.1 billion in 1974 also "cost" \$5 billion of income.

5. From 1969:4 to 1974:2, the growth of M_1 averaged 6.58 percent, and the maximum deviation of M_1 from a smooth trend line connecting those points was \$3.0 billion in 1973:2.

6. Arthur M. Okun, "Unemployment and Output in 1974," *BPEA* (2:1974), pp. 502–03.

7. James S. Duesenberry, "Some Observations on Monetary Policy," *BPEA* (2:1973), p. 512.

8. *Economic Report of the President together with the Annual Report of the Council of Economic Advisers, February 1974*, p. 26.

9. James Tobin, "Monetary Policy in 1974 and Beyond," *BPEA* (1:1974), pp. 221–22.

10. Alternatively, it can be argued that, with monetary conditions so tight during 1974, the money stock exerted more influence on nominal GNP than it had in 1973 or even in 1969; thus inflation led to less upward adjustment of the velocity of money and more downward adjustment of real output.

Postwar Macroeconomics: The Evolution of Events and Ideas

I would emphasize the following salient features of the postwar macroeconomic record:

1. Throughout the postwar era, real economic activity has displayed much more stability than it did in earlier United States history.
2. For the first twenty or twenty-five years of the postwar era—but not since then—that greater stability was accompanied by more rapid progress with especially strong growth of both output and productivity.
3. While the superior real performance from the mid-forties to the mid-sixties was not achieved at the expense of a serious departure from price stability, the record since then shows a dramatic and unprecedented chronic inflation accompanying the deterioration of real performance.
4. In subtle but important ways, both the good news and the bad news of the postwar era reflect the categorical imperative of policymaking established at the beginning of that era—namely the avoidance of an encore of the Great Depression.

The Stability of Real Activity

Throughout the postwar era including the seventies, economic activity has been far more stable than it was in previous United States history. The standard deviation of real GNP around its growth trend in 1946–76 was about one-fourth as large as it had been in 1900–45, and only half as large as in the "golden age" of 1900–16, 1920–29, omitting wartime and depression years in the prewar era (Baily 1978). The contrast in the cyclical chronology is equally striking: the average duration of business-cycle expansions between 1854 and 1937 was twenty-six months, and that of recessions twenty-one months. From 1945 to 1975, expansions averaged forty-eight months in length and recessions, eleven months. Thus, the economy spent only 19 percent, rather than 45 percent, of the elapsed time in recession. The longest and deepest postwar recession (1973–75) was shorter than the median prewar recession and less severe than four of the nine recessions of the 1900–38 period.

This quantum jump in stability—this taming of the business cycle—must, in my judgment, be credited to public policy. It was made in Washington. I suspect that the largest single stabilizing development stemmed from a change that was not designed to enhance macroeconomic stability, namely the increased size of the public sector as a share of GNP. That compositional shift created a large component of the total economy that was not sensitive to cyclical fluctuations and that resisted multiplier-accelerator interactions. On the income side, the counterpart to the growth in the public sector was the increase in marginal tax rates, which cut the size of investment multipliers. The growth of transfer payments also created important automatic stabilizers: unemployment insurance benefits alone have bolstered private purchasing power *during recession periods* by more than the total of discretionary stimulative fiscal actions of the postwar era. The absence of the financial panic element that was a hallmark of prewar recessions reflects, in part, the development of federal deposit insurance and other types of federal financial regulation as well as the willingness and ability of the Federal Reserve to contain the ripple effects of major failures and defaults.

Private decision makers gradually realized that the government had the tools of demand management to prevent catastrophes of depression magnitude. And that recognition helped to alleviate, and ultimately to end, the fears of an encore of the thirties, which were intense at the beginning of the postwar era. The perceived reduction of catastrophe risks, in turn, contributed to less volatile shifts by decision makers in response to those fluctuations that did emerge, as Baily suggests.

Fiscal and monetary policy were geared up appropriately to avoid catastrophes, but their record in dealing with the relatively minor accidents that in fact occurred is mixed. Gordon ably traces that experience in his background paper. I shall merely underline a few of the lessons. Some of the better stabilization performances came early in the postwar era. An appropriately large federal surplus was maintained during 1947 and 1948. In terms of macroeconomic stabilization, the Korean War was by far the best managed military emergency in United States history

—presenting a sharp contrast with the subsequent Vietnam experience. But, during recession periods, fiscal policy was uniformly slow on the trigger. Indeed, it is fair to conclude that no significant discretionary stimulative fiscal action was adopted while the economy was still in recession. A borderline case was the tax cut enacted in March 1975, which was the month of the business-cycle trough. Most of the strongly stimulative fiscal actions were taken in the first year of recovery. On occasions, these worked effectively to promote the restoration of prosperity; on others, they may have overdone the job—providing a stimulus that was too much too late. Antirecessionary expenditure programs like public works seem to have operated with a lag of half a cycle. (It may be easier to stretch the lag to a full cycle than to cut it appreciably!)

The outstanding applications of restrictive budgetary policy occurred in the fiscal years 1957, 1960, and 1974. And all of these were cases of too much too late. At the end of the fiscal years 1957 and 1960, celebrations on the achievement of federal budgetary surpluses were followed immediately by mourning over the onset of recession. The lessons inferred from those experiences contributed to the general acceptance of federal deficits as a normal and appropriate state of affairs in the sixties and the seventies.

Monetary policy as well was too slow on the trigger in reacting to recessions. The growth rate of money remained below average right through the trough of most recessions, even in those cases when (as Gordon emphasizes) it accelerated relative to the peak of the previous expansion. Often, like fiscal policy, monetary policy turned markedly expansionary during the first year of recovery. A generally accommodating stance was maintained for too long during several expansions, followed by shifts to restraint that were too much too late.

The record provides some illuminating examples of bad and good applications of the fiscal-monetary mix. In the face of the massive fiscal stimulus of butter and Vietnam guns, the Federal Reserve in 1966–67 demonstrated that it could do the whole macro job. Tightening enough to generate a virtual cessation of money growth, it achieved a nonrecessionary slowdown that cooled inflation. But the macro success was accompanied by serious micro distortions: a collapse in homebuilding, an acute mortgage famine, a general contraction of availability in credit markets, and major capital losses on bonds and equities. Then in late 1967 and 1968, monetary policy was clearly too stimulative because the Federal Reserve refused to risk an encore of these distortions. A good mix performance is illustrated by the 1964–65 tax cuts, when fiscal policy played an active role and monetary policy carried an accommodative role. That strategy was superior to the alternatives of relying on a unilateral fiscal stimulus or on a unilateral monetary stimulus. In the latter case, in order to provide an equivalent stimulus, interest rates would have had to be reduced substantially, thereby risking an overstimulus to homebuilding and exacerbation of the balance-of-payments problem.

I read the undistinguished record of cyclical stabilization as suggesting ample opportunities for improvement. We have to try harder—not cease the effort.

Deteriorating Growth Performance

Until recently, the greater stability of the postwar era was accompanied by more rapid progress. The average annual growth rate of real GNP was 3.8 percent from 1948 to 1973, far surpassing the average rate of 2.8 percent for 1909–29 and 2.3 percent for 1929–48. Moreover, when allowances were made for the size of the "net gap" under these trend lines connecting prosperity years, the superiority of postwar performance is even clearer: the net gap averaged zero for 1948–73; it averaged 5 percent of GNP in 1909–29 and 12 percent of GNP in 1929–48. Finally, output per hour worked rose at an average rate of 3 percent per year through most of the postwar era, a substantial improvement over the 2 percent par for the course in the earlier periods.

For 1973–78, however, the annual growth rate of real GNP averaged only 2.5 percent. And that growth was accomplished only as the result of an especially rapid increase in the labor force and employment, while the trend growth of output per hour worked apparently slowed to a mere one percent a year. The productivity slowdown has generated a vast amount of interesting economic research, which is often inconclusive. One important consensus finding is that slower growth of capital per unit of labor accounts for *part but only part* of the slowdown. That slower growth of the capital-labor ratio in turn has two components. If the ratio of investment to GNP in recent years had matched its historical average, the capital-labor ratio would have displayed unusually slow growth in view of the especially rapid growth of the labor force. In fact, in the latter part of the 1973–75 recession and for some considerable time in the subsequent recovery, the ratio of business fixed investment to GNP ran considerably below its historical average.

Chronic Inflation

The other outstanding dimension of deteriorating economic performance in recent years is the rapid and accelerating pattern of inflation since the mid-sixties. The chronic inflation that has survived slack and recession is an unprecedented experience for Americans. Fourteen years ago, when the United States economy (and, incidentally, the reputation of economists) looked brightest, Gardner Ackley (1966, p. 176) warned: "It is easy to prescribe expansionary policies in a period of slack. Managing high-level prosperity is a vastly more difficult business and requires vastly superior knowledge." The price record demonstrates that we have not had the skill to manage high-level prosperity.

Actually, in terms of the ability of the federal government to forecast and control the course of *nominal* GNP, demand management has been especially successful in the past decade. The official annual "Troika" forecasts of nominal GNP were distinctly more accurate in the seventies than they had been in the sixties—with an average absolute error of 0.75 percent compared to 1.3 percent. (This brings up to date a fact previously noted by William Fellner. I assure you that the improvement should not be attributed to a lower quality of the people doing the Troika forecasting in the sixties!)

In fact, control over nominal GNP is all that monetary and general fiscal policy can be expected to achieve. They cannot control the "split" of the growth of nominal GNP between its real and its inflation components. But errors in forecasting the split have been serious and costly. In 1970, 1971, 1973, 1974, and 1979, inflation was *under*predicted by a percentage point or more while the growth of real GNP was *over*predicted by a point or more. The year 1974 is the most egregious case: the nominal GNP forecast was nearly perfect, with offsetting errors of about two and a half percentage points each for the GNP deflator and real GNP.

The big errors in assessing the split stemmed initially from continued econometric reliance on the short-run Phillips curve. It was hard to cast aside a tool that had traced the United States record so well from 1954 through the late sixties. And it was easy to ignore the Friedman and Phelps attack on the stability of the short-run Phillips curve, and their prophetic warning (issued at a time when the Phillips curve was still performing admirably) that the curve would come unstuck in a prolonged period of excess demand. Unfortunately, most of the profession (including me) took too long to recognize that. Since 1970, the Phillips curve has been an unidentified flying object and has eluded all econometric efforts to nail it down.

A second major contributor to the split errors was the widespread misassessment of the inflationary significance of supply shocks, such as those in food during 1973 and in fuel during 1974 and 1979. Paradoxically, the theory that correctly predicted the shifting Phillips curve implied incorrectly that the rising prices of these items would be offset by reductions in other prices—with no significant effect on the price level at given utilization rates. Indeed, it is now clear that the shocks generate not merely a "one-shot" rise in the price level but a further inflationary chain reaction through the influence of consumer prices on wages. Here again, the policymakers and much of the profession ignored timely warnings and constructive policy prescriptions, offered, in this case, by Gordon, Perry, and me.

The third major source of split errors was the inadequate recognition of the inertial patterns of wages (and prices) in the sectors governed by implicit and explicit contracts. The experience of 1974–75 reinforced previous evidence that the first-year effect of cutting nominal GNP by $1 is a reduction between 10¢ and 20¢ in the inflation bill and a reduction in output between 80¢ and 90¢. The stark verdict emerges that, unless that split can be improved, an attack on inflation pursued solely by monetary-fiscal restraint would cost roughly $200 billion of production per point of reduction in the inflation rate.

Policymaking has suffered even more from an incorrect qualitative assessment of the broader implications of inflation than from the quantitative errors in forecasting inflation. The costs of perceived inflation are not extra trips to the bank, as most models would have it, but rather a crawl away from money. The entire system of transactions in the United States economy has been built on the dollar as a unit of account and a yardstick. Because the price level at the start of World War II was just about where it had been at the end of the Civil War, people took money seriously. The nominal unit became the foundation of our financial system, our accounting system, our corporate and personal planning and scorekeeping, our tax system, and our explicit and implicit contracts.

The crawl away from money proceeds along many lines: pressures for cost-of-living escalators; the erosion of model-year pricing and orders with guaranteed prices at delivery; the scrapping of pricing formulas that rest objectively on historical costs; the agonizing, slow shift to last in–first out (LIFO) accounting; and the transformation of capital budgeting to incorporate explicit though highly uncertain inflation forecasts.

In asset markets, portfolios shift away from long-term, fixed-interest nominal assets toward the time-honored refuges from inflation—readily resalable tangible assets such as real estate, precious metals, and art objects. But the inflation hedges are far less liquid and involve much higher transactions costs than do nominal assets. And even the most sophisticated investor cannot construct a portfolio whose real value will be neutral with respect to the inflation rate. Moreover, because various categories of prices and wages respond with differential sensitivity to the general price level, inflation is inevitably nonneutral in its micro effects: it must change relative prices and relative wages and must reshuffle real incomes in an arbitrary and haphazard way.

The obsolescence of the capital invested in the dollar as a yardstick and the enforced lottery in the income distribution make inflation extremely unpopular. Yet the government seems incapable of solving the problem; and rationally grounded fears grow that the era of chronic inflation will end ultimately only through either a prolonged deep recession or a prolonged application of stultifying price and wage controls. In this environment of uncertain and pessimistic expectations, is it really a mystery why common stocks are depressed, why capital spending is not ebullient and why it is focused on short-term projects, or why the public's confidence in our basic institutional structure and its future has plummeted?

There are ample grounds for the suspicion (previously voiced by Denison and Fellner) that various aspects of our chronic inflation may account for some of the puzzle of the productivity slowdown. In coping with the uncertain value of the dollar, buyers and sellers face genuine increases in their real transactions costs. Managerial effort is diverted from the promotion of productivity to the development of nonmonetary yardsticks. The search for inflation hedges may distort the composition of investment. Uncertainty shrinks the time horizon and creates an aversion to long-lived projects, which may embody particularly large elements of technical change. Research and development budgets may get squeezed as well in an era of mounting inflation for the same reason that desserts vanish from table d'hôte dinners. These are all conjectures, but they deserve serious investigation in the continuing effort to resolve the productivity puzzle.

A Concluding Perspective

The postwar era began with widespread anxiety about a relapse into another Great Depression. The categorical imperative of policy was to avoid such a relapse; and the success must be measured, not in dollars of real GNP, but in the very survival of United States capitalism. The formulators of the Employment Act of 1946 focused on avoiding catastrophe, but they achieved much more than that: the taming of the business cycle.

Did the crusading zeal to prevent depression bring on the subsequent disease of chronic inflation? Not in the gross ways sometimes alleged. The economy was not generally overheated: Gordon shows a net average gap of real GNP in each of the three postwar decades, relative to his estimates of the "natural" unemployment rate. Nor were investment and saving shortchanged in favor of public or private consumption: the ratio of business fixed investment to GNP compares favorably with the prewar era, and the ratio of gross private saving to GNP in years of prosperity has faithfully obeyed Denison's Law. (I note with envy that that is the one law of an economist that survived the seventies.)

But, in subtle ways, I believe that depression mentality fostered inflation vulnerability. There was an imbalance in policy: it is inconceivable that a four-year recession would have been tolerated in the way that a four-year boom was tolerated in the late sixties. And when an economy is made depression-proof and deflation-proof, private expectations and conventions become asymmetrical, introducing an inflationary bias into the system. Moreover, there was an asymmetry in the development and deployment of the macroeconomics: our analysis of the determinants of employment and output was and remains far superior to our understanding of fluctuations in the price level and their consequences. There was an imbalance, and it must be corrected through greater emphasis on the price level in the economic policymaking (and the economic analysis) of the eighties.

Bibliographical Note

The stability of postwar economic activity and the growing perception of that stability are documented in Martin Neil Baily, "Stabilization Policy and Private Economic Behavior," *BPEA, 1: 1978,* pp. 13–33. The role of monetary policy during business cycles is discussed in George L. Perry, "Stabilization Policy and Inflation." In *Setting National Priorities: The Next Ten Years,* edited by Henry Owen and

Charles L. Schultze (Washington, D.C.: Brookings Institution, 1976), pp. 289–93. The quotation on managing prosperity is from Gardner Ackley, "The Contribution of Economists to Policy Formation," *Journal of Finance* 21 (May 1966): 176.

Fellner's analysis of the accuracy of "Troika" forecasts of nominal GNP can be found in William Fellner, *Towards a Reconstruction of Macroeconomics: Problems of Theory and Policy* (Washington, D.C.: American Enterprise Institute, 1976), pp. 118–24.

Discussions of the contribution to overall inflation from supply shocks appear in Robert J. Gordon, "Alternative Responses of Policy to External Supply Shocks," *BPEA, 1:1975,* pp. 183–204; statement of George L. Perry, in *The 1974 Economic Report of the President,* Hearings before the Joint Economic Committee, 93d Cong. 2d sess. (Washington, D.C.: Government Printing Office, 1974), pt. 2, pp. 542–45: and Statement of Arthur Okun, in *Multinational Corporations and United States Foreign Policy,* Hearings before the Subcommittee on Multinational Corporations of the Senate Committee on Foreign Relations, 44th Cong. 1st sess. (Washington, D.C.: Government Printing Office, 1975), pt. 11, pp. 64–65. Chronic inflation is cited as possibly accounting for the recent slowdown in productivity in Edward F. Denison, *Accounting for Slower Economic Growth: The United States in the 1970s* (Washington, D.C.: Brookings Institution, 1979), pp. 135–36; and William Fellner, "The Declining Growth of American Productivity: An Introductory Note." In *Contemporary Economic Problems: 1979,* directed by William Fellner (Washington, D.C.: American Enterprise Institute, 1979), pp. 4–6.

VI ECONOMIC FORECASTING

A Review of Some Economic Forecasts for 1955–57

A review of aggregative economic forecasts should illuminate discussions of the predictive value of the profession's tools. The evidence presented in this paper is derived from a small sample of quantitative short-term forecasts of gross national product (GNP) and its components for the years 1955–57. The predictions were made by economists employed in nine financial, industrial, and publishing firms in the New York metropolitan area. Most of the predictions were designed exclusively for internal use as a guide to management policy. Annual forecasts in current dollars are considered in the paper. These predictions were prepared within a few months on either side of the onset of the year they cover; the majority were completed in November and December. In a few instances the same firm contributed two forecasts for a single year, one prepared late in the preceding year and one early in the predicted year. Eight forecasts for 1955, nine for 1956, and eleven for 1957 are included. Each of the quantitative predictions was accompanied by a discussion of the evidence underlying and supporting the conclusions; this paper also draws on explanatory material contained in a number of qualitative forecasts which reached conclusions similar to those of the quantitative forecasts under review.

The group of forecasts analyzed below cannot be offered as a representative sample of economic predictions, although it would be exceedingly difficult to define a universe of aggregate forecasts from which an appropriate sample might be withdrawn. The present sample is probably unusually strong in forecasting experience and in resources devoted to prediction. On the other hand, I personally doubt that the voluntary character of the sample produced any distinct bias in favor of successful predictions; but the reader is entitled to be skeptical on this score.

The justification for an intensive analysis of a small group of forecasts lies in the essential homogeneity of current economic forecasting techniques which follow the income-expenditure approach. While there are important differences in tactics among forecasters, their strategies are the same, and their quantitative result display rather small dispersion. Since the income-expenditure approach to forecasting has been thoroughly outlined in the literature,[1] only a brief review is needed here.

Typically, government expenditure is treated as exogenously determined in current dollars. Budgetary information, informal statements of public officials, and recent trend patterns are employed for projections of the government sector. Fixed investment expenditure is related by categories to predetermined flow and stock variables such as the degree of utilization of the existing stock of capital, the state of financial markets, current levels of profits, and corporate liquidity. New orders for durables and construction contract awards may also be given weight. Frequently, anticipations data provided by the Commerce-SEC and McGraw-Hill surveys of business investment plans are weighted heavily. Consumer expenditure and inventory investment are usually treated as endogenous variables. They are thus projected at levels consistent with the predictions of disposable income and sales, respectively. If the forecasters expect changes in capital outlays or government spending, they will project some indirect effects of these events on the rate of consumer spending and probably on inventory investment. It is in this sense that these may be considered endogenous variables. In contrast, many of the forecasters could apparently anticipate considerable changes in government spending or in the saving ratio of consumers and yet make no provision for induced effects of such shifts on capital outlays during the forthcoming year. However, the forecasters emphatically reject the use of stable or normal ratios between personal saving and disposable income or between inventory and sales. Instead, they attempt to diagnose the autonomous strength of demand for inventories and for consumer goods from relevant financial variables, anticipations data, etc.

The income-expenditure approach may be formalized into an econometric model, or it may be used simply as a framework for the informed judgments of the forecasters. The vast majority of economic forecasts, including all those in my sample, are not derived from articulated formal models and do place considerable reliance on judgment in the selection

Table 1 Predicted and actual changes in national product for 1955 (in billions of dollars)

	Actual change	Predicted change			Deviation			Fourth quarter naïve model	
	(1)[a]	Mean (2)	High (3)	Low (4)	Mean (5)	Low (6)	High (7)	Predicted change (8)	Deviation (9)
Gross national product	+34.4	+13.9	+20.4	+10.0	+20.5	+14.0	+24.4	+4.8	+29.6
Personal consumption expenditure	+18.9	+7.4	+11.7	+5.0	+11.5	+7.2	+13.9	+3.7	+15.2
Gross private domestic investment	+14.9	+6.3	+9.1	+4.1	+8.6	+5.8	+10.8	+3.4	+11.5
Residential construction	+3.3	+1.7	+2.9	0	+1.6	+0.4	+3.3	+1.5	+1.8
Other construction	+1.9	+0.1	+0.5	−0.5	+1.8	+1.4	+2.4	0	+1.9
Producers' durable equipment	+2.3	−0.1	+1.2	−1.6	+2.4	+1.1	+3.9	−0.5	+2.8
Change in business inventories	+7.4	+4.8	+6.0	+4.2	+2.6	+1.4	+3.2	+2.4	+5.0
Net foreign investment	0	+0.7	+1.6	0	−0.7	−1.6	0	+1.2	−1.2
Government purchases of goods and services	+0.5	−0.4	+0.8	−2.6	+0.9	−0.3	+3.1	−3.4	+3.9
Federal	−2.1	−2.5	−1.5	−4.6	+0.4	−0.6	+2.5	−4.1	+2.0
State and local	+2.6	+2.1	+2.6	+1.3	+0.5	0	+1.3	+0.7	+1.9

a. In columns 1, 2, 5, 8, and 9 detail need not add to total because of rounding. In columns 3, 4, 6, and 7 detail will not sum to total, since high and low value are selected for each item separately.

and weighting of evidence. At the same time, quantitative techniques are widely employed to extrapolate certain key ratios and regression relationships among variables. The predictive techniques thus fall into the category of "looser frameworks of quasi-mathematical character," to use Fellner's phrase.[2]

Forecasts for 1955

The relevant information for 1955 is presented in Table 1. Each 1955 prediction is interpreted as an expected change, measured by the difference between the level predicted for 1955 and the level then assumed by the forecaster for the 1954 benchmark year. Assumptions made in late 1954 or early 1955 concerning 1954 national product components necessarily differ from the most recent official estimates for 1954 as shown in the July, 1958, issue of *Survey of Current Business*. The device of measuring accuracy by comparison of predicted changes with actual changes is designed to abstract from the unavoidable benchmark inaccuracies. Actual change in column 1 of the table is the difference between 1955 and 1954 levels as shown in the July, 1958, estimates. For each item the arithmetic mean of the predicted change in the eight forecasts for 1955 is recorded in column 2. Predicted change for 1955 in each case is the difference between the level predicted for 1955 and the level assumed by the forecaster for 1954. The range of predicted changes for each separate component in the eight forecasts is shown in columns 3 and 4. The deviations, or forecast errors, tabulated in columns 5, 6, and 7, are the differences between actual change and predicted change; column 5 is column 1 minus column 2, etc. For comparison with the performance of the eight forecasts, columns 8 and 9 present the predicted changes and deviations based on a naïve model which "forecast" 1955 levels as equal to those of the fourth quarter of 1954. The predicted changes of the fourth-quarter naïve model thus equal the difference between the estimates for the fourth quarter of 1954 (seasonally adjusted at annual rates) and those for the full year 1954, as both were first presented in the February, 1955, *Survey of Current Business*. The actual changes in column 1 may be interpreted as the deviations involved in an alternative naïve model which projected all components for 1955 at their levels for the full year 1954, thus predicting zero change for each item.

The most striking characteristic of the table is the predominance of positive predicted changes and positive deviations. The forecasters unanimously envisaged a general expansion of economic activity in 1955. The upswing which actually occurred exceeded the expectations of all. Of the $34.4-billion rise in GNP, about $5 billion are attributable to higher prices in 1955. Since few of the forecasters anticipated any increase in prices, the underestimates of real GNP would be a trifle smaller.

The mean underestimate of $20.5 billion (current) in GNP and even the smallest underestimate of GNP are substantial. Nevertheless, the record is on the whole quite impressive. As of the end of 1954, the national product accounts showed a decline of $14 billion in GNP (at annual rates) from the second quarter of 1953 to the first quarter of 1954; the total then remained remarkably stable over the next two quarters. A mechanical extrapolation of recent trends up to the fourth quarter of 1954 could not have led to a prediction of expanding activity for 1955.

Both the largest gains relative to the naïve models and the largest quantitative underestimates of expansion are found in personal consumption expenditure. Since consumption is treated as an endogenous variable in the sense discussed above, one would like to divide the consumption error into an autonomous and an induced portion. The autonomous portion reflects the error in the relationship between consumption and GNP: it measures the difference between the actual change in consumer spending and the rise that would have been predicted by the forecasters if they had had perfect foreknowledge of total GNP for 1955. The remaining or induced consumption error would measure the implicit multiplier effects on consumption attributable to deviations from the predicted values of other components or to the autonomous error in consumption. Precise determination of the autonomous error is impossible, since the predictions were not based on a formal framework. However, a few relatively crude calculations are enlightening. In each of the forecasts the predicted change in consumption was about half the predicted change in GNP, with a ratio of 53 per cent for the mean of the forecasts.

By extrapolation of the 53 per cent mean predicted marginal ratio over the $34.4-billion actual change in GNP, the calculated rise in consumption amounts to $18.2 billion, or only $0.7 billion less than the actual consumption increase of $18.9 billion. Other calculations on the individual forecasts based on more detailed consideration of the underlying reasoning suggest a somewhat larger autonomous error of about $2 billion. The decline in the saving-income ratio from 7.4 per cent in 1954 to 6.4 per cent in 1955 was typically not foreseen. The consumer sector did not contribute to the success of the forecasts in anticipating expansion. Nevertheless, by any reasonable calculation, the bulk of the $11.5 billion mean underestimate of the rise in consumer spending must be ascribed to induced effects.

Even with the benefit of hindsight, it remains difficult to explain consumer behavior during this period. The most popular current explanation is that the American public fell in love with the 1955 automobile models.[3] This tale of romance hardly supplies an elegant explanation of the strength in consumer demand, but it is consistent with the data: new-auto sales can easily account for the low saving ratio, while sales of non-durables and services were not unusually high. Capital gains associated with the stock-market boom are occasionally mentioned in *ex post* discussions. In the few instances where a decline in the saving ratio was predicted, the forecasters pointed to the optimistic findings of the Survey Research Center's periodic surveys or argued that relatively low acquisitions of durables in the previous year would make demand in 1955 particularly responsive to the expected rise in disposable incomes.

The forecasters anticipated a small rise in net foreign investment, which failed to materialize. They correctly foresaw the decline in federal spending and the rise in state and local outlays, although usually with a slight downward bias for both components of the government sector. In only one forecast did government expenditures account significantly for the underestimate in GNP.

All the economists predicted accurately that the inventory liquidation of 1954 would be reversed in 1955. The inventory forecasts improved upon the full-year naïve model by \$4–\$6 billion and on the fourth-quarter model by \$2–\$4 billion. The positive residuals in the inventory predictions are in part attributable to underestimates of final sales of goods in 1955.

When most of the forecasts were made, stocks in the aggregate were declining without abatement, but the changing composition of liquidated inventories led to optimism. In late 1953 and early 1954, disinvestment of stocks had been concentrated in durable goods manufacturing. Except for the sizable trimming of auto inventories that preceded introduction of 1955 models, the decline in producers' stocks of durables ended after mid-1954. Many forecasters concluded that the adjustment in this sector had been completed, and they viewed the spreading of liquidation to non-durable manufacturing and to trade as a temporary adjustment to the previous weakness of sales. Furthermore, the initial decline in manufacturers' stocks had displayed a very sharp reduction in inventories of purchased materials; a more moderate disinvestment of goods-in-process followed shortly thereafter. By mid-1954 the liquidation in these groups ended; and stocks of finished goods, which had previously been stable, began to fall. It was argued that involuntary accumulation of goods awaiting sale had prevented an earlier trimming of finished goods. Now, since purchased materials and goods-in-process had been set into balance with sales and since finished goods were being adjusted, inventory disinvestment was seen nearing an end. Also buttressing the conclusion were various pieces of survey evidence that business firms no longer deemed their stocks excessive.

Preflow data on housing starts and residential building contract awards convinced the economists that residential construction would show strength during 1955. Relaxed money conditions were expected to support housing during this period. While the housing component contributed to the underestimate of expansion, it also contributed significantly to the bullish tone of the predictions.

For producers' durables and other (i.e., non-residential) construction, the mean of the forecasts displays no particular superiority over either the full-year or fourth-quarter naïve model and is $4.2 billion too low for these two items combined. Thus the principal reasons for the accurate predictions of expanding activity in 1955 and for the uniform underestimates of expansion lie in investment. While inventory investment is the hero, fixed investment must stand as the principal villain. Recent trends in business capital spending as of late 1954 were not encouraging. Furthermore, the McGraw-Hill and Commerce-SEC anticipations data through December pointed to a continued decline. Even the Commerce-SEC annual survey in March indicated a mere 1 per cent rise in capital spending for 1955. Awards of non-residential construction contracts and new orders for durable goods in late 1954 were both above the low levels that had obtained earlier in the year. However, these preflow series remained depressed and were not optimistically interpreted by the forecasters. Since backlogs had been sharply reduced, it was felt that a substantial rise in new orders and contract awards was needed just to maintain the existing rate of production.

Ex post, the upsurge in outlays for fixed capital in 1955 is most plausibly explained as a response to improved sales and earnings experiences; much of the rise appears to have been induced by the concurrent expansion of demand for finished goods and the associated rise in profits.[4] This interpretation is consistent with other postwar evidence that unanticipated changes in sales lead to changes in capital outlays relative to anticipations.[5] Yet the possibility of induced movements in investment spending was rarely mentioned in the *ex ante* discussions of 1955 prospects. The induced-change explanation suggests that the strength of the capital sector was partially predictable in terms of the forecasters' own expectations regarding other components. Because of bullishness about inventories and housing, a mean increase in GNP of $13.9 billion was predicted by the analysts. It is hard to believe that a recovery of the predicted magnitude could have occurred without providing some stimulus to capital outlays.

Business fixed investment was an important source of the underestimate of GNP because the forecasters did not allow for its responsiveness to the buoyancy of other sectors. The role of capital outlays in the 1955 expansion was significant, but it was a distinctly passive part. The recovery must be attributed *ex post* to three active expansionary factors, namely, inventories, housing, and consumption. If producers' capital spending had been properly diagnosed as a passive element, the potential success of the forecasts would have been determined by the accuracy of predictions of the three active forces. Because the expansionary influence of housing and inventories was properly foreseen, the 1955 predictions of fixed investment, and of consumption and inventory accumulation as well, would have been higher and therefore more accurate if allowances had been made for the induced effects on capital spending. However, because the high spending propensity of the household sector was not anticipated, the total of GNP and most of the components—including capital spending—would still have been underestimated to some extent.

Forecasts for 1956

Predicted changes and deviations covering the nine forecasts for 1956 are shown in Table 2. The results resemble those for 1955 in Table 1, since positive predicted changes and positive deviations are again predominant. However, unlike 1955, the mean predicted change in GNP for 1956 is not much better than the fourth-quarter naïve forecast. Because GNP had risen rapidly and consistently during 1955, one could have been quite bearish about the prospective trend of activity during 1956 and still have predicted 1956 GNP well above the 1955 total. Only a very sharp decline during the year could have prevented 1956 from being the "best year ever." Hence it was not much of an achievement to produce a forecast of 1956 GNP which improved upon the full-year naïve assumption of zero change.

Errors in the prediction of price movements weighed heavily in 1956. Since the implicit price-deflator for GNP rose 3.0 per cent, about $12

Table 2 Predicted and actual changes in national product for 1956 (in billions of dollars)

	Actual change	Predicted change			Deviation			Fourth quarter naïve model	
	(1)[a]	Mean (2)	High (3)	Low (4)	Mean (5)	Low (6)	High (7)	Predicted change (8)	Deviation (9)
Gross national product	+21.7	+12.7	+18.0	+6.0	+9.0	+3.7	+15.7	+10.1	+11.6
Personal consumption expenditure	+12.5	+7.6	+11.0	+5.1	+4.9	+1.5	+7.4	+4.9	+7.6
Gross private domestic investment	+4.4	+2.6	+5.4	−1.6	+1.8	−1.0	+6.0	+3.9	+0.5
Residential construction	−1.0	−0.6	+0.3	−1.5	−0.4	−1.3	+0.5	−0.4	−0.6
Other construction	+1.9	+1.0	+1.7	+0.5	+0.9	+0.2	+1.4	+0.4	+1.5
Producers' durable equipment	+3.9	+2.9	+4.2	+1.2	+1.0	−0.3	+2.7	+1.7	+2.2
Change in business inventories	−0.4	−0.9	+0.5	−2.7	+0.5	−0.9	+2.3	+2.1	−2.5
Net foreign investment	+1.8	+0.1	+0.6	−0.1	+1.7	+1.2	+1.9	+0.1	+1.7
Government purchases of goods and services	+3.2	+2.4	+3.7	+0.2	+0.8	−0.5	+3.0	+1.3	+1.9
Federal	+0.3	+0.2	+1.2	−1.9	+0.1	−0.9	+2.2	+0.5	−0.2
State and local	+2.8	+2.2	+2.5	+1.8	+0.6	+0.3	+1.0	+0.9	+1.9

a. In columns 1, 2, 5, 8, and 9 detail need not add to total because of rounding. In columns 3, 4, 6, and 7 detail will not sum to total, since high and low values are selected for each item separately.

billion of the $21.7-billion increase in GNP from 1955 to 1956 are attributable to higher prices. The mean predicted rise in prices was somewhat less than half as large as the actual increase. This would imply an average underestimate of from $6 to $7 billion in the portion of the GNP increase attributable to higher prices and only a $3- or $4-billion underestimate of constant-dollar GNP.

As Table 2 indicates, most of the economists had little difficulty in projecting government spending. On the other hand, the expansionary influence of net foreign investment in 1956 was unanticipated. The actual $1.8 billion rise was produced by a record increase in merchandise exports, which reflected the strength of economic activity abroad. Frequently, net foreign investment has received perfunctory treatment from economic forecasters, who have felt this item was too small and too stable to endanger the over-all accuracy of their predictions of national product.[6] Nevertheless, the minor component did cause trouble in the nine forecasts for 1956.

For both categories of construction and for producers' durable equipment the mean predicted changes of the forecasters were considerably better than either naïve model. The incipient decline in residential construction was foreseen by the group, although its magnitude was understated. Data on new housing starts, contract awards, and mortgage commitments and evidence on the increasing tightness of mortgage markets were invoked to support the prediction of a downturn in home-building. Producers' durables and non-residential construction were accurately identified by most of the forecasters as the principal area of strength for 1956. The mean predicted increase for these two items, amounting to $4 billion, accounts for much of the anticipated rise of GNP and, in particular, explains the mean expectation of a rise over the end of 1955 level. Anticipations data, preflow data on new orders for durable goods and on nonresidential contract awards, the attractive conditions for equity financing, and the high level of 1955 profits all pointed to a continued boom in business outlays for plant and equipment. The McGraw-Hill and Commerce-SEC anticipations surveys were particularly significant in convincing the forecasters of the further rise in fixed investment. The predicted increases were all too small, however, with a mean underestimate of $1.9 billion. Much of the underestimate is attributable to the unexpectedly rapid rise in the prices of capital goods.

Most of the forecasters correctly expected the 1955 rate of investment in inventories to continue with little change in 1956. Inventory-sales ratios were very low in late 1955 and were still declining as the upsurge in sales outweighed additions to stocks. A significant decline in inventory investment was predicted by three forecasters who expected a "topping-out" of the fixed investment boom and a resulting cessation of the incentive to increase stocks.

While distinctly more accurate than either naïve model, the mean predicted change in consumption was $4.9 billion too low. For the mean of the forecasts, this error can be attributed in entirety to the underestimate of fixed and foreign investment; consumer incomes were understated, and, hence, household spending was pegged too low. Actually, the saving ratio rose by 0.9 per cent in 1956 as outlays for durables declined. However, this influence was offset by the unusually large rise in disposable income, amounting to $16 billion of the $22-billion increase in GNP. Corporate profits, which had soared in 1955, remained stable in 1956; consumers therefore received the lion's share of the rise in GNP. Many of the forecasters anticipated neither of these elements and predicted the marginal ratio of consumption to GNP quite satisfactorily. However, two forecasts which were among the most accurate for the investment sector seriously underestimated consumption, anticipating reduced demand for durables and contractionary pressures from instalment debt. They gauged accurately the rise in the saving ratio but did not foresee the relative weakness of corporate profits. The explanation for the actual stagnation of profits must lie in price-cost behavior. But the analysis of how and why the "profit squeeze" of 1956 occurred is still an unsettled issue.

As a group, the forecasters predicted accurately that physical output in 1956 would barely surpass the level of the fourth quarter of 1955. However, they underestimated the prospective rise in the price level and did not accurately foresee the consistent upward movement of current-dollar GNP during 1956. Thus, on the average, the predicted change in GNP was only $2.6 billion better than the fourth-quarter naïve model. At the same time it should be emphasized that the forecasts were consistently and markedly superior to the fourth-quarter naïve model for the individual components of national product. The GNP total may be considered as a sum of eight basic elements: consumption, net foreign investment, federal spending, state and local spending, and four categories of gross private domestic investment, as shown in Table 2. By summing the absolute deviations of the eight items, thus disregarding the sign of the error, one finds the mean of the economic forecasts better than the fourth-quarter naïve model by a decisive $8.1 billion. The error sum for the mean forecast is $10.1 billion compared to $18.2 billion for the naïve model. For none of the eight items is the fourth-quarter naïve model superior to the mean forecast.

The same phenomenon is even more dramatically evident in a comparison with an alternative naïve model. Suppose one had predicted that changes from 1955 to 1956 would simply repeat the changes that had taken place from 1954 to 1955. The predicted change in GNP for 1956 would then have been $34.4 billion, as shown in column 1 of Table 1. This naïve persistence-of-change prediction would have yielded an overestimate of 1956 GNP of $12.7 billion, not much worse than the $9.0 billion mean underestimate of the nine forecasts. The eight individual components, however, present a different picture. The sum of the absolute deviations of this naïve model is $24.5—more than double the $10.1-billion sum for the mean forecast. Such comparisons can hardly inspire confidence in simple extrapolations of recent trends or recent levels of activity.

In this light the forecasts look rather good. On the other hand, one gets a less favorable picture by inspecting the economic prospects envisioned by the forecasters for the fourth quarter of 1956, which they expected to be only slightly above the predicted level for the full year. In fact, GNP for the fourth quarter of 1956 stood $11.3 billion above the full-year rate. Underestimates of the duration of the boom in capital were particularly significant in accounting for the bearishness about the economy at the end of 1956.

Forecasts for 1957

Data on the eleven forecasts for 1957 are shown in Table 3. Unlike the figures for 1955 and 1956, the table displays a balance of positive and negative deviations. The forecasts came very close to the $21.1-billion actual rise in GNP: errors are uniformly small, and the underestimate in the mean forecast is only $1.2 billion. However, the sum of the absolute errors for the eight individual basic components in the mean forecast is $12.5 billion, which exceeds the absolute sum for 1956. Thus the accuracy of the predicted GNP total in 1957 is derived from considerable offsetting of positive and negative errors in the components. A certain amount of such fortuitous cancellation is to be expected in forecasting. The absence of compensating errors in 1955 and 1956 must be deemed unusual, but the extent of the 1957 offsets seems unusually large.

The 1957 level of real GNP was overestimated by about $4 billion, as a $9-billion rise was predicted on the average in contrast with a realized

Table 3 Predicted and actual changes in national product for 1957 (in billions of dollars)

	Actual change	Predicted change			Deviation			Fourth quarter naïve model	
	(1)[a]	Mean (2)	High (3)	Low (4)	Mean (5)	Low (6)	High (7)	Predicted change (8)	Deviation (9)
Gross national product	+21.1	+19.9	+22.8	+15.3	+1.2	−1.7	+5.8	+11.4	+9.7
Personal consumption expenditure	+15.0	+12.6	+15.6	+8.8	+2.4	−0.6	+6.2	+5.2	+9.8
Gross private domestic investment	−2.9	+2.3	+5.6	−2.2	−5.2	−8.5	−0.7	+3.1	−6.0
Residential construction	−0.7	−0.2	+0.9	−1.4	−0.5	−1.6	+0.7	−0.4	−0.3
Other construction	+1.4	+0.9	+2.0	−0.2	+0.5	−0.6	+1.6	+0.2	+1.2
Producers' durable equipment	+0.9	+2.9	+5.4	+0.6	−2.0	−4.5	+0.3	+2.8	−1.9
Change in business inventories	−4.5	−1.3	0	−2.9	−3.2	−4.5	−1.6	+0.6	−5.1
Net foreign investment	+2.1	0	+0.8	−0.7	+2.1	+1.3	+2.8	+1.0	+1.1
Government purchases of goods and services	+6.8	+5.1	+6.7	+3.8	+1.7	+0.1	+3.0	+2.2	+4.6
Federal	+3.7	+2.3	+3.5	+1.3	+1.4	+0.2	+2.4	+1.3	+2.4
State and local	+3.2	+2.8	+3.2	+2.2	+0.4	0	+1.0	+0.9	+2.3

a. In columns 1, 2, 5, 8, and 9 detail need not add to total because of rounding. In columns 3, 4, 6, and 7 detail will not sum to total, since high and low values are selected for each item separately.

$5-billion increase. The portion of the rise in GNP attributable to price change was anticipated at $11 billion as compared with an actual $16 billion. Since prices were already some 2 per cent above the full-year 1956 level by the end of the year, the forecasters were anticipating only slight further inflation during 1957. Once again, price rises were unanimously and markedly underpredicted. This consistent error is hardly surprising in view of the profession's inability *ex post* to account satisfactorily for the inflationary pressures which have marked the period from 1955 to date. The forecasts point to the dire need for a more adequate theory of the determination of the price level.

The $2.4-billion mean underestimate of consumption is principally an autonomous error. The forecasters were typically rather bullish about the household sector, expecting recovery from the slump in outlays for major durables that had marked 1956. However, their estimates of the personal saving-disposable income ratio for 1957 were generally still too high, for personal saving actually contracted a bit, while disposable income rose by $14.6 billion. A slight underestimate of the 1957 disposable income–GNP ratio also contributed to the positive deviation in the mean forecast of consumption.

The forecasters were generally correct in anticipating that residential construction in 1957 would remain at the depressed level of 1956. Preflow data and analyses of mortgage markets led to this conclusion. Higher construction costs were expected to support the dollar magnitude of home-building despite a prospective further decline in the real volume.

Weakness in the volume of contract awards in the second half of 1956 led to satisfactory conservative forecasts of non-residential construction for 1957. However, Commerce-SEC and McGraw-Hill anticipations data suggested that the boom in fixed investment was very much alive, and the forecasters expected producers' equipment outlays to expand further. The maintained strength of orders for manufactured durable goods, accompanied by rising backlogs, reinforced their conclusion. Only a few forecasters of producers' durables were much influenced by the weakening of profits and the tightness of financial markets. The economists overpredicted this component almost unanimously, with an average overestimate of $2 billion.

It was generally expected that the 1956 rate of inventory accumulation would not be maintained in 1957. However, only a moderate tapering-off of investment in stocks was foreseen. Inventory-sales ratios were viewed as still on the low side, though close to "normal." The substantial mean overestimate of $3.2 billion is partially attributable to an overestimate of physical sales of durables but also reflects overly optimistic appraisals of the autonomous strength of demand for stocks.

The Suez crisis produced a further surge in the demand for exports, and once again in 1957 the expansionary influence of net foreign investment surprised the analysts. The predictions of federal spending were consistent with budgetary estimates made at the start of 1957. But the defense outlays of government spurted above the official estimates, so federal outlays were underpredicted.

The mean underestimates of $2 billion each for government, net foreign investment, and consumption were balanced against overestimates of $2 billion in producers' durable equipment and $3 billion in inventory investment. These errors in projecting the composition of GNP and the error in the allocation between rise in prices and increase in output are flaws in the 1957 forecasts.

Another flaw is their failure to anticipate the sharp downturn in GNP which took place in the third quarter of 1957. Forecasts for the fourth quarter were typically about $5 billion too high, with the overestimates concentrated in inventory investment and producers' durables. Because of the upsurge in net foreign investment and federal outlays in early 1957, predicted GNP for the second quarter was on the average $3 billion too low. However, producers' durables were already considerably below the predictions. The incentive to add to capital stock waned in early 1957 as the rise in real GNP terminated. Then the two remaining expansionary influences declined from the second to the fourth quarter, net foreign investment falling by $2.3 billion and federal spending by $1.4 billion. In response to these declines and to the sharp cutback in defense orders, inventory liquidation was initiated in the fourth quarter.

The forecasters failed to sound an alarm for the 1957 downturn at the start of the year. However, their projections did imply a low rate of growth in real GNP and a general tone of weakness in the economy. As a result, certain economists have argued in retrospect that the forecasts made in early 1957 could well have served as an alert warning for both private and public budgeting. They contend that the dangers involved in an increasingly tight monetary policy and a downward reversal of defense outlays should have been evident to policymakers on the basis of economic forecasts.

Econometric Forecasts

The Klein-Goldberger econometric model has been used with certain adaptations as an annual forecasting tool during this period.[7] After performing well for 1953 and 1954, the model predicted only a minor rise in real GNP for 1955, underestimating investment by far more than the forecasts reviewed above. In preparing a forecast for 1956 based on the model, Daniel Suits judiciously adjusted the investment equation upward by the amount of its 1955 error and as a result was more accurate than most of the business economists. The 1957 forecast was more bullish and therefore less accurate then the mean forecast reviewed above.

Like the business economists, the model-builders have had no success in predicting the price level. Both types of forecasts also share a tendency to underestimate the magnitude of changes in GNP, apparently attributing too much inertia to the economy. In the Klein-Goldberger model, inertia is primarily due to the investment equation, which relates demand solely to lagged variables. The consumption equation, which places much weight on consumption of the previous year, also contributes to sluggishness. In brief, the short-run multipliers implied by the model seem inappropriately small. The underestimates in the forecasts studied above can be similarly explained. Trends in sales and earnings within the forecast period are seldom expected to affect planned investment concurrently. Some of the techniques employed to project consumption and inventories also tend to produce low values of the implicit short-run multiplier. If the forecast of autonomous changes is inaccurate, then small multipliers prevent a compounding of error, just as Friedman and Becker have argued.[8] If, however, dynamic adjustments in the economy are in fact rapid and if autonomous changes are successfully predicted, the low multiplier produces a dilution of accuracy.

The Klein-Goldberger model does not include as variables the anticipations and preflow series which are extensively used by business economists as barometers of activity in various sectors of the economy. The usefulness of these "non-causal" indicators was apparent in the above review of the predictive performances. The explicit inclusion of this wider body of data might improve the predictive accuracy of a formal model and might increase its usefulness as a device for formalizing, testing, and refining the techniques currently employed by economic forecasters.

Over-All Appraisal

From the detailed evidence presented above, the reader can form his own overall qualitative judgment of the predictive value of the 1955–57 forecasts. The evaluation should be made in terms of the adequacy of the forecasts as a guide to policy decisions. One rather stringent criterion of success would be the indicated ability of economic forecasts to provide accurate measures of prospective inflationary or deflationary gaps and thus to guide public stabilization policy in keeping the economy at full employment without inflation.[9] Certain optimistic proponents of the Employment Act of 1946 believed that economic forecasts would meet such a test and could, if properly heeded by policymakers, lead to the virtual elimination of fluctuations in aggregate economic activity.[10] The evidence cited above suggests that this was an unduly optimistic view. The forecasters were not sufficiently precise in quantitative terms to keep the economy consistently "on target." Full-employment policy requirements indicated by the predictions would have had a marked inflationary bias in 1955 and 1956, since the forecasts were insufficiently bullish. For 1957 the forecasts did not accurately gauge the dilemma of upward pressure on prices accompanied by downward pressure on output.

An alternative (and perhaps more realistic) measure of success would be the comparative performance of the forecasts relative to various naïve models. In contrast with any specific type of simple naïve projection for the years under review, the forecasts of the economists as a group are substantially more successful. When any naïve model is selected as a yardstick of zero foreknowledge, the forecasters must be credited with a positive amount of insight into the future course of the economy. Public and private economic decisions are forwardlooking and necessarily rest on beliefs about the future course of the economy. Many actual decisions are apparently based on implicit forecasts which simply extrapolate the present economic situation. If such naïve model forecasts are the alternative to explicit economic forecasts, the evidence heartily indorses reliance on the economists' predictions.

Notes

This paper was written as part of the project in Research on Short-Term Economic Forecasting conducted at the Cowles Foundation for Research in Economics at Yale University and financed by the Rockefeller Foundation. I am indebted to Mrs. Wilma W. Heston for her valuable assistance in processing the data presented below. Many thanks are also due to several business economists who generously revealed to me their past forecasts and a number of their trade secrets. In deference to the wishes of some of them, the forecasters who participated must go unnamed. Helpful comments on an earlier draft of this paper were made by Messrs. Don J. Daly, Frank W. Schiff, and Arnold Zellner.

1. See, e.g., V. Lewis Bassie, *Economic Forecasting* (New York: McGraw-Hill Book Co., 1958), Part II; Robert M. Biggs, *National-Income Analysis and Forecasting* (New York: W. W. Norton Co., 1956), chap. xi; Elmer C. Bratt, *Business Cycles and Forecasting* (Homewood, Ill.: Richard D. Irwin, Inc., 1953). For two case studies see the chapters by Kenneth D. Ross and Donald J. Watson in *Business Forecasting in Practice,* ed. A. G. Abramson and R. H. Mack (New York: John Wiley & Sons, 1956).

2. William Fellner, *Trends and Cycles in Economic Activity* (New York: Henry Holt & Co., 1956), pp. 328–29.

3. A variant of this argument credits the auto industry with a clever and successful courtship of the consumer through its merchandising activities and attractive trade-in and instalment-payment conditions.

4. The same conclusion is reached by Bert G. Hickman, "The Contraction of 1953–54," *Review of Economics and Statistics,* XL (February, 1958), 48.

5. See F. Modigliani and H. M. Weingartner, "Forecasting Uses of Anticipatory Data on Investment and Sales," *Quarterly Journal of Economics,* LXXII (February, 1958), 23–54.

6. See, e.g., the comment in Abramson and Mack (eds.), *op. cit.,* p. 171.

7. See University of Michigan, *Annual Conference on the Economic Outlook* for the years 1954, 1955, and 1956. The original model is presented in L. R. Klein and A. S. Goldberger, *An Econometric Model of the United States, 1929–1952* (Amsterdam: North-Holland Publishing Co., 1955).

8. Milton Friedman and Gary S. Becker, "A Statistical Illusion in Judging Keynesian Models," *Journal of Political Economy,* LXV (February, 1957), 64–75.

9. If full employment and price stability are incompatible goals, stabilization policy must be aimed at achieving the socially optimal balance between unemployment and inflation. The critical role of forecasting is unaltered in this event.

10. See the discussion by Paul A. Samuelson, "Economic Forecasting and National Policy," in *The Employment Act, Past and Future,* ed. Gerhard Colm (Washington, D.C.: National Planning Association, 1956), p. 131.

On the Appraisal of Cyclical Turning-Point Predictors

In order to review past economic forecasts and to investigate methods of improving economic predictions in the future, economists require criteria for appraising the predictive accuracy of their forecasts. For quantitative predictions of national product and its components, such criteria have been advanced and discussed. Forecast errors are naturally measurable as dollar deviations between predicted and actual magnitudes. The errors in a number of different forecasts can therefore be readily compared. In addition, "naïve models" which imply persistence of either the rate of change or the level of national product have been accepted as benchmarks for comparison with economists' predictions. There has been little discussion, however, of criteria for appraising the accuracy of cyclical turning-point forecasts, which project reversals in the direction of change of economic activity. This paper advances a method for evaluating turning-point predictions and illustrates the operation of the proposed system on historical data collected by the National Bureau of Economic Research. The assumptions underlying the scoring system and the characteristics of the method are discussed below.

Few claims are made for the system; it is far from ideal. It is offered with the conviction that some objective standard of appraisal is required for turning-point forecasts and that the specification of one possible system may evoke fruitful discussion of the problem. If existing methods of forecasting are to be evaluated and if new methods are to be sought, it must be possible to recognize a good forecast and to distinguish degrees of accuracy. Even if a particular forecasting tool or method is used in combination with other evidence and judgment, it is desirable to determine the predictive contribution of that element of the forecast. It may well be that informed judgment can produce successful forecasting. Still, it is reasonable to inquire whether a particular tool is an aid or a hindrance to the exercise of good judgment. The possibility of employing a method subjectively does not prevent the objective appraisal of that method. Only if predictive techniques can be evaluated objectively can the accuracy of economic forecasting be viewed as a test of methods rather than of men.

In principle, the value of a prediction should be gauged in terms of the uses for which the forecast is desired. In order to obtain guidance for their actions, decision-makers can exercise a choice among a variety of views on future prospects. The most productive forecast among a set of alternatives is the one which would lead to the greatest welfare for the decision-makers. Because the potential uses and users of a forecast cannot be specified generally, this principle of evaluation is difficult to apply. Therefore, appraisals are usually restricted to an examination of the amount and the accuracy of information supplied by the forecast. In the case of predictions of cyclical turning points, the users are offered an assessment of the prospective direction of change of economic activity. The prediction during an expansion that a turning point will occur at some date in the future expresses the belief that the upward movement of the economy will continue until that time and will then be followed by a downward path of business activity.

The making of "up" and "down" or plus (+) and minus (−) forecasts implies that direction of change is crucial to the policy-maker. This proposition may be questioned: if the difference between a change in output of +2 and −2 per cent is important, the difference between +2 and +6 per cent would also be expected to have significance. Even where forecasting is designed principally to alert decision-makers to major prospective swings in the economy, the magnitude (as well as direction) of the expected change will determine whether the signal should be given. These are relevant and interesting issues concerning the purpose and uses of turning-point forecasts, but they can be set aside here. The business-cycle approach does not, after all, restrict the forecaster to predictions of the direction of movements. He can estimate prospective amplitudes after making his turning-point forecast. Thus there is no need to draw a sharp distinction between business-cycle and national-product forecasting. The prediction of cyclical turning points can be appraised separately and yet viewed as a possible first step in the quantitative forecasting of aggregate economic variables.

By one simple test, a method designed to forecast a turning point may be termed a "success" whenever it signals prior to the turn. It must be emphasized that this is thoroughly unsatisfactory as a criterion of accuracy. There is no more difficulty in forecasting that a turn will occur than in predicting that rain will stop. During any contraction it is safe—and hence devoid of content—to advance the prediction that economic activity will rise again. Similarly, even in the stable postwar world, there is little risk in going on the record to assert that another recession will occur. Only when a date is attached to the prediction does it acquire any meaning.

The issue is whether the *timing* of a turning point can be predicted. For some purposes, the date of the next turning point may be the information desired, whether that date is one or forty months in the future. Unlike national-product projections which restrict the forecaster to a fixed forthcoming period, the business-cycle approach permits forecasting over a variable period. However, the planning period of government and business decision-makers dictates emphasis on the prospects for the near future. The length of the usual planning period has been one important determinant of the conventional 12-month period of national product forecasts. The same one-year fixed period is here assumed for the cyclical forecaster. His task is viewed as predicting the signs of monthly changes in general business activity for the coming 12 months. He may predict no turning point over that interval; in that event, his forecast in an expansion is simply 12 +'s; in contraction, 12 −'s. It is assumed that he forecasts, at most, one cyclical turning point which he must date: in an expansion, placing a peak 7 months in the future means predicting 7 +'s followed by 5 −'s for the year. Furthermore, it is assumed that predictions are made each month for the coming 12 months, so that 144 monthly signs (or forecast-months) are predicted each year. The number of correct forecast-months over any period of time provides a measure of accuracy. A percentage score can be readily obtained as the ratio of signs correctly foreseen to total predictions. "Forecast-month" scoring thus rests on the following assumptions:

1. Equal weight is placed on each of the next 12 months; zero weight is attached to months more than a year away. The same penalty is associated with an error concerning the next month as with one for the eleventh month in the future.
2. Type I and Type II errors are weighted equally. The null hypothesis is here taken as the forecast that the current phase will continue. A Type I

error arises if a turning point is forecast when none occurs; a Type II error is made if a continuation of the current phase is predicted and, in fact, a turning point occurs. Equal weighting means that predicting a turn a month too soon carries the same penalty as predicting the turn a month too late.
3. Errors made at any time in dating the turning-point are penalized in proportion to the magnitude of the error: being wrong by 2 months in a given forecast is twice as bad as a deviation of 1 month.

In appraisals of turning-point predictions employing forecast-month scoring, an obvious benchmark is a naïve model in which no turning point is ever predicted. The accuracy of this naïve model can be readily determined. So long as the end of the phase is 12 or more months away, the 12 sign predictions are correct. No turning point occurs during the next year, and none is predicted. However, 11 months before the peak or trough, one error is made out of the 12 months predicted: the first 11 signs are accurate, but the sign forecast for the last predicted month is wrong. In the next month, of the 12 forecast-months, the first 10 predictions are correct, but the last 2 are inaccurate. The following month there are 3 errors. The number of incorrect forecast-months increases by 1 per month until, in the month of the peak or trough, all 12 sign predictions are incorrect. The total number of errors made during the phase is the sum of the digits from 1 to 12, or 78. Thus, for any cycle phase which exceeds 11 months in length, the number of incorrect forecast-months is 78, and the percentage of accuracy depends simply on the length of the phase. In the unusual case of an expansion or contraction shorter than a year, fewer errors are made. For example, the total number of inaccurate forecast-months for a 10-month contraction is the sum of the digits from 3 to 12, or 75,[1] since 3 errors are made in the month immediately following the upturn.

The scoring of naïve forecasts assumes that reference-cycle turning points can be recognized at once and can always be distinguished from "wiggles." Since this simplifying unrealistic assumption is also employed below in evaluating other predictive techniques, no bias is introduced in the comparison of alternative forecasting methods.

The distribution of durations of past cycle phases provides another possible method of predicting turning points. The National Bureau chronology supplies information on the typical duration of past business cycles. It shows, for example, that only 2 of the 25 expansions from 1854 to 1957 lasted less than 15 months. Therefore, after an expansion has proceeded for just 3 months, a forecaster can feel relatively safe in predicting no turning point for the year ahead, providing he is willing to extrapolate past behavior. Suppose, however, that the economy is still expanding 27 months after a trough and that a forecast must be made at that point. Twelve of the 25 recorded expansions lasted less than 27 months; the records of these are irrelevant to the forecast. The significant historical data are confined to expansions of 27 months or longer. The prediction must be based on the conditional distribution of lengths of expansions which survived at 27 months. Of these 13 expansions, only 5 lasted through the next 12 months; the other 8 expansions had durations between 27 and 38 months. In these 8 cases errors would result from reliance on the naïve model at a time 27 months after the trough. The historical data can be used to improve on the performance of the naïve model. Suppose a 12-month forecast was made for each of the 13 expansions surviving 27 months after the trough and that the prediction is for x +'s followed by $(12 - x)$ −'s. The predicted duration is then $(27 + x)$ months. The number of forecast-month errors is then the absolute difference between the actual duration of each phase and $(27 + x)$ for any expansion lasting less than 39 months; for a phase with a duration of 39 months or more, the number of errors made is simply $(12 - x)$. Hence the number of forecast-month errors for the 13 historical expansions is minimized when the predicted turning point is placed at the *median* length of all expansions with durations of 27 months or more. The median is optimal because the total of absolute deviations of a set of items is minimized when those deviations are measured from the median. In this instance the median length of all expansions lasting 27 months or more is 36 months. Thus the median length remaining at 27 months is 9 months. The optimum 12-month forecast is thus for 9 +'s followed by 3 −'s.[2]

In any situation where the median length remaining of past surviving expansions equals or exceeds 12 months, no turning point is predicted for the year ahead. In the earlier example considered, when a forecast had to be made 3 months after the trough, the median length remaining was 24 months. In such instances the prediction for the next 12 months corresponds with the naïve model.

The distributions of lengths of expansions and contractions are recorded in the Figures 1 and 2. In these, National Bureau data are arranged to supply the information required for predictions of median remaining

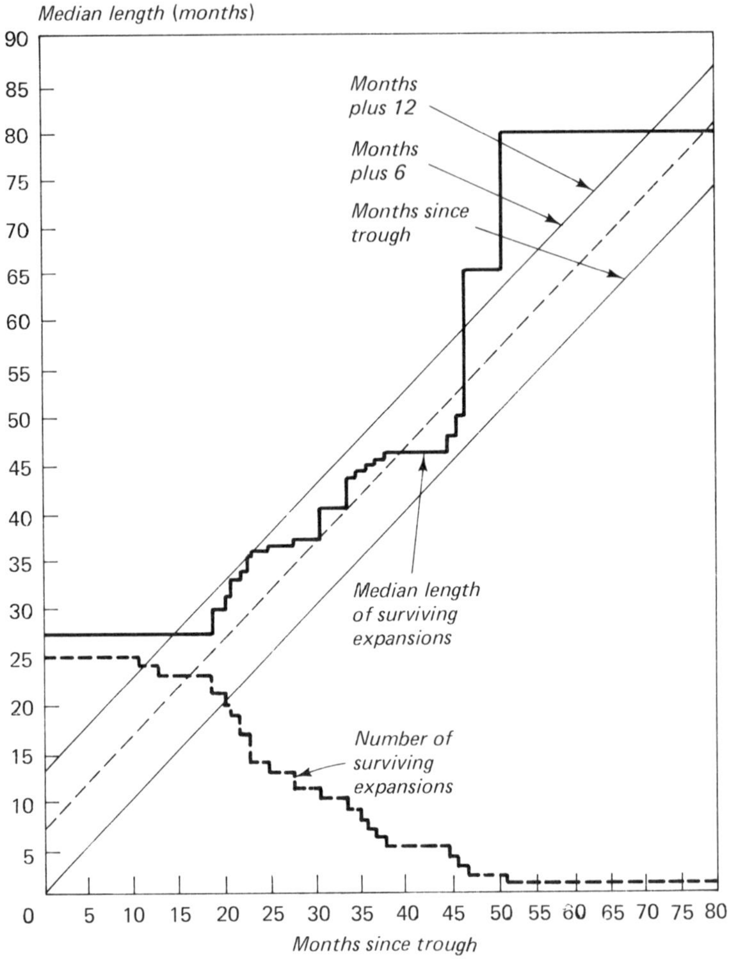

Figure 1 Median length of expansions, December, 1854–July, 1957.

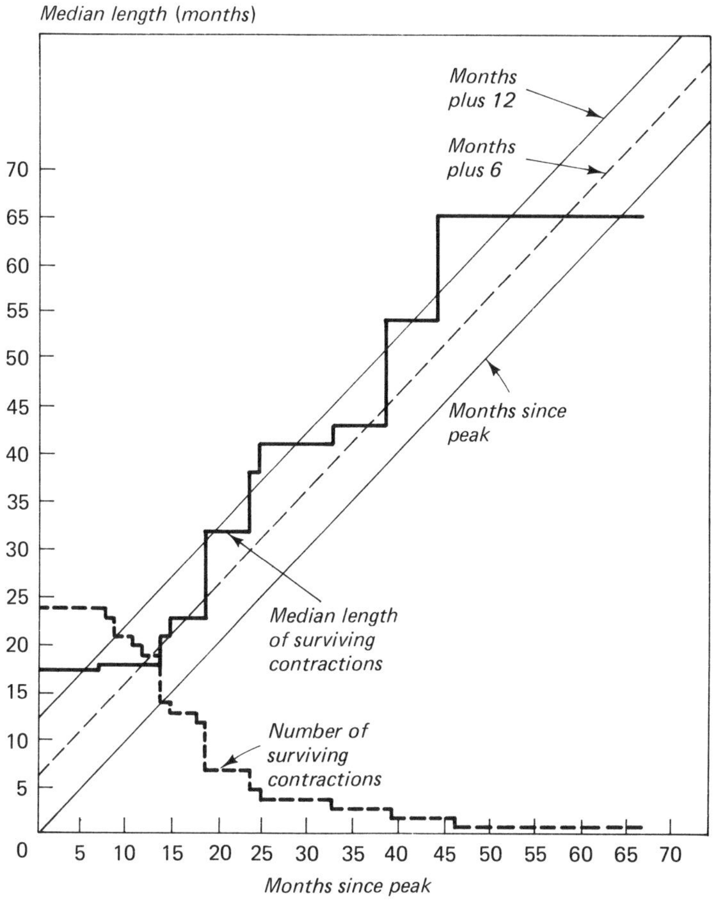

Figure 2 Median length of contractions, June, 1857–August, 1954.

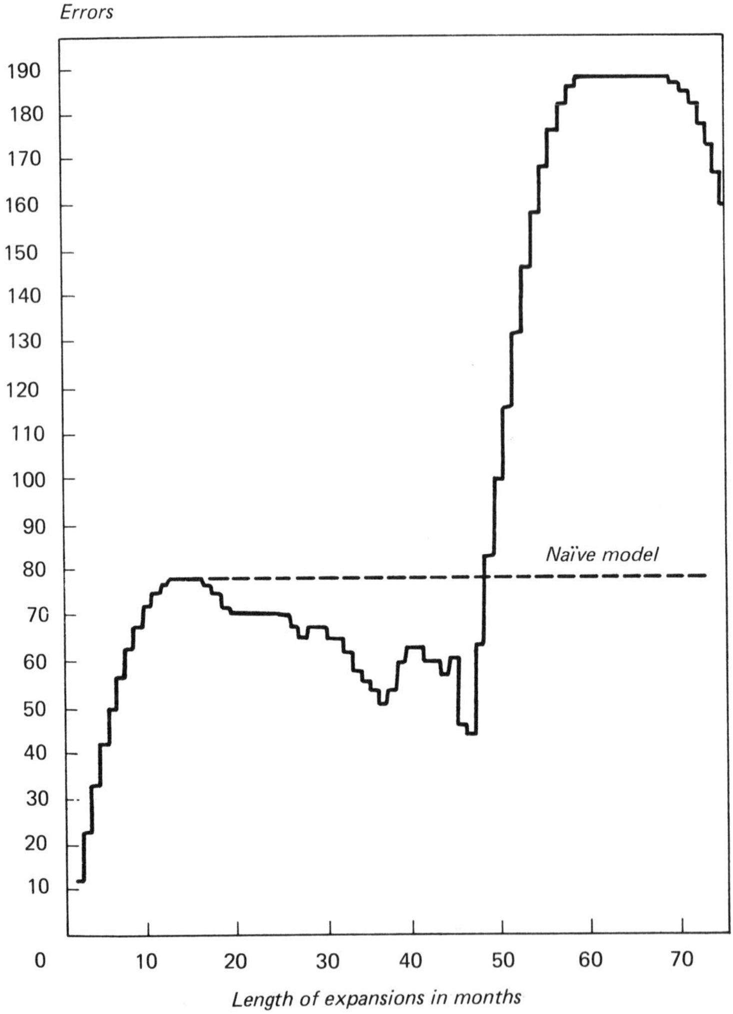

Figure 3 Forecast errors using median remaining-length model, expansions.

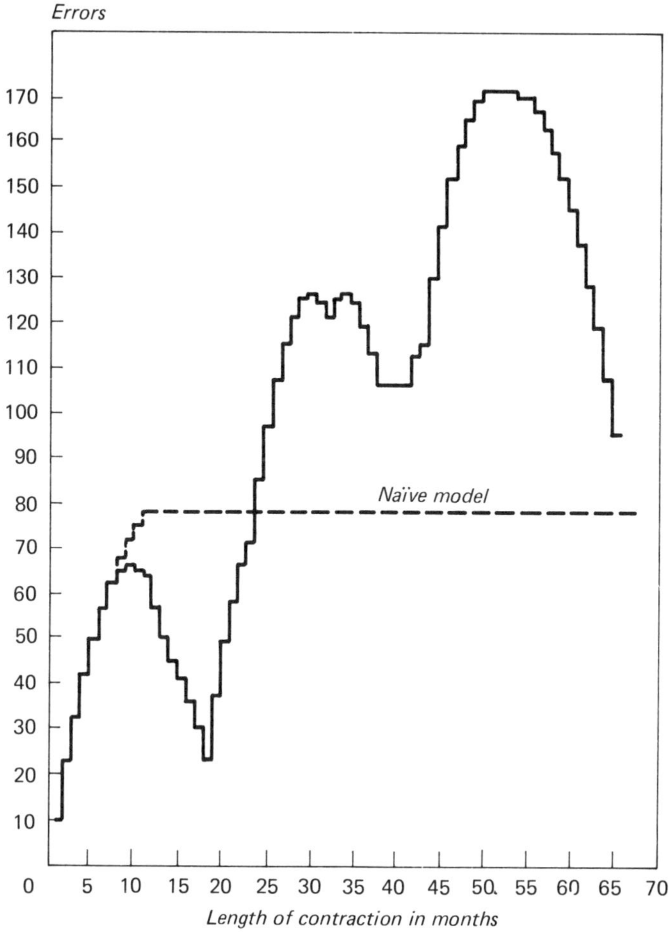

Figure 4 Forecast errors using median remaining-length model, contractions.

length at any point in an expansion or contraction. The figures are constructed to show the median length of all expansions (or contractions) which lasted at least as long as the number of months shown along the horizontal axis. A diagonal line of unit slope is drawn through the origin on each figure. The vertical distance between this 45° line and the median length shown above it is the median length remaining for all surviving expansions (or contractions). For example, 31 months after a trough, the median remaining length of the 10 surviving expansions is 41 – 31, or 10 months. Lines of unit slope with intercepts of 6 months and 12 months, respectively, are also drawn on the diagrams as guides for measuring median remaining lengths. Whenever the curve showing "Median Length of Surviving Expansions" lies above the "Months plus 12" line, the forecast for the coming year coincides with the naïve model.

For 15 months after the start of the expansion and for 6 months after the onset of recession, no turning point is predicted for the next year. Then the median remaining lengths decline to 6–12 months for an expansion in a region of 15–35 months after the trough. During a contraction the corresponding median remaining lengths run 4–13 months over the period 6–24 months after the peak. Over these ranges, as time passes and shorter-lived phases die out, median remaining lengths vary considerably in an unsystematic manner. However, there is no general tendency for the median length remaining to decline. Thus there is little support for the view that old expansions have a short life-expectancy.[3]

The performance of the median remaining-length model is shown for expansions and contractions, respectively, in Figures 3 and 4. The total number of incorrect forecast-months per cycle phase is shown for phases of varying lengths. For very short expansions or contractions, median remaining-length forecasts coincide with the naïve model. For expansions lasting between 15 and 47 months, median remaining-length predictions made 45–70 forecast-month errors in contrast with the 78 of the naïve model. For contractions lasting 6–24 months, the median remaining-length model is superior to the naïve forecast; for durations in the range of 17–21 months, fewer than 40 errors are made. Only for the atypical expansion longer than 47 months or the atypical contraction longer than 24 months is median remaining length inferior. In such long phases the premature forecasts of turning points by the median remaining-length model increase the error total.[4]

Turning-point predictions are most frequently based on the use of leading indicators which are expected to display peaks and troughs in advance of the reference-cycle turning points. Such barometric behavior may be sought in time series of individual economic variables; in a diffusion index which records the percentage expanding of a large number of economic time series; or in a quantitative measure of the rate of change of one or more economic variables. A downturn or upturn in the leading indicator is taken as a signal of a forthcoming reversal in general business activity.

If a leading series is to be used as a turning-point predictor, an expected lead must be attached to the indicator. If the expected lead of a particular series during expansions is 7 months, then, once it displays a downturn, the forecaster should predict a downturn in general business activity 7 months hence. It is assumed here that, in the next month following the signal, the downturn is predicted 6 months in the future; 2 months after the signal, the forecast is for 5 +'s followed by 7 −'s. Thus, once the expected date of a downturn is fixed by the signal, that date is not altered during the period of the expected lead, provided no downturn is experienced. If no reference-cycle turn takes place within 7 months after the signal, the forecaster is assumed to predict an imminent downturn (i.e., 12 −'s) in each succeeding month until the turning point occurs. Whenever no signal has been given by the leading indicator, the forecast is here taken to be equivalent to the naïve model, that is, that no turn will occur within the coming year.

Hypothetical scores for varying expected and actual leads are shown in Table 1. Only when the indicator signals vary prematurely can it be worse than the naïve forecast. For example, when the expected lead of a predictor is 5 months, an actual lead of 18 months produces an error total of 128. On the other hand, if an indicator with an expected lead of 5 months has an actual lead of 1 month, it still reduces the error total to 70 as compared with the 78 errors of the naïve model. When such a case occurs during an expansion, the forecast made in the month of the downturn of the leading indicator is 4 +'s followed by 8 −'s. The downward movement of the reference cycle begins at once because the actual lead is only 1 month; hence, the 4 +'s are errors, but the 8 −'s are correct. All 12 forecast-months of the naïve model would be inaccurate at that point.

If the leading indicator fails to signal prior to a cyclical turning point, the forecaster is still capable of recognizing the turn in the reference cycle. Whenever there is no signal, the indicator produces the same forecast-month error total as the naïve model, usually 78. Hence a lag of 6 months by the indicator is no worse than a lag of 1 month.

Table 1 Scoring of errors for leading series with varying hypothetical leads[a]

Expected lead in months	Actual lead in months																				
	0	1	2	3	4	5	6	7	8	9	10	11	12	13	14	15	16	17	18	19	20
1	78	66	56	48	42	38	36	36	38	42	48	56	66	78	90	102	114	126	138	150	162
2	78	67	55	47	41	37	35	35	36	41	47	55	65	77	89	101	113	125	137	149	161
3	78	68	57	45	39	35	33	33	35	39	45	53	63	75	87	99	111	123	135	147	159
4	78	69	59	48	36	32	30	30	32	36	42	50	60	72	84	96	108	120	132	144	156
5	78	70	61	51	40	28	26	26	28	32	38	46	56	68	80	92	104	116	128	140	152
6	78	71	63	54	44	33	21	21	23	27	33	41	51	63	75	87	99	111	123	135	147
7	78	72	65	57	48	38	27	15	17	21	27	35	45	57	69	81	93	105	117	129	141
8	78	73	67	60	52	43	33	22	10	14	20	28	38	50	62	74	86	98	110	122	134
9	78	74	69	63	56	48	39	29	18	6	12	20	30	42	54	66	78	90	102	114	126
10	78	75	71	66	60	53	45	36	26	15	3	11	21	33	45	57	69	81	93	105	117
11	78	76	73	69	64	58	51	43	34	24	13	1	11	23	35	47	59	71	83	95	107
12	78	77	75	72	68	63	57	50	42	33	23	12	0	12	24	36	48	60	72	84	96

a. Scores apply to expansions or contractions lasting 12 months or more.

The table of errors shows that the value of a leading indicator in forecast-month scoring depends on:

1. The reliability with which it leads, that is, the fraction of all phases in which the signal precedes the reference-cycle peak or trough.
2. The length of the lead. A consistent lead of 3 months produces 45 errors per phase, improving on the naïve model by 12 + 11 + 10, or 33 forecast-months; a consistent lead of 6 months yields only 21 errors per phase.
3. The stability of the lead. An indicator with an expected lead of 4 months which has variable actual leads of 2 and 6 months is inferior to a series with a consistent lead of 4 months.[5]

The expected lead for any indicator should be selected in light of the scoring system. In historical data employed below, the expected lead for each indicator in expansions is taken as the median lead of all cases in which the series displayed a peak prior to the corresponding peak of the reference cycle. The same method is used to derive an expected lead for contractions. It cannot be demonstrated that this is an optimal selection. It is generally true that the expected lead should be established solely from cases where the indicator has led, since the series is never used as a predictor in those instances where it lags (or is coincident with) the reference-cycle turning point. Beyond this principle, the optimum choice for the expected lead will depend on the assumed distribution of actual leads of the indicator. For certain plausible distributions of leads, the median lead is smaller than the ideal expected lead because of the heavy penalty that forecast-month scoring places on very premature signals. It is also here assumed that the expected lead at the time of the signal is independent of the number of months that have elapsed since the preceding reference-cycle turning point. The expected lead is taken to be the same when a downturn of a leading indicator is experienced 3 months after a trough as when it occurs 20 months after a trough. The data provide rough support for the use of the median and for the assumption of independence, but the number of observations on the behavior of any leading series is far too small for a thorough exploration of alternative forcasting rules.

In using the National Bureau's historical data on statistical indicators, one assumes, in effect, that specific-cycle turning points can be identified as soon as they occur and that no "wiggle" of a series is ever misinterpreted as a genuine cycle turn. In fact, distinguishing turns from wiggles may take several months. Of course, the naïve and median remaining-length

Table 2 Performance of alternative indicators of cyclical peaks, 1879–1937 (indicators combined with naïve model monthly predictions for 12-month forecast period)

Expansion	Moore's diffusion index (expected lead = 9)		Business failures (expected lead = 11)		Median remaining-length model errors
	Lead	Errors	Lead	Errors	
March, 1879–March, 1882	26	198	25	167	51
May, 1885–March, 1887	16	78	16	59	71
April, 1888–July, 1890	10	12	23	143	65
May, 1891–January, 1893	5	48	5	58	71
June, 1894–December, 1895	6	39	15	47	72
June, 1897–June, 1899	3	63	*	78	71
December, 1900–September, 1902	9	6	17	71	71
August, 1904–May, 1907	19	114	19	95	58
June, 1908–January, 1910	5	48	4	64	71
January, 1912–January, 1913	10	12	*	78	78
December, 1914–August, 1918	33	282	*	78	61
April, 1919–January, 1920	6	39	5	58	72
July, 1921–May, 1923	9	6	*	78	71
July, 1924–October, 1926	21	138	7	43	65
November, 1927–June, 1929	8	18	4	64	71
March, 1933–May, 1937	8	18	4	64	116
Total forecast-months	4,836				
Total naïve errors	1,242				
Percentage correct forecasts with naïve model		74.3			
Total errors using Moore's diffusion index	1,119				
Percentage correct forecasts using Moore's diffusion index		76.9			
Total errors using business-failures series	1,245				

Percentage correct forecasts using business-failure series		74.3
Total errors using median length-remaining model	1,135	
Percentage correct forecasts using median length-remaining model		76.5

* Indicator failed to signal prior to cyclical turning point.

Table 3 Performance of alternative indicators of cyclical troughs, 1882–1938 (indicators combined with naïve model monthly predictions for 12-month forecast period)

Contraction	Moore's diffusion index (expected lead = 7)		Business failures (expected lead = 8)		Median remaining-length model errors
	Lead	Errors	Lead	Errors	
March, 1882–May, 1885	12	45	12	38	106
March, 1887–April, 1888	2	65	8	10	50
July, 1890–May, 1891	4	48	6	33	65
January, 1893–June, 1894	10	27	13	50	30
December, 1895–June, 1897	10	27	9	14	23
June, 1899–December, 1900	5	38	7	22	23
September, 1902–August, 1904	12	45	13	50	71
May, 1907–June, 1908	7	15	6	33	50
January, 1910–January, 1912	18	117	*	78	85
January, 1913–December, 1914	7	15	6	33	71
August, 1918–April, 1919	5	38	*	68	65
January, 1920–July, 1921	7	15	*	78	23
May, 1923–July, 1924	4	48	9	14	45
October, 1926–November, 1927	10	27	7	22	50
June, 1929–March, 1933	31	273	8	10	141
May, 1937–June, 1938	7	15	3	60	50
Total forecast-months	3,696				
Total naïve errors	1,235				
Percentage correct forecasts with naïve model		66.6			
Total errors using Moore's diffusion index	858				
Percentage correct forecasts using Moore's diffusion index		76.8			
Total errors using business-failures series	613				

Percentage correct forecasts using business-failures series		83.4
Total errors using median length-remaining model	948	
Percentage correct forecasts using median length-remaining model		74.4

* Indicator failed to signal prior to cyclical turning points.

models above were also evaluated as though reference-cycle turning points were recognizable at once, so that the advantage given to leading-series forecasts may not be very large.

Tables 2 and 3 present the results obtained from Moore's diffusion index of all conforming series[6] and from the series on business failures (inverted), which is one of the National Bureau leading series. The period covered is 1879–1938, and the expected leads are derived from observations over this period in the manner described above. The results of median remaining-length and naïve forecasts are presented for comparison. The derivation of expected leads from data of the test period works to the advantage of the National Bureau indicators. Median remaining lengths are drawn from 1854–1957, which, of course, includes the test period. The naïve model alone is not guilty of overworking the data.

For expansions, the data show that the diffusion-index scores best, but its margin over median remaining length is very slight; and these two methods are only a little superior to business failures and the naïve model. Of the four predictive devices, the diffusion index earns the top accuracy score in 11 of the 16 expansions covered. However, it goes astray badly in a few instances. Two premature signals, in 1879–82 and 1914–18, account for nearly two-fifths of all errors made by the diffusion index.

For contractions, there are greater differences in accuracy among the four methods. The percentage accuracy of the naïve model is smaller than in expansions, simply because contractions are shorter. Median remaining length is substantially better than the naïve model, with about one-fourth fewer errors. The diffusion index stands slightly better than median remaining length; again its performance is seriously impaired by two premature signals, in 1910–12 and 1929–33. Greatest accuracy is shown by the business-failures series; its error total is only half that of the naïve model. The business-failures indicator does not signal in 4 of the 16 contractions, while the diffusion index signals in all instances; but business failure earns a higher score because it does not have markedly premature signals.

Tables 4 and 5 show results obtained from historical data on eight leading series for the 1920–54 period with expected leads derived from these years. For expansions, five of the eight indicators are inferior to the naïve model, and only one, hours worked per week, improves substantially on the naïve results. The superiority of the work week emerges

Table 4 Performance of alternative indicators of cyclical peaks, 1921–53 (indicators combined with naïve model monthly predictions for 12-month forecast period; errors = forecast-months with incorrect sign)

Expansion	Expected lead	July, '21– May, '23 errors	July, '24– Oct., '26 errors	Nov., '27– June, '29 errors	Mar., '33– May, '37 errors	June, '38– Feb., '45 errors	Oct., '45– Nov., '48 errors	Oct., '49– July, '53 errors	Total errors	Errors as percentage of naïve model
Business failures (inverted)	6	78*	21	44	44	78*	78*	243	586	107.3
Common-stock prices	5	61	78*	78*	51	78*	272	26	644	117.9
New orders	6	44	41	78*	33	327	33	21	577	105.7
Residential building contracts	15	78*	12	12	78	78*	180	78*	516	94.5
Commercial and industrial building contracts	11	24	23	58	78*	78*	251	78*	590	108.1
Average hours worked per week	7	27	35	78*	65	17	78*	15	315	57.7
No. of incorporations	5	70	56	28	28	78*	272	78*	610	111.7
Wholesale price index	11	73	1	83	73	78*	13	215	536	98.2
Naïve model		78	78	78	78	78	78	78	546	100.0
Median length-remaining model		71	65	71	116	110	54	46	533	97.6
First two indicators	13	63	0	36	68	50	204	180	601	110.1
First three indicators	5	40	56	28	40	78*	272	26	540	98.9
First four indicators	6	63	41	33	54	78*	267	21	557	102.0
First five indicators	5	61	46	40	51	78*	38	26	340	62.3
First six indicators	4	69	50	78*	59	78*	32	78*	444	81.3
First seven indicators	5	78*	26	78*	61	78*	78*	78*	477	87.4

* Indicator failed to signal prior to cyclical turning point.

Table 5 Performance of alternative indicators of cyclical troughs, 1920–54 (indicators combined with naïve model monthly predictions for 12-month forecast period; errors = forecast-months with incorrect sign)

Contraction	Expected lead	Jan., '20– July, '21 errors	May, '23– July, '24 errors	Oct., '26– Nov., '27 errors	June, '29– Mar., 33 errors	May, '37– June, '38 errors	Feb., '45– Oct., '45 errors	Nov., '48– Oct., '49 errors	July, '53– Aug., '54 errors	Total errors	Errors as percentage of naïve model
Business failures (inverted)	7	78*	21	15	17	57	68*	26	27	309	50.4
Common-stock prices	9	78*	6	78*	6	69	68*	55	20	380	62.0
New orders	3	33	57	78*	78*	57	47	44	39	433	70.6
Residential building contracts	6	21	78*	21	54	21	68*	26	78*	367	59.9
Commercial and industrial building contracts	3	39	78*	57	35	78*	68*	56	78*	489	79.8
Average hours worked per week	5	28	78*	78*	28	26	68*	39	40	385	62.8
No. of incorporations	6	21	71	41	78*	78*	68*	20	78*	455	74.2
Wholesale price index	1	66	66	38	66	78*	68*	41	78*	501	81.7
Naïve model		78	78	78	78	78	68	77	78	613	100.0
Median length-remaining model		23	45	50	141	50	65	62	50	486	79.3
First two indicators	7	27	21	15	17	27	68*	28	21	224	36.5
First three indicators	6	21	63	21	23	54	68*	21	21	292	47.6
First four indicators	4	32	69	32	32	59	68*	36	36	364	59.4
First five indicators	3	39	68	57	45	57	68*	39	78*	451	73.6
First six indicators	1	66	66	78*	66	78*	68*	42	78*	542	88.4
First seven indicators	3	78*	78*	78*	78*	78*	68*	45	78*	581	94.8

* Indicator failed to signal prior to cyclical turning point.

because it alone displays no seriously premature signal over the period. All other indicators are marred by a very large error total for either 1938–45, 1945–48, or 1949–53. Thus the favorable verdict for the work week rests on a difference of one observation. Because wholesale prices and new orders had one early signal, their scores are far inferior to the work week's error total. Clearly, the fact that the work week has no premature signals in seven observations does not by any means warrant the conclusion that this indicator has a zero propensity to give premature signals. The data provide no firm ground for selection among the leading indicators.

In an attempt to eliminate the seriously premature signals during expansions, the eight leading indicators were pooled to form another predictive device, that of "first n indicators." Here all eight leading series are treated equivalently, and the nth downturn among the eight indicators is taken as the signal for predicting the reference-cycle peak. If $n = 3$, for example, the signal is given when the third downturn among the leading series is observed, no matter which three of the eight indicators are the earliest to turn down. The expected lead is again taken as the median of actual leads. If $n = 8$, no signal occurs until all eight leading series experience a downturn. In fact, for the seven expansions covered, one or more leading series lagged the reference-cycle peak so the method of first eight indicators coincides throughout with the naïve model. Results for n running from 2 to 7 are shown in Table 4. With first two indicators, there are two bad early signals; one premature signal occurs when the first three and first four indicators are used. None of these improves significantly on the naïve model. However, when forecasts are based on first five indicators, there is no seriously premature signal, and a substantial gain is made over the other predictive techniques. In one expansion, first five indicators lags the cyclical turning point; in the other six cases, it is superior to both the naïve and the median remaining-length models. First six indicators and first seven indicators lag behind at a number of reference peaks and hence do not match first five indicators in predictive accuracy. The favorable performance of first five indicators makes this pooling technique seem promising, but no stronger conclusions are justified.

Contractions again present a very different story on the performance of leading series. As Table 5 shows, each of the eight leading indicators is superior to the naïve model. Median remaining length is considerably more accurate than the naïve method but not so good as six of the eight

Table 6 Performance of indicators combined with median remaining length (monthly predictions of peaks, 1921–53, for 12-month forecast period; errors = forecast-months with incorrect sign)

Expansion	Expected lead	July, '21– May, '23 errors	July, '24– Oct., '26 errors	Nov., '27– June, '29 errors	Mar., '33– May, '37 errors	June, '38– Feb., '45 errors	Oct., '45– Nov., '48 errors	Oct., '49– July, '53 errors	Total errors	Errors as percentage of naïve model
Business failures (inverted)	6	71*	14	44	82	110*	54*	246	621	113.7
Common-stock prices	5	54	65*	71*	89	110*	272	43	704	128.9
New orders	6	38	40	71*	79	429	23	38	718	131.5
Residential building contracts	15	71*	12	12	116	110*	180	46*	547	100.2
Commerical and industrial building contracts	11	24	23	58	116*	110*	251	46*	628	115.0
Average hours worked per week	7	26	34	71*	103	117	54*	37	442	81.0
No. of incorporations	5	63	56	28	74	110*	272	46*	649	118.9
Wholesale price index	11	66	0	83	111	110*	20	216	606	111.0
Naïve model		78	78	78	78	78	78	78	546	100.0
Median remaining-length model		71	65	71	116	110	54	46	533	97.6

* Indicator failed to signal prior to cyclical turning point.

Table 7 Performance of indicators combined with median remaining length (monthly predictions of troughs, 1920–54, for 12-month forecast period; errors = forecast months with incorrect sign)

Contraction	Expected lead	Jan., '20– July, '21 errors	May, '23– July, '24 errors	Oct., '26– Nov., '27 errors	June, '29– Mar., '33 errors	May, '37– June, '38 errors	Feb., '45– Oct., '45 errors	Nov., '48– Oct., '49 errors	July, '53– Aug., '54 errors	Total errors	Errors as percentage of naïve model
Business failures (inverted)	7	23*	21	15	84	47	65*	26	26	307	50.1
Common-stock prices	9	23*	6	50*	75	54	65*	54	20	347	56.6
New orders	3	12	36	50*	141*	42	47	41	39	408	66.6
Residential building contracts	6	6	45*	20	118	20	65*	26	50*	350	57.1
Commerical and industrial building contracts	3	6	45*	42	99	50*	65*	50	50*	407	66.4
Average hours worked per week	5	0	45*	50*	95	25	65*	38	34	352	57.4
No. of incorporations	6	0	43	41	141*	50*	65*	20	50*	410	66.9
Wholesale price index	1	18	38	35	129	50*	65*	40	50*	425	69.3
Naïve model		78	78	78	78	78	68	77	78	613	100.0
Median remaining-length model		23	45	50	141	50	65	62	50	486	79.3

*Indicator failed to signal prior to cyclical turning point.

leading series. Business failures, residential building contracts, common-stock prices, and the work week are particularly successful. Although premature signals create no problem during contractions, the method of first *n* indicators seemed worth exploring. As Table 5 reveals, first two indicators performs impressively with an error total only 36.5 per cent as large as that of the naïve model. When *n* is increased, the degree of accuracy falls consistently.

Tables 6 and 7 show the results obtained from the same set of leading indicators for 1920–54 when the forecasting rules are slightly modified. Here, prior to the leading-series signal, the forecast is derived from the median remaining-length model (based on 1854–1957) rather than the naïve model. There are only slight differences between these results and those of the two preceding tables. Typically, the differences stand in favor of the combination of leading series and the naïve model rather than the combination of leading series and median remaining length. This is somewhat surprising, since, taken alone, median remaining-length forecasts are superior to the naïve model. Logically, if the median remaining-length model is to be employed in the period prior to a signal, the estimate of remaining length at any point should be derived only from those surviving phases in which there has been no signal. However, there are no data on many indicators prior to World War I, and hence such calculations cannot be made on the 1854–1957 chronology.

When forecast-month scoring is applied to leading series, two outstanding characteristics of the system of appraisal become evident. These are that the penalty placed on a failure to signal is relatively light, while the penalty on a premature signal can be very heavy. A leading series is supposed to lead, and its failure to signal deprives the forecaster of the benefit he seeks from reliance on the series. However, if a signal comes too soon and persuades the forecaster to insist incorrectly for a year that a turning point is imminent, the early signal is more harmful than no signal at all, according to forecast-month scoring. This result emerges from the assumptions underlying the system of appraisal. These assumptions apply strictly to a situation where the policy-maker forms a decision for each month of the year ahead and pays a fixed penalty for each decision based on an incorrect sign expectation. Under these conditions the costs of misguided decisions produced by an early signal can easily exceed the penalty resulting when no signal occurs. While this model does not describe the actual forecasting and decision-making situation precisely, it serves as an acceptable approximation and its results seem plausible. Premature signals may in fact do more harm than good. A forecaster who warned of an impending recession throughout 1947 and 1948 deserves lower scores than one who insisted that the postwar boom would continue throughout this period and recognized the 1948–49 recession only when it could be read from current data. Indeed, it is surprising how much emphasis has been placed on the desirability of predicting the turn and how little concern there has been for the danger of forecasting it too soon.

It may be argued, however, that the costs attached to unwarranted bullishness in fact exceed those resulting from unwarranted bearishness and that planning should therefore lean to the conservative side. In this view, preparations made for a slump that is distant may be much less costly than failure to anticipate the slump. By the same reasoning, delayed response to an upturn must be less serious than premature expectation of the expansion. If the argument is accepted, forecast-month scoring can be easily amended to weight Type I errors more heavily in expansions and Type II errors more heavily in contractions. However, the case does not seem convincing. If there is a particular desire to hedge against recession, it should be incorporated in the decision rules by which the forecasts are utilized; it need not color the forecasts. Even without the counsel of learned economists, policy-makers know that booms are followed by slumps. From that knowledge alone, they can take precautions against a downturn. One important but expensive precaution is to retain flexibility of action in the event of an unforeseen downturn. The forecaster of turning points can aid the policy-maker by improving the estimate of the data of the next reversal in economic activity and by reducing the need for costly flexibility. These functions are not fulfilled by premature signals of slumps.

Comparisons of individual leading series with naïve forecasts during expansions show that the indicators are superior to the naïve model for the majority of phases and yet emerge with an overall unfavorable verdict because of one or two extremely bad cases. This is a paradoxical result if the individual cycle phase is viewed as a unit of observation. However, in forecast-month scoring, calendar time is the dimension for measurement, and, in those terms, there is no paradox. By improving on the naïve model in a few critical months, the leading series will save some 30 or 40 forecast-month errors in most expansions. Then, in the atypical case, it will make perhaps 200 errors more than the naïve model by misguiding the forecaster for two years. The over-all unfavorable verdict means that reliance on a leading indicator is harmful for as many forecast-months as it is helpful. The use of time as a yardstick seems appropriate, and forecast-month scoring requires no modification in this regard.

On the other hand, the frequency of very premature signals in expansions depends on the particular forecasting method adopted for the use of leading series. In order to score the indicators, it was necessary to construct a set of forecasting rules. It was assumed above that, once a signal led the forecaster to expect a turning point in June, he continued to place the turn in June until June passed; if still no turning point occurred, he would tenaciously insist that the turning point was imminent until it occurred. It may be argued that this imputes an unreasonable degree of obstinacy to the forecaster and that any sensible economist would in fact reject the evidence of a premature signal after an appropriate waiting period. An effective shutoff device is certainly needed to reduce the costs of early signals, but the leading indicators do not themselves provide such a device. There is no clear means by which the forecaster can decide when to be persistent and when to reject the signal.[7]

In other respects, the quantitative appraisal is probably generous to the leading indicators. They are favored by the 12-month forecast period in comparison with a shorter period which would accentuate even further the problem of premature signals. The selection of expected leads from the same observations on which the leading series are scored also works to the advantage of the indicators. The use of historical specific-cycle turning points as signals is still another factor which bolsters the scores of the leading indicators.

Leading series have earned a rather good score in predicting troughs and a rather poor score in predicting peaks by the criteria of appraisal advanced above. Only the pooling technique of first *n* indicators offered any promise for the successful use of leading series during expansions. But these empirical findings should be carefully qualified. This study has been intended to present and discuss a method of scoring rather than to evaluate comprehensively the predictive accuracy of turning-point indicators. The empirical results cannot be readily applied to an actual forecasting situation. In particular, the findings above rely on historical reference-cycle and specific-cycle dates which are not available to the forecaster in practice. In actual predictions, distinguishing wiggles from genuine turning points is a serious and difficult problem.

Unlike the hindcasting procedure explored above, actual predictions of turning points must determine when a reversal in a leading series is to be taken as a genuine signal and when a reversal in business activity is to be taken as a reference-cycle turn.[8] However, actual forecasting faces, in addition, all of the problems discussed in this paper. It requires a rule for predicting prior to the signal; it must associate an expected lead with the signal; and it needs a shutoff device to reduce the errors produced by premature signals. Moreover, forecasting in practice requires a criterion of accuracy for the selection and evaluation of optimal predictive techniques. Forecast-month scoring is submitted here as one eligible method of appraisal.

Notes

This paper was written as part of the project in Research on Short-Term Economic Forecasting conducted at the Cowles Foundation for Research in Economics at Yale University and financed by the Rockefeller Foundation. I am indebted to Mrs. Wilma W. Heston for her valuable assistance in processing the data presented below. Dr. Geoffrey Moore, of the National Bureau of Economic Research, kindly provided me with data and also offered helpful criticisms. The F. W. Dodge Corporation authorized the release of its data on construction contracts. I am also grateful to Harry Eisenpress, William Fellner, Todd May, Richard Porter, Robert Summers, and James Tobin for their constructive suggestions.

1. Strictly speaking, fewer errors are also made in the preceding cycle phase. Consider the expansion just before the 10-month contraction. In the month of the peak, 12 +'s are predicted, and the last 2 of these are actually correct. However, it seems reasonable not to credit the naïve for these, since it misses the intervening contraction. The same rule is applied to more sophisticated methods discussed below.

2. The discussion assumes that there have been no secular changes in the lengths of cycle phases over time. In fact, the chronology shows that contractions since World War I have been shorter, on the average, than previously (see Geoffrey Moore, *Measuring Recessions* ["Occasional Paper," No. 61 (New York: National Bureau of Economic Research, 1958)], p. 260). A few long wartime expansions also are included in the distribution.

3. Despite its careful statement and qualification, Moore's suggestion to this effect (*ibid.*, p. 262) is not confirmed by the historical data shown in Figure 1. When the three long wartime expansions are excluded, however, Moore's opinion gets some support from a range of short and declining median remaining lengths for 29–36 months.

4. With the three long wartime expansions excluded, the median length of expansions is only 22 months. When this distribution is employed for median remaining-length predictions, the results are roughly similar to those shown in Figure 3. However, the exclusion of the wartime phases reduces the number of forecast-month errors for expansions lasting 20–38 months and increases the number of errors in longer expansions.

5. It may seem paradoxical that an indicator with an expected lead of 4 scores better when it leads by 6 than by 4. But, if the series led consistently by 6, forecasting performance could be improved further by attaching an expected lead of 6 months to the indicator.

6. Geoffrey Moore, *Statistical Indicators of Cyclical Revivals and Recessions* ("Occasional Paper," No. 31 [New York: National Bureau of Economic Research, 1950]), pp. 46–47.

7. If sufficient data were available, it would be possible to construct a system based on the median remaining lengths of phases after a signal was experienced. Then, 5 months after an indicator turned, the forecaster would put the turn at the median remaining length of all phases which survived 5 or more months after the signal of that indicator. A large number of observations would be needed to develop this technique.

8. An interesting exploration of the use of current data for predicting cyclical peaks has been made by Sidney S. Alexander, "Rate of Change Approaches to Forecasting: Diffusion Indexes and First Differences," *Economic Journal,* LXVIII (June, 1958), 288–301. His evaluation of alternative forecasting methods depends on the number of "true" and "false" signals given by the indicators, where false leads are those which reverse themselves. In terms of forecast-month scoring, however, the reversal criterion is not satisfactory. It must be supplemented by consideration of the timing of "false" signals, shutoffs, and "true" signals.

The Predictive Value of Surveys of Business Intentions

Whatever knowledge we have about the future of the economy is derived from evidence on its history and its present state. Some of our information enters into theoretical relationships involving causes and their effects. By understanding how firms and consumers have reacted to certain situations and changes in the past and by quantifying these relations, we expect to predict their reactions in the future to present conditions and recently observed changes. These causal relationships have been the principal traditional concern of economists; they are the study of how the economy works. But the record also gives us some information about the recent and current state of the economy which does not fit into these causal patterns. The new orders and commitments of firms for capital goods are not a determinant of their spending. They are a reflection of decisions to spend. Similarly, investment intentions collected by surveys are symptomatic, and not causal, factors in the outlook.

A prediction of investment based on profits, liquidity, capacity utilization, and other variables that enter into a firm's ability and incentives to invest is genuinely different from one that rests in part on new orders or capital spending intentions. There is a distinct preference among economists for the former kind of relationship. It explains as well as predicts; it relates investment activity to its fundamental causes rather than to their shadows. This preference can be supported on broader grounds than elegance and aesthetics. If the best explanation of investment behavior also provides the best forecasting technique, prediction and explanation need not be separate activities and no diffusion of the profession's resources is required. But it would be pure coincidence if the optimum path to explanation were also the best route to a forecast. If noncausal, symptomatic variables enhance our limited ability to predict, we are obliged to exploit the opportunity. To assess the opportunity, we are first required to determine the predictive value of noncausal series.

A variable has predictive value if it makes a positive contribution to the accuracy of forecasting as an addition to other available information. No survey datum needs to be considered as a potential substitute for anything else we know. Investment intentions data do not stop us from observing profits, sales, or excess capacity and including these in the raw materials used to forecast. The forecaster's tool kit should have plenty of room for both causal and noncausal variables.

The Failure of Sales Expectations

The kit need not contain every recorded time series. Many measures of business expectations do not appear to have direct predictive value, although they have considerable theoretical interest to economists. In some instances, poor predictions can provide indirect assistance in prediction and hence do belong in the forecaster's tool kit. Sales expectations are an interesting example: they do not have direct predictive value; but they are of analytical interest and can be used to improve investment forecasts. Though not everyone would agree, I think the record contains persuasive evidence that sales expectations expressed by individual firms offer a poor forecast of economy-side sales—no better than a simple mechanical extrapolation of recent levels and not able to complement objective economic variables directly.

In January and February of each year, businessmen responding to the Commerce-SEC plant and equipment survey are asked for both their sales and investment expectations covering the full calendar year. While the investment intentions have clear predictive value, the sales expectations do not. The annual predictions of sales by manufacturers covering 1948–61 show no bias—they are as likely to be too high as too low, producing a mean underestimate over the entire period of less than 1 per cent. But the sales expectations have a wide dispersion around the realized sales level. The root-mean-square error of the forecasts is 6 per cent; it represents some improvement over a naïve trend projection of last year's sales, since the actual changes in annual sales have a standard deviation of 8 per cent. But the full-year sales expectations are surpassed in accuracy by a simple extrapolation of the sales level of January (seasonally adjusted). The January sales level predicts better than the firms' expectations for ten out of the fourteen years, and its average absolute error is 4 per cent as compared with 5 per cent for the manufacturers' expectations. According to these observations, the recent data on manufacturers' sales in the statistical tables of the March *Survey of Current Business* have more predictive value than the manufacturers' own sales expectations recorded in the same issue.

It would be easy to assemble a list of results where businessmen score low grades collectively as sales forecasters. I always find such results remarkable in the light of appealing analytical reasons why a collection of the sales expectations registered by individual firms should have predictive value. Firms should be expected individually to have some "feel" of their markets, even though they cannot control their sales volume. In addition, they use substantial resources in systematic attempts to forecast demand. Is there no return to their experience and expenditure? Has the officer of a firm no information to offer on its sales prospects for a year ahead? The individual firm ought to be able to predict its own sales. And, if the sales expectation of the firm is at all superior to a pure guess, proper enforcement of the law of large numbers ought to produce well-behaved sales forecasts in the aggregate. Even if an individual firm can estimate sales only within 20 per cent, twenty-five firms of equal size with independent errors would be expected to pull the aggregate error down to 4 per cent, and four hundred would reduce it to 1 per cent. Even when the example is discounted for the unequal sizes of firms and for positively related errors, the hypothetical results remain impressive.

This analytical argument has a rather obvious shortcoming: its conclusion does not check with the facts. It seems to go astray because of the exceedingly close positive relationship among errors made by individual firms in a given year, despite the fact that they are independently forecasting their own sales. One possible explanation is that each firm, explicitly or implicitly, approaches its sales forecast through a general appraisal of the over-all economic outlook. To be specific, suppose the individual sales forecast is derived by multiplying an estimated market-share by an estimate of the dollar value of the economy-wide market. Then, to the extent that firms are able to diagnose shifts in market-shares in advance, their individual expectations have predictive value at a microeconomic level. Firms that expect increases in sales would be more likely to experience gains than their less optimistic competitors. But this source of forecasting success for the firm makes no contribution to accuracy in the aggregate. Knowing the probable percentage sharing of a sales-pie among firms does not help to determine the likely size of the pie. Under these assumptions, when economists add up sales forecasts of individual firms, their totals are simply a weighted average of the general business outlook of businessmen where the estimated market-shares are the weights. The aggregated sales prediction would then be no better than the economy-wide forecasts that underlie them. And businessmen may collectively assign to themselves more or less than the whole pie. In that event, with the summed weights differing substantially from unity, the aggregated sales expectations would probably be poorer than the average general business forecast expressed by the same firms. The failure of sales expectations as forecasting devices might be attributable to such a process, but, in my opinion, it remains an intriguing puzzle.

Sales expectations might also be expected to display predictive value for another reason. To the extent that sales expectations influence production, employment, and investment decisions, these expectations would have a self-justifying tendency. Any time businessmen were particularly optimistic as a group, their individual actions would buoy up the economy and tend to realize their bullish sentiments. In this view, aggregated sales forecasts would display accuracy, not because businessmen are talented in forecasting, but because firms collectively control their destinies. Entrepreneurial behavior of this type is portrayed in theoretical literature. Also, in the financial press, the sales forecast is taken as a measure of confidence, and confidence is viewed as an autonomous determinant of the path of the economy. The negative findings on the predictive value of aggregated sales forecasts are not decisive evidence, but they do call for some explanation from proponents of these views.

The economist derives some interesting questions and lessons from sales expectations, even though they offer him no direct assistance in forecasting. To see the contributions of survey data which do have predictive value, I turn to the record of investment intentions.

The Success of Investment Intentions

The investment anticipations reported annually in the Commerce-SEC survey have an impressive record of predictive accuracy. For all industries combined, the deviations between actual and planned capital expenditures have averaged 3 per cent in absolute terms for 1948–61 in contrast with the 9 per cent average absolute annual percentage change in expenditures. I know of no naïve model and no "causal" explanation resting on predetermined variables which rivals the anticipations data in accuracy.

The success of the investment intentions is achieved because the large errors made by individual firms shrink in the aggregation process; here, the microeconomic deviations do display a considerable degree of independence. Investment plans came out so well in the total, not because each firm's intentions are fixed and rigid, but because the departures made by individual firms are likely to go in opposite directions. Nevertheless, there are systematic forces producing departures from plans that affect most firms in the same direction. These stem principally from surprises in the course of the economy. The outstanding example occurred when the Korean war broke out: plant and equipment investment in 1950 rose 2 per cent over 1949, in sharp contrast to the planned 11 per cent decline.

The dependence of investment realizations on developments in the economy is most readily observed for manufacturing industry in the relation between percentage deviations of actual from planned investment, on the one hand, and percentage errors in sales expectations, on the other. Generally when sales differ from expectations, investment plans are revised in the same direction. Only in the strike-affected year of 1959 did sales and investment deviations have opposite signs. Bringing the record up to date, I can report that nearly 80 per cent of the variance in the percentage investment deviations for 1948–61 is explained by a linear regression using percentage sales forecast errors as the independent variable. Each 1 per cent deviation in sales is associated with an expected 1.1 per cent revision of investment from plans. I might add that, to my knowledge, no *ex post* measure explains the investment deviations as well as that employing the sales expectations.

Here, the sales expectations reveal the demand assumptions underlying investment intentions and therefore provide indirect assistance in forecasting capital outlays. By collecting both investment and sales anticipations, the survey data hand us a point on an implicit schedule relating prospective capital outlays to the strength of demand in the year ahead. The historical evidence on investment revisions and sales surprises provides some notion of the shape and slope of that schedule. From his analysis of the rest of the economy, the economic forecaster can relate the strength of total demand to the level of the investment schedule. Putting these two parts together, he can use the survey data on sales to make an *ex ante* adjustment on the investment intentions, in effect substituting his own forecast of sales in place of the expectations of the businessmen.

These findings also relate to the influence of business optimism on economic activity. Given the level of investment intentions, optimistic sales expectations must be viewed as an unfavorable factor for capital outlays. The same volume of capital spending plans with lower expected sales means a higher investment demand schedule. Nevertheless, insofar as the sales expectations had an original influence on the investment plans, they still probably have a positive effect on the capital outlays of the year. Excessive optimism about demand tends to come out in the wash, but there is some indication that incorrect expectations retain their influence in part for a considerable time. According to the percentage changes estimated above, a billion dollar sales-surprise for manufacturers alters capital spending by only about 50 million dollars within the same year. A substantial amount of adjustment must be left for future periods.

The annual Commerce-SEC survey is augmented by quarterly surveys for the rest of the year. In these, near the beginning of a quarter, firms report on their anticipated capital outlays for the current quarter and for the next quarter. The first anticipation thus keeps the forecaster six months ahead of available actual data. It still means that as of now no Commerce-SEC anticipations have been reported beyond the first quarter of 1962. It would be very helpful if the plant and equipment survey could keep us briefed over four quarters ahead throughout the year, but the annual planning practices of firms seem to preclude that possibility.

Over the very short-term horizon they cover, the first anticipations are invaluable aids to forecasting. Thanks to the assistance of Richard Attiyeh, I can offer empirical findings on this matter. They employ first anticipations as predictors of quarterly plant and equipment outlays for 48 quarters from 1949-III to 1961-II.

First anticipations (A) explain nearly 97 per cent of the variance of predicted quarterly plant and equipment outlays (I) and yield a standard error of 0.95 billion dollars (at annual rates). The least squares regression estimate of I on A has a small positive intercept and a slope slightly below unity:

$$I = 1.90 + \underset{(.024)}{.923A} \qquad \text{(in billions of dollars)}$$

While no sales expectations are available in the quarterly survey, one can still find a systematic pattern of plan revision related to developments between the time of the survey and the period of the outlays. The predictive value of the first anticipations is significantly enhanced by the addition of another variable, either the change in corporate profits (ΔP) or the change in gross national product (ΔY) in the intervening quarter. The standard error of estimate declines to 0.85 billion dollars for either of the following equations:

$$I = 1.35 + \underset{(.022)}{.929A} + \underset{(.020)}{.070\Delta Y_{-1}} \tag{a}$$

$$I = 1.35 + \underset{(.022)}{.940A} + \underset{(.044)}{.163\Delta P_{-1}} \tag{b}$$

No causal explanation I have unearthed matches the equations above. After a shameless amount of data mining, my best candidate explains capital outlays with GNP, a measure of liquidity flow, and a variable representing excess capacity. The liquidity flow measure (L) is corporate profits after tax plus corporate capital consumption allowances. It fits better than profits alone. Excess capacity (X) is measured by GNP times the excess of the unemployment rate over 4 per cent. While the dollar output gap will be a multiple of this magnitude because of cyclical conformity of productivity and labor force participation, the regression results do not require such an adjustment. The unemployment measure of excess capacity fits slightly better than measures constructed from a trend calculation of potential output or from direct calculations of capital utilization. All the explanatory variables are lagged one quarter, again because they fit best that way. With all of this explanatory artillery, the equation below has a coefficient of determination of 92 per cent and a standard error of 1.52 billion dollars and is thus considerably inferior to the estimation using the anticipations series:

$$I = 1.13 + \underset{(.008)}{.051Y_{-1}} - \underset{(.046)}{.341X_{-1}} + \underset{(.075)}{.249L_{-1}}$$

Instead of and in addition to the investment intentions data, I have tried the "new investment orders and contracts" series (Series 10 in the Census Bureau's *Business Cycle Developments*). Since the lead-time of this series is not obvious, I have employed lags of one- to three-quarters. Taken alone, it does not nearly match the first anticipations series; taken with the anticipations, the new orders series does not add significantly to the accuracy of the explanation. None of these findings bears on the value of new orders and contracts data for detecting cyclical turning points. But for a quantitative prediction of plant and equipment over the short horizon covered by the quarterly anticipations data, I cannot find any profitable use of the orders and contracts series. Other researchers may be able to show that this reflects my limitations and not those of the series in question.

Other Intentions Series and Additional Candidates

Any discussion of business intentions data can easily turn into a testimonal for the Commerce-SEC survey, with kind words for the extra assistance offered by the McGraw-Hill survey. The area of plant and equipment outlays is the only place where business intentions data have become solidly established as valuable forecasting tools. The new Commerce survey of manufacturers' inventory expectations shows some promise of lengthening the list. The August, 1961, *Survey of Current Business* presented a progress report on the accuracy of inventory forecasts made by firms over a six-month period. The raw survey results covering eight quarters were not encouraging but they took on a new and brighter look after corrections and adjustments were made. The manipulations applied to the data are plausible as well as ingenious, but their success in achieving predictive accuracy in future periods remains to be demonstrated. The inventory survey should not be judged by the same high standards of predictive accuracy established by fixed investment intentions.

Sales expectations are also collected in this survey to supply a bench mark for the inventory anticipations. While it is clear that unforeseen changes in sales will affect inventories, the probable quantitative effects, and even their direction, are not obvious. Over a very short period, larger sales will mean depleted stocks; over a sufficiently long period, unforeseen increments in sales will lead to a build-up of inventories to meet greater demand. The unsolved empirical problem is to translate these propositions into calendar time. Survey data may help to quantify the extent of flexibility and the speed of adjustment in inventories. The Commerce data suggest that unexpected gains in sales lead to reduced inventories relative to anticipations over a six-month period. But the evidence is fragmentary and the same pattern is not apparent over a three-month interval.

I believe that in some instances the inventory survey could be complemented by a direct survey of manufacturers' production plans. The inventory and sales expectations combined implicitly yield an approximate estimate of planned production. But the production schedule may be the key decision variable of the firm over a short horizon, and illuminating results might be obtained by requesting a direct forecast of production. Ward's offers a report on automobile production plans which has proved valuable for very short-term forecasting. I should judge that there are considerable opportunities for collecting such intentions data from other manufacturing industries. Homebuilding is another area where "production plans"—in the form of planned starts—might be profitably collected. Experimental efforts in this field have been encouraging. Our ability to predict residential construction might well be improved by a systematic and standardized quarterly survey of builders' plans.

Another challenge to the survey designer lies in the development of new lines of questioning. McGraw-Hill has been venturesome in devising questions on the purpose of new investment (expansion versus modernization) and on the rates of utilization of capacity. Economists might be stunned into silence by the overwhelming conceptual problems if they had to answer such questions; but the survey respondents calmly supply figures which produce a meaningful time series. More work with contingent questions might be profitable. I do not know whether firms can tell us how their capital outlays would be affected, for example, by an investment tax credit or changes in the tax regulations governing depreciation allowances, but such questions would be worth asking.

In conclusion, it seems safe to predict that economists will confront businessmen with old and new questions about their intentions and that the data thus collected will be valuable in forecasting economic activity and in understanding business decision making.

Uses of Models for Policy Formulation

1. Judgmental versus Econometric Forecasts

The invitation to act as a principal speaker at this conference underlines to me that I have become an elder statesman. This encourages me to reminisce as an elder statesman is supposed to do.

I think back to my first post-doctoral research project, which was an effort to interview judgment forecasters of *GNP* to determine how they did it, and how well they did. I encountered several crusty old business economists who were extremely adamant and proud that they had never fitted an equation and never would. Then they began to tell me how they forecasted: they talked about normal ratios of investment to *GNP* and the factors that pull the actual away from the norm and the adjustments they make for each factor. Similarly, they described a normal savings rate for consumers and the process by which the savings rate departs from and returns to the norm. Of course, all the time they were describing equations. But they never, never wrote an equation.

Only slightly later in life did I learn that there is a symmetrical phenomenon on the other side. I met econometric forecasters who always swore by their models and who foreswore the use of extraneous information or judgment. Of course, they shifted their intercepts up now and then, when an equation performed badly for a few quarters in a row. And, especially when the econometrician had a healthy breakfast, he consigned the misbehaving equation to a waste basket and took on the task of writing a new one. But, as he described it, his forecasts were always econometric forecasts, straight out of the model.

In fact, virtually nobody takes econometric forecasts straight out of a model really seriously as the sole guide to a forecast of the near-term future. Quite apart from filling in the exogenous variables, every model builder or model user has to adjust equations. No one would want to advise the makers of business or public policy to rely on forecasts where all the residuals of any model are automatically taken to be zero, regardless of the past history of demand, the presence of major work stoppages, or the like. Nobody would be foolish enough to act that mechanically.

All my observations reinforce Paul Samuelson's suspicion that, inside every model or inside every computer, sits an economist. Indeed, Victor Zarnowitz has offered some evidence pointing in this direction.

One of Zarnowitz's most striking findings is that some models seem to perform worse in *ex post* tests with known exogenous variables than they performed *ex ante* with the model builders guessing at the exogenous components. This finding suggests that the model builder who is feeling bullish allows that to influence his results by plugging in fiscal and monetary variables that are a little more expansionary.

So what is the shouting about? Is there really a difference between judgment forecasts and econometric forecasts as a guide to private and public policy making? The answer, it seems to me, is that the model as a forecasting device is not an alternative to judgment. It is not a product in and of itself. It is a tool in the hands of a trained economist.

2. Models and Forecasting

What one gets when he is given the forecast of a model is the forecasting model and the man who develops that forecast. This is an extra bonus from the use of the model. The real question about the usefulness of the model, to use Paul Samuelson's metaphor, is whether Larry Klein works better when he is hidden inside the computer. That is where the analogy to the chess-playing machine breaks down. The man inside the chess-playing machine presumably could have done as well without the apparatus (unless he had *Modern Chess Openings* tucked away in there). But there are lots of reasons to believe that Larry Klein can perform better when he has his model.

One reason why I suspect he works better that way is that he can get help in a more systematic fashion. The model is a way to create a division of labor among macroeconomists. It is extremely difficult to get useful forecasting input from specialists on housing or business investment or international trade unless they are willing to summarize the evidence about their field in a quantitative way that does not depend on their judgment of the outlook for other segments of the economy. The kind of group research that the Brookings model undertook with specialists and coordinators is thus the heart of any econometric model project. I would be surprised if it is really efficient for a one-man forecasting operation to invest in constructing a fully articulated model.

2.1. Consistency of Forecast Components

On the other hand, in multi-man operations, it is extremely inefficient not to have something formalized. The alternative to a model is really a painful process of compromising and averaging. What happens really helps one to understand the proposition that a camel is a horse created by a committee.

Anybody who has had experience in the government Troika operation knows just what I mean. The forecast emerging from the staff is the most curious compromise of views and is almost inherently inconsistent. I remember commenting once in particular on a forecast of huge inventories that seemed quite inconsistent with a fairly modest forecast of final sales. It was explained to me that the man who was high on inventories conceded his consumption forecast to the man who was low on consumption so they could get a *GNP* total that both could believe. But the resulting composition was something that no one in the world could believe. In short, the division of labor in forecasting can be destructive, and the model can turn it into something constructive.

2.2. Post-Mortem Analysis

A second reason for finding the model useful is its contribution to post-morteming any forecast. Learning from experience means understanding the mistakes of the past. Often a judgment forecaster who looks back must ask himself. 'How could I possibly have believed that six months ago?' The econometric forecaster also has occasions to ask himself that question: but he can usually answer the question, while the judgment forecaster rarely can figure out why he believed what he believed. The econometric forecaster can identify where he went astray—in terms of sectors, in terms of the basic equations, or in terms of the adjustments he made to them.

2.3. Furthering Objectivity

Particularly for a user of forecasts in the field of public policy there is a third advantage to a formalized model, i.e. the protection of objectivity and a safeguard against self-deception. There is an enormous amount of pressure on any government official, especially anyone who advises the President of the United States, to believe that a benevolent providence will do the right thing for the country and for the Administration; that what ought to happen will happen. When he realizes the temptation to let the wish be the father of the thought, he becomes plagued by worries which may make him lean over backwards in an effort to maintain a detached view about something in which he is terribly involved emotionally. Moreover, he finds that staffs don't like to tell their bosses unpleasant news. The practice of beheading messengers who reported lost battles is supposed to have ended with the Persians, but the fear of a resumption remains in the U.S. Civil Service today.

Econometric models have unblemished records for being dispassionate. No econometric model, to the best of my knowledge, has ever developed an attachment to the goals of price stability or full employment or to the Democratic or Republican point of view.

2.4. Cumulating Knowledge

Fourth, the model is a tool for transmitting information from one economist to another and thus for cumulating knowledge. It is a pedagogical tool; it is a research tool; it represents an investment in econometric analysis. All judgment forecasters either die or fade away. Paul Samuelson spoke of the death of some judgment forecasters. More of them fade away before they die. I haven't put together a *GNP* worksheet in several years, reflecting again my role as an elder statesman. Some of the judgment forecasters have some wisdom that disappears and is destroyed when they retire or die. The formal model, on the other hand, preserves knowledge for others to use and build on.

2.5. Saving Time

Finally, the model is a labor-saving device. There are a lot of routine computations in forecasting which everybody will do in much the same way—such as extrapolating Social Security taxes or state and local excises—but the judgment forecaster has to fill in all of those boxes laboriously, while the man with a computerized technique can get them filled in for him.

Because he is freed of some routine chores, the man who uses models has an opportunity to focus on really important areas of uncertainty in the outlook. It should not be an opportunity to go on a vacation, or to depart from the job of forecasting, but rather to concentrate efforts on big issues and big problems and to decide where to make judgment adjustments to the model.

3. Judgment Forecasts with Models

If the econometric forecaster operates that way, he is really using the model as a device for deciding when and where to apply his judgment. He ought then to view the recent performance of the model as an alarm system telling him what sectors are out of line. It should help him to decide when to project any equation for the next quarter with a nonzero residual. The initial results of the model are viewed as a first approximation to the world. The second stage consists of making adjustments reflecting doubts and suspicions that make the initial results ground out of the equations implausible to him.

3.1. Reproducibility

If the model is used that way for forecasting, the procedure sacrifices the objective of reproducibility. For the objective of proving a scientific point or establishing the research value of some particular effort, reproducibility is an important objective. For the purpose of guiding policy, it is not critical. Reproducibility is a matter of convincing others, not of maximizing one's own confidence about the forecast. If I say I have clean hands, that this forecast came out of the computer, and that it uses the same technique that I employed successfully three months ago, that may persuade the user. But the real issue is, do I really believe that forecast? Is it the best judgment I can make?

It is important to distinguish three different dimensions of reproducibility:

1. the reproducibility of any particular forecast as it derives from a model;
2. the reproducibility of coefficients in the equations of the model; and
3. the reproducibility of the equations themselves and the specification of economic relationships in the model.

The reproducibility of the forecast depends on a specified recipe for processing known, or at least estimated, pieces of recent and current data and converting the pieces into a forecast. Reproducibility in that sense means that, if I give you my recipe, you can cook the same dish that I would cook with that recipe. The rules have to be specific enough and binding enough to ensure that everyone who believes the same numbers about the past and has the same access to the *Survey of Current*

Business and the same understanding of the English language will come out with the same predictions.

Once a model is used as I have suggested, as a device for organizing and focusing judgment, no particular forecast will be reproducible in this sense, and any forecast that is kept reproducible will compromise its objective to guide decision-making that depends on the future course of the economy.

3.2. Use of Extraneous Information

It seems to me that the model builders concede departures from reproducibility with excessive defensiveness and apology. They sometimes sound as though it were an act of adultery to look at other pieces of evidence outside their beloved models. Within a week after the President's announcement of his new economic policy last August, I found a bouquet of new econometric forecasts on my desk from all of my best friends. I was particularly interested in the new forecasts of prices. The inflation forecasts were very different, much lower than the previous versions. They were good forecasts, quite interesting and reasonable. But there was no suggestion that these price projections were anything other than standard econometric forecasts, and yet they weren't really econometric in any meaningful sense of the word.

I am unaware of any model that had a dummy variable for presidential announcements. Each model itself had to be predicting exactly the same future path of prices on August 16 as it did on August 14. Nothing had changed any of the variables that were specified in anybody's price equations. The model builders were departing from the recipe book, and it was perfectly sensible for them to do so. But the way those forecasts were written up came dangerously close to violating the Truth in Packaging legislation. What worried me most was the possibility that the model builders may have been kidding themselves (rather than their clients) in thinking somehow they were remaining faithful to the econometric structure, when obviously they were not.

3.3. Revealing Judgment

I am really suggesting that the model builders ought to climb out of that computer. They ought to be glad to stand beside it and pat it affectionately. But they should make clear that they are ready to massage it whenever and wherever it seems appropriate in order to give their clients the best possible assessment of the future outlook of the economy. They should be proud that they are telling their clients what they really believe with the aid of the model. Let me hasten to add that there is a lot of virtue in remaining pure and steadfast if one is explicitly performing an ongoing test of some particular model as a tool. But that is a different purpose from trying to guide decisions that depend on the outlook for the economy.

4. Model Structures and Omitted Variables

If you think for a moment about the message conveyed by any equation in any model, it becomes clear why a sensible model builder should want to amend the results much of the time. Take an automobile demand equation, for example. The equation says: Tell me disposable income for the last three quarters, lagged auto consumption, the existing stock of cars, some interest rate, and a couple of wealth or liquidity variables, and I will tell you what to believe about future expenditures on cars; and nothing else in the world that you could possibly know should make any difference whatsoever in your estimate of automobile expenditures for the next four quarters.

Now, what a foolish equation. How can it be so absurd? How can it have such a limited perspective on what can be relevant in determining the course of automobile expenditures? Anyone working on September 15 to project automobile demand for the fourth quarter of 1971 should have asked himself searching questions about how to assess the impact of the proposed repeal of the automobile excise tax, both while it was pending in the Congress and after it became law. Similarly, he would have had to judge what it meant to consumers that 1972 automobile prices had been rolled back, but might go up again subsequently. Nobody knows how to weight such issues objectively and systematically. But we know zero is the wrong answer. And zero shouldn't be the answer in any forecast meant to guide policy.

That is the key role of judgment—to decide when to depart from the reproducible recipe in light of important pieces of evidence inconsistent with the recipe. Sometimes the evidence consists of changes in what may be called 'latent variables,' influences that we always recognize but which don't normally change from quarter to quarter. When they do change, no time-series regression estimate is available to quantify the impact but neither does the time-series regression model justify zero as the best estimate. Such events must be dealt with by use of judgment.

5. Judgment Forecasters

One problem with judgment is that it is very hard to define the universe of possibly relevant evidence and information. At one point I suspected that every judgment forecaster really did have an implicit set of quantitative relationships in his head, and that somehow they could be elicited. I thought that for every economist who hides inside the computer, there probably was another who was just an outer shell for a computer that did the real work inside. I no longer hold that view of the profession. I believe there really is something different about the judgment forecaster. I interpret him as saying, "I can't write a complete list of all those things that may influence my forecast at any point in time, and I can't state the weights of their influence on me. But I will make sensible decisions about what evidence to include and how much to weight each piece each time I forecast."

Basically, he can envision an essentially infinite universe of possibly relevant information and evidence, and he proposed to sample that universe in a way that he prefers not to specify in advance of any single point in time. We all employ such techniques of empirical inference in everyday life, so the position cannot be wholly unreasonable. It would strengthen the argument if I could point to cases where judgment forecasters have pulled out latent variables and appraised them successfully. But usually it is just an applied econometrician who raises such issues. For example, George Perry focused the profession's attention on demographic factors in labor markets. Nobody would have ever denied their potential importance, but it never seemed worth disaggregating and stressing them until Perry noticed how significantly they had shifted over recent years. Thus, I can't tell you about the fish the judgment forecasters caught which the econometric forecasters had let get away.

I do believe that judgment forecasters recognized the stubbornness of inflation in 1969–71 more promptly than did econometric model builders. The tendency for judgment forecasters to rely more heavily on autocorrelated tendencies of the economy probably serves them well when the economy develops and maintains a tendency that conflicts with the verdict of the model. The record of the profession in price forecasting over the last three years does not look very good, to say the least. One must ask in retrospect, why so many forecasters went down with the ship. It is not hard to understand why the forecasts were generally wrong in 1969, but it is hard to explain why so many econometricians failed to cut their losses and failed to recognize that the structure of their models was not capturing the structure of the economy. I know people who even now claim there wasn't any basic difference. I view that as not only going down with the ship, but insisting on being buried with it. In this case, the apparent reassurance afforded by the formal structure and perhaps the considerations of reproducibility and loyalty to the tool probably hurt, where good judgment was pushing people toward truth by the middle of 1970.

6. Parameter Estimates

Let me say a few words about the reproducibility of coefficients. Minimum variance regression analysis of time series data is a great tool, and anybody who takes the same batch of data and runs it through the same regression program will emerge with the same coefficients. That is reproducibility par excellence.

But aggregate time series data are not the only quantitative evidence in the world. I believe in a number of quantitative relationships that may differ from the results I would get from aggregate time series regression estimates on quarterly data for the United States. Running those equations wouldn't completely change my mind. For example, if I estimated a set of consumption relationships that implied a long-run marginal propensity to consume that was above unity or much below 0.85, I just wouldn't believe that result. I really do have a prior basis, independent of one run on any particular batch of data, to make some judgments about certain economic parameters. Yet, I have found econometric models that imply a long-run marginal propensity to consume as low as 0.65 and as high as 1.1. I doubt that the model builders really believe those results any more than I do.

On the other hand, some econometricians, Klein in particular, have done a lot to augment time series estimates with variables whose parameters are constrained on the basis of cross-section evidence. At one point it seemed as though a major impact of the computer revolution on macroeconometric analysis would be to encourage the use of cross-section parameters in macroeconometric relationships. Then Edwin Kuh published a brilliant article that showed all the serious mistakes that could arise from extrapolating cross-section findings to time series parameters. I believe that unintentionally Kuh scared a lot of econometricians away from that area, when the real message was that they should stick with it but proceed carefully.

Econometric model builders typically constrain the sign of a coefficient. When they get an estimate of -0.1 on a parameter they think should be $+0.1$, they throw it out as a fluke. But when they get $+0.8$ on something they think should be $+0.6$, they feel obliged to use it. There is a strong case for using more constraints so the model emerges with parameters that economists can really believe.

7. Stability of Equation Specifications

It is amusing that the reproducibility of equations has never come to be a criterion of respectability. Nobody has ever suggested that he can spell out a theoretical formulation that will make you specify the equations exactly the way he does with the same variables, the same lags, the same sample period. In some quarters, it is regarded as respectable to throw out an equation but not to amend it. If one changes an intercept or alters a coefficient, that is tampering and unscientific. But if one destroys the equation and fits another one, that is a scientific refinement.

One annual model occasionally showed drastic swings in its economic theory from year to year. As I recall, there were three consecutive years in which the automobile equation was driven first by interest rates, then by liquidity, and then by some real accelerator mechanism. I remember commenting on this to James Tobin, arguing that it shouldn't be called the same model year after year. He said I was really being uncharitable. It really was the same team. The fact that so many of the players changed just meant that its manager traded more than other managers did.

My diagnosis would point toward an effort to formalize decision rules on when to refit or update or refine equations. It would put more stress on the accuracy of individual equations and relatively less on overall forecasting performance. I think it would be an interesting project for one of the critics or connoisseurs to put together an all-star team of equations, combining the best investment sectors, the best monetary sectors, etc. He would probably have to hammer that jig-saw puzzle together, but it would still be a worthwhile enterprise.

8. Policy Formulation

So far I have confined myself to the analysis, uses, and abuses of models for forecasting purposes. Yet, in public policy formulation, best estimate forecasting isn't the sole purpose of the quantified formalized approach. For one thing, the ability to make better policy is more heavily dependent on better hurricane warnings than on more accurate down-the-middle forecasts. The policymaker has a fairly flat utility function on whether *GNP* for this year is \$1,140 or \$1,145 billion. What he really needs is to know that it is not going to be \$1,135 or \$1,155 billion. He needs to appraise the possibility of major surprises. Neither the judgment forecaster nor the model builder has yet been able to offer much help in exploring the relevant range of outcomes—to describe how flat the likelihood function is in comparison with the steepness of the utility function. I understand that users of some commercial forecasting services are encouraged to engage in that kind of experiment, in some sense, by trying their own residuals and seeing how far out they have to go on particular functions to generate a recession catastrophe or an inflationary boom. It seems to me that such efforts deserve to be encouraged.

8.1. Multipliers, Anticipations Data, and Forecasting

Second, the policymaker needs predictions of the impact of particular policy actions that are proposed. As William Brainard has pointed out, how much discretionary economic policy ought to be used depends, not on the accuracy of forecasting private demand, but rather on the accuracy of estimates of the multiplier impact of fiscal and monetary instruments. I don't think any wise man has any claim to judgment about dynamic multipliers. There's no reason to believe that anyone has insight or intuition about how much tax cuts or increased public expenditures, or an increase in the money supply or a reduction in the rate of interest would add to the *GNP*; nor is extraneous evidence likely to help. On the question of multiplier impact, we are stuck with the model; it is the only wheel in town. The answers have to come from a formalized technique. But the model that gives the best answers to add-on multiplier questions may not be the model that will do the best job in predicting the economy. A model designed for forecasting purposes will rely heavily on anticipations data, barometric indicators, and other evidence that is not really 'causal' in affecting the future course of economic variables.

Normally these indicators can be fed into a forecasting model like other exogenous variables. Obviously they are going to be affected by changes in the economy, and their presence impairs the estimates of multiplier add-ons from policy tools. The Wharton model has some ingenious ways of handling this problem by shortcutting the noncausal data or closing a causal link when structural multipliers are wanted. Nonetheless, a versatile model that is meant to engage in overall prediction and structural multiplier estimation does have to pay some cost to achieve that compromise. It is likely to be a little less efficient in each of these tasks than if it specialized in one. The MPS model does specialize; it sacrifices the use of anticipations and barometric data in most cases in order to deal most effectively with the multiplier structure.

8.2. Dynamic Paths and Multipliers

Quite apart from the problems of noncausal variables, the timing of responses to changes in explanatory variables and dynamic multipliers seem to come out of an econometric model as a cheap by-product much as tallow is produced out of a meat slaughter-house. They do not seem to be developed and treated and scrutinized by the model builder with the kind of care that they deserve at the time the model is constructed.

The dynamic multipliers are not subject to direct verification. No matter how many quarters of data are assembled, no test can reveal whether the dynamic multipliers are right or wrong. The estimates of dynamic multipliers are sensitive to seemingly minor changes in individual equations. If one forecasting model retains its three-quarter lag term when the coefficients are 1.2 times their standard errors, it is going to show a much slower process of adjustment than another that tosses out such variables.

The reason some econometricians toss out such variables while others retain them reflects different views on how much one dislikes additional terms in his equations, not any basic convictions about what the multiplier period ought to be. Such incidental decisions may affect R^2 in an equation by only 0.0001 and yet can alter enormously what it implies about how fast or how much a change in government purchases affects the economy. We sorely need more relevant, more realistic, and more focused estimates of these dynamic multipliers. They are the critical elements in the policymaking process. They are the place where the policymakers are most dependent on the model. The multipliers should not come out of that production process as a by-product which is ignored until years later when people are searching for new exercises to play with the model. A model builder with structural intentions and ambitions ought to focus on the multipliers right from the beginning and constrain them to reflect what he really believes and finds reasonable. Bayesian approaches are one route to that objective.

9. Conclusion

Throughout this talk, I keep returning to a central theme. Those of us who labor in the field of quantitative macroeconomics come to have views about economic relationships based on a variety of kinds of evidence. Econometric models are one type of evidence. They are a tool to help us focus on what we really believe about the structure of the economy, to guide us to re-examine and refine these beliefs, and to judge more accurately the future course of the economy and the future impact of economic policy.

VII ECONOMIC POLICY FORMULATION

The Economist and Presidential Leadership

The economists in our universities and research institutions toil in the field of values as well as that of fact and theory. When they come to Washington, they cannot leave their ideologies behind. Indeed, they should not. Political economists necessarily move in the realm of social values, and that is the way they become most useful, especially as advisers to the President. Presidential leadership consists of selecting priorities, making commitments, identifying the aims of the nation, and then working to fulfill them. To exercise this leadership effectively, the President needs the advice of people with diverse professional training.

Nobody comes out of graduate school with a Ph.D. in priority setting or applied political ideology. And yet these are major tasks in the executive's policy making. Some group of people is going to do this job and it should include economists. Unless there is evidence that deep thinking about social problems can be done best by those whose minds are uncluttered by formal training in the social sciences, the economist should not yield this territory entirely to those with no professional background. As Gardner Ackley argued:

> . . . Those in authority get plenty of advice from others who show no great delicacy in distinguishing technical questions within their competence from questions of values. The President hears from other members of his Administration, from businessmen, from labor leaders, from journalists—yes, from economists. If his economic adviser refrains from advice on the gut questions of policy, the President should and will get another one.[1]

To be effective, the adviser must operate with sensitivity and understanding of the President's values and aims. He must know the President's tastes, just as a good wife has to know how her husband takes his coffee. Thus after Kennedy pledged to "start this country moving again,"[2] his economists convinced him that a 4 percent interim target for unemployment was an appropriate translation of that goal.[3] Once that commitment was made, it had broad and pervasive implications for subsequent policy decisions. When President Johnson set forth the vision of the Great Society, his economists shaped the strategies in the war against poverty to fit. They showed how prosperity could contribute to the fulfillment of a great society. They stressed the fundamental compatibility—indeed, complementarity—of material goods and spiritual goals when some of the President's staff urged him to downplay economic considerations in order to emphasize human values. Because President Johnson wished to avoid a Robin Hood or class-struggle theme in social aid to the disadvantaged, it was important to develop programs and justifications that emphasized the long-term benefits to the entire nation from investment in human resources. When President Nixon counseled the nation to lower its voice, his economists followed, in their pronouncements, with a stress on moderation and gradualism. President Nixon's preference for the middle of the road must influence many of the staff efforts to develop program initiatives.

Efforts to flesh out the framework of the President's leadership are of particular importance within the Executive Office of the President. Many of the top officials of other agencies in the executive branch are assigned the role of advocates within the administration. For example, the Secretary of Labor is expected to be a spokesman for manpower programs. An imaginative and energetic secretary ought to be able to generate a volume of high priority manpower programs whose costs would far exceed the amount of resources and legislative energy that can be reasonably allocated to his department. Kermit Gordon, former Director of the Bureau of the Budget, recited the warning of the bureau's very first director, General Charles G. Dawes: "Cabinet members are vice presidents in charge of spending, and as such they are the natural enemies of the President."[4] In point of fact, the members of the Cabinet serve the President by making the strongest possible case for their efforts and their programs. They also serve him by developing a special liaison with private interest groups. This pluralistic system within the administration functions very well. But it does confront the President with some hard choices, which he cannot hope to make all on his own. He needs some staff and some advisers who are not assigned a role of advocacy. Here he is bound to look to the executive office agencies, including the White House staff, the Bureau of the Budget, and the Council of Economic Advisers, to exercise a check on the pluralistic structure of the administration.

To assure this check, our presidents have selected members of the Council of Economic Advisers who were not affiliated with particular interest groups. CEA members have generally moved into public office from a university or nonprofit research institution. To be sure, most of our leading academic economists have taken fees from private groups for consulting or speech making. Moreover, an academic or public service background is no guarantee of objectivity and impartiality, nor does private activity foreclose them. The nation has been served with distinction by economists in public service who previously practiced their profession on behalf of banks, business firms, trade associations, and labor unions. But it is added insurance when the economists sitting closest to the President have a background of concern for the public interest.[5]

The effectiveness of officials in the Executive Office depends entirely on their relationship with the President. They have no programs to run and no responsibilities or powers that they can exercise on their own. The only statutory claim that the Council of Economic Advisers has on the President's eye or ear is the writing of the Economic Report. If the President's attention to the CEA were limited to that once-a-year effort, the Council would be a most uninteresting and ineffective agency. It becomes interesting and effective to the extent that it wins his confidence.

But this confidence must flow two ways. No adviser can expect to have his advice taken all or even most of the time. If he feels in disharmony with the general position and posture of the administration, he ought to leave his job. But if he considers his job worthwhile and is to do it effectively, he must accept certain standards of loyalty. He must agree to confine battling to internal councils and cannot publicly oppose administration decisions once they are made. At most he can hope that, with the President's blessing, he may occasionally launch trial balloons and thus move in the vanguard of administration policy. Loyalty may even dictate that he prepare briefs for others to use with legitimate arguments in favor of positions with which he does not agree. He can and should maintain personal integrity by refusing to say publicly anything that he does not believe even though he cannot say publicly everything he does believe.

Given these constraints, members of the Council of Economic Advisers are clearly recognized as the President's men. If they speak publicly, they will be identified as spokesmen for administration positions. A Council chairman can respond to this dilemma, as Edwin Nourse and Arthur Burns did, by speaking very rarely for the public record. As Nourse strongly expressed his view:

> For the President to permit or encourage intervention of Council members in any manner in the legislative process or in the public promotion of measures or policies is to make them politically expendable and to destroy the unique usefulness of the Council as an institution designed for scientific service to the executive branch.[6]

Most of the other six Council chairmen have not subscribed to this view. They have advocated and explained publicly many administration economic policies and proposals. When the President's case was their case and when the issues could be illuminated by economic education of the citizenry, they have spoken out—as partisans, but as partisans with expertise and professional integrity.

In such cases, both the speaker and the listeners know that the discussion is pursued within, and not above, the political fray. The mere fact that the Council agrees with the President can never be news and can never enhance an administration position. No CEA member has ever claimed to be the spokesman for a purely professional view. Woodrow Wilson once said with obvious facetiousness, "The trouble with the Republican party is that it has not had a new idea for thirty years. I am not speaking as a politician; I am speaking as an historian."[7] Neither presidents nor their advisers can hope ever to convince their audiences that their pronouncements on partisan issues are professional and nonpolitical.

In short, when the President's economists decide to go on public record, they cannot serve two masters. They cannot speak both for the President and for the profession. And they cannot speak for the profession publicly and still maintain confidence and rapport internally with the President. The choice should be clear. It is far more important for society and for the profession to have economists who maintain rapport with the President and thus can have greatest influence on the inside.

A Voice for Consensus

Yet this is not an entirely satisfactory conclusion. One wishes for a more effective way of influencing public and congressional opinion in the areas of professional consensus. There is a role to be played by a Supreme Court of the profession, although a less important one than that actually fulfilled by the Council and the Bureau of the Budget in recent years.

This is not necessarily an either-or choice. One can conceive of another and separate institution outside the administration consisting of economic experts ready to speak up on policy matters involving technical results or widespread professional agreement. Somebody would have to select a group of "outside" economic experts, clearly bipartisan in composition. They could not be self-selected nor should they be named by the President. Perhaps the minority and majority leadership of the Congress could best handle this assignment; they might wish to consult with officers of the American Economic Association for suggestions. Perhaps the majority and minority might each choose six economic experts. This group of twelve could perform the specific and limited function of defining the scope of bipartisan professional agreement. They would make recommendations only when the group was nearly unanimous—perhaps ten signatures out of the twelve might be required on any report. One would expect to hear from the group only rarely on specific pieces of legislation, but it might set forth important principles and positions on both macro- and microeconomic policies. Such a group would probably have supported appropriately restrictive fiscal and monetary actions in 1966–68. It might have done considerable good, and it could hardly have done much harm.

Some risks attend the initiation of any institution in the policy process, no matter how modest its conception and objectives. If too much were expected from the advisory group in terms of either influence or specific recommendations, it could be condemned to failure. If its silence on certain issues would be viewed as incriminating, it might add further to the suspicion that economists are hopelessly divided. If this group would seem to introduce a technocratic element in policy issues or to present a picture of a medieval tribunal of wise men ruling on the theology of social issues, its creation would not serve the nation.

I am confident that it would not endanger the place of the maverick in the profession; he would still find a receptive audience. Nor would it be likely to interfere with the functions of existing institutions; indeed, it would help to clarify the fact that the Council of Economic Advisers simply cannot and should never be expected to fulfill the nonpolitical, purely professional function. In the last analysis, such a group would be beneficial only if it influenced our legislators, directly or indirectly. If they would take such a group seriously and find its judgments helpful, its creation could be a way of resolving a dilemma of the political and nonpolitical role of the economist in public policy.

Whether or not new institutions are created, there will be a continuing challenge to narrow the gap between the judgment of the profession and the law of the land. It must be demonstrated that there *is* a professional view on many matters. The day ought to come when informed noneconomists are no longer surprised that the negative income tax can be strongly advocated by "new economists" like James Tobin and Joseph Pechman and also by Milton Friedman.

To convey the professional view effectively requires the talents of a missionary, an outstanding pedagogue, and a supersalesman; it also takes skillful and sympathetic understanding of opposition views and, especially, of noneconomic considerations in policy choices. These requirements and skills differ from those most vital to successful academic research. The areas of professional consensus are rarely on the frontier of economic inquiry. They are typically built on the foundation of theoretical and empirical results that have been established and accepted by the profession long ago.

The political economist's task can be aided by some types of academic research that can nail down, dramatize, and quantify his message. But the academic researcher will rarely regard these as the most challenging scientific problems. Meanwhile, the political economist will find that much of the exploration on the frontiers of economic knowledge is irrelevant to his task of providing ammunition for the battles waged in a political arena. And so political economy has to be a separate and distinct activity of the profession. It is not science, but it is a source of potential benefit to the nation. And it will remain alive and well in Washington, whichever party occupies the White House.

Notes

1. Gardner Ackley, "The Contribution of Economists to Policy Formation," *Journal of Finance*, Vol. 21 (May 1966), p. 176.

2. *Freedom of Communications*, Pt. 1: *The Speeches, Remarks, Press Conferences. and Statements of Senator John F. Kennedy, August 1 through November 7, 1960*, Final Report of the Senate Committee on Commerce, Prepared by its Subcommittee of the Subcommittee on Communications, S. Rept. 994, 87 Cong. 1 sess. (1961), p. 542.

3. See "The President's News Conference of March 15, 1961," in *Public Papers of the Presidents of the United States: John F. Kennedy, 1961* (1962), p. 187.

4. Kermit Gordon. "Reflections on Spending," in John D. Montgomery and Arthur

Smithies (eds.), *Public Policy,* Vol. 15 (Harvard University, Graduate School of Public Administration, 1966), p. 15 (Brookings Reprint 125).

5. For a contrasting view, see William H. Chartener, "The Business Economist in Government," *Business Economics,* Vol. 4 (January 1969), p. 10.

6. Edwin G. Nourse, *Economics in the Public Service: Administrative Aspects of the Employment Act* (Harcourt, Brace, 1953), p. 500.

7. Albert Shaw (ed.), *President Wilson's State Papers and Addresses* (New York: Review of Reviews Co., 1917), p. 81.

The Formulation of National Economic Policy

When the President handed me a four-line note 11 days ago, designating me Chairman of our three-man Council of Economic Advisers, I became the head of one of Washington's tiniest Federal agencies. Our budget is about three-quarters of a million dollars a year—a little more than it costs to run the Botanical Gardens, but not much more. In addition to the three members of the Council, we have a supporting professional staff of about 16 people. We do not run programs. We do not even collect economic statistics. We really have no operational role. Our job is to serve as an economic consulting service; but, unlike most economic consulting services, we have only a single client—the President of the United States.

The Employment Act of 1946, which established the Council, gave us our basic mandate: to advise the President on how best to fulfill the Act's objectives of maximum employment, production, and purchasing power.

One important aspect of the job is to keep the President fully informed on economic developments and how they bear on Federal policies and the goals of the Employment Act. Another is to insure that the economic implications of all Federal decisions are made clear to the President. He is faced constantly with decisions on programs whose primary objectives may be in the areas of national security or social problems but whose economic aspects are not obvious and might be overlooked. And yet, whenever the Federal Government spends money and acquires resources —which is basically what the Federal Government does—there are economic effects. Frequently the noneconomic objectives of a program can be fulfilled equally in ways that are better for the economy or in ways that are worse for the economy. Our job is to point out the ways in which they can be done better. This gets us into such diverse noneconomic areas as pollution, highway beautification, and communication policy.

At the same time, it is fair to say that the meat and potatoes of the Council's diet is in macroeconomics, in such areas as fiscal and monetary policy, the balance of payments, price-cost stability, and economic growth objectives. It is here that we are called upon most often to advise and inform the President.

For the past 15 years, every member of the Council of Economic Advisers has come to his job from a university professorship. Our qualifications are those of professional economists—indeed of academic, even ivory-tower economists. All the Council members have had some previous experience in the ways of Washington, either as staff economists in some agency or as consultants, and all begin with a strong interest in policy. But our knowledge of policy, at least when we first come to the job, comes in large part from book learning.

By training, however, the Council feels that it is competent to give the President a sound technical judgment, as sound as economists can give, on the economic consequences of alternative policies or actions recommended to him. In many cases, we make a purely technical judgment—I hesitate to say a scientific one, given the state of our science and art.

We try to make these judgments as quantitative, as objective, and as complete as we can. An important part of the judgment is an indication of the degree of confidence we repose in it. In some cases we think we have sufficient experience and scientific knowledge to make fairly confident predictions about the consequences of an action. Other actions are so unique, or the possible reactions to them so hard to assess, that we are obliged to say, "Here is what we think will happen. It is the best judgment we can make, but there are lots of uncertainties." For the policymaker, the degree of uncertainty is in itself an important piece of information.

Whether we are certain or uncertain, in this purely technical sphere the questions we answer are of the same kind as those in the examinations we give our students at the university. In this sphere, we function strictly within the framework of existing economic knowledge, not in the field of values or policy choices.

But sometimes we do get into the area of values and policy choices. Often the line between technical judgment and value judgment is rather fine. If we can say, "This policy is good for economic growth, and good for price stability, and good for the balance of payments, and thoroughly consistent with free market institutions," then we don't have much hesitation about concluding that it is desirable. In such cases we don't insist on the kind of scientific detachment which says, "Here is what will happen, but we don't want to advise you." If a doctor can tell his patient, "You've got a disease that could kill you, and a $6.00 prescription will certainly save your life," it's reasonable for him to say, "You had better go out and buy it." When we can make that kind of an assessment, we are happy to advise accordingly.

Unfortunately, there aren't many $6.00 prescriptions that will save people's lives, in medicine or in economics. Most of the polices we are asked to appraise have some desirable aspects and some that are less so. For the most part, the actions that are clearly desirable have already been taken. After all, we have been in business as a nation for almost 200 years.

New programs and proposals almost inevitably invite mixed views and complicated appraisals. The task becomes particularly difficult when a given policy action looks as though it will promote some objectives but not others—when it may add half a percent to the national output but at the same time raise the price level by one-half of one percent and perhaps cost us something on the balance of payments. In these cases we have to give the President the full range of pros and cons, the good news and the bad news alike.

In addition, the President needs to know how we view the trade-offs among objectives. It is not enough to say, "Here is what this thing will do to the national output, which is good, and here is what it will do to the price level, which is not so good." Somebody has to add up the pluses and minuses and make a judgment on the trade-offs.

The President wants to hear many voices, and the Council's voice is but one of them. So we are drawn into some hard policy choices and even into questions of what is feasible within our democratic legislative process. We also get involved in the task of public education, in convincing the public that a rational economic policy is indeed rational and feasible. As professional educators, we welcome participation in that process. On the other hand, we shy away from making judgments about what will win votes, either on Capitol Hill or in the polling booths. In this area, we claim no expertise and the President has other advisers who are much better qualified.

On nearly every question on which the Council's advice is asked, it is one involving several participating agencies. The President wants and gets independent advice from many financial and economic advisers. It is also useful for him, and for us who advise him, to exchange views in order to identify the sources of any differences of opinion and to ascertain whether there is a basis for consensus.

In this process, there is a clear understanding that the President should not have to adjudicate trivial differences of opinion, the kind that don't really affect the national interest, however they are decided. On the other hand, President Johnson does not want to be given a single recommendation or a majority view simply in order to avoid making a decision. The President's job is making decisions and he likes to make them. Indeed, the President at times exercises his right and responsibility to turn down or amend even recommendations which come to him with the unanimous backing of his aides. In certain cases, he perceives aspects or implications of a decision that are overlooked by his advisers.

There are four organized interagency groups which deal with various aspects of economic advice to the President—the Troika, the Quadriad, the Cabinet Committee on the Balance of Payments, and the newly established Cabinet Committee on Price Stability.

Let me begin with the Troika, which is close to my heart because I have served on all three of its levels. The Troika is a three-by-three group. It involves three agencies—the Treasury, the Budget Bureau, and the Council—and also three levels—a staff level, a middle level (Assistant Secretary of the Treasury, a member of the Council, and an Assistant Director of the Budget), and the senior level (the three agency heads).

The Troika functions in the area of fiscal policy. Its job is to advise the President and keep him informed on the planning and progress of budgetary policies, including both Federal expenditures and taxes. Each quarter, and more often in periods of special stress and strain, the Troika is asked to review the economic outlook and to examine the course of Federal expenditures and revenues.

The quarterly Troika is launched with a staff meeting of participants from the Treasury, Council, and Budget Bureau. At that time they size up pretty well the results of economic activity in the first quarter. They take a look at what has happened to Federal expenditures and review the economic outlook for the remainder of the year and the first half of the next calendar year to complete their estimates for the fiscal year.

The staff takes into account any evident changes in private spending trends and the prospects for Federal expenditures. It may have to take into account some alternative assumptions about what Congress may do with the Administration's continuing proposals for tax legislation. From all this, it spins out a set of quantitative estimates, on a quarterly basis, for economic activity and the Federal Budget.

The middle level of the Troika instructs the staff as to which alternative assumptions it should explore and what different kinds of models or quantitative estimates are desired.

One further assumption that the Troika staff has to make is the future course of developments in the money and credit field. For this, it consults with the Federal Reserve. It must arrive at judgments about how monetary policies will be affecting the course of economic developments, again under a number of possible fiscal policies.

When the staff puts its numbers together, they are reviewed by the middle-level Troika. Usually the middle level drafts the memorandum summarizing the results. What happens from then on depends on the Troika itself—that is, the three agency heads who make up the top-level Troika.

The best of all possible Troika memos for the President is one that says, "Last quarter's analyses were right on the head, and everything is coming out on target. We have nothing new to report." That rarely happens. New developments are likely to result in a new set of estimates and sometimes in new policy recommendations to the President, which may lead to his meeting with the Troika principals. In any case, there is a regular memo to the President reporting on our latest review of the budget.

In the fall, the Troika has no budget to review as it looks into the next year. It therefore becomes a vehicle for formulating rather than merely reviewing budget policy. It is the vehicle for making judgments about how much fiscal stimulus or restraint seems appropriate for the economy and how to implement this through different kinds of tax and expenditure proposals. The President is given a menu of different kinds of fiscal policy that add up to different levels of prospective aggregate demand.

This whole systematic review operation by the Troika was established in 1961. It reflected the general philosophy of the new Administration and its new economic advisers that there should be a continuing and regular review of fiscal policy decisions to determine whether things were going according to plan and whether changes were needed.

Obviously, fiscal policy review didn't begin in 1961. Under the Eisenhower Administration fiscal policy was reviewed, and the review was taken seriously. But the role of policy was conceived differently and policy actions reflected a fire-alarm approach—ready to respond whenever something went wrong or whenever there was a *clear* need to do something to improve the performance of the economy. In the 1960's the system is conceived as not only a fire-alarm, but a fire-prevention system as well. It attempts to diagnose threats to prosperity before they loom on the horizon. It also continuously asks, "Is the Federal Government's budgetary and tax policy as well-geared to the needs of the economy as it can be?"

As you know, this is colloquially referred to as "fine tuning," which is an unfortunate label. No one can hope to manipulate the dials of the economy with the kind of precision that that term implies. A much less pretentions objective is to at least work in the right direction—to turn the right dials, so that we will not play the television set when we want a radio program. But it has been a hallmark of the Kennedy and Johnson Administrations to keep fiscal policy as effectively adjusted as possible so as to promote a sustainable prosperity, and to recognize this need even at times when there is no obvious threat to prosperity.

The Quadriad, the next Federal interagency group that I want to describe, is the Troika plus one—the Federal Reserve. The Quadriad is the group that advises the President on monetary and credit policies and developments. It functions very differently from the Troika. It is less structured and makes no attempt to develop a unified staff presentation. The reason is clear. The Federal Reserve is an independent agency, responsible for making decisions in the money and credit field which are not subject to explicit approval or disapproval by the President. Still, the Federal Reserve wants our views on its actions, and we want to know what it thinks about our fiscal policies. We try, therefore, to achieve mutual understanding, to exchange views and to develop good communications, so that the monetary hand knows what the fiscal hand is doing and vice versa.

There has been one notable exception to that coordination in the past 7 years. That was in December 1965, when the discount rate was increased. The Federal Reserve felt that the need for action was urgent, while the Administration thought a decision on the form of policy restraint to be employed should be postponed for another month until the budgetary and monetary situation could be looked at together. The disagreement was regretted on both sides; and since then we have worked even harder to make sure that we do understand each other. Of course, we may well disagree again in the future, but there will be a better basis for reaching decisions and a clearer understanding on each side.

Let me just briefly mention the Balance of Payments Cabinet Committee, an interagency group chaired by the Secretary of the Treasury. It includes the four Quadriad agencies and also agencies with programs involving significant foreign exchange costs and receipts—the Department of Commerce, the Department of Agriculture, the Department of State, AID, the Special Trade Representative, and the Department of Defense. This is the forum in which balance of payments programs, objectives, and policies are designed and discussed. Obviously, when you have a group this large and many operating agencies, there is a wide range of interests and special concerns. Some agencies are affected more than others by particular measures, such as tying foreign assistance more tightly, or taxing tourists, or tightening up on direct investment controls.

In this Committee, the Treasury's job is the tough one. It tries to prevent the balance of payments program from simply becoming the lowest common denominator of what everybody is willing to do. In the closing weeks of 1967, when we faced a huge fourth-quarter outflow and recognized that we simply had to have an effective program before the magnitude of the deficit became public knowledge, the Treasury took the lead in defining the essential features of a substantial and decisive program that could be presented to the President for his ultimate decision.

I want to conclude with a brief word on the newest of our interagency groups—the Cabinet Committee on Price Stability, which the President mentioned in his Economic Report and actually established by memorandum. He has asked me to coordinate it. This Committee is one part of our machinery for anti-inflationary policy. Think of our battle against inflation this year as having three components—first, fiscal and monetary policies to avoid excess demand; second, continuing efforts to enlist restraint in price and wage decisions by firms and unions which have market power; and, third, the beginning of a new coordinated effort to deal with the full range of effects which particular industries and Government programs have on price stability.

This last element involves the recognition that price stability is a basic long-term problem for every industrial economy. No nation has met this challenge thus far. No nation can really say it has succeeded in reconciling high-level employment and price stability. It is easy to have high-level employment without price stability, and it is easy to have price stability by sacrificing high-level employment. It's awfully hard to have both at the same time. I think this is really the major unsolved problem of overall economic performance; we must find a way to reconcile our employment objective on the one hand with our price stability objective on the other. We have to recognize that what is good for productivity, technology, and competition is good for price stability and for the kind of economy in which price stability and full employment can go hand in hand. We are helped by everything that helps to break bottlenecks and to allow resources to move more freely and respond better to market incentives.

The Committee will look into a number of specific areas, particularly those where market power is not significant on a nationwide basis and hence where the guidepost approach is not the best way to get things done. The problems that we have in the construction area and in medical services are not the problems that come from large firms exercising monopoly power or large unions bargaining on a nationwide basis. They are problems of a different, more structural character. We want to see how we can improve efficiency and reduce costs in these areas and pass the benefits on to the consumers.

We also want to take a look at the whole range of Government programs, recognizing that Federal procurement decisions, stockpile management, manpower training, and research and development programs all have implications for price stability. They are small individually but large cumulatively. It is important that every Federal official and every program manager be aware that his actions do influence prices, and that if everybody works cumulatively toward this objective we will have a better long-term price performance.

VIII

EQUALITY AND EFFICIENCY

Equal Rights but Unequal Incomes

I care not how affluent some may be provided that none be miserable in consequence of it. Tom Paine, 1796

We have a split-level society—one of equal rights but unequal incomes. Our laws bestow upon us the rights to obtain equal justice, to exercise freedom of speech and religion, to vote, to take a spouse and procreate, to be free in our persons in the sense of immunity from enslavement, to leave America if we want, to benefit from public services such as the police and sanitation departments and the schools. These rights are distributed equally and free of charge, not on the basis of one's ability, education, income, or looks. They may not even be bought or sold for money. They confer on Americans membership in a social and political club in which no one is more equal than anyone else.

But the economic club operates under entirely different rules, with rewards and penalties that necessarily generate unequal incomes. In the pursuit of efficiency and material progress, our economic institutions prod us to outdo our neighbors and insist that we must succeed—or suffer. The rewards and penalties of the marketplace create such glaring disparities that the rich can feed their pets better than the poor can feed their children. Thus the society is marked and marred by the conflict between equality and efficiency, between the principles of democracy and the practices of capitalism.

Yet I believe that, for all its faults, the mixed system—equal rights and unequal incomes—reflects a sensible willingness to compromise rather than a hypocritical double standard. If we understand our split-level structure and use that understanding to make the American economic system more humane, democratic capitalism can have a bright future.

Our economic rules are meant to encourage effort and channel it into socially productive activity. In principle, the best-paying jobs are those adding the greatest value to products sold in the marketplace. Pursuing their own choices, workers respond to the signals of what society values most and is willing to pay for. In their search for profits businesses naturally expand the output of an item for which buyers will pay more than the cost of production. It was in 1776, interestingly, that Adam Smith described this incentive system in theory of the invisible hand." Through the market, self-interest—even "greed"—is harnessed to serve social purposes in an impersonal and automatic way. Because producers seek profits, they draw resources into those uses for which consumers will pay the most. They have the incentive to make what the consumer wants and to make it in the least costly way. Nobody is obliged to evaluate what is good for the economy; if he merely pursues his own economic self-interest, he will automatically serve the social interest.

This snapshot of the capitalist economy is, of course, heavily retouched and idealized. Over the years, society has found it necessary to treat the blemishes of real-world private enterprise in many ways—regulation and consumer information to guard against the nefarious or careless producer, special rules for "natural monopoly" situations such as telephones and electric power, where competition cannot work, curbs on productive processes that would despoil the environment or jeopardize public health and safety, and provision of public services that, though vital, do not meet the market's test of profitability. And despite these efforts, the system remains blemished by monopoly, misinformation, misplaced costs and benefits, and, recurrently, by that greatest of all inefficiencies, to much unemployment.

Yet the resemblances between the contemporary American economy and the glorified model are more striking than the contrasts. Most products we buy are made in response to the drive for profit, and most markets are sufficiently competitive to offer some genuine choices among brands and sellers. More often than not, growth and success are the result of the consumers' vote of confidence. From the telegraph and the light bulb to the Xerox machine, frozen food and permanent-press sheets and shirts, most innovations that have raised the American standard of living have been the creatures of a profit-oriented market system.

Despite the "hidden persuaders" of Madison Avenue, nearly half of newly introduced, advertised products are rejected by the consumer and are removed from the shelves. And for all of this corporate profits after taxes take about a nickel out of each dollar of our national product, and all the smaller capitalists who own unincorporated businesses, farms and professional practices take roughly another dime.

Many elements contributed to the American saga of economic progress. Our vast continent teemed with unexplored natural resources; our immigrants (apart from our shame of slavery) came as volunteers driven by venturesomeness and ambition; our social environment was not ossified by feudal hierarchies or medieval traditions. We were a wonderful laboratory for an experiment with Smith's free-market system. Politically we opted to conduct that experiment, and it worked.

The result of the system has been a high standard of living for most Americans. A family with an income at the national average of about $14,000 a year today has a command over goods and services that would have put it well into the top 10 percent of the pyramid in 1948; a family with a $7,000 income—half the average—has a living standard matching that of the average family of 1948. Judged purely as a system of productive efficiency, contemporary American capitalism has to get a high grade. It needs a tune-up, and perhaps even an overhaul, but not a trade-in.

Most Americans want that productive efficiency—a large and growing volume of goods and services. That public consensus becomes especially evident during recessions, like the one we've recently experienced, when a temporary setback in our standard of living has caused anguish from Maine to Hawaii. Only in the eyes of an antimaterialistic minority is the quality of American life impaired by the quantity of our goods. Most of us consider ourselves sensible enough to use our purchasing power to improve the quality of our lives. For the majority, living in one's own home (as two-thirds of American families do) with a garden and an air-conditioner is a characteristic of the good life.

Whether we are truly made better off by the production of more big cars, more cigarettes and more whisky is a real question. But who should answer that question? Society should ban the sale of products, like heroin, that pose a clear and present danger. But on matters of taste, society should—as it does—let each family make its own choices. Indeed, to most of us, the right to select the items for our market baskets, out of a reasonable list of choices, is an essential element of personal freedom.

So is the right to pick our job. The protection of these freedoms is one of the fringe benefits of the market system, along with its productive efficiency.

Another benefit is the limitation on the power of bureaucracy to use economic sanctions against those who disagree with the Government. As an entry on some of the enemies lists compiled during the Nixon Administration, I shudder to imagine my income and status during that era if the Federal Government had been the only employer. Our present economic system guarantees some supply of dissent and criticism. In our profit-seeking newspapers Seymour Hersh can expose the excesses of the C.I.A., and Bob Woodward and Carl Bernstein can unlock the mystery of Watergate.

In these various ways, capitalism does have *something* to do with freedom. It is impressive that no nation with a fully centralized economy has ever had a free press or a free election. But the capitalism-and-freedom connection is often grossly oversold as an argument against any humanizing and equalizing reform. In fact, coercion by Government—as well as freedom—is part of the recipe for a private-enterprise economy. It relies on promarket laws to enforce contracts, ban fraud and require observance of keep-off signs on private property. These laws are necessary and sensible, but nonetheless encroach on freedom as much as do any antimarket Government bans and regulations. Moreover, the preservation of freedom does not require the preservation of every present feature of U.S. capitalism. It does not depend on whether the dividing line between socialized and private industries is drawn at highways, airports, airlines or steel. Nor does it depend on tax breaks or real-estate deals and family trusts. And it certainly does not depend—contrary to the rhetoric of the Secretary of the Treasury—on cutting the ratio of Federal spending to G.N.P. below the present 23 percent figure. Clearly, personal freedoms have been scrupulously protected in Scandinavian countries with huge budgets and have been obliterated by Fascist regimes that espoused fiscal prudence and private enterprise.

The big liability on the balance sheet of capitalism is, of course, the lopsided distribution of its income and wealth—invidious, inhumane and unesthetic. Individuals get their incomes by using or selling their property, by employing labor or by selling their labor to other employers. If their property commands high interest and profit rates and if their skills are deemed valuable, then they get high incomes. But if what they have to sell has no ready and eager market, they wind up at the bottom of the income pyramid. And so the top 1 percent of all families get more income than the entire bottom 15 percent. Moreover, because high incomes permit saving and investing, the top 1 percent have accumulated more wealth than the bottom 70 percent.

This imbalance cannot be defended ethically as the outcome of fair races in which the prizes go to those who make the greatest contribution. First, even if the system is functioning competitively and honestly, the races aren't completely fair. Some people get head starts through family advantages while others suffer handicaps that are no fault of their own. Second, successes and failures in the marketplace cannot be equated with individual merit or demerit. The buggy whip manufacturer who went broke because of the invention of the automobile had not become less deserving or less productive or less ambitious. Although such penalties may be needed to drive talents and funds away from obsolete products, the results are ethically regrettable. And the successes are the product of a whole social system, not merely the individual's contribution Henry Ford's mass-produced automobile was a big winner in a country with a high average income the width of a continent for unimpeded driving, an alert and ambitious work force and a Government that could protect travellers and enforce rules of the road. An Afghan with the same idea might have died penniless.

Finally there is no excuse for unhumane penalties for losers. Whether or not gladiatorial contests were "fair" it was barbaric to feed the losers to the lions. And it is barbaric to starve the losers in the races of an affluent society. Even when the last-place entries do not exert their full effort, impoverishment is not necessarily the most effective way to get them to try harder in the future. We might learn something from primitive hunting societies that gave their slackers an equal share of the catch, but made them eat apart from the rest of the community or gave them a public scolding for goofing off. Or our social rules might draw from our family rules, which only occasionally invoke material rewards and penalties. Indeed, families typically spend more of their time, effort and money on members with physical, mental or emotional handicaps than on those who function well. We don't regard that as an unfair or perverse incentive system. There is an equally strong case for trying to rehabilitate and motivate the losers and even the slackers in the community—although the process is bound to be costly.

In general, the ethical case for unequal incomes is about as weak as the esthetic cases for lawn mowers. But a violin won't cut the grass and the principle of equal sharing wouldn't maintain our standard of living. However attractive it might be ethically to establish the principle of one-person, one-income—along with one-person one-vote and one-person, one-spouse—it would invite economic disaster. If extra income were not offered as an incentive for extra production, then Adam Smith's "invisible hand" would be paralyzed. That means society would need a brand-new set of signals and incentives for work effort and production.

At this point, I see no reliable substitute for the prizes and penalties of the marketplace. Idealistically, altruism looks great; but realistically its demonstrated scope for motivating human behavior is limited. Blind allegiance to the leader or to the state can be an effective motivator, but the consequences are a lot worse than inequality of income. In the absence of some revolution or breakthrough in human motivation and group organization, a commitment to full equality of income would impose the very high price of a less productive and less efficient society. For the vast majority, an equal slice of a shrunken pie would be no bargain if, for example, full equality of income cost us a generation's worth of economic growth (an optimistic guess, in my judgment), four-fifths of our citizens would be made worse off by that trade. Compared with the alternatives, we are better off living with some economic inequality, although it is ethically unappealing, because it is the most practical route to greater economic benefits for the vast majority.

That verdict does not mean that we must accept all the inequality generated by the market. The distribution of income can be and is adjusted by social action. Our main technique of equalization is a readjustment of incomes away from the well-to-do through progressive taxes and to the poor through "transfer" payments such as Social Security, welfare and food stamps. Federal transfer payments provide more than half of the available incomes of those below the statistical poverty line (currently, a little over $5,000 for a nonfarm family of four) and lift millions more above the line. In trying to promote economic equality, we accept some net cost of inefficiency. When we tax the rich by a dollar to help the poor, the latter cannot get a full dollar's worth of benefits. It costs something to collect taxes, to enforce the laws and to administer the programs of aid. Cheating on taxes and on transfer benefits also imposes a cost. Generous benefit payments to the poor may lead some people to work less. Finally, the rich will save and invest somewhat less when their take-home profits are cut by high taxes.

In short, when we carry money from rich to poor through Government programs, we generally have to use a leaky bucket. We can't expect perfection, although we ought to hold the leaks to a minimum. A 20 percent leakage may be quite tolerable (as well as irreducible in some cases) in view of the humanitarian benefit of the 80 percent that doesn't leak out. Many insidious attacks on transfer benefits really prove only that the programs don't meet a standard of zero leakage—and that is an impossible standard of perfection. Despite the leakages, the tax-transfer reshuffle is the best method of equalization we have.

The leaky bucket can essentially end poverty in our affluent society. When that objective was taken more seriously, the number of people with incomes below the poverty line was reduced from 40 million in 1961 to 24 million in 1969; it has changed little since then. The widespread myth that the poverty problem is intractable comforts those who don't want to share the bill for solving it.

Our most successful antipoverty program is retirement benefits for the aged. Nearly all people retiring at age 65 currently are entitled to Federal pensions that can buy an above-poverty-line market basket. Their benefits are generally far greater than the private annuity their payments of Social Security taxes would have bought. The system produces a huge redistribution from today's young to today's aged, but nobody makes a big deal out of that reshuffle; the young, knowing that their turn will come, do not gripe too much; and the aged cash their Social Security checks without guilt, viewing them as a right they have paid for.

Four million families with heads under age 65 were living on incomes below the poverty line in 1974, and they included 10 million children under 18. For most of this group, unlike the aged, the work disincentive of some programs could spring a huge leak in the bucket. For example the leakage would be enormous if the Government simply made up the difference between the poverty line of $5,000 and the actual income of an average-sized poor family. No working member of such a family would continue at his or her miserable job if offered a $5,000 grant with full-time leisure. To preserve work incentives, an efficient system of cash aids must allow poor people to keep a significant fraction of any additional income that they earn from jobs—just as an efficient tax system must let the rich keep a significant part of their high incomes. Designing a sound program is difficult. Should society provide systematic cash support without requiring *some* work effort? If work effort is required, how can it be accompanied by a guarantee of work opportunity, as it logically must be? The most baffling questions concern fatherless families, which include more than half of all poor children. For families headed by mothers—separated, divorced, widowed or never married—would a work requirement deprive the children of maternal care? Would one that exempted mothers with children under school age encourage the creation of more deprived kids? The nasty fact is that society cannot afford to remove the economic penalties that discourage women from getting into dependent positions and that discourage their men from putting them there. But neither can a proud and affluent democratic nation afford to starve the children of broken families.

These problems have no easy solution; but there is plenty of room for improvement over the existing welfare system, which provides neither adequate aid nor adequate work incentives. In particular, the problem of the fatherless family is accentuated by the widespread denial, under the present system, of welfare aid to intact families. According to public-opinion surveys, a majority of Americans would support Federal cash grants to low-income families that preserved work incentives and backed them up with work opportunities. Welfare reform belongs at the top of the nation's agenda for social progress.

While the tax-transfer shuffle requires a compromise between equality and efficiency, some social reforms promote *both* equality and efficiency. One example is the ending of sexual and racial discrimination in jobs. When, through discrimination, black or female workers are excluded from highly productive jobs for which they are qualified, they are forced, in effect, to function with one of the hands tied behind their backs. That is a source of inefficiency as well as inequality. Society opted for equal-employment opportunity a decade ago, placing fair play for workers above the right of employers to discriminate. Measured against our hopes, the rate of progress has been disappointing; but measured against where we started, it has been impressive, both in raising incomes and in proving that public action can change private behavior with virtually no expenditure of public funds. The achievements so far have added at least $10 billion a year to our gross national product. An intensified effort to eliminate job discrimination could give us a good-sized bonus in G.N.P. as well as a bonus of pride and justice.

Elimination of the disadvantages of the poor in trying to borrow money could also increase efficiency and equality of both income and opportunity. When low-income groups are deprived of access to funds, society suffers an inefficiency. This disadvantage curbs investment by the poor in businesses and homes; it limits their ability to accept apprenticeship jobs and educate their children. The unequal access to capital contributes to the vast differences in rates of college attendance by income class. Male high-school graduates in the bottom socioeconomic quarter of the population tend to go on to college at a rate that is 25 percentage points lower than the rate for male high-school graduates in the top quarter—even when the graduates compared are of *equal* academic ability. (For female graduates, the figure is 35 percentage points.)

In all fairness, banks cannot be asked to take the chances of lending to the poor—it is very risky to take the i.o.u.'s of people who lack the collateral and the income to insure their ability to repay their debts. The Federal Government can and must assume these risks. As an example, it might narrow the huge educational-financing gap by establishing a voluntary social-insurance program that would function in a way that mirrors the present old-age program. Young people from lower-income families could get adequate Federal loans to finance their education, repaying them later with a supplementary tax on their postgraduate incomes.

In general, we should strive for greater equality of opportunity—fairer races. Under the existing system of silver spoons and lead weights, the sons of families in the top fifth of the socioeconomic pyramid have average incomes 75 percent higher than those coming from the bottom fifth. Narrowing that differential is an urgent and feasible objective for a capitalistic democracy.

In our split-level system, money, unfortunately, buys a great many things that are not supposed to be for sale in a democracy. Whenever money buys better legal representation for the wealthy, one of our most sacred rights, equality before the law, is violated. Whenever the poor do not have access to adequate health care, the market is granted power over life and death. Whenever money buys political power and influence, the principle of one-person, one-vote is compromised. The uses of money to counterfeit rights can fill a chamber of horrors. Tax reform has been ignored by some liberal politicians who would not risk antagonizing wealth potential campaign contributors; the regional and industrial interests of Howard Hughes have been protected by contributions to both political parties; again and again, 200,000 milk producers have used intensive lobbying and big campaign contributions to beat 200 million consumers in the arena of politics.

A great many actions are required to take our cherished rights off the auction block—once and for all. The recent reform of election-campaign financing is an encouraging first step; it may turn out to be the most important piece of *economic* legislation of our generation. Next, we need a code of fair play for relations between public officials and lobbying groups, one that distinguishes the legitimate persuasion of ideas from the purchase of favors. We need an enormous and costly expansion of legal services for advising and defending the poor, one that honors our commitment to equality before the law. We need additional Government support for voluntary associations of consumers to countervail the super-rich and the special-interest producer groups.

Democratic capitalism is a workable compromise if people see it as a compromise and want to make it work. That means facing the issues of equality as matters of *more* or *less* rather than *all* or *none*. It means recognizing that "profits" and "rich" are neither dirty nor sacred words. It means developing specific measures that offer greater equality at a low cost of inefficiency or shrinkage of the national economic pie. With such measures, we can establish a right to a decent standard of living, end the transgression of money on rights, and reduce the handicaps in the races for jobs and funds. And we can do all that within the framework of efficiency and private enterprise.

Obviously we cannot do all this costlessly or even cheaply. In combination, the measures that I have espoused would add significantly to the Federal budget—and we cannot afford a major expansion today. But economic growth and prosperity can once again swell the revenues of the Federal Government (with tax rates unchanged). Indeed, we need the productive efficiency of a market system to help finance equalization programs without an extra tax burden on the majority of Americans. Progress toward the goal can be swifter if we forgo tax cuts as a regular and steady diet, if we close tax loopholes that now benefit the wealthy (to the tune of perhaps $15 billion a year), and if we shift resources within the Federal budget (perhaps another $15 billion a year) by putting top priority on equalization programs. If we set the goal of the elimination of poverty, we can move in that direction with welfare reform and continuing improvements in Social Security, food stamps, health-care aid and job-creating programs. We will need to set priorities; we will need to pace ourselves; but we will move with a sense of direction and of mission. And when we reach that target, we should raise our sights further by setting half of the nation's average income as the basic minimum of a decent existence—a standard that is now out of reach of about one-fifth of our families.

Unequal incomes would still determine who can buy beachfront condominiums, second cars and college slots for academic underachievers. But they would not block access to first homes, first cars and college slots for solid students; nor would they confer vastly unequal power over legislators and juries. As the British egalitarian R. H. Tawney once stated his reasonable goal: "Differences of remuneration between different individuals might remain; contrasts between the civilization of different classes would vanish."

And that goal can best be reached by modifying and strengthening democratic capitalism. By preserving our basic institutional framework, we can build on its capacity to adapt gradually—and that adaptability is one of its greatest virtues. The vending-machine society espoused by the right would be brittle and inhumane; the collectivized economy proposed by the left would be bureaucratic and inefficient. All things considered, capitalism and democracy, though polar opposites in some respects, really need each other—to put some rationality into equality and some humanity into efficiency.

Further Thoughts on Equality and Efficiency

I have recently expressed in some detail my views on the goal of equality in our society, particularly in relation to the goal of efficiency.[1] I trust that it will come as no surprise to readers of this paper that I have not yet accumulated a brand-new stock of ideas, nor am I yet ready to recant. Rather, I shall use this occasion to elaborate on some of the central issues, presenting them at a level appropriate for an audience of professional, rather than of interested laymen.

Implicit in my book (and more explicit in this paper) is a reliance on a loose notion of "revealed preferences." I look for the rationale—the internal logic—of the institutions that actually operate in contemporary American society. In moving from the realities of institutions back to the principles, preferences, and constraints that could explain them as a reasonably rational and consistent system, my chain of reasoning reverses that of the social philosopher, who starts with his principles and attempts to derive from them the practices of a "good" society. Perhaps that makes me a backward philosopher.

Yet I too am interested in the good society, and I pursue the line of revealed preferences because I think our society is pretty good. At times, however, I depart from this approach to express my personal preferences, some of which are contrary to those of the majority as reflected in the political process. Indeed, a rigorously consistent application of revealed (rational) preferences would be awfully stuffy, since it must always conclude that whatever society does is best for it, or else it would be doing something else. The theory of efficient markets often strains my credulity, and any theory of efficient institutions would shatter it. I believe I can identify accidents of history, lags and imperfections of the democratic political process, misperceptions of costs or benefits, income effects, and technological innovations that result in policies that are suboptimal or inconsistent with majoritarian preferences. But this is a tricky game, no matter how honestly one tries to play it, and the reader should be on guard for any passages in which I might seem to lean on existing practices just because I like them or to find them irrational just because I do not.

The basic observation that requires explanation is that our society accepts far more inequality in the distribution of its economic assets than in the distribution of its sociopolitical assets. In interpreting that seeming inconsistency, I shall once again argue these points:

1. The social preference for equality applies to economic as well as to "noneconomic" assets (although the intensity of those preferences may vary among classes of items).
2. While there may be costs of equalizing distribution in any area, those costs tend to be greater for income (and wealth) than for social and political rights. Hence, it can be rational to tolerate more inequality in the economic realm than elsewhere.
3. The major cost of equalization of income involves the sacrifice of some of the economic efficiency associated with the unaltered determination of incomes in the marketplace.
4. On this reasoning, inequality that is economically inefficient can be explained as rational and justified only if it serves some other social goal (liberty, respect for the market, preference for lotteries, or the like).
5. In general, since equality of income is both desirable and costly, the optimum will involve a compromise—a sacrifice of efficiency to gain more equality than would obtain in the absence of social action, but a tolerance of more inequality than would be preferred in the absence of the costs.
6. While various aspects of the trade-off are amenable to economic analysis and even to empirical quantification, the optimal compromise must be sought through political decision making. And society has clearly stated its choice for that mechanism—democracy untainted by economic inequality.

The Preference for Equality

When an economist is asked to determine what amount of X is optimal for an individual or for a society, he immediately divides the question into two parts: (1) How much does the decision maker in question like

X, in varying quantities? (2) What does it cost to get those varying quantities of X? To noneconomists, this division may appear to be an unnecessary abstraction or complication—or, as Irving Kristol has put it, a flight into "poetry or theology."[2] But it is the only way to use the tools of our trade. The strict separation of preferences and opportunities is essential in organizing the considerations that enter into rational choice.

One application of the economist's approach lies in drawing inferences about preferences from behavior with respect to close substitutes that have sharply different relative prices. Only because of a strong preference do we use any amount of the high-priced item, as we do when we put expensive gold in our teeth and TV sets, and make room for costly lobster in our diets. To a capitalistic nation, accepting the verdict of the marketplace on income distribution is the low-cost diet. That we leave considerable economic inequality on our menu is no more surprising or instructive than is the fact the individuals eat more codfish than lobster. What is striking is that our society takes some steps toward equalization, reflecting a preference for more equality of income among our citizens than the market would generate.

The underlying rationale of the social preference for economic equality has been propounded in many ways. I shall discuss briefly a few of the formulations: (1) my own technique of drawing inferences from the domain of rights; (2) John Rawls's "original position" formulation; and (3) the classical argument based on interpersonal comparisons of utility.

Inferences from Rights

In our political and social arrangements, society diligently pursues equality. American institutions strive for one-person/one-spouse, one-person/one-vote, equal justice, universal freedom of speech and religion, universal immunity from enslavement, and universal and equal claims for such public services as police protection and public education. They also impose on all citizens, at least in principle, some "negative right," or duties, such as responsibility to obey the law, military conscription when imposed, and jury service.[3]

These social and political rights reveal a preference for treating people equally. This preference is embodied in the proposition that all men are created equal, a proposition obviously intended as a social principle rather than an enunciation of a biological fact. That principle in turn fits Rawls's conception that people see equality as a type of "mutual respect . . . owed to human beings as moral persons."[4]

Our institutional rules suggest that the pure preference (abstracting from costs and consequences) for social and political equality is monotonic—that is, more equality is better than less, and complete equality best of all. The costs of equalization can account for society's countenancing of some inequality of rights and its failure to achieve Rawls's "lexical ordering" which would prevent any inequality of other assets from compromising equality in the domain of basic liberties.[5] In the strict sense, precisely equal justice would require every defendant at a criminal trial to have an equal chance of being represented by F. Lee Bailey. Absolute purity of equal suffrage would involve a ban on all resource-using ways of expressing partisan political sentiments. The costs of purity justify the toleration of some impurity and the adoption of criteria for practical rather than perfect equality in the domain of rights.

To be sure, a society might adopt egalitarian sociopolitical practices even though it did not have a preference for equality. If a preferred distribution with structured inequality could be obtained only by very expensive or cumbersome methods, equal rights might be adopted rationally as the less desirable but also less costly alternative—as a purely instrumental rather than a normative choice. Thus, an individual (or a society) might wish votes to be allocated according to competence or spouses according to "need" and yet despair of any satisfactory (low-cost, operational, and objective) means of achieving that allocation. In particular, such an individual or society might see a high risk that any structured inequality would be administered by government officials in ways creating distortion and discrimination among citizens.

On this argument, the nice thing about counting heads is that the calculation is so simple and objective that it defies (or at least resists) deliberate perversion by a bureaucracy. This seems to be the source of the support of equal and universal rights by some libertarians; they turn to equality only out of dire need of an objective rule that constrains the state and the bureaucracy, or in despair of an operational rule for achieving the structured inequality they would prefer. On that line of reasoning, if there were an agreed-upon objective test of political competence, it would be used to allocate votes. I do not believe that "prediction." It is inconsistent with the way society rules out the objective test of voluntary exchange in the assignment of rights and duties, banning trades in votes, jury duty, and conscripted military service and forbidding contracts for indentured service. Deliberately, specialization and comparative advantage are ruled out of the domain of rights. There is no logical escape from the conclusion that Americans have opted for equal rights because we like equality and not because some preferred inequality is difficult to achieve.

If such a preference for equality operates in the social and political realm, it must apply to the economic realm as well. It would be hard, indeed, to imagine any set of consistent social preferences that would give weight to each citizen's freedom of speech (or suffrage, or any other right) and none to his ability to exercise that right in the face of malnutrition or inadequate health care. Starvation would, to put it mildly, compromise "mutual respect." In practice, American society implements its preference by equalizing incomes to some degree at some costs in many ways—conferring entitlements to expensive resource-using rights like public education, imposing progressive taxation, and supplying transfer benefits in the form of social security, food stamps, and welfare. Egalitarian preferences do not—and logically cannot—stop abruptly at the boundary line between economic and noneconomic institutions. The case for economic egalitarianism can be inferred from the equality of sociopolitical rights. Of course, that inference takes as given, rather than seeking to explain, social and political egalitarianism—a delimitation of inquiry that I, as an economist, find convenient and intellectually defensible.

I would not argue that all of the economic inequality society tolerates is necessarily attributable to the perception of the costs of eliminating it. There may be a pure preference to leave some lottery—some inequality—in the income and wealth distribution.[6] Or, as I shall discuss below, there may be some value attached to the market's verdict. Moreover, the concept of complete or perfect economic equality is a will-o'-the-wisp which fortunately we need not chase.[7]

The "Original Position"

John Rawls develops the general case for social, political, and economic equality by invoking a social-contract process: people in an "original position" frame a constitution in ignorance of their class position in the future society and their relative standing with respect to assets and abilities.[8] In particular, they will determine the distribution of the lottery tickets in an urn from which every individual's income will be drawn. From the vantage point of the original position, each participant must view his or her future income as a random drawing from the urn; given the absence of any clues on whether their own tickets will be high or low, all participants would be mutually disinterested. The risk aversion of individuals can then be relied on to produce a preference for equality. It can be safely predicted that the founding fathers and mothers would not design an urn that implied 50 percent probabilities of starvation and of great affluence.

I regard the "original position" as an appealing analytical device for establishing the social preference for equality. Rawls, however, goes far beyond this point by associating with that same process the "difference principle," which insists that "all social values . . . be distributed equally unless an unequal distribution of any . . . is to everyone's advantage"—in particular, to the advantage of the typical person in the least advantaged group.[9] If the difference principle (or "maximin" criterion) is intended as a prediction of how American citizens would behave in a hypothetical original position, I am confident that it is wrong. Contrary to what is implied by the difference principle, very few Americans would prefer an urn *A* whose tickets gave each and every family $14,000 a year to an urn *B* that provided 90 percent of all families with $20,000 and 10 percent with $13,900. As I interpret him, Rawls is really making a different "prediction": that, in the process of discussing the ethics under which the future society should operate, the founders would become impressed with the undesirability of taking advantage of the (unidentified) least fortunate members. Hence, they would adopt a constitutional provision against ever doing so, no matter how slightly and no matter for what benefit and return. I would doubt that prediction as well as the first (and, moreover, the principle is not ethically persuasive to me).

I would even be willing to "predict" various ways in which the original-position group would be willing to lower the minimum income in order to raise mean income, in violation of the difference principle. I suspect that they would behave in Rawlsian fashion insofar as it was necessary to insure against starvation, recognizing that the belly they fill may be their own. I would expect them to demand a large—but still finite—gain in mean income if they were to impose deprivation of a cultural (as well as a strictly physiological) character on the least fortunate members of society. There is even evidence on that issue: a sociological survey shows a widespread perception that the threshold of deprivation lies around half of the average income of the society.[10] I would expect them to show some special concern for the welfare of children. On the other hand, as I noted above, I would not be surprised if even their *ideal* embodied some lottery; for a given average, they might prefer the majority of people to be a little below the mean so that a few could obtain some worthwhile prizes. In principle, psychologists could take some of the conjecture (and some of the fun) out of this range of issues by designing experiments in which people selected the urn from which their "living standard" would be stochastically determined for a short period—if not for the lifetime of a society.

Interpersonal Comparisons?

Both the inferences from rights and the original-position formulation are alternatives to the traditional foundation of economic egalitarianism—a foundation based on interpersonal comparisons of utility.[11] According to that line of reasoning, individuals experience diminishing marginal utility of income, as is demonstrated by their risk-avoiding behavior. When their incomes double, their economic welfare increases but does not double—as is evidenced by the fact that they will not bet their entire income double-or-nothing on the flip of a coin. If each individual experiences diminishing marginal utility of income, then the maximum utility for the whole society must be obtained when the marginal utility of all individuals is equated. And if all individual utility functions are the same, that must occur with complete equality of income.

The last assumption—that all individual utility functions are the same—is the critical one in this chain of reasoning. Since such a proposition about interpersonal comparisons of utility is not empirically verifiable, it must stand as a value judgment—all individuals *should* be treated as though they have the same utility functions. But that in itself is an egalitarian judgment; it "sneaks" an assumed preference for equality into the argument designed to establish that very preference. As Henry Simons once pointed out, that argument could prove treacherous to egalitarians.[12] Imagine a technological breakthrough in utility measurement: a new "utilometer" gives readings consistent with all other observations on any individual and yet different readings across individuals with identical incomes. The social-utility maximizers would then be committed to give especially large incomes to those citizens who are found to be efficient generators of utility. If the empty box of interpersonal comparison were ever filled, the contents might be explosive.

The appeal of the original-position approach is that it can rest its case on diminishing marginal utility without invoking interpersonal comparisons. It focuses on the way one individual would choose among urns that have large or small variances in payoffs, and relies on the well-established diminishing marginal utility of the individual to predict a preference for low variance or equality. But the "intrapersonal" comparison it requires is strained and artificial: Its "veil of ignorance" about one's own capacities introduces an element of split personality. To ensure that the participants are truly disinterested, they are not allowed to "know themselves." But that still seems analytically preferable to interpersonal comparisons.

The new egalitarian literature should render obsolete the approach based on interpersonal comparisons. Yet it is clear why the traditional approach dies hard. With interpersonal comparisons, it becomes possible to rank various Pareto-optimal states (that is, situations where no reallocation can make some better off without making some worse off) in terms of aggregate or social utility, with the higher rankings going to the more nearly equal distributions. By that standard, society misallocates resources when it distributes badly, much as it misallocates resources when it produces badly. It may then legitimately be called "waste" when the garbage of the rich contains better food than the diet of the poor, or when more land is devoted to one private estate than to the homes of a thousand average families.

In contrast, the inferences-from-rights and original-position approaches impose on us an awkward two-stage process of defining optimality. In the first stage, those approaches must accept any and all Pareto-optimal distributions as "efficient" (in terms of preferences revealed through voluntary exchange or dollar-voting)—none involves waste. In the second stage some will be judged better than others insofar as they are more consistent with society's preference for equality—a preference that is exhibited through ballot voting and that is not readily quantifiable in dollars. The analysis must grapple with two sets of considerations—one associated with economic efficiency and the other with the preference for equality. Clearly, this is more cumbersome than the one-step approach of interpersonal comparisons—sufficiently more cumbersome to make me wish I could accept the latter. But I cannot.

The Cost of Equalization

In our capitalistic economy, the marketplace determines the prices of factors of production—labor and various types of physical property. Given the ownership of the productive factors (which is itself strongly influenced by the market over the longer run), the factor prices in turn determine the incomes of the citizenry. That market-determined incomes provide incentives and signals that contribute to efficiency has been the main story told by the economics profession for two centuries. But market-determined incomes also generate the economic inequality we dislike. Equalizing income thus implies modifying, vetoing, or supplanting the market determination, and therein lies its cost.

Doubters raise many searching questions about the efficiency of the real-world (as distinct from the competitive-model) marketplace. Does more real gross national product really mean more welfare? How seriously are consumer choices distorted by misinformers and "hidden persuaders"? How important is monopoly, which confers income as a reward for promoting scarcity rather than productivity? How serious are uncorrected externalities, excess supplies and demands? These issues are crucial, but I will ignore them in this paper—because they are so broad and complex.

All in all, I find the efficiency arguments in favor of the marketplace persuasive. These arguments have both a static and a dynamic component—getting the right things produced today and achieving progress tomorrow. The dynamic component can be further split into two parts: the importance of market incentives to accumulate physical capital (save and invest) and to innovate. I see the dynamic considerations as more important than the static considerations, and innovation as far more significant than accumulation.

Indeed, I believe that concern about accumulation incentives is grossly overemphasized in debates on redistribution.[13] The national saving-and-investment rate is, in fact, a result of political decisions—and should be explicitly faced as such. Society can have the saving-and-investment rate it wants with more or less inequality of income, so long as it is willing to twist some other dials, involving the capital-building component of public budgets, the mix of fiscal-monetary policy, and the taxation of middle-income savers and investors. In the area of innovation, collective action (such as publicly financed basic research) is essential to rescue the market from the appalling inefficiency of private property in knowledge.[14] Yet the market does provide vital incentives for experimentation and innovation that cannot be replaced on a collectivized basis. That is where the really large dynamic costs of any drastic income redistribution are likely to be found.

The basic technique of redistribution actually employed in our society lies in the tax-transfer reshuffle. It appeals to me in principle and in practice. It allows a first-round distribution of income that is dictated by market verdicts and then modifies the results by imposing progressive taxation and by supplying resource-using rights (public goods) to all and transfer benefits (the equivalent of negative taxes) to the poor. With very few exceptions, this second-round redistribution cannot be carried out costlessly: as I like to put it, we can transport money from rich to poor only in a leaky bucket.[15] Some obvious leakages include administrative and compliance costs of implementing both tax and transfer programs, altered and misplaced work efforts resulting from them, and distortion of innovative behavior as well as saving and investment behavior. The most insidious attacks on an equalization program are those that view the discovery of any leakage as prima facie evidence against the desirability of the program. Holding it up to a standard of perfection, or zero leakage, guarantees a negative verdict. A social preference for equality implies a willingness to pay some costs for equalization.

Given (1) a social preference for equality (or at least for more equality than market-determined incomes provide), and (2) a cost of altering the market-determined distribution, society faces a trade-off between equality and efficiency. The resulting optimum will normally be a compromise.[16] Some efficiency will be sacrificed by altering the market's verdict through a second-round redistribution in the direction of greater equality. But some economic inequality will be left because it preserves economic efficiency (or some other social value, a point discussed below). Thus, society will carry the leaky bucket to pursue equality up to the point where the added benefits of more equality are just matched by the added costs of lesser efficiency.

These formal principles have significant implications. For one thing, they put into perspective the often-asked question, "How much equalization of income is enough?" That issue is no different from how large a capital stock or how large a police force or how large a computer is "enough." For all, the optimal "enough" is reached when the next unit costs more than it is worth. So long as benefits and costs are continuous, both fanaticism and complacency about equalization are ruled out of bounds. Second, the principles supply sufficient grounds for society's acting to alter the results of the income distribution. In particular, the preference for equality implies that the overall tax structure must be progressive and not proportional.[17] As Henry Simons suggested long ago, the case for progressive taxes rests on the proposition that inequality is "unlovely."[18] In principle, the necessary and sufficient case for the tax-transfer reshuffle is that simple.

The formal rules do not prescribe what public policy ought to do, but they strongly suggest what public policy questions the country ought to discuss. First, the political dialogue should focus explicitly on the intensities of social preference in favor of equality: I wish that the opinion researchers would give us the public's answers to my leaky-bucket experiment. Second, economists and other social scientists should be striving to measure the leakages and the effective equalization accomplished by various programs of taxation, transfer benefits, and public goods. The effort to quantify the trade-off ought to cover not only existing programs but also such proposals as guarantees of job opportunity, subsidization of low wages, and new forms of subsidy to higher education.

As I read the serious empirical studies of the larger and better-established programs of taxation and income maintenance, I am impressed by the small size of the leakages they find; often 80 or even 90 percent of the contents seem to stay in the bucket. I am also encouraged by the evidence that the programs can be made even more efficient; there are opportunities to plug some of the leaks. Understandably, the leakages seem especially small for aid to the aged, where disincentives to work are not a serious problem. The major leakages in our present old-age security program seem to be confined to its options for early retirement and its structure of minimum benefits (which subsidizes groups like federal workers that do not contribute during most of their careers).

One of the key unsettled empirical issues involves the effects of education on both productivity and wage differentials. The "human capitalists" and the "screeners" in the profession have been slugging it out for years on the social productivity of education.[19] According to either view, a national increase in education reduces the dispersion of labor incomes. But the size of the leakage from such a route to equality depends on how much the investment in education raises productivity. On that issue, the human capitalists are optimistic, while the screeners paint the bleak picture that the investment serves mainly private ends by providing a job-screening device based on relative education. The recent work of Tinbergen offers impressive evidence on the responsiveness of differentials between the wages of the skilled and the unskilled to increases in the supply of educated workers.[20] As he suggests, a policy of saturation of human capital—investment in human capital that is overinvestment relative to any efficiency criterion—may be an important option for reducing the inequality of labor income. Still, the size of the resulting leakage depends on the relative importance of human capital and screening—an issue on which much more research is needed.

As Jan Pen said in his review of my book, "A quantitative guess about the rate of transformation between efficiency and equality still seems beyond the intellectual capacities of our profession . . . ."[21] He is right that this was an especially "sketchy" part of my book; I claim no special expertise in the measurement of leakages or benefits. Hence, my main message remains an appeal to the public and to the profession to sharpen the focus on the trade-off.

The Puzzle of Inefficient Inequality

By the reasoning above, since inequality and inefficiency are both undesirable, society should not be expected to tolerate an arrangement that exacerbates both (unless the arrangement happens to promote some other social goal). Yet, there are uncorrected situations that contribute to both inequality and inefficiency. One of the clearest and most significant is the disadvantage low-income citizens suffer in access to capital. Clearly, the poor face effective interest rates higher than those faced by the rich. This inequality in turn increases the inequality of the income distribution, particularly by discouraging investments in human capital by the poor.[22] The discrimination by lenders can arise from their natural self-interest—the invisible hand; it does not *necessarily* reflect any intended bias on their part. The risk to the lender depends on the borrower's total ability to repay, on the reliability of his signature. Hence, to the lender, a loan to a low-income person is riskier than one to a high-income borrower, even if the former is proposing to use the money for a project with a distinctly higher probability of success. But the risk to society lies in the use of resources for unproductive projects, and this is quite separate from the question of whether the lender is repaid. Thus, a socially efficient allocation of capital would require that funds flow to the particular projects that are most likely to succeed, regardless of the wealth of the prospective entrepreneurs. The market's result, therefore, involves misallocation—inefficiency as well as inequality.

Why does society tolerate such a source of additional inefficiency and additional inequality? Surely, the discrimination does not promote other social values. Indeed, it is not condoned: witness the hortatory speeches by public officials asking bankers to take care of the poor; consider the specific social programs designed to ameliorate this bias—the Federal

Housing Administration, Small Business Administration, student loan programs, and the rest. I think that the real answer lies simply in the limitations of public-sector technology: it is not easy to design effective, low-cost, public programs that would improve the access of low-income groups to capital. Innovations by social scientists in this area could help to reduce both inefficiency and inequality.

The more complex case of job discrimination based on race or sex presents similarities as well as instructive contrasts to discrimination in the access to capital. Both biases misallocate and distort investments in human capital. For example, the woman who knows she will be unlikely to get a management job has no incentive to invest in training to qualify as a manager. But the effect on income inequality of job bias is not necessarily as pronounced as the effect of the lending bias. Because disadvantage in access to capital is geared directly to low income and low wealth, it must increase inequality; that need not be the case for ethnic job discrimination. For example, the average income of Jews exceeded that of other Americans at times when anti-Semitic job discrimination was widespread. In such exceptional cases, equalizing opportunity (and enhancing other social values such as fairness) may actually increase the inequality of income.

Furthermore, job discrimination (unlike the lending bias) could *conceivably* be "perfect," in the same sense that monopolistic price discrimination can be perfect, altering distribution but avoiding inefficiency and leaving social surplus intact. Under conditions of perfect job discrimination, blacks and women (and other victims of prejudice) would get exactly the same jobs they would obtain if not disadvantaged but would merely receive less pay for them. In fact, however, the prevalence of exclusion from good jobs (rather than exploitation involving lower wages) as the technique of discrimination makes substantial inefficiency a by-product of inequality.[23]

Finally, unlike the case with lending, some people *must* have preferences for discrimination when job selections are biased sexually or ethnically.[24] Those discriminators obviously lost welfare when legislation enforcing equal employment opportunity was enacted, at the same time that real GNP was increased and the welfare of the victims of discrimination was enhanced. But I do not believe that the legislation should be interpreted as the embodiment of a new conviction that the welfare gained by others outweighed the welfare lost by discriminators. The legal ban on stealing a loaf of bread does not imply a judgment that the bread stealer would gain less utility than would be lost by the potential victim. The relevant social judgment is that he would be violating the rights of others and that his own utility from such activity should be disregarded. Indeed, any system of law involves decisions that certain types of preferences are inadmissible elements in a social utility function and should not be allowed to influence allocation. The political decision outlawing job discrimination reclassified preferences for discrimination as inadmissible—placing them with preferences in favor of bread stealing. By that interpretation, an appraisal of the social pluses and minuses of equal employment opportunity should not subtract from its total benefits the welfare loss imposed on those with preferences for discrimination. But here again the technology for ruling out such preferences is sorely inadequate, as is evidenced by the inefficient reliance on job quotas for implementing equality of employment opportunity.

In general, a clear case of inequality of opportunity emerges whenever anyone who comes to the marketplace is confronted with a "specially" unfavorable opportunity locus because of his or her personal characteristics rather than any peculiar properties of the package that he or she is offering to buy or sell. Insofar as that discrimination is practiced "imperfectly" and operates to push the person to the lower part of the income distribution, it contributes to both inequality of income and inefficiency of allocation. Wherever the social technology is available, rooting out such inequalities of opportunity offers a promising improvement in both equality and efficiency.

To the extent that inequality of opportunity breeds both inequality of income and inefficiency, there is a clear case for corrective social action that does not depend on a distinct preference for equality of opportunity. Yet, of course, society does have such a preference—a desire for fairness—which reinforces the case for correction. The social goals include both equalizing opportunity and equalizing results. Most Americans would agree that even fair races should not result in inhumane penalties on losers or unreasonable prizes for winners. In any case, the achievement of reasonable equality of opportunity in our society requires narrowing the inequality of results in which the current inequalities of opportunity are so deeply rooted.

The Relativism of the Market's Verdict

Throughout the analysis this far, I have assumed that citizens have preferences about the *result* of the economic process—the distribution of command over goods and services—that are distinguishable from their feelings about the method by which those results were obtained. This is a crucial assumption. Indeed, every serious analysis that urges society to cease modifying the income distribution is based on the contention that the market method is so good, or any method of modification so bad, that the market's verdict should be left intact.

In some important noneconomic areas, we do regard whatever results emerge as untouchable, because they are generated by an explicitly accepted ideal process. I do not believe that the winner of an election is always the best candidate, but I believe that it would be wrong to overturn the results. Similarly, I do not care whether a jury finds a particular defendant guilty or not; I care only that justice be done. And I am prepared to respect the jury's verdict, unless I learn that the intended process was violated by tampering or the like.

Unlike the jury's verdict, the market's verdict is not accepted as necessarily ultimate. The second-round "reshuffle" is established precisely to allow political decision making to second-guess the market. As revealed by our laws, the first-round process is not regarded as sacred, nor the second-round process as sinful.

The Market as Ideal

To be sure, generations ago the marginal productivity theory of factor pricing was invoked by some economists to demonstrate the justice of the income distribution generated by a competitive market economy. I know of no proponent of that view within the economics profession today (though Milton Friedman is ambivalent).[25]

That normative view dissolved in recognition of the enormous distinction between effort and output, of the accidental ("unmerited") variations in the value of marginal product stemming from shifts in demand, and of the dependence of each unit's marginal product on the inputs of other units, which implies the omnipresence of joint inputs (and really makes the social environment a basic joint input in everybody's production process). These considerations effectively rule out the attribution of merit or desert to the market outcome. The results of the first-round income distribution cannot be defended as fair rewards for personal contribution.

The concept of reward for contribution has an even more fundamental defect. It is the logic—perhaps the magic—of capitalism to make distribution a by-product of production; the value of products determines factor prices which in turn determine incomes. Thus, the value of extra marketable output created by the labor and property inputs of any producer is supposed to be returned to that producer in the form of command over marketable output. In that sense, each contributor takes out what he puts in; and it all appears very natural, very fair, and almost inevitable. But that appearance is convincing only in the narrow cultural context of a market economy.

Until the seventeenth century, productive contribution was not viewed as the key to income distribution. For militaristic, marauding, and slave-owning societies, the name of the game was obtaining command over goods and services *without* engaging in the labors of production. In both feudal and monastic societies, the carving up of the pie was governed by rules and customs that did not have much to do with contributions to the baking of that pie. Across the range of human societies, the penalty for slackers was often ostracism, physical punishment, or the threat of divine retribution, rather than deprivation from consumption. The notion that income rewards geared to productive contribution is a natural or self-evident principle is a symptom of market myopia; an excellent treatment for that disease is a careful reading of the works of Karl Polanyi.[26]

An appreciation of the relativism of market rewards can also be gleaned from contemporary noneconomic institutions. Students, soldiers, amateur athletes, club members, friends, and family members are not rewarded with a command over resources geared to their contribution to the "output" of the relevant community. The laissez-faire market economy is unique in presuming that people *should* take out the value of what they contributed.

The Specter of the State

Most contemporary arguments that oppose altering the market's verdict do not rely on enthusiasm for the market, but instead stress the negative aspects of the political second-guessing process. Rather than deifying the market, these theories vilify political decision making. Such arguments are deeply rooted in basic philosophical conceptions of the desirable role of the state. Two modern laissez-faire theories, developed by Friedrich Hayek and by Robert Nozick, can serve to illustrate the nature of the critical issues in this huge area.

According to Hayek, the function of government is to root out the evil of coercion, but the only way it can carry out that mission is "by the threat of coercion. Free society has met this problem by conferring the monopoly of coercion on the state and by attempting to limit this power of the state to instances where it is required to prevent coercion by private persons."[27] Moreover, except in the case of the monopoly of an essential service, market arrangements do not involve coercion, according to Hayek; they may impose hardship on individuals but not "true coercion."[28] Hence, any policies requiring coercion by the state to mitigate such noncoercive hardships would be improper, since they would serve purposes other than preventing coercion by private persons.[29] In Hayek's view, it is clearly appropriate for the citizens to authorize coercion by the state to keep them from killing one another: but it is wrong to empower the state to exercise coercion in order to prevent death by starvation that is imposed impersonally by the market. Our society is not impressed by that distinction, and neither am I.

In his presentation of the case against redistribution, Nozick offers an even more restricted concept of the desirable role of the state. He develops an invisible-hand explanation of the state: it arises from individuals hiring protective agencies to help enforce their rights; as a result of economies of scale, a single protective agency becomes dominant in the territory and thus achieves a monopoly position. Such a state could emerge "without violating anyone's rights," and only such a state can be justified.[30] The resulting "entitlement theory" of distributive justice makes the appropriateness of any distribution of assets depend entirely on the justice of their acquisition and transfer, and not at all on the dispersion of material welfare among individuals.[31]

Like John Locke, Nozick depends heavily on a concept of natural rights. Indeed, he concedes candidly that, to him, it is an assumption rather than a conclusion that "there is some set of principles obvious enough to be accepted by all men of good will, precise enough to give unambiguous guidance in particular situations, clear enough so that all will realize its dictates, and complete enough to cover all problems that actually will arise."[32]

That assumption about natural principles or laws is indispensable to Nozick's theory. The state obviously punishes people for breaking rules. Such law enforcement can be noncoercive (not violating anyone's rights) only if the rules are "natural"—prior to and independent of the state. Thus, it can be argued that, because of natural rights, no one has the right to steal property from his neighbor: hence, when the government enforces laws against theft, it is not infringing on any right.

Frankly, I find the natural-law approach mind-boggling. One of the many questions that mystify me is how John Locke and his disciples acquired the franchise for stipulating the set of natural laws. (Was that "just acquisition"?) Suppose, for a moment, that some intruder into this game advances, as a principle "obvious enough to be accepted by all men of good will," that no citizen of an affluent society should ever be seriously deprived of material sustenance. Thus he can claim that the state is merely enforcing natural law when it carries the leaky bucket. On what basis can he be told that he is wrong? More generally, why should natural laws restrict the state's function to that of a protective association, rather than including a role as an insurance association or a mutual benevolent association?

Varying Normative Attitudes toward the Market

Empowering the political process to second-guess the market does not imply complete neutrality—a purely instrumental attitude—toward the market. People can have preferences about the dispersion of incomes and still have preferences about the process by which income is obtained. Clearly, many Americans are market fans, who like a recognition of success that takes the form of additional command over material output; others are offended by the reliance on greed and competition, rather than fraternity and cooperation, as the key motivating forces in economic life.

The market fans would pay something (but not an unlimited amount) in terms of both efficiency and equality to extend the scope of market determination, while the others would make some sacrifice to narrow it. My own value judgments come out essentially neutral: I like the impersonality of the market process, and I become attached to instrumentalities that work well, but I have some negative feelings about greed and competition.

I prefer exceptionally good plumbers to average plumbers—no matter whether they are better because they are more energetic, or better trained, or better endowed genetically. But I personally want average plumbers to get less steak and smaller homes only insofar as such a structure of rewards and penalties elicits better productive performance. I believe, nonetheless, that the majority of my fellow citizens are market fans. Popular expressions of concern about work incentives, handouts, and welfare ripoffs go beyond regrets about waste in the tax-transfer reshuffle, implying some attachment to the market's principles of distribution. Suppose, for example, that the voters were offered two alternative programs that would achieve exactly the same total GNP with the same income distribution. Program *A* would increase transfer benefits, while program *B* would establish an inefficiently large subsidy for the training of unskilled workers, thus permitting some of them to earn higher pay in the marketplace. Even if it could be demonstrated that the two involved the same government expenditures, the same tax burdens, and the same leakages, I would predict that program *B* would be preferred by an overwhelming majority—both of those who would be taxed to finance the programs and of those who would be recipients of the benefits. Equalization that raises the wage income of the poor is more popular than transfers unconnected to work effort, and it would remain so even if it were demonstrably no more efficient.

The development of such attitudes is easy to understand. Once our laws permit affluence and poverty to coexist, our attitudes must allow the wealthy to enjoy their rewards without personal guilt and must countenance the poverty without social guilt. We become committed to make a judgment that the rich and the poor deserve what they get, or else we would feel morally obliged to narrow the disparities. In effect, the rules of the game legitimatize inequality and, at the same time, reinforce pecuniary incentives with invidious socioeconomic distinctions between productive and unproductive citizens. When it rewards success in the marketplace with social approval as well as with affluence and penalizes failure with social disapproval as well as with deprivation, society marshals a broad set of incentives for market-oriented behavior.

The market ethic has been sold to a mass market. Getting paid is "belonging" in the minds of most citizens. Sociological studies reveal that the poor really do want to work and would strongly prefer higher incomes that come from better-paying jobs rather than from more generous transfer benefits.[33] The surprisingly small disincentive effects of some income-maintenance programs may reflect the motivational force of the market ethic. That, in turn, cuts two ways. On the one hand, fairly generous transfers can be provided without encountering major leakages. On the other hand, the more general and generous the transfer programs become, the more nonmarket income is legitimized, thereby ultimately weakening the market ethic and increasing the size of the leakages. By that reasoning, welfare checks delivered with a smile may be a dangerous product. Indeed, many affluent voters want to keep the frown in transfers that go to people who, in principle, could work. On the other hand, the careful design of a contributory theology—even mythology—in old-age insurance keeps the frown out of that program, as seems appropriate for recipients for whom work disincentives are not a serious problem. Whether or not he shares them, no egalitarian can afford to ignore these market-oriented ethical attitudes when designing and promulgating proposals for carrying the leaky bucket.[34]

Decentralization and Freedom

Beyond the realm of economic efficiency, the market serves a valuable function by diversifying power in the society and, in particular, by providing a counterweight to the power of the state. Following the principles of portfolio diversification, a sound and viable society will not put all its eggs in one basket. It will rely on many mechanisms for decision making, including the formal political process, informal voluntary associations, and organized systems of nonmonetary awards, as well as the market. That is, society strives for balance: giving the market its place and at the same time keeping it in its place.

Trade-Off with Liberty?

By providing for diversification and decentralization, the market contributes to personal liberty. I attach great importance to this contribution, as should be evident in several passages in my book.[35] But I do not see a general trade-off between equality and liberty, so long as equalization is pursued through the tax-transfer reshuffle and the other mechanisms that I recommend—which do not include extended government control over employment or greater public ownership of the means of production. In insisting that the second-round redistribution need not compromise liberty, I believe that I am making the same distinction that Henry Simons intended in the following passage: "What is important, for libertarians, is that we preserve the basic processes of free exchange and that egalitarian measures be superimposed on those processes, effecting redistribution afterward and not in the immediate course of production and commercial transaction."[36] Yet, I have been frequently criticized for my position on this issue. As Irving Kristol put it, ". . . the more fundamental antithesis, the real tradeoff, is not between equality and efficiency but between equality and liberty."[37] I believe that this disagreement is rooted in a confusion between liberty and private property rights.

Of course, the size and scope of redistribution affect the level of tax rates in our society (just as do the size of the defense and highway budgets). And, in a meaningful sense, higher tax rates narrow the scope of private property rights. At one extreme, absolute rights to private property imply zero taxation; and, at the other, 100 percent taxation is just a polite description of confiscation. Thus, there is a trade-off between the size of the tax-transfer reshuffle and the scope of private property rights.

But even by the libertarian's "negative" definition of liberty—"the absence of . . . coercion by other men"[38]—maximum liberty cannot be equated with the maximum scope of private property rights, inasmuch as the latter extends the police power of the state. Private property rights are exercised through voluntary exchange in the marketplace, which in turn depends critically on the state's enforcement of contracts. To be sure, contract enforcement may be viewed as refereeing rather than policing, because it "merely" requires people to abide by their own voluntary decisions. That is a valid distinction, although it must be applied consistently: if laws that require voluntary exchange to be based on truthful statements do not trespass on liberty, then regulations for accurate labeling and advertising, as well as the legal enforcement of contracts, are exonerated from the charge of trespass.

The major exercise of coercion by the state applies, however, to people who are *not* party to the particular contract. The protection of private property rights—the enforcement of the "Keep-Off" sign—is the most pervasive encroachment on liberty (in the sense of minimum coercion) in our society. I want the state to exclude everyone else from the use of my toothbrush, and I would crusade for laws enforcing the private ownership of toothbrushes, but I must concede that such laws represent an extension of coercion by the state. However justified and self-evident the case for promarket coercion may be, it is still coercion. The inability of some libertarians to recognize coercion when it is exercised in behalf of the market is an incomprehensible blind spot in their analysis.

The conflict between liberty and private property is dramatically evident for those private property rights that are created out of thin air by the state—patents and copyrights, common-carrier and broadcasting certificates, and, most significantly, the limited-liability joint-stock corporation. I favor all of these useful institutions, but they all extend the exercise of coercion by the state. When the government grants an exclusive patent to one agent for a promising new antibiotic like Minocin, it is broadening the scope of private property rights; but it is imposing coercion on everybody else—on 99.99999953 percent of the population. By comparison, when the government bans the sale of a dangerous chemical like Kepone, it removes a private property right, opposite to the Minocin case; and it applies coercion to 100 percent of the population—only trivially different from the former case. Clearly, if all society cared about was maximizing liberty (minimizing coercion), the state should keep its hands off both Minocin and Kepone.

The cases of the altered and unaltered income distribution are to me like the Kepone-Minocin pair in these respects: the altered distribution significantly narrows the scope of private property, but does not significantly enlarge the scope of coercion. The trade-off arises between the maximum scope of private property rights on the one hand and both liberty and equality on the other, not between liberty and equality.

Maximizing the scope of private property does not maximize efficiency any more than it maximizes liberty. Within even the narrowest purview of the most abstract model of a competitive economy, efficiency requires public actions to deal with externalities, public goods, pervasive economies of scale, and incentives to destroy competition. The scope of private property rights is clearly reduced by even these minimal requirements, like public ownership of lighthouses and navigable rivers, smoke-abatement action, antimerger legislation, and regulation of the telephone company.

In my view, we can afford to deal pragmatically with the modifications of property rights required both to enhance efficiency and to increase equality, so long as the balance between the political system and the market system stays in the zone that ensures decentralization. When technology opens new areas of potentially important externalities (like the noise of SSTs and the locations of nuclear power plants), and when our affluence and our attitudes enlarge the tax-transfer reshuffle, a gradual expansion of the scope and size of the public sector is a rational response that leaves us well within the safety zone.

Democracy, Discretion, and Demagoguery

There is no Lorenz curve that I or anyone else could unveil as the optimal target for the society. I was not bashful about spelling out my personal preferences in my book, although there is no reason why they should appeal to others. I do, however, hope to persuade others to share my views about the preconditions for optimization—a more focused public dialogue on the intensities of preferences for equality and a greater research effort by social scientists on the measurement of the leakages. In short, I am pleading for us all to face up to the trade-off between equality and efficiency.

In aiming for a crystallization of social attitudes toward the trade-off and in aiming for their implementation, I am counting on effective, enlightened, democratic political decision making. I am well aware that such a course has its dangers.

One is the danger of big and erratic changes in the rules of the game. In a majoritarian political system with two political parties, the tax-transfer reshuffle and the scope of resource-using rights might undergo a drastic overhaul whenever power changed hands. Extreme uncertainty about the future levels and progressivity of taxes, for example, could pose a serious threat to efficiency. Moreover, abrupt shifts would raise questions of fairness to those people who had accumulated wealth with a reasonable expectation that the general levels of taxation imposed on property income and wealth transfer would continue.

Obviously, one sure remedy for the concern that anything might go is the establishment of a principle that nothing goes. But the need for predictability cannot justify that solution. A constitutional amendment that established extremely high and progressive rates for income and estate taxes would provide as much certainty as one that repealed them. In fact, taxes and transfers have been treated as standard kinds of legislation, enactable by simple majorities of both houses of Congress and subject to veto by the President. Yet, those laws have been subject to remarkable continuity rather than to erratic fluctuation. Major structural changes in the tax base or the scope of transfer programs have at times been phased in gradually, often with a grandfather clause. Unlike some other nations, we have not imposed federal taxes on the holding of wealth (as distinguished from property income or the transfer of wealth), in part because the initiation of such a tax might be "retroactive." The political process has displayed a great respect for continuity; on the whole, I find that reassuring.

The much graver danger is that the democratic process may become myopic in confronting the trade-off between equality and efficiency. Much of the gain from a redistributive program is immediate, while many of the efficiency costs are delayed and, indeed, less obvious than the gain. When the lowest 51 percent of families in the distribution have only a quarter of all income and only one-twentieth of all wealth, is there an adequate safeguard against a demogogue who might irresponsibly promise a majority of voters a "fair share" of the pie?

Some market enthusiasts have a recurrent nightmare in which the mob wrecks the bakeries in its quest for bread. As I see it, that nightmare has not materialized in American political and economic life, but I suspect that the security of the wealthy has been ensured because money has bought political power. Indeed, I believe that the use of money to acquire voting rights has blunted the political expression of majoritarian preferences for equality. As a result or recent legislation to curb the counterfeiting of votes, we will get a test of the operation of a more democratic political process.

At the moment, we are experiencing a disturbing divisiveness of attitudes. Recent efforts to curb the market's transgression on equal political rights have frightened those who hold the bulk of the wealth (and think that they therefore hold the bulk of the truth), and have aroused antidemocratic political sentiments. There is a more obvious growth of anticapitalistic sentiments by the nonaffluent. *Profits* and *rich* are often dirty words in the halls of Congress. The rationing and allocative functions of the price system are blithely ignored by many of our legislators. Instead of blending the values of capitalism and democracy, many are pitting them against each other. Instead of compromising, we are polarizing. The nation sorely needs a serious dialogue and a major educational undertaking to develop the enlightened attitudes of compromise, and I hope that this conference will help meet that urgent national need.

Notes

1. Arthur M. Okun, *Equality and Efficiency: The Big Tradeoff* (Washington, D.C.: The Brookings Institution, 1975).

2. Irving Kristol, "The High Cost of Equality," *Fortune*, vol. 92 (November 1975), p. 199.

3. Okun, *Equality and Efficiency*, pp. 6–10.

4. John Rawls, *A Theory of Justice* (Cambridge: Harvard University Press, 1971), p. 511.

5. Ibid., pp. 302–303.

6. See the discussion of why people may like lotteries in Milton Friedman and L. J. Savage, "The Utility Analysis of Choices Involving Risk," *Journal of Political Economy*, vol. 56 (August 1948), pp. 279–304. Their model implies local areas of increasing marginal utility in the individual's utility function.

7. Okun, *Equality and Efficiency*, pp. 70–73.

8. Rawls, *Theory of Justice*, Chapter 4.

9. Ibid., p. 62.

10. Lee Rainwater finds that the public's subjective attitudes correspond to this criterion. See *What Money Buys: Inequality and the Social Meanings of Income* (New York: Basic Books, 1974), pp. 41–63, 110–17.

11. The interpersonal-comparison approach (and its doctrinal history) is discussed in Walter J. Blum and Harry Kalven, Jr., *The Uneasy Case for Progressive Taxation* (Chicago: University of Chicago Press, 1953), pp. 49–63.

12. Henry C. Simons, *Personal Income Taxation* (Chicago: University of Chicago Press, 1938), pp. 10–14.

13. Okun, *Equality and Efficiency,* pp. 98–100.

14. Ibid., pp. 57–60.

15. Ibid., pp. 91–95.

16. In principle, the possibility of a "corner optimum" cannot be ruled out. If the cost of even the first dollar's worth of redistribution exceeded the benefits of its added equalization, zero redistribution would be optimal. At the other extreme, if the benefits of eliminating the last dollar's worth of inequality exceeded the costs of doing so, zero inequality would be optimal. Neither of these extremes appears to have any empirical relevance, unless one invokes a "principle" against any redistribution or any inequality.

17. Again, this assumes that there will be no corner optimum.

18. Simons, *Personal Income Taxation,* pp. 18–19.

19. See the discussion in Paul Taubman and Terence Wales, *Higher Education and Earnings* (New York: McGraw-Hill, 1974), Chapters 1, 2, 9.

20. Jan Tinbergen, *Income Distribution: Analysis and Policies* (Amsterdam: North-Holland, 1975).

21. Jan Pen, "Review/Equality and Efficiency: The Big Tradeoff," *Challenge,* vol. 18 (January-February 1976), p. 61.

22. Okun, *Equality and Efficiency,* pp. 79–82.

23. Taking account of such dynamic influences as the costs and benefits of education and training. I doubt that long-run "perfect" job discrimination is possible; but I also doubt that any perfectly discriminating monopolist can avoid dynamic inefficiency in the face of long-run substitution options.

24. So-called statistical discrimination may provide an exceptional unintended rationale for job bias. For example, an employer finds that women statistically have higher quit rates and he gives preference to applicants who are likely to have low quit rates.

25. See Milton Friedman, *Capitalism and Freedom* (Chicago: University of Chicago Press, 1962), pp. 161–65. For a sampling of libertarian authors who explicitly reject the ethical rationale for income distribution based on marginal productivity, see Frank H. Knight, *The Ethics of Competition and Other Essays* (New York: Harper, 1935), pp. 54–58; and F. A. Hayek, *The Constitution of Liberty* (Chicago: University of Chicago Press, 1960), pp. 93–100.

26. See Karl Polanyi, "Our Obsolete Market Mentality," in George Dalton, ed., *Primitive, Archaic, and Modern Economies* (Boston: Beacon, 1971), esp. pp. 65–67; and *The Great Transformation* (New York: Farrar, 1944; Boston: Beacon, 1957). Another type of historical perspective on the evolution of market ideology in the nineteenth and twentieth centuries is provided by R. A. Gordon, "Adam Smith in the Twentieth Century," in Leonard S. Silk, ed., *Readings in Contemporary Economics* (New York: McGraw-Hill, 1970), pp. 37–44.

27. Hayek, *Constitution of Liberty*, p. 21.

28. Ibid., pp. 136–38.

29. Hayek even manages to justify public services (and the coercive taxation to finance them) as coercion to prevent greater coercion: "We need only remember the role that the assured 'access to the King's highway' has played in history to see how important such rights may be for individual liberty." Ibid., pp. 141–42.

30. See Robert Nozick, *Anarchy, State, and Utopia* (New York: Basic Books, 1974); a brief summary is presented on pp. 118–19.

31. Ibid., pp. 150–53.

32. Ibid., p. 141.

33. Leonard Goodwin, *Do the Poor Want to Work?* (Washington, D.C.: The Brookings Institution, 1972), p. 112.

34. Although I mentioned this range of issues in *Equality and Efficiency* (pp. 48–49, 100, 116), I now think they deserve even greater emphasis. I have benefited from the comments of Daniel Yankelovich at the Public Affairs Outlook Conference of the Conference Board (New York, March 17, 1976).

35. Okun, *Equality and Efficiency*, pp. 21–22, 38–40, 60, 119.

36. Henry Simons, *Economic Policy for a Free Society* (Chicago: University of Chicago Press, 1948), p. 6.

37. Kristol, "High Cost of Equality," p. 200. See also James Grant, "Government in Exile? The Brookings Institution Wields Tremendous Clout," *Barron's*, vol. 55 (October 27, 1975), p. 17; and M. Bronfenbrenner, "Book Reviews, Equality and Efficiency: The Big Tradeoff," *Journal of Economic Literature*, vol. 13 (September 1975), pp. 917–18.

38. Hayek, *Constitution of Liberty*, p. 19.

Our Blend of Democracy and Capitalism: It Works, but Is in Danger

In establishing a capitalistic democracy, the United States has built a society on two differing foundations. The capitalistic foundation attaches top priority to efficiency—operating through market incentives for getting the economic job done in the way that obtains the most useful output from our labor, capital, and natural resources. The democratic foundation, in contrast, emphasizes egalitarian and humanitarian values of cooperation, compassion, and fraternity.

Because our society rests on both of these foundations, we encounter creative tensions and uneasy compromises. As individuals, we attach different weights to the two sets of values, and we reach different conclusions on particular policy issues that define the scope of the marketplace and the scope of the political process. So, inevitably, we disagree and we debate. And the debates are often constructive. In the broad light of history, our nation has displayed remarkable ability to hammer out the needed compromises to balance the two value systems. We have generally avoided big polarizing ideological debates that might have rocked our institutional structure off its democratic and capitalistic foundations. Yet, the threat of polarization has always lurked in the background, and at times has become a clear and present danger.

The polarizers seem particularly hard at work today. By grasping at either the market or democratic value system and ignoring the other, one can readily indict our society for grave defects and grievous crimes. Those who march under the banner of democracy point to the ugly features of capitalism. Our economic contests are motivated by greed and allow the winners to ride roughshod over the losers. There is less nutrition on the tables of many of our poor than in the garbage pails of our rich. Our egalitarian political rights are sometimes contaminated by the power bought by money.

Those who wave the banner of market efficiency see a different set of specters: high tax rates that choke off initiatives; expensive government programs that fail to accomplish their goals; and a maze of regulations that impose large economic costs and that constrain individual liberty.

There is some truth in both of these diagnoses, but both are distorted and partial views that lead to fundamentally wrong and dangerous prescriptions. One would set laudable humanitarian targets and cripple the productive capability essential to hit those targets. The other would probably strengthen our productive capability, but in a manner that could destroy our social cohesion. Despite the appeals of the polarizers, the vital center in American political and social attitudes typically prevails. These centripetal forces stem from the appreciation of the favorable features of both our capitalistic and egalitarian foundations, and from the recognition of their mutual limitations. I want to focus on some of the essential unifying principles that promote consensus—on the broadly shared ideas that help us to maintain our blend of democracy and capitalism.

The Market and the Government Need Each Other

At bottom, most Americans know that our government and our private economy depend on each other. Many of the government's functions in promoting and regulating activity in the marketplace are not controversial; indeed, some are conducted so routinely that they tend to be taken for granted. And the same general, implicit acceptance applies to many of the contributions that our private economy makes to the vitality of our democracy. An explicit recognition and examination of these critical interdependencies helps to put into perspective the adversary relationships and the conflicting issues between the state and the market. The best antidote to polarization is the joint recognition that the pursuit of our human values depends on harnessing materialism and "greed," and that the conduct of our market activity relies on the restrictive legal powers of the state and its "bureaucracy."

Strikingly, the government needs the marketplace in two distinct ways—one as a support and one as a counterweight. As a support for government in a capitalistic system, the private economy is the goose that lays the golden eggs. The marketplace finances the public efforts to educate our youth, protect our shores, and aid our poor. The material resources required to fulfill the objectives of the public sector come from the tax base of a healthy, progressive, private economy.

As a counterweight, the decentralization of power inherent in a private enterprise economy supplies the limitation of government that is essential to the survival of democracy. It is a remarkable uniformity of history that a fully collectivized economy has never produced a single free election or one free press. And that uniformity is not merely an accident or a coincidence. A collectivized economy entrusts government officials with the command over all of society's productive resources. It is natural for them to exercise that enormous power, which allows them to deprive dissenters of their livelihoods and to keep the views of the opposition out of the press and off the airwaves. Why should they put up with democratic processes that threaten their own status and power?

On the other side, the marketplace depends critically on the government and on the exercise of its legal powers to make and enforce the rules of economic activity. The value of contracts, orders, promises to pay, and money itself stems from the power of politicians and bureaucrats to penalize the violators of the rules of the market game. Without the government as referee, there could be no game.

The property rights that are the essence of economic transactions are established and enforced by government in a way that necessarily restricts the actions of all citizens, not just those of the parties to a particular contract. Capitalism works only because the government authorizes the posting of millions of "keep-off" signs—not merely to thwart trespassing and theft in a narrow sense, but to establish ownership; to maintain trademarks, patents, franchises, and copyrights; and to clarify who has the right to sell any particular asset to someone else. The keep-off sign invokes the coercive power of the state: it prohibits some citizens from doing things that they would like to do. In enforcing such restraints, society draws a line between liberty and license, between legitimate access and trespass, between constructive and unconstructive freedoms. If our goals were truly maximum liberty in the sense of minimum coercion by the state, if we really wanted "laissez-faire," we would have a wasteland of chaos rather than a marketplace of economic activity.

Because we want an efficient and progressive economy, we ask the government to intervene in behalf of the marketplace in many ways. As a specific example, consider the joint stock corporation. Upon this inanimate entity the government has bestowed powers and rights normally reserved for human beings—and one outstanding right, eternal life, that is denied to all humans. This political invention has been enormously constructive; it has promoted the development of industrial capitalism and raised the living standards of the masses. The recognition of the corporation as a humanoid creation of the state illuminates a number of specific issues. Isn't it reasonable to expect corporate behavior to conform to our social norms? Is it obvious that a special tax on corporate income is inappropriate "double taxation"?

The government supplies private enterprise with physical and social as well as legal infrastructure. Obviously, public highways and airports have been essential to the development of our industries that manufacture and use motor vehicles and airplanes. Less obviously, public education has contributed much of the human capital employed in private business and has helped to establish a common language and common culture, which have been vital to American economic progress. In short, the successful private entrepreneurs and the successful public officials in our society owe each other a great deal.

The Competitive Marketplace Is Generally the Best System for Organizing Production

Every day for the past two centuries, our economy (as well as those of other advanced Western countries) has confirmed the validity of Adam Smith's theory of the "invisible hand." The competitive marketplace transmits signals to producers that reflect the values of consumers, offering profits for the production of those goods whose value to consumers exceeds their cost to producers. Profitability becomes the magnet that pulls resources into their most productive uses. Thus, in the competitive marketplace, economic self-interest becomes an engine of social welfare.

The market is such an impersonal, decentralized system that its contributions often go unnoticed. We take for granted that the goods we want are generally available in the stores; we don't award prizes for the continual decline in real costs of production generated by incentives for efficiency. And we do not applaud the flow of new products and new services that raise our standards of living.

Yet, when competition works, it creates values for the consumer far greater than the wealth it bestows on successful entrepreneurs and their financial backers. Clearly, an enormous social surplus was created by the dramatic transformation of energy use that Thomas Edison masterminded. We should all wish for a latter-day Edison who might do as much in the energy field today; and the whole country would gain even if he became 10 times as rich as the original Edison did.

To be sure, not every entrepreneurial success in the competitive marketplace represents a shared victory for the consumer. There are con games and rip-offs and deceptive marketing and fraudulent advertising. Because illegitimate business practices can poison the consumer's general confidence in the market, the government enhances the vitality of private enterprise when it can stamp out such practices. Beyond this range, we can all identify results of competitive marketing that seem regrettable and yet acceptable. In one class of such cases, firms operate not by serving the needs of consumers but by playing on their anxieties—for example, by making them worry about whether various parts of their bodies emit the "ideal" scent. I don't care for that smell in the marketplace, but I'd rather tolerate it than pass a law to deodorize it.

The main exceptions to the general presumption of competitive efficiency stem from the presence of vast economies of scale. Monopoly is the only way to capture the potential efficiencies of large-scale production in communication, in the transmission of gas and electricity, and in some areas of transportation. Yet, society simply cannot afford to entrust to a private monopolist the power to enforce scarcity and to collect a huge toll from the consuming public. So government intervention is required. The form of intervention chosen by the United States is different from that adopted by most other nations that regard themselves as capitalistic. They have generally nationalized these industries, while (with the exception of the Post Office) we have relied on the public-utility concept of regulation. The course we have chosen is complex, rigid, bureaucratic, and inelegant and imperfect in a hundred other dimensions. But when the defects of public-utility regulation are weighed against those of unfettered private monopoly and of nationalized operation, our strategy looks remarkably good.

Apart from economies of scale, all of the favorable implications of Smith's "invisible hand" depend on the presence of effective competition and are undermined by monopoly. For monopoly is the very antithesis of competition: it imposes a logic of scarcity rather than of productivity; it enforces rigidity rather than responsiveness, consumer exploitation rather than consumer sovereignty. Yet the very profit-seeking motives that make a competitive market tick also lead producers to try to eliminate competition by collusion, by blocking the entry of new competitors, or by gobbling up or squeezing out existing competitors. A century ago the United States wisely decided to outlaw the freedom to destroy competition, just as it had outlawed the freedom to break contracts and the freedom to trespass. For all its imperfections, our antitrust policy has served the marketplace well and has enhanced our long-run economic performance relative to that of other countries that tolerated collusion and cartelization.

Antitrust policy is confronted by a serious dilemma when monopoly emerges from a competitive race in which one firm has been so much more efficient than others that it grew rapidly in size and market share. Obviously, our regulatory policies should not penalize exceptionally good performance. But, also obviously, even when market share is obtained legitimately and constructively, it can subsequently be abused by practices that block the entry of competitors. In general, the bigness that comes from competitive success can be tolerated as long as new competitors have access to the market. To offer a particular example, I cannot share the concern of consumer groups in the Washington metropolitan area who decry the dominance of two food chains in the grocery business. With a huge number of competitors and extreme ease of entry, their large share of the market strikes me as a testimonial that they are doing something right rather than as a reason for suspecting that they are doing something wrong.

The government's role in preserving competition and curbing monopoly must adapt to changing developments in the marketplace. One important development in the past generation has been the vastly expanded scope of foreign trade. On the one hand, as long as this country pursues a liberal import policy, the presence of effective foreign competitors should permit some relaxation of antitrust policy. On the other hand, the emergence of multinational and state-sponsored corporations introduces new problems and issues. Monopoly has recently raised its ugly head in world markets through the formation of OPEC, the governmentally organized, multinational oil cartel. The world price of petroleum set by OPEC is a politically determined monopoly price, not a market-determined competitive price. Under these circumstances, the oil price in the United States is bounded to be determined by government officials; the only question is how much of a role will be played by Sheiks and Shahs and how much by American Presidents and Members of Congress. A host of valid criticisms can be leveled against U.S. energy policy of recent years, but the charge that our government has interfered with a "free market" is not one of them. OPEC is not what Adam Smith had in mind! And that invalid charge can only weaken the strong case that can be made in favor of greater profit incentives for U.S. energy production.

Our Democracy Should Mitigate Inhumane Penalties of the Market

The incentive system of the marketplace uses both a carrot and a stick, offering large rewards to the outstanding winners of the competitive race and imposing heavy penalties on some of the losers. The operation of the stick is often ugly—indeed, inhumane. The unmitigated verdict of the marketplace would condemn millions to deprivation. When our economy is depressed many skilled workers cannot find jobs. Even when our economy is prosperous there are not enough jobs to go around for the young and others who have not had the opportunity to develop skills. And there are never remunerative jobs for many with severe physical or emotional handicaps. Small farmers are exposed to serious deprivation at the whim of nature. Technological progress exacts its toll; as we recognize Edison's contribution, we must also recognize that it indirectly destroyed the livelihoods of many owners, workers, and investors in the kerosene lamp business.

The cases of serious deprivation cannot be accepted passively or justified complacently in a democratic society. Even if the "losers" are all beaten in fair races, we must ask what is a fair penalty for a loser in a fair contest. And, unlike the citizenry of ancient Rome, we do not consider it fair to throw him to the lions!

In a fundamental sense, moreover, the contests *cannot* be fair over the longer run. Vast disparities in results—living standards, income, wealth—inevitably spawn serious inequalities in opportunity that represent arbitrary handicaps and head starts. In an unmodified market-dominated society, poverty becomes a vicious circle. The children of the poor are handicapped in many ways—their nutrition, their education, their ability to get funds to start business and buy homes, and their treatment on many of the hiring lines for both private and public jobs. Any commitment to a reasonable degree of equality of opportunity requires some correction of the glaring inequalities of results that an unmodified marketplace would decree.

Even more fundamental, poverty cannot be ignored by a society that proclaims democratic values, insisting upon the worth of all its citizens and the equality of their political and social rights. Our commitment to freedom of speech, equality of suffrage, and equality before the law rests on a broader commitment to human values that is violated by the persistence of economic misery in an affluent society. I cannot imagine how a sane society could decide deliberately to guarantee every citizen a fair trial before a judge and jury and at the same time permit some citizens to be condemned to death by the marketplace.

The record of history makes clear that capitalism has no built-in tendency to correct the problem of deprivation and poverty, even though such a self-correcting tendency was predicted by many early advocates of a free market. In a particularly ringing passage, John Stuart Mill proclaimed that he would be a communist if he believed that deprivation and misery were inherent in capitalism. For nearly a century thereafter, America waited for Mill's implied prediction to come true. Then the Federal government began to intervene systematically to correct major areas of economic deprivation, producing evidence that Mill may indeed have been right. Deprivation and misery need not be inherent in a democratic capitalistic society *if* it uses its budgetary resources to eliminate them. Today, one-third of our Federal budget is devoted toward that end, largely through a reshuffle of progressive taxes into benefit payments. If not for that reshuffle, the number of Americans living below the poverty line would be at least double the actual figure.

This is an area of particularly vexing trade-offs. No objective dollar price tag can be placed on the benefit of reducing deprivation and misery; the valuation is a matter of individual judgment and ethical assessment, on which citizens will disagree. And with few exceptions, efforts to shift resources to the poor and disadvantaged have their costs. As I like to put it, society can transport money from rich to poor only in a leaky bucket. The leakages are of two distinct types: direct administrative and compliance costs of the tax and transfer programs; and indirect economic costs of the distortions of incentives to work, save, invest, and innovate. The cost of the leakages must be balanced against the benefits obtained from what is left in the bucket. A program cannot be damned just because it has some leakage, nor can it be blessed simply because something is left in the bucket. Correcting deprivation and preserving economic efficiency are both desirable goals, which unfortunately sometimes conflict with each other. Of necessity, we must live with compromises between the two. We cannot aid low-income groups to the point of destroying the incentive system of the market that marshals the effort and economic activity to fill the bucket. Nor can we tolerate kids with empty stomachs, adults selling apples, and oldsters with begging cups in the name of a greater aggregate of real GNP. There are serious, legitimate grounds for debate and controversy among informed citizens about how much assistance should be provided and how it can be handled with minimum leakage. We need those constructive dialogues and debates, not ideological shouting matches, to formulate policies in this perplexing and crucial area.

The Government Must Look After the Interests of "Third Parties"

It is axiomatic that voluntary transactions in the marketplace are mutually advantageous to both the buyer and the seller—or else they would not be agreed upon by the two parties. But a transaction may harm some third parties whose interests are not reflected in the exchange decision. Only the political process can determine when the interests of third parties are sufficiently weighty to warrant protection.

In some cases the decision is easy. We would all object if our next-door neighbor sold his land for use as a garbage dump. And so zoning laws are enacted by which the government prevents indirect trespassing on our property rights. Similarly, we used the force of law to require vaccinations against smallpox, recognizing the strong interdependence of our exposure to contagious diseases. On the other hand, we do not require homeowners to grow pretty gardens nor do we ban activities that increase the likelihood of catching and spreading colds. In these cases our guide is not a general principle for or against government intervention, but rather a pragmatic weighing of costs and benefits. When the government does not intervene, the value of the unregulated activity—and the freedom to engage in it—is preserved for the participants, but the costs imposed on the nonparticipants are accepted. Regulation or intervention obviously reverses the balance sheet.

The complex environmental decisions that confront us today in the effort to control dirty air, dirty water, and unwarranted noise are similar to those posed by the next-door garbage dump or messy garden. Indeed, it is not obvious that the new problem areas are more vexing, in principle, than those of public health and urban land use that we now handle routinely. They evoke more controversy and divisiveness, in part because we have not shaken down our policies in these new areas, and in part because they are related to technological advances that are still fraught with uncertain consequences. Only recently has anyone had to worry about whether fluorocarbons should go into our air, whether nuclear power plants should be located in our suburbs, or supersonic transports should land at our airports. But, currently, those decisions have to be made—one way or the other. If they are left to the marketplace, the impact on third parties will be ignored and only the benefits and costs to producers and direct consumers will be reflected.

If, however, third party interests are considered through the political process, sometimes they will loom large enough to justify constraining the producers and consumers—thus increasing the scope of government regulation. If we continue to balance benefits and costs pragmatically, we must be prepared for some net increase in the range of third party protections as a by-product of technological advance. I do not welcome that prospect, but I believe it must be faced by improving regulation and collective rule-making, and not by disregarding the impact of technologically created interdependencies on the public at large.

Government Actions Must Be Subjected to the Test of Efficiency

I have emphasized that the competitive market gets its job done, but I have also identified some of its shortcomings—spawning monopoly, imposing inhumane penalties, and disregarding the interests of third parties. Any correction of those shortcomings must come through the operation of the government. But to score a net gain, the public sector must execute its tasks well. The government's cure must not be worse than the market's disease. In fact, Federal, state and local governments do carry out many of their traditional tasks with reasonable efficiency. But the record of performance on the additional tasks that the Federal government has undertaken in the 1960s and 1970s is disappointing.

One source of this disappointment was the veritable explosion of demands for new and complex services from the Federal government—improving neighborhoods, training the unskilled, cleaning up the air and the water, and rooting out discrimination and objectionable lobbying practices. Starting without a background of experience or a base of technological knowledge for the pursuit of these goals, we understandably encountered serious problems in trying to do so much so fast.

Some of the frustrations were not just a matter of the pace, but rather reflected the nature of the public sector and the political decision-making process. The public administrator cannot tune in to the market's signals; he does not get the guidance of the bottom line and the feedback of customer demand that make executives of competitive private firms perform efficiently.

Furthermore, the government suffers as a producer of services from a decision-making process designed to be painstaking and deliberate. Checks and balances of powers, and procedures to ensure due process and accountability are features of the political process for good reasons. They protect us against fraud, conspiracy, and capriciousness. But they also deprive us of flexibility, experimentation, and responsiveness in public administration, and they make political decision-making a costly process.

In addition, as Charles Schultze has explained in *The Public Use of Private Interest*, the pursuit of efficiency in the public sector is impeded by the rule of "we do no direct harm." The political process is generally intended to compensate losers and hence must avoid inflicting losses on citizens. But if it cannot inflict losses, it cannot follow those dictates of efficiency that require exercise of the stick (as well as the carrot). As Schultze notes insightfully, the rule was intended to protect citizens from arbitrary exercise of the powers of government, but it now works in practice mainly to extend the sphere of detailed state control. In order to avoid harming any minority, the government is busily adjudicating all kinds of competing claims, maintaining programs that have either failed or outlived their usefulness, and shunning the use of reward-and-penalty incentives.

A final impediment to efficiency is the greater weight attached to the interests of producers than to those of consumers, particularly in the Congress. In part, this imbalance is a corollary of "do no direct harm"; in part, it stems from the greater wealth and power of producer groups; mostly, in my judgment, it reflects an asymmetry of information and motivation. Every sugar producer knows how his Congressman votes on sugar legislation, while 200 million sugar consumers neither learn the facts nor care deeply enough to evaluate their Congressman on this particular dimension of performance. In principle, this imbalance can be rectified by organized consumer groups, but these generally find issues of health and safety more exciting than those of price supports, tariffs and quotas, restrictive labor practices, or tax shelters.

I doubt that there would be much serious disagreement with my assessment of the shortcomings of government performance in executing its new tasks or with my diagnosis of some of the contributing causes. But there is a highly significant controversy about the lessons to be learned from that record. Many conservatives see a confirmation of their convictions about how little the government can do constructively and a demonstration of the need to abandon some social goals. In contrast, to liberals and many centrists, the record is not only a keen disappointment but also a challenge for reforms to improve government efficiency. Those of us who take up that challenge realize that the tasks we set for government must be revised in light of what it can realistically accomplish at a price the taxpayer can afford. Our past experience should allow us to kill some proposals on the drawing board, to nurture a selected few with more managerial effort, to follow up with a careful evaluation of results, and to phase out the failures.

I see a number of recent, significant, if still incipient, movements toward reform of government efficiency. First, the process by which priorities are weighed in the Congress has been changed for the better by the new budgetary process. With the establishment of the two Budget Committees and of the Congressional Budget Office and the institution of joint resolutions on the budget, our legislators now are facing up to the reality that the whole must equal the sum of the parts in the Federal budget. Second, "sunset" legislation is a promising procedure; if fully implemented, it should ensure that Federal programs do not keep going indefinitely by inertia. Third, despite the unrealism of the implied notion that every dollar of every program can be assessed anew each year, zero-base budgeting may bestow upon us 95-percent-base budgeting, which would be a genuine improvement over the traditional standard of 100 percent. Fourth, the newly enacted reform of the Federal civil service should strengthen carrot-and-stick incentives for our career public administrators.

Many policy-oriented researchers have advanced proposals for applying market-type incentives in public programs designed to correct the shortcomings of the market itself. Schultze's book developed that theme in detail and offered many examples of ways that rewards and penalties could be invoked to make private self-interest serve public purposes more effectively. These include the initiation of fees and subsidies for the curbing of pollution, greater dependence on liability insurance to meet safety and health objectives, the introduction of subsidies to private employers for hiring and training the disadvantaged and the handicapped. Currently, our elected officials are taking seriously proposals to invoke penalties or rewards through the tax system to help break the stubborn, ongoing wage-price spiral. This group of policy innovations calls for the government to apply the carrot-and-stick approach of the marketplace, as a partial substitute for the traditional command-and-control approach of the political process.

Efforts to improve performance in the public sector face many obstacles. Clearly, there is no built-in tendency for the government to become efficient any more than there is for the market to become humane. Indeed, I have noted several ways in which the political process creates inherent limitations on the efficiency of government as a producer of complex services. If we apply benefit-cost analysis rigorously, we will in many cases decide to tolerate market imperfections, rather than trying to correct them through public policy. But many tasks in our capitalistic democracy are going to be executed by government for better or for worse, and our common interest requires that they be done better.

Throughout this essay I have skipped over our serious and intriguing substantive economic problems—inflation and unemployment, poverty and productivity—in order to focus on the problem of polarization. In my judgment, that is a greater threat to our system than any of these substantive problems. And the character of that threat has changed. A decade ago it came mainly from the left—typified by the middle-class youths who emerged from their sports cars to condemn our society for its materialism and greed, for oppressing the masses, and for plundering the planet. Today, in my view, the main threat comes from the extreme right—from those who issue a blanket indictment against all government regulation and intervention, who redefine poverty as the "freedom to fail," and who basically ignore the values of democracy. The worst enemies of U.S. capitalism are a handful of its ardent proponents, who prescribe fiscal-monetary policies that would produce mass unemployment, regulatory policies that would flagrantly violate the legitimate interests of third parties, and "reforms" of government programs that would put vivid pictures of economic misery back on the front pages. The consequences of their program would swing the pendulum of public opinion far to the left. Because I do not believe that we will adopt their program, I expect capitalism to survive and thrive in the United States. And I expect us to continue to pursue the goals of democratic capitalism, striving to make the verdict of the market more humane and the operation of our government more efficient.

Bibliography of Arthur M. Okun

Books and Monographs

The Effects of Open Inflation on Consumer Demand. Ph.D. Dissertation. Columbia University, 1956.

The Battle against Unemployment. New York: W. W. Norton & Co. (1965, 1972 editions).

Challenges in Sustaining Prosperity. Washington, D.C.: U.S. Department of Labor, Manpower Administration, 1967.

Economic Issues for the Future. Seminar on Manpower Policy and Program. Washington, D.C.: U. S. Department of Labor, Manpower Administration, 1968.

Inflation: The Problems It Creates and the Policies It Requires (with Herny M. Fowler and Milton Gilbert). New York: New York University Press, 1970.

The Political Economy of Prosperity. Washington, D.C.: Brookings Institution, 1970.

Equality and Efficiency: The Big Tradeoff. Washington, D.C.: Brookings Institution, 1975.

Curing Chronic Inflation (coeditor with George L. Perry). Washington, D.C.: Brookings Institution, 1978.

Current Issues in Political Economy (with Robert Solomon). Toronto, Ontario: Ontario Economic Council, 1979.

Prices and Quantities: A Macroeconomic Analysis. Washington, D.C.: Brookings Institution, 1981.

Professional Articles

"A Further Note on the Theory of Inflation," *Review of Economic Studies*, vol. 21 (1954).

"A Review of Some Economic Forecasts for 1955–57," *Journal of Business*, vol. 32 (July 1959).

"On the Appraisal of Cyclical Turning-Point Predictors," *Journal of Business*, vol. 33 (April 1960).

"The Predictive Value of Surveys of Business Intention," *American Economic Review*, vol. 52 (May 1962, *Papers and Proceedings*, 1961).

"Money and Business Cycles, Comment," *The Review of Economics and Statistics*, vol. 45 (February 1963 Supplement).

"Invited Dissertations, I," Discussion, in *American Economic Review*, vol. 54 (May 1964, *Papers and Proceedings*, 1963).

"Introduction" and "The Gap between Actual and Potential Output," in Arthur M. Okun, ed., *The Battle against Unemployment*. New York: W. W. Norton & Co., 1965.

"The Role of Aggregate Demand in Alleviating Unemployment," in William G. Bowen and Frederick H. Harbison, eds., *Unemployment in a Prosperous Economy*. Report of 1st Princeton Manpower Symposium, May 13–14, 1965. Princeton: Princeton University Press, 1965.

"The Gap between Actual and Potential Output," in Edmund S. Phelps, ed., *Problems of the Modern Economy*. New York: W. W. Norton & Co., 1966.

"Monetary Policy, Debt Management, and Interest Rates: A Quantitative Appraisal," in Donald D. Hester and James Tobin, eds., *Financial Markets and Economic Activity*. New York: Wiley, 1967.

"The Treatment of Government Lending and Borrowing in the Federal Budget"—Comments in "Proceedings of a Conference Sponsored Jointly by the President's Commission on Budget Concepts and the Brookings Institution, July 31–August 1, 1967," in *Staff Papers and Other Materials Reviewed by the President's Commission*. Washington, D.C.: Government Printing Office, 1967.

"Budget Treatment of Federal Lending and Borrowing—Comment," in Wilfred Lewis Jr., ed., *Budget Concepts for Economic Analysis*. Washington, D.C.: Brookings Institution, 1968.

"Measuring the Impact of the 1964 Tax Reduction," in Walter W. Heller, ed., *Perspectives on Economic Growth*. New York: Random House, 1968. Reprinted in Warren L. Smith and Ronald L. Teigen, eds., *Readings in Money, National Income, and Stabilization Policy*, revised edition, Homewood, IL: Irwin, 1970; and in Norman F. Keiser, ed., *Readings in Macroeconomics: Theory, Evidence and Policy*, Englewood Cliffs, N.J.: Prentice-Hall, 1970.

"The Formulation of National Economic Policy," in Warren L. Smith and Ronald L. Teigen, eds., *Readings in Money, National Income, and Stabilization Policy*. Revised Edition. Homewood, IL: Irwin, 1970.

"The Full Employment Surplus Revisited" (with Nancy H. Teeters), *Brookings Papers on Economic Activity*. 1:1970.

"Inflation: The Problems and Prospects before Us," in *Inflation: The Problems It Creates and the Policies It Requires* (with Henry M. Fowler and Milton Gilbert). New York: New York University Press, 1970. Brookings Reprint 182.

"Notes and Numbers on the Profits Squeeze" (with George L. Perry), *Brookings Papers on Economic Activity*. 3:1970.

"Prosperity without Inflation: Highlights of the Political Economy of Prosperity," *Brookings Research Report*, vol. 102. Washington, D.C.: Brookings Institution, 1970.

"Have Fiscal and/or Monetary Policies Failed?" *American Economic Review*, vol. 62 (May 1972, *Papers and Proceedings*, 1971).

"The Mirage of Steady Inflation," *Brookings Papers on Economic Activity*. 2:1971.

"The Personal Tax Surcharge and Consumer Demand, 1968–70," *Brookings Papers on Economic Activity*. 1:1971.

"Rules and Roles for Fiscal and Monetary Policy," in James J. Diamond, ed., *Issues in Fiscal and Monetary Policy: The Eclectic Economist Views the Controversy*. Chicago: DePaul University Press, 1971. Reprinted in Lloyd G. Reynolds, George D. Green, and Darrell R. Lewis, eds., *Current Issues of Economic Policy*, Homewood, IL: Irwin, 1973. Brookings Reprint 222.

"Introduction," "The Costs of Inflation," and "The Fiscal Fiasco of the Vietnam Period," in Arthur M. Okun, ed., *The Battle against Unemployment*. Revised Edition. New York: W. W. Norton & Co., 1972.

"Fiscal-Monetary Activism: Some Analytical Issues," *Brookings Papers of Economic Activity*. 1:1972.

"Measuring the Impact of the 1964 Tax Reduction," in Martin Schnitzer and Yung-Ping Chen, eds., *Public Finance and Public Policy Issues*. Scranton: Intext Educational, 1972.

"Political Economy: Some Lessons of Recent Experience," *Journal of Money, Credit and Banking*, vol. 4 (February 1972, Part I). Brookings Reprint 236.

"Wage-Price Guideposts—Yes," in Royall Brandis and Steven R. Cox, eds., *Current Economic Problems: A Book of Readings*. Homewood, IL: Irwin, 1972.

"Comments on Stigler's Paper [Micropolitics and Macroeconomics]," *American Economic Review*, vol. 63 (May 1973, *Papers and Proceedings*, 1972).

"Upward Mobility in a High-Pressure Economy," *Brookings Papers on Economic Activity*. 1:1973.

"Income, Inflation and the Policy Alternatives," *The Economists' Conference on Inflation, Report, vol. 2*. Washington, D.C.: Government Printing Office, 1974.

"Three Pitfalls for Presidential Advisors," *Monthly Labor Review*, vol. 97 (March 1974).

"Unemployment and Output in 1974," *Brookings Papers on Economic Activity*. 2:1974.

"A Postmortem of the 1974 Recession," *Brookings Papers on Economic Activity*. 1:1975.

"Inflation: Its Mechanics and Welfare Cost," *Brookings Papers on Economic Activity*. 2:1975.

"On Friedman's and Schwartz' Money and Business Cycles," *The State of Monetary Economics*. A Conference of the Universities–National Bureau Committee for Economic Research. New York: Arno Press, 1975.

"Uses of Models for Policy Formulation," in Gary Fromm and Lawrence R. Klein, eds., *The Brookings Model: Perspective and Recent Developments*. New York: American Elsevier, 1975.

"What's Wrong with the U.S. Economy? Diagnosis and Prescription," *Quarterly Review of Economics and Business*, vol. 15 (Summer 1975).

"Conflicting National Goals," in Eli Ginzberg, ed., *Jobs For Americans*. The American Assembly, Columbia University. Englewood Cliffs, N.J.: Prentice-Hall, Spectrum, 1976. Brookings Reprint 320.

"Consensus and Controversy in Political Economy," in Ryan C. Amacher, Robert D. Tollison, and Thomas D. Willett, eds., *The Economic Approach to Public Policy: Selected Readings*. Ithaca: Cornell University Press, 1976.

"The Economist and Presidential Leadership," in Ryan C. Amacher, Robert D. Tollison, and Thomas D. Willett, eds., *The Economic Approach to Public Policy: Selected Readings*. Ithaca: Cornell University Press, 1976.

"Inflation Adjustment for the Individual Income Tax," comment in Henry J. Aaron, ed., *Inflation and the Income Tax*. Washington, D.C.: Brookings Institution, 1976.

"Did 1968 Surcharge Really Work—Comment," *American Economic Review*, vol. 67 (March 1977).

"Further Thoughts on Equality and Efficiency," in Colin D. Campbell, ed., *Income Redistribution*. Washington, D.C.: American Enterprise Institute for Public Policy Research, 1977. Brookings Reprint 325.

"Business and the Social Order" (with H. M. Williams and M. Olasky), *Columbia Journal of World Business*, vol. 13 (Winter 1978).

"Capitalism and Democracy: Some Unifying Principles," *Columbia Journal of World Business*, vol. 13 (Winter 1978).

"Effectiveness of Monetary, Fiscal, and Other Policy Techniques: Competing Means" (with Robert J. Gordon and C. C. Holt), *American Economic Review*, vol. 68 (May 1978, *Papers and Proceedings*, 1977).

"Efficient Disinflationary Policies," *American Economic Review*, vol. 68 (May 1978, *Papers and Proceedings*, 1977).

"A Reward TIP," in David C. Colander, ed., *Solutions to Inflation*. New York: Harcourt Brace Jovanovich, 1979.

"Rational-Expectations-with-Misperceptions as a Theory of the Business Cycle," *Journal of Money, Credit & Banking*, vol. 12 (Part 2), (November 1980). Brookings Reprint 376.

"Postwar Macroeconomics: The Evolution of Events and Ideas," comment in Martin S. Feldstein, ed., *The American Economy in Transition*. Cambridge, MA.: National Bureau of Economic Research, 1981.

Congressional Testimony

Joint Economic Committee. *The Coordination and Integration of Government Statistical Programs.* Hearings. 90 Cong. 1 sess. Washington, D.C.: Government Printing Office, 1967.

———. *Economic Effect of Vietnam Spending.* Hearings. 90 Cong. 1 sess. Washington, D.C.: Government Printing Office, 1967.

House. Banking and Currency Committee. *Compendium on Monetary Policy Guidelines and Federal Reserve Structure.* Hearings. 90 Cong. 2 sess. Washington, D.C.: Government Printing Office, 1968.

Joint Economic Committee. *Federal Budget, Inflation, and Full Employment.* Hearings. 91 Cong. 1 sess. Washington, D.C.: Government Printing Office, 1969.

———. *Economic Report of the President, Part 2.* Hearings. 91 Cong. 2 sess. Washington, D.C.: Government Printing Office, 1970.

"An Analysis of the Course of Economic Development in the Country During the Past 18 Months" (with Ackley Gardner and Walter W. Heller), Memorandum for the Senate Democratic Policy Committee. 1970.

House. Education and Labor Committee. *Manpower Act of 1969, Part 1.* Hearings. 91 Cong. 2 sess. Washington, D.C.: Government Printing Office, 1970.

Joint Economic Committee. *Economic Report of the President, Part 2.* Hearings. 92 Cong. 1 sess. Washington, D.C.: Government Printing Office, 1971.

———. *President's New Economic Program, Part 2.* Hearings. 92 Cong. 1 sess. Washington, D.C.: Government Printing Office, 1971.

———. *Long-Term Economic Implications of Current Tax and Spending Proposals.* Hearings. 92 Cong. 1 sess. Washington, D.C.: Government Printing Office, 1971.

House. Banking, Finance and Urban Affairs. *To Extend Standby Powers of the President and Authority of the Federal Reserve Board and the Federal Home Loan Bank Board.* Hearings. 92 Cong. 1 sess. Washington, D.C.: Government Printing Office, 1971.

Senate. Appropriations Committee. *Civil Supersonic Aircraft Development (SST) for FY71.* Hearings. 92 Cong. 1 sess. Washington, D.C.: Government Printing Office, 1971.

Joint Economic Committee. *1972 Economic Report of the President, Part 3.* Hearings. 92 Cong. 2 sess. Washington, D.C.: Government Printing Office, 1972.

Senate. Banking, Housing and Urban Affairs. *Economic Stabilization Legislation, 1973.* Hearings. 93 Cong. 1 sess. Washington, D.C.: Government Printing Office, 1973.

———. *Phase IV.* Hearings. 93 Cong. 1 sess. Washington, D.C.: Government Printing Office, 1973.

Joint Economic Committee. *National Priorities and the Budgetary Process.* Hearings. 93 Cong. 1 sess. Washington, D.C.: Government Printing Office, 1973.

———. *Food and Other Consumer Price Increases*. Hearings. 93 Cong. 1 sess. Washington, D.C.: Government Printing Office, 1973.

Senate. Finance Committee. *Proposals to Increase the Income Tax Personal Exemption*. Hearings. 93 Cong. 2 sess. Washington, D.C.: Government Printing Office, 1974.

Joint Economic Committee. *President Ford's Economic Proposals*. Hearings. 93 Cong. 2 sess. Washington, D.C.: Government Printing Office, 1974.

———. *1974 Economic Report of the President, Part 2*. Hearings. 93 Cong. 2 sess. Washington, D.C.: Government Printing Office, 1974.

Senate. Budget Committee. *Economy and Fiscal Policy, 1974*. Hearings. 93 Cong. 2 sess. Washington, D.C.: Government Printing Office, 1974.

Senate. Select Committee on Nutrition and Human Needs. *National Nutrition Policy Study—1974. Part 4: Nutrition and Food Availability*. Hearings. 93 Cong. 2 sess. Washington, D.C.: Government Printing Office, 1974.

House. Ways and Means Committee. *Panel Discussions on the State of the Economy and President's Tax Proposals: Prepared Statements Presented by Participants. Panel No. 2*. Print. 94 Cong. 1 sess. Washington, D.C.: Government Printing Office, 1975.

House. Banking, Finance and Urban Affairs Committee. *Federal Reserve Consultations on the Conduct of Monetary Policy*. Hearings. 94 Cong. 1 sess. Washington, D.C.: Government Printing Office, 1975.

Joint Economic Committee. *1975 Economic Report of the President, Part 3*. Hearings. 94 Cong. 1 sess. Washington, D.C.: Government Printing Office, 1975.

House. Ways and Means Committee. *Energy Crisis and Proposed Solutions*. Print. 94 Cong. 1 sess. Washington. D.C.: Government Printing Office, 1975.

———. *Energy Crisis and Proposed Solutions, Part 1*. Hearings. 94 Cong. 1 sess. Washington, D.C.: Government Printing Office, 1975.

Senate. Select Committee on Small Businesses. *Small Business Tax Reform, Part 2*. Hearings. 94 Cong. 1 sess. Washington, D.C.: Government Printing Office, 1975.

House. Ways and Means Committee. *President's Authority to Adjust Imports of Petroleum; Public Debt Ceiling Increase; and Emergency Tax Proposals*. Hearings. 94 Cong. 1 sess. Washington, D.C.: Government Printing Office, 1975.

Senate. Foreign Relations Committee. *Multinational Corporations and U.S. Foreign Policy, Part 11*. Hearings. 94 Cong. 1 sess. Washington, D.C.: Government Printing Office, 1975.

Senate. Budget Committee. *Second Concurrent Resolution on the Budget—FY76, Vol. 1*. Hearings. 94 Cong. 1 sess. Washington, D.C.: Government Printing Office, 1975.

Joint Economic Committee. *Midyear Review of the Economic Situation and Outlook*. Hearings. 94 Cong. 2 sess. Washington, D.C.: Government Printing Office, 1976.

House. Budget Committee. *FY77 Budget and the Economy*. Hearings. 94 Cong. 2 sess. Washington, D.C.: Government Printing Office, 1976.

Senate. Budget Committee. *First Concurrent Resolution on the Budget, FY78, Vol. 4.* Hearings. 95 Cong. 1 sess. Washington, D.C.: Government Printing Office, 1977.

House. Banking, Finance and Urban Affairs Committee. *Amendments to the Council on Wage and Price Stability Act.* Hearings. 95 Cong. 1 sess. Washington, D.C.: Government Printing Office, 1977.

Senate. Banking, Housing and Urban Affairs Committee. *Anti-Inflation Proposals.* Hearings. 95 Cong. 2 sess. Washington, D.C.: Government Printing Office, 1978.

Joint Economic Committee. *Economics of the President's Proposed Energy Policies.* Hearings. 95 Cong. 1 sess. Washington, D.C.: Government Printing Office, 1978.

House. Ways and Means Committee. *President's 1978 Tax Reduction and Reform Proposals, Part 9.* Hearings. 95 Cong. 2 sess. Washington, D.C.: Government Printing Office, 1978.

House. Budget Committee. *Economic Stabilization Policies: The Historical Record, 1962–76.* Print. 95 Cong. 2 sess. Washington, D.C.: Government Printing Office, 1978.

Senate. Budget Committee. *First Concurrent Resolution on the Budget FY79, Vol. 4.* Hearings. 95 Cong. 2 sess. Washington, D.C.: Government Printing Office, 1978.

House. Banking, Finance, and Urban Affairs. *Amendments to the Council on Wage and Price Stability Act.* Hearings. 96 Cong. 1 sess. Washington, D.C.: Government Printing Office, 1979.

House. Ways and Means Committee. *Real Wage Insurance.* Hearings. 96 Cong. 1 sess. Washington, D.C.: Government Printing Office, 1979.

Joint Economic Committee. *Stagflation.* Hearings. 96 Cong. 1 sess. Washington, D.C.: Government Printing Office, 1979.

Senate. Banking, Housing and Urban Affairs. *Extension of the Council on Wage and Price Stability and Review of the President's Anti-Inflation Policies.* Hearings. 96 Cong. 2 sess. Washington, D.C.: Government Printing Office, 1980.

House. Budget Committee. *Economic Issues for FY81, Part 2.* Hearings. 96 Cong. 2 sess. Washington, D.C.: Government Printing Office, 1980.

General Articles

"Money Can't Be Speech," *Challenge*, vol. 19 (March/April 1976).

"Focus on Jobs and Prices," Videorecording. Washington, D.C.: Public Issues Network, 1976.

"Equal Rights, but Unequal Incomes," *New York Times Magazine* (July 4, 1976).

"Debate—How to Stop Inflation" (with Alan Greenspan), *Fortune*, vol. 95 (April 1977).

"The Great Stagflation Swamp (Remedies)," *Challenge*. vol. 20 (November/December 1977). Reprinted in the *Brookings Bulletin*, vol. 21 (Fall 1977), and *Vital Speeches*, vol. 44 (December 1, 1977).

"Out of the Stagflation Swamp," *Across the Board*, vol. 15 (January 1978).

"Stop the Self-Inflicted Wounds," *Challenge*, vol. 21 (March/April 1978).

"Our Blend of Democracy and Capitalism: It Works, but Is in Danger," *Across the Board* (March 1979). Brookings Reprint 351.

"An Efficient Strategy to Combat Inflation," *Brookings Bulletin*, vol. 15 (Spring 1979).

"Sticks with Two Short Ends," *Challenge*, vol. 22 (July/August 1979).

"The Invisible Handshake and the Inflationary Process," *Challenge*, vol. 22 (January/February 1980). Brookings Reprint 356.

"The Balanced Budget Is a Placebo," *Challenge*, vol. 23 (May/June 1980).

"Notable & Quotable," *Wall Street Journal* (September 8, 1980).

"Uniting against Inflation," *Brookings Bulletin*, vol. 16 (Winter 1980).

Permissions

The editor and The MIT Press wish to thank the publishers of the following essays for permission to reprint them here. The selections are arranged in their order of appearance.

"Inflation: The Problems and Prospects before Us," in Arthur M. Okun, Henry M. Fowler, and Milton Gilbert, *Inflation: The Problems It Creates and the Policies It Requires,* New York: New York University Press, 1970, pp. 3–53. Copyright 1970 by New York University Press. [Brookings Reprint 182. A portion of the material was incorporated into chapter 4 of *The Political Economy of Prosperity*, Washington, DC: Brookings Institution, 1970.]

"The Mirage of Steady Inflation," *Brookings Papers on Economic Activity* 2(1971), 485–498. Copyright 1971 by The Brookings Institution.

"The Great Stagflation Swamp," *Challenge* 20(November/December 1977), 6–13. Copyright 1977 by M E Sharpe Inc. [Reprinted in the *Brookings Bulletin* 21(Fall 1977) and *Vital Speeches* 44(December 1, 1977).]

"Wage-Price Guideposts—Yes," in House. Committee on Government Operations, *Price-Wage Guideposts,* Hearings, 91 Cong. 1 Sess., Washington, DC: Government Printing Office, 1969, pp. 52–54. [Reprinted in Royall Brandis and Steven Cox, eds., *Current Economic Problems: A Book of Readings,* Homewood, IL: Irwin, 1972.]

"A Reward TIP," in Senate. Banking, Housing, and Urban Affairs, *Anti-Inflation Proposals,* Hearings, 95 Cong. 2 Sess., Washington, DC: Government Printing Office, 1978, pp. 15–28. [Reprinted in David C. Colander, ed., *Solutions to Inflation,* New York: Harcourt Brace Jovanovich, 1979.]

"Inflation: Its Mechanics and Welfare Costs," *Brookings Papers on Economic Activity* 2(1975), 351–390. Copyright 1975 by The Brookings Institution.

"The Invisible Handshake and the Inflationary Process," *Challenge* 22(January/February 1980), 5–12. Copyright 1980 by ME Sharpe Inc. [Brookings Reprint 356.]

"Rational-Expectations-with-Misperceptions as a Theory of the Business Cycle,"

Journal of Money, Credit & Banking 12(4) (November 1980, Part 2), 817–825. Copyright 1980 by the American Enterprise Institute. [Brookings Reprint 376.]

"Potential GNP: Its Measurement and Significance," in American Statistical Association, *Proceedings of the Business and Economic Statistics Section, American Statistical Association,* Washington, DC: ASA, 1962, pp. 98–103. Copyright 1962 by the American Statistical Association.

"The Role of Aggregate Demand in Alleviating Unemployment," in William G. Bowen and Frederick H. Harbison, eds., *Unemployment in a Prosperous Economy,* Report of 1st Princeton Manpower Symposium, May 13–14, 1965, Princeton: Princeton University Press, 1965, pp. 67–81. Copyright 1965 by Princeton University Press.

"Upward Mobility in a High-Pressure Economy," *Brookings Papers on Economic Activity* 1(1973), 207–252. Copyright 1973 by The Brookings Institution.

"Conflicting National Goals," in Eli Ginzberg, ed., *Jobs for Americans*, Englewood Cliffs, NJ: Prentice-Hall, 1976. Copyright 1976 by American Assembly, Columbia University.

"Monetary Policy, Debt Management and Interest Rates: A Quantitative Appraisal," in E. Cary Brown and others, *Stabilization Policies*, Research Studies Prepared for the Commission on Money and Credit, Englewood Cliffs, NJ: Prentice-Hall, 1963, pp. 331–380. Copyright 1963 by Prentice-Hall Inc. [Reprinted in Donald D. Hester and James Tobin, eds., *Financial Markets and Economic Activity*, New York: Wiley, 1967.]

"The Full Employment Surplus Revisited," *Brookings Papers on Economic Activity* 1(1970), 77–110 (with Nancy H. Teeters). Copyright 1970 by The Brookings Institution.

"The Personal Tax Surcharge and Consumer Demand, 1968–70," *Brookings Papers on Economic Activity* 1(1971), 167–204. Copyright 1971 by The Brookings Institution.

"Rules and Roles for Fiscal and Monetary Policy," in James J. Diamond, ed., *Issues in Fiscal and Monetary Policy: The Eclectic Economist Views the Controversy*, Chicago: DePaul University Press, 1971, pp. 51–74. Copyright 1971 by DePaul University Press. [Reprinted in Lloyd G. Reynolds, George D. Green, and Darrell R. Lewis, eds., *Current Issues of Economic Policy*, Homewood, IL: Irwin, 1973. Brookings Reprint 222.]

"Measuring the Impact of the 1964 Tax Reduction," in Walter W. Heller, ed., *Perspectives on Economic Growth*, New York: Random House, 1968, pp. 27–49. Copyright 1968 by Random House Inc. [Reprinted in Warren L. Smith and Ronald L. Teigen, eds., *Readings in Money, National Income, and Stabilization Policy*, revised edition, Homewood, IL: Irwin, 1970, and in Norman F. Keiser, ed., *Readings in Macroeconomics: Theory, Evidence and Policy*, Englewood Cliffs, NJ: Prentice-Hall, 1970.]

"Achieving Sustained Prosperity," in Arthur M. Okun, *The Political Economy of Prosperity*, Washington, DC: Brookings Institution, 1970, pp. 31–61. Copyright 1970 by The Brookings Institution.

"Political Economy: Some Lessons of Recent Experience," *Journal of Money, Credit, & Banking* 4(February 1972, Part 1), 23–34. Copyright 1972 by the Ohio State University Press.

"The Conduct of Monetary Policy," in House. Banking, Finance and Urban Affairs Committee, *Federal Reserve Consultations on the Conduct of Monetary Policy*, Hearings, 94 Cong. 1 Sess., Washington, DC: Government Printing Office, 1975, pp. 73–87.

"A Postmortem of the 1974 Recession," *Brookings Papers on Economic Activity* 1(1975), 207–221. Copyright 1975 by The Brookings Institution.

"Postwar Macroeconomics: The Evolution of Events and Ideas," in Martin S. Feldstein, ed., *The American Economy in Transition*, Cambridge, MA: National Bureau of Economic Research, 1981, pp. 162–169. Copyright 1981 by the National Bureau of Economic Research.

"A Review of Some Economic Forecasts for 1955–57," *Journal of Business* 32(July 1959), 199–211. Copyright 1959 by The University of Chicago Press.

"On the Appraisal of Cyclical Turning-Point Predictors," *Journal of Business* 33(April 1960), 101–120. Copyright 1960 by The University of Chicago Press.

"The Predictive Value of Surveys of Business Intentions," *American Economic Review* 52(May 1962), 218–225. Copyright 1962 by the American Economic Association.

"Uses of Models for Policy Formulation," in Gary Fromm and Lawrence R. Klein, eds., *The Brookings Model: Perspective and Recent Developments*, New York: American Elsevier Publishers Inc., 1975, pp. 361–373. Copyright 1975 by American Elsevier, Inc.

"The Economist and Presidential Leadership," in Arthur M. Okun, *The Political Economy of Prosperity*, Washington, DC: Brookings Institution, 1970, pp. 23–30. Copyright 1970 by The Brookings Institution. [Reprinted in Ryan C. Amacher, Robert D. Tollison, and Thomas D. Willett, eds., *The Economic Approach to Public Policy: Selected Readings*, Ithaca: Cornell University Press, 1976.]

"The Formulation of National Economic Policy," *Perspectives in Defense Management* 2(December 1968), 9–12. [Reprinted in Warren L. Smith and Ronald L. Teigen, eds., *Readings in Money, National Income, and Stabilization Policy*, revised edition, Homewood, IL: Irwin, 1970.]

"Equal Rights but Unequal Incomes," *New York Times Magazine* (July 4, 1976). Copyright 1976 by The New York Times Company.

Index